Becoming Aware

A Text/Workbook for
Human Relations & Personal Adjustment

13th Edition

Katie Barwick-Snell

Velma Walker

Kendall Hunt
publishing company

Book Team

Chairman and Chief Executive Officer   Mark C. Falb
President and Chief Operating Officer   Chad M. Chandlee
Vice President, Higher Education   David L. Tart
Director of Publishing Partnerships   Paul B. Carty
Senior Developmental Coordinator   Angela Willenbring
Vice President, Operations   Timothy J. Beitzel
Senior Permissions Editor   Caroline Kieler
Cover Designer   Faith Walker

Cover image courtesy of Bonnie L. Peruttzi, MHR Executive Director, Transition House.

Transition House, Inc., is a private non-profit organization founded in 1982 in Norman, OK. Our Vision is changing lives by creating pathways for mental wellness. Our Mission is improving our community by providing tools for sustaining mental wellness with skills development, supportive care, and advocacy. The hands in the cover photo are of people who are working to overcome a disease that society often sees as a character flaw. We are so proud of the People of Transition House and their commitment to recovery from mental illness. Transition House Executive Director-Bonnie Peruttzi MHR and Mary Hopkins MHR, LPC and the University of Oklahoma Department of Human Relations-Dr. Katie Barwick-Snell are collaborating on a Wellness class for college students to learn more about Wellness issues that impact college students. It has been a great success for the last 3 semesters! For more on Transition House visit www.thouse.org.

Kendall Hunt
publishing company

www.kendallhunt.com
Send all inquiries to:
4050 Westmark Drive
Dubuque, IA 52004-1840

Brief Contents

Contents

CHAPTER 3

Who's in Control? 137

CHAPTER 4

Dealing with Emotions 191

CHAPTER 5

Interpersonal Communication 257

CHAPTER 6

Developing Close Relationships 321

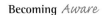

CHAPTER 7

Resolving Interpersonal Conflict 391

CHAPTER 8

Managing Stress and Wellness 441

CHAPTER 9

Values, Ethics, and Choices 499

CHAPTER 10

Life Planning 549

Preface

You will discover that the new thirteenth edition of *Becoming Aware: A Text/Workbook for Human Relations and Personal Adjustment* will assist you in the process of becoming more aware of yourself and others through the most interactive learning process you have found in any textbook.

This new edition is a text/workbook that will give students the opportunity to become active learners in the process of learning about human relations and personal adjustment. Learning should be a "hands on" experience. This new edition will help students explore, experiment, test, and apply the scholarly theories and ideas within the world of human relations and personal adjustment. This text/workbook will allow the learner to think critically, work through problems logically, and make connections with the real world and thus become an active learner. The more you become actively involved within the subject matter of human relations and personal adjustment, the more you will learn. This new edition will give you and the students within the class many new opportunities to get actively involved in learning about yourself and others.

> *The art of teaching is the art of assisting discovery.*
> —MARK VAN DOREN

About the Book

The approach in *Becoming Aware* is humanistic and personal; that is, it stresses the healthy and effective personality and the common struggles we all have in developing a greater awareness of self and establishing more meaningful relationships with others. It especially emphasizes taking risks in accepting personal responsibility for achieving a greater awareness of self and deciding whether and how we want to change our life.

What is more important to us than our personal adjustment and our relationships with other people? This new edition is written for college students of all ages and for all others who wish to explore the world of self-awareness and discover new avenues for personal growth and adjustment and the development and continuance of personal relationships.

The book was written for students who were looking for a practical course: one that dealt with issues in everyday living and would also provide a catalyst for their own personal growth. *Becoming Aware* has been adopted in courses dealing with the psychology of adjustment, human relations, applied psychology, personal growth and awareness, communication, etc. It has also been fortunate to have had numerous adoptions from technical and vocational programs, ranging from nursing to electronics. In addition, instructors in teacher-training courses as well as management-development courses have found *Becoming Aware* a practical guide for their students.

Organization of This Edition

This is a personal interactive book. Within each chapter, the reader is encouraged to examine scholarly, relevant ideas and issues pertaining to their understanding of self and their relationships with others. This is information and skills that are highly sought after in the workplace.

This book is designed to be a personal workbook as well as a classroom text. Each chapter has a minimum of five activities for the reader to pause and reflect on the personal application of the concepts and theories presented in the chapter. Most of the activities will allow the reader to get personally and individually involved in completing the tasks, while a few of the activities will require each person to get involved in a small group process in order to complete the task. It is important for all students to participate in individual projects as well as group activities to retain the knowledge learned. In today's world of business we all have to learn to function as a team (within groups) and as individuals. The better we learn to do it now, the better we will survive in the world.

Active learning is emphasized throughout the text. Each chapter contains a Learning Journal, which will allow the reader to write and assess the personal value or meaning gained from the concepts presented. The activities, as well as the Learning Journals, have perforated pages, specifically designed for more convenient classroom participation in work outside of class that can be used for evaluation and assessment. Additionally, there are numerous thought-provoking quotations, from well-known sources, and over 25 short poems and words of wisdom designed to further promote insightful awareness.

The learning process is an important aspect of this book. The reader gets more involved within the subject matter of the text through the use of chapter test review questions, which will allow the student to relate directly to the important concepts and ideas within each chapter. Reflection questions are designed to help students to develop critical thinking skills and work through problems logically.

To emphasize the need for critical thinking skills, many of the important concepts and ideas are highlighted through use of elements titled—"Think about This"—"Check This Out"—"Consider This"—and "How To."

The sociocultural perspective within the field of human relations and personal adjustment is having a much greater impact on our lives, and it needs to be emphasized more and more. There is continued emphasis on diversity, including additional information on ethnicity, along with culture and gender. You will note the continued emphasis on the elements titled "Focus on Diversity" and "Gender and You."

What's New in This Edition?

The thirteenth edition of Becoming Aware reflects significant updating. Each chapter has been extensively reviewed and updated. New current references, updated glossary terms, and interesting quotations have been added. An engaging new PowerPoint presentation designed to enhance discussion and encourage critical thinking has been developed. You will find new or additional information in the following areas:

* Web-based activities added in selected chapters and updated websites for all chapters.
* Several revised chapter activities and new chapter activities.
* New section: What is human relations?
* New coverage of tolerance, acceptance, and appreciation of differences.
* Broadened discussion of Johari Window to include five dominant patterns of relationships.
* Discussion of gender identity.
* Expanded importance of self-concept with mindset discussion.
* Extended discussion of the Big Five Personality Factors, with the addition of the HEXACO model.
* Enhanced discussion of the Myers Briggs type psychology.
* Increased discussion of strengths-based psychology.
* New Gender and You discussion—Where Did You Learn Your Gender?
* New section: A look at social psychology.
* New discussion of cyberbullying.
* Revamped presentation of guilt and shame.
* Expanded section on helping people grieve with introduction of the Ring Theory.
* New Focus on Diversity: Microaggressions.
* Modernized discussion of technology and communication.
* New discussion of the concept of implicit bias.
* Strengthened discussion of becoming friends with the addition of friendship traits.
* Updated discussion of Internet dating and social networking.
* Broadened discussion of "Should I remain single?"
* New activity: "Take the Marriage Quiz."
* Increased discussion of realities of conflict.
* New information on mistakes to avoid in a conflict.

* New discussion on cross-cultural relationships.
* Updated information on millennials and their stress.
* Revamped discussion of physical effects of stress.
* Revised tips on managing stress.
* Expanded discussion on the nature of prejudice.
* Howard's seven-step method of values clarification.
* Updated discussion of honesty/ethics in professions.
* Steps for intelligent-risk taking.
* Expanded discussion on why goal setting is important.
* New coverage of tips for happiness.

Acknowledgments

We are grateful to the reviewers for their insightful suggestions and innovative ideas: Dr. Barwick-Snell: Thank you to Dr. Joanna Harris, Psychology, East Central Oklahoma University; Dr. Sharon Baker, University of Tulsa; Dr. Tim Davidson; Dr. Janna Martin, University of Oklahoma, Victoria Hoge Tulsa Career Tech Center; Kenneth Catlett, OU Gender and Equity Center; Dr. Cheryl Walker Esbaugh, Dr. Martha Skeeters, OU Women and Gender Studies; Leslie Henderson, McLennan Community College; James Barwick-Snell, LSU; Bonnie Peruttzi and Mary Hopkins, Transitions House; and poet/therapist Colton Snead. I am grateful for all of your insightful suggestions and innovative ideas. Thank you to my OU students Ana Tapia, Oyebola T. Omosebi, Binta Samyang, and Stassi Vullo for your time and talent. A special thank you for Dr. Velma Walker for her writing guidance and mentoring. Finally, I would especially like to thank my family for all the support and ideas they gave me and all the experience and help from my wonderful husband/editor Dr. Daniel C. Snell (a writer of numerous Near Eastern history and religion texts) and my family, James, Abby, & Andrew, and my "other daughters," Jessica, Britney, and Cheyenne. Thanks to all my friends for their support, ideas, contributions, and suggestions.

Finally, we would like to acknowledge those individuals and publishers who kindly gave us their permission to reprint their materials. In several instances, we regret that even after diligent searching, we have not been able to properly credit material being used. Some of the material has been used for many years in classes and workshops with the result that proper identification has been lost, or we no longer are able to provide source information as we would like. Because the material has proved to be of great value, it is included in the book. We trust that eventually we will be able to credit these authors with proper recognition for their work.

Dr. Velma Walker and Dr. Katie Barwick-Snell

About the Authors

Dr. Velma Walker is a Professor Emeritus of psychology at Tarrant County College, Northeast Campus in Hurst, Texas. Although she has specialized in human relations courses for 39 years at the college level, she has also been a counselor and coordinator of student job placement and career information. She has a bachelor's degree in business administration/education, a master's degree in counseling and psychology, and a doctor of education degree, with emphasis in counseling, psychology, and administration. Dr. Walker is also a certified mediator for conflict resolution.

Dr. Walker has given human relations training seminars in the areas of communication, motivation, stress management, time management, and personality lifestyles for educators and business and professional groups for over 36 years. She has also served as a teacher consultant for the Educational Division of the Zig Ziglar Corporation. Dr. Walker is a multiple year honoree in *Who's Who Among America's Teachers*.

After 12 editions of a most enjoyable experience of writing *Becoming Aware*, it is now time to spend more time traveling with my husband of 43 years and more importantly, enjoying time with our six-year-old granddaughter, Reagan. Thank you for your support of *Becoming Aware*, and I am pleased to tell you that Dr. Katie Barwick-Snell, Associate Professor in Human Relations and Women and Gender Studies at the University of Oklahoma, will now be the lead author.

Dr. Katie Barwick-Snell has been a faculty member at the University of Oklahoma, Norman, since the early 1990s. She is currently teaching undergraduate and graduate students in Human Relations, Women and Gender Studies, and in the College of Liberal Studies. She helped develop and implement the undergraduate Human Relations program and was the first academic advisor of the popular undergraduate major in Human Relations. She has won numerous advising and teaching awards. Her B.S. is in Home Economics from Mississippi State University, her M.S. in Human Development from the University of Oklahoma, and her Ed.D. in Occupational and Adult Education from Oklahoma State University. She was on faculty in the former Home Economics Department at USAO in Chickasha, Oklahoma and the former School of Home Economics at the University of Oklahoma. She was also cook on an archeology dig in Syria in the late 1980s and has lived in Australia and Scotland.

She is a long-time volunteer for Norman's Center for Children and Families, the Women's Resource Center Board of Directors, and most recently a community volunteer with Parents Helping Parents, an organization for parents of substance abuse, to offer hope and help to other parents. She has recently become a "parent coach" for the Partnership for Drug-Free Kids drugfree.org/helpline. She is married and has two fantastic grown children, a wonderful son in law, three delightful "other daughters," and three geriatric dogs.

Let us remember: One book, one pen, one child, and one teacher can change the world.
—MALALA YOUSAFZAI

Chapter 1
Getting Acquainted with Ourselves and Others

©Rawpixel.com/Shutterstock.com

[*I sincerely believe that the word* relationship *is the key to the prospect of a decent world. It seems abundantly clear that every problem you will have—in your family, your business, in your personal life, in our nation, or in this world—is essentially a matter of relationships or interdependence.* —Clarence Francis, Business leader]

Think About This...

Think for a minute about your greatest experiences in life. Undoubtedly, you were with another person.
- What would we do without other people?
- What would you do without friends?
- What would it be like?
- Where would you go?
- Would you have fun?
- How do you react in a group? Do you feel shy or do you speak out?
- Would you know what love is?
- Have you ever had a close friend or close relative die? How did you feel when it happened?
- Have you ever experienced or had a close friend or relative experience a divorce? Did they feel lonely? Were they depressed? What did they experience?
- How did you feel when your best friend or lover returned after being gone for a long period of time? Overjoyed? Excited?

I t is obvious that personal relationships and friendships are important to us. We need merely to reflect for a moment on the source of our greatest pleasure and pain to appreciate that nothing else in our life has aroused the extremes of emotion more than the relationships that we have experienced with other human beings.

What is Human Relations?

Human relations (HR) has many meanings to many people, but for this text **human relations** can be defined as the art of developing relationships that improve personal skills and life effectiveness. It offers insight into how you fit into the world and feel about race, class, and gender issues. Basically you have to understand yourself before you can understand others effectively and "**become aware**" of how you fit into the world. In looking at yourself and how you relate to others you can build better relationships and succeed at school and work. Human relations has an emphasis on "soft skills" such as behavior, empathy, co-operation, intergroup development, and interpersonal development. The field of study incorporates sociology, psychology, communications, and other areas like management and human development into the curriculum. Another definition of human relations is the study of improving interpersonal relationships among people or groups of people. As you can see, the basic study of human relations includes a great deal of attention to the emotional needs of oneself as well as the emotional needs of others.

According to Dr. George Henderson, Sylvan N. Goldman Professor of Human Relations at the University of Oklahoma, "Human relations encompasses all the many ways in which people interact with each other to form social units. Unlike social scientists, who are interested primarily in describing **what is**, students of human relations are also concerned with determining **what may be done** to foster positive group interactions." (Henderson, 1996, p.17). He also states that the conflicts that grow out of human relationships may take many forms, positive and negative, such as age and sex rivalry, racism, and, possibly, violence. Microaggressions may also occur as a subtle interaction.

Relationships are the foundation for meaning and success in life.
—DOUGLAS DAFT

Human relations is the study of improving interpersonal relationships among people or groups of people. Dr. Lowell Lamberton defines HR as "the skill or ability to work effectively through and with other people" (Lamberton, 2014, p. 4). Human relations include a desire to understand others, their needs and weaknesses, and their talents and abilities. For anyone in a workplace setting, human relations also involve an understanding of how people work together in groups, satisfying both individual needs and group objectives. If an organization is to succeed, the relationships among the people in that organization must be monitored and maintained (Lamberton, 2014). So, as we can see, the basic study of human relations includes a great deal of attention to the emotional needs of oneself as well as the emotional needs of others.

Human relations begins with self-understanding. The self is about being a total person or individual. You have a **public self**—that is how you communicate about yourself— and what others actually perceive about you—the **private self**—is the actual person that you may be (Dubrin, 2013). In a perfect culture, cultural messages provide scripts for how men and women internally should interact with each other, and therefore, not only gender, but also the gender composition of a friendship, influence a relationship. Women and men regularly face a host of media images that romanticize and sexualize their routine encounters and confront an array of societal expectations and constraints that make a rewarding friendship with someone of the opposite sex challenging (Baumgarten, 2002).

In order to become a healthy and happy person, an individual needs to form close, caring interpersonal relationships. How do we learn to do this? Perhaps the words of John Hope Bryant, founder and CEO of Operation HOPE, will provide some thoughts worth remembering:

> People meet you where you are. If you're open, they tend to be open. If you're closed, they tend to be closed. If you're vulnerable, they tend to be vulnerable. And people are often a little insecure and afraid of themselves. They're afraid to tip their hand. It's just human nature, self-preservation. People will generally only tip their hand when they see you tip your hand. (Bryant, 2009)

George Vaillant is the director of a 72-year study of the lives of 268 men. "In an interview in the March 2008 newsletter to the Grant Study subjects, Vaillant was asked, 'What have you learned from the Grant Study men?' Vaillant's response: **'That the only thing that really matters in life is your relationships to other people.'**" He shared insights of the study with Joshua Wolf Shenk at *The Atlantic* on how men's social connections made a difference to their overall happiness (Shenk, 2009).

Becoming Aware of your Skills - during the reading of this text we will have a video or exercise to do with ways you can get the most of this material. Take a few minutes and watch this video by David Myers discussing study tips with SQ3R or "Testing Effect"

https://www.youtube.com/watch?v=rFIK5gutHKM&feature=youtu.be

David Myers, best-selling introductory psychology author from Worth Publishers, talks about how to make things memorable and study more effectively through the "Testing Effect."

Self-Disclosure

Do You Know Yourself?

Self-awareness is necessary in order to fully understand others. We start the textbook with a review of psychology information which maybe new to you or an **update**. Psychologists have found that a person must gain an understanding of themselves before they can become acquainted with others and understand others. There are some basic questions concerning self-discovery and getting acquainted with others that you can ask yourself. How well do I know myself? Is it easy for other people to get to know me? How well do other people really know me? How much of myself do I reveal to those with whom I want to have a close, personal relationship? How much do I want them to know about me regarding my innermost thoughts, feelings, and actions? You also have to ask yourself, how interested am I in learning the innermost thoughts, feelings, and actions of those with whom I desire to have a close relationship? As you read on, you will discover the importance of revealing the "real you" to other people.

> *If I tell you who I am, you may not like who I am, and it's all that I have.*
> —JOHN POWELL

The revealing of the inner-self is called self-disclosure. This means talking to another person about your innermost thoughts and feelings, your aspirations and dreams, your fears and doubts. It is talking about things of which you are ashamed and proud. Self-disclosure is a crucial part of relationship building. Dr. Sidney Marshall Jourard, a Canadian psychologist from the 1960-70's, is also known for his "Self-Disclosure Theory" of humanistic therapy. The process was originally defined as telling others about yourself. Since then, an extensive amount of information about disclosure has been produced. Decision making behind the act of disclosing private information is an

How do we learn to form close relationships?

© Ann Haritonenko/Shutterstock.com

extremely complicated process, especially when we are considering close personal relationships and family interactions. According to Reiss (2006), sexual self-disclosure is likely to bring about greater bonding between intimates. We know that, although intimacy often increases the possibility of revealing information, there are times when disclosure is counterproductive for the relationship or family.

Why study self-disclosure? The evolution of a relationship, getting acquainted, becoming friends, and developing intimacy, is based on how much you are willing to disclose about yourself and how much the other person is willing to disclose about themselves to you. The more you know about another person and the more he or she knows about you, the more effective and efficient the relationship will be. People who share their ideas, interests, experiences, expectations, and feelings with others will generally have more friends and develop long lasting relationships easier than those who do not (Lynch & Daniels,2000; Delerga et al., 1993). It can be hard when a lack of self-disclosure makes people suspicious and uncomfortable around us. In turn, they will not talk about themselves, and finding those common interests on which to base a relationship will become difficult

> *The unexamined life is not worth living.*
> —SOCRATES

Is self-disclosure important in a relationship? Good self-disclosure skills are fundamental to relationships for many reasons. These reasons include the following:

- **Defining Yourself.** Disclosing personal information lets you be known to others. If you do not define yourself, misunderstandings are more likely to occur. Others may perceive you based on their own interpretation rather than on information you give them.
- **Knowing Yourself.** As you disclose information about yourself, you can get deeper insight and understanding about the kind of person you are. You also give others the opportunity to give you feedback.
- **Getting Acquainted.** Talking about yourself and letting other people talk about themselves gives each of you the opportunity to understand and know the other as an individual. Each is given the opportunity to understand and trust the other. **Reciprocity** (a positive response from the person with whom one is sharing information) often happens. Then the other person who received the disclosure self-discloses in turn.
- **Developing Intimacy.** As you begin to share and receive, a deeper feeling of trust and understanding will evolve and a mutual feeling of closeness will develop.
- **Being Responsible.** Behaving responsibly with that knowledge and not betraying your friend's confidence is another key element in self-disclosure. If you disclose information about a friend without their permission you may lose that friend

> *Only in the part of us that we share, can we understand each other.*
> —ANONYMOUS

Before we can engage in self-disclosure, there must be an atmosphere of goodwill and trust. An individual is not likely to engage in much self-disclosure if the situation involves too much personal threat, or even a threat to anyone with whom he or she is closely associated. According to Wilson (2008) the notion that privacy is "right" has probably been lost on Millennials. Some feel that many people today do not have as much privacy because of social media disclosing information about them. Public self/

FOCUS ON DIVERSITY

RESPECTING DIVERSITY IN RELATIONSHIPS

Researchers often study communication behaviors of various cultures and have noted that self-disclosure tends to be high in mainstream North American society. People from various cultures, including ones within the United States, have learned different communication styles. What Westerners consider openness and healthy self-disclosure may feel offensively intrusive to people from some Asian societies. The dramatic, assertive speaking style of many African Americans can be misinterpreted as abrasive within a Western Caucasian perspective. The best way to understand what another's behavior means is to ask. This conveys the relational message that they matter to you, and it allows you to gain insight into the interesting diversity among us. For Americans, Japanese, and Koreans, self-disclosure was directly associated with online relationship development. However, the relationship between self-disclosure and trust was positive only for Americans (Yum & Hara, 2005). Americans' online relationships might be too open and trusting for other cultures.

> *If I expose my nakedness as a person to you, do not make me feel shamed.*
> —JOHN POWELL

> *If civilization is to survive, we must cultivate the science of human relationships—the ability of all peoples, of all kinds, to live together, in the same world at peace.*
> —FRANKLIN D. ROOSEVELT

private self is the term used for this phenomena. So be careful of disclosing too much on social media. Sociologist Dr. Brene Brown believes that we all need to define our boundaries. Boundaries are not fake walls or divisions but *respect for yourself and your friends* (Brown, 2010).

DO YOU NEED TO DISCLOSE?

Self-disclosure usually involves the sharing of private information, and it is generally of such a nature that it is not something you would normally disclose to everyone who might inquire about it. Therefore, you are not expected to bare the innermost secrets of your soul to casual acquaintances—you can save that information for the significant others in your life. Self-disclosure is a rewarding experience, comparable to those of food and sex (Tamir & Mitchell, 2012). People enjoy self-disclosure if they know other people are listening; talking is a means of catharsis toward good feelings. **Catharsis** is a release of emotional tension that can be achieved through sharing and self-disclosure with others. Self-disclosure promotes attraction. People feel a sense of closeness to others who reveal their vulnerabilities, innermost thoughts, and facts about themselves. The sense of closeness increases if the disclosures are emotional rather than factual. However, if you are to communicate effectively with others, some degree of self-disclosure is required.

It is extremely important to ask ourselves some important questions before disclosing (Punches, 2010):

- Can I trust this person with this information?
- How could this information be used against me? Misconstrued?

- Is this the right time and place to disclose?
- Am I sharing things about myself incrementally and slowly, or too much, too soon?
- How has the person received private information in the past?
- What could happen if I share too much too fast?

GENDER AND YOU

WOMEN DISCLOSE MORE THAN MEN

Several studies have looked at how men and women disclose online. Overall, they have found that women disclose online more than men (Kleman, 2007). When looking at the content of messages, Li (2006) found that computer-mediated communication messages sent by males were more confrontational and autonomous, while female messages were supportive and rapport-building (Sheldon, 2013). Women tend to have more friends and closer relationships than men. These friendships tend to provide them with more social support. Most research shows that women tend to be more openly self-disclosing than males, although the disparity seems smaller than originally believed. Because women tend to value "personal talk" more than men, they tend to share more personal information and feelings with their female friends (Kilmartin, 2010). Previous studies have shown that women disclose to their close friends more than men. Results of testing gender differences in self-disclosure suggest that women disclose to their exclusive face-to-face and exclusive Facebook friends more than men, but men have more intimate discussions with their recently added Facebook friends than women do (Sheldon, 2013).

Males tend to disclose more to strangers than females do, and are more willing to disclose casual things about themselves, such as their work, accomplishments, attitudes, and opinions. Males are also less intimate and less personal than females. Males are expected not to disclose; it's not "manly." In peer/friendship relationships that emphasize competition and challenge, males often avoid revealing weaknesses, and at times associate self-disclosure with loss of control and vulnerability. Research shows that men often become closer by doing things together or doing things for each other, rather than just talking with each other. (Wood, 2010). Byers and Demmons (2010) found that women disclose more than men do, both sexually and non-sexually. However, sexuality is a highly personal and private topic for self-disclosure. Women may be less comfortable than men are in discussing sex, especially their own sexual satisfaction, because the double standard of sex roles inhibits them from admitting to being knowledgeable about sex (Huong, 2010).

What should you reveal to another person? A few examples might be:

- Likes and dislikes
- Fears and anxieties
- Attitudes and opinions
- Tastes and interests
- Ideas about money

- Work perceptions
- Personality choices
- Feelings and reactions about events that have just taken place
- Perceptions of self and others

There are some disadvantages to self-disclosure as well, particularly if there is too much of it. Talking too much about ourselves early in a relationship may not facilitate the development of friendship. People might view your high self-disclosure as an indication that you are too immature, insecure, or phony, or even that you tell everyone such things. Other people like to think that they are special to you (O'Connel & O'Connel, 2005).

What is the greatest risk of self-disclosure? Personal disclosures that are too **general** reduce the sense of openness, thus reducing the feeling of closeness. Disclosures that are too **intimate** often highlight character and personality flaws, thus decreasing likeability. People who make intimate disclosures too early in relationships are often perceived as insecure, which further decreases likeability (Shafer, 2015). Self-disclosure involves taking risks. *The greatest risk is one of rejection—not being liked or accepted.* This may cause us to hide behind a mask—a *facade*—and try to be something we know we are not. In this state, effective communication cannot occur and the growth and maintenance of those deep, special, and meaningful relationships with friends and spouses cannot occur. Risk nothing, gain nothing. You have a choice—to withdraw from honest encounters, to hide your feelings, to falsify your intentions—or to be transparent, open, and real through self-disclosure.

What are the advantages of self-disclosure? Self-disclosure has the potential to improve and expand interpersonal relationships, but it serves other functions as well. One advantage is that *self-disclosure improves relationships.* We prefer to be with people who are willing to disclose to us and we are more willing to be open with them. Self-disclosure is a reciprocal process. Disclosure leads to trust and trust leads to more disclosure, and, thus, the relationship will grow and develop into a mature and long-lasting, loving interaction. There is a strong positive correlation between self-disclosure and marital satisfaction. Research has shown that the more a couple is willing to disclose about themselves, the greater the marital satisfaction and the greater the chance the marriage will last over a longer period of time (Santrock, 2006).

Self-disclosure promotes mental health. The second advantage is that *self-disclosure promotes mental health.* Withholding important information can create stress and thus lead to less-effective functioning and even possible physical problems (Jourard, 1976, Hyman, I. Self 2008). We all need a release, and for many of us "talking-out" our feelings, problems, and thoughts will relieve us of the stresses and anxieties that are interfering with our everyday functioning. This release of emotional tension through talking is known as a ***catharsis***. As many of you have discovered, you feel relieved after sharing your problems with another person. This is the reason counseling and therapy are so effective for many individuals. Also having a wellness plan helps your mental health.

Self-disclosure online. With over 1 billion users and the continued growth in its popularity, Facebook is becoming another avenue for initiating and maintaining interpersonal relationships. A number of studies have found that relationship maintenance and social interaction (Sheldon, 2008; Smock, Ellison, Lampe, & Wohn 2011) are the primary motivations for using Facebook. Social network users tend to rely more on self-disclosures to create a sense of closeness because they do not receive verbal and nonverbal cues that would be otherwise exchanged in face-to-face communications. The veracity of information exchanged online is suspect, thus forcing online daters to spend more time verifying information from their online counterpart. Once veracity has been established, the lack of a physical presence increases the probability of more intimate disclosures online leading to the illusion of a close relationship and, likewise, increases the intensity of the disappointment when a relationship goes wrong (Shafer, 2015). Think about it- Are these relationships illusionary in closeness or are they just too fast? Emoji's are used by millennials and often adults aren't sure how to use them. This has caused some funny disclosures from adults to millennials. ;)

Self-validation. Another advantage of self-disclosure is that periodically we need **self-validation**. If we disclose information such as "I think I may have made a mistake . . ."—with the hopes of obtaining the listener's agreement, you are seeking validation on your behavior—confirmation of a belief you hold about yourself. On a deeper level, this sort of self-validating disclosure seeks confirmation of important parts of your self-concept (Adler & Proctor, 2014).

EIGHT QUICK TIPS FOR INTERPERSONAL COMMUNICATION AND RELATIONSHIP BUILDING (ANNE LOEHR 2016)

When approaching any interaction with another person, try these eight things:

1. Assume the best intentions of the other person. I like the phrase "start new" trust that they have your best interests...
2. Understand the other person's perspective in the situation.
3. Truly listen and ask questions to learn more.
4. Share your perspective in the situation.
5. Find the commonalities.
6. Leverage those commonalities for the common good.
7. Keep communication open as you move forward (to minimize frustration and to create trust).
8. Speak up if things go awry.

The Johari Window

The Johari Window (1969), is a classic tool developed by and named after psychologists Joseph Luft and Harry Ingram, and can be looked upon as a communication window through which you become more aware of yourself and your potential as a communicator, as you give and receive information about yourself and others. It is currently used as an easy tool for trainers to discuss who you think you are. In order for a relationship to develop into a quality relationship, there needs to be trust and mutual sharing of information and feelings, also known as **openness**. An **open communicator** is one who is willing to seek feedback from others and to offer information and personal feelings to others. Open communication involves both giving and receiving. According to the Window, a person's communication behavior can be viewed by looking at the size of each of the four windowpanes—Open Area, Hidden Area, Blind Area, and Unknown Area.

Figure 1.1 THE JOHARI WINDOW

	Known to Self	Unknown to Self
Known to Others	Open	Blind
Unknown to Others	Hidden	Unknown

Adapted from Joseph Luft, *Of Human Interaction*, by permission of Mayfield Publishing Co., Copyright 1969 by the National Press.

See Figure 1.1 for the four areas in the Johari Window:

1. The **Open Area**, which represents information you know about yourself that is also known to others.
2. The **Hidden Area**, which represents all that you know about yourself that is private and not known to others. Information in the Hidden area becomes public primarily through self-disclosure.
3. The **Blind Area**, which represents information about yourself that others can see, but you do not. An example would be a mannerism in speech or gesture of which you are unaware but that is quite obvious to others, such as constantly saying "you know" or constantly playing with your keys.
4. The **Unknown Area**, which represents information that is unknown to both you and others. Yes, this is quite possible. Remember, we are all constantly discovering new things about ourselves: an unrecognized talent, strength, or weakness can develop at any given point in time.

Your Johari Window will look quite different based on the nature of a relationship. For example, your relationship with your very best friend or your significant other will probably have a very large Open area (see Figure 1.2). However, someone you have just recently met will have a very small Open area (see Figure 1.3). As the relationship evolves and you become closer to that person, the Open area will grow, as you share more about yourself. Likewise, as you listen to comments and feedback from this person, the size of your Blind area will decrease.

Figure 1.2 THE JOHARI WINDOW IN A CLOSE RELATIONSHIP

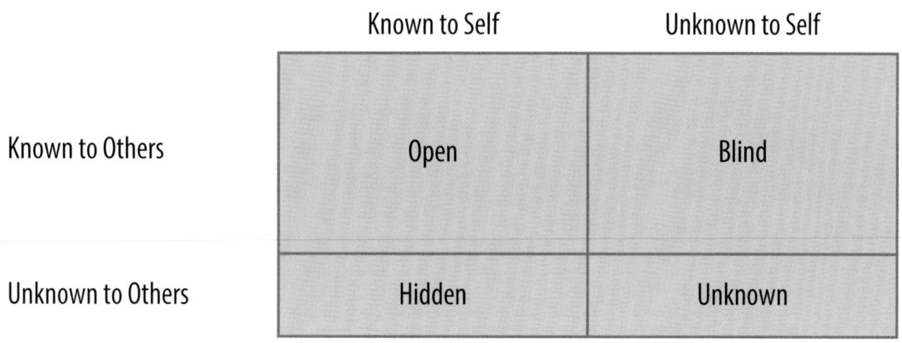

	Known to Self	Unknown to Self
Known to Others	Open	Blind
Unknown to Others	Hidden	Unknown

Adapted from Joseph Luft, *Of Human Interaction*, by permission of Mayfield Publishing Co., Copyright 1969 by the National Press.

Figure 1.3 THE JOHARI WINDOW EARLY IN A RELATIONSHIP

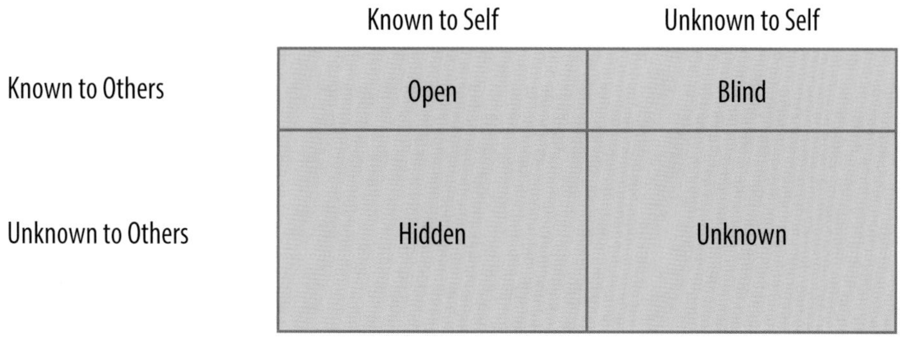

	Known to Self	Unknown to Self
Known to Others	Open	Blind
Unknown to Others	Hidden	Unknown

Adapted from Joseph Luft, *Of Human Interaction*, by permission of Mayfield Publishing Co., Copyright 1969 by the National Press.

The Johari Window *is a simple and useful tool for understanding yourself and others* in a variety of contexts:

- self-awareness
- personal development
- improving communications
- interpersonal relationships
- group dynamics
- team development; and
- intergroup relationships.

It is one of the few tools out there that has an emphasis on "soft skills" such as behavior, empathy, and cooperation; inter-group development; and interpersonal development. It's a great model to use because of its simplicity and also because it can be applied in a variety of situations and environments. Involve other people and ask for feedback about yourself. Be prepared to seriously consider the feedback. That doesn't mean that you have to do everything that's suggested, but you should at least listen and think about it. Then give the person who provided the feedback some acknowledgement or thanks for making the effort. Depending on how confident you are you might prefer to do this as either a group exercise or on a one-to-one basis. Remember that giving effective feedback is a skill and some people may be better at it than others. When receiving feedback, be respectful, listen, and reflect on what has been said. It may be that, upon receiving feedback, you may want to explore the issue further, and that can lead to discovery about yourself.

The Johari window as a tool does have its drawbacks:

- Some things are perhaps better not communicated with others.
- People may pass on the information they received further than you desire or use it in a negative way.
- Some people or cultures have a very open and accepting approach to feedback and some do not. People can take personal feedback offensively, so it's important when facilitating to exercise caution and start gradually.

Johari is a classic model, and, as with other powerful ideas, simply helping people to understand is the most effective way to optimize the value to people. When people really understand it in their own terms, it empowers them to use the thinking in their own way, and to incorporate the underlying principles into their future thinking and behavior.

Now think about it.

There are various ways you can use a Johari Window to evaluate your relationships and increase your self-knowledge. Think about your interactions with family, friends, people at work, school, etc. Generally, your strongest and closest relationships have a very large Open area because being open with the other person and listening to feedback build trust. You will have an opportunity to draw several Johari Windows at the end of this chapter.

Now, think about a particular person with whom you interact: Is it possible that you keep many parts of yourself hidden from this person?

Why are you doing this, and is it healthy for the relationship?

How open are you with people at work, school, acquaintances, friends, your nearest neighbors, and even family members?

In order to reduce the size of the Blind area and the Unknown area in some of your relationships, are there any individuals you may need to ask and be open to receive some honest feedback?

Are there any modifications you need to make in any of your relationships to increase your overall effectiveness?

Now that we understand the importance of self-disclosure in the development of a relationship, we need to understand why relationships are so important. We are all social beings and seek social relationships. We all have a need for other people. Relationships satisfy needs. We are motivated not only to seek the company of others, but to form close and lasting relationships. Many people have difficulty forming relationships and do not seem to have any friends. What happens to these people?

Your greatness is measured by your kindness; your education and intellect by your modesty: your ignorance is betrayed by your suspicions and prejudice and your real caliber is measured by the consideration and tolerance you have for others.
—WM J.H. BOETCKER

Relationship Building

According to Daniel and Lynch (2000) there are many kinds of relationships, and a given kind may fit a given person or couple at one stage of development but not at another. Driven by our personal history, we choose partners who help us meet our present needs, fulfill our expectations, and if we're lucky, work through our issues and grow in the directions in which we need to grow. For a person or couple, recognizing these can open doors to a broader spectrum of ways of being with ourselves and each other.

Five Dominant Patterns of Relationships

Daniel and Lynch found that there are **Five Dominant Patterns of Relationships**. Sharpening and deepening our awareness of we're doing, and how we're doing it, can help us change our behavior in ways that make a relationship more nourishing and supportive, and less toxic and painful. Or it can help us see what we're not going to find in this one. In either case, a clearer perception our present existential reality can help us move toward doing a better job of meeting our own (and often the other person's) needs.

1. **Survival Relationships.** These exist when partners feel like they can't make it on their own. In this type of situation, the choice of a partner tends to be undiscriminating, made out of emotional starvation—almost anyone available will do. This involves relating at its most basic: "Without you I am nothing; with you I am something." Often partners think in terms of what the other person wants them to want, and are out of touch with what they themselves want. They may have little tolerance for independence and aloneness, and "go everywhere together and do everything together."

2. **Validation Relationships**. A person may seek another's validation of his or her physical attractiveness, intellect, social status, sexuality, wealth, or some other attribute. Many teenagers and young adults who are looking for a sense of

identity form relationships based on physical or sexual validation. If no deeper basis for connecting materializes and the partners drift apart, there is a strong chance that the needs for validation have been met and the partners have begun seeking something different. At that point, the relationship has done its work. The partners have learned to validate in themselves the qualities they were insecure about and they are ready to connect along other dimensions.

3. **Scripted Relationships.** This common pattern often begins when the partners both are just out of high school or college. They seem to be "the perfect pair," fitting almost all the external criteria of what an appropriate mate should be like. The marriage involves living out their traditional sex role expectations for the roles they learned they were supposed to play. He has the "right" kind of job and she is the "right" kind of wife and they have the "right" kind of house or apartment or condo in the "right" place. Partners in these relationships need to look at all the things they›ve wanted to do in life but haven't, because these things didn't fit their stereotypes about themselves and their expectations about their partners. They need to learn to communicate at an emotional level, to disclose their feelings and listen to those of their partner. They may need to learn to work less and play more.

4. **Acceptance Relationships**. This is what many of us thought we were getting into when we entered a relationship, including many people in the three categories above. In an acceptance relationship we trust, support, and enjoy each other. And within broad limits, we are ourselves.

5. **Individuation-Assertion Relationships.** These relationships are based on the assertion of each person's wants and needs, and on respect for the other person's process of personal growth. Often they are focused on partners' struggles with what is missing or lacking in terms of self-discovery, becoming whole, and developing their potentialities. They require each person's acknowledgment and appreciation of their differences.

For some couples in other forms of relationships, it's easier to move into an acceptance relationship, while for others it's easier to move into an individuation/assertion relationship. In a scripted relationship where partners have very different interests but genuinely care for each other, loosening the role expectations and creating space for each person to follow his or her own pursuits is one way to step out of chronic power struggles.

Living Alone. The experience of living alone deserves a few words in the context of relationships. The reasons people live alone include:

- First, some processes are "loner" processes, such as grieving, or exploring oneself in a variety of contexts with a variety of people.
- Second, people may keep their distance from others because of fears and insecurities. Some kind of counseling or therapy is often appropriate here.
- Third, they may keep their distance because of a desire to learn to stand alone and be independent, or to work through issues which caused trouble in a past relationship before moving into a new one.
- Fourth, a person may be available, but face a supply-and-demand inequality of acceptable partners. In this case, a network of supportive friends can be invaluable.

- Finally, someone may be fulfilled enough on his or her own and feel no strong need for a partner. Some highly creative artists fall into this category. A network of supportive friends can be valuable.

FOCUS ON DIVERSITY

PUT YOURSELF IN SOMEONE'S SHOES: A DIVERSITY THOUGHT

My mother would always remind me, "Put yourself in the other person's shoes. Don't think you know how they feel and what they have to go through daily." We have added to this text a number of concepts and ideas that you may not believe in or agree with. They include sensitive ethnic, cultural, and gender issues. It is so important to consider different sides of the issue in a contemplative, analytical way. Our world needs more people to feel open to others and meet new people who are not like them. This is the only way we will end the racial and gender turmoil, such as violence against women or violence against police or anything else that becomes fodder for the news media. Unless we can educate ourselves about others, be aware of information about sociocultural issues from more than one perspective, develop relationships, and "walk in another's shoes" we will not be truly educated.

Loneliness

Have you ever felt lonely? What causes loneliness? Answer the questions on the following page before you continue to read this section.

The lack of relationships can create *loneliness*.

Loneliness occurs when a person has fewer interpersonal relationships than desired or when the relationships are not as satisfying as desired. Loneliness is one of the most serious problems in our society today, "Loneliness isn't a feeling to be ashamed of, but simply a way for your body to tell you that you need more connections just like hunger means you need food," says Shasta Nelson, founder of Girlfriend Circles.com, a women's friendship matching site, and author of *Frientimacy: How to Deepen Friendships for Lifelong Health and Happiness (2016)*. Research shows that when a person reports feeling lonely, their close family and friends are 52 percent more likely to say they're lonely too, and others can "catch" loneliness up to three degrees of separation (i.e., your friend's friend's friend), according to a study in the *Journal of Personality and Social Psychology.*

Loneliness is **not** something that happens only when we are physically alone. It can also happen when we are with people. Online friends, followers, or "likers" don't necessarily add up to much when you crave fulfilling interaction, and satisfying, long-term relationships are not a mystery to be left up to chance (or technology). The good news is that, according to relationship coach Kira Asatryan, loneliness has a reliable antidote: the feeling of closeness. We can and should cultivate closeness in our relationships using the steps outlined in this book: knowing, caring, and mastering closeness.

Check this out   WHAT DO YOU KNOW ABOUT LONELINESS?

TRUE OR FALSE?

_____ Loneliness is more predominant during adolescence.
_____ Loneliness varies with the time of day and day of the week.
_____ Loneliness may be a sign of personal problems.
_____ Loneliness may be the cause of depression, suicide, and other mental disorders.
_____ The elderly are less lonely than most groups of individuals.
_____ Loneliness is not the same as aloneness.
_____ Most people assume other people have more friends than they do.

Based on research and literature all of the above statements are mostly true and we will address them in the following information.

The truth is that between two-thirds and three-fourths of Americans believe there is more loneliness in today's society than there used to be, report dissatisfaction in their current friendships, and feel they have fewer meaningful relationships than they did five years ago. Another statistic comes from a study, published in the *American Sociological Review,* that looked at two decades of social isolation in the United States. To the question of how many confidants one has, in 1994 the common answer was two to three confidants; as of 2004 the answer was closer to zero. (Nelson, 2016) Much more than half of the world's populations are chronically depressed or lonely, and everyone will experience some type of depression at some point in their lives. But the good news is you don't have to go it alone (Creole 2016).

You can learn strategies to alleviate the symptoms of depression and loneliness. Talk to your medical doctor about these feelings and they can decide if you need a counselor, a support group, or maybe medication. With so many people in the world who are depressed and taking antidepressants there is no shame. Another treatment for both loneliness and depression is pet therapy, or animal-assisted therapy, as it is more formally known. Studies and surveys, as well as anecdotal evidence provided by volunteer and community organizations, indicate that the presence of animal companions such as dogs, cats, rabbits, and guinea pigs can ease feelings of depression and loneliness among some sufferers. Beyond the companionship the animal itself provides there may also be increased opportunities for socializing with other pet owners. Many university classes will allow therapy pets in the classroom to give support and ease anxiety for their owners.

Maybe the biggest problem with loneliness is that we walk around thinking we are the only ones suffering from it.
—JEANNE MARIE LASKAS

Can people be lonely in the presence of others? The answer is a resounding **yes**, and the feeling can be dreadful. Mara commented, "You can be in the center of a crowd and be dreadfully lonely." Some people can feel lonely even when surrounded by others. Debbi, whose husband had left her, said, "I have periods of loneliness now, but it's nothing compared to how lonely I felt when my husband was sitting in the same room with me." Being married offers no protection from the dangers of loneliness: Studies indicate that roughly 20% of the general population suffers from chronic loneliness at any given time, and in one recent study of older adults, 62.5% of people who reported being lonely were married and living with their partner. In addition to the emotional anguish loneliness creates, it also has devastating effects on our mental and physical health. Loneliness depresses our immune system functioning, increases inflammatory responses that put us at greater risk for cardiovascular disease, and can literally shorten our longevity. On the mental health front, loneliness puts us at risk for depression and anxiety and causes us to distort our perceptions such that we view ourselves, our lives, and our relationships more negatively—which in turn, influences our behavior in damaging ways (Winch, 2013).

Being lonely is not the same as being alone. Some people prefer solitude and are content with fewer social interactions. Many of us have a need to be alone at times in order to maintain our mental health. Loneliness is a highly subjective and personal feeling. Guy Winch in his article "Together But Lonely" (sometimes referred to as Living Together Lonely LTL) offers three strategies to overcome loneliness. The first is to take the initiative and ask your partner about something they care about and really listen. The second is to try to make shared memories. You might try certain activities that require little effort, like a walk in the neighborhood. And lastly try to take their perspective. Often couples that have been together a while assume they know what the other is thinking (Winch, 2013).

Who is lonelier? Loneliness is found in all groups. Loneliness is most prevalent among teenagers, unmarried young adults, the divorced, and the widowed. Actually, traditional college students who are among thousands of peers who suffer more loneliness than any other group (Wiseman et al., 2006). Though we may know a lot of people, that doesn't mean we feel we have meaningful connections. But if we don't acknowledge our need—and admit that we lack meaningful connections, that we feel disconnected—we limit our chances of getting our needs met. In other words, if we don't identify the problem, we can't do anything about it. To admit we wish for more meaningful friendships is the first step to inviting us to then ask the all-important question, "What could I do to develop more fulfilling relationships in my life?" (Nelson, 2016). Everyone needs a confidant. A confidant is a person with whom one can share problems and worries and who gives one feelings of being understood and accepted (Wills & Ainette, 2012).

Preventing and reducing loneliness is crucial to well-being and good health. Social relationships protect people against loneliness. Friendship qualities like intimacy and frequency of contact may vary throughout a person's lifespan (Nicolaisen & Thorsen, 2016).

Loneliness makes a person vulnerable to many different situations. This may include more depression, use of drugs as an escape, and higher blood pressure. There is even some evidence that points to loneliness as being associated with higher risks for heart disease, lessened longevity, and increased risk for recurrent illness (Hafen et al., 2005).

Weiss and Schneider also found that new connections are impacting not only society as a whole, but more specifically communication in relationships and across generations (2014).

Attract what you expect. Reflect what you desire... Become what you respect..and Mirror what you admire.

Zhou, Sedikides, Wildschut, and Gao (2008) found they can counteract loneliness with nostalgia by increasing perceived social support similar to what you had in your early years. Think about how your music from when you were young makes you feel or play music for your parents or grandparents from their high school or college years and see if it lifts their spirits. Renowned scientists Christakis and Fowler present compelling evidence for our profound influence on one another's tastes, health, wealth, happiness, beliefs, and overcoming loneliness, as they explain how social networks form and how they operate (2009).

What Should a Relationship Provide?

Once a friendship is established through **self-disclosure and reciprocity**, the glue that binds is **intimacy**. According to Beverly Fehr's research, people in successful same-sex friendships seem to possess a well-developed, intuitive understanding of the give and take of intimacy (1999). "Those who know what to say in response to another person's self-disclosure are more likely to develop satisfying friendships," Fehr says (1999). Hefty helpings of emotional expressiveness and unconditional support are ingredients here, followed by acceptance, loyalty, and trust. Our friends are there for us through thick and thin, but rarely cross the line: A friend with too many opinions about our wardrobe, our partner, or our taste in movies and art may not be a friend for long (Karbo, 2016). Once a friendship is established through self-disclosure and reciprocity, the glue that binds is intimacy. understanding of the give and take of intimacy.

Relationships with others lie at the very core of human existence.
—ELLEN BER-SCHEID AND LETTIA PEPLAU

Why do our society and many other cultures put so much emphasis on marriage? Why are there clubs for single people, escort services, singles bars, dating services, and social networking websites, people advertising for partners in local newspapers, and using 1-900 telephone services to meet new people? Why—because people are lonely. We have a strong need for relationships. The following needs must be satisfied in order to have a fulfilling life and overcome feelings of loneliness.

Emotional attachments. We all need to know that no matter what the situation is or whatever we do, good or bad (for better or worse, in sickness or in health), that there will be someone around to take care of us or help us out. As long as we know this, we feel comfortable and secure. A child who knows that mother or father is available whenever he or she needs one of them will feel secure enough to explore the world around them. They will be willing to take some chances and risks in life. A child who is insecure and not sure if the parents will be available when needed will be clinging and unsure of other people. How would you feel if you were told by your parents, "If you ever get in trouble with the law," or "If I ever hear about you taking drugs," or "If you ever get someone pregnant or get pregnant, don't step a foot back in this house?" Most people who have been told this when they were young feel very insecure and lonely since they are not sure anyone will be there in a time of need.

Where do we get emotional attachments? Most people will receive their emotional attachments from their parents, and pets, especially during their early years of development. And if you think about it, many individuals continue to rely on their parents for this support for most of their lives. This is why you will hear stories about married couples who, when they are having marital problems, will go back to their parents' home, because parents still provide that individual with the feeling of security. As we tend to mature and start to "cut the apron strings," becoming more independent, we begin to find this emotional support from others—our best friend, boyfriend, girlfriend, spouse, pastor, etc. For some people, their dog or cat will provide them with this feeling of security.

People and animals have a long history of living together and bonding. Perhaps the oldest evidence of this special relationship was discovered a few years ago in Israel—a 12,000-year-old human skeleton buried with its hand resting on the skeleton of a 6-month-old wolf pup. "The bond between animals and humans is part of our evolution, and it's very powerful," says Dr. Ann Berger, a physician and researcher at the NIH Clinical Center in Bethesda, Maryland. Today animal companions are more popular than ever. The pet population nationwide has been growing dramatically for nearly a half century, from about 40 million pet cats and dogs in 1967 to more than 160 million in 2006. About two-thirds of U.S. households now own at least one pet. (NIH, 2016)

Inanimate objects can also be a source of security. Items such as teddy bears, dolls, or imaginary companions are examples. Other sources could be certain belief systems, religious beliefs, or a philosophy of life and even confidence within one's self may satisfy the need for emotional attachments for some people. A young child's blanket or teddy bear is a source of security for some. As you know, if you take the blanket or bear away from some children even for a short time just to be washed, the child will go into a rage and become very insecure and lonely.

Whosoever is delighted in solitude is either a wild beast or a god.
—FRANCIS BACON

What happens to a person who has been relying solely on their spouse for the satisfaction of this need, especially when the spouse announces that the relationship is over? This person will become insecure, lonely, and vulnerable. A newly divorced or separated individual who has lost his or her emotional support is very open and vulnerable to another person or belief system that tends to show support for the individual. This is why many individuals will possibly end up in a negative relationship, some type of cult or so-called religion, or gang that purports to provide emotional support.

Social ties. *Social ties* provide us with the feeling of belonging—a feeling that we are part of a group and have an identity. During early childhood this feeling of belonging and developing an identity is, for most children, provided by their parents. This is expressed with statements like, "I'm a member of the Smith family or Adams family or Sanchez family." Later in childhood, the peer group becomes more important to them than the family, especially during adolescence. Special groups, clubs, teams, and religious organizations such as Girl Scouts, Boy Scouts, Bluebirds, Indian Guides, Little League, church youth groups, pep clubs, gangs, and fraternal organizations provide many young people with a feeling of identity. Have you ever observed a child walking down the street in their scout uniform or team uniform? They really think they are "special." The uniform makes them feel like they are part of a group and they have an identity. We all need an identity.

How does the person feel who is not able to join a club or be a member of a team? This person feels "left out" and feels that there is something missing in their life. They will do whatever it takes to satisfy this need. The end result of not having this need satisfied is the same as for those whose emotional attachment needs are not satisfied. This person will feel lonely, depressed, and vulnerable.

Who provides you with a feeling of belonging?

How can we satisfy this need? *Social ties* may be satisfied through positive as well as negative means. Social ties may be satisfied through marriage—a legal bond that makes you feel like you belong to another person and have a recognized identity. A person's job or career may also give some people a feeling of identity or belonging. Ask a person the question, "Who are you?" and the response is generally, "I'm a student, a banker, a plumber, a salesperson, an attorney," etc. These titles give the individual an identity, and the organization the person works for gives the person a feeling of belonging.

© Phovoir/Shutterstock.com

During the high school and college years, a person's identity may be found in many different ways. Some students find their identity by being on an athletic team, by being an excellent student, playing in the band or orchestra, dating a cheerleader, being in a sorority or fraternity, or just working a job to pay the bills. If a student does not find his or her identity or feeling of belonging through "normal" or acceptable means, they will attempt to satisfy this need through other means, such as drugs, non-traditional clothing, a unique hairstyle, promiscuous behavior, gang activity, delinquent behavior, or some people delve into the world of the Internet or social media and can narrow their world.

Emotional support and social ties are not only important to young people, but they are vital to all of us and will continue to be important throughout our lives. We will be in a constant state of stress and anxiety if our emotional support and social ties change too much. Divorce, death of a loved one, changing jobs or being fired from a job, retirement, breaking up with a boyfriend or girlfriend, or a serious illness may be the cause of our needs changing. People with adequate social support are also less likely to suffer from depression, anxiety, and numerous physical problems. And, in a four-year study of 823 people, Dr. Robert Wilson (2007), senior neuropsychologist, Rush University Medical Center, reported that seniors who feel disconnected from other people are twice as likely to develop an Alzheimer's-like form of dementia as those who are not lonely.

> *You can make more friends in two months by being interested in other people than you can in two years trying to get others interested in you.*
> —ZIG ZIGLAR

The discussion of emotional support and social ties should demonstrate to all of us that we should not rely only on one person or one source for the satisfaction of our emotional and social needs. We all need to work at developing a good support system. Yet, is there anything we can do to enhance our personal, meaningful relationships?

MUTUAL REWARD THEORY (MRT)

The Mutual Reward Theory (MRT) states that a relationship between two people is enhanced when there is a satisfactory balance of rewards between them (O'Neil & Chapman, 2008). Actually, if any meaningful relationship is to remain healthy over a long period of time, the individuals involved must benefit from the relationship. The more equally the rewards balance out, the stronger and more permanent the relationship becomes. The relationship will quickly weaken if one individual suddenly realizes that he or she has been contributing significantly more than he or she has been receiving.

Now that we understand the need for relationships, many of us still find it difficult to get to know other people and develop good relationships. Why do we fear getting acquainted?

The Fear of Getting Acquainted—Shyness

> *Having enjoyed the friendship of many people in many places for many years—I have learned that, in the main, people are as we choose to find them.*
> —DORIS SCHARY

Meeting people and forming relationships should be fun, but for a lot of people it is a difficult process full of stress and anxiety. "It seems so easy for other people, but for me, it's one of the most difficult things I do in life." Because of the complexity of our society, we have made the process of getting acquainted and developing relationships an involved process. "How can I make meeting people and forming relationships more fun and less stressful? Why do I feel so uncomfortable meeting people?" You may want to answer the questions in the box on page 23.

Am I shy? How did you answer the questions? If your answer to any of the questions is that you feel uncomfortable, anxious, inhibited, and excessively cautious, then you showed signs of shyness. Do not feel bad—shyness is universal. You have lots of company. Nearly one of two Americans claims to be shy. What is more interesting, the incidence is rising, and the use of the computer and technology may be turning our society into a culture of shy people (Carducci & Zimbardo, 2016). It affects the young and old, men and women, celebrities and people like you and me. It is a very common problem. The consequences of shyness may be devastating. If you mistake having alone time for shyness, remember that everyone needs alone time but some need more of it.

How common is shyness? Researcher Dr. Bernardo Carducci (2000) in his popular book, *Shyness: A Bold New Approach*, makes it very clear that between 75 and 95 percent of people have felt shy at one point in their lives. In fact, Dr. Carducci has compiled the following statistics on the pervasiveness of shyness:

- About 80 percent of American college students report they have been shy at some point in their lives.
- Almost 50 percent of our population says that they're shy.
- About 89 percent of shy people claim that they've been shy all their lives.
- Of people who are not shy now, 75 percent have been shy at some point in the past.
- Only 11 percent of our population claims that they are not shy now and have never been shy in the past.
- About 21 percent of shy people feel shy daily or almost daily, while almost 60 percent of the people who say that they're shy feel shy at least once a week.
- About 78 percent of shy people believe that they can overcome shyness, while 3 percent say that they cannot.

Dr. Carducci also comments that the three most common shyness-provoking situations are: 1) being around strangers, 2) the presence of people in positions of authority by virtue of their role or knowledge, and 3) being with members of the opposite sex, either one-on-one or in a group (2000).

What is shyness? We're all a little shy at times when meeting other people. It's hardly surprising that shyness can often interfere with how we interact in social situations. For some people, however, shyness can lead to social anxiety and a crippling fear that results in deliberate isolation to avoid associating with others (Vitelli, 2013). **Shyness** refers to a tendency to withdraw from people, particularly unfamiliar people (Stein & Walker, 2009). Shyness involves *feelings, physical reactions,* and *thoughts* that create a state of anxiety, discomfort, and inhibition. Extremely shy individuals are typically low in self-esteem and largely preoccupied with what others think of them. Driven by a fear of rejection, shy people often engage in self-sabotage to prevent themselves from growing closer to others and avoid social situations when possible (Stein & Walker, 2009).

> A man who talks only of himself and thinks only of himself is hopelessly uneducated.
> —MURRAY BUTLER

> It's a shame when the things that are on your mind and in your heart never reach your lips.
> —ANONYMOUS

What are the consequences of shyness? Often starting in early childhood, shy children are at greater risk of being bullied and rejected by their peers. Those friendships they do succeed in making are often of lower quality than the friendships made by children who are less shy. Shy children are more likely to internalize problems such as depression, anxiety, and loneliness. There are also gender differences with shy boys being more likely to have socio-emotional difficulties than shy girls. This is probably due to shyness being less socially acceptable for boys than for girls since boys are expected to be more dominant and self-confident (Vitelli, 2013). For some people shyness may become a "mental handicap" that is as crippling as the most severe of physical handicaps. Its consequences can be devastating. What are the consequences of shyness? (Zimbardo, 1990; Carducci & Zimbardo, 2015; Duffy, 2007/2008).

1. *Shy people become preoccupied with themselves and thus become self-conscious. Because of this, they are not aware of other people's feelings and needs.*
2.. *Shyness makes it difficult for us to become acquainted with new people and thus make new friends.*

Something to Think About

HOW DO YOU FEEL IN THE FOLLOWING SITUATIONS?

- Meeting people for the first time.
- Asking someone for a date.
- Giving a talk in front of a group of people.
- Going to a party or going to a dance or nightclub.
- Asking someone for help—for example, your boss or professor.
- Being interviewed or participating in a discussion group.
- Situations requiring assertiveness—for example, asking for your money back.
- Showing your body in a nonsexual context.

3. *Shyness keeps us from experiencing new situations.* This could affect our career prospects or higher education. Shy young adult are also less likely to date, get married later (if at all), and are less likely to enter into stable relationships according to Vitelli (2013). Through different relationships, most young adults learn what they are looking for in a permanent partner and also become more experienced in handling a stable relationship. For shy people who do not gain these experiences, their ability to form permanent intimate relationships later in life may be impaired (Vitelli, 2013).
4. *Shyness prevents people from standing up for their own rights and as individuals, keeps them from expressing their own feelings and beliefs.*
5. *Shy people tend not to demonstrate their personal strengths and capabilities. As a result, they prevent others from making positive evaluations.* If you have two em-

Mutual confidence is the foundation of all satisfactory human relationships.
—NAPOLEAN HILL

ployees, equal in all abilities except that one is shy and the other is not shy, which of the two would you promote? In most situations the non-shy person would be promoted because we are more aware of his or her potential than that of the shy person.

6. *Some people are not really shy—they are presenting respect from their culture or they might need time to know you before they interact.*

What is the difference between a shy and non-shy person? It may come as a surprise to many of you that the major difference between the two individuals is a matter of *self-evaluation.* How do you compare yourself to others? Do you see yourself as capable, intelligent, or as attractive as the person next to you? If the answer is no, then would you interact with them? Or, if you did have to interact with them, how would you feel? Would you feel inferior or inadequate? Many people would feel this way. Why? As we stated earlier, shyness is a matter of self-evaluation—how you compare yourself with others. Actually this should tell you how ridiculous shyness really is, since we are all capable human beings. Just because the other person is a doctor, lawyer, teacher, or engineer does not mean that person is superior to you. The other person may have more formal education than you or more money than you, but you may have more common sense, or real-life education. You are just as good as the other person.

> *Shyness is a series of choices that gradually cement into a lifestyle.*
> —BERNARDO CARDUCCI

Technology and shyness. Technology is continually redefining how we communicate. We are not engaging in as many face-to-face interactions on a daily basis. How often do you call a friend or colleague when you know they are not in so you can leave a message on their machine? How often do you see a bank teller or gas station attendant? Voice mail, faxes, banking online, text messaging, and e-mail give us an illusion of being "in touch," but what is to touch but the keyboard?

Today's teens and college students are what researchers call "digital natives," or the "iGeneration," a generation constantly connected to the Internet and Facebook, texting and instant messaging. Certainly, there are positive and negative effects of social networks. However, research by Larry Rosen (2011), a social media researcher at California State University, indicates that the online social networking experience can give shy kids an easier experience building relationships, by speaking through a keyboard instead of in person. The electronic age was supposed to give us more time, but ironically it has stolen it from us. Technology has made us time-efficient and redefined our sense of time and its value. It is not to be wasted, but to be used quickly and with a purpose. Office encounters have become barren of social interaction. They are information-driven, problem-oriented, and solution-based. No pleasantries. No backs slapped. We cut to the chase: I need this from you. Says Zimbardo, "You have to have an agenda." Some people don't even bother to show at the office at all; they telecommute (2016).

Carducci and Zimbardo also state "that the dwindling opportunities for face-to-face interaction put shy people at an increasing disadvantage. They no longer get to practice social skills within the comfort of daily routine" (2016, pg 7). Dropping by a colleague's office to chat becomes increasingly awkward as you do it less and less. Social life has shrunk so much it can now be entirely encapsulated in a single, near-pejorative phrase: 'face time,' denoting the time employees may engage in eyeball-to-eyeball conversation. Electronic hand-held video games played solo now crowd out the time-honored social games of childhood. "Even electronically simulated social interactions can't substitute—they do not permit people to learn the necessary give and take that is at the heart of all interpersonal relationships" (2016, pg 7).

If technology is ushering in a culture of shyness, it is also the perfect medium for the shy. The Internet and World Wide Web are conduits for the shy to interact with others; electronic communication removes many of the barriers that inhibit the shy. You prepare what you want to say. Nobody knows what you look like. The danger, however, is that technology will become a hiding place for those who dread social interaction. The first generation to go from cradle to grave with in-home computers, faxes, and the Internet is a long way from adulthood. We will have to wait at least another 20 years to accurately assess shyness in the wake of the new electronic age. But to do so, we must find a group of infants—shy and non-shy—and follow them through their life, rather than observe different people, from different generations, in different periods of their lives. Only then will we see the course of shyness over a lifetime (Carducci & Zimbardo, 2016).

What causes shyness? Actually, there is no one cause of shyness but many diverse causes including brain chemistry and reactivity (inborn temperament), harsh treatment from teachers or classmates, overprotective parents, faulty self-perceptions, poor adaptability, intolerance for ambiguity, physical appearance, life transitions (such as going to school, divorce, a new job), and even cultural expectations. Furthermore, some people are simply more sensitive about their behavior and are more easily embarrassed than others (Carducci, 2000; Casriel, 2007). According to Vitelli, research into shyness has suggested different causes including genetic influences, prenatal influences, environmental factors (including the effects of emotional abuse in childhood), or as the result of a traumatic social episode. While usually not severe enough to merit a diagnosis of social phobia or social anxiety, shyness can have a powerful effect on a person's sense of well-being along with being linked to depression or other emotional problems due to isolation (2013). Research is ongoing between many cultures and whether different cultures accept shyness and parent children to be shy (Gudino and Lau, 2010).

Overcoming shyness. How can a person overcome shyness? It would be naive to pretend that shyness can be overcome easily. It is important, however, to emphasize that shyness can be overcome successfully. There are three steps in the process of dealing with shyness (Zimbardo, 1990; Pelusi, 2007). These steps are: 1) Analyzing your shyness, 2) Building your self-esteem, and 3) Improving your social skills.

Analyzing Your Shyness

- Try to pinpoint exactly what social situations tend to elicit your shy behavior. Or are you shy because your culture wants you to be respectful and it is mistaken for shyness like Native American or Asian cultures?
- Try to identify what causes your shyness in that situation. Use a diary or journal to keep track of the times you experience this feeling.
- Have a friend or relative give you feedback. Discuss how you interact with others and how you can improve.

Building Your Self-Esteem

- Recognize that you ultimately control how you see yourself.
- Set your own standards. Do not let others tell you how to live your life.
- Set realistic goals. Do not set your goals too high or too low. Many people demand too much of themselves.
- Talk positively to yourself. Tell yourself that you can do it and that you are a good person.
- Learn to take rejection. Rejection is one of the risks everyone takes in social interactions. Try not to take it personally; it may have nothing to do with you.

Improving Your Social Skills

- Follow a role model. Select someone you respect and observe how they interact. Imitate their behavior.
- Learn to listen. Smile.
- Talk to one new person every day about something.
- Volunteer at a place of interest to you.
- Reinforce yourself for each successful interaction.
- Use your imagination. Rehearse in your mind new situations—how you will respond.
- Practice with a friend—interviews, dating situations, etc.
- Find your comfort zone. Not all social situations are for everyone. Go where your interests are. You might be happier at an art gallery, book club, or on a volleyball team than you are at a cocktail party or bar.

It takes time to change. Do not expect to overcome shyness overnight; it is a gradual process.

According to psychologist Bernardo Carducci (Casriel, 2007), conversation with strangers typically moves through five stages:

1. Opening line (keep it simple) and introductions,
2. Trying out topics and exploring for common ground,
3. Closing, in which you tell the person that you're going,
4. Summing up what you learned, and
5. Possibly exchanging contact information.

> *Most of us feel that others will not tolerate emotional honesty in communication. We would rather defend our dishonesty on the grounds that it might hurt others; and having rationalized our phoniness into mobility, we settle for superficial relationships.*
> —JOHN POWELL

Remember, once you internalize these steps, you will always have a mental map of where to go next. Actually, shy people who are determined to develop their social skills can force themselves to interact despite the nervousness it provokes, and they can also end up garnering great satisfaction from the effort even if the bashfulness remains (Rodgers, 2006).

As we begin to reach out and meet new people in the process of overcoming shyness, we attempt to sift through the millions of people in the world to select the individuals that will eventually become our friends and lovers. How do we do this? We begin the process of getting acquainted and finding friends through *perceptual awareness*.

Perception refers to how we mentally organize and interpret the world around us. Because we all have different backgrounds and experiences, we perceive the world around us in different ways—and thus many of us misinterpret and misunderstand the people around us. We need to increase our perceptual awareness.

Perceptual Awareness

How can we prevent misunderstandings due to the inaccuracy of our own perceptions? Serious problems can arise when people accept their misinterpretations as if they were a fact of life while we tend to get upset with others when they jump to conclusions about our own behavior.

> A friend says, "You really look tired today!" (You were feeling great until they said that.)
>
> "What's the matter with you today?" (Who said anything was wrong?)
>
> "Why are you mad at me and not talking to me?" (You are concerned about your final exam that you are not prepared for.)

How can we become more aware of our misinterpretations and make people more aware of their personal perceptions? The **perceptual awareness process** will provide us with a technique that will help us deal with these misperceptions. What is this process?

- Make note of the **behavior you are observing**. Describe the behavior.
- **Interpret the behavior**. Why is that person acting that way? (Write down at least two interpretations.)
- Ask yourself what you would do in the same situation and look at their **point of view**. Put yourself in the other person's "shoes."
- Ask for **clarification** about how to interpret the behavior. Do not jump to conclusions. Ask the person why they are acting that way or ask someone else how they would interpret the situation.

You must find a way to get in the way and get in good trouble, necessary trouble. To save this little piece of real estate that we call earth for generations yet unborn. You have a moral obligation, a mission and a mandate when you leave here to go out and seek justice, for all. You can do it, you must do it.
—CONGRESSMAN JOHN LEWIS

Fair isn't everybody getting the same thing... Fair is everybody getting what they need in order to be successful.

The perceptual awareness process will help us understand others more accurately instead of assuming that our first impression is correct. Our goal is a mutual understanding and acceptance of others.

Now, let us take a closer look at how we perceive the people we meet and interact with on a regular basis through the process called **people perception**. This section will be somewhat longer.

CONSIDER THIS

APPLICATION OF THE PERCEPTUAL AWARENESS PROCESS

Your roommate, Stephanie, has been quiet for the last two days and has not been talking to you (Behavior). You are sure that she is mad at you (First interpretation). She may have had a fight with her boyfriend (Second interpretation). Why would I be acting that way? (Put yourself in that situation.) Ask Stephanie, "Why have you been so quiet recently?" (Request for clarification).

Jim stomped out of the room and slammed the door (Behavior). Jim must have not liked what I said and got mad (First interpretation). Jim sure must be in a hurry and accidently slammed the door (Second interpretation). "Why would I have acted that way?" (Put yourself in that situation). "Jim, how did you feel when you left the room yesterday?" (Request for clarification).

Think of some situations you have been in and go through this process.

People Perception

Imagine yourself alone at a large party that you are attending. You look around and see nothing but unfamiliar faces. As you look at each individual, you immediately make a judgment of what you think each person is like. Your perception of each individual is based on many things, such as your past experiences, prejudices, and stereotyping. Since your past experiences, prejudices, and stereotypes are different from those of others, your perception of each individual will be different from other people's interpretations. You may perceive someone as serious and studious while someone else may perceive the same individual as depressed and slow intellectually. Sometimes we discover that our perception is not always accurate. Initiating interactions is a valuable skill to have. Being open-minded is the best way to approach it. Some recent psychological studies indicate that our perception may be distorted at the time of perception because we are using our own past experiences, prejudices, and stereotyping to make the interpretation.

As we encounter people daily, we form an impression or perception of them. The term **social perception** describes the way we perceive, evaluate, categorize, and form judgments about the qualities of people we encounter (Nevid, 2015). These *social perceptions* have a critical influence on our interactions. In fact, they are more important in guiding our feelings, thoughts, and behaviors than the actual traits or attitudes of the people around us. The factors that seem to influence our social perceptions are *first impressions, stereotyping*, and *prejudices*.

First impressions. First impressions can have a tremendous influence on our perception of others. The initial impression we have of another person may have a strong impact on our future interactions with them. If you go to a party and see someone that looks just like the boss that fired you last week, what is your impression of that person? What is the likelihood of you approaching that person? You will most likely avoid that person even though they seem to be very friendly and not at all like your boss. The **primacy effect** occurs when the first impression carries more weight than any subsequent information. That first impression of the person that looks like your previous boss will be difficult to change even if you see them in a new and different situation (Myers, 2013).

Our first impressions are formed quite rapidly—often within a matter of seconds. Research indicates that negative first impressions are often quickly formed and hard to overcome. This is why they say "getting off on the wrong foot" may be particularly damaging to a person (Hutson, 2016). The opposite tends to be true of positive first impressions, which are often hard to earn but easily lost. If the person you are going out with for the first time is late, what is your first impression? Would you think that he or she is unreliable and must be a flake since this is your first encounter—a negative first impression? Many of you would feel this way and this impression will be difficult to change. If your new date is on time are you willing to say that this person is reliable and conscientious? Research indicates that, indeed, an early wrong is the greater offense and can permanently cripple a relationship, even after repeated apologies (Hutson, 2016). Most of us will take more time to make that judgment even though the first impression was positive.

First Impressions—What do you notice first? While you are walking down the street one day, you notice a person whom you have never seen before. In your mind you immediately form an impression of what you think this person is like. What had the greatest impact on the formation of your opinion? Was it the way the person was dressed, their hairstyle, their size or shape, their facial expression, or their physical attractiveness? In the article "6 Myths about Men and Women and Relationships," Gwen Seidman indicated that data reveals that *both* men and women think looks are important, with men rating it somewhat higher than women (Seidman, 2012). Some people feel that we seem to be influenced more by *physical appearance* than anything else. This may be due to the fact that mass media puts too much emphasis on these factors and, thus, has a great influence on our perception of the world. Wilbourne feels that in the psychology of impression management, it's all about those first few seconds of an interaction. You know you'll be judged, as you judge in turn, by what happens the moment you and a stranger see each other for the first time (Hutson, 2016).

Connection is critical because we all have the basic need to feel accepted and to believe that we belong and are valued for who we are. —DR. BRENÉ BROWN

You never get a second chance to make a first impression —GARY WILLIAMS

Other factors that seem to have an impact on our first impressions of others include what the individual is doing (their behavior) at the time you perceive them and what the *interactional possibilities* are with that person (whether or not they would be a good date, tennis partner, or study partner). If you see someone acting weird the first time you see them, what kind of person do you think he or she is? What will you think of that person the next time you see them? Most of us would continue to perceive them as weird, because of what we observed them doing the first time we saw them. If you see someone who you think would be fun to date, will you approach them? If you think the person sitting in the corner would help you study psychology, will you ask them to help you? If you perceive someone as "stuck-up," or with an "attitude," will you approach them? Based on your first impression of these individuals, you have already determined how you will respond or not respond to them. You are making your decision based on how you perceive the *interactional possibilities* (Aronson et al., 2015).

What about the impression you leave on the World Wide Web, your webpage and Facebook? Do you realize that any information you post on those sites is quite public and long-lasting? Do you realize that the public can see all the pictures taken in various stages of sobriety, etc. on Facebook? Do you realize that what you post may be the **first impression** someone has of you further down the road? Do you realize that employers might check the Internet to see what you have posted on various websites? The lesson is just think carefully—the Internet is available to millions of people—just think before you post.

Tolerance, Acceptance and Appreciation of Differences

Tolerance of people is a goal worthy of having when you are making friends. Tolerance is defined is a fair, objective, and permissive attitude toward those whose opinions, beliefs, practices, or racial or ethnic origins differ from one's own; freedom from bigotry (2016 Random House Dictionary). The following discussion can help you examine your attitudes and commit to any positive change. Keep your mind open to new ideas. Classifying people into social groups is called *social categorizing.* The categories are often based on characteristics such as race, ethnicity, class, and gender. You can find yourself over-categorizing, and that is called **stereotyping**. (See the discussion below on stereotyping.) Social justice issues like racism, sexism, feminism, heterosexism, classism, ableism, and privilege need to be thought about so you can address societal issues with knowledge. Definitions are found in the glossary. Check out the Heroic Imagination Project that psychologist Phillip Zimbardo has researched. It is called the **Heroic Imagination** Project and it provides lessons and tools to encourage "**everyday heroism**," or the power of individuals or networks of individuals to neutralize negative social influences—the genesis of the Heroic Imagination Project and its mission is to teach young people how to "stand up, speak out and act courageously in challenging situations." (Zimbardo, 2017).

THE "HOW" OF POSITIVE SOCIAL CHANGE:

- **The Power of One** — How to **be the first** and specific in helping others in need;
- **The Power of Two** — How to **be an ally** to others who are doing the right thing;
- **The Power of Three** — How to **use group psychology to promote prosocial behavior.**

Prejudices Our perception of other people may be influenced and distorted by our prejudices. Prejudices predispose us to behave in certain ways toward other people and groups. ***Prejudice*** is when we prejudge a person or group of people prior to having all known information and facts (2007, Gale). Being prejudiced does not always have a negative meaning, it can also be positive. You see someone dressed as a nurse. You automatically perceive that person as kind and generous, even though you do not know anything else about the individual. When prejudice is negative, it can even lead to ***discrimination***, which involves your negative behavior (unfair treatment) toward members of a group.

Stereotyping Many people think people with red hair have hot tempers, that all police officers are mean, that all Irish people drink a lot, that all Japanese are intelligent, and that all Jewish people are rich. These are all *stereotypes*—preconceived, inaccurate, rigid beliefs about individuals or groups of people. The habit of stereotyping people is so common that almost any personal characteristic leads to the formation of stereotypes and ***labeling***. For example, what are your feelings about overweight people, old people, short people, black people, women, or gays? Leo Buscaglia once said, "a loving person does not label others" (Hanna, 2008). Labeling can happen often and is mainly what you see. "The eye can be the most inaccurate, most inconsistent, and the most prejudicial organ we have in the body. What is truly essential is invisible to the eye" (Buscaglia, 1982, p. 94).

Did you know that tall people are more apt to get hired first and get paid more than short people? Did you know that attractive students tend to get better grades than less attractive students? Are you aware that women are paid about seventy percent of what men are paid for doing the same job? Is this because tall people are better qualified than short people, attractive students are more intelligent than the less attractive students, and women are not as good employees? No, it is because we have allowed our prejudices and stereotyping to influence our behavior. We must learn to overcome these influences and accept people as they are and not how we learned to perceive them (Fiske, 2014). We will have more to say about prejudice and stereotypes and how they affect our values in Chapter Nine.

Now that you have become knowledgeable about how challenging situations work — like the bystander effect and negative peer pressure, you are obligated. You are obligated to use this knowledge constructively in your daily lives, whether in opposing evil or in inspiring heroic actions.
—DR. PHILLIP ZIMBARDO

Inaccuracy in social perceptions. This is both a cause and an effect of prejudice. We will examine a few sources of inaccuracy that we discussed earlier that contribute to prejudice in important ways.

- *Stereotyping.* Stereotyping seems to contribute more than any other factor in determining our prejudices. Many people subscribe to derogatory stereotypes of various groups. Although studies suggest that racial stereotypes have declined over the last fifty years, they are still not a thing of the past (Plous, 2002). The **stereotype content model** (SCM) is a psychological theory arguing that people tend to perceive social groups along two fundamental dimensions: warmth and competence (Fiske, Cuddy, Glick, & Xu, 2002). The SCM was originally developed to understand the social classification of groups within the population of the United States. However, the SCM has since been applied to analyzing social classes and structures across countries and history (Fiske, 2012).

> *A Study Skills Moment. Take a few minutes to watch this video that will help you stay motivated to read all of this book to "Become more Aware of yourself and others"*

A Weekly Habit That Will Help You Stay Motivated All Semester by Thomas Frank

https://www.youtube.com/watch?v=PlTrxpNaZI8

- *First Impressions.* One of the problems with the power of first impressions is that many people's first impressions of minorities come not from actual interactions, but from the media or disparaging remarks made by parents, neighbors, and others. Thus, many impressionable children develop unfavorable opinions toward Hispanics, African Americans, **people with disabilities,** or **lesbian, gay, bisexual, and transgender (LGBTQ) people** before they have any opportunity for rewarding interactions with members of these groups. Even though these negative first impressions may eventually be overridden by contradictory experiences, the primacy effect probably contributes to prejudice. Judging a book by its cover is a pervasive consequence of our initial reactions to other people—reactions that encourage often inaccurate stereotypes about races and ethnic groups other than our own, women, old people, overweight people, and many other negatively stigmatized social groups (Pingitore et al., 1994). Psychologist Dr. Susan Fiske developed a **continuum model of impression formation** which describes the process by which we form impressions of others. Impression formation is framed as depending on two factors: The available information and the perceiver's motivations (Fiske, Lin, & Neuberg, 1999). According to the model, these two factors help to explain people's tendency to apply stereotyping processes in preference to individuating processes when forming social impressions.

- *Categorizing.* People frequently categorize others on the basis of *inherited traits* (culture, gender, ethnicity, physical features) or *acquired traits* (education, occupation, lifestyle, and customs). *In-group—out-group bias* explains the tendency to hold less favorable opinions about groups to which we do not belong, often over-emphasizing the negative aspects *(out-groups)*, while holding more favorable opinions that are often exaggerated about groups to which we do belong *(in-groups)* (Hewstone et al., 2002). The tendency of people to favor their own group, known as "in-group bias," has been found in cultures around the world (Aberson, Healy, & Romero, 2000). We perceive people like ourselves to be members of the "in-group" and those who are different to be part of the "out-group." We tend to have more favorable attitudes toward "in-group" members than "out-group" members. We tend to explain the behavior of people in the "out-group" on the basis of their membership in the group. Jamie is slow, not very athletic, and obese, so Jamie must be just like all fat people. In contrast, my best friend, Larry, is slow and also obese, but I do not categorize him into the "out-group," because I perceive Larry to be a unique person. Therefore, he's part of my "in-group." Keep an open mind and avoid categorizing people.

What is your impression of this person?

As we continue the process of **people perception**, we discover that it is common for us to make many mistakes in our perceptions of others. We have found that our prejudices and our stereotypes often lead to unfair treatment of others. We will now take a look at one characteristic that seems to have the greatest impact on our perception of others without substantial evidence to support its accuracy—another distortion in perception. Perception is an interesting subject. The better we get to know someone, the more beautiful he or she becomes in our eyes. We often perceive the people we love as being beautiful, regardless of what anyone else may think.

You can see a lot by observing. —YOGI BERRA

Another important aspect of *people perception* is the judgment we make about why people behave as they do. Our responses to other people are strongly influenced by these judgments, and we are constantly attempting to understand the reasons for other people's behavior. This leads us to the *attribution process.*

Physical attractiveness. Are you more likely to seek out an attractive person as a friend or someone who is perceived as less attractive? If you were an employer, would you be more likely to hire the most attractive applicant? Do you perceive physically attractive people to be more poised, likeable, sexy, competent, happy, interesting, and socially skilled than people of average or unattractive appearance? Many of you would answer no to these questions, but when it comes time for you to act on these questions it could be a different story. Research indicates that physical attractiveness has a profound influence on our impression of others and our interactions with them (Berscheid 2000; Baron et al., 2012).

In general, people tend to believe that what is beautiful is good (Atwater et al., 2013). This stereotype seems to start early in life. When preschool children were asked to pick whom they liked best and who they thought was the best behaved in their class, they selected both categories of their classmates with the same group of children adults judged to be the most attractive physically (Berscheid, 2000).

We have all been told, "Beauty is only skin deep, and it's what's inside the person that counts." A person's character and behavior are more important than looks. Most of us would probably agree that physical attractiveness should not be a major factor in interpersonal attraction. Then, why is physical beauty such a powerful influence in attracting us to others?

One reason is that we all want to be accepted and liked, and we perceive attractive people as being more friendly, liked more by others, and thus, if we hang around them more we will also be perceived in the same way. People tend to see themselves as being more similar to attractive people than to unattractive people. Another reason is that, beginning early in life, we have been told that beautiful things are good and that ugly things are bad, so we have generalized this belief to include our perception of people. Later, we discover that attractive people tend to receive more positive reinforcement than less attractive individuals, and, thus, they will be more likely to feel good about themselves. Finally, if they feel good about themselves, other people will also perceive them as more positive and they will continue to receive more and more reinforcement. As a result of such cultural conditioning, most people do associate physical attractiveness with a wide variety of desirable characteristics (Myers, 2013).

People's attractiveness is surprisingly unrelated to their self-esteem. One reason may be that, except after comparing themselves with super-attractive people, few people view themselves as unattractive. As time goes by, we become accustomed to our own face and perceive it on a positive basis (Gosling, 2016).

What about dating? When selecting a date, does physical attractiveness influence your selection? Research has shown that people desire to date the most attractive person possible. But when given the opportunity to choose a date, people tend to choose someone of attractiveness nearly equal to their own (Berscheid, 2000). We may desire the more attractive date, but we are afraid that they would reject us. In order to maintain a positive self-concept, we are more likely to select someone we think would be more likely to say "yes." That person will most likely be someone whom we perceive as equal to us in physical attractiveness. The *matching hypothesis* proposes that people of similar levels of physical attractiveness gravitate toward each other (Worchel et al., 2000). There seems to be evidence to support this in regard to selecting friends, dating partners, and marriage partners. Look around you; look at your friends and mates. Are they similar to you?

What traits are important to you? Your best friend wants to get you a date. Your friend asks you to list the three most important characteristics you would like that date to have. What are the three characteristics you would list? Take a minute and write down the three characteristics that are most important to you in a date. Most people would say *intelligence*, *friendliness*, and *sincerity* are the most important qualities. But when you actually make your selection, you base your selection on physical appearance.

Are attractive people really better adjusted, smarter, or more assertive than unattractive people? Physical attractiveness is not correlated with intelligence, mental health, or even self-esteem. However, our tendency is to perceive beautiful people as healthier and just plain better than others (Flora, 2004).

The more aware we are that characteristics, like physical attractiveness, influence our perceptions of others, the less chance that these characteristics will have on influencing our perceptions of others. Thank goodness that *beauty is in the eye of the beholder* and what is beautiful to one person is not considered beautiful to another person. This gives all of us a fair chance.

What is the attribution process? What would you do and think in the following situation? Class is over and you are walking to your next class and you see your boyfriend or girlfriend on the other side of campus talking to a member of the opposite sex. Many of you would feel your emotions take control of your mind and body and react aggressively toward your partner and accuse them of flirting with the other person. Are you jealous? What would you say when your boyfriend or girlfriend finds you talking to a member of the opposite sex? It tends to be a different story when the *shoe is on the other foot*, doesn't it? Why? **Attribution theory** shows that we frequently over-estimate the influence of a person's personality and under-estimate the impact of the situation he or she is in (Worchel et al., 2000). In the situation above, you attributed your girlfriend's or boyfriend's behavior to his or her personality and not being a trustworthy person. You forgot to consider the *situation* she was in. Remember, yesterday she was sick and missed her classes and she was talking to the other person in order to get the notes for class. Your response to this event was inappropriate because you did not consider the situation your girlfriend was in. Have you ever done this? We are more likely to respond this way to people we do not know than people we do know. Hopefully, you are secure enough in your relationship with your boyfriend or girlfriend that you would trust them talking to a person of the opposite sex. Attribution is concerned with how we make sense of our world because we wonder why people say and do the things they do (Reeder, 2013).

- *Attribution Error.* When we observed Juan for the first time, he was studying by himself in the cafeteria using a laptop computer. What is our first impression of Juan? What label do you give him? He must be a loner. He must be an intellectual. He must be a "nerd." Are we right about our perception of Juan? The next day we are walking by the soccer field and we notice a very fast aggressive player scoring a goal and we discover that it is Juan. Was our first impression of Juan correct? We then further discover that Juan is also a very outgoing individual with lots of friends. We definitely made an error based on our first impression. Remember, a person's behavior at a given time may or may not reflect their personality—but we tend to assume that it does.

    Inaccuracy in our perceptions tends to persist because first impressions can be very difficult to overcome. Evidence tends to demonstrate that we tend to see what we expect to see in our interpersonal interactions. Now that you are more aware of how your perceptions are influenced, we hope that you can begin to accept people as they really are.

The greatest discovery in our generation is that human beings, by changing the inner attitudes of their minds, can change the outer aspects of their lives.
—WILLIAM JAMES

Another variable that has a powerful influence on our perception of others and our interaction with them is *the power of expectations*.

Predicting the future is usually the work of astrologers or others who claim to be a prophet. In reality, each of us predicts what will be, and we also make it come true. A self-fulfilling prophecy is "an expectation that helps to bring about the predicted events, which consequently strengthens the expectation" (Myers, 2013). Psychologists are aware that these expectations can affect the behavior and outcome of others.

The self-fulfilling prophecy. We see what we want to see; we become what others expect of us. This is the premise of the ***self-fulfilling prophecy***. This is such a powerful force in our life that it not only determines how you see yourself in the present, but can actually influence your future behavior and that of others. A *self-fulfilling prophecy* occurs when a person's expectations of an event makes the outcome more likely to happen than would otherwise have been true. *Self-fulfilling prophecies* occur all the time, although you are not always aware of them. For example,

- You hate math, but you register for a math class anyway, knowing that you will have difficulty learning the material. You end up dropping out because you're failing the course.
- You expected to become nervous and not do well in a job interview, and later you did actually become nervous and your interview suffered.
- Your boss assigns you a new task saying that you will have difficulty completing it. You proved him right and did not complete it.
- A parent keeps telling his daughter that she is a brat. She proves him right and keeps causing problems.
- You anticipated having a good (or terrible) time at a social affair and your expectations came true.

> *If you think you can do something, or you think you cannot, you are usually right.*
> —HENRY FORD

In each of these cases, there is a good chance that the event happened because you expected it to happen. Rosenthal and Jacobson (2003) found that teacher expectations can have a tremendous effect on his or her students. For example, a teacher was told that certain students had more intellectual potential than the other students in the class. The class was given a test prior to the teacher's first day of class and another test a few months later. The results were surprising, because all of the students started with about the same potential. The students who were recognized as having "high potential" by the teacher improved at a much higher rate than those recognized as "average" students—apparently as a result of the teacher's higher expectations.

Types of self-fulfilling prophecies. There are two types of self-fulfilling prophecies. The *first type* that we will discuss is imposed by one person on another, so that the expectation of one person seems to control another's action. We described this in the Jacobson and Rosenthal study of a teacher's expectations of their students. The teacher expected certain students to do well, and as a result they did better than the low-expectation students. To put this phenomenon in context with self-concept, we can say that when a teacher communicates to a student the message "I think you're bright," the student accepts that evaluation and changes their self-concept to include it. In contrast, we realize that the reverse is also true for students whose teachers send the message "I think you're stupid." Can you think of some examples of this type of self-fulfilling prophecy that you have observed?

- A coach telling a player he is not sure if he will make the team.
- A parent telling his daughter that she is a brat.
- A doctor telling her patient that he may not live much longer.
- A teacher telling his student that he is not college material.
- A coach telling a player that she is too short to play basketball.

How would these comments influence a person's behavior?

The *second category* of self-fulfilling prophecy is the self-imposed prophecy that occurs when your own expectations influence your behavior.

Expectations are the basis of the self-fulfilling prophecy. We find that expectations are the foundation of our success, but they can also be the basis of our failure. If we believe that we can succeed, we can do it. If we believe that we are incompetent and not capable, we will be a failure. Which do you want to become—a failure or a success? This type of self-fulfilling prophecy becomes a vicious circle (Schultz & Oskamp, 2000). A thought about oneself is carried out in behavior, which then brings about an even stronger confirming thought. You, a shy person, will fulfill your own prophecy. If the descriptor is a positive one which increases your self-esteem, the self-fulfilling prophecy is a friend. Too often, though, our thoughts are limiting and serve as our enemy. Figure 1.4 demonstrates this vicious circle.

Self-fulfilling prophecies are powerful. They can have a positive or negative impact on our self-concept, or they can influence us in the business world, or in how our family operates. What kind of effect has the self-fulfilling prophecy had on you?

> *Get on good terms with yourself and see how quickly others get on good terms with you.*
> —NAPOLEAN HILL

Figure 1.4

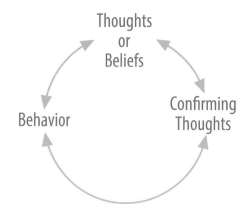

Person to Person: Positive Relationships Don't Just Happen, 5th Edition by Sharon L. Hanna © 2008. Adapted by permission of Prentice Hall, Upper Saddle River, NJ.

Can I Change My Image?

Can I change how others perceive me? Can I change my expectations? It is not easy, but you can change. How can you do this? You are constantly projecting yourself to others as being a capable, good, bad, inferior, successful, dumb, happy, sad, depressed, or superior type of person. Do you like the way others perceive you as a person? You can change your image through *impression management*.

Impression management. There is a strong correlation between the *self-fulfilling prophecy* and *impression management*. If you project yourself as being a successful person, others will perceive you as being successful, and if they expect you to be successful, you become more successful. ***Impression management*** refers to our conscious effort to present ourselves in socially desirable ways (Worchel et al., 2000; Santrock, 2006).

> *A man without a smiling face must not open a shop.*
> —ANCIENT CHINESE PROVERB

Have you ever been interviewed for a job? How did you dress? Did you project yourself in a positive way? Did you relate to this person differently than you do with your friends? Most of you would dress differently for the interview. You would make sure that you say the "right" things and respond positively to the interviewer. You are doing what we call *impression management*. You are attempting to portray yourself in a way that you think the interviewer expects you to be. *Impression management* is necessary if we want people to like us, respect us, hire us, or buy something from us.

How can you influence the impressions you make on others?

> *We inherit our relatives and our features and may not escape them, but we can select our clothing and our friends, and let us be careful that both fit us..*
> — VOLNEY STREAMER

What kind of image do you project? How do others perceive you? Remember, if you do not like how others perceive you, you can change the image. You can change the way you dress, the way you act, your hairstyle, your posture, whatever it takes to change the image. You can do it. "People are sensitive to how they are seen by others and use many forms of impression management to compel others to react to them in the ways they wish" (Giddens, 2005). An example of this concept is easily illustrated through cultural differences. Different cultures have diverse thoughts and opinions on what is considered beautiful or attractive. For example, Americans tend to find tan skin attractive, but in Indonesian culture, pale skin is more desirable (Norris, 2011). As we begin to understand the process of people perception, we are now ready to begin the process of getting acquainted. What are the stages in the development of a friendship?

How To Make Favorable Impressions

How can you influence the impressions you make on others? Most of us make a conscious effort to influence the way others think of us. When we present ourselves to others, we usually try to make ourselves look better than we really are. We spend billions of dollars rearranging our bodies, our faces, our minds, and our social skills.

To increase your odds of making a good first impression, Valerie White and Ann Demarais (2005), authors of *First Impressions: What You Don't Know about How Others See You*, offer these tips:

1. Make eye contact at least half to two-thirds of the time (any more than this and you may come on too strong). And pay attention to your body language. Lean toward others when they speak. Nod every now and then.
2. Smile, even if you aren't in the mood. Just going through the motions of showing some teeth may make you—and others—feel better, says the research.
3. Be careful about "oversharing," i.e., disclosing too much personal information about yourself. Keep it light. Keep it positive.
4. Try a little flattery. People warm to others who pay them compliments even if they know they're false. But, it is best when done sincerely.
5. Got a prepared opening line as an ice-breaker? Ditch it, or you risk coming across as shallow, aggressive, and calculating ...so ask the interviewer about the job so you might gain insight into questions to ask.
6. Check your impulse to use the other person's name repeatedly. Once or twice might work, but overplaying the name game can make you seem "salesy" and forced.
7. Think a neutral, inscrutable style makes you appear thoughtful, deep, or cool? Forget it. Aloof behavior like kicking back at the table, crossing your arms, or showing zero emotion makes you look bored or arrogant.

Remember that first impression techniques that work in one cultural setting may not work in another. For example, the nonverbal "thumbs up" gesture, which means in the United States that everything is OK, or that we would like to hitch a ride, means something very different in Greece—an insult similar to a raised middle finger. In the Native American culture of the Sioux, it is considered courteous to open a conversation with a compliment. In some Eastern European countries, if one person expresses great admiration for another's wristwatch, courtesy dictates that the watch is given to the admirer. When interacting with people from different backgrounds and different cultures, you need to remember that they may be interpreting the situation or event differently than you.

Our values can also color "the facts." Our preconceptions can bias our observations and interpretations. Sometimes, we see what we are predisposed to see. Even the words we use to describe a person or an event can reflect our values.

Developing New Relationships

Unfortunately, it is not easy to meet or get acquainted with others. If we wait for others to initiate the encounter, we may become very lonely. It is up to you, and only you, to initiate the encounter and get the ball rolling in order for your friendships to grow and develop into long-lasting relationships. It also seems that there may be a growing acceptance of cross-sex friendships, particularly among younger groups, a tendency that is similarly indicative of a greater flexibility in friendship ties (Monsour, 2002). In the past, cross-sex friendships were comparatively rare, at least outside of couple friendships. Indeed for many people they still are. Yet the transformations there have been in young adulthood, including patterns of household and partnership formation, education, leisure, and employment, and have resulted in a range of more gender-integrated activities than was typical for previous generations. These changing patterns of social involvement, the relatively greater elision of male and female worlds, have in turn rendered cross-sex friendships more acceptable and provided routine environments, especially employment, for fostering such friendships. Thus, while gender remains a significant status division, the reality of which continues to be reflected in friendship networks, its power in shaping friendship eligibility is less marked than it was (Allan, 2008). So you might want to look for men and women to be your friends—not just your own sex.

If we understand the steps that are involved in initiating new relationships, we will be more likely to begin to incorporate them into our everyday life. What are these steps?

Steps in initiating new relationships. Here are four steps you can take to initiate new relationships.

> *Friendship improves happiness; it abates misery, doubles our joy and divides our grief.*
> —JOSEPH ADDISON

1. **Communication** underlies all relationships, but in order to communicate with others we must first make contact with them. Whatever the nature of the situation, an encounter will usually begin with some communicative act that invites a response from another person. In order to do this, we must develop good communication skills. We find that the people who seem to have lots of friends also seem to have good communication skills. These skills can be learned. The communication chapter will help you learn these skills.

2. **Be Active** may give you the opportunity to get acquainted with someone you would like to get to know. By allowing the people you want to get to know you to see you more often. The more familiar you become with someone the more apt you are to interact with that person. The first time you walk by a stranger what do you do? Most of us would ignore the stranger. The next time you walk by the stranger you may smile. The next time you see one another you say, "Hi," and from then on the more you encounter this person the more you begin to interact. All of a sudden—you're friends.

Have you heard the story about people marrying the person next door? You are constantly being *exposed* to that person. You see each other on a regular basis and without any real effort on your part; all of a sudden you are friends and begin dating. The more we see someone, the less we will be influenced by first impressions.

Where did you meet your friends? Was it school, church, near where you live, at your place of employment, the grocery store, or at the athletic club? Research reveals that most people are more likely to like, and even marry, an individual who lives, works, or goes to school within close proximity to them. ***Proximity—geographical nearness***—is perhaps the most powerful predictor of friendship. Of course, *proximity* also provides opportunities for fights, assaults, rapes, and murders. But much more often it instigates liking.

If you live in a college dormitory, your friends are more likely to live down the hall than across campus. Your earliest friends were probably children who lived next door or even in the same neighborhood.

What about the saying, *absence makes the heart grow fonder?* As long as you isolate yourself from other prospective dates or mates, the saying is accurate. But, for most of us the saying goes, *"Absence makes the heart grow fonder for someone else."* There is another saying that is appropriate here, *"When I'm not with the one I love, I love the one I'm with."* What happens when friends and lovers move away? Eventually most of these relationships will slowly dissolve to nothing more than a periodic phone call or card.

> Often the deepest relationships can be developed during the simplest activities.
> —GARY SMALLEY

Does familiarity breed contempt? Evidence shows that familiarity does not breed contempt, it breeds fondness. The more we are exposed to novel stimuli—a new person or new product—our liking for such stimuli will increase. This phenomenon, called the ***mere-exposure effect***, explains in part why we are attracted to people in close proximity to us (Wood et al., 2013).

Social networks. If it seems as though you are having difficulty getting acquainted with others, you may want to join a singles club, or even try a social networking website. Actually, the Internet has tremendously expanded opportunities for people to meet and develop relationships through social networking services, e-mail, blogs, chat rooms, and news groups. Facebook was the first social network to surpass 1 billion registered accounts and currently sits at 1.59 billion monthly active users. Eighth-ranked photo-sharing app Instagram has over 400 million monthly active accounts. Meanwhile, blogging service Tumblr had more than 555 million active blog users on their site in July 2016, according to Statista.com (Shafer, J. 2016).

See Table 1.1 for more detail on who uses social networking sites.

Be careful when joining a club, dating service, or social networking website—check their references. How long have they been established? How much will they cost you? Talk to other friends who have joined or used their services. You want to make sure that you can benefit from their services and not let them take advantage of you.

Table 1.1

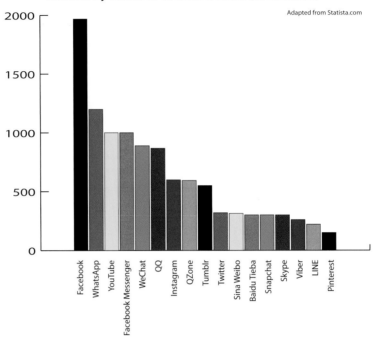

Most famous social network sites worldwide as of April 2017, ranked by number of active users (in millions)

Adapted from Statista.com

The other two steps in initiating relationships are:

3. **Social skills** enable you to create situations to meet new people and to maintain their friendship. How can you learn these skills? Practice makes perfect. Practice the skills you observe other people using that enable them to interact well among others. Practice role playing with a friend—your friend will also be able to provide you with beneficial feedback that will enable you to change. Practice different situations in your mind. Picture yourself asking someone out for a date or imagine yourself being interviewed for a job. The more you practice, the better you will be able to handle the situation. Practice verbal and nonverbal skills. Another idea would be to have someone record video of you in different situations. This is a lot of fun and provides great feedback when you watch yourself on film.
4. **Classes** in communication skills, human relations, or acquiring assertiveness skills will provide you with new techniques and skills that you can apply in developing new relationships while improving your present relationships.

These are just a few steps you can use in initiating new relationships. What about meeting and interacting with people from different cultures? If you see someone who is struggling to make friends or being "bullied" because they do not dress in the most "in" clothing, PLEASE step up and say Hi or at least smile at them. You never know what someone is facing. You might end up with a great friend. You may find that you get to know yourself better and to get to know another person with a shared giving and taking regarding what we know about ourselves—*self-discovery*.

How we can have successful interactions with people from other cultures. In the world today, it is important that we learn to relate successfully with people from other cultures. *"Culture" refers to a group or community with which we share common experiences that shape the way we understand the world.* It includes groups that we are born into, such as gender, race, national origin, class, or religion. It can also include groups we join or become part of. For example, we can acquire a new culture by moving to a new region, by a change in our economic status, or by becoming disabled. When we think of culture this broadly we realize we all belong to many cultures at once. And building relationships with people from different cultures, *often many different cultures*, is key in building diverse communities that are powerful enough to achieve significant goals. Relationships are powerful. Our one-to-one connections with each other are the foundation for change. We need to move beyond prejudicial thinking that affects our interactions with different types of people. We all want to experience success in our efforts in developing intercultural relationships.

People must feel that they are having successful relationships with people from other cultures. In order to work with people from different cultural groups effectively, you will need to build sturdy and caring relationships based on trust, understanding, and shared goals. You must show respect, seek out activities of mutual interest, work cooperatively on projects, spend part of your free time with others, and so forth. In short, relationships should be warm and cordial, and you should look forward to your intercultural interactions.

> *Friendship is a plant we must often water.*
> —GERMAN PROVERB

WAYS TO MAKE A FRIEND

Where and how do adults make friends?

- **"STEP OUTSIDE YOUR BOX"** Sign up for a group travel adventure; people tend to bond more easily when out of their comfort zone. The experience will provide an instant group of people with whom you share a unique memory. Try new things alone or with friends.
- **TAKE A CLASS** in something you love; enthusiasm is contagious.
- **GET A DOG** (a pet is also good for your health) and show up every morning at your local dog park. People love to chat about their pooches.
- **TAKE A FRESH LOOK** at your neighbors, coworkers, classmates, fellow gym bunnies—the people you meet and greet on a regular basis. If you've been standoffish, say hello. If you've traded hellos for months, engage them in conversation.
- **SMILE**

Karbo (2016)

How Do You Build Relationships With People From Other Cultures?

In the Community Toolbox developed by The Kansas Health Foundation there are many ways that people can learn about other people's cultures and build relationships at the same time. (http://ctb.ku.edu/en/table-of-contents/culture/cultural-competence/culture-and-diversity/main)

Here are some steps you can take.

- Make a conscious decision to establish friendships with people from other cultures.
- Put yourself in situations where you will meet people of other cultures.
- Examine your biases about people from other cultures.
- Ask people questions about their cultures, customs, and views.
- Read about other people's cultures and histories.
- Listen to people tell their stories.
- Notice differences in communication styles and values; don't assume that the majority's way is the right way.
- Risk making mistakes.
- Learn to be an ally.

Make a conscious decision to establish friendships with people from other cultures.

Making a decision is the first step. In order to build relationships with people different from yourself, you have to make a concerted effort to do so. There are societal forces that serve to separate us from each other. People from different economic groups, religions, ethnic groups, and races are often isolated from each other in schools, jobs, and neighborhoods. So, if we want things to be different, we need to take active steps to make them different.

You can join a sports team or club, become active in an organization, choose a job, or move to a neighborhood that puts you in contact with people of cultures different than your own. Also, you may want to take a few minutes to notice the diversity that is presently nearby. If you think about the people you see and interact with every day, you may become more aware of the cultural differences that are around you.

Once you have made the decision to make friends with people different from yourself, you can go ahead and make friends with them in much the same way as with anyone else. You may need to take more time, and you may need to be more persistent. You may need to reach out and take the initiative more than you are used to. People who have been mistreated by society may take more time to trust you than people who haven't. Don't let people discourage you. There are good reasons why people have built up defenses, but it is not impossible to overcome them and make a connection. The effort is totally worth it.

Put yourself in situations where you will meet people of other cultures; especially if you haven't had the experience of being a minority, take the risk.

One of the first and most important steps is to show up in places where you will meet people of cultures other than your own. Go to meetings and celebrations of groups whose members you want to get to know. Or hang out in restaurants and other gathering places that different cultural groups go. You may feel embarrassed or shy at first, but your efforts will pay off. People of a cultural group will notice if you take the risk of coming to one of their events. If it is difficult for you to be the only person like yourself attending, you can bring a buddy with you and support each other in making friends.

Examine your biases about people from other cultures.

We all carry misinformation and stereotypes about people in different cultures. Especially, when we are young, we acquire this information in bits and pieces from TV, from listening to people talk, and from the culture at large. We are not bad people because we acquired this; no one requested to be misinformed. But in order to build relationships with people of different cultures, we have to become aware of the misinformation we acquired.

These feelings must be perceived as positive and be reciprocated by those culturally diverse individuals. Some people report that they have many friends and that these friends are gracious and cordial, but others report that those same people are abrasive, unfriendly, and should be avoided.

We discover that most intercultural interactions often involve tasks of some kind. The tasks that people want to accomplish while interacting with people from other cultures involve such things as: community projects, completing a degree in school, wanting to start or maintain a joint venture, completing forms that have to be filled out, visiting a foreign country and finding your way to a strange location, communicating with someone you cannot understand, dealing with government agencies, medical facilities, or legal hassles. These tasks need to be accomplished in an efficient manner and within a reasonable amount of time.

People should also experience minimal stress due to the fact that they are dealing with individuals from other cultures rather than from their own culture. Life is stressful enough, and successful intercultural relations suggest that there should be no additional stress brought on by the fact that the others with whom people work and/or interact are from a different cultural background (Community Toolbox developed by The Kansas Health Foundation, 2016).

As we close this chapter, perhaps the words of Winston Churchill are worth remembering:

> You haven't learned life's lesson very well if you haven't noticed that you can give the tone or color, or decide the reaction you want of people in advance. It's unbelievably simple. If you want them to take an interest in you, take an interest in them first. People will treat you as you treat them.

> *When I meet someone from another culture, I behave in the way that is natural to me, while the other behaves in the way that is natural to him or her. The only problem is that our "natural" ways do not coincide.*
> —RAYMONDE CARROLL

Chapter Review

Our greatest pleasures and our most traumatic experiences have evolved around relationships.

- *Human Relations* can be defined as the art of developing relationships that improve personal skills and life effectiveness.
- *Self-Discovery*—to get to know yourself and to get to know another person requires a shared giving and taking regarding what we know about ourselves.
- The revealing of the inner self is called *self-disclosure*.
- The evolution of a relationship is based on how much you are willing to disclose about yourself and how much the other person is willing to disclose about themselve to you—the process called self-disclosure.
- Good self-disclosure skills are fundamental to relationships for many reasons: defining yourself, knowing yourself, getting acquainted, developing intimacy.
- The greatest risk of self-disclosure is rejection.
- There are many advantages of self-disclosure: improves relationships, promotes mental health, self-validation, social control, impression management.
- The *Johari Window* illustrates how self-disclosure operates and will allow you to become more aware of yourself and your potential as a communicator.
- The size of the window pane in the Johari Window may vary depending on your communication behavior and the quality of your relationship.
- *Loneliness* is one of the most serious problems in our society today—it is a feeling of longing and emptiness that is caused by the lack of emotional attachments and social ties.
- Loneliness makes a person vulnerable to many different situations, including the use of drugs and alcohol, suicide, medical problems, sexual promiscuity, mental illness, and negative relationships.
- What should a relationship provide? *Emotional attachments and social ties* must be satisfied in order to have a fulfilling life and overcome the feeling of loneliness.
- Most people will receive their emotional attachment from: parents, relatives, mates, friends, pastors, animals, blankies, and teddy bears.
- *Social ties* provide us with the feelings of belonging, a feeling that we are part of a group and have an identity.
- *Shyness* is universal; it involves feelings, physical reactions, and thoughts that create a state of anxiety, discomfort, and inhibitions.
- The consequences of shyness may be devastating. If you mistake having alone time for shyness remember everyone needs alone time but some need more of it.
- The major difference between a shy person and a non-shy person is a matter of *self-evaluation*.
- There are three steps in the process of overcoming shyness—1) Analyzing your shyness; 2) Building your *self-esteem*; 3) Improving your social skills.
- The perceptual awareness process will help us understand others more accurately instead of assuming that our first impressions are correct.
- When thinking about sensitive ethnic, cultural, and gender issues, it is important to consider different sides of issues in a contemplative, analytic way as the *perceptual awareness* process explains.
  - *Technology* changes may diminish actual personal interaction. Or they may be helpful in meeting new people.

- *Social perception* describes the way we perceive, evaluate, categorize, and form judgments about the qualities of people we encounter.
- The factors that influence our *social perceptions* are: *first impressions*, *stereotyping*, and *prejudices*.
- First impressions can have a tremendous influence on our perceptions of others. The initial impression we have of another person may have a strong impact on our future interactions with them. The *primacy effect* occurs when the first impression carries more weight than subsequent information.
- The inaccuracy of social perception is both the cause and effect of prejudice. *Stereotyping* seems to contribute more than any other factor in determining our prejudices.
- The *attribution process* allows us to make sense out of other people's actions, figure out their attitudes and personality traits, and, ultimately, gain some control over subsequent interactions with them through our increased ability to predict their behaviors.
- The *self-fulfilling prophecy* is a powerful force in our life that not only determines how you see yourself in the present but can actually influence your future behavior and that of others. (We see what we want to see; we become what others expect of us.)
- You can change. *Impression management* allows you to consciously present yourself in socially desirable ways.
- Developing new relationships is not always an easy process. The steps involved in initiating new relationships include communication and exposing yourself. The *mere-exposure effect* explains why we are attracted to those who are in close proximity.
- The *Mutual Reward Theory* (MRT) states that a relationship between two people is enhanced when there is a satisfactory balance of rewards between them.

You can learn to make your social life rich and rewarding by taking an active role in changing yourself. Your knowledge and beliefs about relationships will influence your enjoyment. You learn from experience, so take charge of your life, and take a few risks and chances. Enjoy life and appreciate each and every relationship you have.

Test Review Questions: Learning Outcomes

1. Describe the risks involved in getting acquainted with others.
2. Describe what a person can do to overcome shyness.
3. Why do we need to study self-disclosure? Why is self-disclosure important in a relationship?
4. What are the greatest risks of self-disclosure? Explain.
5. What are the advantages of self-disclosure? Explain.
6. What is the purpose of the Johari Window? How can the Johari Window be of benefit to you?
7. What is loneliness? What effects will loneliness have upon an individual?
8. How can a person overcome the effects of loneliness?
9. Define emotional attachments and social ties and explain their importance in relationship to loneliness.
10. Explain what shyness is and discuss the consequences of shyness.
11. What would you tell someone to help them overcome shyness? Can social networks help?
12. Explain the perceptual awareness process.

13. Why do we need to study people perception?
14. Explain how first impressions, stereotyping, and prejudices influence our perception of others.
15. How does physical attractiveness influence our perception of others?
16. Explain the attribution process.
17. What is the self-fulfilling prophecy? What influence can it have on a person?
18. Explain how you can change your image. Why should we study impression management?
19. What are the qualities necessary to have a close, personal relationship with another person?
20. Explain the Mutual Reward Theory (MRT).
21. Explain the four steps in initiating new relationships.
22. How can we have successful interactions with people from other cultures?
23. Does technology enhance social connections? How? How not?
24. Define Human Relations.
25. Identify the three most common shyness-provoking situations according to Dr. Bernardo Carducci
26. Explain what LTL means.

Key Terms

Attribution Error
Attribution Theory
Categorizing
Catharsis
Continuum Model of Impression
Confidant
Depression
Discrimination
Diversity
Emotional Attachments
First Impressions
Human Relations
Impression Management
Intercultural Communication/
    Interactions
In-Group—Out-Group Bias

Johari Window
    Open Area
    Blind Area
    Hidden Area
    Unknown Area
Living Together Loneliness (LTL)
Loneliness
Matching Hypothesis
Mere-Exposure Effect
Mutual Reward Theory
Openness
Open Communicator
People Perception
Perceptual Awareness Process
Physical Attractiveness
Public Self and Private Self

Prejudice
Primacy Effect
Proximity
Self-Disclosure
Self-Discovery
Self-Esteem
Self-Evaluation
Self-Fulfilling Prophecy
Self-Validation
Shyness
Situational Shyness
Social Networking
Social Perception
Social Ties
Stereotyping
Tolerance

Reflections: Critical Thinking

1. Discuss the risks involved in getting acquainted with others.
2. Describe what a person can do to overcome shyness.
3. Why is self-disclosure so important in a relationship and what are the advantages of self-disclosure?
4. What is the purpose of the Johari Window? How can the Johari Window be of benefit to you?
5. What effects will loneliness have upon an individual?
6. How can a person overcome the effects of loneliness?
7. What is the self-fulfilling prophecy? What influence can it have on a person?
8. What are the qualities necessary to have a close, personal relationship with another person?
9. If you knew someone was moving to a new town and did not know anyone in that town, what would you tell this person about meeting and getting to know others? Explain the three steps in initiating new relationships.
10. Describe Impression Management and give examples of how it can be used. How have you applied it in the past?
11. Give some examples of how first impressions have influenced your interactions with others. Were they accurate or inaccurate?
12. Why is the Mutual Reward Theory (MRT) important in relationships?
13. How can we have successful interactions with people from other cultures?
14. Explain how a person can be married or move to a foreign country and still feel lonely.
15. Why are Human Relations skills needed?
16. What are public self and private self?
17. How would you explain self-esteem? Why would you want to build it up? What about lose it?
18. How do you explain Tolerance, is that different from Stereotyping? Does mere-exposure effect have a part of these explanations?

Web Resources and Web Activities

TRY THESE ACTIVITIES

www.shyness.com/

The Shyness Institute offers this Web site as "a gathering of network resources for people seeking information and services for shyness." It is an index of articles, associations, and agencies that work with shyness.

www.kevan.org/johari

An interactive Johari Window in which you are asked to describe yourself from a list of adjectives and you can also ask friends and colleagues to describe you and then see the results.

The Loneliness Workbook: A Guide to Developing and Maintaining Lasting Connections by Mary Ellen Copeland

http://www.peopleandpossibilities.com/interview.html

Read about and take the Leo Buscaglia Love Quiz

http://www.counselling.cam.ac.uk/selfhelp/selfleafpdf/loneli/view

This resource from University of Cambridge is an informational pdf. It reviews what you can do about loneliness, worry, and anxiety, among many other emotions. Remember that many of these feelings are very common.

www.authentichappiness.sas.upenn.edu/testcenter.aspx

University of Pennsylvania Questionnaire Center with Emotion Questionnaires like Compassionate Love Scale, which measures your tendency to support, help, and understand other people. Other scales measure Depression and Happiness.

http://psychcentral.com/quizzes/loneliness.htm

The Loneliness Quiz based on the UCLA Loneliness Quiz

www.seventeen.com/love/love-quizzes/a27362/commitment-quiz/

Commitment Quiz - Are You Ready for a Serious Relationship?

http://dating.about.com/library/readytolivetogether/blReadyToLiveTogetherQuiz.htm

Are You Ready to Live Together? A Quiz

https://www.psychologytoday.com/blog/resolution-not-conflict/201312/why-am-i-still-single-quiz

Why Am I Still Single? A Quiz

http://www.theatlantic.com/magazine/archive/2009/06/what-makes-us-happy/307439/

What Makes Us Happy?

http://www.understandingprejudice.org/

Social Psychology Network- Check out the Exercises and Demonstrations

http://heroicimagination.org/

VIDEOS TO WATCH

http://friendship.about.com/od/Improve_Your_Behavior/tp/TED-Talks-to-Improve-Your-Friendships.htm

https://www.youtube.com/watch?v=MtLVCpZIiNs&feature=youtu.be

Sherry Turkle- Alone Together

https://www.ted.com/talks/meaghan_ramsey_why_thinking_..

Meaghan Ramsey: Why thinking you're ugly is bad for you | TED Talk ...▶ 12:02

https://youtu.be/_0hxl03JoA0

The lethality of loneliness: John Cacioppo at TEDxDesMoines

https://www.youtube.com/watch?v=whjDeFZDEUk

Codependency & Pathological Loneliness: Why We Stay w/ Narcissists. The Lonely Hurt! Expert

http://www.ted.com/talks/guy_winch_the_case_for_emotional_hygiene

Guy Winch talks about Emotional first aid

https://www.youtube.com/watch?v=iCvmsMzlF7o

The Power of Vulnerability by Social worker Brene Brown

http://www.ted.com/talks/thandie_newton_embracing_otherness_embracing_myself?language=en

Embracing Others Embracing Self by Thandie Newton

https://www.youtube.com/watch?v=OMGUzXknoVQ

What Social Anxiety Feels Like

https://www.youtube.com/watch?v=2U-tOghblfE

Nicholas Christakis: The hidden influence of social networks

https://www.youtube.com/watch?v=08cYINwQYts

Leo Buscaglia - Speaking of Love

http://documentaryheaven.com/discovering-psychology/

The power of the situation—social psychology

Getting Acquainted Interview

PURPOSE

To interview another person in order to get to know them well enough to introduce them to the rest of the group.

INSTRUCTIONS

1. Each individual should make a list of 10 interview questions that you would not mind someone asking you.

2. Choose a partner and exchange your list of questions with the person.

3. During the next 10 to 20 minutes you have in which to interview each other, each of you should write out your partner's answer as you ask them questions.

4. At the end of interview time, you and your partner join the larger group (if the group is larger than 20, you may want to divide into smaller groups). Each individual will introduce their new friend to the rest of the group using the information you received in the interview. Each partner may correct or modify the information.

DISCUSSION

1. What was the value of this activity?

2. What did you learn about your partner that you did not know prior to the interview?

3. How is an interview different from an ordinary discussion?

4. Do you believe that the information you have gained from your partner is accurate? Is this the same impression you had of your partner when you first saw this person?

5. Were your answers honest, or were you attempting to impress your partner? Explain.

6. Because of this experience in class, will you be willing to talk with this person in the courtyard, sit with this person in the cafeteria, or do something social with this person outside of school?

Name _____ Date _____

Who Am I Presentation

PURPOSE

To enable each person to know something about all the other people in the class—including the teacher.

INSTRUCTIONS

1. Construct outside of class a Who Am I Presentation by pasting or gluing fragments, pictures, or words torn out from magazines, newspapers, and so on onto a large poster board (or other chosen object) to form an abstract "picture" or composition. You may also create any of these words/pictures that you use. OR

2. You may develop your Who I Am Presentation using a computer generated creative approach, or another creative approach that is JUST **you**. (If in doubt, just check with the instructor.)

3. Each individual is asked to compose the presentation around the following ideas—this is what you will be graded on.

    a. Use at least three people who are the most influential in your life. What cultures impact your life?

    b. Use hobbies and interests you have.

    c. Use three words you would like to have said about you.

    d. Use the part of your personality of which you are most proud.

    e. Use the part of your personality that may create difficulties in your relationship with others.

    f. Use an accomplishment of which you are most proud.

    g. Use your likes and dislikes.

    h. Use the goals and values you have for your life.

    i. Use your background, family, and friends.

    j. Use your greatest lesson learned in life.

4. Give your presentation to the class, commenting on the various pictures or meanings reflected. The timeframe is approximately five minutes.

DISCUSSION

1. If you were to do your presentation again, what changes would you make?

2. What was the most difficult part of this assignment? Why?

Name _____ Date _____

First Impressions

PURPOSE

To utilize feedback in discovering how accurate your judgments are about people. To discover how first impressions influence our perceptions of others.

INSTRUCTIONS

1. Without speaking, select a person you do not know in the class and sit together.

2. Without verbally communicating with your partner, write down predictions and/or impressions about the person for the following items:

   a. Estimated Age: _____

   b. Major: _____

   c. Estimated Education: Did not complete high school _____
   Completed high school _____ Some college _____ College degree _____

   d. Nationality or Culture: _____

   e. Political Preference: _____

   f. Occupation: _____

   g. Marital Status: Married _____ Separated _____ Divorced _____
   Single _____ Widowed _____

   h. Children: Yes _____ No _____ How many? _____

   i. Interests:

_____	Sports, what type	_____	Gambling
_____	Camping	_____	Shopping
_____	Movies	_____	Artistic
_____	Gardening	_____	Music, what type?
_____	Dancing	_____	Reading, what type
_____	Politics	_____	Travel
_____	Exercising	_____	Writing
_____	Civic Activities	_____	Cooking
_____	TV	_____	Other

j. List any personality traits or characteristics that might describe this person:

1)

2)

3)

4)

5)

DISCUSSION (WITH YOUR PARTNER):

1. Compare your impressions of each other. Discuss where you were correct and where you were incorrect.

2. As you compare your impressions/predictions with your partner for each item, be sure to comment on what clues or cues led you to make the prediction. In other words, why did you predict what you predicted? For example, did any of these concerns have an influence on your observations, impressions, and predictions?

   a. Clothes/appearance

   b. Anything you remembered from the first day of class

   c. Eye contact or lack of eye contact

   d. Sex and age of partner

   e. Mannerisms when you first began to observe each other

   f. Stereotyping according to ethnicity and race

   g. Your own belief system and values—what you want your partner to believe

   h. What other concerns had an impact?

3. Honestly, did first impressions because of overall appearance have anything to do with your observations and predictions?

DISCUSSION (WITH ALL OF THE CLASS MEMBERS):

1. How does this exercise apply to our everyday interactions with others?

2. How can we change our impressions of others?

Evaluating Stereotypes

PURPOSE

To clarify what stereotypes you have been taught about other groups and evaluate how the process of stereotyping works.

INSTRUCTIONS

The instructor will post the following list of words on sheets of paper around the room.

Republicans	Democrats
Male	Female
Old people	Teenagers
Blondes	Redheads
African American	Asian American
Native American	Hispanic American
Midwestern	Southern
Protestants	Jews
Higher income	Lower income
Lawyers	Car salespeople

1. Each member of the class is to circulate around the room, read the various categories, and write at least one stereotype he or she has heard under each heading. Be sure to not repeat anything that is already written.

2. After the members of the class have finished writing, they are then asked to go around the room and read all the stereotypes under each category and make note of any of particular interest.

3. The instructor will either divide the members into small groups or conduct a class discussion surrounding the following discussion questions.

DISCUSSION

1. What are your personal reactions to comments written under each heading of stereotypes?

2. How accurate are the stereotypes of their identities?

3. What have you learned about stereotyping others?

Name _____ Date _____

Where Does It Come From?

ASSESSING YOUR EMOTIONAL ATTACHMENTS AND SOCIAL TIES

INSTRUCTIONS

Refer to the definitions of Emotional Attachments and Social Ties in the chapter and then look at the following list. If the item provides you with no support, put a "0." If the item provides you with minimal support, put a "1" in the appropriate space, or if you feel that the item provides you with a lot of support, put a "2" in the appropriate space. For example, for Significant Others, you may have a 2 under Emotional Attachment and a 1 or 0 under Social Ties.

You may also want the people who are important to you to take this inventory and review their means of emotional attachment and social ties. If you have young children, you may want to review the inventory for them to make sure they have adequate means of support.

Attachment	Emotional Ties	Social
Significant Others: boy or girlfriend, husband or wife, parents, etc.	_____	_____
Friends: school-mates, co-workers, close friends, neighbors, etc.	_____	_____
Extended Family: aunts and uncles, grandparents, brothers and sisters, in-laws, etc.	_____	_____
Support Groups: singles clubs, men's groups, women's groups, 12 step groups, etc.	_____	_____
Teams: sport teams, hobby groups, singing groups, athletic club members, square dance groups, etc.	_____	_____
Service Groups: Rotary, Kiwanis, sororities and fraternities, Elks, Masons, Scouts, etc.	_____	_____
Racial, Ethnic, and Nationality Groups: associations, clubs, etc.	_____	_____
Vocational Groups: unions, firefighters, police associations, etc.	_____	_____
Religious Organizations: church, Bible study group, men's or women's groups, etc.	_____	_____

Community Groups: neighborhood associations, protection groups, etc. _____ _____

Total _____ _____

Scoring

Add your total points under each column. You should have a score of at least five in each column. The higher the score, the better. If your score is below a five in either column you may want to seek help in adding to your means of emotional attachments and/or social ties. Be prepared to discuss in class.

Discussion

1. Explain from where you receive your emotional attachments. How important are these sources to you?

2. Explain from where you receive your social ties. How important are they to you?

3. What would you tell a friend who is lonely how to change in order to find emotional attachments and social ties?

Name _____ Date _____

Internet Search Activity

INSTRUCTIONS

Heterosexism is the existence of advantages and rewards on heterosexuals solely as a result of their sexual orientation. Many of the things that heterosexuals take for granted may be unavailable to gay or bisexual people. Make a list of the advantages a heterosexual "straight" has.

If you are "straight," what advantages do you enjoy that gay people are less likely to enjoy? Think hard—many of the things that heterosexuals take for granted are not equally available to everyone. Examples include displaying a picture of one's loved one without fear of retaliation or ridicule; not having to hide parts of one's life from family, friends, and coworkers; or having the loved one be legally recognized as the next-of-kin.

When you have made your list, go to www.yahoo.com or www.google.com and type "heterosexism" into the search box. What items could be added to your list as a result of your search? Why do you think you didn't see them earlier?

Draw Your Own Johari Window

PURPOSE

To gain a better understanding of yourself and examine the degree of overall "openness" of your communication.

To understand self-disclosure as a situational concept—you respond (communicate) differently in different situations.

To provide insight into your "open self," "blind self," "hidden self," and "unknown self."

INSTRUCTIONS

Draw your own Johari Window for each of the following situations:

1. When you are with your closest friend.

2. When you are with your parent or parents.

3. When you are in this class.

4. When you are at a social gathering with people you do not know very well.

In addition to the above activity, you may want to explain the purpose of the Johari Window to the following individuals: your best friend, one of your parents, another member of this class, and a new acquaintance, and have them draw the Johari Window as they perceive you. This will give you an idea of how others perceive you.

DISCUSSION

1. Compare your windows in the different situations. Do they differ? Why?

2. How could you become a more "open" communicator?

3. How do others perceive you? Do you agree with their perception of you?

4. What could you do to change other people's perception of you?

Getting Acquainted

LEARNING JOURNAL

Select the statement below that best defines your feelings about the personal value or meaning gained from this chapter and respond below the dotted line.

I learned that I . . .   I was surprised that I . . .

I realized that I . . .   I was pleased that I . . .

I discovered that I . . .   I was displeased that I . . .

Chapter 2
Self-Awareness

©ESB Basic/Shutterstock.com

An individual's self-concept is the core of their personality. It affects every aspect of human behavior: The ability to learn, the capacity to grow and change, the choice of friends, mates, and careers. It is no exaggeration to say that a strong, positive self-image is the best possible preparation for success in life. —Joyce Brothers

Think About This...

In my memories of when I was a "little" kid, between the ages of two and four, it seemed like everything I would attempt would be a "No, No," "No" to this, and "No" to that, and "No" to everything. For awhile I almost thought my name was "No No." I soon learned that my life was much easier if I just sat and watched television.

Life was not much fun because I was afraid to try anything since I thought I would get in trouble. I didn't think I was a very good kid since most of the people around me kept telling me that I wasn't capable of doing anything. I thought it was because I was "no good" and "inferior," but in reality I just wasn't old enough to do what I wanted to do. I didn't realize that.

When I turned six, I was excited because it was time to go to school like the "big kids." It was a new life, and I needed a change. It didn't take long for me to realize that I was not as good as the rest of the kids.

They laughed at my overalls and shiny shoes. When it came time to select teams, I was the last to be picked since I was short, skinny, and wore glasses.

I wanted to be liked by the other students and my teachers, so I became the "class clown." I needed attention and I got it, but it was the wrong type of attention. I became depressed and felt inferior to the people around me, so I withdrew into my own little world and isolated myself as much as I could. I would sit in the back of the room at school, and at home I would go to my room and draw.

My early school years were not fun. In middle school I got mixed up with the "wrong crowd." I wanted to be accepted, so I thought I had to be like everyone else. I wanted to be part of a group with an identity so I got involved in a gang. In the meantime I tried a few drugs and got in trouble. It wasn't a happy time in my life.

In ninth grade, I registered for an art class, not knowing what art was all about. The teacher asked the students to draw a picture. I turned mine in and the teacher thought it was great. The teacher thought that I had talent, but I knew better. I have been told that I am "dumb, inferior and not capable of accomplishing anything," so why try. My teacher encouraged me and kept telling me how good I really was, so I kept trying. All of a sudden the other students were also telling me that I was good and I began to believe it. I became motivated to succeed in the field of art. I overcame my depression and anxiety, set some goals, found some friends who accepted me for being me and not because of my size or looks.

I am now a professional artist and feel good about myself and my life. I like people and accept them as they are and will allow them the freedom to grow and develop as individuals. I hope you will too.

"Self-Image" Development

Reviewing the story above, we realize that people acquire a sense of self throughout their life. It is an ongoing process that evolves from our experiences and interactions with others within the environment. Significant adults in our life also provide us with feedback as to who we are. This is the beginning of *self-image development*. In this chapter you can learn ways in which you can identify and better understand your *real self* and learn strategies to improve your self-esteem.

Self-image is the mental picture, generally of a kind that is quite resistant to change, that depicts not only details that are potentially available to objective investigation by others (height, weight, hair color, gender, IQ score), but also items that have been learned by that person about themselves, either from personal experiences or by internalizing the judgments of others. A person's self-image is their answer to the question "What do you believe people think about you?"

Was I born this way? Are you born with a self-image or is it acquired? Most psychologists say that it is acquired. During infancy, early emotional experiences form the basis for its development . Our *self-image* is affected by all the experiences we have had—successes and failures, compliments and "put downs," happy times and sad times, personal thoughts and experiences, our own expectations and others' expectations of us, and the way other people have reacted to us, especially in our early adulthood. As you can see, a person's self-concept is not a singular mental self-image, but a multifaceted system of related images and ideas. A more technical term for self-image that is commonly used by social and cognitive psychologists is **self-schema**. Self-schemas are also considered the traits people use to define themselves; they draw information about the self into a coherent scheme (Schacter, 2011).

Who are you? How many times have you asked yourself that question? Before we go on, take a few minutes and try to answer the question by writing ten brief statements that begin with *I am* _____. After you have completed your list, examine it to find ways that your self-image has evolved. It may have developed from your social world with statements such as: I am a Roman Catholic, I am a student, I am an adult, I am a mechanic; or it may refer to the nature of your interactions with others with statements such as: "I am a friendly person," "I am a shy person," "I am a family-oriented person," "I am a political activist." Still other statements may refer to traits that you attribute to yourself either because other people have attributed them to you or because you have seen that you stand out in those ways in comparison to other people: "I am short," "I am good at math," "I am conscientious." You probably will not find any self-statements in your list that do not stem in one way or another from your social environment. We will now begin to explore many of the theories and ideas of how you have become the person you are. Let us take a look at how other people influence our feelings about ourselves.

We learn who we are from the way we are treated by the important people in our lives.

©wavebreakmedia/Shutterstock.com

Since we are talking about self-awareness, let's understand what the terms are because it causes much confusion… more terms are in the Glossary in the back of the book.

Ableism - Discrimination or prejudice against individuals with disabilities.

Cultural Difference - To be highly skilled in interpersonal relations you must recognize and appreciate individual and demographic (group or category) differences as well as cultural differences. People from the same demographic group often come from many different cultures, respectfully navigating these differences calls for cultural sensitivity, political correctness *also called "PC,"* cultural intelligence, and respect for all workers and cultures.

Gender/Gender Identity - A person's innate, deeply felt psychological identification as a man, woman, transgender, or somewhere on the spectrum, which may or may not correspond to their sex assigned at birth. People are called cisgendered, gender queer, transgendered, or gender fluid.

Sex Roles - People are born male or female and their society teaches them how to be masculine or feminine. Also called sex-role stereotyping.

Intersectionality - This term started in the 1980s when a lawyer, Kimberly Crenshaw, realized we did not have a way to talk about the experiences of people of color (racial discrimination) and different experiences of men and women (gender discrimination)…looking at the intersections of who we are. Intersectionality refers to the reality that we all have multiple identities. It also gives us a way to talk about impressions and privilege that overlap and reinforce each other. Black men and black women endure bother racial discrimination and black women and white women both have gender discrimination. A video is included in the back of this section that explains intersectionality visually.

Bias - Unreasonably hostile feelings or opinions about a social group; prejudice.

Implicit Bias - **Implicit is** unquestioning or unreserved; absolute: implied, rather than expressly stated: implicit agreement. **Bias** a particular tendency, trend, inclination, feeling, or opinion, especially one that is preconceived or unreasoned: unreasonably hostile feelings or opinions about a social group; prejudice. So **implicit bias** would be an unquestioning preconceived notion or opinion of a social group: predjudice.

Bisexual - Traditionally bisexual has referred to romantic or sexual attraction to two, and not more than two, genders, specifically male and female. However, the term is increasingly being used to refer to a level of sexual fluidity in which an individual moves bidirectionally along a spectrum of sexuality. This newer sense accounts for attraction to people who do not fall within the gender binary.

Disabilities - Is the consequence of an impairment that may be physical, cognitive, intellectual, mental, sensory, developmental, or some combination of these that results in restrictions on an individual's ability to participate in what is considered "normal" in their everyday society. Many people would rather be referred to as a person with a disability instead of handicapped.

Disabled - Having a physical or mental condition that limits movements, senses, or activities.

LGBTQ - An acronym that originated in the 1990s and replaced what was formerly known as "the gay community." The acronym was created to be more inclusive of diverse groups. **LGBTQ** stands for lesbian, gay, bisexual, transgender, and queer (and/or questioning) individuals/identities.

Privilege - a right or benefit that is given to some people and not to others. A special opportunity to do something that makes you proud. The advantage that wealthy and powerful people have over other people in a society. (Gender + Equality Center - The University of Oklahoma, 2017)

Who are the significant others in your life? Who is important in your life? How have they affected your self-image? To whom are you a significant other? Think about the kind of influence you are having on their self-image. Is it a positive or negative effect? You may be surprised to find that if you are a parent, a spouse, a boyfriend or girlfriend, a teacher, a son or daughter, a brother or sister, or a person that can have any impact on another individual, you are a significant other.

A parent says to a child, "You better not try that, I don't think you can do it." You tell your husband, "Can't you ever do anything right?" A teacher tells a student, "Everyone else in the class understands it, what's wrong with you?" A son tells his mother, "You're a 'rotten' parent, you made me this way." Have you heard any of these comments? If we hear these comments too often, we soon begin to believe them, especially if the person saying them is important or significant to us.

From all of these numerous experiences, we construct a mental blueprint of the sort of person we believe we are. Once an idea or belief about ourselves goes into this mental picture, it becomes "true" as far as we are personally concerned. We generally do not

Do you ever compare yourself to other people?

© Blaj Gabriel/Shutterstock.com

question its validity, but proceed to act upon it as if it were true. Most of our actions, feelings, responses, and even our abilities are consistent with this contracted self-image. If we see ourselves as incapable when we enter a math class, we will most likely experience difficulty and failure. If you view yourself as well qualified and capable as you are interviewed for a job, the interviewer will evaluate you on a positive basis, and this will improve your prospects of getting the job. Do you remember from Chapter One what this process is called? This is often called the *self-fulfilling prophecy*. For further discussion on the self-fulfilling prophecy, refer to Chapter One.

Do you ever compare yourself to other people? How does this comparison influence your feelings about yourself?

> *One isn't born one's self. One is born with a mass of expectations, a mass of other people's ideas—and you have to work through it all.*
> —V. S. NAIPAUL

Gaining self-knowledge from our perceptions of others: social comparison. How many times have you asked yourself such questions as, "Am I as good looking as Jake?" "Can I play tennis as well as Anne?" "Am I as smart as Marti?" We gain self-knowledge from our own behavior; we also gain it from others through *social comparison*, the process in which individuals evaluate their thoughts, feelings, behaviors, and abilities in relation to other people. Social comparison helps individuals evaluate themselves, tells them what their distinctive characteristics are, and aids them in building an identity. We tend to compare ourselves with others of our own sex; males compare themselves to other males and females compare themselves to other females. Students who are questioning their gender become quite confused from the societal, social, and family messages they are given. Social comparison allows us a way to decide if we are the *same or different, inferior or superior (Festinger, 1954; Kassin et al., 2016)*.

Same or different? How did you learn about your ethnicity or that you are male or female? A child who is told that he is a different color than his schoolmates begins to see himself as different. A 6'4" female student compares herself with her female schoolmates and perceives herself as weird. "All my friends are from Vietnam just like I am and this makes me feel like I'm part of the group, I'm the same as they are." This perception of sameness or difference in relation to others has a great influence on how we perceive ourselves (Flora, 2005).

Inferior or superior? How often do we label ourselves or others? We tend to decide whether we are superior or inferior by comparing ourselves to others. Are we attractive or ugly? A success or failure? Intelligent or dumb? It depends on those against whom we measure ourselves. In school we compare ourselves with other students, "I'm not as smart as José," or "I'm more intelligent than Gretchen." In sports we tend to compare ourselves with other athletes, "I'm a better racquetball player than Steve," or "Ben's a better quarterback than I am."

> *Our main task in life is to give birth to ourselves.*
> —ERICH FROMM

Social comparison theory has been modified over the years and continues to provide an important rationale for why we affiliate with others and how we come to know ourselves (Kimmel & Aronson, 2011).

The importance of self-concept. When our *self-concept* is intact and secure, we feel good. When it is threatened, we feel anxious and insecure. When it is adequate and one that we can be wholesomely proud of, we feel self-confident. We feel free to be ourselves and to express ourselves. When it is inadequate and an object of shame, we attempt to hide it rather than express it—we withdraw inside ourselves. If we have strong, positive feelings about ourselves, we want and feel that we deserve a good loving relationship, or a good job, and even a feeling of freedom—whatever we think of as the highest good for us. On the other hand, if we have a poorly developed, negative, or inferior self-image, we may expect very little for ourselves. We may settle for second or third best because we feel that is all we deserve. In essence, we project to others the way we feel about ourselves. If we cannot like and respect ourselves, how can we ever hope other people will see us as worthy individuals who have something to contribute to the world in which we live?

To gain a better understanding of how the self-image evolves over a life span, we need to study some of the traditional theories of personality that will provide us with a foundation of how we become aware of who we really are.

> *To be at peace with ourselves, we need to know ourselves.*
> —CAITLIN MATTHEWS

Personality Development

Throughout our lives, we will be attempting to understand other people, such as our boyfriends or girlfriends, our bosses, our husbands or wives, or our teachers. In addition, we will also be attempting to understand ourselves. The following theories will help us gain an understanding of ourselves and the people around us. We will consider a variety of theories that will help you in the journey of finding yourself and answering the question, *Who am I?*

The theory that has had the greatest impact on the field of psychology was developed by Sigmund Freud. This classic theory has created a lot of controversy, not only within the realm of psychology, but also within our everyday lives—in literature, movies, child-rearing practices, the feminist movement. Let us take a look at some of Freud's ideas—**The Psychodynamic Approach**.

Sigmund Freud. Freud's theory of personality development provided the foundation for many other personality theories. Freud (1965) states that a person's personality is made up of three distinct but interrelated parts: the id, ego, and superego.

What is this thing called an id? The *id* is composed of the basic biological drives that motivate an individual. This includes the hunger drive, the thirst drive, sexual impulses, and other needs that assure survival and bring pleasure. The id operates according to the *pleasure principle*, which demands immediate gratification of its urges, and some people believe this often leads to the lack of impulse control—much like preschooler throwing a temper tantrum. Freud has received much of his criticism because of the emphasis he puts on the sexual impulses, pleasure drives, and their control over our behavior (Larsen & Buss, 2014).

When does the superego develop? The *superego* begins to develop after the age of four and is acquired from the environment around us. It consists of our values, morals, religious beliefs, and ideals of our parents and society. Another name for the super-ego would be our *conscience*. The superego tells us what is right and wrong, what we should do and should not do—our *moral compass*. This is the part of our personality that makes us feel guilty and experience anxiety when we do things we should not and allows us to reward ourselves or pat ourselves on the back when we doing something good. As you can observe, the id and the superego are in conflict. Each characteristic is trying to take control of your life. Remember the cartoon with the man with the devil on one shoulder and the other shoulder held an angel and they were both giving him advice? You could use the following analogy—the id is the "devil" and the super-ego is "an angel," each attempting to control your life. If the id or the superego takes control of your life you may develop some form of personality disorder.

The ego to the rescue. Thank goodness for the ego and the fact that it develops before the superego. The ego begins to develop the first time a child understands the word No. With that first "no," the ego has begun to develop and begins to moderate and restrain the id by requiring it to seek gratification of its impulses through realistic and socially acceptable means. The *ego, the reality principle,* is the rational, logical, and realistic part of your personality that attempts to maintain balance between the id and superego. The conflict between the id and the superego causes anxiety, which, in turn, leads the ego to create defense mechanisms to control the anxiety. Defense mechanisms will be discussed in Chapter Eight.

Most psychologists today think that Freud put too much emphasis on the biological drives, specifically the sex drive—the id. For example, Alfred Adler, a charter member of Freud's inner circle, argued that the foremost human drive is not sexuality, but a striving for superiority. Also, Erik Erikson, an original follower of Freud, realized that the biological drives are important, but that the effects of the environment on our development and us are as important, if not more important. Let's take a look at Adler's and Erikson's theories.

Adler's Individual Psychology Theory

To Alfred Adler, personality arises from our attempts to overcome or compensate for fundamental feelings of inadequacy. Adler was responsible for coining the popular term **inferiority complex**, a concept, he argued, that underlies and motivates a great deal of human behavior. From his point of view, it is our natural drive for superiority that explains motivation, not sexual gratification as envisioned by Freud. Adler viewed striving for superiority as a universal drive to adapt, improve oneself, and master life's challenges. He felt that young children understandably feel weak and helpless in comparison to more competent older children and adults. These early inferiority feelings supposedly motivate individuals to acquire new skills and develop new talents (Nevid & Rathus, 2012).

Adler also noted that everyone has to work to overcome some feelings of inferiority. **Compensation** involves efforts to overcome imagined or real weaknesses, limitations, or inferiorities by developing other areas of our personalities. Adler believed that compensation is entirely normal. However, in some people, inferiority feelings can become excessive, resulting in what is called an inferiority complex, exaggerated feelings of weakness and inadequacy. Adler thought that either parental pampering or parental neglect could cause an inferiority problem. He also believed that early childhood experiences exert momentous influences over adult personality.

Adler was careful to explain that an inferiority complex can distort the normal process of striving for superiority. He felt that some people engage in overcompensation in order to conceal their feelings of inferiority. Instead of working to master life's challenges, people with an inferiority complex work to achieve status, gain power over others, and acquire the trappings of success (fancy clothes, impressive cars, or whatever looks important to them). Unfortunately, they tend to flaunt their success in an effort to cover up their underlying inferiority complex (Adler, 1998).

Birth order. It was also Adler who first focused attention on the possible importance of *birth order* as a factor governing personality. Although his theory created many studies on the effects of birth order, the studies failed to support his hypothesis. In recent years, there has been some revived interest in the relationship between birth order and personality, but the research findings have continued to be somewhat inconsistent (Weiten et al., 2014). Yet, the topic is very interesting to discuss. How do you think birth order has influenced your personality development?

> *Your only obligation in any lifetime is to be true to yourself.*
> —RICHARD BACH

> *Shame corrodes the very part of us that believes we are capable of change.*
> —BRENÉ BROWN

What is wrong with me?

©Shayneppistockphoto/Shutterstock.com

Erik Erikson. Erikson has identified *eight stages of psychosocial development* that each individual experiences through his or her life. Each stage is characterized by specific tasks that must be mastered. If these tasks are not satisfied, an unfavorable outcome throws us off balance and makes it harder to deal with later crises. As each stage is completed, we continue to build toward a positive, healthy development and a satisfying life. Those who are plagued with unfavorable outcomes will continue to face frustration and conflict while striving to develop as a person. A brief description of Erikson's eight stages of psychosocial development follows (Feldman, 2013).

ERIKSON'S EIGHT STAGES OF PSYCHOSOCIAL DEVELOPMENT

1. **Trust vs. Mistrust.** During the first years of life, a child is completely dependent on others for the satisfaction of his or her needs. If these needs are satisfied on a consistent basis, the child will feel comfortable and secure. If the child's needs are not satisfied on a regular basis, *mistrust* will develop, and this may become the core of later insecurity and suspiciousness. This child will become *mistrusting* and fearful of others and have difficulty developing close, trusting relationships with others in the future.

2. **Autonomy vs. Doubt.** During ages one through three, a child is attempting to become more independent. They are learning to walk, talk, explore, and become toilet trained. The people around him or her, especially the parents, help the child to develop a sense of independence and autonomy by encouraging him to try new skills and by reassuring him or her if he fails. Consistent discipline is also important during this time. If the parents are inconsistent, overprotective, or show disapproval while the child is attempting to do things on their own, they will become doubtful, unsure, and ashamed. If a child is told by a *significant other* that they should be able to read or be toilet trained, they may wonder, "What is wrong with me? My parents say I should be able to do that but I can't do it." This child will feel doubtful and shamed and thus feel negative about their capabilities. A child who has accomplished some of these tasks and is given encouragement and positive reinforcement will feel confident and independent.

3. **Initiative vs. Guilt.** During the ages of four through five, the child moves from simple self-control to an ability to take control. This is the *questioning and exploring stage* when a child wants to try anything and everything. The child becomes very curious about the world around them. If they are encouraged to take the *initiative* and explore the world, the child will feel good about themselves and will continue to be curious in the future. If the parents inhibit the child's activities and curiosity, the child will feel *guilty* whenever they take the initiative and this can cause the individual to become passive. Why try to do something if your parents keep showing disapproval? This often instills learned helplessness.

4. **Industry vs. Inferiority.** Assume that the child is between the ages of six and twelve and is excited about life and motivated to solve problems and accomplish tasks. These are the early school years when the child should be making new friends, joining clubs and teams, and succeeding in school. When a child has a task to complete, such as a homework assignment, or cookies to sell, or a wood car to make, the child should

attempt to accomplish the task with encouragement from others. The parents should not intervene and complete the task for the child. Otherwise, the child will quickly learn that the parents will always complete the task, so why try? Or possibly the child will feel inferior and incapable because his or her parents always ended up completing the tasks for them. Many parents feel like they are being responsible parents by helping their children learn, but, in reality, they are hindering their development. During this stage, the child is becoming involved in the outside world, and other people such as teachers, classmates, and other adults can have a great influence on the child's attitude toward himself or herself. If someone is there to bail you out then they are "helicopter parents" and then why do you need learn independence?

5. **Identity vs. Role Confusion.** Between the ages of twelve and twenty, a person is caught between childhood and adulthood. The major task to accomplish during this stage is to answer the question, "Who am I?" Adolescence is a turbulent time for many individuals. Mental and physical maturation brings on new feelings and new attitudes of which people are unsure. Should these new feelings and attitudes be expressed or inhibited—especially one's new-found sex drive?

Our identity evolves from our self-perceptions and our relationships with others. People need to see themselves as positive, capable, and lovable individuals as well as having the feeling that they are accepted by others. Otherwise, they will experience **role confusion**, an uncertainty about who they are and where they are going. Role confusion may lead to a constant searching for acceptance and a feeling of belonging. This search for identity can lead people to unhealthy relationships and to alternatives such as drugs and gangs.

The beginning of the adult years. Freud did not put much emphasis on the adult years, but Erikson noticed that we continue to go through different stages as we age.

6. **Intimacy vs. Isolation (20–40 years).** Now that we feel good about ourselves and have an *identity*, we are ready to form meaningful relationships and learn to share with others. During the young-adult years, we must develop the ability to care about others and express a willingness to share experiences with them. Marriage and sexual intimacy do not guarantee these qualities. Failure to establish intimacy with others leads to a deep sense of *isolation*. The person feels lonely and uncared for in life. A person who satisfies this stage is capable of developing close, intimate, and sharing relationships with others and feels comfortable and secure in these relationships. New research indicates that young adults are choosing not to marry or marrying later in life, suggesting that they are building close relationships with friends.

7. **Generativity vs. Self-Absorption (40–65 years).** Until middle age, we seem to be preoccupied with ourselves. Even the intimacy stage is primarily for the self to prevent loneliness. Now we are ready to look beyond the self and look to the future, not only for ourselves, but also for others. This seems to be the best time to establish a family because we are concerned about the development and welfare of others. This is the time in our life when we feel productive and are concerned for the benefit of humankind.

What about the individual who does not feel productive and also feels like they are not accomplishing any goals in life? This person feels trapped. Life loses its meaning and the person feels bitter, dreary, unfulfilled, and stagnant. This person becomes preoccupied with the self, personal needs, and interests.

Daniel Levinson (1986) has written extensively about stages of adult development. However, most of Levinson's research and work were based on the study of men. According to Levinson, if people do not go through a *mid-life transition stage,* they may live a life of *staleness and resignation.* Some individuals, approximately two to five percent of the population (McCrea & Costa, 2005), will experience a painful and disruptive struggle, which is called the *mid-life crisis.* This is similar to the adolescent identity crisis (Erikson stage of identity versus role confusion), where the individual seeks a new identity or to find an identity. Since these individuals have not satisfied their goals they had set for themselves, they experience frustration. It is not uncommon for individuals to divorce their spouses, quit their jobs, buy a convertible, and attempt to start all over again.

8. **Integrity vs. Despair (65 years–death).** Old age should be a time of reflection, when a person should be able to look back over the events of a lifetime with a sense of acceptance and satisfaction. This is the type of person who has tried to live life to its fullest. The individual who wishes they could live life over again, and also feels cheated or deprived of any of the breaks in life will live a life of regret and failure. This is the person who keeps saying, "What if . . .?" or "If I had taken that opportunity" and because of this, feels depressed and will be unhappy the rest of their life. However, newer research indicates that it is possible to resolve this issue and move into acceptance and end life with integrity.

What dreams do you have for your life?

© rzozel9/Shutterstock.com

As most people continue through this stage, they re-evaluate the meaning of life for themselves and ideally find a new meaning that will help reduce fear and anxiety and help prepare them for facing death.

 **Check this out**   **THERE'S A REVOLUTION GOING ON!**
(MANY CHANGES HAVE TAKEN PLACE)

There is a revolution going on in our "life-cycle" development. People are leaving childhood sooner, but they are taking longer to grow up and much longer to die. Look at some of the "happenings" that we have been hearing about in the news and on social media.

- Nine-year-old boys carrying a gun to school
- Nine-year-old girls developing breasts and pubic hair
- 16-year-olds divorcing their parents
- 35-year-old men still living at home with their parents
- 40-year-old women are just getting around to pregnancy
- 50-year-old men are forced into early retirement
- 55-year-old women can have egg donor babies
- 65-year-old women receiving their doctorate degrees
- 70-year-old men reversing aging by 20 years with human growth hormones
- 80-year-olds running marathons
- 85-year-olds remarrying and still enjoying sex
- More and more people reaching the age of 100

There seems to be a shifting of all the stages of adulthood. Adolescence is being prolonged. Adulthood begins around 30. Most baby-boomers do not feel "grown up" until they are into their forties. When our parents turned 50, we thought they were old! Fifty is what 40 used to be; 60 is what 50 used to be. Middle age has already been pushed far into the 50s (Sheehy, 2006). So what's next? What are your thoughts?

All of us need to continue to evaluate our lives on a regular basis. As long as we do this, we will not experience any traumatic transitions that will disrupt our life (Gibbs, 2005). As you observe the above eight stages you notice that there is a positive and negative aspect of each stage. Are you able to identify the stage you are in right now? Are you able to identify the stages some of your friends are in? Erik Erikson was one of the first psychologists to put some emphasis on the fact that we continue to go through developmental stages throughout our lives. Freud emphasized that the first six years of life were the most important years.

> *Do not be too timid and squeamish about your actions. All life is an experiment.*
> —RALPH WALDO EMERSON

What traits do you think this woman possesses?

©John Roman Images/Shutterstock.com

Trait Theory

Your friends ask you to tell them about your brother. You tell them he tends to be domineering, anxious, optimistic, intelligent, and athletic. Are these terms you have used to describe other people? Many of us use terms like moody, smart, stupid, restless, impulsive, passive, careful, aggressive, quiet, reliable, shy, outgoing to describe people. The words you use to describe other people (and yourself) are called **traits**, relatively stable and consistent personal characteristics. Trait theorists are interested in measuring how people differ (which key traits best describe them), and then in measuring how much they differ (the degree of variation in traits within the individual and between the individuals).

GENDER AND YOU

MEN OR WOMEN: WHO'S THE BETTER LEADER?

According to a 2014 Pew Research Center study, Americans believe, in general, that women in high political offices are better than men in several different capacities. For instance, when it comes to working out compromises, 41 percent say women are better at it than men (27 percent say men are better). Thirty percent say women work harder to improve the quality of life for Americans, as opposed to 22 percent who say men work harder at it. Thirty percent also believe that women stand up for beliefs despite political pressure, as opposed to 19 percent for men. Women are rated as being more honest and ethical with 37 percent compared to 30 percent for men. Finally, women are perceived as being more persuasive than men, at 25 percent. Men rated eighteen percent for persuasiveness.

Adapted from Pew Research Center. Survey conducted Nov. 12-21, 2014.

Becoming *Aware*

Personality Types

The Big Five. Because trait and type theories, gained popularity in the1980's by well-known psychologists, such as Gordon Allport, Raymond Cattell, and Hans Eysenck,because they follow a common sense approach, researchers today still find them attractive. However, rather than speaking of hundreds of traits or of a few types, many theorists now agree that there are five broad categories. These five major dimensions of personality have become known as the *Big Five* (McCrae & Costa, 2005; 2008). (You can easily remember the five factors with the following mnemonic device by using the first letters of each of the Big Five traits, which spell OCEAN.)

Many researchers are now convinced that the best way to describe personality and individual differences is to find where people stand on the following dimensions: 1) openness to experience, 2) conscientiousness, 3) extraversion, 4) agreeableness, and 5) neuroticism. Like Cattell, McCrae and Costa maintain that personality can be described adequately by measuring the basic traits that they've identified. Their bold claim has been supported in many studies by other researchers, and the five-factor model has become the dominant conception of personality structure in contemporary psychology (John & Srivastava, 2008). This is indicated, in part, by the fact that these dimensions are ones to which most people in many different cultures refer in describing themselves.

Table 2.1   THE "BIG FIVE" PERSONALITY FACTORS

TRAIT	DESCRIPTION OF HIGH SCORER	DESCRIPTION OF LOW SCORER
Openness to experience	Imaginative	Practical
or	Prefers variety	Prefers routine
Not open	Creative	Uncreative
Conscientiousness	Responsible	Negligent
or	Organized	Disorganized
Undirected	Dependable	Undependable
Extraversion	Talkative	Quiet
Or	Expressive	Reserved
Introversion	Active	Passive
Agreeableness	Good-natured	Irritable
or	Helpful	Stubborn
Antagonistic	Trusting	Suspicious
Neuroticism	Worrying	Calm
or	Anxious	Self-controlled
Emotional stability	Insecure	Secure

Adapted from McCrae & Costa (2005; 2008).

Trait theories allow us to describe personality, but they do not necessarily help us understand how we developed these traits (Cloninger, 2007). Yet, the above traits are stable across the life cycle; if you're curious when young, you're likely to be curious when older. Five decades of research on the determinants of the Big Five suggests that the heritability of each trait is in the vicinity of 50 percent (Krueger & Johnson, 2008). What about describing people in terms of temperament and personality type?

HEXACO The HEXACO personality inventory model includes six dimensions of human personality: Honesty-Humility, Emotionality, Extraversion, Agreeableness, Conscientiousness, and Openness to Experience. Along each of these six dimensions, the four cardinal virtues (wisdom, courage, temperance, and justice) are represented. The "H" in the H factor stands for "Honesty-Humility," one of the six basic dimensions of the human personality. People who have high levels of H are sincere and modest; people who have low levels are deceitful and pretentious. It isn't intuitively obvious that traits of honesty and humility go hand in hand, and until very recently the H factor hadn't been recognized as a basic dimension of personality. But scientific evidence shows that traits of honesty and humility form a unified group of personality traits, separate from those of the other five groups identified several decades ago. The H factor explores the scientific findings that show the importance of this personality dimension in various aspects of people's lives: their approaches to money, power, and sex; their inclination to commit crimes or obey the law; their attitudes about society, politics, and religion; and their choice of friends and spouse. Drs. Lee and Ashton provide ways of identifying people who are low in the H factor, as well as advice on how to raise one's own level of H. (Ashton & Lee, 2007)

http://hexaco.org/ gives you basic information and materials for the HEXACO Personality Inventory-Revised, an instrument that assesses the six major dimensions of personality.

Mindset - A term from the dictionary *is the established set of attitudes held by someone.* Another definition is that mindset is a simple idea discovered by world-renowned Stanford University psychologist Carol Dweck in decades of research on achievement and success—a simple idea that makes all the difference in the social psychology and education worlds. Let's take a look at that new concept. Dr. Carol Dweck found that teaching a growth mindset creates motivation and productivity in the worlds of business, education, and sports.

In 2007 Psychologist Dr. Carol Dweck studied the effect of praise on students in a dozen New York schools. Her seminal work—a series of experiments on 400 fifth-graders—paints the picture most clearly. Dweck sent four female research assistants into New York fifth-grade classrooms. The researchers would take a single child out of the classroom for a nonverbal IQ test consisting of a series of puzzles—puzzles easy enough that all the children would do fairly well. Once the child finished the test, the researchers told each student his score, and then gave him a single line of praise. Randomly divided into groups, some were praised for their *intelligence*. They were told, "You must be smart at this." Other students were praised for their *effort*: "You must have worked really hard." Why just a single line of praise? "We wanted to see how

sensitive children were," Dweck explained. "We had a hunch that one line might be enough to see an effect."

Having artificially induced a round of failure, Dweck's researchers then gave all the fifth-graders a final round of tests that were engineered to be as easy as the first round. Those who had been praised for their effort significantly improved on their first score—by about 30 percent. Those who'd been told they were smart did worse than they had at the very beginning—by about 20 percent.

Dweck had suspected that praise could backfire, but even she was surprised by the magnitude of the effect. "Emphasizing effort gives a child a variable that they can control," she explains. "They come to see themselves as in control of their success. Emphasizing natural intelligence takes it out of the child's control, and it provides no good recipe for responding to a failure." Then the students were given a choice of test for the second round. One choice was a test that would be more difficult than the first, but the researchers told the kids that they'd learn a lot from attempting the puzzles. The other choice, Dweck's team explained, was an easy test, just like the first. Of those praised for their effort, 90 percent chose the *harder* set of puzzles. Of those praised for their intelligence, a majority chose the *easy* test. The "smart" kids took the cop-out. Why did this happen? "When we praise children for their intelligence," Dweck wrote in her study summary, "we tell them that this is the name of the game: Look smart, don't risk making mistakes." And that's what the fifth-graders had done: They'd chosen to look smart and avoid the risk of being embarrassed.

In a subsequent round, none of the fifth-graders had a choice. The test was difficult, designed for kids two years ahead of their grade level. Predictably, everyone failed. But again, the two groups of children, divided at random at the study's start, responded differently. Those praised for their effort on the first test assumed they simply hadn't focused hard enough on this test. "They got very involved, willing to try every solution to the puzzles," Dweck recalled. "Many of them remarked, unprovoked, 'This is my favorite test.'" Not so for those praised for their smarts. They assumed their failure was evidence that they weren't really smart at all. "Just watching them, you could see the strain. They were sweating and miserable."

In follow-up interviews, Dweck discovered that those who think that innate intelligence is the key to success begin to discount the importance of effort. *I am smart,* the kids' reasoning goes; *I don't need to put out effort.* Expending effort becomes stigmatized—it's public proof that you can't cut it on your natural gifts. Repeating her experiments, Dweck found this effect of praise on performance held true for students of every socioeconomic class. It hit both boys and girls—the very brightest girls especially (they collapsed the most following failure). Even preschoolers weren't immune to the inverse power of praise (Bronson, 2007).

"Parents should praise children for their effort, their concentration, their strategies," Dweck said. This view creates a love of learning and a resilience that is essential for great accomplishment. Virtually all great people have had these qualities. Teaching a growth mindset creates motivation and productivity in the worlds of business, education, and sports. It enhances relationships—praising brains and talent does not foster self-esteem and accomplishment but jeopardizes them (Dwerk, 2007).

WHAT IS YOUR MINDSET? THINK ABOUT HOW YOUR PARENTS PRAISED OR ENCOURAGED YOU AS A CHILD.

Achievement and success—a simple idea that makes all the difference. Dweck found that children's performance worsens if they always hear how smart they are. Kids who get too much praise are less likely to take risks, are highly sensitive to failure, and are more likely to give up when faced with a challenge. What do you have? Can you tell what your friends have?

In a fixed mindset, people believe their basic qualities, like their intelligence or talent, are simply fixed traits. They spend their time documenting their intelligence or talent instead of developing them. They also believe that talent alone creates success—without effort. They're wrong.

In a growth mindset, people believe that their most basic abilities can be developed through dedication and hard work—brains and talent are just the starting point. The key is be specific about the praise you give.

While there are many personality type indicators and/or tests available, perhaps the best known is the Myers-Briggs Type Indicator® (MBTI®). It is based on the theory of Carl Jung's psychological types. In essence, we have mental or psychological preferences for performing certain tasks. (It is a fun, entertaining test for a classroom activity and, even though questions exist about the use of the test—see "Something to Think About," below, giving the MBTI has proven to stimulate the conversation around the idea and use of personality tests.) According to type psychology, there are 16 basic personality types consisting of four dimensions. We will now discuss these four different dichotomies or dimensions (Myers & Myers, 1995).

Extroversion (E) or Introversion (I). People who prefer extroversion like variety and action in their work and everyday activities. They are sociable, naturally communicate energy and enthusiasm, and are particularly good at interacting with people. Extroverts prefer having people around them most of the time, and it is not unusual for them to act quickly, sometimes without thinking. Extroversion is characterized by breadth of activities (as opposed to depth), surgency from external activity/situations, and energy creation from external means (Olson, 2012). Surgency is a trait aspect of emotional reactivity in which a person tends towards high levels of positive affect. It has been linked to the Big Five personality traits of extroversion. The trait is marked by pronounced engagement with the external world. Extroverts enjoy interacting with people, and are often perceived as full of energy. They tend to be enthusiastic, action-oriented individuals. They possess high group visibility, like to talk, and assert themselves (Canadian Research & Development Center of Sciences and Cultures, 2012).

Introverts like having a great deal of time for quiet activities so they can concentrate, develop ideas, and reflect on the day. In fact, one of their strong gifts is their natural ability to reflect on decisions they need to make, so it is rare for them not to think through something very carefully before making a decision. Introverts are collectors of thoughts, and solitude is the place where the collection is curated and rearranged to make sense of the present and the future (Helgoe, 2010). They keep their energy and enthusiasm inside, prefer working alone, and are quite comfortable with just a few very close friends.

Sensing (S) or Intuition (N). Individuals who prefer sensing are practical and realistic and like to use facts, details, and examples to help them solve problems. They may distrust and ignore their inspirations, preferring to just continue with what is, with some fine tuning. Sensing types like established ways of doing things, usually proceed step-by-step, and rarely make errors of fact.

People who prefer intuition enjoy solving new complex problems and are good at seeing the big picture, new possibilities, and new ways of doing things. It is common for them to rely heavily on insights and imagination. They often follow their inspirations, good or bad, and often may make errors of fact. Intuitive types prefer change, sometimes radical, to continuation of what is and often proceed in bursts of energy, with slack periods in between.

Thinking (T) or Feeling (F). Thinkers prefer to use logical analysis and deep thought to make decisions, being careful to review the pros and cons of any decision they need to make. They tend to be brief, concise, firm-minded, and can give criticism when appropriate. It is normal for them to be convinced by cool, impersonal reasoning and tend to use emotions and feelings as the only cognitive data to weigh in the decision-making process.

Feelers tend to use personal values to make their decisions, while taking time to consider how much they care and how much personal investment they have for each of the alternatives. These individuals are sociable and friendly, prefer harmony with others, dislike telling people unpleasant things, and tend to be sympathetic and appreciative. They are convinced by personal information, enthusiastically delivered.

Judgment (J) or Perception (P). Individuals who prefer a judging lifestyle tend to live in an organized, structured, planned way, desiring to regulate life and control it. They prefer to "plan their work and work their plan," and like to get things settled and finished. These individuals create lists to keep them on schedule and often focus on the task to be done. It is important to note that judging does not mean being judgmental of others—only as it refers to how one prefers to live their individual life.

Those who prefer a perceptive approach tend to live in a flexible, unstructured, and spontaneous manner. They prefer to leave things open for last-minute changes and dislike deadlines, schedules, and may postpone tasks that need to be done. It is common for these individuals to present views as tentative and modifiable. Perceptive individuals use lists to remind them of all the things they have to do someday.

> If a man does not keep pace with his companions, perhaps it is because he hears a different drummer. Let him step up to the music which he hears, however measured or far away.
> —HENRY DAVID THOREAU

> The merit of the MBTI is that it enables us to expect specific personality differences in particular people and to cope with the people and differences in a constructive way.
> —ISABEL MYERS

something to Think About

The MBTI is only one type of personality test. There have been questions concerning the validity of the MBTI personality inventory. The MBTI does poorly on reliability, says Annie Murphy Paul in *The Cult of Personality Testing*. Also research shows "that as many as three-quarters of test takers achieve a different personality type when tested again, and the sixteen distinctive types described by the Myers-Briggs have no scientific basis whatsoever." In a recent article, Roman Krznaric adds that, "if you retake the test after only a five-week gap, there's around a 50% chance that you will fall into a different personality category." As management researchers William Gardner and Mark Martinko write in a comprehensive review, "Few consistent relationships between type and managerial effectiveness have been found." As Susan Cain explains in *Quiet*, "more than a thousand studies conducted by scientists worldwide" suggest that introverts "are more sensitive than extroverts to various kinds of stimulation, from coffee to a loud bang to the dull roar of a networking event." The vast majority of us are ambiverts: in Dan Pink's words from *To Sell is Human*, most people are "neither overly extroverted nor wildly introverted."

If you are interested in taking the Myers-Briggs questionnaire, your college counseling service may have a version you can take, or you may have an opportunity in a class or seminar. The book *Please Understand Me* (Keirsey & Bates, 1998), offers a questionnaire that provides scores in the four categories. Also, the Web Resources at the end of the chapter may be of help. I have included videos about the MBTI, the Harry Potter MBTI versions, and also a video debunking the MBTI test.

THE ART OF PEOPLE: 11 SIMPLE PEOPLE SKILLS THAT WILL GET YOU EVERYTHING YOU WANT.

"Sometimes you'll get your way, sometimes you won't"

"While you can't control the outcome you can choose your attitude."

"Choose positivity."

"Choose gratitude."

"Enthusiasm is contagious."

"Put yourself second."

"Walk in others' shoes before taking action."

"Open your ears—you might connect to someone by really listening not just wait your turn to talk."

(Kerpen, 2016) Art of people book.com

Author Dave Kerpen believes it's actually those with the best *people skills* who win the day. Those who build the right relationships, and those who truly understand and connect with their colleagues, their customers, their partners. Those who can teach, lead, and inspire (Kerpen, 2016). In a world where we are constantly connected, and social media has become the primary way we communicate, the key to getting ahead is being the person others like, respect, and trust. Because no matter who you are or what profession you're in, success is contingent less on what you can do for yourself, but on *what other people are willing to do for* you. Dave Kerpen in his book *The Art of People* feels that the key to gaining influence and getting what we want is to be the person **others** like, respect, and trust. A self-assessment is available at the end of the chapter so you can evaluate yourself.

Now, it is time to return to our discussion of other theories that will help us understand how we have evolved into the individuals we are today.

Strengths-Based Psychology

In 1998, Tom Rath (2007) began working with a team of Gallup scientists led by the late Father of Strengths Psychology, Donald O. Clifton. Their goal was to start a global conversation about what's right with people rather than focusing so much on people's shortcomings. They believed that people have several times more potential for growth when they invested energy in developing their strengths instead of correcting their deficiencies.

Based on Gallup's 40-year study of human strengths, they created a language of the 34 most common talents and developed the Clifton StrengthsFinder assessment to help people discover and describe these talents. They have continued to conduct research on their findings, and *StrengthsFinder 2.0* picks up where the first version left off. The language of 34 themes remains the same, and the results yield a much more in-depth analysis of an individual's top five strengths and talents. There is an access code at the back of Rath's book, *StrengthsFinder 2.0*, which directs you to the online assessment and Strengths Discovery and Action-Planning Guide based on your *StrengthsFinder 2.0* results. The access code is valid for one user only.

While there may be other strengths tests, free or fee-based, available, at the end of this chapter be sure to review the web resources activity: *Brief Strengths Test*, or *VIA Survey of Character Strengths*, which measures 24 strengths and is free online. You can get an analysis of your scores for your personal evaluation.

There now are several major approaches in the helping professions to facilitate personal growth based on capacity and not limitations. Positive psychology (Martin Seligman), the strengths perspective in social work (Dennis Saleebey), and solution oriented therapies (Milton Erickson; Steve de Shazer) are some of the most prominent schools of thought. Davidson (2014) developed a model from these traditions with eight (8) principles that can be used for an individual's personal growth or as a guideline for helping others. To make the model easier to remember, Davidson uses an acronym: STRENGTH.

Table 2.2 THE STRENGTH MODEL

S Be "solution-focused" instead of going over and over describing what is wrong. As a helper, listen to problems with empathy and then collaborate to discover new possibilities and do things differently.
T Do a "trajectory preview." Imagine a better future and use that preferred scenario to activate hopes and dreams. Use your new vision of what you want as a way to keep on track with what you will do.
R Begin "resource development." Identify resources that will promote successful outcomes and, with supportive people, put in the effort to access those resources.
E Conduct an "exceptions analysis." Emphasize overlooked strengths and remember what has helped in the past. Under-utilized skills and previous solutions pave the way for exceptions to current problems.
N Practice "Noticing positives." Get in the habit of thinking more about what is already good and what is getting better. This helps motivate a person to build on strengths and to recognize progress being made.
G Concentrate on "goal setting." Select a few short-term goals that are likely to lead to quick, small solutions, while also identifying some longer-term goals based on emerging strengths and accomplishments.
T Do a "tenacity review." Remind yourself of times when you have been determined and reinforce a positive image of your abilities to endure difficult times.
H Focus on "human capacity development." Identify skills to develop competence and rely on maximizing the potential within the self, while drawing on strengths of family, group, traditions, and culture.
(Davidson 2014)

Carl Rogers: Self-Theory—Humanistic Approach

Carl Rogers (1995) defines the development of the self-concept in terms of *self-actualization*, which is defined as the fulfillment of one's own unique potential. The key to self-actualization is the self-concept. Rogers maintains that the way we regard ourselves depends largely on the kind of regard given by others. In the ideal situation, love is given freely and does not depend on any specific aspects of behavior. Rogers calls this **unconditional positive regard** (Pastorino & Doyle-Portillo, 2012). Unconditional acceptance leads to unimpaired growth and the development of positive characteristics. Individuals who have received unconditional positive regard have a positive realistic self-concept, high self-esteem and feelings of self-respect. Rogers believes that a fully-functioning person lives totally in the present and is continually changing to make full use of their potential.

The difficulties in functioning are caused by a lack of *unconditional acceptance* by others starting at birth. Many parents make their affection and approval conditional on certain kinds of behavior. If the child does what the parent says, the parent will love the child. If the child does not live up to parental expectations, the parent may show disapproval and withhold affection. Consequently, the child attempts to live up to his parents' expectations but cannot always be successful. This is the beginning of an unrealistic self-concept.

In order to become a self-actualized individual, we must accept ourselves as we are, the positive and the negative, with the potential to grow as a person and to accept others as they are, rather than wishing that they were somehow different. We all need to learn to place a high value on the individuality and uniqueness of ourselves and others.

CONSIDER THIS

THE SELF-ACCEPTING PERSON

- The self-accepting person is a participant in life rather than a spectator.
- He is inclined to be objective, spontaneous, emotional, and intellectually honest.
- He tries to understand the interpersonal and environmental problems he faces, but he also accepts his limitations in gaining true insight concerning them.
- He works out the best adjustment to life of which he is capable, often without fully understanding all that is involved.
- However, he is willing to experience the pleasures and discomfort of self-revelation: i.e., he accepts the mixed pain and joy that accompanies each change in his attitude and feeling toward himself and others.
- His claims on life are, for the most part, reasonable. If he wants to be a member of the Country Club and yet cannot afford it, he finds other social and recreational outlets in keeping with his budget.
- The self-accepting person without special talent or ability is able to emotionally share in the gifts of others without undue regret about his own inborn deficiencies.
- He does not brood about missed opportunities, lost causes, errors, and failures. Rather, he looks on them for what they can contribute to his doing things differently or better in the future.
- He does not get stuck in the rut of irrational feelings of love, hate, envy, jealousy, suspicion, lust, and greed, because he lets each feeling spell out its special message for him.

From *Self-Acceptance* by McDonald, Smith, and Sutherland. Copyright by The Hogg Foundation for Mental Health. The University of Texas, Austin, Texas.

Viktor Frankl: Search for Meaning

VIKTOR FRANKL (1998) STATES:

> As humans, we are capable of self-awareness, which allows us to reflect and to decide. With this awareness, we become free beings who are responsible for choosing the way we live and thus influence our own destiny.

This awareness of freedom and responsibility gives rise to existential anxiety, which is a basic human condition. Whether we like it or not, we are free, even though we may seek to avoid reflecting on this freedom. The knowledge that we must choose leads to anxiety. Facing the inevitable prospect of eventual death gives the present moment significance, for we become aware that we do not have forever to accomplish our projects.

Our task is to create a life that has *meaning* and *purpose*. (Meaning, purpose, and self-actualization will be discussed in more detail in Chapters Nine and Ten.) As humans, we are unique in striving toward creating purposes and values that give meaning to living.

This is an existential view of human nature that states that the significance of our existence is never fixed once and for all. Rather, we continually recreate ourselves through our goals. Humans are in a constant state of transition, emerging, evolving, and becoming. Being a person implies that we are discovering and making sense of our existence.

Life has taught me so many lessons, it's hard to decide which one is of the greatest value, but one of the most important is this: Nobody will believe in you unless you believe in yourself.
—LIBERACE (1919–1986), PIANIST

Virginia Satir: Self-Worth

I am me and I am okay.
—VIRGINIA SATIR

Virginia Satir (1988; 2001) indicates in her writing that the crucial factor in interpersonal relations—what happens inside people and between people—*is the picture of the individual worth that each person carries around.* A person who can appreciate his or her own self-worth will be able to see and respect the worth of others. She describes a human being who is living humanly as a person who understands, values, and develops his or her body, finding it useful and beautiful. This is a person who is honest about himself or herself and others, who is willing to take risks, to be creative, embrace change, who is feeling, loving, playful, authentic, and productive. She says that the person who is living humanly can stand on his or her own two feet, can love deeply and fight fairly and effectively, and can be on equally good terms with both his or her tenderness and his or her toughness.

Self-worth is learned, and the family is where it is basically acquired. There is always hope that your life can change because you can always learn new things. Human beings can learn, grow, and change all their lives. Every person has a feeling of worth, positive or negative. The question is, which one is it—positive or negative?

36 oz.—
27 oz.—
18 oz.—
9 oz.—

Pot of Self-Worth

Do you have high or low self-worth? If you have low self-worth or know someone with low self-worth, you can change or help the other person change. Do not blame other people for your problems or faults. You are already that way, but you can change. Look to the future. For others to change, a nurturing environment needs to be provided, and for you to change, a new environment is also needed. You will be able to develop and grow in an atmosphere where individual differences are appreciated, mistakes are tolerated, communication is open, and rules are flexible—this is a nurturing environment. Satir describes the main points that help human beings change and grow:

How many ounces are in your pot today?

1. Communication of feelings: all feelings are honorable—Express your feelings— no one knows how you feel if you do not disclose your feelings to them.
2. Belief that a person is able to grow and change—If you believe you can change, you can.
3. Restoring the use of the senses—take in the world and see freely, touch freely, and hear freely.

What is in the pot of self-worth? Satir uses this *pot concept* to refer to how you feel about yourself, your self-worth. For example, assuming the maximum capacity of a pot of self-worth is 36 ounces, how many ounces would be in your pot today? And, what is it full of?

Suppose your *"pot"* is full of a feeling you have had since childhood, such as hostility toward one of your parents because they abused you. Your inner thoughts say, "I must be a bad person since my parents always beat me. I'm no good. I must have deserved the abuse." Your pot of self-worth is low because of your past experience. You are experiencing "self-defeating" thoughts. You can learn to change these feelings. You can change your "self-talk," and tell yourself that you are a "good person." You can read a good self-help book that may help you or you may seek professional counseling.

Does your pot of self-worth change? Your self-worth pot is constantly changing. One day you get an "A" on a test and you feel great, your pot of self-worth is full of good feelings. The next day you call someone on the phone for a date and you get turned down. Now your pot of self-worth is low—it has a lot of negative feelings in it. Knowing that you are a "good" person no matter what happens to you, will help you maintain a full pot of good feelings and help you succeed in life.

You must learn to free yourself of any rule decreeing that some feeling you have is not a human feeling. Then you are free to function fully and free to make choices about what you want for your life.

How Do Our Thoughts and Our Environment Relate to the Development of Our Personality?

In Chapter Three we will discover how learning theory relates to the development of our personality, but in the meantime we will discover how our thoughts and our relationships with other people interrelate.

How Did I Get to Be the Person I Am Today?

Cognitive theories of personality point out that there are important individual differences in the way people think about and define situations. Cognitive theories stress the mental processes through which people turn their sensations and perceptions into organized impressions of reality. They emphasize that people actively choose their own environments to a great extent. People choose to enter those situations that they expect to be reinforcing and to avoid those that are unsatisfying and uncertain. As many of you have observed, some members of minority ethnic groups "stick together" on college campuses. Oftentimes it is that these members are uncertain about whether they would be accepted if they ventured into different ethnic friendships. Most of us tend to avoid relationships that we anticipate as unsatisfying by not attempting to start them and by continuing with familiar ones instead.

The cognitive emphasis to personality is the interaction of a person's thoughts and behavior. It considers the uniqueness of human beings, especially of their thought processes. It also assumes that human beings are decision makers, planners, and evaluators of their own behavior. Many contemporary researchers claim that people can change their behavior, their conception of themselves, and their personalities in a short time if they are willing to change their thoughts. More often than not, we hope our cognitions are rational and sensible, thus enabling us to live and make decisions in emotionally healthy ways. But many times, our cognitive processing is irrational and not sensible, and we may be totally unaware of it.

Talk to yourself. Use positive self-talk. It has been said that there is nothing wrong with talking to yourself, but if you should ever start answering back, then it is time to be concerned. Although going around talking to yourself in public may cause people to wonder about you, holding an inner dialogue is not only very useful, but also quite normal.

In fact, the inner conversations we have with ourselves can have a powerful effect on our emotional well-being and our motivation. Developing an awareness of precisely what we are saying to ourselves and about ourselves can help us understand why we react the way we do to various people and events in our lives.

© mimagephotography/Shutterstock.com

Does positive thinking influence your behavior?

Building self-esteem is easier with the help of positive self-talk (self-talk is discussed in depth in Chapter Eight). You may have discovered that negative self-talk can have a tremendous influence in the development of someone's feelings about themselves—a poor self-concept. Research shows that talking to yourself positively can make you feel much better.

Thinking positively and optimistically. You may recall the words of a popular song by Bobby McFerrin, "Don't worry, be happy," and it continues, "Cause when you worry, your face will frown and that will bring everything down." Does this kind of thinking influence your behavior? Indeed it does. A positive mood improves our ability to process information more efficiently, increases optimism, and raises self-esteem. A positive attitude enhances our sense of controlling our environment, and acting on this optimism can actually lead to more control over our circumstances. Since many of us are not positive thinkers and are more pessimistic than optimistic, how can we change this behavior?

Let's take a brief look at what is called **cognitive restructuring**—the process of modifying thoughts, ideas, and beliefs. Cognitive restructuring can be used to increase positive and optimistic thinking. This is also known as **self-talk**—the unspoken, mental speech we use when we think about something, solve problems, and make plans. Self-talk is very helpful in cognitive restructuring. Positive self-talk will allow you the freedom to build the confidence you need in order to reach your potential. David Sarwer is a psychologist and clinical director at the Center for Weight and Eating Disorders at the University of Pennsylvania. He says that, in fact, a mirror is one of the first tools he uses with some new patients. He stands them in front of a mirror and coaches them to use gentler, more neutral language as they evaluate their bodies ("Why Saying

Chapter 2: Self-Awareness

Is Believing—The Science Of Self-Talk," NPR, 2014). Take a look at what you may be saying to yourself in Table 2.3.

Is there a relationship between the self-fulfilling prophecy and positive self-talk? When you keep telling yourself, "I'm no good," "I'll never amount to anything," "I'm a liar," "Nobody likes me," "Nobody will ever love me," "I will never be able to pass math," etc., you will discover that it unconsciously affects your attitude and behavior. This is why it is so important to monitor your self-talk.

You need to become aware of your self-talk. Several strategies are listed below that will help you monitor and fine tune your self-talk.

Table 2.3   WHAT DO YOU TELL YOURSELF?

POSITIVE SELF-TALK	NEGATIVE SELF-TALK
I sure am a good person.	I am not a very good person.
I know I can do it.	I cannot do anything right.
"I am a harder worker than most people think."?	I sure am stupid.
I know, if I try hard enough, I can pass that math class.	I will never be able to pass math.
If I do not ask, I will never know if Cassandra will go out with me.	Cassandra would not want to go out with me.
I sure feel good.	I feel depressed.
Sabi and Angie are two of my good friends.	Nobody likes me.
What can you say to yourself to make you feel more confident?	

> *Your biggest competitor is your own view of your future.*
> —WATTS WACKER AND JIM TAYLOR

Mental health experts have discovered that this process has had a tremendous influence on the development of positive self-esteem for many people. Our thoughts have a great influence on our behavior, but we also need to look at the importance of external events and see how they are interrelated. Ethan Kross is a psychologist at the University of Michigan. He studies the pronouns people use when they talk to themselves silently, inside their minds. He finds that a subtle linguistic shift—shifting from I to your own name—can have really powerful self-regulatory effects ("Why Saying Is Believing—The Science Of Self-Talk," NPR, 2014).

Cognitive and Social Learning Theories

Two somewhat different theories combine an emphasis on cognitive processes and a focus on social learning processes. Some psychologists believe that we learn many of our behaviors either by conditioning or by observing others and modeling our behavior after them. Like cognitive and social psychological theorists, they emphasize the importance of mental processes: How we think and feel about the situations we are in affects our behavior. So instead of focusing solely on how our environment controls us (learning theory), social-cognitive theorists focus on how we and our environment interact: How do we interpret and respond to external events? How do our schemas, our memories, and our expectations influence our behavior patterns?

Human beings are driven by neither inner forces nor environmental factors but rather by monitoring the impact of their behavior on other people, on the environment, and on themselves. We learn from our own experience and also learn vicariously by observing other people. We can also evaluate our own behavior according to personal standards and provide ourselves with reinforcers, such as self-approval or disapproval. You expect to get at least a "B" in your psychology class, but the night before the final exam you go to a party instead of studying. You only get a "C" for your grade. You tell yourself how dumb you were for not studying and feel disappointed in yourself.

> It is our choices that show what we truly are, far more than our abilities.
> —HARRY POTTER

Bandura's (2001) theory explains the complex interaction of individual factors, behavior, and environmental stimuli. Each factor can influence or change the others, and the direction of change is rarely one-way; it is reciprocal or bidirectional. This is an interactive, reciprocal perspective that has inspired researchers to study how the environment shapes personal factors, such as self-control and self-concept, and how these, in turn, influence behavior.

 Check this out PERSONAL INFLUENCES ON BEHAVIOR

The following categories of cognitive variables may have a tremendous influence on your behavior. Can you identify how these relate to your life?

1. **Expectancies.** What we have learned from our past experience leads us to form different expectations that help to determine our reactions to future events. You expect that your marriage will be the perfect relationship. When you discover that your spouse does not live up to your expectations, how do you feel? You expect to get a "D" in your calculus class, and you receive a "C." How do you feel? Think back on some of your experiences. How have your expectations affected your life?
2. **Competencies.** Each of us has a different combination of abilities and skills that shape our responses to events. Juan and Kyla are both asked to give a speech at a local event. Juan thinks he is a good speaker, so he accepts, but Kyla does not feel competent as a

public speaker, so she refuses the offer. What are your competencies and how have they influenced your behavior?

3. **Personal Values.** Our sense of priorities and values also shape our decisions and actions. You refuse the offer for a job in a store where they sell pornographic magazines, but accept the job as a sales clerk in a store that sells religious goods. Your values influenced your decision.

4. **Encoding Strategies.** We also have different ways of perceiving and categorizing experiences that shape our responses. One mother gets very angry at her teenager when she sees his messy room, while another mother takes it in stride and realizes that it is a stage most teenagers go through.

5. **Self–Regulatory Systems.** We also formulate goals, plans, and strategies that influence our actions. You decide to take a physics class because you are majoring in science, and even if you decide to drop science as your major, physics will help you in your other future pursuits. Another student decides that physics would be a waste of time and would not be beneficial (Mischel, 2007).

What is reciprocal determinism? We have repeated this statement many times, but we cannot recall who we should credit for it: "We react to others as others react to us; others react to us as we react to them." "Behavior, internal personal factors, and environmental influences all operate as interlocking determinants of each other" (Bandura, 2004). *Reciprocal determinism* is the interacting influences between person, behavior, and environment. You respond to a new acquaintance as a happy, positive person, and they respond back to you on a positive basis. Your new acquaintance sees you as a friendly, happy person, and you feel good about yourself because they responded back to you on a positive basis. You have a new friend. You were reinforced positively for being friendly, and in the future you will most likely respond positively to other new acquaintances. Your younger sister would like to be just like you, a friendly, happy person. Everytime she tries to be nice and friendly to new people she seems to be rejected. She feels bad and thinks that people must think she is ugly or inferior, so she withdraws from people and becomes shy. She was not reinforced positively for being friendly and she interpreted that response as an indication that she must be inferior or inadequate. Her behavior is being influenced by her environment and she interprets the situation as positive or negative. Someone else may have interpreted the situation differently. They may say to themselves that those other people were sure weird, and do not perceive their reaction as a negative response.

How do environments and people interact? We are both the products and the architects of our environment. Let's take a look at some specific ways in which people and environments interact.

Figure 2.1

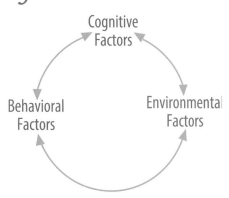

RECIPROCAL DETERMINISM

1. Our personalities shape how we interpret and react to events. A shy person is most likely to interpret a frown on someone's face as a negative response, even though the person is not feeling well.

2. Our personalities help create situations to which we react. You think your roommate is mad at you and you respond negatively to your roommate, and, thus, your roommate responds angrily toward you. Now you are being reinforced correctly for your response, you think. Originally your roommate was not mad at you, but because of your response your roommate now is mad. Has this ever happened to you?

3. Different people choose different environments. The type of party you go to, the friends you associate with, the music you listen to, the type of shows you watch on television, the places you hang out, the reading you do for pleasure—all are environments that you have chosen based on your beliefs, attitudes, and moods. The son of one of our colleagues was trying to decide which college to attend. He made his choice based on his liberal political beliefs. Most of the students attending that college will have similar political beliefs and will thus reinforce one another for having those beliefs. A person with a conservative orientation may not feel as comfortable at that college.

As you continue to read this book you will see how your thoughts, behavior, and environment interact to influence your behavior. You may want to refer to self-efficacy and social learning theory in Chapter Three.

We now have some insight into how our personalities have evolved over a period of time. We have looked at a variety of theories that contribute to our development. What theory do you feel has had the greatest influence on you, or do you think that

> *The person whom you're with most in life is yourself and if you don't like yourself you're always with somebody you don't like.*
> —MARC LEWIS

What kind of environment makes you happy?

© mimagephotography/Shutterstock.com

each theory has some valid points that you could use to justify how your personality developed? An interesting project would be for you to write your own personality theory that best describes your development.

Now we need to take a look at the importance of the "self"—your self-concept, self-image, and self-esteem. What kind of influence do these have on your behavior and how does the "self" develop?

THE SELF

There is new thinking about the self. The *self* is one of psychology's most vigorously researched topics. Every year it is amazing to see all the new studies that appear on "self-esteem," "self-awareness," "self-monitoring," and "self-efficacy."

One example of new thinking about the self is the *concept of "possible selves."* Your possible selves include your visions of the self you dream of becoming—the rich self, the thin self, the educated self, the successful self, and the admired self. They also include the self you fear becoming—the unemployed self, the addicted self, the failure self, and the unloved self. Such selves motivate us by laying out specific goals to pursue and the energy to work toward them. As they say: "Those who dream most, achieve most."

The nature of the self. One of the main factors differentiating humans from other animals is awareness of *"self."* As human beings, we can think, feel, and reflect on who we are. We form an identity and attach a value to it.

The Person That Is Me

If ever you should meet me
    the image you may see
is just a mere reflection
    of the person that is me.

    The person I am really,
the one deep down inside,
    is made of many feelings
that I sometimes try to hide.

Feelings of doubt and worry,
    wondering how I will fit in.
Feelings of hope and longing,
    that someday I might win.

    Feelings of frustration
for answers I don't know.
    Feelings for my loved ones.
Relationships that grow.

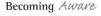

Feelings of loss and loneliness,
  of memories left behind.
Feelings of excitement.
  For what I have yet to find.

So remember when you meet me
  the image you may see
  is just a mere reflection
  of the person that is me.

Tom Krause

Excerpt "The Person That Is Me" from the book *Touching Hearts—Teaching Greatness* by Tom Krause. Used with permission of Universal Press Syndicate.

- Who are YOU?
- Where are you headed?
- Does it make a difference that you exist?

Over 2,000 years ago, the Greek philosopher Socrates advised all seekers of wisdom to *"know thyself."* What Socrates realized and we have discovered since is that the most vibrant, compelling, and baffling reality we can know is, *the self.* It is difficult to define and even more difficult to measure or even investigate. Yet, such awareness of *self* is vital in knowing how people adjust to life.

Many ideas about *the self* have sprung from the humanistic-existential perspective, discussed earlier. Carl Rogers (1995) has summarized a number of important characteristics of the self as follows:

1. It is organized and consistent.
2. It includes one's perceptions of all that comprises "I" or "me."
3. It includes the relationship among I or me and other people and features of life, as well as the value and importance of these relationships.
4. The self is available to consciousness (we can become aware of it), but it is not always conscious at any given moment.
5. The shape of the self is constantly changing, yet always recognizable.

We are human. We wrestle with our humanness. Some of us struggle with insecurity or inferiority, some deal with emotional problems, while others face mental or sexual problems. Poverty, illness, and physical disability can also test us. Many feel the pain of gender, racial, or ethnic prejudice. It is as if each of us is given a special task or challenge to work on as part of life and part of what will enhance our growth as an individual. It is the joy of discovering ourselves as human beings, our personal growth, sharing our love with others, and the contribution we make to others' lives that makes the process of life so exciting. The journey inward is life. Each of us must find our own way.

When I stand before God at the end of my life, I would hope that I would not have a single bit of talent left and could say, I used everything you gave me.
—ERMA BOMBECK

I often marvel that while each man loves himself more than anyone else, he sets less value on his own estimate than on the opinions of others.
— MARCUS AURELIUS, A.D. 121–180 MEDITATIONS

©amixstudio/Shutterstock.com

Find Your Real Self

The ***personal self-image*** is the part of the self that includes physical, behavioral, and psychological characteristics that establish uniqueness. It also includes gender, racial or ethnic identity, age, and status. Your personal self-image, who you think you are, is literally a package you put together from how others have seen and treated you and from your conclusions as you compared yourself to others. Your *sense of identity* is the end result of the interaction between your uniqueness and how others have reacted to it. It is the package you call *me*. But it is not the *real self.*

It is never who you are that hangs you up, but rather who you *THINK* you are. To discover your ***real self***, it is important to separate the *real you* from your *personal self-image*. Lining up your self-picture to fit the "real you" is of the utmost importance. There is probably no more exciting journey than that of *real self*-discovery. Once your *self-belief system* is accurate, you are free of the low self-esteem trap. You are free to be the *real you*.

Where did your "personal self-image" come from? Your personal self-image includes past teachings about yourself. As a child, you build your *sense of self* based on what others told you about you. If you were exposed to large doses of *put downs* and *belittlers,* your personal self-image does not feel very pleasant. If you grew up in a very positive climate, your *me* package feels good to live in. Your personal self-image is simply a belief system you have constructed about yourself. These past learnings jell into a *self* which may or may not be accurate. But once past learnings are part of your *self-image*, you see the package you have put together as accurate, regardless of the facts.

Tom, for instance, was repeatedly told as a child that he was dumb because he was slow to learn to read. Because he bought that label, he ignored or denied any evidence of his academic ability and creativity. "Dumb" and "smart" do not mix, they are mutually exclusive. Tom held onto those negative messages he received from significant people in his life, such as his parents and teachers. He also ignored any contrary evidence because it did not fit the "dumb" profile.

As an adult, Tom's past learning limited the accuracy of his "Personal Self-Image." He saw only evidence of being academically inferior. Years later, despite a college degree and a successful career, Tom still sees himself as "dumb."

Each of us identifies whatever qualities we learn to place after the words *I am*. Like Tom, we see such traits as truths about ourselves. These truths or *self-beliefs* literally screen out any messages to the contrary. In this way, past teachings can limit our options. If your self-worth is low or shaky, you are still believing things about yourself that are untrue negative ideas programmed into you about *you*.

> There was a prisoner who spent years in his cell totally unaware that the door was unlocked. At any point he could have walked out. But because he assumed there was a lock on the door, he remained trapped. His false belief limited his behavior.

Becoming aware of the self. Once you become aware that you are not locked into a prison of self-doubt, a whole new set of choices will open up. You become aware of new ways to see yourself, new ways you can behave, and new ways to relate. Of course, such choices and behaviors have been available to you all along. The problem has been you did not fully appreciate your capabilities and potential.

> *My Mother said to me, "If you become a soldier, you'll be a general. If you become a monk, you'll end up as the pope." Instead, I became a painter and wound up as Picasso.*
> —PABLO PICASSO

FOCUS ON DIVERSITY

WHAT IS YOUR CULTURAL ORIENTATION?

Answer the following questions Yes or No:

	Yes	No
1. I like to live close to my good friends and family.	___	___
2. To be superior, a person must stand up for herself or himself.	___	___
3. I enjoy meeting and talking to my neighbors every day.	___	___
4. If the group is slowing me down, it is better to leave it and work alone.	___	___
5. The larger the family, the more family problems there are.	___	___
6. It is reasonable for a son to continue his father's business.	___	___
7. I can count on my relatives for help if I find myself in any kind of trouble.	___	___
8. In the long run, the only person you can count on is yourself.	___	___
9. There is everything to gain and nothing to lose for classmates to group themselves for study and discussions.	___	___
10. If you want something done right, you have to do it yourself.	___	___

If you answered "yes" to questions 1, 3, 6, 7, and 9, you are more than likely from a collectivist orientation. If you answered "yes" to 2, 4, 5, 8, and 10, you are more than likely from an individualistic orientation. What does this mean?

Lack of awareness, of course, is the same as having no choice. It is up to you to increase your awareness about the real you, so you can experience inner freedom. By increasing your awareness about yourself, you increase your choices in life. Carl Rogers (2002) described such a person as a *fully functioning person* who feels inwardly free to move in any direction. Being a fully functioning person can be a reality for you. If you strive for such an inner freedom, little can hold you back.

What about people from different ethnic groups and cultural backgrounds? Will this difference have an influence on an individual's self-concept?

Self-Esteem

How to appreciate your true self. This chapter began with a description of the nature of self. Remember that as human beings, we have the ability to reflect on who we are. We are aware of a unique *identity*. But we are not only aware of *ourself*; we attach a value to that *self*. So we can decide whether we will accept or reject *ourself*, whether we are *OK* or *not OK*, whether we are good or bad. You are either a *self-hater, self-doubter,* or a *self-affirmer*.

So this unique human ability we have—the ability we have to attach a value to our self—can lead to self-rejection and tremendous emotional pain. The term **self-esteem** refers to the overall evaluation of oneself, whether one likes or dislikes who one is, believes or doubts oneself, and values or belittles one's worth. How you evaluate yourself is crucial to your psychological adjustment.

Does your cultural orientation influence your self-esteem?

> *There is over-whelming evidence that the higher the level of self-esteem, the more likely one will treat others with respect, kindness, and generosity. People who do not experience self-love have little or no capacity to love others.*
> —NATHANIEL BRANDEN

Individualism vs. Collectivism

Over the years, social scientists have observed that cultures differ to the extent to which they value individualism and the virtues of independence, autonomy, and self-reliance, or collectivism and the virtues of interdependence, cooperation, and social harmony. In a collectivist society, a person is first and foremost a loyal member of a family, team, company, church, state, and other groups. In an individualist culture, however, personal goals take priority over group allegiances. In what countries are these different orientations most extreme? The United States, Australia, Great Britain, Canada, and the Netherlands, in that order, are the most individualistic. People from Venezuela, Colombia, Pakistan, Peru, Japan, Taiwan, and China are the most collectivistic (Matsumoto, 2007).

© Rawpixel.com/Shutterstock.com

What groups do you belong to?

> *There is as much difference between us and ourselves, as between us and others.*
> —MICHEL DE MONTAIGNE, ESSAYS, 1588

Individualism and collectivism are so deeply ingrained in a culture that they mold our very self-conceptions and identities. Take a brief look at Table 2.4 and see how each culture may influence your personality and self-esteem.

Table 2.4 INDIVIDUALISM VS. COLLECTIVISM

	INDIVIDUALISM	COLLECTIVISM
Concept of self	Independent (identity from individual traits)	Interdependent (identity from belonging)
Relationships	Many, often temporary or casual; confrontation acceptable	Few, close and enduring; harmony required
Attribution	Behavior reflects one's personality and attitudes	Behavior reflects social norms and roles
Coping methods	Changes reality	Accommodates to reality
Morality	Defined by individuals (self-based)	Defined by the group (duty-based)
Life task	Discover and express one's uniqueness	Maintain connections, fit in
What matters	My personal achievement and fulfillment; rights and liberties	We-group goals, and solidarity; social responsibilities and relationships

Adapted from Myers (2012) and Matsumoto (2007).

The benefits of self-esteem.   How we feel about ourselves is important. Research studies reveal the benefits of positive self-esteem and the hazards of self-righteous pride. High self-esteem—a feeling of self-worth—pays dividends. People who feel good about themselves have fewer ulcers, fewer sleepless nights, succumb less to pressures to conform, are less likely to use drugs, are more persistent at difficult tasks, and are just plain happier (McKay & Fanning, 2000).

A study in 1951 by Leaky showed that when a student's self-esteem changed, so did performance. A later study found a positive correlation between self-esteem and grade-point average. Self-esteem was also related to teacher ratings of students and observations of classroom behavior. Students with higher levels of self-esteem generally performed at higher academic levels and got along more positively in the classroom. In terms of academic performance, a student's IQ score may not be as important as the self-esteem rating. Self-confidence permits a child to perform; whereas brilliance may be trapped in low self-esteem (Krueger & Vohs, 2003).

Briggs also stated that "self-esteem is the mainspring that slates every child for success or failure." Self-esteem has a direct influence on the feeling of self-worth, on human relations, productivity, integrity, stability, and uncertainty. "Self-esteem is the armor that protects a person from the dragons of life: drugs, alcohol, unhealthy relationships, and delinquency" (McKay & Fanning, 2000).

Another benefit of self-esteem is the ability to accept criticism and rejection. Those with high self-esteem tend to view criticism as constructive. They do not interpret a "no" as rejection. Instead, these individuals usually learn and "return with a more polished act."

Clearly, self-esteem influences all aspects of life; in fact, it is the foundation upon which happiness and well-being are built.

The costs of low self-esteem. Low self-esteem exacts costs. People who do not feel good about themselves are vulnerable to depression and failure. Those whose self-image falls short of what they think they ought to be are vulnerable to anxiety. Most counselors will agree that most of the clients that they encounter that are unhappy, frustrated, and in a state of despair are individuals that have impairments in self-acceptance and self-esteem. There seems to be a correlation between self-esteem and life problems, but the opposite can also be true, that life problems may be the cause of low self-esteem. People who are negative about themselves also seem to be thin-skinned and judgmental (Cole et al., 2004).

If you feel good about yourself, you are more apt to succeed in whatever you do. Both Abraham Maslow and Carl Rogers emphasize the point that a "healthy" self-image pays dividends. Accept yourself, and you will find it easier to accept others. See Table 2.5 for the benefits.

> Have patience with all things but first with yourself. Never confuse your mistakes with your value as a human being.
> —ST. FRANCIS DE SALES

> All of us have inferiority complexes.
> —JOHN POWELL

Becoming *Aware*

Table 2.5   HIGH SELF-ESTEEM VS. LOW SELF-ESTEEM

HIGH SELF-ESTEEM TRAITS	LOW SELF-ESTEEM TRAITS
Perceives reality	Avoids reality to avoid anxiety
Relatively undefensive	Defensive
Gives credit to others when it is due	Envies others and puts them down
Natural	Plays a role
Task centered	Self-centered
Enjoys being alone	Oriented toward approval of others
Self-reliant	Dependent
Feels kinship with humankind	Us vs. Them
Relationships are intimate	Relationships are casual
Non-judgmental of others	Critical of others
Accepts self	Strives to be perfect and avoid mistakes
Well-developed value system	Values not clarified
Philosophical sense of humor	Hostile
Accepts compliments	Rejects compliments or qualifies them
Cooperative with others	Views self as different from others
Makes growth choices	Makes fear choices
Dares to be unpopular	Conforming
Experiences without self-consciousness	Considers what others think

Adapted from Bandura (2004) and McKay & Fanning (2000).

What is the self-serving bias? Social psychologists have found that most people are not realistic in evaluating themselves, their capabilities, or their behavior. The ***self-serving bias*** is a person's tendency to evaluate their own behavior as worthwhile, regardless of the situation. Most people consider themselves as more intelligent, more sensitive, more considerate, more likely to succeed, and more of a leader than they consider most other people. We tend to be self-enhancing and we often exaggerate positive beliefs about ourselves (Nier, 2004).

People tend to take credit for their successes and blame others for their failures. That is, people assume that good things happen to them because they deserve them and that bad things happen to other people because they deserve them. When something bad happens to you, you may blame it on bad luck or circumstances. When something bad happens to others, you may blame it on their carelessness or reckless behavior (attribution theory). The combination attribution error and self-serving bias helps some people maintain their self-esteem and appear competent. Be careful because this may inhibit some people from having realistic goals, thus setting them up for disappointment.

Psychologists have focused on two possible explanations for the development and role of the self-serving bias. First, a self-serving bias meets people's need for self-esteem and need to feel good about themselves in comparison to other people. It allows people to deal with their limitations and gives them the courage to venture into areas they normally might not explore. Self-serving biases allow people to present themselves to other people in a positive light. Psychologists explain self-serving bias as being partly due to an attempt to "save face" and protect self-esteem in the face of failure (Nier, 2004). We all need to feel good about ourselves, and the self-serving bias allows us to do this.

MY DECLARATION OF SELF-ESTEEM

I am me.

I was uniquely created. There's not another human being in the whole world like me—I have my very own fingerprints and I have my very own thoughts. I was not stamped out of a mold to be the duplicate of another.

I own all of me—my body, and I can do with it what I choose; my mind, and all of its thoughts and ideas; my feelings, whether joyful or painful. I am not defined by what I have or what I own.

I own my ideals, my dreams, my hopes, my fantasies, my fears.

I reserve the right to think and feel differently from others and will grant to others their right to thoughts and feelings not identical with my own.

I own all my triumphs and successes. I own also all my failures and mistakes. I choose what I do and am responsible for my own behavior. I will permit myself to be imperfect. When I make mistakes or fail, I will know that I am not the failure—I am still OK—and I will discard some parts of me that were unfitting and will try new ways.

I will laugh freely and loudly at myself—a healthy self-affirmation.

I will have fun living inside my skin.

I will remember that the door to everybody's life needs this sign: Honor Thyself.

I have value and worth.

Review again Table 2.5 illustrating characteristics of low self-esteem and high self-esteem.

Just knowing what traits a person *of high self-esteem* has is not enough for most of us to embark upon the philosophical, emotional, and behavioral change necessary to increase our self-esteem. On the following pages is a list of strategies that provide a good start. This list is by no means complete because this process is ongoing and will continue your entire lifetime. Also remember that this is not an easy process. It not only takes work but requires the inner strength to put up with the anxiety that goes along with making change and making mistakes. Remember too, that not all these strategies will work for you. Think of this list as a menu from which you choose what you like, what fits, and from which you reject what you do not like and what does not fit. So, here goes. This is no easy fix, just an aid or guideline for you. And just because you are willing to try to judge yourself less often means you are a courageous person.

> *The self-portraits that we actually believe, when we are given freedom to voice them, are dramatically more positive than reality can sustain.*
> —SHELLY TAYLOR—POSITIVE ILLUSIONS

> *If you accept your limitations, you go beyond them.*
> —BRENDAN FRANCIS BEHAN

STRATEGIES TO IMPROVE SELF-ESTEEM

1. **Recognize That You Are in Control of Your Self-Image.** The first thing you must do is recognize that you ultimately control the way you see yourself. You have the power to change your self-image. You have the choice to accept or reject feedback. Your self-image resides in your mind and is a product of your thinking. Although others may influence your self-concept, you are the final authority.

   People with low self-esteem tend to be more accepting of negative feedback about themselves than of positive feedback. Are they in control of their self-image? As people become aware of this they can begin to take control and learn to reject the negative feedback and take control of their own self-image.

2. **Be Able to Accept All Parts of Your Physical Appearance Now!!!** Describe your age, height, weight, facial appearance, skin, hair, and specific body areas such as chest, waist, and legs. Then accept your body. Treasure it. It is what you have and it works. Say to yourself, "You are all I have and I will take care of you." Judy started working on appreciating her body by completing an appearance inventory as follows:

   - ■ + large brown eyes
   - ■ + clear, young looking skin
   - ■ − fat stomach
   - ■ − fat hips
   - ■ slim legs
   - ■ 5'5"
   - ■ + nice teeth
   - ■ − too many fat cells

   Then she went back over her list and put a plus next to descriptions that represented strengths to her, a minus by items she wanted to change, and did not mark the items she considered to be neutral. She also re-worded those minus statements to more accurate less judgmental statements:

Minus Statement	Less Judgmental
Fat belly	32-inch waist
Fat hips	40-inch hips
Too many fat cells	Slightly overweight

Remember, *people with low self-esteem* put off *self-acceptance* until they get that perfect body. It is imperative you treasure your body the way it is now.

3. **Affirm Your Strengths.** As a result of cultural and parental conditioning, you may find it anxiety provoking to give yourself credit for your assets. It is now time, however, to toot your own horn. Get a BIG piece of blank paper. List all your strengths. Think of all parts of your *Real Self-Image*.
   - Your physical appearance
   - How you relate to others
   - Your personality
   - How others see you
   - Your work/school/daily task performance

It takes a concentrated effort to make this list. If you are having difficulty thinking of strengths, think of how your best friend would describe you in each of these areas. Your list of strengths will be long if you are willing to put forth the effort and willing to experience the anxiety. Once you have listed many of the qualities in yourself you appreciate, that does not mean you will remember them. Remembering your strengths, particularly at the times when you feel most down on yourself, requires a system. The following three strategies may help you really believe in your positive qualities:

A. *Daily affirmations (positive sayings).* Write affirmations for yourself each day using your name. Make them believable, comforting, and supportive. And repeat them to yourself in front of the mirror.

B. *Reminder signs and notes.* Many people who post positive messages report they reinforce and strengthen their personal sense of adequacy.

C. *Active integration.* Recall specific examples and times when you clearly demonstrated your strengths. Transform your strengths into specific memories. This process will help to convince you that your list of positive qualities actually applies to you.

How do you describe yourself?

© Syda Productions/Shutterstock.com

4. List Your Faults. There is nothing wrong with having faults. Every human being has them. The problem is not with your faults, but how you overrate them. The problem is that people use their faults for destructive self-attack and to condemn themselves. There are four basic rules to acknowledging weaknesses:
   A. *Use non-pejorative language*—language that does not make a bad situation worse. Go through your list and eliminate all the words that have negative connotations. Banish certain words from your self-descriptive vocabulary; for example: fat, ugly, dumb, blabbermouth.
   B. *Use accurate language*. Confine yourself to the facts.
   C. *Be specific rather than general*. Eliminate words such as always, never, anything.
   D. *Find exceptions or corresponding strengths*. This is essential for any item you feel particularly bad about.
5. Attain Legitimate Accomplishments and Successes. Accomplishing worthwhile activities is a major contributor to self-esteem. It is also important to remember that accomplishments do not have to be *big*. They just have to be something that you achieved through hard work and commitment. Social science research suggests this sequence of events: Person establishes a goal . . . person pursues the goal . . . person achieves the goal . . . person develops esteem-like feelings (Cole et al., 2004).
6. Make the Growth Choice Rather than the Fear Choice. Reject rigidity. Take responsibility to direct your own life. If you are dissatisfied with your life as it is now, be willing to accept change. You promote your growth or fail to do that every time you make a decision. We are constantly making decisions whether to be honest or to lie, to try new things or be safe, to be open or be defensive. If you make each decision a choice for growth, you manifest courage.
7. Shed Perfectionistic Demands. Perfectionists, experts now know, are made and not born, commonly at an early age. Concern with mistakes and doubts about actions are absolute prerequisites for perfectionism. Real-world success hinges less on getting everything right than how you handle getting things wrong. There's a difference between excellence and perfection. Excellence involves enjoying what you do. Perfection means not being satisfied—no matter what (Marano, 2008).
8. Become More Synergistic. Maslow describes this as being *involved with others*. Become involved with other people and your work and leisure time will become more valuable to you. Make a commitment. Alfred Adler (1998) points out that we greatly promote our health and functioning by cooperation with others.
9. Observe People You Admire. Identify at least five qualities that you aspire to and admire in others. Become a careful observer. Think of how you can adapt their behavior to fit your own personal style.
10. Keep a Diary. Record what you enjoy about your day. You may be doing things out of habit rather than because you enjoy them. By keeping a diary, you may discover that some of your activities do not make you happy. If this is the case, then you can actively make the attempt not to do these things any longer.
11. Keep a Sense of Humor. Laugh easily, enjoy a good joke, have fun in life. Some of us do not know how to play. We take our life and ourselves too seriously. Perhaps we grew up in families in which there was not much fun and hap-

That you may retain your self-respect, it is better to displease the people by doing what you know is right, than to temporarily please them by doing what you know is wrong.
—WILLIAM J.H. BOETCKER

You will always be in fashion if you are true to yourself, and only if you are true to yourself.
—MAYA ANGELOU

The best way to find yourself is to lose yourself in the service of others.
—MOHANDAS K. GANDHI

Do you take time for
pleasures in life?

© Nikola Solev/Shutterstock.com

piness. Remember to keep a balance in your life between work and play. Take time for the pleasures in life.

12. **Do Not Be Afraid to Make Mistakes.** You will make thousands of mistakes during your lifetime if you plan to live up to your creative potential. Do a personal mistake check, and then increase the number of mistakes you make each day by 10 percent. You will take more risks, stretch, grow, and enjoy life more. You learn through experience. If you do not try something you may lose out on a lot of experiences in your life.

Everyone makes mistakes; do not worry about them. Forgive yourself for making mistakes. If you do not make mistakes, you're not trying. You learn from your mistakes. Remember "friends" who run you down, even in jest, are not friends. Omit them

So, there you have it. The twelve strategies listed here to help you to improve your self-esteem will give you a good start. As your work progresses, you may come up with a few of your own that are not listed here. Just remember that as a child you were told all about who you were. Your sense of self came from others. As an adult, it is up to you to develop a realistic positive sense of self. To do this, you must be dedicated to the effort for a lifetime. It is not enough to just say you will love yourself. Your assumptions about yourself and about your world must be positive, healthy, realistic ones.

The Real Journey

At the beginning of the 20th century, sociologist Charles Cooley described the American identity as a "looking-glass self." Our sense of ourselves, wrote Cooley, is formed by our imagination of the way we appear in the eyes of others. Other people are a looking glass in which we see not merely our own reflection but a judgment about the value of that reflection. ("Each to each a looking glass/reflects the other that doth pass," he wrote.) If we are lucky, we feel pride in that imagined self; if not, we feel mortification (Elliott, 2004).

Growth and change are not a destination, but rather a journey. All through our lives, if we are to function fully, we will continue to grow and change. Self-esteem is really so much more than just feeling good about oneself. Researchers are quick to assert that excessive pride can be dangerous, and too few people really know how to be humble. Remember, **narcissism** is the tendency to regard oneself as grandiosely self-important. Self-esteem is about having respect for yourself and others. Self-esteem is about trusting your ability to make appropriate choices and cope effectively with adversity. According to self-esteem researcher Dr. Nathaniel Branden (2007), author of *The Psychology of Self-Esteem,* building self-esteem requires a lifelong commitment to six principles and daily practices:

BRANDEN'S SIX PILLARS OF SELF ESTEEM

Self-esteem = self-efficacy + self-respect.
—NATHANIEL BRANDEN

- **Living consciously.** Maintain an unflinching willingness to face reality even when it is painful. Become aware of how you treat yourself and how others are treating you.
- **Self-acceptance.** Experience and take responsibility for your thoughts, feelings, and actions. Avoid putting yourself down.
- **Self-responsibility.** Realize that you alone are responsible for your life and well-being. You are responsible for your own choices.
- **Self-assertiveness.** Have the courage to stand up for who you are. Do not pretend to be someone you're not to avoid someone else's disapproval.
- **Living purposefully.** Identify your goals and the actions needed to attain them. Organize your priorities to meet those goals.
- **Personal integrity.** Demonstrate personal integrity by telling the truth, honoring commitments, and dealing with others justly and considerately. Conduct your life by merging what you know, what you profess, and what you do.

Authors Linda Sanford and Mary Ellen Donovan (1993) describe the power of self-esteem as follows:

> Our level of self-esteem affects virtually everything we think, say and do. It affects how we see the world and our place in it. It affects how others in the world see and treat us. It affects the choices we make—choices about what we will do with our lives and with whom we will be involved. It affects our ability to take action to change things that need to be changed.

Chapter Review

Life is a journey. All through our lives, if we are to function fully, we will continue to grow and change.

- People acquire a sense of self throughout their lives; it is an ongoing process that evolves from our experiences and interactions with others.
- If we are to have a strong self-concept, we need love, respect, and acceptance from the significant others in our lives. Who are the significant others in your life and what impact have they had on your self-concept?
- The self-fulfilling prophecy has a great influence on a person's image of himself or herself.
- As we compare ourselves with others (social comparison) we gain a better understanding of ourselves, be it positive or negative.
- When our self-concept is intact and secure, we feel good. When it is threatened, we feel anxious and insecure.
- **Dwerk's theory of mindset.** Some of the less-bright students are real go-getters, thriving on challenge, persisting intensely when things get difficult, and accomplishing more than they expected. The right mindset and being praised for trying harder, not for how smart they were, made a difference according to Dwerk. The students who have learning goals—who are concerned with increasing their competence and abilities while mastering new tasks over time—make better grades. Dwerk found that the best mix is a combination of (a) valuing learning and challenge and (b) valuing grades but seeing them as merely an index of your current performance, not a sign of your intelligence or worth.
- **Freud's theory of personality development** provides the foundation of many other personality theories. Freud stated that the personality is made up of three distinct, but interrelated, parts: the id, the ego, and the superego. The **id** is composed of the basic biological drives that motivate an individual, including the pleasure-seeking part of your personality. The **ego** is the rational, logical, and realistic part of your personality. The **superego** consists of our values, morals, religious beliefs, and ideals of our parents and society.
- To **Adler**, personality arises from our attempts to overcome or compensate for fundamental feelings of inadequacy. Adler was responsible for coining the popular term "**inferiority complex**," a concept, he argued, that underlies and motivates a great deal of human behavior. While he believed that everyone has to work to overcome some feelings of inferiority, Adler believed that some people overcompensate in order to conceal their feelings of inferiority.
- Most recent research studies do not seem to support Adler's idea that birth order is a possible factor regulating personality.
- **Erik Erikson** identified **eight stages of psychosocial development** that each individual needs to satisfy throughout their life. They are:
  1. Trust vs. Mistrust,
  2. Autonomy vs. Doubt,
  3. Initiative vs. Guilt,
  4. Industry vs. Inferiority,
  5. Identity vs. Role Confusion,
  6. Intimacy vs. Isolation,
  7. Generativity vs. Self-Absorption, and
  8. Integrity vs. Despair.

- The **Myers-Briggs Type Indicator** covers four dimensions: Extroversion (E) or Introversion (I), Sensing (S) or Intuition (N), Thinking (T) or Feeling (F), and Judgment (J) or Perception (P).
- Some psychologists have developed a personality theory that identifies personality traits that many of us use to describe other people (and ourselves). These are called **traits**, which are relatively stable and consistent personal characteristics. This is known as the **Big Five Model of Personality**.
- Your personality evolves from the Big Five, these traits include the **OCEAN** traits: Openness, Conscientiousness, Extroversion, Agreeableness, and Neuroticism.
- The **HEXACO Personality Dimensions Inventory** model includes six dimensions of human personality: Honesty-Humility, Emotionality, Extroversion, Agreeableness, Conscientiousness, and Openness to Experience. Each of these six dimensions represent the four cardinal virtues (wisdom, courage, temperance, and justice).
- **Strengths-Based Psychology** is based on the work of Tom Rath and a team of Gallup scientists who set out to start a global conversation about what's right with people rather than focusing so much on people's shortcomings. Their work was originally led by the late Father of Strengths Psychology, Donald O. Clifton.
- **Carl Rogers' Self-Theory** defines the development of the self-concept in terms of self-actualization, which is defined as the fulfillment of one's own completely unique personality. Unconditional positive regard (unconditioned acceptance) leads to unimpaired growth and the development of positive characteristics.
- **Viktor Frankl** states that our task is to create a life that has meaning and purpose.
- **Virginia Satir's Self-Worth theory** indicates that what happens inside people and between people is the picture of the individual worth that each person carries around.
- Cognitive theories of personality point out that there are important individual differences in the way people think about and define situations.
- **Building self-esteem** is easier with the help of **positive self-talk** and thinking positively and optimistically.
- **Cognitive restructuring**, the process of modifying thoughts, ideas, and beliefs, can be used to increase positive and optimistic thinking.
- **Self-talk** is the unspoken, mental speech we use when we think about something, solve problems, and make plans. Positive or negative self-talk may have an influence on your self-concept.
- Reciprocal determinism is the interacting influences between person, behavior, and environment.
- Your personal **self-image** is the part of the self that includes physical, behavioral, and psychological characteristics that establish uniqueness.
- There are many benefits to positive self-esteem, including better health, feeling happy, etc.
- There are many costs to low self-esteem, including poor health, not as happy, more frustration, poorer work performance, etc.
- The **self-serving bias** is a person's tendency to evaluate his or her own behavior as worthwhile, regardless of the situation.
- **Individualistic societies** value independence, autonomy, and self-reliance. **Collectivistic societies** value interdependence, cooperation, and social harmony.
- Individualism and collectivism are so deeply ingrained in a culture that they mold our self-concepts and identities.
- There are many **strategies to improve self-esteem**, including:
  1. Recognize that you are in control
  2. Accept your physical appearance—just the way you are
  3. Affirm your strengths
  4. List your faults

5. Attain legitimate accomplishments and successes
6. Make a growth choice rather than a fear choice
7. Shed perfectionistic demands
8. Work well with others
9. Observe role models
10. Keep a diary
11. Keep a sense of humor
12. Do not be afraid to make mistakes

- Self-esteem researcher and author Dr. Nathaniel Branden says that building self-esteem requires a life-long commitment to six principles and daily practices: living consciously, self-acceptance, self-responsibility, self-assertiveness, living purposefully, and personal integrity. Remember, **narcissism** is the tendency to regard oneself as grandiosely self-important. This attitude is dangerous.

Personal growth and self-awareness involve accepting ourselves and enjoying our relationships with others. Only "you" can make the choice whether you will live an enjoyable and fulfilling life or one of stagnation.

Test Review Questions: Learning Outcomes

1. Why do we need to study about the development of the "self"?
2. Explain how significant others influence a person's self-image.
3. Define and explain Carol Dwerk's theory of mindset. What do you have?
4. Explain Alfred Adler's theory of personality development and the inferiority complex.
5. What do the latest research findings suggest about birth order as a possible factor regulating personality?
6. Describe Erikson's Eight Stages of Psychosocial Development.
7. Briefly explain the four dimensions of the Myers-Briggs Type Indicator.
8. Explain how the Big Five Model of Personality has influenced your perception of others using the "Big Five" Traits.
9. Define Strengths-Based Psychology.
10. Describe how Carl Rogers' Self-Theory influences the development of your personality.
11. Describe, briefly, Viktor Frankl's Search for Meaning theory.
12. Briefly describe Virginia Satir's Theory of Self-Worth.
13. Define Reciprocal Determinism and explain how our thoughts and our environment influence the development of our personality.
14. Explain how cognitive and social-learning theories explain your self-image.
15. Describe the cognitive variables that influence your behavior.
16. Define collectivism and individualism and explain how they may influence an individual's self-concept.
17. What are the costs of low self-esteem? Explain.
18. What are the benefits of having high self-esteem? Explain.
19. Define the Self-Serving Bias and explain how it influences your behavior.
20. Briefly explain the twelve strategies that will help you improve your self-esteem.
21. Define narcissism and explain how Nathaniel Branden's views of building self-esteem are exactly the opposite from narcissism.

22. Briefly describe Davidson's STRENGTH model for helping yourself and others.

Davidson's Strengths is modeled from Positive Psychology traditions. It can be used for an individual's personal growth or as a guideline for helping others. The word Strength is an acronym:

S --Be Solution oriented

T --Do a Trajectory preview

R--Begin Resource development

E-- Conduct a Exceptions analysis

N-- Notice positives

G--Concentrate on goal setting

T-- Do a tenacity review

H-- Focus on human capacity development

Key Terms

Agreeableness

Autonomy vs. Doubt

Cognitive Restructuring

Collectivism

Compensation

Conscientiousness

Ego

Extroversion or Introversion

Generativity vs. Self-Absorption

HEXACO

Id

Individualism

Industry vs. Inferiority

Inferiority Complex

Initiative vs. Guilt

Integrity vs. Despair

Interpersonal Relations

Intersectionality

Intimacy vs. Isolation

Judgment or Perception

Mid-Life Crisis

Mid-Life Transition Stage

Mindset

Myers-Briggs Type Indicator

Narcissism

Neuroticism

Openness

Personal Self-Image

Pot of Self-Worth

Real Self

Reciprocal Determinism

Search for Meaning

Self-Awareness

Self-Esteem

Self-Image

Self-Perception

Self-Serving Bias

Self-Talk

Self-Theory

Self-Worth

Sensing or Intuition

Significant Others

Social Comparison

Stages of Psychosocial
  Development

STRENGTH Model

Strengths-Based Psychology

Superego

Thinking or Feeling

Trait

Trust vs. Mistrust

Unconditional Positive Regard

Reflections: Critical Thinking

1. Do we have a choice in determining who we become? Explain.
2. How do our interactions with others help in discovering who we are?
3. Who are the significant others in your life? What impact have they had on your life? Were they a good influence or a bad influence?

4. How does striving for perfection lead to emotional pain?
5. How does social comparison influence our self-image?
6. How have the id, ego, and superego influenced your behavior?
7. How has the concept of inferiority complex impacted your personality development?
8. Discuss the relationship between your life and Erikson's Stages of Development.
9. Discuss your personality type on the Myers-Briggs Type Indicator. Do you think it is open to being wrong or lacking?
10. Why is it so difficult to make changes in our self-concept?
11. Discuss the cultural influences on a person's development.
12. Which theory of personality seems to explain your own development best?
13. How can excessive pride be dangerous?
14. How do you think birth order has influenced your personality development?
15. Do you think tests for Personality Type are true and enlightening? Or are they a bunch of bunk?

Web Resources and Web Activities

ACTIVITIES

http://www.mindsetonline.com/testyourmindset/results.php

Carol Dwerk's website—try the mindset test and see how you can change it.

http://mindsetonline.com/testyourmindset/step1.php

Carol Dweck's mindset website—find out what your mindset is.

http://nymag.com/news/features/27840/

How not to talk to your kids: The inverse power of praise, *New York Magazine*

http://www.selfgrowth.com/topics.html

This site provides much information about self-improvement and personal growth.

www.keirsey.com

This Web site is dedicated to personality/trait differences. For a free sample you can click on the temperament sorter icon and read the results about yourself.

http://www.webheights.net/lovethyself/home.htm

A resource directing visitors to books, online articles, and programs to enhance the self-worth of adults and children.

www.authentichappiness.sas.upenn.edu/testcenter.aspx

Brief Strengths Test or VIA Survey of Character Strengths—measures 24 character strengths.

http://links.upworthy.mkt5937.com/ctt?kn=8&ms=MTIyNjkyNzQS1&r=NzM1N-jU0NTc2NTcS1&b=0&j=NTgzNjM3Njk0S0&mt=1&rt=0

Here are 5 things you may regret at the end of your life, from a nurse who works with the dying.

HEXACO Personality Dimensions Inventory http://hexaco.org/hexaco-online

On this website you can complete the HEXACO Personality Inventory-Revised (HEXACO-PI-R).

VIDEOS

http://www.ted.com/talks/carol_dweck_the_power_of_believing_that_you can improve

Carol Dweck: The power of believing that you can improve

https://www.youtube.com/watch?v=w6dnj2IyYjE

Intersectionality

https://www.youtube.com/watch?v=n2kUpKP18z8

Khan Academy on Intersectionality

https://www.youtube.com/watch?v=FeLpvgAVtU8

Self Esteem—Understanding and Fixing Low Self-Esteem

https://www.youtube.com/watch?v=nHSZ3_VMgjU

Introduction to the Myers-Briggs Personality Test

https://www.youtube.com/watch?v=Q5pggDCnt5M

Why the Myers-Briggs test is totally meaningless

—myers briggs personality types documentary

https://www.youtube.com/watch?v=vNlmFXOpGI0

Which HARRY POTTER Character Are You?

https://www.youtube.com/watch?v=9MGaL2lwBv4

Doctor Who MBTI Myers Briggs Type Indicator - YouTube

https://www.youtube.com/watch?v=jOl37t_E_cA

What a recent TED talk teaches us about our hidden stereotypes--and their pernicious effects. With candor and directness, Russell draws on her own experiences as a highly successful model to expose modern manifestations of racism and sexism, where physical appearance dictates who gets seen and heard in the mass media, and how they're perceived.

https://www.ted.com/talks/cameron_russell_looks_aren_t_everything_believe_me_i_m_a_model?language=en

Cameron Russell: Looks aren't everything. Believe me, I'm a model.

The "Big Five" Test

PURPOSE

To survey the "Big Five" Personality Traits.

INSTRUCTIONS

1. Using the numbers on the scale from 1 to 5, indicate how true each of the following terms is in describing you.

    1 = Not at all true of me: I am never this way.
    2 = Mostly not true of me: I am rarely this way.
    3 = Neither true nor untrue of me, or I can't decide.
    4 = Somewhat true of me: I am sometimes this way.
    5 = Very true of me: I am very often this way.

1.	_____ imaginative		14.	_____ soft-hearted
2.	_____ organized		15.	_____ nervous
3.	_____ talkative		16.	_____ insightful
4.	_____ sympathetic		17.	_____ responsible
5.	_____ tense		18.	_____ energetic
6.	_____ intelligent		19.	_____ warm
7.	_____ thorough		20.	_____ worrying
8.	_____ assertive		21.	_____ clever
9.	_____ kind		22.	_____ practical
10.	_____ anxious		23.	_____ outgoing
11.	_____ original		24.	_____ generous
12.	_____ efficient		25.	_____ self-pitying
13.	_____ active			

INSTRUCTIONS FOR SCORING

To compute your score for each of the five scales, simply add your scores for the items that contribute to each of the scales.

Openness to Experience: 1, 6, 11, 16, 21   Your Score _____

Conscientiousness: 2, 7, 12, 17, 22   Your Score _____

Extroversion: 3, 8, 13, 18, 23   Your Score _____

Agreeableness: 4, 9, 14, 19, 24   Your Score _____

Neuroticism: 5, 10, 15, 20, 25   Y   our Score _____

Note: Be sure to review Table 2.1 for a description of high and low scores. Also, review the next page for mean scores of men and women. High scores on neuroticism are not desirable. Discuss this with your instructor.

Mean scores for men and women on each of the scales are listed below:

	Men	*Women*	*Your Score*
Openness to Experience	*20.3*	*19.4*	
Conscientiousness	*18.8*	*20.2*	
Extroversion	*18.8*	*19.0*	
Agreeableness	*18.8*	*22.2*	
Neuroticism	*16.3*	*18.5*	

DISCUSSION

1. Review the descriptions in the text of the five types and answer the following: Do you agree or disagree with your scores? Why or why not?

2. How do you think you could start to improve the areas where you scored the lowest?

Brody, N., & Erhlichman, H. (1998). *Personality Psychology: The Science of Individuality*. Upper Saddle River, NJ: Prentice Hall.

I Am a Person Who

PURPOSE

To become more aware of how you are perceived by others and how accurate you are in your perceptions of others.

INSTRUCTIONS

1. You have two forms—one for you and one for another person. Each person responds to the first scale by circling the number on the continuum that indicates the way you present yourself to others. Do not mark this the way you see yourself but the way you feel you come across to others.
2. Give the second form to a friend and have him or her evaluate you.
3. Looking at both scales, identify any discrepancies between the two. Ask your friend to discuss the discrepancies in terms of: "I see you this way because . . ."

I AM A PERSON WHO . . .

Personal warmth	|	|	|	|	|	|	|	|	|	Aloofness, coldness
Neat appearance	|	|	|	|	|	|	|	|	|	Careless appearance
Cheerful disposition	|	|	|	|	|	|	|	|	|	Unhappy disposition
Sincerity, genuineness	|	|	|	|	|	|	|	|	|	Insincerity, artificiality
Insecurity in behavior	|	|	|	|	|	|	|	|	|	Confidence in behavior
Reluctancy to talk with others	|	|	|	|	|	|	|	|	|	Eagerness to talk with others
Desire to listen	|	|	|	|	|	|	|	|	|	No interest in listening
Primary concern for self	|	|	|	|	|	|	|	|	|	Primary concern for others
Ability to express ideas and feelings	|	|	|	|	|	|	|	|	|	Difficulty in expressing ideas and feelings
Awareness of what is happening	|	|	|	|	|	|	|	|	|	Lack of awareness of what is happening
Difficulty in making other people comfortable	|	|	|	|	|	|	|	|	|	Ease in making other people comfortable
Talk too much	|	|	|	|	|	|	|	|	|	Talk too little
Not intelligent	|	|	|	|	|	|	|	|	|	Intelligent
Excitement, enthusiasm	|	|	|	|	|	|	|	|	|	Dullness, apathy

Note: If you want more than one person to evaluate you, make several copies of this form.

Personal warmth										Aloofness, coldness
Neat appearance										Careless appearance
Cheerful disposition										Unhappy disposition
Sincerity, genuineness										Insincerity, artificiality
Insecurity in behavior										Confidence in behavior
Reluctancy to talk with others										Eagerness to talk with others
Desire to listen										No interest in listening
Primary concern for self										Primary concern for others
Ability to express ideas and feelings										Difficulty in expressing ideas and feelings
Awareness of what is happening										Lack of awareness of what is happening
Difficulty in making other people comfortable										Ease in making other people comfortable
Talk too much										Talk too little
Not intelligent										Intelligent
Excitement, enthusiasm										Dullness, apathy

DISCUSSION

1. Many times we feel we present particular characteristic to others because that is the way we see ourselves. What does this activity show us about our awareness and honesty in conveying our true self to others?

2. Did you have a realistic perception of yourself as compared to how the other person perceived you? Discuss the differences between your perceptions and the other person's perceptions.

3. Discuss how our perceptions of another person affect our interactions with them.

Adjective Checklist

PURPOSE

To provide an opportunity for the class members to reveal themselves to the other group members and to receive feedback on how the other group members perceive them.

INSTRUCTIONS

1. Review the list of words and place a (+) next to the adjectives you think best describe you and a (–) next to the adjectives which are least descriptive of you.
2. Divide into groups of three or four.
3. Each member then shares, with the group, at least four adjectives that are most descriptive and least descriptive of them.
4. Another option is to ask a friend (using the other person's adjective checklist), to place a (+) next to the adjectives they think best describe you and a (–) next to the adjectives they think are least descriptive of you.

_____ accepting	_____ simple	_____ silly
_____ self-accepting	_____ proud	_____ selfish
_____ anxious	_____ adaptable	_____ carefree
_____ aggressive	_____ dependent	_____ determined
_____ original	_____ effervescent	_____ spontaneous
_____ happy	_____ thoughtful	_____ tense
_____ vain	_____ lazy	_____ certain
_____ controlling	_____ dependable	_____ sentimental
_____ irritable	_____ mystical	_____ unpredictable
_____ worried	_____ inconsiderate	_____ patient
_____ rigid	_____ understanding	_____ extraverted
_____ brave	_____ sarcastic	_____ hostile
_____ responsible	_____ dreamy	_____ questioning

_____ remote	_____ loving	_____ serious
_____ shy	_____ ambitious	_____ modest
_____ warm	_____ authoritative	_____ mature
_____ withdrawn	_____ calm	_____ unsympathetic
_____ bitter	_____ conforming	_____ immature
_____ independent	_____ confident	_____ objective
_____ naive	_____ intelligent	_____ religious
_____ complex	_____ observant	_____ organized
_____ sensitive	_____ obsessive	_____ unorganized
_____ insensitive	_____ relaxed	_____ sympathetic
_____ nervous	_____ intuitive	_____ temperamental

DISCUSSION

1. What did you find out about yourself as a result of this activity?

2. What is the one adjective that causes you the greatest amount of difficulty in relationships with other people? Explain.

Becoming *Aware*

Other Person's Adjective Checklist

INSTRUCTIONS

1. Review the list of words and place a (+) next to the adjectives you think best describe your friend and a (–) next to the adjectives which are least descriptive of your friend.

_____ relaxed	_____ intelligent	_____ effervescent
_____ intuitive	_____ observant	_____ thoughtful
_____ serious	_____ obsessive	_____ lazy
_____ modest	_____ self-accepting	_____ dependable
_____ mature	_____ anxious	_____ mystical
_____ unsympathetic	_____ aggressive	_____ inconsiderate
_____ immature	_____ original	_____ understanding
_____ objective	_____ happy	_____ sarcastic
_____ religious	_____ vain	_____ dreamy
_____ organized	_____ controlling	_____ silly
_____ unorganized	_____ irritable	_____ selfish
_____ sympathetic	_____ worried	_____ carefree
_____ temperamental	_____ rigid	_____ determined
_____ accepting	_____ brave	_____ spontaneous
_____ ambitious	_____ responsible	_____ tense
_____ authoritative	_____ simple	_____ certain
_____ calm	_____ proud	_____ sentimental
_____ conforming	_____ adaptable	_____ unpredictable
_____ confident	_____ dependent	_____ patient

_____ extraverted

_____ hostile

_____ questioning

_____ remote

_____ shy

_____ warm

_____ withdrawn

_____ bitter

_____ independent

_____ naive

_____ complex

_____ sensitive

_____ insensitive

_____ nervous

_____ loving

The Rosenberg Self-Esteem Scale

PURPOSE

The scale below is a widely used research instrument that taps respondents' feelings of general self-esteem.

INSTRUCTIONS

Using the scale below, indicate your agreement with each of the following statements.

1	2	3	4
Strongly Disagree	Disagree	Agree	Strongly Agree

_____ 1. I feel that I am a person of worth, at least on an equal basis with others.

_____ 2. I feel that I have a number of good qualities.

_____ 3. All in all, I am inclined to feel that I am a failure.

_____ 4. I am able to do most things as well as most other people.

_____ 5. I feel I do not have much to be proud of.

_____ 6. I take a positive attitude toward myself.

_____ 7. On the whole, I am satisfied with myself.

_____ 8. I wish I could have more respect for myself.

_____ 9. I certainly feel useless at times.

_____ 10. At times I think I am no good at all.

SCORING

To calculate your score, first reverse the scoring for the five negatively worded items (**3, 5, 8, 9,** and **10**) as follows: 1 = 4, 2 = 3, 3 = 2, 4 = 1. Then sum your scores across the 10 items. Your total score should fall between 10 and 40. A higher score indicates higher self-esteem.

Total Score _____

DISCUSSION

1. Do you agree or disagree with your score? Why or why not?

2. From the strategies to improve self-esteem discussed in the text, what do you think you need to do to improve your self-esteem?

Adapted from *Society and the Adolescent Self-Image* by M. Rosenberg, Princeton University Press.

Becoming *Aware*

Name _____ Date _____

Do Gender Roles Still Exist?

PURPOSE

Discover how you and others perceive gender roles and issues.

INSTRUCTIONS

In the spaces below, list 10 characteristics and behaviors that you associate with being male and female in our society. Note whether you think each is traditional or not used anymore.

1. You may either do this activity individually or with a partner. An interesting alternative would be to divide your pairs by sex; males with males and females with females. This will help the class see whether there is a distinct perceived difference or not.

Males	Females
1. _____	1. _____
2. _____	2. _____
3. _____	3. _____
4. _____	4. _____
5. _____	5. _____
6. _____	6. _____
7. _____	7. _____
8. _____	8. _____
9. _____	9. _____
10. _____	10. _____

2. Before you go on, make two copies of the list and set them aside for now.
3. Look at the list of the 20 different characteristics, both male and female, and circle the ones that best apply to you. You may discover that you identify with some characteristics of the opposite sex. How many of them did you select?
4. Divide into small groups of 3 to 5 individuals and answer the following questions.

DISCUSSION

1. Did the females in the group circle more of the male characteristics than males circled of the female characteristics? If so, why?

2. Are there some characteristics of the opposite sex that you wish could be attributed to members of your sex? Which ones are they? Why would you like them attributed to your sex?

3. Do you feel our definitions of gender roles are preventing you from behaving or developing in the ways you would prefer? Explain.

4. How have gender role expectations influenced your personality development?

5. How could we best make society more accepting of varying gender roles?

6. Now give the copy of the list that you previously made to someone who knows you well and ask them to circle the characteristics that best apply to you, using gender neutral characteristics. When they have completed the list, compare your list with theirs. How we see ourselves is not always how others see us. How closely did your list match your friend's? What might the differences tell you about yourself?

7. Give the other copy of the list to someone who knows you well who is at least ten years or more older or younger than you, and do the same as in previous question. Is there a difference because of age? If there is a difference, why?

Name _____ Date _____

Human Relations Position Paper

PURPOSE

To analyze your present position, based upon your past experiences and learning, in order to have a better idea of the direction in which you want to move in the future.

INSTRUCTIONS

1. A Human Relations Position Paper should represent a critical analysis of those factors that have brought you to this point in your life and have made you what you are. It should also include your plans for the future.
2. No one but you and your instructor will read your position paper unless, of course, you choose to show it to someone else. Your instructor considers it completely confidential.
3. As a guide for preparing your position paper, the following outline is suggested. This is intended only as a guide, and you may add or delete whatever items you choose.
4. Anything that helps you arrive at your position and chart your course of action (from poetry to pictures to words) is acceptable.
5. Your instructor will determine the length of this paper. We suggest five pages.

** Retain a copy of this to review in ten years. How far have you come?

HUMAN RELATIONS POSITION PAPER OUTLINE

I. The Person I Am (Include the influential factors which have contributed to making you what you are).
   A. Influence of Family Background
      1. Relationship with parents
      2. Relationship with siblings
      3. Socioeconomic setting
      4. Family's expectations
      5. Other
   B. Adolescence
      1. School experience
      2. Peer group (left out/included—Why?)
      3. Successes/Failures and their effect
      4. Influential adults other than parents
      5. Other
   C. Personal Sexuality
      1. Dating experiences and their effects

2. "Facts of life" information or misinformation and its effect
3. My "role" in life and how people understand me
4. My attitudes toward the opposite sex
5. Other
D. Goals for Future
1. How have I arrived at my goals?
2. Occupational choice—Why?
3. Feelings of personal adequacy or inadequacy
4. Degree of flexibility
5. Influential people
6. Other
II. Where Do I Go From Here?
A. Summary of Present Position
1. How do I see myself/how do others see me?
2. How well do I communicate?
3. Value system
4. Accepting relationships with others
5. My view of a meaningful occupation
a. What I expect
b. What's expected of me
c. My chances for success
6. How I view my sexuality
a. In relation to marriage
b. "Role" expectations
c. Understanding of needs
B. Plans for Future
1. What is the Good Life for me?
a. How I will achieve it
b. How it relates to my value system
c. How it relates to my chosen occupation
2. What are my priorities for the future?
3. Do I want to "go it alone" or build relationships with others?
a. How I will do this
4. Do I want to share my life with someone else in marriage?
a. My responsibilities
b. What I expect of others
5. What will my biggest problems be?

Name _____ Date _____

Self-Awareness

LEARNING JOURNAL

Select the statement below that best defines your feelings about the personal value or meaning gained from this chapter and respond below the dotted line.

            I learned that I . . .   I was surprised that I . . .

            I realized that I . . .   I was pleased that I . . .

            I discovered that I . . .   I was displeased that I . . .

....

Chapter 3
Who's in Control?

© Anže Malec/Shutterstock.com

Not Today
It's funny, to me, though.
The times I don't think I will survive are the times I learn to live.
And no matter how hard it's raining, the rain will stop.
The sun will come back out.
The hurt will heal. The holes will be filled.
So when life forgets to knock on your door and decides
instead to knock you down and kick you, you stand up.
You dust yourself off and with the dirt of pain and broken heartedness
all over your cheeks, smile and say, "not today." —Colton Snead 2016

Think About This...

- "How am I ever going to stop smoking?"
- "I've tried hundreds of times to lose 15 pounds. I lose 5 pounds then gain back 10 pounds. How can I lose weight and make sure that I can keep it off?"
- "I need to study more. My grades aren't too good. How can I get myself to sit down and study more?"
- "I would sure like to have more dates; I haven't had a date for two months. How can I get more dates?"
- "I've been married for three years and the relationship is not as exciting as it was before. What can I do to improve the relationship or is it time to get out?"
- "My boss is always so critical. Why can't she be more positive?"

Most of us have either asked one or more of these questions or we have heard many of our friends ask them. Now the question is "If I want to change, can I?" "Am I in control of my own behavior or is someone or something else in control of me?" "How can someone change?" As we all know, change is not easy.

B. F. Skinner (2002), a well-known psychologist, has indicated in much of his writing that all of our behavior is controlled and that there is no such thing as "free will." Do you agree? This is a philosophical question that people have been discussing for years. We will not attempt to answer this question in this book, but we will be referring to it, directly or indirectly, throughout the book.

Who is in control? You? Me? Someone else? Our environment? Psychologists have come up with a number of theories to explain how we can develop the capacity to control our own behavior and to influence other people's behavior. Many psychologists believe that learning theory is the answer to all our questions. Learning theory underlies all relationships—good, bad, happy, and sad ones.

Self-Control or External Control

Self-control is often considered to be the opposite of external control. In self-control, individuals set their own standards for performance, and will then reward or punish themselves for meeting or not meeting these standards. On the other hand, in external control, someone else sets the standards and delivers or withholds the rewards or negative consequences.

Both Angie and Beth took a psychology test last Friday. Angie studied two hours every night for the last five nights and it paid off for her; she received an "A" grade. Angie knows that she earned her grade; it took a lot of work. On the other hand, Beth only studied two hours total for her test and she also received an "A" for her grade. Beth knows how hard she really studied and that she was really lucky to receive such a good grade. How hard will Beth study for her next test? Who will be more motivated to study, Beth or Angie? Which person will be most likely to succeed in school and everyday life?

Perceived locus of control. People differ markedly in their feelings about their capacity to control life situations. Some people feel that they are in control of their own destinies. Their general expectancy about what happens to them and what they achieve in life is due to their own abilities, attitudes, and actions. In contrast, other people see their lives as being beyond their control. They believe that what happens to them is determined by external forces, whether it is luck or fate, other people, "Mother Nature," or the stars. Much has been written on the self-perceived ability of individuals to change the nature of their lives (Rotter, 1990; Judge & Bono, 2001). While many psychologists interpret ideas such as "locus of control" and "self-efficacy" as individually variable personality characteristics, they may actually reflect worldviews of a nation, ethnic group, or geographic community. How might these worldviews affect the self-perceived ability of individuals to change the nature of their lives? According to psychologists (Rotter, 1990; Zukerman et al., 2004), these two types of people are said to be identified as having either an *internal* or an *external* "locus of control." Angie would be said to have an **internal locus of control** and Beth would have an **external locus of control**.

Internals perceive that their efforts make a difference when they are facing a difficult situation, so they try to cope with it. They take whatever action seems appropriate to solve the problem. "I didn't make an A on that test…I guess I will study longer next time."

Externals perceive that their efforts will not make a difference, so naturally they do not attempt to cope with threatening situations. "This test is rigged. I will not make an A… why bother?"

The difference in perceived locus of control is important for personal adjustment to the world. People who believe they can control events in their environment will respond to stress quite differently from those who believe the opposite. Rotter indicates that these attitudes are learned from experience prior to the age of nineteen. If you discover that your efforts are repeatedly rewarded, you will believe that you will be able to exert control over your outcomes in the future. If you discover that your efforts are to no avail, you will become resigned to the lack of control.

> *Luck is a matter of preparation meeting opportunity.*
> —OPRAH WINFREY

> *For a change, Lady Luck seemed to be smiling on me. Then again, maybe the Fickle Wench was just lulling me into a false sense of security while she reached for a rock.*
> —TIMOTHY ZAHN

Can you control events in your environment? Do you feel that you are in control in your environment?

Are You an Internal or External?

What implications does research on the locus of control have for you? The most important point is that there is a link between your beliefs about locus of control and your behavior. If you believe your experience is beyond your own control, you may expend less effort than you could. You may not try as hard as you are able, because you believe that your efforts will not make a difference. You may satisfy yourself with poor performance, figuring there is nothing you can do to improve the situation. Certainly some situations are more out of your control than others are, but your overall attitude about challenging situations will affect every aspect of your life.

© *CandyBox Images/Shutterstock.com*

Are internals or externals more successful? Internals seem to be more successful in more aspects of life than externals. Although an internal locus of control does not ensure success, those who believe they can influence the events in life tend to be the best life managers. These people are more likely to consider the possibility of doing something differently in their lives than people with an external orientation.

Internals are more curious than externals about ways to improve their lives. They see that education and knowledge are personal power. They are more likely to read about problem areas in their lives and attend workshops and classes related to solving these problems. Internals are also better listeners than externals (Worchel et al., 2000). They are more likely to ask questions, give others time to speak, and accurately interpret what others are saying. Internally oriented individuals tend to get better grades and score higher on standardized academic tests than externals (Schultz & Schultz, 2012).

Concerning relationships, internals tend to fare better than externals, especially considering the fact that internals tend to be better listeners and are more willing to work at improving their relationships. During stressful times in life, internals are more likely to seek social support than externals. Numerous studies have found that having an internal locus of control is associated with positive functioning and adjustment (Roden, 2004). Another study found that the less internal locus of control an individual perceives, the greater the likelihood for stress and depression (Kormanik & Rocco, 2009).

Take a look now at the following Consider This.

> *For the weak, it is impossible. For the fainthearted, it is unknown. For the thoughtful and valiant, it is ideal.*
> —VICTOR HUGO

CONSIDER THIS

INTERNALS AND EXTERNALS

How would you respond in this situation?

Event
Wanda's boyfriend and Jeff's girlfriend just announced to each of them that the relationship is over.

Cognitive Response
Jeff's response: "What did I do wrong?" "What can I do to get her back?" "Why doesn't she like me anymore?" "I'll do anything for her." "My whole life is ruined."

Wanda's response: "My boyfriend has sure been depressed lately," "He sure has changed in the past few months," "I really like him, but I could tell that things weren't going well between us recently," "I know it will be tough, but I know I can get along without him."

Imagine what you would say to yourself if your mate were to tell you today that your relationship is over.

Perceived Control or Lack of Control

Jeff continues to call his girlfriend to find out what he can do to get her back. He sends her gifts, pleads with her, but his efforts are to no avail. Whatever he does seems to have no effect on her. He does not have any control over the situation.

Wanda seems to understand that she has no control over her boyfriend's behavior, but she does have control over her own life. She accepts the fact that the relationship is over and she needs to get on with the rest of her life.

Outcome

Jeff develops a negative feeling about himself and his life. He sees himself as no good, not worthy, and that nobody will ever love him, so what is the use of living. He becomes depressed, passive, and develops *learned helplessness*. That is the assumption—based on past failures—that one is unable to do anything to improve one's performance or situation and he just gives up.

Wanda's not happy with the situation, but realizes that she does not have any control over her boyfriend, so she looks to the future. She sets new goals and actively begins to work to achieve them ("There are other fish in the sea.").

Who's in Control?

We would define Jeff as an "external" because he feels that he is not in control of his own destiny, that outside forces are determining his fate, and that whatever effort he puts into changing the situation will not make any difference.

Wanda would be defined as an "internal," since she perceives herself as in control of her destiny and her success is dependent upon her efforts and not on others. She also realizes that she does not have control over other people's behavior.

Personal control versus learned helplessness. Helpless, oppressed people often perceive that control is external and this perception may deepen their feelings of resignation. This is what Martin Seligman (2006) and others found in experiments with both animals and humans. When dogs are strapped in a harness and given repeated shocks, with no opportunity to avoid them, they learn a sense of helplessness, now called "learned helplessness."

When people are faced with repeated traumatic events over which they have no control, they too, will come to feel helpless, hopeless, and depressed. You can see the importance of parents teaching their children to have the feeling of some control over their lives and their behavior. Parents who do everything for their children are not doing their children a favor; the children are beginning to show learned helplessness, because "Daddy will take care of it." Seligman's research now shows that people's *cognitive interpretation* of aversive events determines whether they develop learned helplessness (Weiten et al., 2012).

Is your life out of control? *Learned helplessness* is the passive behavior produced by the exposure to unavoidable aversive events. For example, in concentration camps, prisons, work environments, or nursing homes where people are given little control, they will experience a lowering of morale, a feeling of increased stress, depression, and a feeling of helplessness. Increasing control—allowing workers to have some participation in decision making, allowing inmates to make decisions when they want to watch TV or exercise, letting nursing home patients make choices about their environment—noticeably improves morale along with mental and physical health. Perceived control is vital to human functioning. Thus, for young and old alike, we should create an environment that enhances a sense of control and self-efficacy (Aronson et al., 2012).

Are you an *internal* or an *external*? Which of these do you want to be? Can you change your behavior? Who's in control?

What is it about school or my job that contributes to my belief that I am not in control of my life?

© *Pressmaster/Shutterstock.com*

God grant me the serenity
to accept the things I cannot change;
courage to change the things I can;
and <u>wisdom</u> to know the difference

REINHOLD NIEBUHR, The Serenity Prayer

How can we take control? In the following paragraphs, we will give you some helpful hints on taking control of your life. In order to increase the probability of you developing an internal locus of control, you will want to work on the following items (Watson & Tharp, 2006; Santrock, 2006):

1. *Consider changing aspects of your environment.*
   Ask yourself some of the following questions: What types of people in my life contribute to my locus of control beliefs? What is it about school or my job that contribute to my belief that I am not in control of my life? How do my current friends, acquaintances, and other people in my life contribute to my locus of control? What can you do about these situations in order to take control of your life?

2. *Try new activities rather than the usual safe and secure ways of doing things.*
   Take some risks, do something different, try a new restaurant, do not travel the same route home or to school each day, try new food, wear different clothes, or anything that will help you break old habits that may be harming you. **Externals** have difficulty trying something new and breaking old habits. Trying and enjoying something new will help you see that you can control aspects of your life.

3. *Begin to assume more responsibility for tasks at home, work, and school.*
   Volunteer to do things that you do not usually do. Join a committee, volunteer to help someone, and offer to take responsibility for some tasks to be completed. Start slow and then keep adding on responsibilities. You will feel much better about yourself and see that you are in control.

4. *Notice new things so you are in the present. You become engaged and mindful*
   Dr. Ellen Langer has determined that the mindless following of routine and other automatic behaviors leads to much error, pain, and a predetermined course of life. Mindful living helps you to have an increase of learning, and decrease in accidents. You notice new things when you are in the present. Mindfulness, which is derived from Zen Buddhism, is basically a skill one can use to better tolerate and cope with emotional distress. You become engaged. Working on your mindfulness with even small amounts of meditation or just "being in the moment" will help you when you have those aggravating negative thoughts running through your head that will not leave you alone. For example "I failed that test"... "I could kick myself for not studying more"... "My dad is going to ream me out for this"... "My teacher made it too hard"... "I failed that test..."

      Dr. David Allen, a professor of psychiatry, believes that mindfulness is relevant to the first part of of the Serenity Prayer—"accepting things that one cannot change." What about changing the things that need changing? How do we know which things can be changed and which ones cannot and how does one go about changing them? He explains that people feel emotional pain for the same reason they feel physical pain: It is a signal to the person that something in the *environment* is wrong and needs attention. Sometimes this needs the help of a trained therapist.

It is important to note that the newest findings from neuroscience show that the prefrontal cortex plays a major role in our ability to restrain our behavior and impulses (Wargo, 2009). Actually, this research demonstrates that because the prefrontal cortex matures later than other brain systems (around the mid-20's), adults should be better than children at controlling themselves. Likewise, other research shows when our self-control is depleted and our brain becomes fatigued by too much restraint, we may, in fact, experience even less control than we ordinarily would (Ackerman et al., 2009; Wargo, 2009).

Read Table 3.1 to decide whether you want to become an external or internal.

As you continue to read this chapter you will discover new ways to take control of your life. One of the ways that you will discover to take control of your own life is by developing a high level of **self-efficacy** *(which is your* belief that you can do anything you put your mind to!).

Table 3.1 CHARACTERISTICS OF EXTERNALS AND INTERNALS

EXTERNALS	INTERNALS
More susceptible to depression.	Not very susceptible to depression.
Not likely to vote in elections.	More likely to vote and get involved in politics.
Not too likely to complete school, or college.	Likely to complete high school, college, and graduate school.
Not too likely to change habits.	Willing to take action to change bad habits.
Tend to be susceptible to anxiety.	Not too susceptible to anxiety.
Does not adapt well to stress.	Copes better with stress.
Gives up easily.	Willing to continue trying in spite of failure; persistent.
Will not spend much time on a task.	Willing to work on a task for a long time.
Does not like new challenges and does not handle them well.	Willing to meet new challenges and handles the pressure.
Tends to just let things happen and not too curious.	Will seek out information to help solve problems.
Does not earn as much money as an internal.	Tends to be more successful and earns more money.

Seligman (2006).

What is self-efficacy? **Self-efficacy** is our belief about our ability to perform behaviors that should lead to expected outcomes. Believing that you can control your behaviors is fundamental to self-management. Individuals having high self-efficacy for particular behaviors or skills are likely to work longer and try more strategies to develop these skills than those with low self-efficacy (Bandura, 2008). When self-efficacy is high, we feel confident that we can execute the responses necessary to earn reinforcers. When self-efficacy is low, we worry that the necessary responses may be beyond our abilities.

Perceptions of self-efficacy are subjective and specific to different kinds of tasks. For instance, you might feel extremely confident about your ability to handle difficult social situations, but very doubtful about your ability to handle academic challenges. Perceptions of self-efficacy can influence which challenges we tackle and how well we will perform them. One thing is certain: good outcomes increase self-efficacy; they fuel an appetite for future risk (Webber, 2010).

Gender and self-efficacy. Men and women develop differently, both physiologically and socially. This difference affects their self-efficacy. As children, girls are more likely than boys to play in small groups in which interpersonal awareness is more likely to be heightened. In contrast, boys are more likely than girls to play in large groups where opportunities for discussion are minimized. In addition, boys, more than girls, may be encouraged to become involved in competitive, achievement-related activities (Deaner et al., 2012). Research that has manipulated a person's view of performance on various tasks shows that a person's sense of self-efficacy is related to the person's fulfillment of culturally mandated, gender-appropriate norms (Hockenbury & Hockenbury, 2010). Men more than women focus on independence and distinctiveness; while some women more than men focus on interdependence and good relationships. From these different focuses, both men and women derive a sense of self-efficacy. Can you identify any culturally mandated gender-appropriate norms that have been expressed to you in your environment? It seems today we are sending mixed messages to our children about gender roles. We will explore that later.

Why do women tend to focus on interdependence and good relationships?

© mimagephotography/Shutterstock.com

You can take control! To realize your aims, you should try to exercise control over the events that affect your life (Bandura, 2008). You have a strong incentive to act if you believe that control is possible—that your actions will be effective. Perceived self-efficacy, or belief in your personal capabilities, regulates human functioning in three major ways:

1. **Mood or affect.** The amount of stress or depression a person is experiencing in threatening or difficult situations depends largely on how well they think they can cope in that situation.

2. **Motivational.** Motivation will be stronger if individuals believe they can attain their goals and then adjust them based on their progress.

 Check this out   RATE YOUR SELF-EFFICACY

Remember that self-efficacy is the extent or strength of one's belief in one's own ability to complete tasks and reach **goals**.

Place a check mark in the column that best applies to you for each item: (1) not at all true, (2) barely true, (3) moderately true, and (4) exactly true.

Items	Self-Rating 1	2	3	4
1. I can always manage to solve difficult problems if I try hard enough.				
2. If someone opposes me, I can find the means and ways to get what I want.				
3. I am certain that I can accomplish my goals.				
4. I am confident that I could deal efficiently with unexpected events.				
5. Thanks to my resourcefulness, I can handle unforeseen situations.				
6. I can solve most problems if I invest the necessary effort.				
7. I can remain calm when facing difficulties because I can rely on my coping abilities.				
8. When I am confronted with a problem, I can find several solutions.				
9. If I am in trouble, I can think of a solution.				
10. I can handle whatever comes my way.				

Becoming *Aware*

Total Score: _____

Scoring

Total your score for the 10 items. Total scores can range from 10 to 40. The higher your score, the more general self-efficacy you are likely to have. If you scored 31 or higher, you likely have a reasonably strong sense of self-efficacy. If you scored 20 or lower, you may want to think of ways that you can improve your self-efficacy.

Scale adapted from Santrock (2006).

This measure has been used internationally for more than two decades. Researchers have found that it is linked to adaptation after life changes and is an indicator of quality of life at any point in time (Scholtz et al., 2002).

3. **Cognitive.** People with positive thoughts, feelings, beliefs, and high aspirations will have high self-efficacy. Could it be possible that people have at least two ways of explaining defeats and various setbacks? Let us take a closer look.

Two Explanatory Styles

Optimism is defined as a generalized tendency to expect positive outcomes, while *pessimism* is defined as a general tendency to envision the future as unfavorable. To understand why someone becomes an optimist or a pessimist, it helps to understand what distinguishes them. Optimistic people tend to feel that bad things won't last long and won't affect other parts of life. Pessimists tend to believe one negative incident will last and undermine everything else in their lives.

Also important, researchers say, is the story or causal attributions you construct about why things happen—your *explanatory style*. Psychologist Martin Seligman (2006) suggests that people who have an *optimistic explanatory style* tend to use external, unstable, and specific explanations for negative events. People who have a *pessimistic explanatory style* use internal, stable, and global or pervasive explanations for negative events.

More than any other major personality trait, optimism is a matter of practice.
— KATHLEEN MCGOWAN

To pessimists, the "movie of life" is a documentary that has an unchangeable script. Optimists grab the story line and become directors. They edit, refocus, and add color to concoct a brighter, happier picture. This hopeful, in-control attitude shields them from outside influences and inner emotional turmoil (Vaughan, 2000). Positive thinkers feel powerful. Negative thinkers, Seligman says, feel helpless because they have learned to believe they're doomed, no matter what.

Are you an optimist or a pessimist? Are you an Eeyore or a Winnie the Pooh? Do you look at the bright side and expect good things to happen, or do you tend to believe that if something can go wrong, it will?

Health, happiness and success. Studies show that optimists are better at coping with the distress associated with everything from menopause to heart surgery. Furthermore, scientists at UCLA discovered that optimists have more disease-fighting T cells. Not surprisingly, positive thinkers live longer. Mayo Clinic researchers recently compared the scores of a personality test taken by 839 men and women three decades ago with their subsequent mortality rates. Those who had a pessimistic explanatory style in their young years had a significantly higher risk of dying than their optimistic peers (Newman, 2001). Optimism as it relates to stress will be discussed in Chapter Eight. Optimistic thinking tends to lead us to a more successful, happier, and healthier life.

Optimism is also a remarkable predictor of achievement and resilience. For example, studies have found that optimistic Olympic-level swimmers recover from defeat and later swim even faster, whereas pessimistic swimmers, following defeat, get slower (Seligman, 2006). When faced with serious problems—such as deciding about a risky operation, coping with traumatic events, or overcoming drug abuse or alcoholism—optimists tend to focus on what they can do rather than on how they feel. They keep their sense of humor, plan for the future, and reinterpret the situation in a positive light.

© ESB Professional/Shutterstock.com

Optimistic thinking tends to lead us to a more successful, happier, and healthier life.

Are You an Optimist or a Pessimist?

Pat Pessimist and Otis Optimist were invited to a social function. Both are single and looking for a date. Pat sees an attractive person across the room and decides to approach the person and introduce himself and see where it could lead. As he approaches her, she notices him approaching and immediately looks the other direction. Pat immediately interprets this as rejection and thus turns away and goes to the bar for a drink. Otis notices a different female and approaches her. She sees him coming toward her and she immediately turns away and begins a conversation with another person. Otis decides that she must not want to meet him and he heads to the bar.

If you were in this situation what would you say and do? Let's see what Pat and Otis did.

Pat Pessimist: I guess I'll just have a couple more drinks and then go home and watch TV alone. (After rejection, becomes passive and withdraws)

Otis Optimist: Wait a minute, there's another good-looking one over there; why not try her? (After rejection, perseveres, doesn't stop trying)

Pat Pessimist: Women just don't seem to be interested in me. I don't know what to say, and they don't like the way I dress. It must be my hair. (Global, pervasive explanation)

Otis Optimist: I bet she's engaged anyway. She's probably shy and not too interesting. (Specific explanation)

Are you an Otis or a Pat?

Optimists, by definition, expect to eventually recover from adversity, and they expect to be successful at whatever they do, so they work much harder to reach their goals than pessimists do. Thus, another self-fulfilling prophecy is created. Suzanne Segerstrom, a University of Kentucky psychologist, indicates that optimism leads to increased well-being because it leads you to engage actively in life, not because of a miracle happy juice that optimists have and pessimists don't (Neimark, 2007).

Learned optimism. Martin Seligman (2006) defines ***learned optimism*** as a learned way of explaining both good and bad life events that in turn enhances our perceived control and adaptive responses to them. In learned optimism, the real emphasis is on interpreting life events in a reasonably accurate way to enhance our perceived control and, thus, our adaptive responses. According to Seligman (2006), people can train themselves to make optimistic explanations by the following three steps:

1. Think about situations of adversity (being turned down for a date, doing poorly on a test, losing a sports competition);
2. Consider the way you normally explain these events, and, if it is pessimistic (Nobody likes me, I'm not very smart, I really choked in the game);

> *The people who trigger us to feel negative emotion are messengers. They are messengers for the unhealed parts of our being.*
> —TEAL SWAN

Dispute these explanations by looking closely at the facts (She probably had plans with her family, I need to spend more time studying, My opponent played a great game).

Practice this exercise over and over again. And, be sure to consider the following advice from David Myers (1993), author of *The Pursuit of Happiness*:

> The recipe for well-being requires neither positive nor negative thinking alone, but a mix of ample optimism to provide hope, a dash of pessimism to prevent complacency, and enough realism to discriminate those things we can control from those we cannot.

Courage is the most import- ant of all the virtues because without cour- age, you can't practice any other virtue.
—MAYA ANGELOU

THE BOTTOM LINE

Face it, nobody owes you a living.

What you achieve or fail to achieve in your lifetime, is directly related to what you do, or fail to do.

No one chooses his parents or childhood, but you can choose your own direction.

Everyone has problems and obstacles to overcome, but that too is relative to each individual.

Nothing is carved in stone; you can change anything in your life, if you want to badly enough.

Excuses are for losers: Those who take responsibility for their actions are the real winners in life.

Winners meet life's challenges head on, knowing there are no guarantees, and give all they've got.

And never think it's too late or too early to begin. Time plays no favorites and will pass whether you act or not.

Take control of your life. Dare to dream and take risks . . .

Compete.

An optimist is the one who sees an oppor- tunity in every difficulty. A pessimist is one who sees a dif- ficulty in every opportunity.
—L.P. JACKS

How did you become an internal or external? Where did your high level or low level of self-efficacy come from? How did you learn to become a pessimist or optimist? How can you take control of your life? These are not easy questions to answer. In order to understand yourself better and to discover different ways to improve your life, psy- chologists have developed many different theories. Many of these theories evolve from or revolve around learning theory.

Social Learning Theory

Albert Bandura is one of several behaviorists who have added a cognitive flavor to learning theory. Bandura points out that humans obviously are conscious, thinking, and feeling beings. He feels that some psychologists like B. F. Skinner ignore these cognitive processes. An important aspect of *social learning theory* that may have an important impact on our lives is *observational learning*—the fact that much of personality is learned in social situations through interactions with and observations of other people, including family members (Mischel, 2004).

Observational learning. This occurs when an individual's behavior is influenced by the observation of others, who are called models. Observational learning requires that you pay attention to someone who is *significant* to you, a parent, or a friend. You observe their behavior and understand its consequences, and then store this information in your memory.

Some role models are more influential than others. Children and adults tend to imitate people they like and respect more so than people they do not. We also are especially prone to imitate the behavior of people whom we consider attractive or powerful, such as rock stars, movie stars, sports heroes, or politicians. It is a bit scary to discover that we are also more likely to model ourselves after the individual who is the most aggressive, especially if that aggression leads to positive reinforcement. If you observe your mother yelling at your father in order to get him to do something, and he does do it, you are more likely to yell at someone the next time you want something. Prior to that experience, you most likely would have not yelled at someone in order to get your way. A five-year-old boy goes to the store with a seven-year old. The older boy picks up a candy bar and does not pay for it and on the way home shares it with his friend. Did he get positive reinforcement for stealing? What is the likelihood of the younger boy attempting to pocket a candy bar the next time he goes to the store? What we learn through modeling is not always positive. That is why our parents keep saying, "Do what I say, not what I do."

According to **social learning theory**, modeling has a great impact on personality development. Children learn to be assertive, conscientious, self-sufficient, aggressive, fearful, and so forth by observing others behaving in these ways.

Many of you are familiar with the classic cartoon TV program called *The Simpsons*. Matt Groening, the creator, decided it would be funny if the Simpsons' eight-year-old daughter Lisa played the baritone sax. Do you think this would have an influence on the audience of this program? Sure enough, across the country little girls began imitating Lisa. Cynthia Sikes, a saxophone teacher in New York, told the *New York Times* (January 14, 1996) that when the show started, she got an influx of girls coming up to her saying, "I want to play the saxophone because Lisa Simpson plays the saxophone." Groening says his mail regularly includes photos of girls holding up their saxophones. Can you think of other ways that the media has influenced your behavior?

> *Children need models more than they need critics.*
> —JOSEPH JOUBERT, *PENSÉES*, 1842

> *What a child doesn't receive he can seldom later give.*
> —P. D. JAMES

HOW DOES LEARNING THEORY INFLUENCE YOUR LIFE?

When you do something you enjoy, what is the likelihood that you will do it again?

If you try something and fail at it, what are the chances that you will attempt it again?

If you ask someone out for a date five times and the answer is "NO" each time, are you going to ask again?

If you make a nasty comment to a classmate who responds by telling the teacher, will you make that comment next time?

If someone you do not know very well embarrasses you in front of a large group, are you going to avoid that person in the future?

If you drink something that tastes good, will you drink it again?

You hate green peas because you were forced to eat them as a kid. Do you eat them now?

All of these situations can be explained by learning theory.

In order to understand learning theory, we need to define the term learning. **Learning** is defined in psychology as a relatively permanent change in behavior as a result of experience or practice (Gardner, 2002).

Before you can begin the process of learning, you have to pay attention. Are you aware of all the different types of stimuli that get your attention?

WHAT GETS YOUR ATTENTION?

What gets your attention?

You are concentrating on reading a book and the phone rings. What do you do? A person whom you perceive as attractive enters the room. Do you notice that person? What gets your attention? Before you can learn something, you have to pay attention to it. Attention is the most important aspect of learning because we have to pay attention to something before we can respond. Another aspect of attention that may surprise you is that **you can only pay attention to one thing at a time**. You cannot watch TV and study at the same time. Again, to what do you pay attention? We find that there are three kinds of stimuli that attract our attention. They are *novel stimuli, significant stimuli,* and

Becoming *Aware*

conflicting stimuli. We find that these three different kinds of stimuli are not only important to learning, but also vital to our relationships with others.

Novel stimuli. We tend to pay attention to people, places, or things that are new, different, unique, or original. You tend to pay more attention to the student who is new to your school than a student who has been going to your school for the past few years. When reading the newspaper, you tend to notice an advertisement that is in color more than in black and white, because the color ad is unique. The person with a Mohawk haircut will generally be noticed before someone with a "normal" hairstyle. A person wearing the latest in fashion will tend to get more attention than someone wearing last year's style of clothing. Why? Because it is unique, different, or *novel*. The more familiar we become with the "new" person, the "unique" hairstyle, or the "latest" fashion, the less we are apt to pay attention. We tend to begin to take them for granted. When you begin to date someone, you tend to give the individual a lot of special attention, but what happens after you have been dating that same individual for years? Many times you find that you begin to habituate or get bored with that individual when the novelty wears off and you no longer pay as much attention to him or her.

What else gets your attention?

Significant stimuli. So, you like to listen to music? Do you like ice cream? Are you interested in sex? Do you like money? If your answer to all of these questions is yes, then all of these things are *significant* to you and you will pay attention to them. If you are a teacher and want to get your students to learn, you better make sure the material is *significant* to your students. Otherwise, you may find it difficult to keep your students' attention. You need to make the material relate directly to your students' needs, wants, interests, and desires, and if you do this, you will be surprised to discover that your students are paying attention and learning.

Do you get bored in relationships after the novelty wears off?

How important is this in a relationship? When you first start dating someone, do you consider your date's needs, wants, interests, and desires when deciding where to go and what to do? If you do, you will find that your date will respond more positively to you, and you both will be much happier. If you send your mate flowers for the first time and he or she likes them, will you receive more attention? Are the flowers *significant*? Are the flowers *novel*? Since they are both *novel* and *significant*, they should increase the attention paid to you by your friend. You reinforce your mate, and your mate reinforces you. It tends to make life more interesting to you and your friends.

If you want a relationship to continue on a positive basis over a long period of time, you must make sure that you provide *novel* and *significant* stimuli in the relationship—otherwise the relationship will become stale and boring. This is why that old saying is appropriate here; *the grass always looks greener on the other side of the fence.* You wonder why your boyfriend, girlfriend, husband, wife or significant other is always interested in others? You wonder why students are not paying attention to the teacher? Could it be that the other people are novel and maybe even more significant?

Conflicting stimuli. What if we were to tell you that, "All of your behavior is controlled!"; "There is no 'God'!"; "It is all right to steal!" And "It's okay to cheat on your spouse, boyfriend, or girlfriend?" Are these statements in conflict with any of your beliefs?

We have discovered that you will not only pay attention to *novel* and *significant* stimuli, but also to anything that is in conflict with your values, needs, or morals. It has been found that in many relationships the only time that two people pay attention to one another is when they are in conflict—arguing, fighting. We do not recommend this form of stimuli in order to get attention because it can create more problems than it solves. If this is the only time you find that you and your partner pay attention to one another, you might want to change this by seeking counseling, reading a good self-help book, or changing your behavior in order to provide more novel or significant stimuli in your relationships.

With all the technology and equipment we have today and with all the activities available to us, many of us still get tired of just sitting around. We get bored with life.

Make life more exciting! We all seek change in our lives. Kids get bored, teenagers get bored, and adults get bored. If you take your kids to the zoo every Saturday, eventually they will not enjoy going any longer. If you take your date to the movies every Friday night, it just is not as exciting as it used to be. You have your favorite dessert, a hot fudge brownie sundae, every night for two months. Believe it or not, even that sundae will not be enjoyed as much as it was when you could have it only once a month. Using novel and significant stimuli in your life will help you and those around you have an exciting, non-boring life.

We learn throughout life. We all need to change in order to adapt to the world that we must live in. What we have learned in the past is not always the best for us in the future. Consider using novel and significant stimuli and sometimes conflicting stimuli

© g-stockstudio/Shutterstock.com

Are you bored?

as you relate to others in business situations, in relationships, in family situations, and in teaching-learning environments—which is the laboratory of life. If you do, you will discover that your life and the life of the people around you will improve.

Now that we have your attention, it is time to learn.

Learning Theory

Why study learning theory? Learning theory is the basis of all interactions—we are applying it constantly and it is constantly being applied on us, most of the time without our knowledge. Learning theorists believe that our behavior, including our personality, is shaped through operant conditioning and observational learning. If you have a better understanding of learning theory, it will help you understand the relationships you have with others and hopefully you will be able to improve the relationships you are involved in and help you acquire new relationships.

An understanding of learning theory will also allow you to understand yourself as well as others. You will learn how to manage your own behavior as well as discover ways in which you can influence other people's behavior.

WHAT ARE THE CONSEQUENCES?

Reinforcement. In behavioral terminology, pleasant or unpleasant stimuli that strengthen a behavior are called ***reinforcers***, and their effect is called ***reinforcement***. The simplest type of reinforcer, called ***primary reinforcer***, is a pleasant or unpleasant one to which we respond automatically without thinking (food, drink, heat, cold, pain, physical comfort or discomfort). For example, a kiss is a *primary reinforcer*, it can be pleasant or unpleasant, depending on who is doing the kissing, your sweetheart, or Dracula. The vast majority of our reinforcers, however, are not primary reinforcers, but ***conditioned or secondary reinforcers***—stimuli to which we have attached positive or negative value through association with previously learned conditional reinforcers. For example, money is a secondary reinforcer. When you were a youngster and someone gave you a dollar bill, what did you do with it? Most likely you tried to eat it or make an airplane out of it. In order for the dollar to gain reinforcing value, you had to take it to the store and trade it for candy or food and at that time you realized it had reinforcing value. Other secondary reinforcers would be a smile, a grade you receive in school, a trophy, etc. Negative consequences need not be physical punishment but giving options that have consequences. If you need help with negative consequences the book *Parenting with Love and Logic: Teaching Children Responsibility* by Jim Fay and Foster Cline (1990) has a formula that involves three things: the child makes a mistake, the adult responds with empathy and compassion instead of anger, and the child learns from the consequences of his or her actions.

> *Failure is positive reinforcement.*
> —ANONYMOUS

> *Live long and prosper.*
> —MR. SPOCK

Positively reinforce the good responses— not the bad ones.

> *Everything should be made as simple as possible, but not simpler.*
> —ALBERT EINSTEIN

© Creativa Images/Shutterstock.com

GENDER AND YOU

WHERE DID YOU LEARN YOUR GENDER?

How do we acquire our gender roles? Being a boy or a girl, for most children, is something that feels very natural. At birth, babies are assigned male or female based on physical characteristics. This refers to the "sex" of the child. When children are able to express themselves, they will declare themselves to be a boy or a girl (or sometimes something in between); this is their "gender identity." Most children's gender identity aligns with their biological sex. However, for some children, the match between biological sex and gender identity is not so clear. Gender role socialization operates through learning processes of reinforcement and punishment, observation, and self-socialization. But these days it is not as cut and dry as it was in the past. Times have changed.

Our expectations of "what girls do" and "what boys do" have changed. Girls frequently excel at sports and school subjects traditionally thought of as masculine. Boys frequently excel in artistic subjects once traditionally thought of as feminine. All children show some behaviors that were once thought of as typical for the opposite gender—no one shows exclusively male or female traits—and this is normal. For some young children, expressing a wish to be or identifying as another gender may be temporary; for others, it is not. Only time will tell. Some children who are gender non-conforming in early childhood grow up to become transgender adults (persistently identifying with a gender that is different from their birth sex), and others do not. Many gender non-conforming children grow up to identify with a gay, lesbian, or bisexual sexual orientation (i.e., attracted to the same or both genders as opposed to feeling they are a different gender). There is no way to predict how a child will end up identifying him or herself later in life. This uncertainty is one of the hardest things about parenting a gender non-conforming child. It is important for parents to make their home a place where their child feels safe and loved unconditionally. **Research suggests that gender is something we are born with; it can't be changed by any interventions. It is critically important that children feel loved and accepted for who they are.**

Should you use negative consequences? Psychologists suggest that you do not need to use negative consequences as a means of disciplining your children, because positive reinforcement is the most effective and best means of controlling someone's behavior.

Positive reinforcement is generally much more effective than any other form of reinforcement. You will discover that if you use positive reinforcement on yourself and in your relationships with others you will be much happier and those around you will be much happier. Your own life, your business relationships, and your personal life will be richer and much more positive and effective.

Life is change. Growth is optional. CHOOSE WISELY.

> *I expect to pass through this life but once; therefore if there be any kindness I can show or any good thing that I can do for any fellow being, let me do it now, not defer, or neglect it, for I shall not pass this way again.*
> —ANONYMOUS

Self-Control in Everyday Living

A look at social psychology. In "Becoming Aware" of yourself you will find that ***social psychology*** is the scientific study of how people's thoughts, feelings, and behaviors are influenced by the actual, imagined, or implied presence of others, As you learn more about the field, social psychologists such as Carol Dweck at Stanford in the field of "mindsets"; Claude Steele, Gregory Walton, and Geoff Cohen at Stanford University in the fields of "stereotype threat, belonging, and values affirmation"; Timothy Wilson of University of Virginia in the field of "core narratives"; and Peter Gollwitzer of New York University in the fields of "action triggers" and "implementation and goal intentions" are theorist who might influence you. Social psychology is a discipline that has traditionally bridged the gap between psychology and sociology. It looks at the individual and group dynamics which are at work in Human Relations (Moscovici, 2006).

Do you have Grit? *Grit* is defined as "perseverance and passion for long-term goals. It is a positive trait based on an individual's passion and perseverance. People with grit also possess "zeal" and "persistence of motive and effort." This characteristic derives from a person's research coupled with a powerful motivation to achieve their respective objective. This perseverance of effort promotes the overcoming of obstacles or challenges that lie within a gritty individual's path to accomplishment, and serves as a driving force in achievement realization. *Grit: The Power of Passion and Perseverance*, (2016) by Angela Duckworth, is an excellent resource on grit. Another social psychologist, Dr. Carol Dwerk, also has been doing research about mindset, which you learned about in Chapter Two.

All of us are engaged in a variety of everyday activities simply to survive. We must eat, drink, sleep, and take care of basic biological needs. It turns out that all of these activities can pose challenges to successful personal adjustment to our environment, and we must be careful to control them and not let them control us. For some people, their eating habits, drug use, sleeping habits, or alcohol use control their lives.

What other challenges do we have that seem to control our everyday lives? Do any of you need to study more? Would you like to stop smoking?

Would you like to exercise more? Do you watch TV too much? Are you shy? Would you like to make more friends? These and many of your other habits that you would like to change can be modified. You can do it! Find out how. Implementation intentions, a term coined by Peter Gollwitzer, is a specific type of intentional statement that defines when and where a specific behavior will be performed. "If- then" This will possibly help you avoid procrastination by initiating a goal action. **It's time to make your own implementation intention for an important goal intention in your life.** (Pychyl, 2008 & 2010).

Psychologists have also devised a number of different theories to explain how we develop the capacity for self-control. There is one technique that has been very success-

© KENNY TONG/Shutterstock.com

What challenges do we have that seem to control our everyday lives?

ful for many individuals (Martin & Pear, 2010). This technique includes the application of learning theory to improve your self-control. If you stop and think about it, self-control—or the lack of it—underlies many of the personal challenges that we struggle with in everyday life. *What we learn can be unlearned.* Before we learn about the self-change program, perhaps the wonderful words from psychologist Robert Leahy (2006), the author of *The Worry Cure,* might be worth remembering:

> If you want to whip yourself into shape, or renovate your apartment, don't wait until you feel ready, because no such time will come. Instead, commit to doing something that you don't want to do each day. After all, if your goal is to lose 15 pounds, you'll have to consistently deny your desires in order to achieve it. Resourceful people are not having fun all of the time. But they do feel empowered when they force themselves to do what is needed. (Flora,Carlin (Nov 2016) Psychology Today)

STRATEGIES TO SELF-CHANGE: A FIVE-STEP PROGRAM

Step 1: Identify the behavior to be changed.

Step 2: Observe the behavior to be changed.

Step 3: Set your goal.

Step 4: Design your program.

Step 5: Monitor and evaluate your program.

It's the friends you can call up at four a.m. that matter.
—MARLENE DIETRICH

A Self-Change Program

Identify the behavior to be changed. The first step in any systematic program in self-modification is to identify the specific behavior that you would like to change. Many of us tend to be vague in describing our problems and identifying the exact nature of the behavior we want to change. You must be specific and clearly define the overt behavior to be changed. For example:

- I want to lose weight
- I want to stop smoking
- I need to spend more time studying
- I want to exercise more
- I would like to have more friends
- I need to stop procrastinating

Which of the statements above is too vague and would not be easy to observe? Can you measure and observe how much you exercise? Definitely. But, can you observe yourself procrastinating? You need to identify what things you are not doing, so you can get them completed in a timely manner.

Sometimes you need a little support! Drug abuse, physical abuse, eating disorders, and other serious negative habits that are detrimental to your health can be changed through this process of self-modification—with a lot of willpower. But, we have found that it is easier to change these serious habits with the benefit of professional help and support. So, please seek professional help, or if you know anyone else having a serious problem, please help him or her find professional help. Talk to your instructor, counselor, pastor, or therapist. There are 12-step programs for drug/alcohol, physical abuse, weight issues… in many areas and they are free. Many meet weekly and you can find a sponsor at the meetings who will help you.

Observe the behavior to be changed. The second step in your self-modification project is to observe the behavior to be changed in order to discover your **operant level** (baseline), the number of responses prior to beginning the project. People are often tempted to skip this step and move ahead. In order to evaluate your progress you must not skip this step. You need to know the original response level, the starting point. You cannot tell whether your program is working unless you have a baseline for comparison. While observing your behavior in order to find your *operant level*, you need to monitor these three things: 1) the initial response level of the target behavior, 2) the events that precede the target behavior, 3) the typical consequences (reinforcement or punishment).

1. **Initial Response Level.** You need to keep track of each and every response of the targeted behavior that occurs within a specified period of time—usually five to seven days. Write down on a piece of paper attached to your cigarette package each and every cigarette you have each day for a week. Keep a diary of the number

of dates you have within a three-week period, the amount of time you study each day for five days, the number of times you yell at your kids, the amount of time you spend exercising each day for six days, or whatever the targeted behavior happens to be. As soon as you can identify a *pattern of behavior,* you are ready for the next step. If you discover that you do not exercise, there is nothing to observe, you are ready to begin. Your *operant level* for exercise is "0," no responses prior to conditioning. You may discover that your *operant level* for cigarette smoking is "23 cigarettes" per day, "42 minutes" of studying each day, "3,100 calories" each day, or "2 dates" per month. Now to the next step.

2. **Events That Precede the Target Behavior.** The events that precede the target behavior can play a major role in governing your target response. Where you study may affect how much time you actually study. When you study at the library, you find that you study more than when you study at home on the kitchen table or on your bed. You discover that you smoke more when you drink coffee. You may find that you may have to give up coffee in order to stop smoking because coffee seems to create the urge to smoke. You find that you eat the greatest number of calories late at night after you have a couple of beers; the beers seem to stimulate the hunger drive. Once you are able to pinpoint the events that seem to cause the behavior, you can design your program to circumvent or break it down.

3. **Consequences.** Finally, you need to identify the reinforcement that is strengthening the targeted behavior or the punishment that is decreasing or suppressing it. We eat because we like food—the food becomes reinforcing within itself; just like smoking, we enjoy it. It is easier not to study than to study. Bad habits are self-reinforcing. I do not have to worry about being turned down for a date if I do not ask anyone out. Most of the behaviors we would like to change are being reinforced and are very difficult to change.

Set your goal. The most important factor in the third step is that when you set your goal, make sure that it is a realistic goal that can be accomplished. Losing twenty pounds in four weeks is not realistic, but four to five pounds could be realistic. Studying five hours a day, seven days a week is not realistic for many students, but studying three hours a day five days a week would most likely be accomplished by most students, depending on how many courses you are taking and how many hours you work per week. Try to set behavioral goals that are both challenging and realistic. You want your goals to be challenging, so that they lead to improvement in your behavior. **Setting unrealistically high goals—a common mistake in self-modification—often leads to unnecessary discouragement.**

Design your program. Now that you have identified the targeted behavior to be changed, found your operant level (remember it is intentional actions that have an effect on the surrounding environment), and set your goal, you are ready to design your program.

You have now discovered that many of your bad habits and behaviors that you have identified to change are self-reinforcing. In order for you to change, you must find something that is more reinforcing to you than the previous reinforcement. You must

> *Sometimes we miss a workout or eat something that isn't ideal, but if you had a flat tire on your car would you get out and puncture the other three? Of course not! If you slip, shake it off and do better the next day!*
> —JILLIAN MICHAELS

find something that will motivate you and make you want to change. If you intend to reward yourself for increasing a response, you need to find an effective reinforcer. What is reinforcing to one individual may not be reinforcing to another. Your choice will depend on your unique personality and situation. How can you discover what is reinforcing to you?

Select reinforcers. What is reinforcing enough to you to motivate you to change? Is it money, sex, free time, concert tickets, praise, or tickets to the ball game? An easy way to discover what is reinforcing to you is to observe your own behavior for a while (Watson & Tharp, 2006).

- Observe what you enjoy doing for a few days.
- Observe what you spend your money on each week.
- What kind of praise do you like to receive: from yourself and from others?
- What are your major interests?
- What do you do for fun?
- What people do you like to be with?
- What do you like to do with those people?
- What would be a nice present to receive?
- What makes you feel good?
- What would you like to do for your next vacation?
- What would you buy if you had an extra $20? $50? $100?

> *We form habits and then our habits form us.*
> —RALPH WALDO EMERSON

Any or all of the above could be used as reinforcers to motivate you to change. As B. F. Skinner's early research demonstrates, reinforcement—*not punishment*—is necessary for permanent change. Reinforcement can be intrinsic, extrinsic, or extraneous. According to Dr. Carol Sansone, a psychology professor at the University of Utah, one type of reinforcement must be present for self-change, two would be better than one, and *three* would be best (Goldberg, 2002).

Administer the reinforcers. Receiving the reinforcement has to be contingent upon you first making the appropriate response. Once you have chosen the reinforcer, you then have to set up reinforcement contingencies. Your reinforcement contingencies will describe the exact behavioral goals that must be met and the reinforcement that may then be awarded. Do not administer too much reinforcement and receive it too often. If you receive too much of something or receive it too often, you soon get bored or habituate to it. If a chocolate milkshake was used as reinforcement five times a day for three weeks, you would soon get tired of having milkshakes and habituate to them. They will soon lose their reinforcing value.

Generally, rapid reinforcement works better than delayed reinforcement. If we delay reinforcement, we discover that we do not realize what behavior is being reinforced. You may find it easier to have a friend or relative administer the reinforcement. It may also commit you more to your project if you make up a behavioral contract for you to sign and give to your friend.

Trying to modify behavior is a difficult task. Sometimes it helps to have someone we can talk to or who might assist us to do this. It is difficult to change some of our actions by ourselves. We might benefit from a person who can offer advice or encouragement. Or, we might need another person to know about our plan because it keeps us honest and committed to our project. It is sometimes easy to fool yourself about your progress, but another person may not be as easily deceived.

What do you do for fun?

CONSIDER THIS

A SAMPLE CONTRACT

Target behavior: I want to lose five pounds in the next six weeks.

Contract between: Sally Sane

Amy Abler (roommate of Sally Sane)

Agreement: Sally Sane—I agree to stop eating candy bars and drinking pop between meals. I will write down each and every candy bar and soda pop that I consume for the next seven days. I will weigh myself each day and record it. After the observation period, for the following two weeks, I will eat only one candy bar each day and two cans of pop. During the second two weeks, I will eat one candy bar every other day and one soda pop each day. On the final two weeks, I will have only one candy bar and one soda pop every three days. From that day following I will substitute pieces of fruit and vegetables and glasses of water for my snacks between meals.

Agreement: Amy Abler—I agree to help Sally Sane lose five pounds and stop eating candy bars and drinking pop between meals. I will review her program with her weekly and do whatever I can to help her reach her goal.

Consequences: Sally Sane—For each week that I reach my goal, I will buy a movie I want or the jewelry I really want... If I fail to reach my goal during the week, I do not get the movie I want and I will have to clean the apartment without Amy's help. When I reach my final goal, I will receive two tickets to the concert that I have wanted to attend.

Consequences: Amy Abler—I will praise Sally for keeping her schedule and offer encouragement. I will review her program with her weekly and give her feedback. If she reaches her goal by the end of the six weeks, I will clean the apartment the next two weeks without Sally's help.

Signed: _____ Date: _____

Just Do It!

Be careful the environment you choose for it will shape you; be careful the friends you choose for you will become like them.
—W. CLEMENT STONE

Monitor and evaluate your program. Now that you have designed your project, you are ready to "do it." As you begin the project, you need to monitor your progress as you begin to achieve your goal. Monitoring your progress will allow you to assess if your plan is working. Start with your operant level (baseline) and continue to accurately record the frequency of your targeted behavior so you can evaluate your progress. If your behavior shows improvement, keep up the good work; however, if there is no improvement or you begin to regress, you need to reevaluate your reinforcers, since they do not seem to be motivating you to improve. You may need to strengthen your reinforcement or the delay between the time you emit the behavior and the time you receive the reinforcement may be too lengthy. Do not reward yourself when you have not actually earned it. Many people end up giving themselves the reinforcers no matter what they do. They rationalize it by saying, "I needed that new dress anyway" or "I just need a vacation, even though I'm not going to stop smoking." Another problem you may have in not reaching your goal is that you are trying to do too much too quickly by setting unrealistic goals.

When set into action, self-modification programs often need some fine-tuning. So do not be surprised if you need to make a few adjustments. Often, a small revision or two can turn a failing program around and make it a success. Don't give up!

A bad habit never disappears miraculously— it's an undo-it-yourself project.
—ABIGAIL VAN BUREN

A happy ending. Why won't people break old habits and begin new ones? Actually, a *habit* is the intersection of *knowledge, skill,* and *desire. Knowledge* is the what to do and the why. *Skill* is the how to do. And *desire* is the motivation or the want to do. In order to make something a habit in our lives, we have to have all three. In other words, you have to want to break a habit, have a desire to learn a new way of doing something, and have the ability to do the task the new way. All of this, of course, takes time and energy because you must engage in a particular behavior at least 30 consecutive days before it becomes a habit. Furthermore, it may take six weeks to a year for the habit to become reality (Aamodt & Raynes, 2001).

Often a new and improved pattern of behavior becomes self-maintaining. When you feel good about yourself and know that you are successful, it becomes self-reinforcing. Responses such as eating right, not smoking, exercising regularly, or studying diligently may become habitual so that they no longer need to be supported by an elaborate program. But you may find it important to periodically reinforce yourself for *doing the right thing* and not slipping back to your old patterns of behavior. You did a good job! Keep up the good work!

History will never accept difficulties as an excuse.
—JOHN F. KENNEDY

As you work on your self-change program, just remember the words of novelist Louis L'Amour:

Today is wide open. I will decide on a course of action and move ahead. All around me help is available for the asking.

> Up to a point, a [person's] life is shaped by environment, heredity, and movements and changes in the world about [them]; then there comes a time when it lies within [their] grasp to shape the clay of [their] life into the sort of things [they wish] to be . . . Everyone has it within [their] power to say, "This I am today; that I shall be tomorrow."

Chapter Review

We learn throughout life. What we learn is not always positive, but we have also learned that we can take the negative and turn it into a positive and rewarding experience.

- Self-control is the opposite of external control.
- In **self-control**, the individual sets his or her own standards for performance, and will then reward or punish themselves for meeting or not meeting these standards. On the other hand, in **external control**, someone else sets the standards and delivers or withholds the rewards or punishment.
- People differ markedly in their feelings about their capacity to control life situations.
- People who perceive that their efforts make a difference when they are facing a difficult situation and take whatever action seems appropriate to solve the problem are referred to as **Internals.**
- People who perceive that their efforts do not seem to make a difference and they seem to be controlled by such things as luck or fate are referred to as **Externals.**
- **Learned helplessness** is the passive behavior produced by the exposure to unavoidable aversive events.
- **Operant level** is intentional actions that have an effect on the surrounding environment,
- **Self-efficacy** is our belief about our ability to perform behaviors that should lead to expected outcomes.
- Men and women develop differently, both physiologically and socially. This difference affects their self-efficacy.
- **Optimism** is defined as a generalized tendency to expect positive outcomes, while **pessimism** is defined as a general tendency to envision the future as unfavorable.
- Psychologist Martin Seligman (2006) suggests that people who have an **optimistic explanatory style** tend to use external, unstable, and specific explanations for negative events.
- Optimists, by definition, expect to eventually recover from adversity, and they expect to be successful at whatever they do, so they work much harder to reach their goals than pessimists do.
- People who have an **optimistic explanatory style** tend to use external, unstable, and specific explanations for negative events.
- People who have a **pessimistic explanatory style** tend to use internal, stable, and global explanations for negative events.
- **Learned optimism** is a learned way of explaining both good and bad life events that in turn enhance our perceived control and adaptive responses to them.
- According to **Social Learning Theory**, **modeling** (imitation) has a great impact on personality development.
- **Learning** is defined as a relatively permanent change in behavior as a result of experience or practice.
- **Self-efficacy**, or belief in your personal capabilities, regulates human functioning in three major ways: *Mood or affect, Motivational, and Cognitive.*
- **Grit** in psychology is a positive, non-cognitive trait based on an individual's passion for a particular long-term goal or end state, coupled with a powerful motivation to achieve their respective objective. This perseverance of effort promotes the overcoming of obstacles or challenges that lie within a gritty individual's path to accomplishment, and serves as a driving force in achievement realization.
- Before you can begin the process of learning, you have to pay attention. We find that there are three kinds of stimuli that attract our attention: 1) **Novel stimuli**, 2) **Significant stimuli**, and 3) **Conflicting stimuli**.

- Another aspect of attention that may surprise you is that you can only **pay attention to one thing at a time.**
- Why study learning theory? Learning theory is the basis of all interactions—we are applying it constantly, and it is constantly being applied to us, most of the time without our knowledge.
- In most of our daily interactions, we are using operant conditioning. **Operant conditioning** is based on the premise that we are controlled by the consequences of our behavior. It relies on the **law of effect**, which states that behaviors followed by positive consequences are more likely to be repeated, and behaviors followed by negative consequences are less likely to be repeated.
- **Reinforcers** strengthen behavior. A **primary reinforcer** is a pleasant or unpleasant stimulus that has immediate reinforcing value: food, water, heat, pain, etc. A **secondary reinforcer** is a stimulus to which we attach positive or negative value through association with previously learned conditioned reinforcers.
- Positive reinforcement, negative reinforcement, and punishment all have a tremendous impact on our life. **Positive reinforcement** is defined as anything that increases a behavior by virtue of its presentation. **Negative reinforcement** is defined as anything that increases a behavior by virtue of its termination or avoidance
- We can change! We all have bad habits and things that we would like to change. If you apply the Self-Change Program to your daily life, you will discover that you will be able to modify your behavior.

Test Review Questions: Learning Outcomes

1. Define "perceived locus of control" and explain the difference between an internal and an external.
2. Explain what learned helplessness is and how it can influence someone's life.
3. What are the recommended "helpful hints" mentioned in the text for developing an internal locus of control?
4. What is learned optimism? What does Seligman suggest for learning to be more optimistic?
5. What is self-efficacy? Explain how you can increase your self-efficacy.
6. Define optimism and pessimism and explain how optimistic explanatory and pessimistic explanatory styles can influence someone's behavior.
7. Define Social Learning Theory and explain the importance of imitation (modeling) in a person's development. If you are a teacher and want to get your students to learn, you better make sure the material is *significant* to your students.
8. Explain the importance of novel, significant, and conflicting stimuli in our life.
   Why is it important to study learning theory in relation to understanding yourself and in your relationships with others? Explain.
9. **Define** grit and explain if you have it.
10. What are primary and secondary reinforcers?
11. What is a self-change program? What are the steps involved in a self-change program? Explain.
12. Explain why the perseverance of effort called grit promotes the overcoming of obstacles or challenges.

Key Terms

Behavioral Contract

Consequences

External Locus of Control

Grit

Initial Response Level

Internal Locus of Control

Law of Effect

Learned Helplessness

Learned Optimism

Learning

Mental Health

Modeling

Negative Reinforcement

Novel Stimuli

Observational Learning

Operant Conditioning

Operant Level

Optimism

Optimistic Explanatory Style

Pessimism

Pessimistic Explanatory Style

Positive Reinforcement

Primary Reinforcer

Punishment

Reinforcement

Reinforcer

Secondary Reinforcer

Self-Change Program

Self-Control

Self-Efficacy

Significant Stimuli

Social Learning Theory

Target Behavior

Violence

Reflections: Critical Thinking

1. Why do you think it is important to study learning theory in regards to human relations?
2. Do you feel you are in control of everything in your life?
3. What are the benefits of having an internal locus of control? What are the benefits of having an external locus of control?
4. What do you think determines whether you become an internal or external?
5. What do you think causes learned helplessness?
6. What is self-efficacy and how can you increase your self-efficacy?
7. Discuss the benefits of being an optimist compared with being a pessimist.
8. Who has been a role model in your life? What influence have they had on you?
9. Are there any positive role models in our society? Who are they and what characteristics do they have that make them a positive role model?
10. Name some negative role models. What influence are they having on our youth today?
11. What can you do to your relationships to make them more interesting and exciting?
12. If you were a teacher, what would you do in order to keep your students' attention?
13. Using operant conditioning, how would you change one of your bad habits? Explain.
14. Why is mindfulness helpful to some people?

Web Resources and Web Activities

Accomplishment, however small, nurtures good feelings!

VIDEOS

https://www.youtube.com/watch?v=YMPzDiraNnA

Learned helplessness

https://www.youtube.com/watch?v=4XQUJR4uIGM

Ellen Langer: Mindfulness over matter

https://www.youtube.com/watch?v=nXixMXDPv6g

Dr. Ellen Langer on Mindfulness and the Psychology of Possibility.

https://www.headspace.com/andy-puddicombe

Andy Puddicombe is a meditation and mindfulness expert and an accomplished presenter.

https://www.ted.com/talks/angela_lee_duckworth_grit_the_power_of_passion_and_pers...

Angela Lee Duckworth: Grit: The power of passion and perseverance.

https://www.youtube.com/watch?v=BzuawrFE1xM

The Happiness Project with Gretchen Rubin.

https://www.youtube.com/watch?v=HTfYv3IEOqM

The effect of trauma on the brain and how it affects behaviors, a presentation by John Rigg at TEDx-Augusta 2015. In his work with trauma patients, Dr. Rigg has observed how the brain is constantly reacting to sensory information, generating non-thinking reactions before our intelligent individual human brains are able to process the event and formulate a self-driven response.

https://www.ted.com/talks/cameron_russell_looks_aren_t_everything_believe_me_i_m_a_model?language=en

Cameron Russell: Looks aren't everything. Believe me, I'm a model.

https://www.youtube.com/watch?v=PTlmho_RovY

Killing Us Softly 4: Image of women.

https://www.youtube.com/watch?v=WLMJHdySgE8

Violence: A family tradition, a presentation by Robbyn Peters Bennett at TEDxBellingham on November 23, 2013. Robbyn Peters Bennett, LMHC, CMHS is a psychotherapist, educator, and child advocate who specializes in the treatment of trauma-related mental health problems resulting from the effects of early childhood stress, abuse and neglect.

ACTIVITIES

A Simple WayTo Break A Bad Habit Why is it so hard to stop smoking or lose weight when we know these habits are bad for us?

- **9 Interesting TED Talks on Breaking Bad Habits &...**
blog.hubspot.com/marketing/habit-research-ted-talks

  Apr 13, 2016 ... 9 TED Talks on Forming Better Habits. Judson Brewer: "A Simple Way to Break a Habit". Length: 9 min. 24 sec. Why do we overeat, smoke, ...

http://www.uky.edu/~eushe2/Bandura/BanEncy.html

  Reading on Self-efficacy

http://www.upworthy.com/how-lady-dynamite-hilariously-nails-comedy-about-serious-mental-illness?c=upw1&u=781e1b682edf6d11d917cd528b9824421641e9e5

  This funny TV show helps us all understand mental health better.

http://www.successconsciousness.com/index_000006.htm

  This is a Web site about conscientiousness and self-discipline. For example, it suggests that will power is not something that exerts us but rather something that is easy. After a discussion of these topics, the reader is provided with exercises to reinforce and improve one's self-discipline.

www.mindtools.com/

  This site provides practical suggestions for problem solving, memory improvement, increasing creativity, and much more.

http://www.upworthy.com/5-things-i-didnt-want-to-hear-when-i-was-grieving-and-1-thing-that-helped?c=upw1&u=781e1b682edf6d11d917cd528b9824421641e9e5

  5 things I didn't want to hear when I was grieving and 1 thing that helped.

www.authentichappiness.sas.upenn.edu/testcenter.aspx

  Optimism Test measures optimism about the future.

What Controls Your Life?

PURPOSE

This is a device to measure your attitudes toward rewards and punishments: Do you feel that they come as a result of your own behavior or from outside sources? We have reproduced this device below so that you can measure yourself and determine your own beliefs. Read each set of two statements and decide which statement seems to you more accurate and place a check mark (✓) next to it. Read and answer carefully. There are no right or wrong choices. They are based on your personal judgments. Try to respond to each pair of statements independently, apart from your responses to other pairs of statements.

1. _____ a. A great deal that happens to me is probably a matter of chance.
   _____ b. I am the master of my fate.

2. _____ a. It is almost impossible to figure out how to please some people.
   _____ b. Getting along with people is a skill that must be practiced.

3. _____ a. People like me can change the course of world affairs if we make ourselves be heard.
   _____ b. It is only wishful thinking to believe that one can really influence what happens in society at large.

4. _____ a. Most people get the respect they deserve in this world.
   _____ b. An individual's capabilities often pass unrecognized no matter how hard he or she tries.

5. _____ a. The idea that teachers are unfair to students is nonsense.
   _____ b. Most students do not realize the extent to which their grades are influenced by accidental happenings.

6. _____ a. If you do not get the right opportunities, one cannot become a good leader.
   _____ b. Capable people who fail to become leaders have not taken advantage of their opportunities.

7. _____ a. Sometimes I feel that I have little to do with the grades I get.
   _____ b. In my case, the grades I make are the results of my own efforts; luck has little or nothing to do with it.

8. _____ a. Heredity plays the major role in determining one's personality.
   _____ b. It is one's experiences in life that determine what one is like.

9.   _____ a.   It is silly to think that one can really change another person's basic attitudes.

         _____ b.   When I am right, I can convince others.

10.   _____ a.   In my experience I have noticed that there is usually a direct connection between how hard I study and the grades I get.

         _____ b.   Many times the reactions of teachers seem haphazard to me.

11.   _____ a.   The average citizen can have an influence in government decisions.

         _____ b.   This world is run by the few people in power, and there is not much the little guy can do about it.

12.   _____ a.   When I make plans, I am almost certain that I can make them work.

         _____ b.   It is not always wise to plan too far ahead because many things turn out to be a matter of good or bad fortune anyhow.

13.   _____ a.   There are certain people who are just no good.

         _____ b.   There is some good in everybody.

14.   _____ a.   In my case, getting what I want has little or nothing to do with luck.

         _____ b.   Many times, we might just as well decide what to do by flipping a coin.

15.   _____ a.   Promotions are earned through hard work and persistence.

         _____ b.   Making a lot of money is largely a matter of getting the right breaks.

16.   _____ a.   Marriage is largely a gamble.

         _____ b.   The number of divorces indicates that more and more people are not trying to make their marriages work.

17.   _____ a.   In our society, a person's future earning power is dependent on their ability.

         _____ b.   Getting promoted is really a matter of being a little luckier than the next person.

18.   _____ a.   Most people do not realize the extent to which their lives are controlled by accidental happenings.

         _____ b.   There is really no such thing as luck.

19.   _____ a.   I have little influence over the way other people behave.

         _____ b.   If one knows how to deal with people, they are really quite easily led.

20.   _____ a.   In the long run, the bad things that happen to us are balanced by the good ones.

         _____ b.   Most misfortunes are the result of lack of ability, ignorance, laziness, or all three.

21. _____ a. With enough effort, we can wipe out political corruption.
    _____ b. It is difficult for people to have much control over the things politicians do in office.

22. _____ a. A good leader expects people to decide for themselves what they should do.
    _____ b. A good leader makes it clear to everybody what their jobs are.

23. _____ a. People are lonely because they do not try to be friendly.
    _____ b. There is not much use in trying too hard to please people—if they like you, they like you.

24. _____ a. There is too much emphasis on athletics in high school.
    _____ b. Team sports are an excellent way to build character.

25. _____ a. What happens to me is my own doing.
    _____ b. Sometimes I feel that I do not have enough control over the direction my life is taking.

Scoring Key for Project: For each of the responses below, give yourself 1 point.

ITEM #	RESPONSE				
1	a	10	b	19	a
2	a	11	b	20	a
3	b	12	b	21	b
4	b	13	a	22	b
5	b	14	b	23	b
6	a	15	b	24	a
7	a	16	a	25	b
8	a	17	b		
9	a	18	a		

Total Points _____

Your total number of points indicates the degree to which you view control as external or internal. **The higher the score (above 15) the more you perceive control as external.** Remember, this means that you perceive yourself as not being in control of your own destiny, that outside forces are determining your fate, and whatever effort you put into something, it will not make any difference. **The lower the score (below 15) means the more you perceive control as internal.** This means that you perceive yourself as being in control of your own destiny and your success is dependent upon your efforts and not on others.

You may also find it helpful to review Table 3.1: Characteristics of Externals and Internals.

DISCUSSION

1. What are the benefits of being an Internal?

2. What are the advantages of being an External?

3. If you decided that you would rather be an Internal than an External, how would you go about changing yourself?

4. What did you learn from this activity?

Are You an Optimist or a Pessimist?

PURPOSE

The following scale, a version of the Life Orientation Test, can help raise your awareness about whether you are the type of person who tends to see the proverbial glass as half full or half empty.

INSTRUCTIONS

Using numbers 0 to 4, indicate your responses to the following items in the spaces provided. Then check the scoring key.

4 = strongly agree
3 = agree
2 = neutral
1 = disagree
0 = strongly disagree

_____ 1. In the uncertain times, I usually expect the best.

_____ 2. It's easy for me to relax.

_____ 3. If something can go wrong for me, it will.

_____ 4. I'm always optimistic about my future.

_____ 5. I enjoy my friends a lot.

_____ 6. It's important for me to keep busy.

_____ 7. I hardly ever expect things to go my way.

_____ 8. I don't get upset too easily.

_____ 9. I rarely count on good things happening to me.

_____ 10. Overall, I expect more good things to happen to me than bad.

Total Score _____

Scoring Key

The first step is to reverse the scoring for items 3, 7, and 9. In other words, change a 4 to a 0, a 3 to a 1, a 1 to a 3, and a 0 to a 4. A 2 remains a 2. Next, add your score for items 1, 3, 4, 7, 9, and 10 to obtain an overall score. (Do not score items 2, 5, 6, and 8. These items are considered "fillers" and are not scored as part of the test.) Total scores can range from **0 to 24.**

Now, you can compare your score to those of a sample of 2,055 college students. Higher scores indicate greater optimism while lower scores indicate greater pessimism. The average (mean) score in the college sample was **14.33.** About two-thirds of the sample scored from **10 to 19.** Scores greater than **14** reflect relatively higher levels of optimism. Psychologists believe that people can change their attitudes—that optimism can be learned.

Discussion

1. Do you agree with your score? Why or why not?

2. If you scored low on optimism, what do you think you need to do to change your attitude?

3. Psychologists believe that optimism can be learned. How do you feel about this belief?

Source: Based on Scheier, Carver & Bridges (1994).

Becoming *Aware*

Life's Lessons

PURPOSE

To review the messages used by significant others to help you change behavior and learn some important lessons in life.

INSTRUCTIONS

Thinking about individuals who were most beneficial in helping you change some behavior and learn some lessons in life?

1. Parents:

    What did you learn?

2. Friends/ friends parents/ teachers/instructors/the school system:

    What did you learn?

3. Have you tried meditating? Watch the YouTube videos mentioned in the text and give it a try.

4. What do you think about the violence videos? Is Katz right that violence is too pervasive in our society? What did you learn?

DISCUSSION

1. To whom are you a significant (influential) other? Explain any contributions you think you have made to their life. What did they learn?

2. What did you learn?

What Kind of Reinforcement Do You Use?

PURPOSE

To learn the value of reinforcement.

INSTRUCTIONS

1. You can either answer the following questions individually or with a partner. After you have completed the questions, get into larger groups and answer the discussion questions.

2. Put yourself in the following roles and state how you think each form of reinforcement and/or negative consequences will influence the person involved. Also explore learned helplessness.

   a. Parent—Discuss how or if you would use the following forms of positive reinforcement, negative reinforcement, and negative consequences in the training and education of your child. What impact will it have on your child?

      Money

      Hugs and kisses

      Spanking

      Compliments

      Gifts

      Allowance

"Time-out"

Video games and TV

Encouragement

Special outings—zoo, miniature golf, science museum, movie theater.

b. If you are a teacher, what kind of positive reinforcement, negative reinforcement, and negative consequences would you use? What effect do you think each of these would have on your students? Would it be motivating for the student or would it have a detrimental effect? Explain how or if you would use the following:
Compliments

"Time-out"

Sitting them in the corner

The "star" or "point" system

Taking away recess time

Encouragement

Negative comments

"Student of the Week"

Grades

Sending them to the principal's office

No after school activities

(1) Which of the above would have the greatest effect on your students' motivation, positive and negative? Explain.

c. If you were an employer, what would be the best way to motivate your employees? How would you use the following?
A plaque for accomplishments

A salary increase; how much is needed in order to motivate them? 1%, 5%, 10% or more?

Positive comments

Larger work area

New job title

Extra time off

Flex-time

Special commendations

Criticism

Feedback on undesirable behavior

Bonus

Commission

Fines

Probation

a. Which of the above do you think would motivate your employees the most? Explain.

b. Which of the above would be most detrimental to your employees' motivation and morale? Explain.

DISCUSSION

1. Considering all of the above situations:
   a. Which forms of reinforcement seem to be most effective? Explain.

   b. Which forms of negative consequences seem to be most effective? Explain.

   c. Which forms of reinforcement do not seem to be very effective? Explain.

2. Can you think of any types of reinforcement and/or negative consequences that could be used in any of the above situations that would be more effective than what has been previously mentioned? Explain what it is and in what situation it would be most effective.

3. Some people say that physical punishment is the best way to control another person's behavior. Other people say that physical punishment should never be used. What do you think? How is this different than negative consequences?

Name _____ Date _____

Self-Change Project

PURPOSE

To understand how learning theory applies to your life.

INSTRUCTIONS

Review the section on Learning Theory, specifically the Self-Change Program. This program will explain how you can apply this to your life.

1. Identify the behavior you would like to change.

    _____

2. Observe the target behavior for 5 to 7 days to get the baseline (operant level). (Make a record every few hours of the behavior you are changing.)

    Day 1 _____

    Day 2 _____

    Day 3 _____

    Day 4 _____

    Day 5 _____

    Day 6 _____

    Day 7 _____

3. What is your goal and the date to be completed?

    _____

    _____

4. Identify your reinforcers, long-term reinforcement, and short-term reinforcement. What will motivate you to change?

_____

_____

_____

_____

_____

5. Make a plan. What are you going to do to change the behavior?

_____

_____

_____

_____

_____

6. Change the behavior. (This can take anywhere from one to six weeks.) Keep records of the daily activity relating to the project. Record the daily activity in a separate notebook.

7. What are the results?

_____

_____

_____

_____

DISCUSSION

1. What kinds of changes would you like to make yourself?

2. What is motivating (reinforcing) enough to get you to change your behavior?

3. What could people use as reinforcers in order to facilitate the behavior change?

4. How could you apply the methods of the Self-Change Project to other aspects of your life (job, children, spouse, mate, and so on)?

Name _____ Date _____

Who's in Control?

LEARNING JOURNAL

Select the statement below that best defines your feelings about the personal value or meaning gained from this chapter and respond below the dotted line.

I learned that I . . .   I was surprised that I . . .

I realized that I . . .   I was pleased that I . . .

I discovered that I . . .   I was displeased that I . . .

....

Chapter 4
Dealing with Emotions

© wavebreakmedia/Shutterstock.com

It's unfortunate that we're never really taught how to show emotion in ways that help our relationships. Instead, we are usually told what we should not do. However, too little emotion can make our lives seem empty and boring, while too much emotion, poorly expressed, fills our interpersonal lives with conflict and grief. Within reason, some kind of balance in the expression of emotion seems to be called for. —Gerald Egan, You and Me

Think About This...

HOW WOULD YOU FEEL IN THESE SITUATIONS?
- You have just turned on the TV and the screen is filled with shootings of police and protestors. You are sad and afraid. No! Perhaps you are just in shock and extremely depressed.
- It has finally happened! You have found that special person, and the two of you are discussing marriage. You are sooo—in love.
- Once again, your boss said some critical, unfair things to you today. You are really angry.
- The telephone rings, and you learn that one of your best friends has been killed in an accident. You are filled with sadness and grief.
- Your spouse has just come in and told you, quite unexpectedly, that he or she wants a divorce. You are very, very hurt. No! Maybe you're angry.

Would your feelings and emotions be similar to the feelings and emotions that other people have when they are having the same experiences? How do you feel when you are in love? Can you easily verbalize the words: "I love you?" Do you verbally express your anger, or do you save your "bad" feelings and explode at a later date? Could you talk about your feelings if your best friend or someone very close to you died? How would you deal with your feelings if your spouse walked out?

We know that our emotions play an important part in making our relations with other people pleasant and joyful, or sad and painful. We also know that what we respond to emotionally is learned. For example, we learn what situations or people stimulate our feelings of anger; we learn what situations produce stress or anxiety for us; we learn what kinds of situations leave us with a sense of guilt; and we learn which experiences help us to feel joyful and pleasant.

Because emotional responses and expressions are learned, we can learn how to change emotional patterns that are self-defeating or harmful to our growth toward self-actualization. We can also learn how to develop ways to become more emotionally expressive.

In our society, people often experience alienation or lack of ability to express emotions. And it sometimes appears that many of us have almost forgotten how to cry or laugh or express genuine feelings for ourselves and others. Therefore, we hope this chapter will help you become a more emotionally mature person and help you better understand the reasons behind some of your emotional reactions to certain people or situations. And we hope that you will be able to get ideas about ways you can manage emotional patterns that are giving you trouble in living with yourself and others.

What Are Emotions?

If someone asked you to explain *emotions,* what would you say? In all probability, you would say, "They are the different feelings I have." You might even give these feelings a label such as anger, love, hate, and so on. Now, suppose someone asked you to explain the term *feelings.* Would you be likely to say, "They are the different emotions I have?" And, you might even give these emotions a label, such as anger, love, or hate. The point is, it is quite difficult to separate the two; therefore, we will use the two interchangeably.

Actually, Dr. Daniel Goleman (2006), author of *Emotional Intelligence,* defines emotion in this way:

> "I take emotion to refer to a feeling and its distinctive thoughts, psychological and biological states, and range of propensities to act." Richard Carl-

son (2007), in the *New York Times* bestseller, *Don't Sweat the Small Stuff . . . and it's all small stuff*, says: Your "feelings act as a barometer, letting you know what your internal weather is like." Therefore, we are going to think of **emotions** as feelings that are experienced.

Without emotions, we would be little more than drab, colorless machines that run the same way day after day. We would not know the happiness of success or the pangs of disappointment. We would not experience joy from the companionship of others and would feel no grief at their loss. We would neither love nor hate. Pride, envy, and anger would be unknown to us. We would not even be able to understand the joys and sorrows of others. The definition of **emotion** is a feeling state that involves certain components: physiological changes, subjective cognitive states, and expressive behaviors

Fortunately, we are not machines; we are humans. Therefore, each of us, young or old, male or female, is capable of having and expressing many different emotions. Although it is true that individuals experience and express their emotions in many different ways, psychologists generally agree that emotions are very complex experiences, with at least four common characteristics: physiological or internal changes, behavioral expressions, cognitive interpretations, and motivational tendencies (Wood & Wood, 2014). We will now look more closely at these characteristics, as well as briefly discuss the effect our moods have on our emotional reactions.

> *The feelings or emotional aspects of life lie pretty close to the value and significance of life itself.*
> —J. B. WATSON

> *Real strength is not just a condition of one's muscle, but a tenderness in one's spirit.*
> —MCCALLISTER DODDS

Characteristics of Emotions

Why do you feel so tired when you're depressed?

Physiological or internal changes. Let us assume that you are walking alone at night when suddenly a large object jumps in front of you. Would your neck muscles tighten? Would your stomach possibly feel "funny"? Would you be able to hear the sound of your heartbeat, even when you later discovered that the "large object" was just a box blowing in the wind? Would you still be breathing faster? What would be happening inside of you? How do you feel inside when you are nervous, frightened, or angry?

As the question suggests, a main characteristic of emotional states is that they involve physiological changes.

When our emotions are aroused, there are physiological changes over which we have no control. In strong fear and anger, you do not tell your adrenal glands to pump adrenaline into the bloodstream so that you will have extra energy. These physiological changes in the nervous system are nature's way of preparing you to react faster, harder, and for longer periods

© Oleg Golovnev/Shutterstock.com

of time. In essence, your whole body is mobilized for action—you are physiologically ready to run or fight.

When you experience strong feelings, the internal changes in your body contribute to your feelings. For example, in grief or depression, there is a reduction of pulse rate, breathing, and muscular strength. Consequently, you feel tired.

Behavioral expressions. Even though emotions are felt internally, they often lead to observable expressions. These expressions may come in the form of a blush, trembling hands, sweating palms, or a tremor in the voice. Behavioral expressions can also include crying, laughing, cursing, kicking a chair, or even hitting another person. Sometimes people will deny they are feeling anything, even though their external and behavioral expressions indicate something else. We will discuss some suggestions for verbally expressing feelings later in the chapter.

Cognitive interpretation. While it is true that there is some connection between physical behavior and emotional states, in most situations, our emotions cannot be separated from our mental lives. Cognitive appraisals are an essential part of the experience. Realistically, individuals are constantly appraising the events they experience for their personal implications: Do I care about what is happening? Is it good or bad for me? Can I do anything about it? Is this matter going to get better or worse? Can I cope? Psychologist Arnold Lazarus (2000a) believes that the cognitions involved in emotion range from your immediate perceptions of a specific event to your general philosophy of life. For example, do you see the glass as half empty or half full?

Cognitive appraisals also help explain why people differ in the intensity of their emotions. Cognitive therapists Albert Ellis and Robert Harper (1998) and Dienes et al. (2011) believe our thoughts, beliefs, and prior experiences will color the way we view an event and, thus, profoundly influence our emotional reaction to that event. Two people confronted with the same situation may interpret it in a different way and, therefore, respond with different feelings.

Actually, we go through life describing the world to ourselves, giving each event or experience some label. We make interpretations of what we see and hear; we predict whether they will bring danger or relative safety. Sometimes, these thoughts are very powerful, and as you will discover in Chapter Eight, they can create most of the major stresses we experience in life.

Motivational tendencies. Emotions themselves may function as motives, directing you toward pleasant situations and away from those that are emotionally unsatisfying, anxiety provoking, or painful. In fact, the root of the word *emotion* means *to move*, indicating the close relationship between motivation and emotion (Kagan, 2009). In essence, when you are feeling a particular way, you are going to do certain things because of that feeling, in spite of that feeling, or to avoid or change that feeling. Another way of saying this would be: You do what makes you feel good, and you avoid what makes you feel bad. UCLA psychologist Gary Emery (2000) explains this further:

> *We experience life's pains and pleasures through our emotions.*
> —LIFE 101

> *Nothing can make you frustrated. Nothing can make you depressed. Nothing can make you angry. For that matter, nothing can make you happy, either. All your emotions are produced from your own mental interpretations.*
> —ANDREW BERNSTEIN

- **Pleasure** motivates you to move toward something. Your pleasure feelings, for example, motivate you to move toward a certain crowd of people ("They think my jokes are funny!"); you continue to interact with these people until it no longer feels good ("They made fun of me because I don't drink").
- **Anxiety** motivates you to run or escape from a possible loss ("I had to run for my life").
- **Anger** motivates you to fight against a perceived loss ("I had to fight for my life"). You yell or you attack someone to get rid of your angry feelings, even though you know your outburst will make matters worse.
- **Sadness** motivates you to shut down and withdraw after a loss. If you lose money in the stock market, your sad feelings motivate you to be much more cautious playing the market and protect the money you have left.

Moods. Before we leave our discussion of the characteristics of emotions, we need to briefly discuss the effect our moods have on how we respond emotionally. Your **moods** are a general feeling tone, and they have a definite influence on your emotions. Stated another way, Gardner (2002) says, "Our mood generally informs about the general state of our being." Even though we do not like to admit it, our moods are often evident to others: For example, "Don't ask Mr. Jones for a day off—he's really grouchy" or "Mrs. Smith is in such a good mood today, I bet we can talk her out of the test today."

Think for a moment and try to recall how your moods affect your emotions. Are you ever grouchy for no reason at all? Do you know what puts you in a bad mood? Often, we do not know what event or events put us in a particular mood; hence the old saying, *I just woke up on the wrong side of the bed.*

Now that we have a better idea of what emotions are and how they affect us, we will discuss some of the emotions which cause us the most difficulty.

Do you get upset by things that you can't control?

Types of Emotions

At this point, you may be asking, "Just how many emotions are there?" We really do not know the answer to this question, because our emotions include many subjective factors and individual differences. Our language is rich with words to describe our emotions. Table 4.1 gives a partial list of some common emotions we experience.

In a way, this list only represents labels we give to our feelings. Perhaps we need to explain these labels further. One way we can do this is to identify emotions or feelings as either primary, mixed, mild, or intense.

Primary and mixed emotions. Psychologists who study emotions have made up lists of certain basic emotions. Robert Plutchik (2003) identified eight *primary emotions*: joy, acceptance, fear, surprise, sadness, disgust, anger, and anticipation. The emotion wheel (see Figure 4.1) illustrates that these *primary emotions* are inside the perimeter of the circle. He suggests that these primary feelings can combine to form other *mixed emotions*, some of which are listed outside the circle: love, submission, awe, disappointment, remorse, contempt, aggressiveness, optimism.

Table 4.1   SOME EMOTIONS: HOW DO YOU FEEL TODAY?

accepted	envious	insecure	sad
afraid	exhilarated	intimidated	sentimental
aggravated	fearful	isolated	self-reliant
angry	friendly	jealous	shy
annoyed	frightened	joyful	sincere
anxious	glad	lazy	sorry
ashamed	grieving	lonely	supported
bitter	guilt-free	loved	surprised
calm	guilty	loving	tense
cautious	happy	optimistic	terrified
cheerful	helpful	out of control	tired
comfortable	hopeless	overcontrolled	trusting
confident	hostile	pessimistic	uneasy
confused	humiliated	powerful	unsure
contented	hurried	powerless	uptight
defeated	Hurt	puzzled	vulnerable
defensive	impatient	regretful	wanted
depressed	inadequate	relieved	weak
embarrassed	incompetent	resentful	worried
energetic	inferior	restless	overwhelmed

Psychologist Gary Emery (2000), however, indicates that there are only four basic emotions: mad, sad, glad, and scared. He suggests that all the other emotions we experience are just derivatives of these basic four. For example, too much sadness becomes depression, too much gladness becomes mania, too much fear becomes panic, and too much anger becomes rage.

Although you may not agree with the specific primary and secondary emotions just identified, you would probably agree that it is possible to experience several different emotions at the same time. For example, consider the following example:

> You are going to have some friends over for hamburgers. Your date is going to help you get ready for your guests and also act as a host for the evening. An hour before your date is due at your house, you get a call that he has an unexpected guest from out-of-town arriving and will be unable to join you and your friends. Your date tells you that this is just an "old friend" he used to date, and she is only going to be in town for the evening.

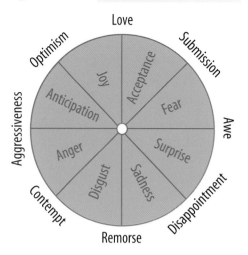

Figure 4.1 THE EMOTION WHEEL

PRIMARY AND MIXED EMOTIONS.

Now, would you just be angry? No, you would probably be hurt, jealous, and even embarrassed that you are the only one without a date. The point is, an emotional event can create a wide range of feelings. We generally communicate only one feeling, however, usually the most negative one. In this case, it would probably be your anger. Could your anger become a problem for you? Let's see!

Intense and mild emotions. We have discussed that it is human to have and express emotions and that our emotions have a lot to do with how much pleasure and enjoyment we get out of life. Our emotions can have negative effects, however, and cause problems for us. For example, strong emotions such as fear, depression, anger, and hate can disrupt our functioning and ability to relate to other people.

Generally, our emotions begin to have negative effects when they are viewed as being excessive in *intensity* and *duration* (Ellis, 2001). For example, if intense emotions linger, your ability to get enjoyment from life may be decreased. It is perfectly normal to be sad when someone close to you dies. However, if you are still depressed about this three years later, this sustained, intense emotion may be a problem for you. For example, other people may want to avoid being with you, because you are so sad and probably feeling sorry for yourself!

How about another example? Have you ever had to get up in front of a group and give a speech? How did you feel? A "little bit" of anxiety before a speech can help you prepare and do a more effective job in delivery. Total fear, however, will probably cause you to be unable to concentrate on preparing adequately for the speech. In some cases, intense anxiety can cause you to stammer and forget important aspects of your speech.

Now, let us answer the question concerning your date who did not show for dinner: When could your anger become a problem for you? It would be normal for you to be angry if you were left in this situation. If this anger becomes so bad that you awoke for "nights on end" and "stewed" about your anger, or even tried to harm your date and his "guest," then your intense anger or rage would be a problem for you.

Consequently, we say that when mild, emotions can be *facilitative*—they assist us in preparing for the future, solving problems, and in doing what is best for us. However, intense, sustained emotions can be *debilitative*—they disrupt our overall functioning (Ellis, 2001). For example, we may experience difficulty in performing certain tasks, such as passing a test or giving a speech, and in solving problems—"stewing" over that date who did not show up for dinner.

What are we trying to say? Essentially, emotions can serve a purpose in one situation and in other situations may serve as a hindrance. Specifically, what emotions cause us the most difficulty?

Living with Problem Emotions

> *Of all the passions, fear weakens judgment most.*
> —CARDINAL JEAN-FRANÇOIS-PAUL-GONDI DE RETZ

Some emotions cause more difficulties than others: fear, anxiety, anger, guilt, grief, and love are such emotions that are experienced often and with mixed reactions.

FEAR

We all experience the emotion of fear. It can take many forms, serve many purposes, and create many different responses. It is important to distinguish *fear* from *anxiety* (Ellis, 2000).

> A specific situation or object elicits *fear*, whereas *anxiety* is objectless. Therefore, we speak of **fear** when we think we know what we're afraid of and **anxiety** when we're unsure.

Types of fear. You may feel the emotion of fear as a type of warning that danger is near. This warning may take the form of an external "cue," or it may reflect your learning. For example, if you walked into your house and a burglar carrying a gun met you in the hallway, you would feel frightened. This feeling of fear was caused by an external force. Sometimes fear reactions are learned through past associations. You might be afraid of thunderstorms because your father had a tendency to believe that lightning could result in a tornado. After all, his mother had been killed in a tornado when he was quite young.

How do you feel when you have to speak in front of a group?

© ESB Professional/Shutterstock.com

Although most of the above examples reflect physical dangers, we also have fears of being left out of the crowd, of being ridiculed, of being a failure, or of being rejected. For example, if you have ever been rejected in a relationship, you may be afraid of getting involved in another relationship again. Actually, this is a good example of where you are really experiencing mixed emotions. Is it fear you are feeling, or is it hurt? Could it be that you want to protect yourself from getting hurt again? This type of fear or hurt is one that takes time to work through. After all, do you really want your "bad feelings" from one relationship to "rob" you of the opportunity to have a healthy and satisfying relationship with someone else?

Some people have a personal fear of failure. Have you been wanting or at least considering a financial, personal, or scholastic risk? What is the worst that could happen if you did experience a disappointment? Could you cope with that? Remember that even if you do fail, some good can come from it. How did you learn to walk? You did not just jump up from your crib one day and waltz gracefully across the room. You stumbled and fell on your face and got up and tried again. David M. Burns (2008) makes some valid points in the following thoughts:

> At what age are you suddenly expected to know everything and never make any more mistakes? If you can love and respect yourself in failure, worlds of adventure and new experiences will open up before you, and your fears will vanish.

How do you handle your fears? Because fear and anxiety are closely related, below are some suggestions for dealing with these emotions. First of all, let us get a clearer picture of the sometimes-troublesome emotion of anxiety.

> *Remember that fear always lurks behind perfectionism. Confronting your fears and allowing yourself the right to be human can, paradoxically, make you a far happier and more productive person.*
> —DAVID M. BURNS

ANXIETY

As we mentioned earlier, when the basis for our fear is not understood, we are experi-encing anxiety. Actually, ***anxiety*** is an unpleasant, threatening feeling that something bad is about to happen. Rollo May (1973) in his classic book, *Man's Search for Himself,* states:

> Anxiety is the feeling of "gnawing" within, of being "trapped and over-whelmed." Anxiety may take all forms and intensities, for it is the human being's reaction to a danger to his existence, or to some value he identifies with existence. . . . It is the quality of an experience which makes it anxiety rather than the quantity.

How to Face Your Fears and Anxieties

1. **Admit your fears.** It is one thing to mask your anxieties with physical and creative activities; but if these activities become avoidance techniques, anx-iety eventually increases.
2. **Take risks.** Fear does not go away unless you take chances to make your dreams come true. You will gain new strength and improved self-esteem with each accomplishment.
3. **Acknowledge the positive.** Anxious people tend to overlook their own strengths. When you are scared, make a conscious effort to remember some past positive experiences instead of focusing on your failures.
4. **Avoid catastrophic thinking.** Ask yourself what the worst possible outcome of the situation could be. Having faced the worst possibility makes it easier to deal with what does come.
5. **Stay in the present.** Much anxiety is the result of projecting yourself into future situations. Stay focused in the present—here and now—because that is all you can control anyway.
6. **Have patience.** If you are overwhelmed at the thought of confronting an anxiety triggering situation, take it one step at a time. Do not get in a hurry.

Types of anxiety. Many times the basis of our anxiety is so vague it is very difficult to explain what we are really feeling. As Rollo May suggests above, anxiety may occur in slight or great intensity. It may be mild tension before going for an important job in-terview; or it may be mild apprehension before taking an examination. These are com-mon examples of ***preparation anxiety***, which help us get energized to deliver our best.

The emotional tension that we commonly refer to as anxiety also functions as a signal of potential danger. For example, "I better study for that test, or I will flunk!" However, when the quality of the threatening experience is blown way out of proportion to the actual danger posed, and to the point that our anxiety hinders daily functioning, it becomes *"neurotic" anxiety*. A common example of this is when a student loses his "cool" over a test: "I can't do it—I just know I am going to flunk" and *goes totally blank.* Is this normal anxiety or neurotic anxiety?

Worry is also a form of anxiety (Leahy, 2005). For example, it is normal for people to worry about future events they are going to be involved in and whose outcome they are uncertain about. However, some people worry and lose sleep, lose sleep and worry even more, over "things" that never happen. Does this ever happen to you? In recent years, researchers have learned that there is a genetic component to anxiety; some people seem to be born worriers (Gorman, 2002).

The difference in normal and "neurotic anxiety" may be in one's ability to handle or cope with the anxiety-producing situation. Just ask yourself, "Am I in control of this situation, or is the anxiety controlling how I react to this situation?"

The fears that resulted from the World Trade Center bombing have been minimal for some individuals, and for others the anxiety has led to extreme overreactions. In the wake of the most horrendous bombing attack in American history, it is healthy to feel some fear. Dr. Brad Schmidt (2002), an expert on fear, reminds us, "Just don't allow that fear to defeat you."

> *There is a great difference between worry and concern. A worried person sees a problem, and a concerned person solves a problem.*
> —HAROLD STEPHENS

ANGER

Anger is a signal that tells us that we do not like what is going on. *Anger* refers to a feeling of extreme displeasure, usually brought about by interference with our needs or desires. Anger is an emotion characterized by antagonism toward someone or something you feel has deliberately done you wrong. Anger can be a good thing. It can give you a way to express negative feelings, for example, or motivate you to find solutions to problems. But excessive anger can cause problems. Increased blood pressure and other physical changes associated with anger make it difficult to think straight and harm your physical and mental health (APA, 2016).

Therefore, anger can range from mild to very strong (Parker Hall, 2008). Carol Tavris (1989) has identified several forms of anger:

> *Never answer an angry word with an angry word. It is the second one that makes the quarrel.*
> —W. A. NANCE

- **Hate** may be thought of as intense anger felt toward a specific person or persons.
- **Annoyance** is used to describe a mild form of anger.
- **Rage** describes intense anger and implies that the anger is expressed through violent physical activity.
- **Hostility** is a mild form of anger/hate directed to a specific person or group; often it is unintentionally conveyed to others either verbally or nonverbally.

- **Resentment** is chronic anger that may be entirely subjective. It is a combination of the emotions and actions and thought patterns resulting from our unresolved anger at an injustice. *Resentment comes from anger just as smoke comes from fire.*

Remember, anger is a completely normal, usually healthy, human emotion. However, when it gets out of control and turns destructive, it can lead to problems—problems at work, in your personal relationships, and in the overall quality of your life. And, it can make you feel as though you're at the mercy of an unpredictable and powerful emotion (Nay, 2010). There is nothing like walking on egg shells and being afraid someone will snap at you. Anger most often begins with a loss or the threat of a loss, such as (Lerner, 2005):

- **Loss of self-esteem.** We get angry when we think we have failed or "let ourselves down."

HOW TO CONTROL YOUR ANGER

Anger Do's and Don'ts

- Do speak up when an issue is important to you.
- Do take time out to think about the problem and clarify your position.
- Do speak in "I" language. "I feel."
- Do try to appreciate the fact that people are different.
- Do recognize that each person is responsible for his or her own behavior.
- Do try to avoid speaking through a third party.
- Don't strike while the iron is hot.
- Don't use "below-the-belt" tactics.
- Don't blame the other person.
- Don't tell another person what she or he thinks or feels or "should" think or feel.
- Don't participate in intellectual arguments that go nowhere.
- Don't expect change to come about from hit-and-run confrontations.

Lerner (2005).

- **Loss of face.** Public exposure of one's failures or inadequacies can be both humiliating and infuriating.
- **Threat of physical harm or violence.** Anger helps activate our instinct for self-preservation.
- **Loss of valued possessions, skills, or abilities.** Regardless of who is to blame, losing something we are proud of can cause both hurt and anger.
- **Loss of a valued role.** If we lose a part of our life, such as a job, which is important to our identity, we may feel angry at having the role removed.
- **Loss of valued relationships.** Anger is often a response to the loss of an important relationship.

Now stop and think for a moment about the times you have experienced genuine anger. Do you agree that your anger began with some loss or even the threat of a loss you incurred? Which type of loss just described were you dealing with?

From these losses, then, there are four *psychological reactions* to anger. They are:

1. Seeing yourself as a victim,
2. Feeling discounted or ignored,
3. Feeling powerless, and
4. Looking for justice and revenge.

In dealing with these psychological reactions to anger, it is important to remember three characteristics of anger.

- **Anger is neither right nor wrong.** Everybody gets angry. Haim Ginott (2003) confirms this but provides some limits, too:
  You have the right to get angry, but you do not have the right to attack other people or their character traits.

- **Anger can be released in a right or wrong way.** It is important to remember that anger released in inappropriate ways destroys relationships. This most often occurs when we *displace* our anger toward important people onto other relationships. In this way, anger at a boss gets deflected onto our spouse, anger at a spouse onto our child, and so on. Because we trust them to accept us as we are, we often unconsciously choose our strongest relationships as a "dumping ground" for our anger (Simon, 2005). On the one hand, it's negative, but then it also has some of the features of positive emotions. Researchers have found that associating an object with anger actually makes people want the object—a kind of motivation that's normally associated with positive emotions. "People are motivated to do something or obtain a certain object in the world because it's rewarding for them. Usually this means that the object is positive and makes you happy," says Henk Aarts of Utrecht University in the Netherlands (APA, 2010).

- **You are vulnerable when angry.** You may say or act in ways that are totally uncharacteristic of you. Sometimes anger causes more anger. Uncontrolled anger leads to bitterness, hatred, and even violence. If your local newspaper carries a brief synopsis of the daily police reports, we encourage you to take notice of the assaults and even murders that occur because people are angry and lose control of their emotions. Sometimes people even strike out at others with aggressive behavior.

Aggression. *Aggression* is any behavior that is intended to hurt someone, either verbally or physically (Weiten, 2010). Curses and insults are much more common than shootings or fistfights, but aggression of any kind can be a real problem. Why do people behave in such fashion? Some psychologists believe that aggression is largely learned in humans. Albert Bandura (2008), a proponent of social learning theory, indicates that aggressive models in the subculture, the family, and the media all play a part in increasing the level of aggression in our society. Bandura and other researchers also believe that violence in films, television, video games, and other media not only desensitizes us to violence (that is, makes it less bothersome) but also induces aggressive thoughts, feelings, and behavior in children and adults (Anderson et al., 2007).

Expressing anger. Anger is like fire. Sometimes it can be useful, sometimes it can be destructive, sometimes it can feel that we just can't get a spark started although we

> *Anyone can become angry. That is easy. But to be angry with the right person to the right degree, at the right time for the right purpose, and in the right way: This is not easy.*
> —ARISTOTLE

> *If you are patient in one moment of anger, you will escape a hundred days of sorrow.*
> —CHINESE PROVERB

> *A clear understanding of the significance of our misdeeds is emotionally healthier than hopeless misery afterward.*
> —DR. THEODOR REIK

feel like we're sitting on a powder keg. We're all human and we all have anger, whether others see us as angry and bitter or smiling and carefree (Howie, 2015). The question now might be: How do I express my anger? Carol Tavris (1989) suggests that we have been told that, if we ventilate our anger, we will experience the following:

- Improved communication and closeness with the target of our anger,
- Physiological relief and catharsis,
- Resolution of problems instead of brooding about them, and
- We will just feel better because we got "rid" of the anger.

Tavris goes on further to say that sometimes we get the benefits of this list, but most frequently, we get exactly the opposite:

- Decreased communication and feelings of closeness with the target of our anger,
- Physiological arousal and even higher blood pressure,
- The problem becomes worse, and
- We frequently just rehearse the anger and get angrier.

The question then is, how can I ensure the benefits and avoid the "exact opposites"? Psychologist Harriet Lerner (2005) feels that the expression of anger provides maximum results when the *Do's and Don'ts* under How to Control Your Anger (above) are followed. Also, you will find the discussion dealing with resolving interpersonal conflict through the use of "I" messages in Chapter Seven helpful in dealing with your anger.

Anger is a very powerful emotion and one that requires a balance between spontaneous expression and rational control. It is helpful to remember that when you are angry at someone, you are the one with the problem; therefore, you must be the one to correct the problem.

How about learning to shift your anger from an emotional level to an intellectual level? Redford Williams, director of the Behavioral Medicine Research Center at Duke University Medical Center in Durham, North Carolina, suggests asking yourself four questions whenever you feel angry: 1) Is this important? 2) Is my anger appropriate? 3) Is the situation modifiable? and 4) Is it worth taking action? Such evaluation helps convert your anger into rational thought. The anger is then under your control. Williams further suggests that if the answers to those questions are all "yes," decide what result you want, make a plan, and follow it. Even one "no" means you need to change your angry reaction and move on (Foltz-Gray, 2002).

Cyberbullies Increasingly Target Peers Online

Mary Aiken is in the new field of *cyber psychology.* Anger against friends and others is a concern in cyberbullying. The illusion is that the cyber environment is safer than real life and connecting to people online is safer than meeting them in person. She feels that "people behave differently when they are interacting with technology than they do in the real world" (Aiken, 2016 pg 21). She observed we are more altruistic online than in giving face to face. Another thing she thinks happens is that people are more trusting of others they meet online and can quickly disclose too much information. She has observed human behavior is often amplified and accelerated online (Aiken, 2016 pg 36). You can see this with the changing role of selfies and sexts, and flirting on social networks. Bullying and stalking have become quite common since people feel anonymous.

Bullying is when one person picks on another person again and again. Usually children who are being bullied are either weaker or smaller, are shy, and generally feel helpless. Experiencing bullying is challenging and upsetting. It's one of those situations that may negatively impact a person's mental health and can alter the path a person takes, depending on how the situation is handled.

As more of life has become digital and online, bullies have gone there too. The problem with online bullies is that they are faceless and often harder to identify and stop, than bullies who are off-line in the classroom. The negative effect, though, is no less significant, on children and on adolescents. In fact, online bullying—**cyberbullying**— is the most common negative situation that can happen to any of our kids while they are spending time in the online space.

Robert Preidt (2016) found that cyberbullying among teens is highly likely to involve current or former friends and dating partners. Researchers analyzed data from a 2011 survey of nearly 800 students in grades 8 through 12 at a public school in a New York City suburb. About 17 percent had been involved with cyberbullying in the previous week, the study found. Nearly 6 percent of those students were victims; about 9 percent were aggressors; and about 2 percent were both. Cyberbullying usually occurred through Facebook or texting, the study author said. "A common concern regarding cyberbullying is that strangers can attack someone, but here we see evidence that there are significant risks associated with close connections," lead author Diane Felmlee said in an American Sociological Association news release. Felmlee called "the large magnitude of the effects of close relationships on the likelihood of cyberbullying" surprising (2016, pg 243).

"We believe that competition for status and esteem represents one reason behind peer cyberbullying. Friends, or former friends, are particularly likely to find themselves in situations in which they are vying for the same school, club, and/or sport positions and social connections," she explained (2016, pg 243).

"In terms of dating partners, young people often have resentful and hurt feelings as a result of a breakup, and they may take out these feelings on a former partner via cyber aggression. They might also believe they can win back a previous boyfriend or girlfriend, or prevent that person from breaking up with them or dating someone else, by embarrassing or harassing him or her," Felmlee suggested (2016, pg 243).

Ybarra and Mitchell (2006) found, in earlier research, that cyberbullying among teens and preteens had increased by 50 percent in the preceding five years as youths increasingly chronicle their lives on Web logs, or "blogs," and socialize online through chat rooms, instant-messaging and such Web sites as Facebook.com. Examples included receiving unnerving messages relating to their appearance or containing disturbingly personal details or threats of being assaulted at school. Others said harassers threatened to spread rumors about them or post embarrassing photos of them online.

Being Bullied

Evans and Chapman (2014) suggest a relationship between being called gay, lesbian, and queer and the most extensive experiences of bullying including physical, cyber, and relational victimization. Youth who experience social and emotional bullying, and youth who experience all forms of social and physical bullying,(including being bullied by being called gay, lesbian, or queer) are at a high risk of experiencing all forms of bullying behavior, highlighting the importance of increased support for this vulnerable students. (2014 pg 649.) This has also been similar to the research of Diane Felmlee and Robert Faris (2016) in the Social Psychology Journal. They found approximately 17 percent of the NY students reported some involvement in cyber aggression within the past week. LGBTQ youth were targeted at a rate over four times that of their heterosexual peers, and females were more frequent victims than males. Rates of cyber aggression were 4.3 times higher between friends than between friends of friends (pg.243).

Two interpretations of their survey findings are possible.

First, the victims of bullying may comprise youth who are particularly susceptible to bullying and are bullied in several different ways. In this case, the actual or perceived sexual orientation of the victim does not affect the bullying; homophobic name calling is one technique in the bullies' arsenal of bullying tactics (Evans and Chapman, 2014).

A second possibility is that the victim openly identifies as LGBT or is perceived by others to be LGBT, and therefore, the youth is bullied by being called gay, lesbian, or queer due to their actual or perceived sexual orientation. The youth in the 2014 survey (whether they identified as LGBT or not) had nearly equal probabilities of reporting that they were bullied (87% and 90%, respectively), indicating that most youth who have experienced the behaviors assessed in the study define those behaviors as bullying. (American Journal of Orthopsychiatry 2014, Vol. 84, No. 6, 644 – 652).

So what do you do when you are bullied? It may be hard to do, but tell someone! Start with your loyal friends then parents …

- **Try not to react to the bully and not give into their demands.** A bully likes scaring others and often tries to get the victim to cry or become visibly upset in other ways. Save all e-mails, IMs, and texts.

- Form strong friendships for yourself (you need a loyal friend).
- Have your parents try to talk to the other parents and determine what may have gone on.
- Talk to school staff and have your parents or other advocate be prepared to help if school staff are not sure how to get involved.

The 2016 book, *The Cyber Effect*, by Mary Aiken, examines the escalation of cyberstalking, and organized cybercrime in the Deep Web. Aiken provides horrifying statistics and incredible-but-true case studies of hidden trends like fetishes and cranking that are shaping our culture and raising troubling questions about where the digital revolution is taking us (2016 pg 23). She also covers a wide range of subjects from the impact of computer screens on the developing child to the explosion of teen sexting, and how fast addictive behaviors are growing such as online gaming, shopping and pornography. Dr. Aiken examines the escalation of cyberchondria (which is anxiety produced by self-diagnosing online), cyberstalking, and organized cybercrime in the Deep Web (2016) pg 188d. *Dr. Aiken quotes from her 2016 book:*

> *"At this moment in time we can describe cyberspace as a place, separate from us, but very soon that distinction will become blurred. By the time we get to 2020, when we are alone and immersed in our smart homes and smarter cars, clad in our wearable technologies, our babies in captivity seats with iPads thrust in their visual field, our kids all wearing face-obscuring helmets, when our sense of self has fractured into a dozen different social-network platforms, when sex is something that requires logging in and a password, when we are competing for our lives with robots for jobs, and dark thoughts and forces have pervaded, syndicated, and colonized cyberspace, we might wish we'd paid more attention. As we set out on this journey, into the first quarter of the twenty-first century, what do we have now that we can't afford to lose?"* (Aiken, 2016 pp. 303-304)

GUILT AND SHAME

Two other powerful emotions that can rule our lives are guilt and shame. **Guilt**, in its simplest form, is the remorse over having done something morally, socially, or ethically wrong. Although shame is an emotion that is closely related to guilt, it is important to understand the difference. **Shame** can be defined as a painful emotion caused by consciousness of guilt, shortcoming, or impropriety. David Burns (1999) indicates that, when we feel guilt, *it is about something we did or did not do*. When we feel shame, *it's about who we are as a person*. Shame is often a much stronger and more profound emotion than guilt. Shame and vulnerability researcher Dr. Brené Brown has studied the power of these intensely painful feelings. Brown says shame is the most primitive human emotion we all feel—and the one no one wants to talk about (Brown, 2007). "I think shame is lethal," she says. "I think shame is deadly. And I think we are swimming in it deep." Brown explains that feelings of shame can quietly marinate over a lifetime. "Here's the bottom line with shame," she says. "The less you talk about it, the more you got it. Shame needs three things to grow exponentially in our lives: secrecy, silence, and judgment" (2012 pg 188). By keeping quiet, Brown says your shame will grow

Guilt is feeling bad for what you have done or not done, while shame is feeling bad for who you are, measured against some standard of perfection or acceptability.
—HAROLD KUSHNER

exponentially. "It will creep into every corner and crevice of your life," she says. The antidote, Brown says, is **empathy**. She explains that, if you talk about your shame with a friend who expresses empathy, the painful feeling cannot survive. "Shame depends on me buying into the belief that I'm alone," she says. Here's the bottom line: "Shame cannot survive being spoken," Brown says. "It cannot survive empathy."(2012 pg 68)

Experts in human behavior report that unjustified, excessive guilt and shame can sour our enjoyment of living, disrupt our social and business lives, worry, dishearten, and even humiliate us. They can cause fears and anxieties and even torment a person to the point of suicide. As you can see, tragedy and much human suffering have been triggered by needless feelings of guilt and shame. Are guilt and shame bad, however? Andrew Rosenthal (2009), founder of Happier.com and researcher with Martin Seligman has an answer for us:

> I would not want to enhance one's ability to block out the sense of shame or guilt; these emotions help stabilize society and provide disincentives for destructive behavior. Without shame or guilt, we would fail to learn effectively from mistakes. These fundamental *emotions are at the core of what it means to be human*. (Rosenthal, 2009)

"Shame [is] highly correlated with addiction, depression, eating disorders, violence, bullying and aggression. Guilt? Inversely correlated with those." Therefore, the ability to change the self-talk—and believe it—can dramatically affect the outcomes of those measures and others (Brown, 2007 p. 13).

HOW TO DEAL WITH GUILT

- **Examine why you feel guilty.** Take a long inward look, seeking the reason for your feelings. It is important to remember that powerful guilt feelings are sometimes pushed far beneath the layers of our conscious thinking. In such cases, professional help may be needed to help bring them to the surface. The point is to find out exactly why you feel guilty.

- **Determine whether you really need to feel guilty.** Reappraise all the rules that have been set down for you during your lifetime. Take a whole new look at the principles, not created by yourself, but prescribed by parents, friends, society, and others. Are these principles realistic and valid for you at your stage of life and relevant in the society in which you now live and work?

- **Do what is right for you.** Make decisions that sound "good" to you. No one can tell you how you should live your life. You must make your own decisions about what is right and what is wrong. Do not live your life by listening to what other people say you should or should not do. Obviously, you will have to accept the consequences of your choices, but be your own person.

- **Forgive yourself.** Learn to accept the fact that perfection is an unattainable ideal. Mistakes happen. If you have done something morally or ethically wrong, accept it and forget it. Apologize if you can or correct the misdeed in whatever way is proper. Say nothing if you will hurt someone else grievously, recognizing that "telling all" is actually asking for punishment to ease your sense of guilt. It is possible to feel sorry about something without feeling guilty. The point is that you will need to tell yourself and also internalize that you have done something wrong, that it was wrong, and that it is now behind you.

GRIEF AND BEREAVEMENT

Coping with losing a loved one is one of life's more difficult, yet inevitable tasks. ***Grief and bereavement***, sometimes even referred to as mourning, can be defined as "to be deprived." In *mourning*, we use our memory to recall the deceased and what was great about them and then try to move on in our own lives (Simonini, 2011). The grief process consists of 1) freeing ourselves emotionally from the loss, 2) readjusting to life without this loss, 3) resuming ordinary activities and forming new relationships (Dickenson & Leming, 2007).

Grief has long been broken down into stages. One cycle made famous by Elisabeth Kübler-Ross, M.D. (1997) uses stages of denial, anger, bargaining, depression, and acceptance. However, researchers have shown that stages don't always apply. Camille Wortman, Ph.D. and Roxane Cohen Silver, Ph.D. have found that there are individual patterns of grieving. For example, some people suffer profound grief, some interminable grief, and others show no distress at all. Furthermore, while some people recover in a year, some individuals find the second year to be much worse, and others have difficulty for several years. It all depends on the individual, the relationship of the loss, and the circumstances surrounding the loss (Greenberg, 2003). There is no correct way to grieve (Freeman, 2005). It is interesting to note that some individuals even use a deceased person's Facebook page to express their grief, and connect with the person they lost.

Dealing with the loss. While there are individual differences in how people grieve, some common reactions might be sense of shock and disbelief, especially when death occurs unexpectedly. When we've been anticipating a person's death, the initial response may be subdued, often accompanied by a sense of relief. In general, there are often memories of the deceased, and feelings of expected sadness to various degrees of depression are very, very common. Negative emotions, such as anger and guilt, may even surface, particularly if the loss was due to suicide. For example, we may even ask: Why did that person abandon me? What could I have done differently? Regardless of the circumstances surrounding the loss, we may have feelings of guilt over things we said, did, or feel we should have done while the person was still alive. It is not even uncommon to have "survivor's guilt," that is, feeling guilty simply because we are still alive and the other person is not.

It is important to emphasize that we never get over the loss of someone to whom we feel especially close. We just learn to adjust to the loss. We get used to the loss, and we "reinvest" in a new reality. ***Grief work***, the process of freeing ourselves emotionally from the deceased and readjusting to life without that person, takes time. You will need a strong support system of family and friends to aide you in your progress. (Some of the suggestions below may be helpful in assisting a grieving friend.) People who are fortunate to work through their grief may eventually find it becomes a positive growth experience—sometimes called ***good grief*** (Welshons & Dyer, 2003).

> *Forgiveness In all of recorded history, no one has ever determined to everyone's satisfaction whom to blame when an argument occurs. But it is a known fact that being the first to take the blame quickly puts the fire out and that with a touch of humor most problems can be worked out in a civil manner. . Forgiveness... Pass It On. Forgiveness*
> —THE FOUNDATION FOR A BETTER LIFE (VALUES.COM)

> *We cannot become separate people, responsible people, connected people, reflective people without some losing and leaving and letting go.*
> —JUDITH VIORST

Granger Westburg (2004), author of *Good Grief*, explains the results of **good grief** as the *following*:

1. We come out of a grief experience at a slightly higher level of maturity than before.
2. We come out of grief as deeper persons, because we have been down in the depths of despair and we know what it's like.

HOW TO ASSIST A GRIEVING FRIEND

- Don't force your method of grieving: Respect what the person wants.
- Avoid minimizing the loss: Never tell the person to "get over it." Be patient.
- Be a better listener: Be aware of your feelings; and know you can't solve the problem.
- Be with the mourner: Say—"I'm sorry about your loss." "I'm here for you."

3. We come out of it stronger, for we have had to learn how to use our spiritual muscles to climb the rugged mountain trails.
4. We come out of it better able to help others. We have walked through the valley of the shadow of grief. We can understand.

HOW TO HELP PEOPLE GRIEVE

In helping others you often find people who need to grieve. Whether it is a loss of a close friend or loss of a parent, knowing how to handle the situation is a simple technique developed by clinical psychologist Susan Silk and negotiator Barry Goldman to help people help others. It works for all kinds of crises: medical, legal, financial, romantic, and even existential. Susan Silk calls it the ***Ring Theory***.

> **Draw a circle.** This is the center ring. In it put the name of the person at the *center of the current trauma*. For Katie's aneurysm, that's Katie. Now draw a larger circle around the first one. In that ring put the name of the person <u>next closest</u> *to the trauma*. In the case of Katie's aneurysm, that was Katie's husband, Dan. Repeat the process as many times as you need to. In each *larger ring put the next closest* people. Parents and children before more distant relatives. Intimate friends in smaller rings, less intimate friends in larger ones. When you are done you have a "Kvetching"/ Complaining Order. It looks like a target.

> Here are the rules. **The person in the center ring** can say anything they want to anyone, anywhere. They can kvetch and complain and whine and moan and curse the heavens and say, "Life is unfair" and "Why me?" That's the one payoff for being in the center ring. **We need to give them room to grieve.**

Everyone else can say those things too, but only to people in **larger rings.** The person in the center will have a hard time processing your complaints so let them have time to grieve in their own way. And don't lament to them.

When you are talking to a person in a **ring smaller** than yours, someone closer to the center of the crisis, the *goal is to help*. Listening is often more helpful than talking. If you are going to say something, ask yourself if what you are about to say is likely to provide comfort and support. If it isn't, don't say it. Don't, for example, give advice. People who are suffering from trauma don't need advice. They need comfort and support. So say, **"I'm sorry"** or **"This must really be hard for you"** or "Can I bring you a pot of soup?" Don't say, "You should hear what happened to me" or "Here's what I would do if I were you." And don't say, "This is really bringing me down."

If you want to scream or cry or complain, if you want to tell someone how shocked you are or how horrible you feel, or whine about how it reminds you of all the terrible things that have happened to you lately, that's fine. It's a perfectly normal response. **Just do it to someone in a bigger ring.**

Comfort **IN**, dump **OUT.**

There was nothing wrong with Katie's friend saying she was not prepared for how horrible Katie looked, or even that she didn't think she could handle it. The mistake was that she said those things to Katie's husband Dan. She dumped **IN.**

Complaining to someone in a smaller ring than yours doesn't do either of you any good. On the other hand, **being supportive** to her principal caregiver may be the best thing you can do for the patient. Most of us know this. Almost nobody would complain to the patient about how rotten she looks. Almost no one would say that looking at her makes them think of the fragility of life and their own closeness to death. In other words, we know enough not to dump into the center ring! Ring Theory merely expands that intuition and makes it more concrete: Don't just avoid dumping into the center ring; *avoid dumping into any ring smaller than your own.* Remember, you can say whatever you want if you just wait until you're talking to someone in a larger ring than yours. And don't worry. You'll get your turn in the center ring. You can count on that. (Silk & Goldman, 2016)

Love

Countless volumes have been written about the subject of love. Yet, do we really understand the true meaning of love? You will have the opportunity to explore love as it relates to more intimate relationships in Chapter Six. Therefore, our discussion in this chapter will be limited to the learned attitudes that interfere with our ability to give and receive love, as well as the use and misuse of love.

Learned attitudes. Certainly, our ideas about love are shaped by childhood experiences. If your parents hug you and tell you how great you are, hugs and praises become a part of your vocabulary of love. If they slap you and tell you are stupid, however, you

Our ideas about love are shaped by childhood experiences.

may conclude that, in some odd way, abuse is part of a loving relationship. Why would you do this? From a child's perspective: "These people are my parents; parents love their children; therefore, the way my parents love me is loving behavior."

We also grow up assuming that others will find the same things lovable that our parents did. For example, if we are lucky, our parents love us unconditionally and continue to love us even when they do not love our behavior or when we disagree with them. Consequently, we grew up believing that we deserved to be loved just because we are who we are.

If, however, our parents loved us only when we were compliant and undemanding, we may have mistakenly learned that compliance was loving behavior. Therefore, we assume that we should not make demands on those we love. In essence, our parents' loving us only when we pleased them taught us that we must always be pleasing or risk losing love.

Use and misuse of love. There are also problems we encounter through the misuse of the emotion, love. Because love is such a powerful and yet complicated emotion, we may even have a tendency to "smother" other people because we "love" them. Do we love them in the appropriate manner?

> You may find yourself feeling confused about the relationship, off balance or like you are "walking on eggshells" all the time. This is the kind of abuse that often sneaks up on you as you become more entrenched in the relationship. I am talking here about psychological abuse, which is also known as mental or emotional abuse. Psychological abuse occurs when a person in the relationship tries to control information available to another person with intent to manipulate that person's sense of reality or their view of what is acceptable and unacceptable. (Feuerman, 2016)

Becoming *Aware*

Psychiatrist Dr. Foster Cline (2006) makes an interesting comment about the misuse of love: "Love becomes a problem when it gets in the way of our allowing individuals the right to experience the consequences of their choices." For example, what about the countless hours spent in enabling a child or spouse who has a drug or alcohol problem? Why do we find it difficult for those we love to suffer the consequences of their choices? The answer is simple: We love them, and we do not like to see those we love suffer—we want to spare them their pain.

Remember, to let go is not to care for, but to care about.

Letting Go

To let go does not mean to stop caring,
It means I can't do it for someone else.

To let go is not to cut myself off,
It's the realization I can't control another.

To let go is not to enable,
But to allow learning from natural consequence.

To let go is to admit powerlessness,
Which means the outcome is not in my hands.

To let go is not to try to change or blame another,
It's to make the most of myself.

To let go is not to care for,
But to care about.

To let go is not to fix,
But to be supportive.

To let go is not to judge,
But to allow another to be a human being.

To let go is not to be in the middle arranging all the outcomes,
But to allow others to affect their own destinies.

To let go is not to be protective,
It's to permit another to face reality.

To let go is not to deny,
But to accept.

To let go is not to nag, scold, or argue,
But instead to search out my own shortcomings and correct them.

To let go is not to adjust everything to my desires,
But to take each day as it comes, and cherish myself in it.

To let go is not to criticize and regulate anybody,
But to try to become what I dream I can be.

To let go is not to regret the past,
But grow and live for the future.

To let go is to fear less and love more.   —Author unknown

> To be loved because of one's merit, because one deserves it, always leaves doubt; maybe I did not please the person whom I want to love me, maybe this or that—there is always a fear that love could disappear. Furthermore, "deserved" love easily leaves a bitter feeling that one is not loved for oneself, that one is loved only because one pleases, that one is, in the last analysis, not loved but used.
> —ERICH FROMM

The reality is that love can mean letting go of the responsibility we sometimes impose on ourselves to "take care" of those we love. It is in the best interest of those we love to let them assume the responsibility for making their choices and the consequences of those choices. When we jump in and smother them, we take away their choices and their freedom to be self-sufficient human beings. In essence, we have done them a major injustice, quite the opposite of what we really believe we are doing. This is extremely difficult for people to accept, and it takes a great deal of time to work through this emotional understanding of the true meaning of love.

Another misuse of love is when we find ourselves or others using love as a control agent—"If you loved me, you would do this . . ., or you wouldn't do this." Do we really understand what we are saying? This is obviously a strong form of manipulation and can totally destroy whatever love and caring there may be in a relationship.

Although there are many definitions of love, in the final analysis, love may truly be the desire to see another individual become all he or she can be as a person—with room to breathe and grow; and it may be caring as much about another person's well being as we do our own. This is true whether our love be for a spouse, friend, child, or co-worker.

© Masson/Shutterstock.com

Some people show their feelings by buying presents or doing nice things for those they love.

Expressing love. Certainly, there are many types of love relationships. Depending upon the relationship involved, the true meaning of love will be expressed in various ways. Some people have trouble saying the words, "I love you!" Instead, they show their love by buying presents or doing nice things for those they love. Obviously, for one who says, "I love you" frequently, it is difficult to understand why another person cannot "spit" the words out. People, however, express their emotions in different ways. Although it is true that adults who did not know love as a child have a greater difficulty learning how to express love, it is never too late to develop or expand our ability to love. As women surpass men on college campuses, the threat felt by thin-skinned males often reveals itself in the relationships where they feel most exposed. "Boys are not only more invested in ongoing romantic relationships but also have less confidence navigating them than do girls," writes the sociologist Robin W. Simon in *The Journal of Health and Social Behavior*. That's problematic, because "romantic partners are their primary sources of intimacy," whereas young women confide in friends and family (Reiner, 2016).

HOW TO EXPAND YOUR ABILITY TO LOVE

- **Express yourself.** You have positive feelings, so put them into words: "Our relationship means a lot to me," "I like being with you," "I love you."
- **Love yourself.** Self-love is the opposite of selfishness, not the same thing. If you do not love yourself, you cannot love someone else.
- **Be tolerant.** You can love and be loved without sharing exactly the same opinions, values, and personality traits. Do not make constant agreement your main criterion for love. This is unrealistic.
- **Hang in there.** You are vulnerable and there is always the risk of hurt, but do not give up at the first sign of trouble. Relationships can be difficult but rewarding.
- **Learn to be alone.** You cannot be happy until you can be happy being alone. Do not ask another person to be your "security blanket." If you love someone, give the person room to breathe and grow while you keep your distance.
- **Grow up.** Immature love says, "I love you because I need you"; or "I love because I am loved." Mature love says, "I need you because I love you"; or "I am loved because I love."
- **Practice.** The more you practice developing a loving attitude, the more love you will attract. The more frequently you say, "I really care about you," "I love you," the more comfortable you will become in expressing these loving words.

From *The Art of Loving* (Fromm, 2006) and Love: What Life Is all About (Buscaglia, 1996).

Now that we have a better idea of how some of our more common emotions affect us, we will discuss how we got to be feeling persons. The chapter concludes with a discussion on learning how to express emotions, as well as the benefits to be derived in achieving a balance between emotional expression and emotional control.

Development of Emotions

From early infancy, human beings display tendencies toward responding emotionally. Most authorities agree with Jungian philosophy's classical theory that heredity does predispose us toward fairly specific emotional tendencies (Jung, 1923). For example, one child develops a natural tendency to react calmly to most emotional stimuli, whereas another shows a tendency to react quickly and intensely to all emotional stimuli.

An infant's first emotional expression is crying. For several months, babies will continue to show their excitement by crying when they feel like doing so. After a few weeks, they have learned to distinguish and respond to two basic emotions—*distress* and *delight*. Bodily discomfort (a wet diaper or hunger) brings forth the earliest unpleasant reaction, known as **distress**. **Delight**, the earliest pleasant reaction, appears several weeks after distress, in the form of smiling, gurgling, and other babyish sounds of joy.

Soon, we become more aware of the world within us and the world outside us. Consequently, we learn from others and our own experiences other emotional responses such as love, anger, frustration, fear, jealousy, and so on. We learn which emotions will bring us rewards and those that will bring us punishment.

Through our family, school, and social experiences, we learn various ways of dealing with our emotions. We also receive messages on how to express and deal with some of our emotions. For example, we may hear: "Don't make a scene by crying"; "There is nothing to be afraid of"; "Don't let everybody see how angry you are"; "Cheer up, there is no reason to feel bad"; "Be strong and endure your pain"; or even, "Control yourself; don't let others know how excited you are." It is even possible that you heard the statement, "Big boys don't cry." Consequently, we may grow up thinking that girls and women can cry, but boys and men must not do so. Could these messages have anything to do with the cultural stereotype of the unexpressive male and the more expressive female? See Gender & You on the following page. Do you agree or disagree with the findings? This is an example of how sexist behavior is learned and can be unlearned in the same manner. Men can be brought up to learn to show their feelings more and to be more emotionally aware (Rolls, 2010).

With modeling and messages from our parents, society, and our peers, is it any wonder that we grow up confused about *what to do with our feelings?*

Emotional Intelligence

Have you ever wondered why some people with high academic IQs are "poor pilots of their private lives," while those with modest academic IQs may do surprisingly well? Why do some "really bright people" make disastrous choices in business and in their personal lives? Are we either emotional beings or rational beings? Could it be possible to have an intelligent balance of the two, whereby the head and heart are in harmony with each other? Most people understand what academic or intellectual intelligence means, but what does it mean to use emotion intelligently?

Women tend to be more emotionally empathetic than men—that is, better able to pick up the emotions of others. Men tend to be faster than women at returning to normal after experiencing distressing emotions. "Some universities offer counseling services for men of color and gay men, and some sponsor clubs through which male members explore the crisis of sexual violence against women. Only a precious few colleges offer ways for all men to explore their shared struggles. And these don't exist without pushback. But wouldn't encouraging men to embrace the full range of their humanity benefit women? Why do we continue to limit the emotional lives of males when it serves no one?" (Reiner, 2016) The concept of emotional intelligence was originally developed by John Mayer and Peter Salovey (2004) and Daniel Goleman has made it more popular. **Emotional intelligence** consists of the ability to monitor,

GENDER AND YOU

DO WOMEN EXPRESS MORE EMOTIONS THAN MEN?

Women are more likely than men to express positive emotions like love, liking, joy, and contentment. Women have a hard time expressing anger.

Women are more likely than men to express feelings of vulnerability like fear, sadness, loneliness, and embarrassment. Men have difficult expressing sadness.

Men rarely express positive emotions and feelings of vulnerability, especially to their male friends, although they may be more expressive to the woman they love. Men are less bashful about revealing their strengths.

While men experience emotions much like women, men tend to be not as emotionally expressive as women. Men's emotional behavior often masks their emotional inclinations. And, men often express their feelings through actions and activities rather than words. Goldsmith & Fulfs (1999); Goleman (2007).

---

access, express, and regulate one's own emotions; the capacity to identify, interpret, and understand others' emotions; and the ability to use this information to guide one's thinking and actions. Emotional intelligence includes four essential abilities:

1. *First*, people need to be able to accurately perceive emotions in themselves and others and have the ability to express their own emotions.
2. *Second*, people need to be aware of how their emotions shape their thinking, decisions and coping behavior.
3. *Third*, people need to be able to understand and analyze their emotions, which may have important social implications.
4. *Fourth*, people need to be able to regulate their emotions so they can minimize negative emotions and make effective use of positive emotions (Mayer et al., 2009). Daniel Goleman, an emotional intelligence writer, quotes, "If your emotional abilities aren't in hand, if you don't have self-awareness, if you are not able to manage your distressing emotions, if you can't have empathy and have effective relationships, then no matter how smart you are, you are not going to get very far." (http://cultureofempathy.com/references/Experts/Daniel-Goleman.htm)

Actually, emotional intelligence (EI) has become a popular phrase in homes, schools, and businesses due to a book, *Emotional Intelligence: Why It Can Matter More Than IQ* (Goleman, 2006). The author, a Harvard-educated psychologist, believes that emotional intelligence is involved in some of the most important things in our lives, such as managing bad moods, maintaining hope after setbacks, getting along with people, and making important decisions. People who are high in emotional intelligence have the ability to use their emotions wisely, and they appear to have a deeper understanding of their emotional lives (Goleman, 2011).

In fact, emotional intelligence may be a more important contributor to success in life than IQ. However, more research is needed in this area as well as continued research into the meaning of emotional intelligence. At present, ways to cultivate emotional intelligence are being explored in classrooms and workplaces. Emotional intelligence is an assortment of mental abilities and skills that can help you to successfully manage both yourself and the demands of working with others.

Developing your own EI enables you to:

1. Know yourself reasonably well.
2. Control your own emotions.
3. Show empathy with the feelings of others.
4. Use social skills in an effective as well as simply pleasant way. (Walton, 2013)

In any case, we are *both* emotional and rational beings, and we need an intelligent balance of the two (Gibbs, 2001; Duffy, 2007/2008). Be sure to review the Fully Human Being for additional insights into emotional intelligence.

Social Emotional Learning (SEL) is comprised of the skills we use to recognize and manage our own emotions and being able to recognize emotions in others. This concept arose out of research about Emotional Intelligence Methods for improving social skills. **Social Emotional Learning** emphasize learning personal and social skills and setting personal goals (Ng'andu, 2015). There is a movement to inspire mindful social emotional learning with children and adults by setting competencies. Casel.org has a coordinated framework for educators, families and communities to promote SEL and academic learning.

THE FULLY HUMAN BEING

The fully human being is aware of the vitality of his senses, emotions, mind, and will; and he is neither a stranger to, nor afraid of, the activities of his body and emotions. He is capable of the whole gamut of emotions: from grief to tenderness. What I mean, is that the fully human being experiences the fullness of his emotional life; he is in touch with, attuned to his emotions, aware of what they are saying to him about his needs and his relationships with others.

— Carl Rogers, *On Becoming a Person*

FEELING AWE – THE EMOTION TO BALANCE AND BECOME FULLY HUMAN

Awe may be the the secret emotion to help you get your balance and feel better. In fact, Paula Spencer Scott believes that feeling awe may be the secret to health and happiness. It is really not secret but not always talked about as a needed emotion. Awe has been researched by Dacher Keltner, a pioneer in the study of emotions. He consulted on the video about emotions, *Inside Out,* released in 2015. (That video did a great job of talking about the "big six" emotions: happiness, sadness, fear, anger, disgust, and surprise). Keltner started Project Awe in 2013, a three-year research project funded by the Sir John Templeton Foundation. **Awe** is the "take your breath away feeling" or it might be your "spine tingle" that you feel when you see something or experience something that can be new, like a sunset over the Rockies or just a beautiful cluster of butterflies.

The definition of *awe* is 1. an overwhelming feeling of reverence, admiration, fear, etc., produced by that which is grand, sublime, extremely powerful, or the like: in *awe* of God; in *awe* of great political figures. 2. Archaic. power to inspire fear or reverence. **(https://www.merriam-webster.com/dictionary/awe)**

- Keltner believes **we are wired to feel awe**. Awe binds us together in a collaborative way. It helps us to realize we are a small part of something larger like the solar system.
- Awe helps us **see things in new ways** and **makes us more receptive to details.**
- Awe can **make us nicer and happier**. It makes us act more generously, ethically and fairly.
- Awe can **help us fight depression**. Researchers are looking into whether a lack of access to nature and other opportunities for feeling awe might add to the stresses and health damage that come from living in urban blight or poverty (Scott, 2016).

THE COSTS OF DENYING EMOTIONS

What kinds of messages did you get about expressing or controlling your emotions? Were you taught to express your emotions openly, or did you grow up believing that you should "stop showing" your emotions, even though you continued to experience them? That is right! As long as you live, you continue to experience emotions. Why? You already know the answer: you are a human, not a robot or a machine. You will be given several opportunities in the activities at the end of this chapter to review how you express your emotions.

> *When feelings are avoided, their painful effects are often prolonged, and it becomes increasingly difficult to deal with them.*
> —ANDREW SALTER

How, then, do people deal with the emotional aspects of their life? There are only two choices: *deny* them or *express* them. Because over control poses our biggest problem in expressing emotions, we will begin by looking at two common ways we deny our emotions.

Repression. The most common form of overcontrol is repression. In *repression*, the self automatically excludes threatening or painful thoughts and feelings from awareness. By pushing them into the subconscious, we are able to manage the anxiety that grows out of uncomfortable situations.

Perhaps the most destructive aspect of repression is that although we realize we are hurting when we have repressed our true feelings, we do not know why. We have hidden the source of pain in the "dungeon" of the subconscious. Repressed emotions unfortunately do not die. They refuse to be silenced and continue to influence our whole personality and behavior. For example, when we repress guilt feelings, we are forever, though subconsciously, trying to punish ourselves. We will not allow ourselves success or enjoyment because we are so unworthy. For example, rather than accepting compliments, we "qualify" them or quickly give all the credit to someone more deserving than us!

Repressed fears and angers may be acted out physically as insomnia, headaches, ulcers, and so on. If such fears and angers had been consciously accepted and expressed, however, there would be no necessity for the sleeplessness, the tension headaches, or ulcers. In his book *The Language of Feelings,* David Viscott (1990) indicates that feelings always follow a predictable pattern when you suffer one of three major kinds of loss: *1) the loss of someone who loves you or the loss of their love or your sense of lovability; 2) the loss of control; 3) the loss of self-esteem.*

The predictable pattern then becomes:

- When a loss threatens, you feel anxious.
- When a loss occurs, you feel hurt.
- When hurt is held back, it becomes anger.
- When anger is held back, it creates guilt.
- When guilt is unrelieved, depression occurs.

Viscott goes on to say that if you take care of your fear, hurt, and anger, the guilt and depression will take care of themselves. In other words, they will be nonexistent, just like the sleeplessness, the tension headaches, or ulcers. When a person is especially sensitive to one type of loss, however, he or she tends to bury the unpleasant feelings associated with the loss.

Suppression. Sometimes people suppress rather than repress their emotions. In *suppression*, people are usually conscious of their emotions, but deliberately control rather than express them. For example, you might say, "I'll never let her know that I'm jealous." Why would you say this? You might be afraid that your emotional admissions could be used against you; maybe she would bring it up later. Then you would probably always wonder if she might distance herself from you because of the feelings you confided. Obviously, these are all threats to your self-esteem, so why take the risk? After all, what you do not say cannot be used against you.

Although suppression of emotions is a healthier way of handling feelings than is repression, habitual suppression may lead to many of the undesirable effects of repression. Furthermore, chronic suppression of feelings interferes with rational, problem-solving behavior. When people have unexpressed feelings that are "smoldering" within, they cannot think clearly. Consequently, they may have difficulty studying, working, or even socializing with others. More importantly, when you consistently suppress your emotions, you may eventually explode and do things or say things total-

When you deny what is real, When you hide from life's pains, When you shut out the world, Only fantasy remains.
—DAVID VISCOTT

Buried emotions are like rejected people; they make us pay a high price for having rejected them. Hell hath no fury like that of a scorned emotion.
—JOHN POWELL, 1995

Becoming *Aware*

ly uncharacteristic of you. Obviously, this makes the problem(s) much, much worse. As you can see, chronic suppression can be just as unhealthy as repression (Duffy & Atwater, 2014).

Now we are left with the other choice of dealing with our feelings—expressing them. But, is this not difficult when we have been holding them back for so long? Let us see.

> *Highly sensitive people are too often perceived as weaklings or damaged goods. To feel intensely is not a symptom of weakness; it is the trademark of the truly alive and compassionate. It is not the empath who is broken, it is society that has become dysfunctional and emotionally disabled. There is no shame in expressing your authentic feelings. Those who are at times described as being a "hot mess" or having "too many issues" are the very fabric of what keeps the dream alive for a more caring, humane world. Never be ashamed to let your tears shine a light in this world.* —ANTHON ST. MAARTEN

Getting Out of Emotional Debt

Everybody gets into emotional debt from time to time. Gary Emery (2000) defines **emotional debt** as a condition of imbalance in which feelings are trapped instead of expressed. As we have already stated that keeping feelings from being expressed naturally employs defenses and drains energy. The more feelings are held in, the less energy you have to be yourself. Obviously, this interferes with your ability to interact with others.

Accepting and learning to handle and express emotions are the marks of maturity. You are a feeling being. If you are to have the joy of positive emotions, you also must accept the reality of your negative emotions without guilt, self-condemnation, or repression of the emotion. Furthermore, a person who can control his own emotions (especially negative ones like anger and anxiety) without denying them will be able to tolerate others' upsets, not prompted to run from them—and be able to help (Marano, 2011).

> *The greatest lesson I ever learned was to accept complete responsibility for what I was feeling.* —GEORGE B. SHAW

Do you want to begin to learn how to express your emotions in a healthy way?

Guidelines for Dealing with Your Emotions

Emotions are a fact of life, and communicating them certainly is not a simple matter. It is obvious that showing every feeling of anger, frustration, and even love and affection could get you in trouble. However, withholding emotions can be personally frustrating and certainly affect your relationships. Therefore, the following suggestions can help you to decide when and how to express your emotions (Adler & Proctor, 2014).

Listen to your body. What is happening inside of you? What are those butterflies in your stomach telling you? Why is your heart pounding? Remember, physiological changes are a part of your emotions and what you are feeling. Those internal changes speak to you very clearly; do not ignore them.

Identify your feelings. Just ask yourself, "What am I really feeling?" Is it fear, anger, frustration? Give your feelings a label if you can. If you have difficulty with an exact label, use the techniques in the next suggestion to help you express your feelings. Remember to name all the feelings you are having. Try to identify your primary feeling and then your secondary feeling. Above all, do not deny or suppress your feelings.

Personalize your feelings. There are times when you can name the feeling: "I'm feeling hurt," "I love you," "I'm angry." There are times, however, when it is easier to describe the *impact* the feelings are having on you: "I feel like I'm being dumped on," "I feel used," "I feel he cares for me." Metaphors with a *colorful description,* such as "I'm sitting on top of the world," "I feel like my world has caved in," "I'm down in the dumps," can be used. Feelings can also be expressed by describing what action you feel like taking: "I feel like giving up," "I feel like telling him off," "I just want to jump for you."

Own your feelings. Your feelings are yours; no other person can cause or be responsible for your emotions. Of course, we feel better assigning our emotions to other people: "You made me angry," "You frightened me," "You made me jealous." The fact is that another person cannot make you *anything.* Another person can only stimulate the emotions that are already in you, waiting to be activated. The distinction between *causing* and *stimulating* emotions is not just a play on words. The acceptance of the truth involved is critical. If you think other people can make you angry, when you become angry you simply lay the blame and pin the problem on them. You can then walk away from your emotional encounter learning nothing, concluding only that the other people were at fault because he or she made you angry. Then, you do not have to examine your own feelings because you gave all the responsibility for your feelings to the other people.

Decide what you will do with your feelings. This is oftentimes very difficult, because there are many factors to consider. Careful consideration of the following suggestions may be of assistance to you:

- **Timing and Appropriateness of Place.** We are all familiar with the thought: *there is a time and a place for all things.* This is particularly true when expressing emotions because you want to get your message across. You also want your message to be heard, and you hope your message is understood. As we will discuss in Chapter Five, your receiver will probably be more receptive to your message if he or she is not distracted by outside stimuli and if the receiver has the energy and time to listen.
- **How Much Emotion to Express.** Young children may squeal with delight or cry with anguish in the grocery store, at church, or wherever they so please. Adults, however, are expected to exert control over their emotional expressions. This does

not mean that adults should not express emotion spontaneously. Instead, it means that adults feel an emotion, understand it, and decide how intensely to express it. For example, regardless of how intensely an adult feels he or she wants to laugh and get excited in church, this is just considered taboo, if you are the only one laughing. Also, regardless of how sad you feel that your daughter is marrying this "certain" boy, it might not be a good idea to cry loudly and profusely through the entire wedding. A quiet sob would be much more appropriate.

- **Significance of Relationship.** There is some risk involved in expressing feelings. In an encounter with a store clerk, an acquaintance, or a distant relative, expressing your feelings may do nothing more than relieve tension. In other words, you might be able to get away with "telling this person off." If you value another person's friendship, however, you may want to carefully consider just "telling this person off." You may find that this relationship means so much to you, you need to be very careful in expressing your feelings. Maybe, you can soften your approach. After all, you want the net effect to be a closer, more meaningful relationship. It is important to realize you are going to be interacting with this person in the future; you can avoid the store clerk if you so choose.

- **Words and Mannerisms.** You already know some ways to personalize your feelings. You will also want to consider the appropriate verbal and nonverbal techniques to use in getting your message across. This will be discussed in more detail in Chapter Five. Careful selection of words means that you use tact and deal with facts instead of interpretations, judgments, or accusations.

- **Recognize the Difference between Feeling and Acting.** At times you may be so angry that you feel like "punching someone in the nose." In this instance, it would be more constructive to talk about your feelings, rather than act upon your feelings. One point should be made clear: Allowing ourselves the freedom to feel and observe our emotions does not necessarily mean that we should act on those emotions. As a small child, you might punch someone in the nose when you get angry. Although this is not necessarily appropriate, you might just get a spanking or a "time out" period. As an adult, however, if you "punch" someone in the nose, you might get a ticket to jail or even get killed in extreme cases. To live effectively in our world requires that we be sensitive to situations and adjust our emotional expression accordingly. Remember, we used the term *adjust,* not *deny.*

Although it is true that people express their emotions differently and respond to situations differently, the truth is that sometimes, as stated, it is just not possible to openly express what you really feel. In these instances, you need to choose some indirect ways to express your feelings. As you already know, feelings do not just go away. Here are some suggestions for these times:

1. Ventilate or share your feelings with someone you trust.
2. Choose some type of physical or creative activity to help release your "pent-up" emotions.
3. Work to maintain a positive or realistic perspective of the situation.
4. As much as possible, keep a sense of humor.

> *An emotion without social rules of containment and expression is like an egg without a shell: a gooey mess.*
> —CAROL TAVRIS

> *Do you collect emotional trading stamps—that is, collecting feelings, rather than dealing with them?*
> —ANN ELLENSON

You are probably thinking or saying to yourself, "I'll never remember all these guidelines." If this is true for you, perhaps the "shorthand technique" developed by Gary Emery (2000) and illustrated below in Consider This will be a quick way for you to remember the key concepts in expressing your feelings.

CONSIDER THIS

FEEL—THE SHORTHAND TECHNIQUE

F   Focus on your feelings.
E   Express them constructively.
E   Experience them.
L   Let them go.

Emery (2000).

UNDERSTANDING CULTURE AND EMOTION

Research shows that certain basic emotions are experienced by people around the world. The ability to feel and recognize happiness, sadness, surprise, anger, disgust, and fear seems to be universal, regardless of a person's background or where they are born (Gudykunst & Young, 2002). Culture plays a key role in moderating our expression of emotion and in helping us cognitively appraise situations in appropriate ways. Paul Eckman found that different cultures have different display rules: norms about when, where, and how much we should show emotions. The Focus on Diversity on the following page gives examples of some of these cultures' display rules (Adler & Proctor, 2011; King, 2010).

We are emotional human beings. Understanding our emotions, how they affect us, and developing ways of handling them can be beneficial for all of us. Understanding how different cultures express emotions can certainly eliminate some potential communication problems. Learning to constructively express and utilize our emotions is a lifelong process; we learn by doing.

Benefits of Expressing Your Feelings

Many emotional responses feel good to us. Feelings of love, tenderness, and warmth toward other people give us a sense of well-being. Emotional responses involved in happy or joyful experiences in life are also enhancing to us, as are emotional responses found in humor or laughter that tend to help us feel good about being alive.

However, the real benefit of having good feelings can only be found if one chooses to truly experience emotions and share them with others.

As we have stated several times in this chapter, strong feelings that are not expressed or dealt with rarely go away. Instead, you may begin to collect your feelings and cash them in at a later date for a free mad, temper tantrum, or an angry outburst at someone else. Also, bottled-up anger may "leak out" in the form of a lack of cooperation, silence, coldness, cynicism, or even sarcasm. Obviously, none of us would really want these types of behaviors to occur.

FOCUS ON DIVERSITY

CULTURAL DISPLAY RULES

- Russians control their expression of emotions much more than Americans. And, happy or not, Russians rarely smile in public.
- Japanese culture emphasizes the suppression of negative emotions in public.
- African Americans display emotion with more liveliness than whites, showing more changes in facial expression, voice pitch, and body movements.
- If you see someone eating a hamburger, you are not likely to respond emotionally, unless you are in India where cows are sacred.
- In Native American culture, emotions ranging from expressing affection, being curious, or even expressing unhappiness are much less public than in Anglo cultures. For example, expressing love is displayed by helping and caring for people they love.
- Americans say, "I love you" more frequently than members of most other cultures.
- Asians tend to express positive emotions (e.g., happiness) and powerful emotions to a lesser extent than whites from the United States and Canada.
- How might these differences in display rules lead to communication problems?

Duffy & Atwater (2011); Weiten (2010); Adler & Proctor (2011); King (2010).

The authors believe that, after you have carefully considered your options and the consequences involved in expressing your feelings, and *choose to take the risk,* you are likely to derive several long-term, positive benefits. Below are three, although there are many others.

1. **You Will Develop Positive Feelings about Yourself.** You cannot possibly understand that part of yourself which you deny or repress. Furthermore, you cannot possibly appreciate yourself when you know you are not being honest with yourself and others. Once you begin to openly and honestly deal with your feelings in

© Monkey Business Images/Shutterstock.com

The real benefit of having good feelings can only be found if one chooses to truly experience emotions and share them with others.

> The things that most clearly differentiate and individuate me from others are my feelings and emotions.
> —JOHN POWELL

> The top eight hits on the "hurt parade": disappointment, rejection, abandonment, ridicule, humiliation, betrayal, deception, and abuse.
> —SIDNEY AND SUZANNE SIMON

a constructive way, you will automatically experience increased feelings of self-esteem. People who feel good about themselves are not afraid of their emotional responses. That is, they trust themselves and their emotions. Obviously, this type of dual trust leads to a sense of inner harmony and freedom—you do not have to *pretend* any longer.

2. **Your Relationships Will Grow Stronger.** The expression of feelings is vital to effectively building meaningful relationships. How can others know what you are feeling if you never tell them? How can another person really get to know you if you only talk about the "weather" or "surface" type issues?

    Other people may have dark hair as you do or drive a Ford as you do, but others will not experience fears, frustrations, love, and joy in the same way as you do. So, you must tell others how you feel, what your "gut" is saying, if you really want to establish and maintain meaningful relationships.

    Often, when you begin expressing your feelings, others will be more likely to express some of their own. Consequently, you each know more about each other. When two people can share their feelings in an open, honest, and caring way, their relationship will deepen, even if these feelings are sometimes negative.

3. **Pressure Is Relieved.** Experts in psychosomatic medicine believe that the most common cause of fatigue and actual sickness is the repression of emotions. We all experience frustrations and anxieties in our daily lives. For example, our goals may be thwarted, our self-esteem and integrity may be threatened, and our abilities to handle situations may seem overwhelmed. As we have seen, our health and our relationships are negatively affected when we deny "what we are really feeling." When we are able to express what we have kept "bottled up" inside us, we normally feel better. Consequently, we naturally reduce some of the stress we are feeling. We will discuss stress and its effects more fully in Chapter Eight.

Sometimes in the process of expressing and dealing with our feelings, we even go through a healing process, known as *forgiveness*. Let us see what this process involves.

Forgiveness—The Healing Process

Have you ever been hurt or experienced a painful injustice from:

- Parents
- Lovers
- Children
- Spouses (former and present)
- Brothers and sisters
- Grandparents
- Friends
- Co-workers
- Employers
- People of the opposite sex, other races, or religions
- Ourselves
- Whole systems (schools, government, criminal justice system, the media)

Do you harbor bitter, angry, resentful feelings toward these people? Have you tried to "even the score" with any of these people or wished that harm would come to those who have hurt you?

Actually, we have all experienced some hurts and had some painful past experiences but many of these no longer influence our life. On the other hand, there may be some hurts that we still hang onto. We have not forgiven the people who hurt us, but more important, we have not let go of the pain. Sidney and Suzanne Simon (2014), authors of the book, *Forgiveness: How to Make Peace with Your Past and Get On with Your Life,* explain that the pain has not let go of us:

> Many of us wake up each morning and fill an enormous suitcase with pain from our pasts. We stuff it with grudges, bitterness, resentment, and self-righteous anger. We toss in some self-pity, envy, jealousy, and regret. We load that suitcase with every injury and injustice that was ever done to us; with every memory of how others failed us and how we ourselves have failed; and with all the reminders of what we have missed out on and what we can never hope to have. Then, we shut that suitcase and drag it with us wherever we go. (Simon & Simon, 2014 pg. 43)

Throughout our lives, we have all heard the following statements:

- Forgive and forget,
- Let bygones be bygones,
- Turn the other cheek, and
- Kiss and make up.

However, it is oftentimes very difficult to forgive the people who caused us real pain. Instead, we believe that the people who hurt us should pay for the pain they caused—they *deserve to be punished, not forgiven*. Sometimes we may even say, "I'll work at forgiving when they say they are sorry. I will work at forgiveness when somehow they communicate to me that they realize and regret what they have done."

In all probability, the people who hurt you have not made up for what they did to you, and even if they wanted to, they probably could not really do that. Furthermore, no amount of *punishment* they may have endured could relieve your pain or evaporate your resentment. What if they never apologize? What if they are never sorry? What if they are never even capable of knowing what they did to you? Then what? Then what do you do? Do you continue to let them dictate the quality of your life (Larsen, 1992)?

Forgiveness has nothing to do with them. It's natural and certainly tempting to blame others or unfortunate circumstances for feelings of anger, guilt, depression, anxiety, shame, or insecurity. But look at the word *blame*. It is just a coincidence that the last two letters spell the word *me*. Other people or unfortunate circumstances may have caused you to experience some pain but only *you control whether you allow that pain to go on*. You may not have had any power or control over what happened to you when you were 5, 10, or 15 years old, but you do have a choice now whether you are going to keep on carrying that hurt and resentment with you (Enright, 2001).

What can you do to make those feelings go away? What can you do to get those people who hurt you off your *blame list*? Forgiveness is not done as a favor to the people who hurt you or because someone once told you that forgiving was the good or right thing to do. Forgiveness is something you do for *yourself*, for your own health, happiness, and emotional well-being. You forgive so that you can let go of the pain and finally get rid of the excess emotional baggage that has been weighing you down and holding you back.

Rabbi Harold Kushner author of *When Bad Things Happen to Good People* (2004;) and *Overcoming Life's Disappointments (2007),* explains what is meant by carrying around emotional baggage that has been weighing one down:

> When I would counsel a divorcée still seething about her husband's having left her for another woman years ago and having fallen behind on child support payments, she would ask me, "How can you expect me to forgive him after what he's done to me and the children?" I would answer, "I'm not asking you to forgive him because what he did wasn't so terrible; it was terrible. I'm suggesting that you forgive him because he doesn't deserve to

When you grant forgiveness, you are simply re-moving yourself from the justice equation.
—CRAIG ETHEREDGE

To forgive is to set the prisoner free and then discover the prisoner was you.
—ELLIS COSE

When we forgive, we free ourselves from the bitter ties that bind us to the one who hurt us.
—CLAIRE FRAZIER-YZAGUIRRE

have this power to turn you into a bitter, resentful woman. When he left, he gave up the right to inhabit your life and mind to the degree that you're letting him. Your being angry at him doesn't harm him, but it hurts you. It's turning you into someone you don't really want to be. Release that anger, not for his sake—he probably doesn't deserve it—but for your sake, so that the real you can re-emerge."(2007)

University of Wisconsin's Robert Enright (2001), head of the recently established International Forgiveness Institute, reminds people that forgiving does not mean letting the guilty party off the hook. It is not excusing, forgetting or even reconciling—it is giving up resentment to which you are entitled and offering compassionate understanding to someone who may not deserve it. The paradox, he says, is that "by giving this gift to the other, it is the gift-giver who becomes psychologically healed."

Benefits of forgiveness. "Holding on to hurts and nursing grudges wears you down physically and emotionally," says Stanford University psychologist Fred Luskin (2007), author of *Forgive for Love*. Luskin, director of the Stanford Forgiveness Project, applied his method to help families in Northern Ireland recover emotionally from the murder of loved ones, some of whom had been killed more than 20 years earlier. Rather than agonizing over the past, his subjects were able to enjoy the present. Feelings of hurt, measured by using psychological tests, had fallen more than half. They were also less likely to feel depressed and angry. Their health also improved. On average, they saw stress-related symptoms like backaches and stomach pain dip by almost 35 percent.

To heal, some people take fate's raw material and transform it. Judy Keane, 54, whose husband of 31 years, Richard, was killed at the World Trade Center, felt she had to move forward. Despite her anguish, she did not want to become more rigid and hostile. Keane responded by starting a foundation in her husband's name that will open a sports center in her Connecticut town. Her goal is to offer programs built on Richard's philosophy for coaching kids: in true sports, kids learn how to deal with life.

Forgiveness is truly a journey of hard work and an exercise in personal power. Lewis Smedes (2007) reminds us that "you will know that forgiveness has begun when you recall those who hurt you and feel the power to wish them well." If this is difficult for you to imagine, Robert Enright (2001), in his insightful book, *Forgiveness Is a Choice*, says, "forgiveness is feeling free of negative energy." If you remain angry, the hostility will reverberate through all your relationships. When we're angry, we cannot help but inflict pain on children, spouses, close friends, and coworkers.

We will probably never understand why we were hurt. But forgiving is not having to understand. Understanding may come later, in fragments, an insight here and a glimpse there, after forgiving. But we are asking too much if we want to understand everything at the beginning.
—LEWIS SMEDES

Human pain does not let go of its grip at one point in time. Rather it works its way out of our consciousness over time. There is a season of sadness, a season of anger, a season of tranquility, and a season of hope.
—ROBERT VENINGA, *GIFT OF HOPE: HOW TO SURVIVE OUR TRAGEDIES*

CONSIDER THIS

THE HEALING PROCESS

While a variety of strategies can be used in the forgiveness process, at least some of these important stages will be involved:
- Exploring the anger you have
- Deciding to forgive
- Working on forgiveness
- Discovery and release, whereby one learns a great deal about oneself, the other person, and relationships.

Adapted from Enright (2001); Cose (2005).

Consider the words of columnist Berta Sisemore (2009):

> Forgiveness is truly a gift to ourselves. Holding onto resentment and thoughts of revenge keeps us bound to the offense committed against us, whereas forgiveness allows us to live freer and grants one greater peace of mind.

Chapter Review

We would all agree that emotions are a crucial part of being human. Indeed, we experience life's pains and pleasures through our emotions.

- **Emotions** are feelings that are experienced, with at least four common characteristics: physiological or internal changes, behavioral expressions, cognitive interpretations, and motivational tendencies.
- Although authorities do not always agree on the exact number of basic emotions, there appear to be both primary and mixed emotions. Primary and mixed emotions suggest that many feelings need to be described in more than a single term.
- Generally, our emotions begin to have negative effects when they are viewed as being excessive in intensity and duration. When mild, emotions can be facilitative—they increase our functioning. When emotions are intense, or sustained, they are debilitative—they disrupt our overall functioning.
- Some emotions cause us more difficulty than others. Some of these are fear, anxiety, anger, guilt, grief, and love.
- Although there are gender differences with respect to several potential causes of anger, both males and females report physical and verbal aggression as the most anger-provoking behaviors they could encounter.
- **Anger** most often begins with a loss or the threat of one, such as: loss of self-esteem, loss of face, threat of physical harm or violence, loss of valued possessions, skills, or abilities, loss of a valued role, or loss of valued relationships.
- Four psychological reactions to anger are: 1) seeing yourself as a victim, 2) feeling discounted or ignored, 3) feeling powerless, and 4) looking for justice and revenge.
- Three characteristics of anger are: 1) anger is neither right nor wrong, 2) anger can be released in a right or wrong way, and 3) you are vulnerable when angry.
- When we feel **guilt**, it is about something we did or did not do. When we feel **shame**, it's about who we are as a person.
- The **grief process** consists of: 1) freeing ourselves emotionally from the loss, 2) readjusting to life after this loss, 3) resuming ordinary activities and forming new relationships. There are individual patterns of grieving.
- In **mourning**, we use our memory to recall the deceased and what was great about them and then try to move on in our lives. In helping others you often find people who need to grieve. The **Ring Theory** often helps by buffering the main griever.
- With modeling and messages from our parents, society, and our peers, it is not surprising that we grow up confused about what to do with our feelings.
- We are both emotional and rational beings, and we need an intelligent balance of the two. **Emotional intelligence** consists of the ability to monitor, access, express, and regulate one's own emotions; the capacity to identify, interpret, and understand others' emotions; and the ability to use this information to guide one's thinking and actions.
- Because over control poses our biggest problem in the expression of emotions, there are two common ways we deny our emotions—repression and suppression.
- **Repression** is a defense mechanism consisting of the exclusion of painful, unwanted, or dangerous thoughts and impulses from the conscious mind. **Suppression** is a defense mechanism by which people are conscious of their emotions, but deliberately control rather than express them.
- It is helpful to remember the following suggestions when deciding when and how to express your emotions: Listen to your body, personalize your feelings, identify your feelings, own your feelings, and decide what you will do with your feelings.

- Different cultures have different **display rules**—norms about when, where, and how much we should show emotions. These differences, if not understood, can lead to communication problems.
- Several long-term, positive benefits can be derived from learning to express emotions: You will develop positive feelings about yourself, your relationships will grow stronger, and pressure is relieved.
- Sometimes in the process of expressing and dealing with our feelings, we may even go through a healing process, known as **forgiveness**. Forgiveness is something you do for yourself, for your own happiness, health and well-being.
- **Social Emotional Learning (SEL)** comprises the skills we use to recognize and manage our own emotions and being able to recognize emotions in others. This concept arose out of research about emotional intelligence. Methods for improving SEL emphasize learning personal and social skills and setting personal goals. **Happiness** is an emotion that gives you a sense that life is good—a state of well-being that outlasts yesterday's moment of elation, today's buoyant mood, or tomorrow's feeling of sadness.(David Myers, Pursuit of Happiness)
- The competition for status and esteem represents one reason behind peer cyberbullying. Friends, or former friends, are particularly likely to find themselves in situations in which they are vying for the same school, club, and/or sport positions and social connections,

As we go through adulthood, we have the opportunity to experiment with a full range of behaviors and full range of emotions. Hopefully, we learn to express our emotions in constructive ways and to control those emotions and expressions that might be destructive to ourselves and others.

Test Review Questions: Learning Outcomes

1. What are emotions? Explain their four characteristics.
2. Describe how cognitive appraisals can be a part of an emotional experience.
3. What are the eight primary emotions? What is the difference in primary and mixed emotions?
4. Differentiate between mild (facilitative) and intense (debilitative) emotions. When do our emotions begin to have negative effects?
5. What is the difference in fear and anxiety? Define preparation anxiety and neurotic anxiety.
6. Anger most often begins with what kinds of losses or threats?
7. What are the four psychological reactions to anger? What are the three characteristics of anger? What are at least six do's and don'ts to remember in the expression of anger?
8. Explain the difference between guilt and shame.
9. What seems to be three causes of aggression in our society?
10. Discuss the common reactions people have in coping with a loss.
11. Define and discuss the mourning process. What is the Ring Theory?
12. Compare and contrast the importance of intellectual IQ and emotional intelligence.
13. Name and define the two common ways we deny our emotions.
14. What is the difference between repression and suppression?
15. List and discuss the five guidelines for dealing with your emotions. What is the shorthand technique for dealing with emotions?
16. Define the term "cultural display rules" and be able to give examples of some ways these rules are expressed in different cultures.

17. Discuss the three common benefits of learning to express emotions.
18. Why do we need to consider going through a forgiveness process?
19. What important stages are involved in the forgiveness process?
20. Identify the four questions to ask yourself when attempting to shift your anger from an emotional level to an intellectual level.
21. What is SEL?
22. Is happiness an emotion? Why?
23. What is awe and how can it affect your life? What things do you like to do to produce awe in your life?

Key Terms

Aggression
Anger
Annoyance
Anxiety
Awe
Cyberbullying
Cyberpsychology
Cultural Display Rules
Debilitative Emotions
Delight
Distress
Emotional Debt
Emotional Intelligence
Emotions

Empathy
Facilitative Emotions
Fear
Forgiveness
Good Grief
Grief and Bereavement
Grief Work
Guilt
Happiness
Hate
Hostility
Intense Emotions
Love
Mild Emotions

Mixed Emotions
Moods
Neurotic Anxiety
Preparation Anxiety
Primary Emotions
Rage
Repression
Resentment
Ring Theory
Social Emotional Learning (SEL)
Shame
Suppression

Reflections: Critical Thinking

1. Why do our emotions often color our point of view and affect our opinions?
2. How were you taught to express and deal with your emotions?
3. Do you believe that feelings follow a predictable pattern when we suffer a loss? If so, explain the process for you.
4. Of the problem emotions discussed, which one(s) present the greatest problem for you?
5. How do you deal with guilt and shame in your life?
6. When someone close to you dies, what do you want others to do for you?
7. Which part of the Shorthand Technique for expressing your feelings will be the most difficult for you? Why?
8. Which one of the four psychological reactions to anger is the most difficult for you to deal with?
9. What can be done to decrease aggression in our society?
10. Do you believe there is really emotional intelligence?
11. Discuss any "cultural display rules" you have experienced.

12. How do you deal with forgiveness in your life?

13. How do we measure social and emotional learning? Why is it important?

14. What is authentic happiness?

15. Do you agree that violence against women is a man's issue?

16. Why is cyberbullying so prevalent?

17. Explain why you would use the Ring Theory.

18. Why should you pursue experiencing awe? Is this something everyone can do?

Web Resources and Web Activities

GAMES

http://rippleeffects.com/

http://thesocialexpress.com/

Games for the kid in all of us to practice and learn social emotional skills. Explore the resources. They are easy to read and you might find these games can help you too… Take a test drive and walk through each program.

https://www.youtube.com/watch?v=T516vKoP06cInside out sneak peek

Take a personality test with the *Inside Out* cast.

ACTIVITIES:

www.authentichappiness.sas.upenn.edu/testcenter.aspx

The PANAS Questionnaire measures positive and negative effect(s) of different feelings and emotions. The Transgression Motivations Questionnaire measures forgiveness.

http://www.apa.org/topics

Explores various topics on emotions and feelings.

http://www.schooltools.info/resources-1/2016/7/8/how-do-we-measure-social-and-emotional-learning

How do we measure social and emotional learning?

http://www.apa.org/topics/anger/control.aspx

Controlling anger before it controls you

Awe

http://www.varietiescorpus.com/learn

Emotional honesty

New York Times *Teaching Men to Be Emotionally Honest* By ANDREW REINER APRIL 4, 2016

http://www.eiconsortium.org/reports/technical_report.html

A report issued for research on Emotional Intelligence in Organizations.

http://blog.online.saintleo.edu/degree-programs/10-useful-ted-talks-for-online-psychology-degree-students

Depression: the secrets we share.

VIDEOS

https://www.youtube.com/watch?v=KTvSfeCRxe8

Violence against women: It's a men's issue, by Jackson Katz.

https://www.youtube.com/watch?v=qsEPUth4ovU

Anger, Rage & Relationships, an interview with Sue Parker Hall.

https://www.youtube.com/watch?v=juET61B1P98

The Adventure of Grief: Dr. Geoff Warburton.

https://youtu.be/PBzEwf1k59Y

There is power in grieving intentionally and purposefully. Telling her own story of loss, Elaine Mansfield explains the use of ritual as a tool for empowerment for life's most challenging times

https://www.youtube.com/watch?v=jz1g1SpD9Zo

Awe-https://www.youtube.com/ShotsOfAwe

Empathy.

http://movies.disney.com/inside-out

Fun Disney movie about emotions: *Inside Out*.

https://www.youtube.com/watch?v=HTfYv3IEOqM

Daniel Goleman: "Social Intelligence." |

https://www.youtube.com/watch?v=esPRsT-lmw8

The most important lesson from 83,000 brain scans by Daniel Amen.

https://www.youtube.com/watch?v=3aYWvujaT6M

Falling in Love Is the Easy Part by Mandy Len Catron, TED Talks.

https://www.youtube.com/watch?v=ecb6ExBaW80

Brené Brown on Boundaries, Empathy and Compassion.

http://www.ted.com/talks/brene_brown_listening_to_shame

Listening to shame by Brené Brown.

https://www.youtube.com/watch?v=H_8y0WLm78U

Monica Lewinsky: The price of shame. She takes a look at our "culture of humiliation and why it leads to bullying.

http://www.helpguide.org/articles/depression/dealing-with-depression.htm

Overcoming depression.

https://www.youtube.com/watch?v=apbSsILLh28

What Really Matters at the End of Life by BJ Miller, TED Talks.

http://tedxtalks.ted.com/video/Hacking-the-adolescent-brain--2;search%3Acyberbullying

Hacking the adolescent brain to stop cyberbullying byt Trisha Prabhu, TEDxNaperville.

http://tedxtalks.ted.com/video/Beat-bullying-why-young-people;search%3Abullying

Beat bullying; why young people hold the key, by Alex Holmes.

https://www.youtube.com/watch?v=-FyVetL1MEw

Be The Warrior Not The Worrier: Fighting Anxiety and Fear by Angela Ceberano, TEDxBedminster

http://tedxtalks.ted.com/video/The-Upsides-of-Anger-Dan-Moshav;search%3Aanger%20management

Dan Moshavi explores the upsides of an often misunderstood emotion: Anger. Dan Moshavi is a Professor of Management in the Barowsky School of Business at Dominican University of California.

https://www.youtube.com/watch?v=KTvSfeCRxe8

Violence against women – it's a men's issue by Jackson Katz.

https://www.youtube.com/watch?v=PTlmho_RovY

Killing Us Softly 4:Image of women

https://www.youtube.com/watch?v=WLMJHdySgE8

Violence - a family tradition by Robbyn Peters Bennett at TEDxBellingham, November 23, 2013. Robbyn Peters Bennett, LMHC, CMHS, is a psychotherapist, educator, and child advocate who specializes in the treatment of trauma-related mental health problems resulting from the effects of early childhood stress, abuse, and neglect.

Am I Emotionally Intelligent?

PURPOSE

To get a sense of your emotional intelligence.

INSTRUCTIONS

Respond by placing a check mark (✔) next to each of the items below, using the following scale:

1 = very much unlike me   2 = unlike me   3 = neutral   4 = like me   5 = very much like me

	1	2	3	4	5

Emotional Self-Awareness

1. I am good at recognizing my emotions.
2. I am good at understanding the causes of my feelings.
3. I am good at separating my feelings from my actions.

Managing Emotions

4. I am good at tolerating frustration.
5. I am good at managing my anger.
6. I have positive feelings about myself.
7. I am good at coping with stress.
8. My emotions don't interfere with my ability to focus and accomplish my goals.
9. I have good self-control and am not impulsive.

Reading Emotions

10. I am good at taking the perspectives of others (such as students and parents).
11. I show empathy and sensitivity to others' feelings.
12. I am good at listening to what other people say.

Handling Relationships

13. I am good at analyzing and understanding relationships.

14. I am good at solving problems in relationships.   _____ _____ _____ _____ _____
15. I am assertive (rather than passive, manipulative, or
    aggressive) in relationships.   _____ _____ _____ _____ _____
16. I have one or more close friendships   .   _____ _____ _____ _____ _____
17. I am good at sharing and cooperating.   _____ _____ _____ _____ _____

SCORING AND INTERPRETATION

Add up your scores for all 17 items. My total emotional intelligence score is _____.

If you scored 75–85, you probably are very emotionally intelligent, someone who is emotionally self-aware, manages emotions effectively, knows how to read emotions, and has positive relationships with others. **If you scored 65–74,** you probably have good emotional intelligence but there probably are some areas on which you still need to work. Look at the items on which you scored 3 or below to see where you need to improve. **If you scored 45–64,** you likely have average emotional intelligence. Give some serious thought to working on your emotional life. Examine your emotional weaknesses and strive to improve them. **If you scored 44 or below,** you likely have below-average emotional intelligence. You might contact the counseling service at your college for some recommendations.

DISCUSSION

1. Do you agree or disagree with your score and the interpretation? Why or why not?

2. What, if anything, do you think you need to do to improve your emotional intelligence?

Adapted from John Santrock, 2006, Human Adjustment. New York: The McGraw-Hill Company.

Name _____ Date _____

Emotional Expressivity Scale

PURPOSE

To assess your degree of emotional expression.

INSTRUCTIONS

Using the following scale, place the number on the line that best describes your agreement with the following statements:

5 = Strongly Agree   4 = Agree   3 = Neither Agree nor Disagree   2 = Disagree   1 = Strongly Disagree

_____ 1. I think of myself as emotionally expressive.
_____ 2. People think of me as an unemotional person.*
_____ 3. I keep my feelings to myself.*
_____ 4. I am often considered indifferent by others.*
_____ 5. People can read my emotions.
_____ 6. I display my emotions to other people.
_____ 7. I don't like to let other people see how I am feeling.*
_____ 8. I am able to cry in front of other people.
_____ 9. Even if I am feeling very emotional, I don't let others see my feelings.*
_____ 10. Other people aren't easily able to observe what I am feeling.*
_____ 11. I am not very emotionally expressive.*
_____ 12. Even when I am experiencing strong feelings, I don't express them outwardly.*
_____ 13. I cannot hide the way I am feeling.
_____ 14. Other people believe me to be very emotional.
_____ 15. I don't express my emotions to other people.*
_____ 16. The way I feel is different from how others think I feel.*
_____ 17. I hold my feelings in.*

SCORING

Recode these statements:* 2, 3, 4, 7, 9, 10, 11, 12, 15, 16, and 17 with the following:

$$5 = 1 \qquad 4 = 2 \qquad 3 = 3 \qquad 2 = 4 \qquad 1 = 5$$

After you recode the negative items, sum all the scores together. **My Score:** _____

Range of Emotional Expressivity = 17–85 (17 is the lowest expression of emotions and 85 is the highest expression of emotions).

DISCUSSION

1. Do you agree with your results? Why or why not?

2. What do you think you need to do to be more emotionally expressive?

Name _____ Date _____

Identifying Feelings

PURPOSE

To determine how you deal with various feelings and emotions.

INSTRUCTIONS

Complete the "feelings" survey below by circling the number that expresses how well you deal with each feeling listed.

1. Can express easily and completely in any situation
2. Can express most of the time
3. Can express some of the time—with difficulty
4. Can express rarely—with reservation
5. Cannot express this emotion

Caring	1 2 3 4 5	Love	1 2 3 4 5
Concern	1 2 3 4 5	Sadness	1 2 3 4 5
Depression	1 2 3 4 5	Fear	1 2 3 4 5
Anger	1 2 3 4 5	Tension	1 2 3 4 5
Disappointment	1 2 3 4 5	Hurt	1 2 3 4 5
Excitement	1 2 3 4 5	Pride	1 2 3 4 5

Complete the sentences below:

1. I very much care about _____

2. The thing that depresses me most frequently is _____

3. I feel tense when _____

4. The thing that hurts me most is _____

5. I am excited about _____

6. I take pride in _____

7. I am disappointed with _____

8. The thing that frightens me most is _____

9. I get angry when _____

10. I am concerned about _____

11. I feel sad when _____

12. Love is a feeling _____

DISCUSSION

1. Is there a feeling that you absolutely cannot deal with? If so, what?

2. Which feeling do you think you deal with most successfully? Why?

3. How important are feelings to you in your interactions with others?

4. How can you learn to express your emotions in a positive way?

How I Express My Feelings

Purpose

To identify how you personally express a variety of emotions/feelings.

Instructions

Being as spontaneous as possible, complete the following sentences:

1. When I'm angry, I express it by . . .
2. When I'm worried, I express it by . . .
3. When I'm sad, I express it by . . .
4. When I'm happy, I express it by . . .
5. When I feel like a failure, I express it by . . .
6. When I'm afraid, I express it by . . .
7. When I feel successful, I express it by . . .
8. When I feel affectionate, I express it by . . .
9. When I feel guilty, I express it by . . .
10. When I feel lonely, I express it by . . .
11. When I feel hurt, I express it by . . .
12. When I feel rejected, I express it by . . .

Discussion

1. Which of these feelings would you like to be able to express in a different manner?

2. Explain what steps you would take to learn how to express the feelings identified in Question 1.

3. Which of these feelings are the most difficult for you to express?

4. Which of these feelings are the easiest for you to express? Why?

Anger Inventory

PURPOSE

To learn how you confront and/or handle your anger.

INSTRUCTIONS

Complete these statements as quickly as you can. Circle T for True, F for False. Your first response is usually going to be the best.

1. I concern myself with others' opinions of me more than I like to admit.	T	F
2. It is not unusual for me to have a restless feeling on the inside.	T	F
3. I have had relationships with others that could be described as stormy or unstable.	T	F
4. It seems that I wind up helping others more than they help me.	T	F
5. I sometimes wonder how much my friends or family members accept me.	T	F
6. At times I seem to have an unusual amount of guilt even though it seems unnecessary.	T	F
7. At times I prefer to get away rather than to be around people.	T	F
8. I realize that I do not like to admit to myself how angry I feel.	T	F
9. Sometimes I use humor to avoid facing my feelings or to keep others from knowing how I really feel.	T	F
10. I have a problem of thinking too many critical thoughts.	T	F
11. Sometimes I can use sarcasm in a very biting way.	T	F
12. I have known moments of great tension and stress.	T	F
13. When I feel angry, I sometimes find myself doing things I know are wrong.	T	F
14. I like having times when no one knows what I am doing.	T	F
15. I usually do not tell people when I feel hurt.	T	F
16. At times I wish I had more friends.	T	F
17. I find myself having more bodily aches and pains.	T	F
18. I have had trouble in the past in relating with members of the opposite sex.	T	F
19. Criticism bothers me a great deal.	T	F
20. I desire acceptance by others but fear rejection.	T	F
21. I worry a lot about my relationships with others.	T	F
22. I believe I am somewhat socially withdrawn.	T	F
23. I believe I am overly sensitive to rejection.	T	F
24. I find myself preoccupied with my personal goals for success.	T	F
25. I often have felt inferior to others.	T	F
26. There are times when I like to convince myself that I am superior to others.	T	F
27. Even though I do not like it, I sometimes am phony in social settings.	T	F
28. I do not seem to have the emotional support I would like from my family or friends.	T	F

29. I would like to tell people exactly what I think.   T   F

30. My concentration sometimes seems poor.   T   F

31. I have had sleep patterns that do not seem normal.   T   F

32. I worry about financial matters.   T   F

33. There are times when I feel inadequate in the way I handle personal relationships.   T   F

34. My conscience bothers me about things I have done in the past.   T   F

35. Sometimes it seems that my religious life is more of a burden than a help.   T   F

36. There are times when I would like to run away from home.   T   F

37. I have had too many quarrels or disagreements with members of my family.   T   F

38. I have been disillusioned with love.   T   F

39. Sometimes I have difficulty controlling my weight, whether gaining or losing too much.   T   F

40. At times I feel that life owes me more than it has given me.   T   F

41. I have had trouble controlling my sexual urges.   T   F

42. To be honest, I prefer to find someone to blame my problems on.   T   F

43. My greatest struggles are within myself.   T   F

44. Other people find more fault with me than they really should.   T   F

45. Many of the nice things I do are done out of a sense of obligation.   T   F

46. Many mornings I wake up not feeling refreshed.   T   F

47. I find myself saying things sometimes that I should not have said.   T   F

48. It is not unusual for me to forget someone's name after I have just met him/her.   T   F

49. It is difficult for me to motivate myself to do things that do not have to be done.   T   F

50. My decisions are often governed by my feelings.   T   F

51. When something irritates me, I find it hard to get calmed down quickly.   T   F

52. I would rather watch a good sporting event than spend a quiet evening at home.   T   F

53. I am hesitant for people to give me suggestions.   T   F

54. I tend to speak out when someone wants to know my opinions.   T   F

55. I would rather entertain guests in my own home than be entertained by them.   T   F

56. When people are being unreasonable, I usually take a strong dislike to them.   T   F

57. I am a fairly strict person, liking things to be done in a predictable way.   T   F

58. I consider myself to be possessive in my personal relationships.   T   F

59. Sometimes I could be described as moody.   T   F

60. People who know me well would say I am stubborn.   T   F

Total number of T's _____ + **Total number of F's** _____ = **Total number** _____

SCORING AND EVALUATION

Go back and count the number of "Ts" you circled. This will tell you how great your need is to confront your anger. For example:

1. **Less than 15:** You probably have pretty good control over your anger (or else you were using a lot of denial). Look back over the questions you responded to with a "T" and you will be able to focus on those items as areas for further improvement.
2. **Between 15 and 30:** You are probably in the normal range. You are willing to admit that you have anger within you and you know you have plenty of room to grow. You will need to be careful as you learn to handle your anger in more effective ways.
3. **Between 31 and 40:** You have probably experienced more than your share of problems. Chances are you have had more dissatisfying moments than you would like to admit.
4. **Greater than 41:** You probably need to work diligently at keeping your anger under control.

DISCUSSION

1. Do you agree with the description of how you confront your anger? Why or why not?

2. As you analyze your results, what do you think you need to do to confront and/or handle your anger?

Do Women Express More Emotions than Men?

PURPOSE

Is the cultural stereotype of the unexpressive male and the more expressive female true?

INSTRUCTIONS

Divide the class between the males and the females, with the males on one side, and the females on the other.

Beginning with one of the following statements, have one gender give their views on the following statements, and then have the other gender respond until all statements have been addressed.

1. Is it true that women are more likely than men to express positive emotions like love, liking, joy, and contentment and that women have a hard time expressing anger? Why or why not?

2. Is it true that women are more likely than men to express feelings of vulnerability like fear, sadness, loneliness, and embarrassment and that men have difficulty expressing sadness? Why or why not?

3. Is it true that men rarely express positive emotions and feelings of vulnerability, especially to their male friends, although they may be more expressive to the woman or man they love? Why or why not?

4. Is it true that men are less bashful about revealing their strengths? Why or why not?

5. Is it true that while men experience emotions much like women, they may tend to mask their emotional inclinations? Why or why not?

6. Is it true that men often express their feelings through actions and activities rather than words? Why or why not?

7. Is it true that women are better able to "pick up" (read) the emotions of others? Why or why not?

8. Is it true that men tend to be better than women at returning to normal after experiencing distressing emotions? Why or why not?

9. What is a "Real Man"? Give your definition.

10. Discuss violence in families and against women. What can be done to help men control anger against women?

POST-ACTIVITY DISCUSSION QUESTIONS:

1. Is there a difference in the way men and women express emotions? If so, how?

2. Is it possible that the real difference in the expression of emotions between men and women is just an individual personality difference?

3. What do you plan to teach your male children and your female children about the expression of emotions?

Develop a "Wellness Toolbox" to Deal with Mental Health

DEVELOPING A WELLNESS TOOLBOX | MENTALHEALTHRECOVERY

mentalhealthrecovery.com/info-center/developing-a-wellness-toolbox/

Come up with a list of things that you can do for a quick mood boost. The more "tools" for coping with depression, the better. Try to implement a few of these ideas each day, even if you're feeling good.

- Spend some time in nature
- List what you like about yourself
- Read a good book
- Watch a funny movie or TV show
- Take a long, hot bath
- Take care of a few small tasks
- Play with a pet
- Talk to friends or family face-to-face
- Listen to music
- Do something spontaneous

Other information you might find interesting and helpful:

According to the latest statistics from the National Alliance on Mental Illness, 43.8 million Americans, or 18.5% of the national population, experience mental illness every year. Mental illness is a broad term defined by the Mayo Clinic as any disorder that affects one's mood, thinking, or behavior. When mental illness influences family life, work, education, and other aspects day-to-day life, the condition is known as a psychiatric disability.

- 43.8 MILLION AMERICANS, OR 18.5% OF THE NATIONAL POPULATION, EXPERIENCE MENTAL ILLNESS EVERY YEAR.

A recent report from Johns Hopkins University notes that psychiatric disabilities are not caused by singular life events; rather, they are persistent conditions that may have a significant, lifelong impact. Those diagnosed with a psychiatric disability may mitigate the effects of their condition with medication and/or ongoing psychotherapy. Even with treatment though, many psychiatric disabilities will persist in some form.

- College students with psychiatric disabilities face unique educational challenges. Dedicated mental health counselors and disability coordinators are available on most campuses, and students can typically seek medical attention. Many students, however, do not know how to get help for their problems. (http://www.bestcolleges.com/resources/college-planning-with-psychiatric-disabilities)Suicide Facts at a Glance 2015 (n.d.). Retrieved October 23, 2015, from http://www.cdc.gov/violenceprevention/pdf/

suicide-datasheet-a.pdf - See more at: https://www.nami.org/Learn-More/Mental-Health-By-the-Numbers#sthash.yCoO1hWO.dpuf

NAMI-Want-to-know-how-to-help-a-friend.pdf at https://www.nami.org/NAMI/media/NAMI-Media/Infographics/NAMI-Want-to-know-how-to-help-a-friend.pdf

KNOW THE 10 COMMON WARNING SIGNS

1. Feeling very sad or withdrawn for more than two weeks
2. Seriously trying to harm or kill oneself or making plans to do so
3. Severe out-of-control, risk-taking behaviors
4. Sudden overwhelming fear for no reason
5. Not eating, throwing up or using laxatives to lose weight; significant weight loss or weight gain
6. Seeing, hearing or believing things that are not real
7. Repeatedly using drugs or alcohol
8. Drastic changes in mood, behavior, personality or sleeping habits
9. Extreme difficulty in concentrating or staying still
10. Intense worries or fears that get in the way of daily activities.

ADDITIONAL RESOURCES

- National Institute of Mental Health (NIMH): The leading federal agency in the field of mental health research, NIMH is one of 27 branches of the National Institutes of Health. The NIMH website is a compendium of news, published reports, academic journals, data tables, and other academic resources.
- National Alliance on Mental Illness (NAMI): Founded in 1979, NAMI is the nation's largest grassroots organization in the country that supports people living with mental illness. NAMI maintains a toll-free hotline to provide advice and medical referrals. Representatives from the organization also work closely with lawmakers nationwide to ensure fair and equal protection for people with mental health issues.
- Treatment Advocacy Center (TAC): This nonprofit organization has worked to promote mental health treatment and fight social stigma related to mentally ill individuals for nearly 20 years. TAC also collaborates with researchers to publish the latest developments in medication and treatment for mental illnesses.
- MentalHealth.gov: This website maintained by the U.S. Department of Health and Human Services maintains an up-to-date listing of toll-free hotlines accessible to people living with mental illness.
- Shining a Light on Mental Illness: an Invisible Disability: This blog post from the World Bank explores various issues faced by people living with mental illness. Links to other related blogs and websites are included.

Name _____ Date _____

Learning to Forgive

This activity is to do alone and it is at your own pace.

WHY IT WORKS

Forgiveness is a long and often-challenging process. These steps may help along the way by providing concrete guidelines. Specifically, they may help you: to narrow and understand whom to forgive; to name and describe your pain; to understand the difference between forgiving and excusing or reconciling; and by thinking about the person who has caused you pain in a novel way, you may begin to feel some compassion for him or her, facilitating forgiveness and reducing the ill will you hold toward this person. (These steps also attune you to residual pain from your experience, and encourage you to find meaning and some positivity in it. You may want to get a counselor or therapist to help you to forgive someone who deeply harmed you—particularly as a young person or child. The difference between forgiveness and reconciliation is very, very important. In our culture, we often try very hard to be "good," hoping that will right past pains when just realizing our own feelings are valid and understandable given the circumstances is equally as important in the process. In addition, simply addressing the issue honestly and openly with the person who harmed you may, in fact, cause them pain, particularly if they have been living in denial.)

We suggest that you move through the steps below based on what works for you.

1. Make a list of people who have hurt you deeply enough to warrant the effort to forgive. You can do this by asking yourself, on a 1-to-10 scale, How much pain do I have regarding the way this person treated me?, with 1 involving the least pain (but still significant enough to justify the time to forgive) and 10 involving the most pain. Then, order the people on this list from least painful to most painful. Start with the person lowest on this hierarchy (least painful).

2. Next to the person's name consider one offense by the first person on your list. Ask yourself: How has this person's offense negatively impacted my life?

   Reflect on the psychological and physical harm it may have caused. Consider how your views of humanity and trust of others may have changed as a result of this offense. Recognize that what happened was not okay, and allow yourself to feel any negative emotions that come up.

3. When you're ready, make a decision to forgive. Deciding to forgive involves coming to terms with what you will be doing as you forgive—extending an act of mercy toward the person who has hurt you. When we offer this mercy, we deliberately try to *reduce* resentment (persistent ill will) toward this person and, instead, offer them kindness, respect, generosity, or even love.

   It is important to emphasize that forgiveness does not involve excusing the person's actions, forgetting what happened, or tossing justice aside. Justice and forgiveness can be practiced together.

   Another important caveat: To forgive is not the same as to reconcile. Reconciliation is a negotiation strategy in which two or more people come together again in mutual trust. You may not choose to reconcile with the person you are forgiving.

4. Start with cognitive exercises. Ask yourself these questions about the person who has hurt you: What was life like for this person while growing up? What wounds did they suffer from others that could have made them more likely to hurt you? What kinds of extra pressures or stresses were in this person's life at the time he or she offended you? These questions are not meant to excuse or condone, but rather to better understand the other person's areas of pain, those areas that make them vulnerable and human. Understanding why people commit destructive acts can also help us find more effective ways of preventing further destructive acts from occurring in the future.

5. Be aware of any little movement of your heart through which you begin to feel even slight compassion for the person who offended you. This person may have been confused, mistaken, and misguided. They may deeply regret their actions. As you think about this person, notice if you start to feel softer emotions toward them.

6. Try to consciously bear the pain that they caused you so that you do not end up throwing that pain back onto the one who offended you, or even toward unsuspecting others, such as loved ones who were not the ones who wounded you in the first place. When we are emotionally wounded, we tend to displace our pain onto others. Please be aware of this so that you are not perpetuating a legacy of anger and injuries.

7. Think of a gift of some kind that you can offer to the person you are trying to forgive. Forgiveness is an act of mercy—you are extending mercy toward someone who may not have been merciful toward you. This could be through a smile, a returned phone call, or a good word about him or her to others. Always consider your own safety first when extending kindness and goodwill toward this person. If interacting with this person could put you in danger, find another way to express your feelings, such as by writing in a journal or engaging in a practice such as compassion meditation.

8. Finally, try to find meaning and purpose in what you have experienced. For example, as people suffer from the injustices of others, they often realize that they themselves become more sensitive to others' pain. This, in turn, can give them a sense of purpose toward helping those who are hurting. It may also motivate them to work toward preventing future injustices of a similar kind.

Once you complete the forgiveness process with one person on your list, select the next person in line and move up that list until you are forgiving the person who hurt you the most.

Adapted from Baskin, T.W., & Enright, R. D. (2004). Intervention studies on forgiveness: A meta-analysis. *Journal of Counseling and Development, 82*, 79-90.

Name _____ Date _____

Dealing with Emotions

LEARNING JOURNAL

Select the statement below that best defines your feelings about the personal value or meaning gained from this chapter and respond below the dotted line.

I learned that I . . .   I was surprised that I . . .

I realized that I . . .   I was pleased that I . . .

I discovered that I . . .   I was displeased that I . . .

. . . .

Chapter 5
Interpersonal Communication

© Liderina/Shutterstock.com

Communication is the lifeblood of every relationship. When open, clear, sensitive communication takes place, the relationship is nurtured. When communication is guarded, hostile, or ineffective, the relationship falters. When the communication flow is largely obstructed, the relationship quickly deteriorates and ultimately dies. Where communication skills are lacking, there is so much lost love—between spouses, lovers, friends, parents, and children. For satisfying relationships, it is essential to discover methods that will help us to at least partially bridge the interpersonal gaps that separate us from others. —Robert Bolton, People Skills

Think About This...

- Friends say, "We can't communicate anymore. We aren't even on the same wavelength."
- Kids say, "I can't talk to my parents. They just don't understand me."
- Parents say, "I can't talk to my kids. They won't even listen to me."
- Marriage partners say, "We can't talk to each other. We just don't have anything meaningful to talk about."
- Students say, "We can't discuss our lack of understanding with Mr. Jones. He thinks he has explained the chapter perfectly well. There is no use in us trying to talk to him."
- An employer learns that her secretary is leaving and just can't believe she didn't tell him she was so unhappy. She replies, "I've tried to many times in the past, but we just can't communicate."
- You think, "Every time I think we are having a romantic dinner my partner keeps glancing at the cellphone like someone's call is more important than me. I should be the one to focus on!"

H ave you ever said to another person, "We just can't communicate?" Has another person ever said that to you? Actually, you were both communicating at some level, but you were not connecting. What, then, is communication?

Mary Kassian (2014) indicates that the Greek word for communication is *koinonia*, which means sharing; making known; exchanging thoughts, feelings, and information; joining together; having fellowship with; forming a connecting link; and sharing. How important is this?

Because communication underlies all relationships, and the process of communication is such a complex topic, we want to begin by providing some organizational structure for our discussion. The first half of the chapter deals with the communication process, including the verbal and nonverbal aspects of communication. The remaining part of the chapter is devoted to learning how to improve our listening and responding skills.

Why Do We Need to Communicate?

Without communication, we, as humans, would not be able to survive. We need to find out about the world we live in; we need to know how to interpret the experiences we have; we need to release tension; we need to find out about other people; we need to know how to get information from others; we need to know how to let others know what is going on inside of us.

Communication has been described as *the process of conveying feelings, attitudes, facts, beliefs, and ideas between individuals, either verbally or non-verbally* in such a way that the message intended is received. On the surface, then, communication appears to be such a simple act. After all, our daily lives are filled with one communication experience after another. When we are with other people who are aware of our presence, it is impossible not to communicate. No matter what we do, we send out messages that say something about ourselves.

This points to the fact that communication is perhaps the most important factor in determining the kinds of relationships we have with others. Furthermore, communication is the way relationships are created, maintained, and destroyed. The ability to send clear messages and to be heard is central to any ongoing relationship—husband and wife, parent and child, employer and employee, friends, siblings. In her classic book *Making Contact,* Virginia Satir (1995) confirms this:

> I see communication as a huge umbrella that covers and affects all that goes on between human beings. Once a human being has arrived on this earth, communication is the largest single factor determining what kinds of relationships he makes with others and what happens to him in the world about him. How he manages his survival, how he develops intimacy;

how productive he is, how he makes sense, how he connects with his own divinity—all are largely dependent on his communication skills.

However, as much communicating as we do, most of us are not all that efficient in performing this simple act. Perhaps, the trite, but true, statement—*keep the communication channels open*—indicates the complexity, rather than simplicity, of communication. Be open, honest, and flexible when you communicate (Hannah et al., 2008).

Nonviolent Communication holds that most conflicts between individuals or groups arise from miscommunication about their human needs, often due to words that aims to induce fear and shame. International peacemaker, mediator, author and founder of the Center for Nonviolent Communication, Dr. Marshall Rosenberg, has shared Nonviolent Communications training with hundreds of thousands of people worldwide through his books, videos and in-person training courses from *The Nonviolent Communication Training Course* (2006).

> *Whether clear or garbled, tumultuous or silent, deliberate or fatally inadvertent, communication is the ground of meeting and the foundation of community. It is, in short, the essential human connection.*
> —ASHLEY MONTAGU

Why Is Communication Difficult?

Do you generally communicate what you mean or intend? Do you generally interpret messages in the same way the sender intended? Think about the following statement: When two people talk, six possible messages can get through:

1. *What you mean to say.*
2. *What you actually say.*
3. *What the other person hears.*
4. *What the other person thinks they hear.*
5. *What the other person says about what you said.*
6. *What you think the other person said about what you said.*

We are all concerned with the ability to communicate real meaning and understanding. Some people think that communication is really the sending and receiving of messages, because both elements must be present for communication to take place. They think that communication originates with the sender, and they believe that the message sent is the one that is received. They expect their listeners to act in accordance with the intentions of their message, and they are often bewildered, hurt, or angry when their listeners do not do so. Add to the mix is the use of technology that promises instant access to everyone and everything, along with real-time response.

As we can see, the fundamental transaction of the message sent and received does not presuppose that communication has occurred. In essence, if I speak and you listen, I may be transmitting information, but that is all. If I speak, however, and you listen, and we understand, then we are communicating effectively. Therefore, effective communication exists between two people when the receiver interprets the sender's message the way the sender intended it (Johnson, 2014).

Effective communication is not just an event, but a process—a process that requires the cooperation and understanding of both parties. What kind of cooperation are we talking about?

What Is Involved in the Communication Process?

In any given situation, there are three commonly accepted parts to the communication process. There is always: 1) *a sender of the message,* 2) *a receiver of the message* and 3) *the content of the message.* The message can be either verbal or nonverbal. Could it be possible that there are really more than three parts to the communication process (De Vito, 2012; Hamilton, 2014)?

Let us look at a simple diagram (see Figure 5.1) of what is involved in a communication transaction. Assume that Jill wants to inform John, her husband, that she would like to remodel the house.

Step one: *The idea.* Here the sender creates an idea or chooses a fact to communicate. Jill says to herself, "I think I'll ask John if we can remodel the house."

Step two: *Encoding.* The sender, in attempting to get his or her message across, forms a mental picture of that message and then organizes and translates this picture into symbols that will make the sender's idea receivable. Symbols involve such things as the selection of words, tone and pitch of voice, nonverbal method, or even types of supportive materials. Jill says, "John, there is something I would like to talk to you about after dinner and when the children are in bed." Later, Jill says, "I would like for us to remodel the house this summer."

Figure 5.1 COMMUNICATION PROCESS

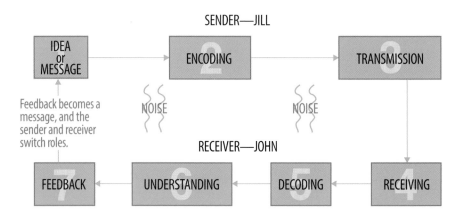

Step three: *Transmission.* This refers to the means by which the encoded communication is to be made, or the channel through which the message must pass from the sender to the receiver. *Communication channels* can be a face-to-face discussion, something in writing, the telephone, or even radio or television. In this instance, Jill chose to talk to John face to face.

Step four: *Receiving.* John can only receive the message if he is attentive to Jill. He must not be reading the newspaper or watching the news.

Step five: *Decoding.* This is done by the receiver. The message that has been transmitted by the sender must be interpreted and translated into meaning. By decoding, the listener has now formed his or her own mental picture of what the sender said. In our example, decoding is not complete until John hears the whole message. The opening comment, "John, there is something I would like to talk to you about," is a good way to get John's attention and help him listen for the whole message. John hears the complete message from Jill.

Step six: *Understanding.* If the receiver has decoded accurately, the mental picture he or she has formed of what the sender said will match. Consequently, the message has been understood correctly. In our example, John does not have any trouble understanding that Jill wants to remodel the house this summer.

There is always the possibility that the listener may have misinterpreted the speaker's words, however, thus forming a totally different mental picture. This would mean that communication did not properly take place. Too often, this type of communication breakdown occurs, resulting in all sorts of problems, ranging from not knowing what to study for an exam to painful relationship situations.

There is a means of preventing, or at least reducing, this type of communication problem by checking and decoding for accuracy and thus improving the quality of your communication. This method is called feedback.

Step seven: *Feedback.* Feedback, the process by which the sender clarifies how his or her message is being received and interpreted, is really the only means for determining whether there is mutual understanding between the sender and receiver.

In our example, John understands Jill's request, but he does not agree. He acts, or gives feedback, by telling Jill that she will have to wait six more months until his promotion and salary increase will become effective. Jill understands John's position and tells him, "Okay, but I am counting on us starting November 1." As you can see from this illustration, as well as in Figure 5.1, *feedback* becomes a message, and the sender and receiver switch roles (Reece & Brandt, 2010).

Noise. Before we leave the communication diagram, it is important to note that noise can occur at every stage of the communication process. **Noise** includes anything that interferes with communication and distorts the impact of the message. *External noise* includes such elements in the physical environment as temperature, a show on television, music on a stereo, loud traffic, children or roommates screaming, or any oth-

> *To keep your character intact you cannot stoop to filthy acts. It makes it easier to stoop the next time.*
> —KATHARINE HEPBURN

er external event or distracting influences. *Internal noise* includes such things as a headache, lack of sleep, daydreaming, preoccupation with other problems, or even a preconceived idea that the message is going to be unimportant or uninteresting (Hamilton, 2014).

One- and Two-Way Communication

As we have just discussed, since there are so many sources of error or distortion in a message, it is wise for both the sender and receiver to provide adequate feedback to one another in an effort to gain understanding and rapport. This completes the process of *two-way communication*, with the *key element being feedback*. One-way communication frequently results in our making inaccurate inferences or assumptions (Reece & Brandt, 2010).

One-way communication is sometimes referred to as *passive listening*, because there is an *absence of verbal feedback*. Examples of one-way communication might be a class which is *strictly* lecture oriented, or a certain person you know who tends to dominate and control conversations, with little interest shown in your ideas or concerns. Even written messages can become avenues for two-way communication. For example, "I'll follow up with a phone call to you within a week to hear your ideas on this proposal," or "Send me your ideas on this proposal, and then we will get together for lunch and discuss our mutual concerns."

Without a doubt, many of the difficulties that arise in communication stem from the fact that we fail to remember that communication is really a two-way process. Open two-way communication facilitates understanding in communication, which in turn helps such things as developing a fulfilling relationship and being able to work together effectively (Johnson, 2008).

After having reviewed the complete communication process, it becomes apparent that "breakdowns" can occur at any step. Sometimes these "breakdowns" are caused by a *communication barrier*—something that stops, blocks, prevents, or hinders. In communication, we may be hindered by a number of barriers that seem to arise from natural human differences and others that are the result of personal habits or attitudes. All or most can be eliminated, changed, or minimized. Review Table 5.1 for a partial listing of barriers to interpersonal communication. Which barriers sometimes prevent you from achieving clear, open communication?

The remaining sections of this chapter will discuss ways to minimize these barriers and reduce communication "breakdowns." We will begin with a discussion of nonverbal communication.

Table 5.1   BARRIERS TO INTERPERSONAL COMMUNICATION

Background and experience	Hidden agendas
Health and physical condition	Stereotyping
Feelings and emotions	Physical environment
Word meaning and usage	Preoccupation—technology?
Listening only for words	Closed mind
Jumping to conclusions	Being self-centered
Making snap judgments	Failure to listen—technology?
Failure to seek clarification	Unclear messages
Disregarding feedback	Highly charged, emotion-laden words
Defensiveness	Talking too fast
Incongruent verbal and nonverbal behavior	Generalizations
Lack of eye contact	Language level

> *If you and I can honestly tell each other who we are, what we think, judge, feel, value, love, honor and esteem, hate, fear, desire, hope for, believe in, then and only then can each of us grow.*
> —JOHN POWELL

Nonverbal Communication

The science or study of nonverbal communication, called *kinesics*, comprises a great deal of the meanings between people. Most experts on the subject of nonverbal communication agree that between 65 and 70 percent of our communication is by nonverbal means. Thus, nonverbal communication is an extremely important medium of communication. Actually, nonverbal communication relates to verbal communication in three ways:

1. Nonverbal communication can reinforce the verbal message.
2. Nonverbal communication can replace the verbal message.
3. Nonverbal communication can contradict the verbal message.

When the nonverbal message contradicts the verbal message, a *double bind* exists. Usually, however, the nonverbal message is more accurate and is believed over the verbal message. How about deception? How is this when you use technology? Do you appear not to listen?

© VICOTOR TORRES/Shutterstock.com

Can you tell what his body language is saying?

Deception. It is a difficult task to identify deception in others, with the ability to judge whether someone is lying around 50 percent (Burgoon & Levine, 2010). There is no bulls-eye that "tells" that a person is lying. A lack of eye contact, quavering voice and descriptive vagueness are all signs of lying, but they can also be signs of anxiety or personal quirks. The most reliable signals of deception pertain to the cognitive effort and emotion that surround the lie itself. A person who lies may exhibit discomfort (Perina, 2011).

Microexpressions, fleeting facial expressions that last only a fraction of a second, are oftentimes helpful signals. These are often caught by only the most astute observers. Many people try hard to control their facial expressions, but deceivers may blink more or smile more in an effort to deceive. Some individuals are so good at monitoring and controlling their faces that their true feelings are difficult to detect. However, while liars can control certain facial expressions when facing scrutiny, they can't suppress them completely or every time; therefore, monitoring inconsistencies becomes key (Burgoon & Levine, 2010).

Signals of deception—often called *body leakage*—where body postures rather than the face leak the truth can be extremely revealing. Individuals who choose to deceive can sometimes concentrate so much on controlling their words and facial expressions that they pay less attention to their bodies, which actually reveal their true feelings. In the verbal realm, changes in word usage, word flow, or voice pitch may signal the extra cognitive horsepower lying demands (Perina, 2011).

Conscious Nonverbal Communication

Senders of conscious nonverbal communication are aware that they are sending a message and the general meaning of that message. For example, the individuals extending a hug know that they are embracing someone and that action is normally perceived as indicating affection.

Receivers of conscious nonverbal communication are aware that they received the message and the meaning intended by the sender. The receiver of a hug, for example, generally realizes that the message is a sign of affection.

FOCUS ON DIVERSITY

MICROAGGRESSIONS

Microaggressions are the everyday verbal, nonverbal, and environmental slights, snubs, or insults, whether intentional or unintentional, which communicate hostile, derogatory, or negative messages to target persons based solely upon their marginalized group membership (Sue 2010). Such incidents have become a commonplace experience for many people of color because they seem to occur constantly in our daily lives.

They are subtle but offensive comments or actions directed at a minority or other nondominant group that unintentionally or unconsciously reinforces a stereotype, such as: "I don't see you as black" or "you run like a girl." When a white couple (man and woman) passes an Hispanic man on the sidewalk, the woman automatically clutches her purse more tightly, while the white man checks for his wallet in the back pocket. (Hidden message: Hispanics are prone to crime and up to no good.) Whether they are meant to be offensive or said to be not hurtful, they are offensive to the receiving party and others who may see or hear them. Sometimes the sender does not realize the receiver is offended.

The term **racial microaggressions** was first coined by psychiatrist Chester Pierce, MD, in the 1970s. But the concept is also rooted in the work of Jack Dovidio, PhD (Yale University) and Samuel Gaertner, PhD (University of Delaware) in their formulation of **aversive racism**: many well-intentioned whites consciously believe in and profess equality, but unconsciously act in a racist manner, particularly in ambiguous situations (Sue, 2010).

Subliminal Nonverbal Communications

Subliminal messages are communicated to the subconscious mind of the receiver. Receivers of subliminal messages are not consciously aware of the message. However, these messages are important.

- Gut reactions are frequently based upon your subconscious reading of subliminal nonverbal communications.
- Police and military uniforms subliminally communicate the authority of those wearing them.
- Well-dressed executives project success and credibility.
- Poor dress transmits messages of failure and a lack of credibility.

Although subliminal messages do not create awareness on a conscious level, they still influence the receiver. In fact, subliminal messages are often more powerful than conscious messages. The advertising world is replete with examples of the value of subliminal nonverbal messages.

- Young, beautiful people are often seen in advertisements to communicate the subconscious message that the advertised product is associated with youth and beauty.
- Companies pay large sums of money to have their products appear in movies. While these appearances are not typical product advertisements, the mere association of the product with the movie transmits subliminal messages that will influence viewers.

Do you know how you communicate nonverbally? Do you know how other cultures communicate nonverbally? Let's look at some possible ways.

Facial expressions and eye contact. More than any other nonverbal factor, facial expressions can communicate more emotional meaning more accurately. For example, the face:

- Communicates evaluative judgment.
- Reveals the level of interest or lack of it.
- Can exhibit the level of intensity of the emotions.
- Reveals the amount of control we have over our expressions.
- Shows whether we understand or not.

Through our facial expressions, we reveal a great deal about our feelings and responses to other people as we nonverbally convey shock, sadness, anger, happiness, worry, and so on. This is confirmed by researcher Paul Eckman (2007):

> The rapid facial signals are the primary system for expression of emotion. It is the face you search to know whether someone is angry, disgusted, afraid, sad, etc. Words cannot always describe the feelings people have; often words are not adequate to express what you see in the look on someone's face at an emotional moment.

Nonverbal communication can also be controlled by a knowledgeable person.

- A person who knows that people telling falsehoods often blink their eyes can take special care not blink when telling a falsehood.
- A person who knows that a hug indicates friendship can consciously hug his/her worst enemy as trick to put the person off guard or as part of an effort to improve their relationship.

What can you say about this expression?

The eyes are the most expressive part of the face and have considerable effect on communication. We may use eye contact in a positive way to:

- Invite interaction with another by looking directly at them.
- Show friendship and positive regard by extended mutual eye contact.
- Demonstrate believability or honesty.
- Demonstrate interest by extended eye contact.
- Signal turn-taking in normal conversation.

Many times we avoid eye contact when we want to hide feelings, when we are tense, when we are interacting with someone we dislike, or when attempting to end social contact. However, it is important to note here that nonverbal expressions have different meanings in various cultures. Therefore, it is wise to be careful about assigning your culture's meanings for eye behavior to all people. See Focus on Diversity—Facial Expressions and Eye Contact.

Listen first and acknowledge what you hear, even if you don't agree with it, before expressing your experience or point of view; if you don't agree, it is even more important to listen first and acknowledge what you hear.

Vocal qualities. *Paralinguistics* is the study of vocal cues such as pitch, rate, tone, or fluency. Almost everyone distinguishes meanings by noting differences in vocal qualities. For example, the statement "What a vacation I had" can have at least two different meanings, depending on the tone of voice of the speaker. The ambiguous phrase might mean that it was a most enjoyable weekend. With different qualities, however, the listener would assume that it was quite unpleasant (Hamilton, 2014).

FOCUS ON DIVERSITY

FACIAL EXPRESSIONS AND EYE CONTACT

Researchers indicate we can move people from culture to culture and they know how to make and read the same basic expressions: anger, fear, sadness, disgust, surprise, and happiness. The six appear to be hardwired in our brains (Matsumoto, 2004).

The mouth is a very expressive part of the face, and not just for the words that come out of it. However, reactions in the eyes are harder to control. So while Americans, big on personal expression, look to the mouth to read each other, the relatively subdued Japanese rely more on those revealing orbs (Perina, 2006).

For example, in the United States we encourage eye contact as an indicator of honesty and interest. People in some other societies believe that they should look down when talking to another person to indicate deference and respect. White Americans consider a reluctance to make eye contact as rude, disrespectful, and hostile, as well as conveying disinterest. However, looking someone in the eye is often perceived as a sign of disrespect or rudeness by people from many Asian, Latin American, Native American, and Caribbean cultures. Many African Americans, especially from the South, observe this custom, too (Baruth & Manning, 2011).

FOCUS ON DIVERSITY

VOCAL QUALITIES

White Americans often use a loud voice and a warm, hearty greeting when they meet each other. However, Asian Americans are more likely to greet each other calmly and quietly. Native Americans speak more softly and at a slower rate than white Americans do (Santrock, 2006).

The nonverbal messages communicated by the sound of the human voice can provide valuable information during meetings. Look at Table 5.2 and try to accentuate the one word in the sentences which appears in *boldface italics*. Just put extra emphasis on that one word as you read out loud. Each sentence is exactly the same, but watch what happens when you place emphasis on the different words.

With practice, we can all learn to notice the pitch and timbre of a person's voice, the rhythm of speech, and the rapidity of expression. These vocal qualities help us to tune into the mood of the speaker, as well as to understand how different cultures use vocal qualities in their communication.

Table 5.2 CAN THE WAY YOU SAY SOMETHING ALTER WHAT YOU MEAN TO SAY?

Accentuate the one word in each sentence that appears in *boldface italics*. What are the different possible meanings?
I didn't say she stole the money.
I *didn't* say she stole the money.
I didn't *say* she stole the money.
I didn't say *she* stole the money.
I didn't say she *stole* the money.
I didn't say she stole the *money*.

Gestures and other body movements. Because movements and gestures of other parts of the body are also closely tied to culture, it is extremely misleading to isolate a single body movement (such as crossing the arms) and give it a precise meaning. Regardless of your intentions, however, your gestures and body movements may be given specific meanings by others.

For example, the way a person stands may indicate self-confidence, status, friendliness, or enthusiasm. Various types of gestures may be used to indicate feelings of restlessness, nervousness, or perhaps the need to emphasize a meaning. Frequent

Becoming *Aware*

hand movements, for example, often communicate a positive, enthusiastic attitude. However, movements such as the constant pencil tapper or the doodler may indicate nervousness and boredom. Even weak or overly strong handshakes will be given some significance by many people. They can communicate enthusiasm, or they can communicate uneasiness.

You will be given an opportunity in one of the exercises in this chapter to evaluate your gestures and body movements. Pay very close attention to what you learn about yourself.

FOCUS ON DIVERSITY

GESTURES AND OTHER BODY MOVEMENTS

Gestures are not universal. For example, white Americans view a firm handshake as a sign of strength and power. However, Native Americans view a firm handshake as aggressive and disrespectful (Atkinson, 2004). Furthermore, the sign shown in Figure 5.2, which in our culture usually means "OK," has other meanings in other cultures. In Japan, it can mean "coins." In France and Belgium, it means "worthless" (as in "zero worth"). In Greece and Turkey, it is a vulgar sexual invitation.

Another example of how a simple gesture can be subject to misunderstanding and offense is noted in Figure 5.3. The sign of the University of Texas football team, the Longhorns, is to extend the index finger and the pinkie. In Italy and other parts of Europe, this gesture means a man's wife has been unfaithful to him—a serious insult (Tavris & Wade, 2011)! Without a doubt, tourists should be very careful about their gestures.

Figure 5.2

In many cultures, but not all cultures, the circle made with the thumb and forefinger means everything is "OK."

© *Kendall Hunt Publishing Company*

Figure 5.3

Be careful where you make this gesture.

© *Kendall Hunt Publishing Company*

Touching. Some people use the language of touch more easily and readily than others. Actually, *one of the most meaningful methods* of nonverbal communication can be that of touching. There are times in our lives when it is difficult to express our feelings through words. We may use a hug, a pat on the shoulder, or a clasp of the hand to communicate meaning without words. Touching is risky, however, because this form of nonverbal communication may violate the personal space of others. Because there is indeed a complex language of touch, researchers Heslin and Alper (1983) have suggested a number of factors to consider:

What is this touch communicating?

- What part of the body does the touching?
- What part of the body is touched?
- How long does the touch last?
- How much pressure is used?
- Is there movement after contact is made?
- Is anyone else present?
- What is the situation in which the touch occurs?
- What is the relationship between the persons involved?

FOCUS ON DIVERSITY

TOUCHING

There are cultural and gender differences in the language of touch. For example, there is a strong taboo against strangers touching in Japan, which is reflected in the sufficient distance maintained by most Japanese in public. Latinos tend to touch one another while communicating, whereas white Americans tend not to touch one another while communicating (Santrock, 2006).

Kenneth Blanchard (2006) confirms the ideas of Heslin and Alper: *There is a very simple rule about touching—when you touch, don't take.*

Think for just a moment and respond to these questions. How do you feel when a friend touches you on the shoulder? How do you feel when your boss touches you on the shoulder? How do you feel when a family member touches you on the shoulder? How do you feel when a stranger touches you on the shoulder? When the balance of power is off, like a boss and employee, touch could be considered a microaggresion or actual sexual assault by the person of less power.

We would guess that you will have many different answers to these questions, which just illustrates that we feel differently and interpret differently the language of touch.

Personal space and distance. Our own personal space is an invisible bubble around us that allows us to feel safe. As we said earlier, if this bubble is violated, we are uncomfortable and may become defensive. Usually, only intimates can violate the space without making us uncomfortable. Sometimes, violation of this space by another can demonstrate that person's dominance of the situation.

FOCUS ON DIVERSITY

PERSONAL SPACE AND DISTANCE

French people maintain very small personal spaces in trains, buses, cafes, and even in their homes, and they increase their involvement with other people by using more direct body postures and eye contact. In consequence, when Americans visit Paris, they are sometimes shocked when strangers approach so closely and stare right into their eyes. Furthermore, when Americans attempt to protect their invaded personal space, Parisians interpret their retreat as a lack of good manners (Dresser, 2005).

Many times you can tell how people feel toward one another by observing the distance between them. Anthropologist Edward T. Hall (1992) defined four distances that we use in our everyday lives (see Figure 5.4). These are:

- *Intimate distance*, which begins with skin contact and ranges out to about 18 inches. This is reserved for close friends and loved ones, or other people to whom you feel affectionate.
- *Personal distance*, from 18 inches to 4 feet. This is where you may carry on a friendly conversation or sometimes even a heated argument.
- *Social distance*, from 4 to 12 feet. This is reserved for social interactions that are businesslike or impersonal.
- *Public distance*, ranging out from 12 feet. This is reserved for speaking to a large audience.

Too often we underestimate the power of a touch, a smile, a kind word, a listening ear, an honest compliment, or the smallest act of caring, all of which have the potential to turn a life around.
—LEO BUSCAGLIA

Hall is careful to note that these distances pertain to Americans only and may be quite different for people raised in other cultures. For example, Americans are quite comfortable conducting business at a distance of approximately three to four feet, but people from the Middle East, Italy, Greece, and other southern European cultures stand

Figure 5.4 ZONE AND DISTANCE

Zone 1	Zone 2	Zone 3	Zone 4
Intimate distance	Personal distance	Social distance	Public distance
0"–18"	18"–4'	4'–12'	12'+

Appropriate people and situations			
Parents and children, lovers, spouses/partners	Close friends	Co-workers, social gatherings, friends, work situations	Speaking to groups

Hall (1992) and Weiten et al. (2012).

much closer. Therefore, it is easy to see how feelings of uneasiness can occur without either individual possibly knowing why (Hall, 1992).

Physical environment and territory. What characteristics in a physical environment make you feel comfortable or uncomfortable? What do you think your room, house, or car communicates to others? Do you prefer a neat and "tidy" room, house, or car, or do you prefer the more "lived-in" look? What meaning do you give to a spotless house or to a friend's constantly clean car? How about your desk at home or work? Is it free of papers, or does it look like *someone works there every minute of the day and*

Whom do you allow within your intimate distance?

© *Monkey Business Images/Shutterstock.com*

Becoming *Aware*

night? Interestingly enough, physical environments not only reveal characteristics of the owner of the territory but also actually affect how a person communicates.

Clothing and personal appearance. What we wear and how we groom ourselves are also important means of nonverbal communication. We send messages about our economic level, level of success, social position, educational background, moral character, and sometimes just our personal preferences. We also may send messages that suggest, "Notice me." For example, there is a tremendous amount of pressure in schools to wear the "in" brand of jeans, shoes, dress, and so on.

Although it is natural to make assumptions about clothing and personal appearances, it is equally important to note that this area of nonverbal communication is filled with ambiguity. A stranger, wearing worn, ill-fitting clothes, might normally be a stylish person or even a millionaire. Maybe today he or she is on vacation, going to do some "dirty" work, just wants to be comfortable, or it is considered stylish in their community. This points to the fact that as we get to know others better, the importance of clothing and personal appearance decreases.

What kind of messages do you think you send about the clothing you wear and the manner in which you groom yourself?

Silence. Silence is *communication*. Silence may convey relaxation, contentment, fatigue, anxiety, frustration, uncertainty, shyness, avoidance, or thoughtful analyses. Sometimes, what we do not say has more impact than what we do say. For example, silence can be used to convey negative messages such as "I'm angry with you," "I'm not OK," or positive messages of, "It is nice just to be alone," "I understand."

> *Do not the most moving moments of our lives find us all without words?*
> —MARCEL MARCEAU

Nonverbal communication, everything in the communication context except the actual words being uttered, is sometimes very clear and unambiguous. Also consider the culture the person has lived in. In the Arabic world a click sound means NO; it is not derisive but a shortcutting communication. If an Indian person is wagging their head it conveys happiness with the situation.

 If you are a woman and men whistle at you as you walk down the street you might find it offensive and scary or you may feel positively that they like your style. At times it can be difficult to decipher. Mark Knapp and Judith Hall (2009), authors of *Nonverbal Communication in Human Interaction*, remind us that as we become aware of nonverbal messages in our everyday lives, we need to think of them not as facts, but as clues that need to be checked out. Furthermore, we can be more effective in communicating messages if we support words with appropriate forms of nonverbal communication.

HOW TO IMPROVE NONVERBAL COMMUNICATION

The following don'ts can dilute the most compelling words.
- Pointing a finger
- Pounding your fist
- Placing hands on hips
- Licking your lips
- Looking at the floor
- Playing with pocket change
- Playing with rubber bands or paper clips
- Twirling your mustache
- Clicking pens
- Repeatedly adjusting your glasses
- Assuming a stern facial expression
- Repeatedly touching your hair

Pachter (2006).

Verbal Communication

Verbal communication—words and language—is generally considered the primary means of communication. We gather, share, give, and receive information through words, and establish, continue, or terminate relationships through words. Words can make us feel good or miserable; they can make us lose our tempers or keep our cool; they can persuade us to take action or convince us not to move; they can be clear and concise or ambiguous and confusing; more importantly, *they cannot be unsaid once they are said.*

Actually, the way we use words may communicate much more than the actual words used. As we have already discussed, our tone of voice and the emphasis placed on our words may reveal far more than our choice of words. As we can see, it is the meaning and understanding behind words that is the essence of communication. And, *meanings are in people—not words.* Let us look at some barriers or ways that meanings can go astray.

Semantics. *Semantics* is the study of meaning and changes of meanings in words. It is virtually impossible to communicate effectively if the people conversing do not understand the same terminology, or if they hold different meanings for the same word. For example, consider the common expressions:

> I'll be back in a little while.
> I'll be back in a few minutes.
> I'll be back about 5:00 P.M.

What or when is *a little while* or *a few minutes*? Do we mean a little late, or do we mean 5, 10, or 30 minutes? Does "about 5:00 P.M." mean exactly 5:00 P.M., or does the expression mean between 5:00 and 6:00 P.M.? What do you mean when you use these expressions?

Also, certain occupations have their "jargon" too: realtors talk about going after "listings"; individuals working in finance and credit talk about a "class 2-A credit rating." Do you know what these statements mean? Any profession, avocation, or field of specialization will develop such word usages or even "slang" words. This often splits persons inside the group from those outside the group in that they will use the same language terminology to mean different things or they are not up on the latest slang.

> *Our language is funny—a fat chance and a slim chance are the same thing.*
> —J. GUSTAV WHITE

FOCUS ON DIVERSITY

SEMANTICS?

Two first-time visitors to Montreal, Quebec (the French-Canadian province), entered a restaurant for dinner. After looking over the menu, the husband suggested they order the shrimp cocktail *entrée*. He said to his wife, "A whole shrimp dinner for $11.95 Canadian is quite a deal. I guess it's because Montreal is a seaport." When the entrée arrived, the visitors were sadly disappointed because they were the size of an *appetizer*.

The husband asked the server why the entrées were so small in Montreal. With a smile, the server replied, "You folks must be Americans. In French-speaking countries the word entrée is just the beginning of the meal, like the word enter. In the United States, it's just the reverse—the entrée is the main meal. Are you now ready to order your main meal?"

Even English-speaking countries have different meanings for the same word. For example, in the United States, "Let us *table* that motion" means: "Let us put it aside." In England, the same phrase means: "Let us bring it up for discussion."

Maybe the meaning only rests in the "eyes of the beholder." The beholder leaves the listener to guess what he or she means, while the beholder operates on assumptions that he or she is, in fact, communicating. The listener, in turn, proceeds on the basis of what he or she guesses. Mutual misunderstanding is an obvious result.

Often we have needs that we do not express to each other and, if that happens, someone gets their feelings hurt. If you can actually provide your need and your feeling to the other person they can better understand you. "The following list of needs is neither exhaustive nor definitive. It is meant as a starting place to support anyone who wishes to engage in a process of deepening self-discovery and to facilitate great-

> *I know you believe you understand what you think I said. But I am not sure you realize that what you heard is not what I meant.*
> —ANONYMOUS

er understanding and connection between people" (https://www.cnvc.org/Training/needs-inventory). It is provided by the Center for Non-Violent Communication (https://www.cnvc.org/Training/needs-inventory).

The following are words we use when we want to express a combination of emotional states and physical sensations. This list is neither exhaustive nor definitive. It is meant as a starting place to support anyone who wishes to engage in a process of deepening self-discovery and to facilitate greater understanding and connection between people. There are two parts to this list: feelings we may have when our needs are being met and feelings we may have when our needs are not being met. Use them in your communications—it will help.

FEELINGS WHEN YOUR NEEDS ARE SATISFIED

AFFECTIONATE
compassionate
friendly
loving
open hearted
sympathetic
tender
warm

ENGAGED
absorbed
alert
curious
engrossed
enchanted
entranced
fascinated
interested
intrigued
involved
spellbound
stimulated

HOPEFUL
expectant
encouraged
optimistic

CONFIDENT
empowered
open
proud
safe
secure

EXCITED
amazed
animated
ardent
aroused
astonished
dazzled
eager
energetic
enthusiastic
giddy
invigorated
lively
passionate
surprised
vibrant

GRATEFUL
appreciative
moved
thankful
touched

INSPIRED
amazed
awed
wonder

JOYFUL
amused
delighted
glad
happy
jubilant
pleased
tickled

EXHILARATED
blissful
ecstatic
elated
enthralled
exuberant
radiant
rapturous
thrilled

PEACEFUL
calm
clear headed
comfortable
centered
content
equanimous
fulfilled
mellow
quiet
relaxed
relieved
satisfied
serene
still
tranquil
trusting

REFRESHED
enlivened
rejuvenated
renewed
rested
restored
revived

FEELINGS WHEN YOUR NEEDS ARE NOT SATISFIED

AFRAID
apprehensive
dread
foreboding
frightened
mistrustful
panicked
petrified
scared
suspicious
terrified
wary
worried

ANNOYED
aggravated
dismayed
disgruntled
displeased
exasperated
frustrated
impatient
irritated
irked

ANGRY
enraged
furious
incensed
indignant
irate
livid
outraged
resentful

AVERSION
animosity
appalled
contempt
disgusted
dislike
hate
horrified
hostile
repulsed

CONFUSED
ambivalent
baffled
bewildered
dazed
hesitant
lost
mystified
perplexed
puzzled
torn

DISCONNECTED
alienated
aloof
apathetic
bored
cold
detached
distant
distracted
indifferent
numb
removed
uninterested
withdrawn

DISQUIET
agitated
alarmed
discombobulated
disconcerted
disturbed
perturbed
rattled
restless
shocked
startled
surprised
troubled
turbulent
turmoil
uncomfortable
uneasy
unnerved
unsettled
upset

EMBARRASSED
ashamed
chagrined
flustered
guilty
mortified
self-conscious

FATIGUE
beat
burnt out
depleted
exhausted
lethargic
listless
sleepy
tired
weary
worn out

PAIN
agony
anguished
bereaved
devastated
grief
heartbroken
hurt
lonely
miserable
regretful
remorseful

SAD
depressed
dejected
despair
despondent
disappointed
discouraged
disheartened
forlorn
gloomy
heavy hearted
hopeless
melancholy
unhappy
wretched

TENSE
anxious
cranky
distressed
distraught
edgy
fidgety
frazzled
irritable
jittery
nervous
overwhelmed
restless
stressed out

VULNERABLE
fragile
guarded
helpless
insecure
leery
reserved
sensitive
shaky

YEARNING
envious
jealous
longing
nostalgic
pining
wistful

Source: Center for
Nonviolent Communication

HOW TO IMPROVE VERBAL COMMUNICATION

- Speak with enthusiasm
- Enunciate
- Use inflection
- Avoid antagonistic words
- Use short, simple sentences
- Adjust the volume of your voice to the situation
- Adjust your speaking rate to the situation
- Keep the door open for feedback

That words are powerful may seem obvious, but the fact is that most of us, most of the time, use them lightly. We choose our clothes more carefully than we choose our words, though what we say about and to others can define them indelibly.
— JOSEPH TELUSHKIN

"Everyone has a Story"

I used to get bored with people
so easily and
so quickly.
Then I began seeing them
as more than people—
as beautiful
and interesting.
As worth more than my judgments.
As people with a story to tell.
I began seeing them.
I began listening.

— COLTON SNEAD, 2016

Technology. Digital culture expert and MIT professor Sherry Turkle (2016) reports on the various ways humans have adapted their sense of self and relationships to the digital age. In her opinion, this period has seen a decline in the face-to-face communication needed for self-reflection, empathy, and intimacy. Turkle has done extensive research to examine what is lost and gained as digital communication becomes more pervasive (2012). There are intersections between emotion and technology, such as apps for computers and phones designed to find romantic partners and algorithms that assess psychological states. Turkle believes that technology communication encourages a "friction-free" style of communication, defined by self-editing and the immediate gratification of a "Facebook like." She suggests that this approach degrades the quality of performance at work and school, and that democracy is undermined as citizens accept the surveillance provided by social media as a new way of life (2016).

The phones or cybermedia you carry put social media on a 24-hour cycle. We all know that with phones, the amount of time you spend on them increases when you are bored or lonely. Navigate your cyber landscapes, and learn how to evaluate those spaces and differentiate potentially damaging content from potentially enlightening content. You can search Twitter for people who use that platform to speak of justice and equity. Please check out videos, apps, and blogs that present ideas you are learning in this class and push beyond snarky tweets.

Please <u>think before you type</u> and engage respectfully on digital media. Your cellphones and any digital media can promote thought and meaning rather than mindlessness and negativity. At the end of the chapter I have linked to a couple of YouTube videos from the TED app that you might enjoy. One is Marshall Davis Jones reading his poem "<u>Touchscreen</u>," and considers how social media can affect personal communication and interpersonal relationships. "<u>Lost Voices</u>" by Darius Simpson and Scout Bostley opens up your thoughts to serious topics of racial and gender equality in this country. Slam poetry as a genre is both entertaining and socially conscious. Generally short, averaging three minutes each, these videos fit right into easily consumable content.

Assumptions. To *assume* is to accept as fact without any evidence of proof (Milliken, 2011). Often, we make the mistake of assuming that others will understand more than we actually say to them. "If it is clear to me, it must be clear to you also." This assumption is one of the most difficult barriers to successful human communication. In personal relationships, for example, we may expect our intimates to be able to read our minds because they know us so well. "She ought to know how I feel," you may say to yourself, even though you have said nothing about your feelings.

A story is told of a family ruckus that occurred when the father sent his son to the lumberyard for a *longer* board. The young man thought he knew what his father wanted—but the longer board he brought back was still three feet too short. His father became angry and accused the boy of being stupid and not listening. The father had simply assumed that since he knew what he meant by *longer*, his son would also know. Could it be possible that Dad had not bothered to make himself clear or to check his meaning with his son?

Self-concept. The most important single factor affecting our communication with others is our self-concept. Chapter Two showed that a strong self-concept is necessary for healthy and satisfying interactions. On the other hand, if we have a weak self-concept, we may feel inadequate and lack the confidence to converse with others. As a result, we feel our ideas are not worth communicating and we become guarded in our communication attempts.

> The real art of conversation is not only to say the right thing in the right place but to leave unsaid the wrong thing at the tempting moment.
> —LADY DOROTHY NEVILL

In circumstances where we feel insecure or unsafe, it is extremely easy for us to feel that our self-image is being threatened. As a result, our defenses are immediately aroused. It is so easy to take an innocent remark and reply with, "What did you mean by that?" We may distort questions into accusations. Our replies become immediate justifications.

For example, a husband may ask his wife, "Did you happen to get my blue shirt from the cleaners?" His intention may be informational. If the wife feels insecure, she may respond as if the issue was her inability to meet his needs. She may say, "No, I didn't. I can't think of everything, you know, when I've got the kids with me and time is getting short, and I can't even find a decent roast that we can afford. I suppose you think my getting your shirt is more important than preparing a good meal." The wife assumes an accusation is made. This accusation may be seen as an "intended putdown." Does the husband really mean to cut the wife down, or does the wife just feel insecure?

Emotion-packed phrases. As we can see, words stated may not be as important as the way in which we *catch* these words. Because it is highly possible for us to operate on different mood levels, an experience we have had during the day may cause us to react with words that we do not really mean. Sometimes, our mood level combined with certain emotion-packed phrases really sets us off.

Some of these emotion-packed phrases are as follows (Ekman, 2007):

> *After all I've done for you . . .*
> *I wish you would say what you mean . . .*
> *After you have been here as long as I have . . .*
> *When I was your age . . .*
> *Do you know what you are doing? . . .*
> *You aren't upset, are you? . . .*
> *Talk to me later . . .*
> *Do you understand me? . . .*
> *I wouldn't do that . . .*
> *You wouldn't understand . . .*
> *Are you sure that's right? . . .*
> *Any very opinionated statement . . .*

Have you ever reacted to one of these emotion-packed phrases? It takes a great deal of practice to learn to listen, to not be distracted by emotion-packed phrases. The key here is to *respond* to the statement and not *react* to the statement. After all, when you *respond,* the rational, thinking, logical part of you is communicated, but when you *react,* the emotional, feeling, irrational part of you is communicated. Sociolinguist professor Deborah Tannen (2001) in her powerful communication book, *You Just Don't Understand,* offers some helpful advice:

The most important thing is to be aware that misunderstandings can arise and with them tempers, when no one is crazy and no one is mean and no one is intentionally dishonest. We can learn to stop and remind ourselves that others may not mean what we hear them say.

As we can see, there are numerous ways that words can go astray. What about communicating with e-mail, text messaging, and other forms of technology?

Many people perceive a style difference as the other person's personal failing. If we could see style differences for what they are, then a lot of blaming and negative feelings could be eliminated. Nothing hurts more than being told your intentions are bad when you know they are good, or being told that you are doing something wrong when you know you're just doing it your way.
—DEBORAH TANNEN

Technology and Communication

There has been a tremendous increase in electronic and wireless communication technology. Communicating by e-mail, text messaging, blogs, instant messaging, chat rooms, videoconferencing, or using the latest communication device, have reduced the traditional memos, letters, phone calls, and face-to-face conversations. Text messaging is a global phenomenon and is increasing dramatically as more people own a smartphone. Use of cell phones while talking and driving is banned in 37 states and the District of Columbia while text messaging is banned for all drivers in 46 states and the District of Columbia according to the Insurance Institute for Highway Safety (webpage June 2016). Texting and looking up information and maps while driving have caused numerous accidents and very distracted drivers.

Digital connectivity offers many potential benefits, from connecting with peers to accessing educational content, but we need to be careful not to abuse and overuse it. Parents have also voiced concerns about the behaviors teens engage in online, the people with whom they interact, and the personal information they make available. Indeed, these concerns are not limited to parents. Some lawmakers have raised concerns about issues such as online safety; many people worry with the rise of connectivity; there is concern that many people use mobile apps or Internet sites and do not see what harm it can be doing to others. More mobile applications are created every day for finding people to date or to "hook up with" (have sex) or for "catfishing" (to fabricate an online dating identity) or for cyberbullying (such as sharing personal photos to others without the person's consent).

In a 2015 survey, the Pew Research Center found that:

> …college graduates and the relatively affluent are especially likely to know people who use online dating or to know people who have entered into a relationship that began online. Nearly six-in-ten college graduates (58%) know someone who uses online dating, and nearly half (46%) know someone who has entered into a marriage or long-term partnership with someone they met via online dating. By comparison, just 25% of those with a high school diploma or less know someone who uses online dating—and just 18% know someone who has entered into a long-term relationship with someone they met this way…

> Those who have tried online dating offer mixed opinions about the experience—most have a positive outlook, even as they recognize certain downsides. Overall, men and women who have used online dating tend to have similar views of the pros and cons—with one major exception relating to personal safety. Some 53% of women who have used online dating agree that it is more dangerous than other ways of meeting people, substantially higher than the 38% of male online daters who agree with this statement. (http://www.pewinternet.org/2016/02/11/15-percent-of-american-adults-have-used-online-dating-sites-or-mobile-dating-apps/)

There have been concerns regarding the overuse of technology and its impact on face-to-face communication, so much so that Emily Drago in her Strategic Communications class at Elon University created a survey to observe students' technology use and habits while with others as well. She found that 38 of 100 students (38%) while with others used no technology; the other 62% were either texting, talking on the phone, or using a computer or tablet.

In an effort to determine what impacts technology has on face-to-face communication, the survey asked students to rank the following statement on a scale from strongly agree to strongly disagree: "It bothers me when my friends or family use technology while spending time with me." Seventy-four percent of respondents said that they either agreed or strongly agreed with this statement, while only 6% disagreed. Among respondents, 20% neither agreed nor disagreed.

Another survey question asked students whether they believed the presence of technology, while spending time with others, affects face-to-face interpersonal communication negatively. "An overwhelming 92% of respondents believed technology negatively affects face-to-face communication, and only 1% did not. Only 7% of respondents neither agreed nor disagreed" (Drago, Spring 2015).

MIT psychologist Sherry Turkle observes in her book, *Alone Together: Why We Expect More from Technology and Less from Each Other* (2012), "The Net teaches us to need it." She found that couples need to reclaim life's unstructured moments of reflection and openness to each other and not fill the time with digital intrusion. According to the Pew Research Survey cited above, 42 percent of cell-phone-owning 18-29 year olds in a serious relationship say their partner has been distracted by mobile devices while they were together, which is more than the 25 percent of all couples reporting such problems. The survey reported 18 percent of young adults argue over the amount of time spent online (Marano, 2016).

REMEMBER, BEFORE YOU SAY OR WRITE SOMETHING YOU MIGHT THINK ABOUT IT. DON'T REGRET NOT THINKING.

Read your messages again before you send them. If they do not fit the reminders of THINKING, you might need to adjust what you are saying.

T..... Is it **True?**
H.... Is it **Helpful?**
I..... Is it **Inspiring?**
N.... Is it **Necessary?**
K.... Is it **Kind?**
I...... Is it **Not Inappropriate?**
N... Is it **Needed?**
G...... Is it **Good?**

If your answer is yes, go ahead, but if your answer is no, **stop.**
(adapted from Alan Redpath)

Gender and Communication

For just a moment respond to the following questions with either T or F.

_____ 1. Women are better at interpreting nonverbal cues while listening.

_____ 2. Men generally do most of the talking in mixed-gender groups.

_____ 3. Women are more willing to ask for help than men.

_____ 4. Men are more likely to interrupt more often.

_____ 5. Women are more likely to initiate confrontations in relationships than men.

_____ 6. Men are less likely to be verbally expressive.

According to research, if you answered true to all of these statements, you were correct (Hamilton, 2014; Wood, 2009).

Actually, these are just some of the possible differences in communication styles between males and females. Also, men often talk about sports, money, facts, business, and events, while doing something else, and often without looking at each other. Women, on the other hand, talk about feelings, relationships, and people face to face, sitting down. See Gender & You—Communication: Different Languages, for more differences in the way men and women communicate.

> *Listening is the most used skill and the least taught!*
> —JANNA MARTIN

Sometimes, our communication attempts go astray because we fail to listen. We will now discuss the skills of listening and the qualities essential for improving person-to-person communication.

GENDER AND YOU

COMMUNICATION: DIFFERENT LANGUAGES

In the national best-seller, *You Just Don't Understand: Women and Men in Conversation*, Deborah Tannen (2001) contends that males and females are typically socialized in different "cultures." That is, males are likely to speak and hear a language of "status and independence" while females are likely to speak and hear a language of "connection and intimacy." Stated in another way, men use language to challenge others, to achieve status in a group, to convey information, and to keep from getting pushed around. On the other hand, women use language to achieve and share intimacy with others, to promote closeness and equality in a group, and to prevent others from pushing them away. It is not so much that men want to dominate women as that they simply have different ways of communicating. She states that "communication between men and women can be like cross cultural communication, prey to a clash of conversational styles." The influence of gender differences begins very early in childhood and can shape the communication style of the adult (Tannen, 2001). Yet, there are some researchers who feel that some of the differences in male and female communication styles are really not due to biological sex at all. In fact, the idea of "different cultures" is a myth (MacGeorge et al., 2004). After all, it is just about individual personality differences. At any rate, it is important to be cautious about putting all men and all women into some type of category.

Listen to the Pew research on multi-racial Americans sharing their views, experiences and perspectives. http://www.pewresearch.org/multiracial-voices/ What do you think?

Listening (What Did You Say?)

How many times have you had a conversation with people and not heard a word they said? Do you sometimes ignore others when they are talking? How many times have you had a conversation with someone, and you felt they were not paying attention to you? Actually, listening is a form of *paying attention,* which is an active process involving much more than hearing and seeing.

According to Stephen Covey (2013), when another person speaks, we are usually "listening" at one of four levels. We may be *ignoring* another person, not really listening at all. We may practice *pretending.* "Yeah. Uh-huh. Right." We may practice *selective listening,* hearing only certain parts of the conversation. Or we may even practice *attentive listening,* paying attention and focusing energy on the words that are being said. Very few of us ever practice the fifth level, however, the highest form of listening, *empathetic listening*—listening with the intent to *understand.* We will discuss listening with the intent to understand in greater detail later in the chapter.

Have you ever had a conversation with someone who wasn't paying attention?

© Kzenon/Shutterstock.com

Becoming *Aware*

Communication experts describe listening as our primary communication activity. According to one study, college students spend about 11 percent of their communicating time writing, 16 percent speaking, 17 percent reading, but more than 55 percent listening, with 27.9 percent spent on media listening, and 27.5 percent spent on interpersonal listening (Emanuel et al., 2008). It is interesting to note that while universities often require classes that evaluate competence in writing and speaking, few highlight listening as an important communication skill.

Unfortunately, few people are good listeners. Researchers claim that *75 percent of oral communication* is ignored, misunderstood, or quickly forgotten (Bolton, 1986). It just seems that the speaker's words go *in one ear and out the other.* Yet, the quality of your friendships, the closeness of your family relationships, and your effectiveness at work depend to a great extent on your ability to listen (O'Neill & Chapman, 2008).

Is there really a difference in hearing and listening? *Hearing* is a word used to describe the physiological sensory process by which auditory sensations are received by the ears and translated to the brain. *Listening*, on the other hand, is an intellectual and emotional process that integrates physical, emotional, and intellectual inputs in a search for meaning and understanding (Barker & Watson, 2000).

In fact, Cheryl Hamilton (2014), author of *Communicating for Results*, says there are Five Stages of Listening, where listeners . . .

1. Sense — Hear what is important to them
2. Interpret — Assign meaning to what is seen, heard, and felt
3. Evaluate — Determine speaker credibility and message importance
4. Respond — React to speech usually through nonverbal cues
5. Remember — Retain parts of message in memory

Is it possible to hear what another person is saying without really listening to him?

> *We have been given two ears but a single mouth, in order that we may hear more and talk less.*
> —ZENO OF CITIUM

Barriers to Listening

Do you have any habits, attitudes, or desires that may screen out what is really said? Are you ever too busy to really listen? What kinds of things prevent you from really listening? Let us examine some possible barriers to listening.

> *Listening is as important as talking. If you're a good listener, people often compliment you for being a good conversationalist.*
> —FORMER GOV. JESSE VENTURA

Listen

When I ask you to listen to me and you start giving advice, you have not done what I asked.

When I ask you to listen to me and you begin to tell me why I shouldn't feel that way, you are trampling on my feelings.

When I ask you to listen to me and you feel you have to do something to solve my problems, you have failed me, strange as that may seem.

Listen! All I asked was that you listen, not talk or do—just hear me. And I can do for myself; I'm not helpless.

When you do something for me that I can and need to do for myself, you contribute to my fear and weakness.

But when you accept as simple fact that I do feel what I feel, no matter how irrational, then I quit trying to convince you and can get about the business of understanding what's behind this irrational feeling.

And when that's clear the answers are obvious and I don't need advice.

Irrational feelings make sense when we understand what's behind them. So, please listen and just hear me, and if you want to talk, wait a minute for your turn, and I'll listen to you.

–Author Unknown

Internal psychological filter. Each of us has an internal psychological filter through which we process all the information we receive. This filter consists of prejudices, past experiences, hopes, and anxieties. Everything that we hear, see, or read is interpreted through this filter. For example, the style of a speaker's clothing, facial expressions, posture, accent, color of skin or hair, mannerisms, or age can cause you to make prejudgments and tune him or her out—all because of what is in your filter.

The further we go through life, the more clogged that filter can get. Regardless of what we intend to say, what is ultimately heard depends on what is in the filter of the listener. If your filter contains memories of many painful past experiences, then you may perceive hurt where none is intended. If your filter contains a reservoir of unexpressed anger from the past, then you may hear anger in what others say, regardless of their intent. In *Principle Centered Leadership,* Stephen Covey (2005) summarizes the *root* of most communication problems as being *perception problems:*

> None of us see the world as it is but as we are, as our frames of reference or "maps" define the territory. And our experience-induced perceptions greatly influence our feelings, beliefs, and behavior.

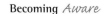

Hidden agenda. Sometimes we enter a conversation or situation with a special interest in mind, a grudge which we want to bring into the open, or even a "chip on our shoulder." Consequently, we may hear the message in accordance with our own needs. Either consciously or unconsciously, we may sabotage a meeting or direct a conversation in such a way as to further our own needs and motives.

Preoccupation and lack of interest. The communication failures arising from the gap between what the senders meant and the receivers understood does not usually arise from word usage or lack of verbal ability. Many times we are so preoccupied that we just do not listen to what others are saying. We may allow our mind to wander while we are waiting for the speaker to make his or her next point. Perhaps, we need to remember that the *rate of speech* is about 100–150 words per minute and the *rate of thought* is about 400–600 words per minute. Also, we may be so preoccupied with what we have to say that we listen to others only to find an opening to get the floor to say what we want to say. Sometimes, our fast-paced lifestyle contributes to our not taking the time to really listen to others. We may not even be interested or care enough to listen.

> *Listening is a magnetic and strange thing, a creative force. The friends who listen to us are the ones we move toward, and we want to sit in their radius. When we are listened to, it creates us, makes us unfold and expand.*
> —KARL MENNINGER

HOW TO IMPROVE YOUR LISTENING SKILLS

- Be receptive and attentive
- Allow the speaker to speak freely; limit your lip
- Listen to the speaker and ignore distractions
- Avoid preoccupation with your own thoughts and what you want to say next
- Use verbal following or minimal encourages (**minimal encourages** are brief indicators to the speaker that you are following their thoughts; e.g., "mm-hmm," nods, or repeating one or two of the speaker's words)
- Avoid all judgments, initially
- Try to listen for more than just the spoken words
- Use feedback and reflect on what the speaker said

Adapted from Hamilton (2014) and Fisher-Sykes (2005).

A story is told of a very busy business executive who every morning rushed through the office and asked his secretary, "How are you?" She always said, "Fine, thank you." After all, is not that what we expect others to say to such a question? Rushing through the office, the executive replied, "That is great." One day, the secretary decided to really "test" the executive's ear. When the usual question came the next morning, the secretary said, "Terrible, terrible, thank you." The executive, still rushing into his office replied, "That is great." The executive's ear had really been tested.

> *The word <u>listen</u> contains the same letters as the word <u>silent</u>.*
> —ALFRED BRENDEL

It seems as though the capacity to listen effectively is a "natural gift" for some people. This "natural gift" has been referred to as *sensitivity*. However, the ability to listen can be cultivated by anyone who wants to develop this capacity. It requires a conscious alertness that can become a *habit* with practice.

Styles of Responding

How do you respond when others want to discuss their problems or innermost feelings with you? Do you ask a lot of questions? Are you judgmental, or supportive? Do you ever criticize?

Noted psychologist Carl Rogers (1995) indicates that a major barrier to building close relationships is the very natural tendency we have to *judge and evaluate the statements made by others.*

Sometimes we overuse one style, rely on the style too early in the conversation, or fail to know when and how to use a style that will be of most benefit to the sender and thereby create a better relationship. Let us discuss six of the more common styles of responding: 1) Evaluative or Judging, 2) Advising, 3) Interpretative, 4) Supportive, 5) Questioning, and 6) Understanding (Adler, et al., 2015).

> *Don't judge any person until you have walked two moons in their moccasins.*
> —NATIVE AMERICAN PROVERB

Evaluative or judging. This type of response shows that the receiver is making a judgment about the motive, personality, or reasoning of the sender. The evaluation indicates the sender's statement is either "right" or "wrong." The response may be positive, "You're right on target," or unfavorable, "You shouldn't feel that way." In both cases, the receiver appears to be qualified to suggest to the sender what he or she might or ought to do.

Since evaluative or judgmental responses often lead to defensiveness, it is best to begin your responses with "I feel . . .," rather than "You are . . ." Evaluative or judgmental responses are best accepted when you have been specifically asked to make a value judgment and when you want to disclose your own values and attitudes. In the early stages of relationships, it is generally best to avoid evaluative or judgmental responses.

Criticizing. Even though criticizing is often a part of the evaluative or judging response, it is also a commonly used and even misunderstood response pattern. Therefore, we have decided to discuss it separately. Sometimes, you may want to give someone some constructive feedback, but you are afraid they will perceive it as criticism. After all, have not you perceived feedback as really just criticism? Criticism often has a negative connotation and may not be pleasant, but it can be helpful when it leads to productive changes. If you want to give constructive criticism or feedback, rather than destructive criticism or feedback, it is wise to remember these points (Groder, 1997):

- **Emphasize Behavior Rather than Personalities.** Concentrate on what a person does or says rather than who you think the person is. The use of choice adjectives oftentimes leads to labeling the person rather than the behavior. This causes defensiveness. There is a big difference between saying, "John is lazy" and in "John works slowly."

- **Refrain from Using "You" Messages.** The use of "You" messages creates a feeling of blame and accusation. It is more appropriate to say, "I felt hurt today when . . ." rather than use, "You were cruel today when . . ."
- **Focus on Actual Observations Rather than Judgments.** Reporting what actually occurred is giving objective feedback. However, reporting on what you think about what actually occurred is giving subjective, value-laden feedback. It is one thing to say, "I really liked the house better the way it was decorated," and quite another to say, "The house looks terrible now."
- **Do Not Criticize When You Are Angry or Upset.** Other people will hear only your anger and not your message. "Cool down" until you can express yourself with facts. It is acceptable to say, "I need to think this through and get back with you later."
- **Concentrate on Sharing Ideas Rather than on Giving Advice.** It is less threatening to say, "Here are some ideas for you to think about . . ." rather than, "Well, you would be wise to do . . ." Sharing ideas gives options to others; advising implies, "My solution is the best way."

When others respond to you with criticism, it is easier to handle if you can learn to deal with it *intellectually* and not *emotionally. Remember to respond and not to react.* Rather than hearing criticism as a personal attack, it might be helpful to remember some suggestions from Harriet Lerner (2002):

- **Listen.** Do not panic and get defensive when someone criticizes you. Calm listening helps you think clearly.
- **Analyze.** Is the criticism factually correct or is the critic mostly venting anger? If the critic is really just venting, you can sympathize with his or her feelings without accepting the content of what they say.
- **Decide What to Do.** If the criticism is accurate, what can you do to remedy the situation and prevent recurrences? If you decide to change your behavior as a result of the criticism, let your critic know.
- **Practice.** Make an honest effort to consistently practice the new routine or behavior until it feels natural or becomes a habit.

Advising. This is responding to others by offering a solution. Sometimes this type of response is helpful and sometimes it is not. For example, we may have the tendency to tell others how we would behave in their place. They may not want to hear what we would do; they may just want us to listen to their thoughts. Giving advice also means that you may get blamed if the advice is followed and *does not work. In giving advice, it is helpful* to remember to be sure: 1) your advice is correct, 2) the other person really wants your advice, 3) the other person is willing to accept the responsibility for choosing to follow your advice.

> *I've learned that people will forget what you said, people will forget what you did, but people will never forget how you made them feel.*
> —MAYA ANGELOU

> *Criticism, like rain, should be gentle enough to nourish one's growth without destroying one's roots.*
> —THE BEST OF BITS & PIECES

Foster Cline (Cline & Fay, 2006), a nationally known psychiatrist, frequently suggests two magic sentences that will keep you from appearing dogmatic when offering advice:

I wonder if it would be helpful to . . . rather than, if I were you, I would . . .
Do you think it would be beneficial to . . . rather than, you really should . . .

When giving advice, it is important to remember some advice from Paula Englander-Golden and Virginia Satir (1991):

We maximize our chances of being heard when we express our caring friendship and support while expressing our hopes, wishes, and a specific suggestion that our friend can consider.

Interpretative. In this response, the receiver tries to tell the sender what his or her problem really is and how the sender really feels about the situation. The receiver implies what the sender might or ought to think. Consider these statements:

I don't think you really mean to say that.
Maybe you are really feeling . . .
It sounds to me that what is actually bothering you is . . .

Giving an interpretative response can often offer a person another way of looking at his or her situation. It can produce great insight. Interpretative responses are best received when they are made as suggestions rather than as absolutes and when they are offered with integrity and empathy.

Supportive. This response shows the receiver's intent is to reassure, comfort, or minimize the intense feelings of the sender. There is an implication that the sender should not feel as he or she does. Statements such as, "Now, it is okay. It is all going to be better," or "Mary, you don't have anything to worry about. I know you can pass your test," are examples of supportive responses. Consider this exchange:

Sender: I could die here, and no one would even notice.

Receiver: Now, now, it's okay. It's all going to be better. I will help you.

This reply may not have acknowledged the content or emotion of the original statement and may get you involved in a situation you wished you had avoided. It might be more helpful to simply say, "Let's talk about why you feel this way."

Supportive statements are best received when they are sincere and help others to feel accepted and motivated to try to solve their problems. Sometimes, supportive statements can be made in a joking manner and result in the sender feeling "put down" and "worse off" than before.

Questioning. This response indicates that the receiver wants to probe the sender for additional information and to discuss the issue further. The receiver often implies that the sender might benefit from discussing the issue in more detail. Typical statements might be:

I've learned that it is best to give advice in only two circumstances: When it is requested and when it is a life-threatening situation.
—ANDY ROONEY, COMIC COMMUNICATOR

The greatest compliment that was ever paid me was when one asked me what I thought, and attended to my answer..
—HENRY DAVID THOREAU

What is your understanding of why your husband lost his job?
How do you feel about that?

Questioning is a way to get additional information so that you can understand the situation in more detail. Actually, if you do not understand the situation, it is extremely important that you try to ask questions for clarification before you respond to the situation. We have a tendency to ask questions that often fail to give us adequate information. Let us distinguish between two types of questions: *closed questions and open questions. Closed questions* often result in yes, no, or a very short response. *Open questions*, on the other hand, provide space for the speaker to explore his or her thoughts.

Let us look at a typical example between a boss and an employee who have been having conflict with a valued customer. The employee enters the boss's office, and the boss replies:

Closed question: Do you want to see me about the Smith account?

Open question: What's on your mind, Linda?

In short, closed questions are like multiple choice or true/false test questions, whereas open questions are like essay questions.

It is also important that you ask questions about the issue raised, rather than asking questions about irrelevant issues. You do not want to lead the sender to possibly more problems and forget the original issue.

Another important aspect of questioning is to remember to avoid *interrogating and manipulating* the other person. Too many questions do precisely that.

If you have reviewed the Communication Spoilers and given some thought to the styles of responding discussed above, you may be thinking to yourself, "I am confused. It seems that all these responses can spoil my attempts at listening and communicating. Is there another type of response that will be more effective for me?"

Understanding. This response indicates that the receiver is seeking to fully understand what the sender is actually saying. Stephen Covey (2013), author of *The 7 Habits of Highly Effective People,* believes that understanding is the key to achieving effective interpersonal communication. Covey makes a profound point about understanding:

If I were to summarize in one sentence the single most important principle I have learned in the field of interpersonal relations, it would be this: Seek first to understand, then to be understood.

Because this is the most effective way of responding to others and requires the specific skills of active listening, sometimes referred to as empathetic listening, we will now discuss the meaning and development of these skills.

> Some people are born more Tigger-ish, and others are born more Eeyore-ish.
> —GRETCHEN RUBIN

> I am not who you think I am, I am not who I think I am, I am who I think you think I am.
> —CHARLES H. COOLEY

Implicit Bias. One of the key aspects of interpersonal communications that can happen in your verbal and non-verbal response is implicit bias. Being diligent in your communications is key to dealing with it. "Implicit bias refers to the attitudes or stereotypes that affect our understanding, actions, and decisions in an unconscious manner. These biases, which encompass both favorable and unfavorable assessments, are activated involuntarily and without an individual's awareness or intentional control" (Kirwan Institute, 2016).

A Few Key Characteristics of Implicit Biases

- Implicit biases are **pervasive**. Everyone possesses them, even people with avowed commitments to impartiality such as judges.

- Implicit and explicit biases are **related but distinct mental constructs**. They are not mutually exclusive and may even reinforce each other.

- The implicit associations we hold **do not necessarily align with our declared beliefs** or even reflect stances we would explicitly endorse.

- We generally tend to hold implicit biases that **favor our own in-group**, though research has shown that we can still hold implicit biases against our in-group.

- Implicit biases are **malleable**. Our brains are incredibly complex, and the implicit associations that we have formed can be gradually unlearned through a variety of debiasing techniques. (Kirwan Institute for the Study of Race and Ethnicity.osu.edu, 2016)

Active Listening—Empathetic Listening

The reality of the other person is not in what he reveals to you, but in what he cannot reveal to you. Therefore, if you would understand him, listen not to what he says but rather to what he does not say.
—KAHLIL GIBRAN

In *active listening* you see the expressed idea, attitude, or problem from the other person's point of view, to sense how it feels to the sender, and to achieve the sender's frame of reference in regard to the thing he or she is talking about. This really means that you are listening with the whole body and that you are paying careful attention to the person who is talking. How is this achieved?

As a vehicle of communication, listening must focus on the other person, not just on what the other person is saying. This has been referred to as *listening with the third ear*. The third ear hears what is said between the lines and without words, what is expressed soundlessly, and what the speaker feels and thinks. It is listening in such a way that it creates an atmosphere of communication; others will be able to hear us because they feel we have heard them, that we are in touch with them and not just what they are saying. How can you learn to listen with the third ear?

Robert Bolton (1986) and Thomas Gordon (2000) have written extensively about the requirements of active listening. We will now discuss four of these: 1) develop a pos-

© Monkey Business Images/Shutterstock.com

Are you an effective listener?

ture of involvement, 2) make use of door openers, 3) keep the other person talking with minimal encouragement, and 4) respond reflectively.

Develop a posture of involvement. This means you practice the habit of inclining your body toward the speaker rather than leaning back in the chair or slouching around on the floor or on the sofa. It also means you position yourself at a comfortable distance from the speaker so that you can have close eye contact. Usually, about three feet is a comfortable distance in our society. Effective eye contact expresses interest and a desire to listen. You will also need to turn the TV or stereo off and remove any environmental distractions. Remember that to actively "listen" means to move with the speaker.

Make use of door openers. This is really just an invitation for the other person to say more. These responses do not communicate any of the listener's own ideas or judgments or feelings; they merely invite the other person to share his own ideas, judgments, or feelings. Some examples might be:

> Tell me more about that . . .
> Let's talk about it . . .
> Go ahead, I'm listening . . .
> Sounds like you have a lot of feelings about that . . .
> This seems like something that is important to you . . .
> I'd like to hear some more about that . . .
> Can you tell me what's going on . . .?
> Sounds like this is difficult for you to talk about . . .

I won't look for love today. I will just give it. It will bless me tenfold. Love is not getting, but giving. It is sacrifice. And sacrifice is glorious!
—JOANNA FIELD

Most people feel encouraged to talk with the use of door openers. More importantly, people feel worthy, respected, significant, and accepted when we invite them to share their feelings and ideas.

Keep the other person talking with minimal encouragement. Minimal encouragement (Bolton used the term "minimal encourages") are brief indicators to the other person that you are still listening. Some examples you can use are:

- "Mm-hmmm"
- "Really?"
- "You did, huh."
- "How about that!"
- "Go on."
- "I see."
- "Oh."
- "And?"
- "Interesting."
- "I hear you."

Another way to use minimal encourages is to repeat the last word or two of the speaker's comment. When the speaker says, "I just don't know what to do; I guess I'm confused," the listener may respond, "Confused?" Generally, the speaker will then express more about his or her confusion.

Respond reflectively. Thomas Gordon (2000) explains responding reflectively in this way:

> In active listening, the receiver tries to understand what the sender is feeling or what his message means. Then, he puts his understanding into his own words and feeds it back for the sender's verification. The receiver does not send a message of his own—such as an evaluation, opinion, advice, logic, analysis, or question. He feeds back only what he feels the sender's message meant—nothing more, nothing less.

As you can probably see, when you use active listening, you really respond reflectively in two ways. *First, you paraphrase or state the essence of the other's content in your own words, focusing on facts and ideas rather than the emotions the sender is expressing.*

Paraphrasing responses usually begin with phrases such as:

> What I hear you saying is . . .
> Correct me if I'm wrong . . .
> Do I understand you correctly that . . .

Let us look at this exchange:

> **Sender:** "My psychology professor is really piling the assignments on, and I'll never get caught up. Does she think psychology is the only course I am taking?"

Receiver: "Do I understand you correctly that she is giving you too much work and doesn't realize you have three other college courses?"

Sender: "Oh she knows I have other courses, but it is just the end of the semester, and she is shoving it all in at the last minute."

Receiver: "It doesn't seem fair, is that it?"

Sender: "It really isn't, but I'll just have to buckle down and get the work done. I need this course on my degree plan."

Sometimes people confuse paraphrasing with parroting. However, *parroting* means to repeat exactly the speaker's words.

Secondly, when possible, mirror back to the speaker the emotions they are communicating. The most difficult part of learning to respond reflectively is to listen for the feeling of the other person. The format is simple when you learn to listen for feeling words. For example:

"You sound _____ about _____."

- Angry
- Frustrated
- Worried
- Upset
- Excited
- This
- That
- The other thing
- All of this
- These

Let us look at some examples:

Sender: "I could die here, and no one would even notice."

Receiver: "You sound really frustrated."

Sender: "Oh, I just get to thinking that no one really cares about me."

Receiver: "So, maybe you aren't frustrated, but just a little angry."

Sender: "Yeah, I suppose I am a little angry. I just wish I knew how my family really cares about me."

You will note that in both of these examples, the receiver actively demonstrates that he or she genuinely wants to understand the sender and to hear more of the problem. The receiver does not make evaluative or judgmental responses regarding either the sender or the content. Instead, the receiver just paraphrases or mirrors back what the

Next to physical survival, the greatest need of a human being is psychological survival—to be understood, to be affirmed, to be validated, to be appreciated.
—STEPHEN COVEY

sender has said. By maintaining an objective stance, the active listener encourages a sharing of ideas and paves the way for a freer exchange of other points of view.

Active listening is an excellent tool to use in "heated discussions." The next time you get into an argument with your wife, husband, friend, or a small group of friends, just stop the discussion for a moment and, for an experiment, generate Carl Rogers' (1995) communication rule: ***Each person can speak up only after he or she has restated the ideas and feelings of the previous speaker accurately and to that speaker's satisfaction***. This is the heart of active listening.

Do you see what this would mean? It would simply mean that before presenting your point of view, it would be necessary for you to achieve the other speaker's frame of reference—to understand his or her feelings so well that you could summarize them for him or her. Sounds simple, doesn't it? If you try it, however, you will discover that it is one of the most difficult things you have ever tried to do. Nevertheless, once you have been able to see the other person's point of view, your own comments will have to be drastically revised. You will also find that with this type of listening and response, there is an attitude of open, two-way communication.

Something to Think About When a Relationship Ends

- Sleep more. Take care of yourself.
- Do things you enjoy and surround yourself with special friends.
- Think About It: we all have friends or lovers we loved and lost.
- The best way to deal with it is to enjoy the good memories and try not to repeat the bad ones. Remember: "better loved and lost than never loved before."
- Often relationships and friendships revolve around activities we do like work, school, church. Volunteering is a good way to meet people because you share your common interests.
- If your friendships last for years they are very special: you are special too.
- Happiness can become your new project.

WHICH STYLE OF RESPONDING DO YOU USE?

Of the styles of responding we have discussed in this chapter, how often do people use each response? Carl Rogers (1995), a noted psychologist, conducted a series of studies on how individuals communicate with each other in face-to-face situations. *(You will note that Rogers studied five styles, whereas we included six in our discussion. That is because Rogers considered the advising response style to be closely related to the evaluative or judging style.)* He found that the categories of evaluative or judging, interpretative, supportive, questioning, and understanding statements encompass 80 percent

Becoming Aware

of all the messages sent between individuals. The other 20 percent of the statements are incidental and of no real importance. From his observations of individuals in all sorts of different settings—business, home, people at parties and conventions, and so on—he found that the responses were used by individuals in the following frequency: 1) *evaluative or judging* was most used, 2) *interpretative* was next, 3) *supportive* was the third most common response, 4) *questioning* the fourth, and 5) *understanding* was the least-used style in human communication. Finally, he found that if a person uses one category of response as much as 40 percent of the time, then other people see him as *always* responding that way.

Although we would classify this last statement as a process of oversimplification, the question to ask yourself is, What style of responding to others do I use most often? Obviously, depending on various situations, you use all of the styles as you constantly interact with others. It would be beneficial to pay careful attention and become aware of how you respond to others. Then, you be the judge: are you pleased with the way you respond to others?

Human relations is also a systematic study of the ongoing process of shared interactions that occur among people in all aspects of their lives.

Person-to-Person Communication

How do we integrate all that we have discussed in this chapter to improve our communication with those with whom we live and work? In the late 1950s, psychologist Carl Rogers (1957) hypothesized that there were three qualities essential to constructive communication: 1) *genuineness,* 2) *acceptance and respect of others, and* 3) *empathy.* Since then, numerous research studies have been conducted that support Rogers's theory.

Genuineness. This means being honest and open about one's feelings, needs, and ideas. *Genuineness* means being what one really is without front or facade. The authentic person experiences feelings and is able to express those feelings when appropriate. A genuine person can spontaneously be himself with another so they know him as he truly is: "What you see is what you get." Being a genuine person involves the search and constant improvement directed toward self-awareness, self-acceptance, and self-expression. Robert Bolton (1986), a human performance and communication skills consultant in New York, summarizes genuineness in this way:

> Genuineness is essential to all vital relationships. To the degree that I lack authenticity, I am unable to relate significantly to any other person. I must dare to be me to be able to relate to you.

> *When we put ourselves in the other person's place, we're less likely to want to put him in his place.*
> —FARMER'S DIGEST

> *To be persuasive, we must be believable; to be believable, we must be credible; to be credible, we must be truthful.*
> —EDWARD R. MURROW, JOURNALIST

Acceptance and respect of others. This refers to the decision to offer an atmosphere largely uncontaminated by evaluations of the other's thoughts, feelings, or behaviors. In a way, it can even be described as attitude of neutrality toward another person or persons. It also means that we **respect** the other person's capacity and right to self-direction, rather than believing that his or her life would be best guided by us. ***Acceptance*** is not synonymous with approval. You can accept another person's feelings and still not approve of his behaviors. It is even possible to be accepting and confrontational at the same time. Menninger and Holzman (2010) of the Menninger Clinic in Topeka, Kansas, speak of this quality in the following way:

> I believe this quality is demonstrated by a person's patience, fairness, consistency, rationality, and kindliness for the other person—accepting the other person as he or she is.

> For much of the nation's history, America has discussed race in the singular form. But the language of race is changing. With the rise of interracial couples, combined with a more accepting society, America's multiracial population has grown at three times the rate of the general population since the beginning of the millennium. The U.S. Census Bureau says 2.1% of American adults check more than one race. Using a broader definition that factors in the racial backgrounds of parents and grandparents, a new Pew Research Center report finds that 6.9% of U.S. adults, or nearly 17 million, could be considered multiracial today. Intermarriage and the children of such marriages—particularly white and black—haven't always been accepted by society. It was less than 50 years ago that the U.S. Supreme Court, in the case bearing the evocative title *Loving v. Virginia*, struck down laws prohibiting mixed-race marriages that had been in place in 16 states, all in the South. In 2013, 12% of new marriages were interracial, and today very few Americans see this as a bad thing for society (Pew Research Center, 2015).

> Multiracial Americans are no longer rare in number. They're front and center in our culture—represented on television, in professional sports, in music and politics, even in the White House. (Pew Research Center, 2015). Listen to some multi-racial people tell their stories. The link is in the Resources section for this chapter. http://www.pewresearch.org/multiracial-voices/

Empathy. You will recall, when we were discussing the tremendous benefits of the understanding response style, we referred to specific methods that foster empathetic listening. You may also recall that in Chapter Four we referred to *empathy* as one of the key qualities of emotional intelligence. In fact, Carl Rogers (1995) indicates that empathy is the most effective agent we know for fostering personal growth and improving a person's relationships and communications with others. What, then, is this quality, *empathy*?

Empathy refers to the ability to understand how another person feels and how he or she perceives the situation. To see things from the other person's point of view, Sam Horn (1997), author of the communication book, *Tongue Fu! How to Deflect, Disarm and Defuse Any Verbal Conflict*, recommends using the Empathy Phrases:

How would I feel?
How would I feel if I were in their shoes?
How would I feel if this were happening to me?

It is important to note that empathy is not sympathy (Ciaramicoli, 2001). *Sympathy* is an involuntary feeling—the passive experience of sharing another person's fear, grief, anger, or joy. *Empathy* is an active process in which you try to learn all you can about another person rather than having only a superficial awareness. With sympathy, you view the other person's situation from your point of view. With empathy, you view it from the other person's perspective (Adler & Proctor, 2015). Milton Mayeroff (1990) describes what it means to *learn all you can about another person*:

> To care for another person, I must be able to understand him and his world as if I were inside it. I must be able to see, as it were, with his eyes what his world is like to him and how he sees himself. Instead of merely looking at him in a detached way from outside, as if he were a specimen, I must be able to be with him in his world, "going" into his world in order to sense from "inside" what life is like for him, what he is striving to be, and what he requires to grow.

As we have discussed, genuineness, acceptance and respect of others, and empathy are actually attitudes that foster improved relationships with people. The dictionary defines an *attitude* as a "mental or emotional orientation to some object." When these three attitudes are missing, a person's relationships are diminished. When these attitudes are present, the relationships can flourish. However, they have little or no effect on a relationship until they are communicated to the other party. Since these three attitudes are strengthened and nourished every time they are expressed, the question you might want to ask yourself now is: When do I plan to start practicing the art and skills of genuineness, acceptance and respect of others, and empathy?

To end this chapter, Dale Carnegie, Author of How to win friends and influence has these words of wisdom (Carnegie, 2010):

Six Ways to Make People Like You

1. **Become genuinely interested in other people.** "You can make more friends in two months by being interested in them, than in two years by making them interested in you." The only way to make quality, lasting friendships is to learn to be genuinely interested in them and their interests.

2. **Smile.** Happiness does not depend on outside circumstances, but rather on inward attitudes. Smiles are free to give and have an amazing

Five Phrases to Live By:
"Thank you"
"I love you."
"How are you?"
"What do you need?"
"I'm sorry."
—RABBI RIEMER

We must practice the skill of listening instead of speaking, of acknowledging and celebrating difference instead of recoiling from it, of putting ourselves, as squarely as we can, into the experience of others.
—ANDRE CAROTHERS

ability to make others feel wonderful. Smile in everything that you do.

3. **Remember that a person's name is, to that person, the sweetest and most important sound in any language.** "The average person is more interested in their own name than in all the other names in the world put together." People love their names so much that they will often donate large amounts of money just to have a building named after them. We can make people feel extremely valued and important by remembering their name.

4. **Be a good listener. Encourage others to talk about themselves.** The easiest way to become a good conversationalist is to become a good listener. To be a good listener, we must actually care about what people have to say. Many times people don't want an entertaining conversation partner; they just want someone who will listen to them.

5. **Talk in terms of the other person's interest.** The royal road to a person's heart is to talk about the things he or she treasures most. If we talk to people about what they are interested in, they will feel valued and value us in return.

6. **Make the other person feel important – and do it sincerely.** The golden rule is to treat other people how we would like to be treated. We love to feel important and so does everyone else. People will talk to us for hours if we allow them to talk about themselves. If we can make people feel important in a sincere and appreciative way, then we will win all the friends we could ever dream of.

All the mistakes I have made, all the follies I have witnessed, all the errors I have committed have been the result of action without thought.
—ANONYMOUS

Chapter Review

We all share the common problem of trying to combat communication breakdowns. When we stop to think of how many ways we can misunderstand each other, it seems a wonder that any effective communication can take place.

- **Communication** is the process of conveying feelings, attitudes, facts, beliefs, and ideas between individuals, either verbally or nonverbally. Communication is effective when the message we intend to convey is the message that is actually received.
- In any given situation, there are three commonly accepted parts to the communication process. There is always: 1) a sender of the message, 2) a receiver of the message, and 3) the content of the message. There are several elements involved in a communication transaction: the idea, encoding, transmission, receiving, decoding, understanding, and feedback.
- **Feedback** is really the only means for determining whether there is mutual understanding between the sender and receiver. Feedback completes the process of two-way communication. In one-way communication, there is an absence of active verbal feedback.
- A large percentage of our communication is by **nonverbal** means. This can include facial expressions and eye contact, vocal cues, gestures and other body movements, touching, personal space and distance, physical environment and territory, clothing and personal appearance, and silence.
- Nonverbal communication can relate to verbal communication in three ways: Nonverbal communication can reinforce, replace, and contradict the verbal message. When the nonverbal message contradicts the verbal message, the nonverbal message is generally more accurate.
- The ability to identify deception in others is around 50 percent. **Microexpressions**, fleeting facial expressions that last only a fraction of a second, are oftentimes helpful. Signals of deception are often called **body leakage**, where body postures rather than the face leak the truth.
- **Microagressions** are the everyday verbal, nonverbal, and environmental slights, snubs, or insults, whether intentional or unintentional, which communicate hostile, derogatory, or negative messages that target persons based solely upon their marginalized group membership.
- The meanings of various kinds of nonverbal communication can vary from culture to culture. Communication can be enhanced when these meanings are understood.
- We share, give, and receive information through words and establish, continue, or terminate relationships through words—verbal communication. The meaning and understanding behind words are the essences of communication.
- There are several barriers or ways that meanings can go astray: semantics, assumptions, self-concept, and emotion-packed phrases.
- Men and women often use different styles in communication. That is, males are likely to speak and hear a language of "status and independence" while females are likely to speak and hear a language of "connection and intimacy."
- **Listening** is a form of paying attention, which is an active process involving much more than hearing and seeing. When another person speaks, we are usually listening at one of four levels: ignoring, pretending, selective listening, and attentive listening. Very few of us listen with the intent to understand—**empathetic listening**. Some of the barriers to listening include: internal psychological filter, hidden agenda, preoccupation, and lack of interest. **Noise** can occur while sending and receiving a message.
- There are five stages of listening: to sense, interpret, evaluate, respond, and remember.

- There are at least six common styles of responding to others: 1) Evaluating or judging, 2) advising, 3) interpreting, 4) supporting, 5) questioning, and 6) understanding.
- The most common form of responding to others is evaluating or judging, and the least-used style in human communication is the understanding style.
- Criticizing is often a part of the evaluating or judging response. It is extremely important to remember to give and receive criticism intellectually, rather than emotionally.
- The understanding style requires the specific skills of active listening, sometimes called empathetic listening—seeing the expressed idea, attitude, or problem from the other person's point of view. The requirements of active listening or empathetic listening are to develop a posture of involvement, make use of door openers, keep the other person talking with "minimal encouragement," and respond reflectively.
- Researchers and theorists in the behavioral sciences have identified three qualities or attitudes that, when communicated to others, foster improved relationships with people. These qualities are genuineness, acceptance and respect of others, and empathy.
- **Implicit bias** refers to the attitudes or stereotypes that affect our understanding, actions, and decisions in an unconscious manner. These biases, which encompass both favorable and unfavorable assessments, are activated involuntarily and without an individual's awareness or intentional control.

Test Review Questions: Learning Outcomes

1. Define communication. Why do we need to communicate?
2. What are the three commonly accepted parts to the communication process? What is involved in a communication transaction?
3. Define feedback and explain why it is so important. Describe the difference in feedback in one-way and two-way communication.
4. What are the three ways nonverbal communication relates to verbal communication? When the nonverbal message contradicts the verbal message, which message is usually more accurate?
5. How likely is it that deception can be detected in others? Define microexpressions, microaggressions, and body leakage.
6. What are at least five different types of nonverbal communication? Which form of nonverbal communication communicates more emotional meaning more accurately? Define paralinguistics and give at least two examples in sentence form. Define the four distances Edward T. Hall discovered in his research.
7. Give at least five examples of cultural differences in nonverbal communication.
8. Explain at least four barriers or ways that meanings can go astray in verbal communication.
9. What are some examples of emotion-packed phrases? What is the key to remember in dealing with these phrases?
10. Compare and contrast at least six differences in the communication styles of men and women.
11. What is the difference in listening and hearing? List and discuss the five different levels of listening we may employ when another person speaks.
12. Name and describe the five stages of listening.
13. What are the barriers to listening? What is the difference between external and internal noise?
14. Give at least four techniques for improving nonverbal communication, verbal communication, and listening skills.

15. Define and give examples of the six common styles of responding to others. What is the most used responding style in human communication? What is the least-used responding style in human communication?
16. What are the suggestions to remember when giving and receiving criticism?
17. Give examples of the four requirements for active listening or empathetic listening.
18. What are the three qualities or attitudes, when communicated to others, that improve relationships with people?
19. Explain the empathy phrases. What is the difference between empathy and sympathy?

Key Terms

Active Listening
Advising Response
Assume (Assumptions)
Attentive Listening
Body Leakage
Closed Questions
Communication
Communication Barriers
Communication Channels
Communication Process
Decoding
Door Openers
Emotion-Packed Phrases
Empathetic Listening
Empathy
Encoding
External Noise
Feedback
Genuineness
Hearing
Hidden Agenda

Implicit Bias
Ignoring while Listening
Internal Noise
Internal Psychological Filter
Interpretative Response
Intimate Distance
Judging Response
Kinesics
Listening
Listening with the Third Ear
Microagressions
Microexpressions
Minimal Encourages
Noise
Nonverbal Communication
One-Way Communication
Open Questions
Paralinguistics
Paraphrase
Parroting

Parts of a Communication
    Transaction
Passive Listening
Personal Distance
Pretending while Listening
Public Distance
Questioning Response
Reacting to Others
Responding Reflectively
Responding to Others
Selective Listening
Semantics
Social Distance
Supportive Response
Symbols in Communication
Sympathy
Two-Way Communication
Understanding Response
Verbal Communication
"You" Messages

Reflections: Critical Thinking

1. Discuss the causes for communication breakdown. In your opinion, what presents the biggest problem?
2. Many times nonverbal messages are more honest and revealing than what is verbally expressed. Why? Give examples of nonverbal communication to support your answer.
3. Discuss the signals you rely on to try to detect deception in others.

4. Discuss some examples of semantics in your field of work—occupational jargon.
5. Is it possible to give constructive criticism without causing the other person to become defensive? How?
6. Of the techniques discussed for improving listening skills, which technique will be most difficult for you to use?
7. Of the six common styles of responding to others, which style of responding is the most difficult for you to use? Why?
8. Discuss any examples of cultural differences you have experienced in verbal or nonverbal communication.
9. Is it possible that the differences in communication styles of men and women, as discussed in this chapter, have more to do with basic personality styles, rather than gender?
10. What are the key qualities in the communication skills of others that impress you the most?
11. Which part of the empathy phrase is more helpful for you and why?
12. Have you ever felt you were not chosen for a job or a team because of implicit bias?
13. Explain implicit bias.
14. How has technology impacted your life? What about your friends and family?

Web Resources

VIDEOS

http://www.tolerance.org/youth-united

Teaching Tolerance website: Teaching Tolerance, Diversity, and Justice.

http://kirwaninstitute.osu.edu/research/understanding-implicit-bias/

Understanding Implicit Bias: Kirwan Institute for Bias Free Communication.

http://www.pewresearch.org/multiracial-voices/

Multiracial in America.

https://www.ted.com/talks/julian_treasure_5_ways_to_listen_better? language=en

Julian Treasure: 5 Ways to Listen Better.

https://www.youtube.com/watch?v=CWry8xRTwpo

TED Talk: How Body Language and Micro Expressions Predict Success

www.youtube.com/watch?v=xAIFGBlEsbQ

Microaggressions in Everyday Life, a YouTube TED Talk

https://www.youtube.com/watch?v=WDbxqM4Oy1Y

How To Skip the Small Talk and Connect With Anyone, by Kalina Silverman

https://www.youtube.com/watch?v=GAx845QaOck

Marshall Davis Jones: "Touchscreen." National slam poetry contest winner.

https://www.youtube.com/watch?v=lpPASWlnZIA

Darius Simpson and Scout Bostley, "Lost Voices"

https://www.*ted*.com/*talks*/amy_cuddy_your_body_language_shapes_who_you_are?..

Amy Cuddy: Your body language shapes who you are, **a** *TED Tal**k***

Body Language- amy cuddyhttps://youtu.be/jvZdsy9HHpM

https://www.youtube.com/watch?v=PnDgZuGIhHs

Love has no Labels.

ACTIVITIES:

www.authentichappiness.sas.upenn.edu/testcenter.aspx

Brief Strengths Test or VIA Survey of Character Strengths. A self-test that measures 24 character strengths.

https://tbytmedia.com/

Think before you type. Think Before You Type Media Group is a media outlet affiliated with Think Before You Type, Inc. (TBYT), an anti-cyberbullying and positive self-esteem non-profit organization.

https://implicit.harvard.edu/implicit/takeatest.html

Take the Implicit Bias test from Harvard.

http://greatergood.berkeley.edu/quizzes

Quizzes, all based on scientific research, to learn more about yourself, your emotional makeup, and how you relate to others.

http://nonverbal.ucsc.edu/

This web site gives you a chance to learn more about nonverbal communication. You can even test your own ability to "read" samples of real nonverbal communication.

http://www.mindtools.com/CommSkll/ActiveListening.htm

Learning how becoming a better listener can increase your productivity and improve your relationships.

http://www.newconversations.net

A free 100-page guide to better communication skills for work, family, and friendships.

Check out **Connected** by Nicholas Christakis and James Fowler
http://connectedthebook.com/pages/authors.html for powerpoints etc to further your knowledge.

Personal Communication Concerns

PURPOSE

To review individual communication concerns and problems.

INSTRUCTIONS

Following is a list of 15 problems many individuals have as they try to communicate effectively. Read the list and rank your top five individual concerns from 1 to 5, with 1 being your top choice.

_____ A.   I often speak before I really think.
_____ B.   I usually speak rather than really listen to others.
_____ C.   I feel that I am shy.
_____ D.   I let others do most of the talking.
_____ E.   I would rather communicate in writing rather than speaking face to face.
_____ F.   People tell me that I speak too fast.
_____ G.   I often misunderstand what people say to me.
_____ H.   People often misinterpret what I say.
_____ I.   When talking, I gesture more than others.
_____ J.   I often interrupt others while they are talking.
_____ K.   I feel uncomfortable looking into someone's eyes when talking.
_____ L.   When meeting others, I tend to get very nervous.
_____ M.   I have trouble when speaking to people in authority positions.
_____ N.   I feel that others lose interest in what I am saying.
_____ O.   I often find myself playing games with others instead of expressing how I really feel.

DISCUSSION

1.   List your top 5 communication concerns and share them with a small group of 4 or 5 classmates.

2. What steps can you take to begin working on these concerns?

3. What suggestions can the group give you for working on your personal concerns?

Adapted from Communication Research Associates (2016). *Communicate! A Workbook for Interpersonal Communication.* Dubuque, IA: Kendall Hunt Publishing Company.

How Well Do You Know Women and Men?

PURPOSE

To see how well you understand gender differences.

INSTRUCTIONS

Place a check mark (✓) in either the T or F blank at the end of each statement.

1. Women's language is more direct than men's.   T _____ F _____
2. Men seek assistance from others more than women.   T _____ F _____
3. Women try to change others more than men.   T _____ F _____
4. Men are more jealous than women.   T _____ F _____
5. Women boast about their successes more than men.   T _____ F _____
6. Respect is a major issue in the female world.   T _____ F _____
7. Men need more "space"—private time—than women.   T _____ F _____
8. Women respond better to stress than men.   T _____ F _____
9. Men seek approval from others more than women.   T _____ F _____
10. Winning through intimidation is a male skill.   T _____ F _____
11. Women are more decisive than men.   T _____ F _____
12. Men like to give orders more than women.   T _____ F _____
13. Women are more apologetic than men.   T _____ F _____
14. Men tell more jokes and stories than women.   T _____ F _____
15. Women usually dominate public discussions.   T _____ F _____
16. Men accept words at face value more than women.   T _____ F _____
17. Women take more physical risks than men.   T _____ F _____
18. Men talk about their feelings more than women.   T _____ F _____
19. More women than men are worriers.   T _____ F _____
20. Men would rather talk about things than people.   T _____ F _____
21. Women avoid verbal confrontation more than men.   T _____ F _____
22. Men nag—repeat requests—more than women.   T _____ F _____
23. Women interrupt others more than men.   T _____ F _____
24. Men gossip about others as much as women.   T _____ F _____
25. Women want to be married more than men.   T _____ F _____
26. Men talk on the phone more than women.   T _____ F _____
27. Women are more facially animated than men.   T _____ F _____
28. Men's postures lean toward others more often than women's.   T _____ F _____
29. Women have about one-tenth as much testosterone as men.   T _____ F _____
30. Men talk about health matters more than women.   T _____ F _____

What's Your Score? The answers are below.

Here are the answers to the test you took. Give yourself one point for each correct answer.

1. False	9. False	17. False	25. True
2. False	10. True	18. False	26. False
3. True	11. False	19. True	27. True
4. False	12. True	20. True	28. False
5. False	13. True	21. True	29. True
6. False	14. True	22. False	30. False
7. True	15. False	23. False	
8. True	16. True	24. False	

Excellent	**28–30 Correct**
Good	**25–27 Correct**
Fair	**21–24 Correct**

DISCUSSION

1. Do you think there are "true" gender differences in the way men and women communicate? If so, what are the differences?

2. Is it possible the differences could be just more personality differences, rather than biological sex differences? Why or why not?

Excerpted from *The Opposite Sides of the Bed* by Chris Evatt © 1992, 1993, 1994 Chris Evatt, foreword © 1993 by John Gray with permission from Red Wheel/Weiser LLC Newbury, MA and San Francisco, CA. www.redwheelweiser.com

One Way/Two Way

PURPOSE

To demonstrate how descriptive communication can be interpreted differently by other people and also to show the superior functioning of two-way communication.

INSTRUCTIONS

1. A sender is selected to give information to the class.
2. The sender is given a drawing, made up of designs of geometric figures. The participants are given a blank sheet of paper; they are instructed to label one side Diagram I and the other side Diagram II.
3. The sender turns his or her back to the rest of the group and tries to describe verbally how to reproduce the geometric model. This is Diagram I.
4. Participants may neither ask questions nor give audible responses; participants may not talk or compare sketches with the other group members.
5. After 10 or 15 minutes, repeat the exercise with the sender facing his group, and giving directions for Diagram II. Participants should use the other side of their paper designated as Diagram II.
6. Participants may ask any questions they desire. Senders may respond verbally, but no gestures, please.
7. When Diagram II has been completed, the sender shows the participants the two diagrams, and they are to tell him or her how many figures they drew correctly.

NOTE: Instead of selecting one sender for the entire group, triads may be formed, with one student being the sender, one student being the receiver, and one student being the observer. The sender and receiver will place their desks or chairs back to back, with the observer nearby. The observer should record the length of time required for completing Diagram I and Diagram II. The observer will also give feedback to the sender and receiver when the diagrams are complete. For example, what contributed to the diagrams being accurate or inaccurate? Were there any unusual terms used by the sender? How long did it take to complete each diagram?

DISCUSSION

1. What assumptions might you make about one- and two-way communications? Which takes longer? Which is more accurate?

2. Explain which is more frustrating for the sender. For the receiver.

3. What parallels does this exercise have in your everyday life? Does this exercise tell you anything about the way you listen?

Gender and Communication

PURPOSE

To understand the gender differences in language and communication style so that communication can be more effective.

INSTRUCTIONS

1. Individually respond to the questions below, being as specific as possible.
2. Divide into groups of five. Select a spokesperson for the group. Each group member will share his or her responses to the questions below, with the spokesperson taking notes to present to the entire class.

QUESTIONS

1. List three differences in how men and women communicate, listen, and understand various types of communication issues. (Women and men complete both responses.)

Women

Example: *They (We) just want to talk about feelings and relationships.*

Men

They (We) just want to talk about sports and business events.

2. What would you suggest the "other sex" do to facilitate their communication with you? (Women complete women responses and men complete men responses.)

Women

Example: *I would like him to express his feelings more.*

Men

I would like her to become more interested in sports and cars.

3. What would you like the "other sex" to learn and understand about the way you communicate? (Women complete women responses and men complete men responses.)

Women	Men
Example: *I just want him to listen— not try to solve my problems.*	*I don't like to feel pressured into talking about my feelings and problems.*

DISCUSSION

1. What have you learned most about the communication style of men?

2. What have you learned most about the communication style of women?

3. What do you think you need to do to communicate more effectively with the "other sex"?

Name _____ Date _____

Empathetic Listening

PURPOSE

To develop an understanding of the importance of active listening.

INSTRUCTIONS

1. Find a partner, and then move to a place where you can talk comfortably. Designate one person as **A** and the other **B**.
2. Find a subject on the list below on which you and your partner apparently disagree, or you may select a current events topic, a philosophical or moral issue, or perhaps simply a matter of personal taste.
    A. Abortion
    B. Death Penalty
    C. Single Parenting
    D. Teenage Pregnancy
    E. Homosexuality
    F. Euthanasia
    G. Education Standards
    H. Drug/Alcohol Abuse—How to Prevent Their Use
    I. Internet Regulation
    J. Cohabitation
    K. Divorce/Children
    L. Prison Reform
    M. Other . . .
3. **A** begins by making a statement of the subject. **B**'s job is then to paraphrase the idea back, beginning by saying something like, "What I hear you saying is . . ." It is very important that in this step **B** feeds back only what he/she heard **A** say without adding any judgment or interpretation. **B**'s job is simply to understand here, and doing so in no way should signify agreement or disagreement with **A**'s remarks.
4. **A** then responds by telling **B** whether or not his or her response was accurate. If there was some misunderstanding, **A** should make the correction and **B** should feed back his/her new understanding of the statement. Continue this process until you are both sure that **B** understands **A**'s statement.
5. Now it is **B**'s turn to respond to **A**'s statement, and for **A** to help the process of understanding by correcting **B**.
6. Continue this process until each partner is satisfied that he/she has explained himself/herself fully and has been understood by the other person.

DISCUSSION

1. As a listener, how accurate was your first understanding of the speaker's statements?

2. How did your understanding of the speaker's position change after you used active listening?

3. Did you find that the gap between your position and that of your partner narrowed as a result of your both using active listening?

4. How did you feel at the end of your conversation? How does this feeling compare to your usual emotional state after discussing controversial issues with others?

5. How might your life change if you used active listening at home, at work, or with friends?

Name _____ Date _____

Are You an Active Listener?

PURPOSE

To assess your active listening skills and establish goals for improvement.

INSTRUCTIONS

1. Before responding to the statements below, make a copy and have a person with whom you talk regularly answer these questions about you.
2. Select the response that best describes the frequency of your actual behavior. Place the letters A, U, F, O, or S on the line before each of the 15 statements.

Almost Always	Usually	Frequently	Occasionally	Seldom
A	U	F	O	S

_____ 1. I like to listen to people talk. I encourage them to talk by showing interest, by smiling and nodding, and so on.

_____ 2. I pay closer attention to speakers who are more interesting or similar to me.

_____ 3. I evaluate the speaker's words and nonverbal communication ability as they talk.

_____ 4. I avoid distractions; if it is too noisy, I suggest moving to a quiet spot, turning off the TV, and so on.

_____ 5. When people interrupt me to talk, I put what I was doing out of sight and mind and give them my complete attention.

_____ 6. When people are talking I allow them time to finish. I do not interrupt, anticipate what they are going to say, or jump to conclusions.

_____ 7. I tune people out who do not agree with my views.

_____ 8. While the other person is talking or the professor is lecturing, my mind wanders to personal topics.

_____ 9. While the other person is talking, I pay close attention to the nonverbal communications to help me fully understand what the sender is trying to get across.

_____ 10. I tune out and pretend I understand when the topic is difficult.

_____ 11. When the other person is talking, I think about what I am going to say in reply.

_____ 12. When I feel there is something missing or contradictory, I ask direct questions to get the person to explain the idea more fully.

_____ 13. When I do not understand something, I let the sender know.

_____ 14. When listening to other people, I try to put myself in their position and see things from their perspective.

_____ 15. During conversations I repeat back to the sender what has been said in my own words (paraphrase) to be sure I understand correctly what has been said.

KEY FOR SCORING

For items 1, 4, 5, 6, 9, 12, 13, 14, and 15, give yourself: 5 points for each A, 4 for each U, 3 for each F, 2 for each O, and 1 for each S statement. Place the numbers on the line to your response letter. For items, 2, 3, 7, 8, 10, and 11 the score reverses: 5 points for each S, 4 for each O, 3 for each F, 2 for each U, and 1 for each A. Place these score numbers on the lines next to the response letters. Now add your total number of points. Your score should be between 15 and 75. Place your score on the continuum below.

Poor Listener 15 _____ 25 _____ 35 _____ 45 _____ 55 _____ 65 _____ 75 _____ Good Listener

Generally, the higher your score, the better your listening skills.

Note: To improve active listening, items 1, 4, 5, 6, 9, 12, 13, 14, and 15 should be implemented, whereas items 2, 3, 7, 8, 10, and 11 should be avoided.

DISCUSSION

1. Explain how you did on the items to be implemented for improved active listening.

2. Explain how you did on the items to be avoided for improved active listening.

3. How did your perception of your listening skills compare to those of the individual who rated you? Do you agree or disagree?

4. After comparing your perception of your listening skills with those of the individual who rated you, in what areas do you feel you could improve to become a more effective active listener?

Interpersonal Communication

LEARNING JOURNAL

Select the statement below that best defines your feelings about the personal value or meaning gained from this chapter and respond below the dotted line.

I learned that I . . .   I was surprised that I . . .

I realized that I . . .   I was pleased that I . . .

I discovered that I . . .   I was displeased that I . . .

. . . .

Chapter 6
Developing Close Relationships

© wavebreakmedia/Shutterstock.com

[
The 10 Most Important Words in Any Loving Relationship
1. *Trust*   2. *Intimacy*   3. *Communication*   4. *Commitment*   5. *Love*
6. *Friendship*   7. *Patience*   8. *Humor*   9. *Flexibility*   10. *Forgiveness*
— Gregory J. P. Godek, *Love*
]

Think About This...

David is a junior in college. He has had a lot of dates, but has never had a "real, serious" intimate relationship with a member of the opposite sex. David has many close friends and is very active in school activities. He likes to ski, play tennis, watch movies, and listen to all types of music. David would like to become a lawyer and is majoring in political science.

Ashley is a sophomore in college and has dated the same person since her junior year in high school. Ashley was a cheerleader and her boyfriend was captain of his football team. They seem to be "made" for each other. They had the same friends, went to dances together, and studied together. Ashley does not seem to have any other friends since she was always with her boyfriend. Ashley also seems to be depressed. There seems to be something missing in her life, but she is not sure what it is. Presently, Ashley's boyfriend is attending college in another state. She misses him, so she writes and calls him often.

Ashley would like to become a judge, so she is in a pre-law program with emphasis in history. She likes to play tennis and racquetball, water ski, and listen to all types of music. Her boyfriend likes to play and watch football. Ashley only watches football if her boyfriend is playing. He likes ice hockey and plays basketball with the boys. He enjoys going to rock concerts. Her boyfriend is majoring in computer science. When Ashley and her boyfriend get together they are very active and busy, but they do not seem to really talk.

It's the first day of a new term and classes are just beginning. David walks into his European History class and sits down and notices an attractive female sitting three chairs away. It so happens that the attractive female is Ashley. David says to himself, "I would like to get to know her. Just looking at her makes my heart beat faster." Now the dilemma, how does he get to know her and what are the chances of him developing a close intimate relationship with her, especially since she already has a boyfriend?

We will continue following the development of this relationship throughout this chapter.

The Development of a Relationship

Relationships evolve, they do not just happen. They take *time* and *effort*. The first step in a relationship is *becoming aware* of the other person—*first impressions*. At this time we evaluate the person, using our past experience, prejudices, and stereotyping to make a judgment about whether or not to take the next step. David is impressed with Ashley's physical appearance—he perceives her as being attractive. Remember, beauty is in the eye of the beholder; not all people would perceive her as beautiful. Now that David has *become aware* of Ashley, he needs to decide how he is going to take the next step, that is, *making contact,* or getting acquainted with her. This is a difficult step for many individuals.

What would you recommend for David to do in order to get to know Ashley? The *mere exposure phenomenon* may work in this situation (Wood et al., 2014). The more familiar we are with someone or something, the greater the chance of liking them. The more Ashley sees David, the greater the chance of her interacting with him and liking him. David could improve his odds of *making contact* with Ashley by sitting in the chair next to her *(proximity)* or by making sure that he stands near the door every day so she has to pass by him to enter the classroom *(exposure)*. Do not be too aggressive in this process or you may threaten the other person. During the first week or so, David may not even want to say anything—do not make it too obvious.

> *Be slow in choosing a friend, slower in changing.*
> —BENJAMIN FRANKLIN

The third step is *disclosure.* As we become friends, we are more willing to disclose more about our personal lives—our hopes, dreams, and fears. As we begin to disclose information about ourselves, we are demonstrating to our partner that we trust them and they in turn will disclose to us. Thus, the relationship will become stronger and

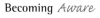

more intimate. As David begins to open up slowly to Ashley, and Ashley to David, the relationship will begin to develop. David could begin by asking Ashley questions about European History, then talk about school-related subjects, ask about her hobbies and interests, and tell her about his interests. As they continue disclosing information about themselves to each other, their interest in one another will continue to grow.

Do all the terms and concepts mentioned so far sound familiar? They should; we discussed all of thm thoroughly in Chapter One. That was a review of how a relationship develops over a period of time, and now we will discover how the relationship will continue to evolve into a more intimate relationship.

Becoming Friends

Friends provide us with the *emotional support* and *social ties* that are vital to our well-being. A good friend will always be there when they are needed. We can rely on their support no matter what happens to us. They also provide us with a feeling of belonging and a feeling that we are part of a group. We need an identity, and our friends help us in the development of finding who we are. Good friends satisfy these needs. Relationships rely on mutual interactions. It is important to examine our own contribution to the dynamics of a friendship. It is only our own behavior that we can change, and there are certain personal characteristics that are essential to cultivate in order to build healthy, lasting friendships.

Texting is the most common and frequent way that teens communicate with all types of friends, from the ones they've just met to more established relationships). But teens haven't abandoned phone calling yet. A 2015 research study by the Pew Research Center surveyed teens about technology and friendship and found that phone calls are an important way that teens connect, particularly with their closest friends. Teens with close friends said they reach their friends by text messaging with 80% of teens naming it as one of their top three choices and 49% saying it is the *most common* way they keep in touch. Phone calls are second with 69% of teens saying that this is the favored way to keep in touch with their best

Who are your good friends?

© William Perugini/Shutterstock.com

friends, and only 13% used it just for keeping in touch occasionally. Pew Research Center focus-groups reinforce the notion that teens use different channels of communication depending on the closeness of a friendship. Phone calls are reserved for more intimate relationships. Anderson found teens saying, "if they are just friends', not best friends, you don't really have anything to talk about." (Anderson 2015)

The 13 Essential Friendship Traits

How much do you agree with each statement?
I am trustworthy.
I am honest with others.
I am generally very dependable.
I am loyal to the people I care about.
I am easily able to trust others.
I experience and express empathy for others.
I am able to be non-judgmental.
I am a good listener.
I am supportive of others in their good times.
I am supportive of others in their bad times.
I am self-confident.
I am usually able to see the humor in life.
I am fun to be around.

These traits fall into three general categories, each representing an essential aspect of relational behavior. If you find that you disagree with many of the statements, you may struggle to develop meaningful, lasting friendships (Degges-White Suzanne , March 2015).

According to Dr. Degges-White (2015), there are three friendship traits:

Traits of Integrity

These qualities, represented by the first five traits on the list above, are related to core values held by most cultures—**trustworthiness**, **honesty**, **dependability**, **loyalty**, and, as an interrelated quality, **the ability to trust others**.

Traits of Caring

These qualities, represented by the traits listed as numbers 6 to 10 above, include **empathy**, **the ability to withhold judgment**, effective **listening skills**, and **the ability to offer support** in good times and bad. These traits require personal insight, self-discipline, and unconditional positive regard for our friends.

Becoming *Aware*

Traits of Congeniality

This group, representing by the final three traits listed above, includes **self**-confidence, **the ability to see the humor in life**, and **being fun to be around**. This trio of traits has also been associated with overall well-being and happiness in life.

Before You Can Increase Your Friendship Quotient, You Must Admit That the Need Exists

Remember: Everyone brings a different level of the 13 traits to their relationships. However, the very best friends offer a generous helping of this baker's dozen.

Remember from Chapter Two that Carl Rogers believed in the importance of unconditional acceptance from a friend—*accept me as I am—not how you want me to be.*

Can men and women be friends? Researchers tell us that men and women can be friends. However, do we really believe them? A survey of more than 1,450 members of the Match.com dating site revealed that we are an optimistic bunch (Chatterjee, 2016). See Consider This below.

> *In my own relationships, I know that I should break up with someone who doesn't encourage me to be strong and make my own choices and do what's best in my life, so if you're dating someone who doesn't want you to be the best person you can be, you shouldn't be dating them.*
> —VERONICA ROTH

CONSIDER THIS

CAN MEN AND WOMEN BE FRIENDS?

A survey of more than 1,450 members of the Match.com dating site revealed the following:

1. Do you believe men and women can be platonic friends?
   Yes: 83%   No: 11%   Unsure: 6%
2. Have you had a platonic friendship that crossed the line and became romantic or sexual?
   Yes: 62%   No: 36%   Unsure: 2%
3. Who is more likely to misinterpret the intimacy of friendship for sexual desire?
   Men: 64%   Women: 25%   Unsure: 11%
4. Is it possible to fall in love with someone who first enters your life as a friend?
   Yes: 97%   No: 4%   Unsure: 2%
5. Do you hope that when you do fall in love, your partner will have started out as your friend?
   Yes: 71%   No: 9%   Unsure: 20%
6. Who is better at keeping sex out of a platonic relationship?
   Men: 13%   Women: 67%   Unsure: 20%

Camille Chatterjee (2016).

Can you trust your friends? If not, are they friends? Keeping confidence and trust are almost synonymous. Trust and respect are things people need to earn and should not be given away lightly. There are three questions that need to be answered that will help us make decisions about whether to trust someone or not:

1. **How predictable is the individual?** A predictable person is someone whose behavior is consistent—consistently good or bad. An unpredictable person keeps us guessing about what might happen next. Such volatile people may make life interesting, but they do not inspire much in the way of confidence.
2. **Can I depend upon them?** A dependable person can be relied upon when it counts. One way to tell is to see how a partner behaves in situations where it is possible to care or not to care.
3. **Do I have faith in that person?** Through "thick and thin" you know you can rely on this person. They make us feel "safe."

Similarities. Is it true that "opposites attract"? Or is it true that "birds of a feather flock together"? Look around. Do most of your friends have different interests, beliefs, and political preferences from you, or are they similar? Research indicates that similarities attract. We tend to select friends who are similar to us in many different aspects, including ethnic background, social status, interests, income level, occupation, status, educational level, and political preferences (Myers, 2015). Similarities are also important in the selection of a mate. There is a correlation between length of marriage and the similarities between the two people. The more similarities there are between the two spouses, the longer the marriage tends to last.

What would it be like if your friends always disagreed with you? You are a Republican and they are Democrats; you are pro-life and they are pro-choice; you are religious and they are not; you are conservative and they are liberal; you smoke and they do not; they like rock music and you like classical music; you like to participate in sports and they would rather hang out and smoke. Are you going to have fun together or is there going to be a lot of conflict? Research studies have found that there are two critical similarities that are important within a relationship: they are *similar beliefs* and *similar attitudes* (Taylor & Peplau, 2009). When considering a long-term commitment between you and another person, ask yourself, what do we have in common? Are our beliefs and attitudes similar? If they are not, you may discover that over a period of time, conflict is more apt to develop between the two of you.

So, similarity breeds content. *Birds of a feather do flock together* (Hyde & DeLamater, 2014). Surely you have noticed this upon discovering a special someone who shares your ideas, values, and desires—a soul mate who likes the same music, the same activities, even the same foods you do. So, how do I find someone who has something in common with me?

Male and female friends. Chatterjee (2016) believes that male-female friendship can be tricky, but both benefit from cross-sex buddyhood. "The belief that men and women can't be friends comes from another era in which women were at home and men were in the **workplace**, and the only way they could get together was for romance," explained Linda Sapadin, a psychologist in Valley Stream, New York. "Now they work together and share **sports**, interests, and **socialize** together." This cultural shift has encouraged psychologists, sociologists, and communications experts to put forth a new message: Though it may be tricky, men and women can successfully become close friends.

The media has added to the confusion with movies and television implying that sex always comes between friends, making true friendship hard to do. Don O'Meara, Ph.D., at the University of Cincinnati-Raymond Walters College, published a landmark study in the journal *Sex Roles* on the top impediments to cross-sex friendship. "I started my research because one of my best friends is a woman," said O'Meara. "She said, 'Do you think anyone else has the incredible friendship we do?'" He decided to find out, and after reviewing the scant existing research, O'Meara identified the following challenges to male-female friendship: defining it, dealing with sexual attraction, seeing each other as equals, facing people's responses to the relationship, and meeting in the first place.

CHALLENGE # 1 DEFINING THE RELATIONSHIP: FRIENDS OR LOVERS?

Platonic love does exist, O'Meara asserted, and a study of 20 pairs of friends published in the *Journal of Social and Personal Relationships* (Sapadin, 2014) lends credence to the notion. Distinguishing between romantic, sexual and friendly feelings, however, can be exceedingly difficult.

CHALLENGE # 2 OVERCOMING ATTRACTION: LET'S TALK ABOUT SEX

A study published in the *Journal of Social and Personal Relationships*, Sapadin (2014) asked more than 150 professional men and women what they liked and disliked about their cross-sex friendships. Topping women's list of dislikes: sexual tension. Men, on the other hand, more frequently replied that sexual attraction was a prime reason for initiating a friendship, and that it could even deepen a friendship. Either way, 62 percent of all subjects reported that sexual tension was present in their cross-sex friendships.

CHALLENGE #3 ESTABLISHING EQUALITY: THE POWER PLAY

Friendship should be a pairing of equals.

CHALLENGE #4 THE PUBLIC EYE: DEALING WITH DOUBTERS

Society may not be entirely ready for friendships between men and women that have no sexual subtext.

Do opposites attract? Or is it birds of a feather flock together?

© Nestor Rizhniak/Shutterstock.com

CHALLENGE #5 THE MEETING PLACE: FINDING FRIENDS

These obstacles may seem numerous and formidable, but male-female friendship is becoming not only a possibility but also a necessity

Where do I go to find friends? You need to go to those places where you will find other people who have similar interests and needs. *Proximity*, or physical nearness, is a major factor in the development of friendships. When you were a young kid, most of your friends came from the local neighborhood where you lived, then from the local school you attended. This is what we mean when we say proximity—you get to know the people you are near or close to in regards to location. Rather than picking our friends based on intentional choice and common values and interests, our friendships may be based on more superficial factors like proximity or group assignments (2008).

So, where do you go to meet people? Where have you met most of your friends? Should you go to church? What about bars and sports bars? What about political events, if you are interested in politics? Should you consider the Internet?

Internet dating/Social Networking. There was a time when online dating or the posting of personal ads in newspapers was seen as a crutch used only by those desperate for a date. Times have changed.

In the U.S., matchmaking has taken off as a huge industry only in this decade, with close to 1500 Internet sites such as Match.com, Zoosk, Elite Singles, GayDating, Pink-Wink, and eHarmony (Pew, 2016). A national survey by Pew Research Center, conducted June 10-July 12, 2015, among 2,001 adults, found that:

12% of American adults have ever used an *online dating site*; up slightly from 9% in early 2013, and 9% of American adults have ever used a *dating app on their cellphone*. The share of Americans who use dating apps has increased threefold since early 2013—at that point just 3% of Americans had used these apps. The share of 18- to 24-year-olds who report having used online dating has nearly tripled in the last two years. Today 27% of these young adults report that they have done so, up from just 10% in early 2013. Also, the share of 55- to 64-year-olds who use online dating has doubled over the same time period (from 6% in 2013 to 12% in 2015).

As was the case in previous Pew Research Center surveys of online dating, college graduates and the relatively affluent are especially likely to know people who use online dating or to know people who have entered into a relationship that began online. Nearly six-in-ten college graduates (58%) know someone who uses online dating, and nearly half (46%) know someone who has entered into a marriage or long-term partnership with someone they met via online dating. By comparison, just 25% of those with a high school diploma or less know someone who uses online dating—and just 18% know someone who has entered into a long-term relationship with someone they met this way.

Those who have tried online dating offer mixed opinions about the experience —most have a positive outlook, even as they recognize certain downsides. But despite these reservations, those who have personally used online dating themselves —or know someone who does—tend to have much more positive attitudes compared to those with little direct exposure to online dating or online daters. For instance, just 55% of non-users agree that online dating is a good way to meet people, while six-in-ten agree that online dating is more dangerous than other ways of meeting people.

Overall, men and women who have used online dating tend to have similar views of the pros and cons—with one major exception relating to personal safety. Some 53% of women who have used online dating agree that it is more dangerous than other ways of meeting people, substantially higher than the 38% of male online daters who agree with this statement" (Pew Research Center, 2016).

Also, online matchmaking sites in the U.S. are eyeing millions of singles in China, India, and beyond. Since it is true that some of these sites focus on helping people find suitable marriage partners, other sites focus on less committed involvements, and some even focus on specific populations—people over 50, parents without partners, Christian and single, and so on (Overstreet, 2007). So, be sure to research thoroughly and think carefully about how different sites work before you decide to join a site. And, be quite cautious of what personal information you post as well as specific arrangements for meeting in person.

> Let's check in on David and Ashley. Do they have anything in common? To begin, they are both taking European History—that is a good start. They are both in the pre-law program and enjoy studying history and political science. They both like to ski and participate in individual sports like ten-

nis. After having coffee with David, Ashley thinks to herself, "David seems to be quite intelligent, he is very likable, I hope we get to meet again." They seem to have a lot in common—a lot more in common than Ashley and her present boyfriend. These similarities give David and Ashley a lot to talk about. Does David have a chance to start dating Ashley? Wait and see.

© Syda Productions/Shutterstock.com

Where do you go to find friends?

Do opposites attract? What about the saying *opposites attract?* They do for a period of time, until the novelty wears off, and then you will discover that these dissimilar beliefs, interests, and attitudes cause more conflict than attraction. You may find someone from a different culture exciting and interesting, primarily because of the novelty. You may interpret this interest as attraction, but over time you may discover that you do not have anything in common and the excitement and interest will wane.

Another interesting phenomenon is the fact that some people are initially and spontaneously repulsed by strangers who are very dissimilar to themselves (Bordens, 2013). This is referred to as the *repulsion hypothesis*. Attitudes and values that contradict our own are physiologically arousing. Just as we implicitly assume that people who are similar to us will probably like us and treat us well, so we implicitly assume that people who are very different from us will probably dislike us and treat us poorly. Thus, initial dissimilarities can cut a relationship short. Can you think of some examples where you have experienced this?

But, what about people we know who have been married for years and seem to be totally different and seem to be happy together? Even though they seem to be opposites, they are very compatible. Why?

In the article "Love and Power," Gottman says, "In 200 years, heterosexual relationships will be where gay and lesbian relationships are today." That's a long time to wait for change, but it reflects his findings that couple interactions are far more direct and kind among same-sex partners than the power struggles that arise among heterosexual ones. Rather than rely on cultural assignment of gender roles, gay men and women must come up with their own ways to divide labor and share decisions. Having to actively decide who does what pulls for greater consciousness of fairness and equality, even after children arrive. Lesbian parents—family responsibilities among gay men are too new to have undergone similar study—are "dramatically more equal in sharing of child-care tasks and decision making than heterosexual parents," researchers report (Marano, 2016).

Do they complement each other? People with *complementary needs* seem to be drawn to each other. You notice that one of your friends is very outgoing and her boyfriend is very shy. This does not seem consistent with the idea that similarities attract. Why do they get along so well? We discover that differences in which one person's strengths compensate for the other person's weaknesses may lead to mutual attraction (Strong et al., 2014). The personalities seem to complement each other. In most relationships, each person supplies certain qualities that the other partner is lacking. Does your partner supply these missing characteristics? "A relationship has to feel fair. And that requires flexibility and responsiveness to emotions. People try to get their partner's attention or interest, or open a conversation or share humor or affection. We look at what proportion of the time a partner turns toward such a bid or a need. The turning towards needs to be at a very high level."   Fairness has one critical element, says University of Washington sociologist Pepper Schwartz—respect. In interviewing thousands of couples around the world she found that the American definition of a good relationship is "best friend." (Europeans prefer "passionate lover.") Best friends are egalitarian, and what most characterizes good friendship is respect—equal dignity (Marano, 2014).

Social exchange theory. According to *social exchange theory*, **we measure our actions and relationships on a cost-benefit basis**. People maximize their rewards and minimize their costs by employing their resources to gain the most favorable outcome (Strong et al., 2014). We generally think of rewards and costs as tangible objects, like money. However, in personal relationships, resources, rewards, and costs are more likely to be things such as love, companionship, status, power, fear, loneliness, and so on. As people enter into relationships, they have certain resources—either tangible or intangible—that others consider valuable, such as intelligence, warmth, good looks, or high social status. Individuals consciously or unconsciously use their various resources to obtain what they want, as when they "turn on" the charm. Have you ever wondered what a friend of yours sees in his or her partner? Your friend is so much better looking and more intelligent than the partner. (Attractiveness and intelligence are typical resources in our society.) However, it turns out that the partner has a good sense of humor, is considerate, and is an accomplished artist, all of which your friend values highly.

Reciprocity. "Flattery will get you . . . everything or nowhere?" Which is true? What have you heard? The evidence on **reciprocity indicates that we tend to like those who show that they like us and that we tend to see others as liking us more if we like them** (Baron et al., 2012). Thus, there does seem to be an interactive process in which liking leads to liking and loving leads to loving.

If our self-esteem is low, we are more susceptible to flattery, especially if the compliment is from someone of higher status. A person of high self-esteem may not be so easily swayed by positive treatment. Do you like to receive compliments? How do you feel about the person that is giving the compliments? Do they have a positive or negative influence on you? Do you now understand why some people seem to be greatly influenced by people who are nice to them, especially if that person is perceived as important to them?

David has been complimenting Ashley a lot the last few weeks. He tells her how nice she looks, that he likes her dress, he likes her hairstyle, etc. Will this influence her feelings toward David, especially since she has been depressed lately? The story continues.

We have discovered the importance of a friend and now we will see how the relationship evolves into a more intimate level as we begin the process of dating and mate selection.

Dating and Mate Selection

The changing roles of men and women, economic pressures, and the fragility of the environment have caused relationships to be stress tested on a daily basis. Even within this stressful context, however, relationship development and mate selection continue to thrive. The basis of mate selection is courtship—the interesting processes in which two people get together and hopefully stay together. So, what makes someone desirable to us? What are the traits we find attractive in potential dates and mates?

What makes someone desirable? What attracts men and women to their potential mate? In part, romantic at traction is a mystery. Scientists may not know everything about why people are drawn to the people that they are, but they know something. Every culture has standards for courtship and marriage. Without really thinking about it, most of us dutifully follow our cultural dictates. As we discussed the development of friendships and relationships in the previous pages of this chapter and in Chapter One, we will discover that the same characteristics that are important in finding friends are also very important in date and mate selection. As Brené Brown (2007) writes, "Our imperfections are what connect us to each other and to our humanity. Our vulnerabilities are not weaknesses; they are powerful reminders to keep our hearts and minds open to the reality that we're all in this together."

Most of us are looking for dates, mates, and friends who are similar to us (similarities). We seek out others who are about our own age, who are from the same socioeconomic class, religion, and educational level. They cannot be too tall or too short, too fat or too thin in comparison to us. Such preliminary screening cuts out a surprising number of potential partners. But most of us want more. Generally, we want someone who we perceive as good looking (physical attractiveness), personable, warm, a good sense of humor, someone we can trust, and who is intelligent. We also want someone whose views match our own. Other important variables that most of us also consider are reciprocity, personality fit, and most important, our own self-concept (self-confidence).

Review Gender & You—What Characteristics Do I Desire in a Potential Mate, and decide how you would rate the characteristics. Are there any other gender mate preferences?

Every year, more women than men become college-educated. The disparity is already prevalent across North America and Europe, and the trend is beginning to spread across the world more widely. Many causes can be speculated, like gradual gender discrimination barriers lifted or it could be more women have better grades and college application qualifications; the disparity is creating an unintended mating crisis among educated women. Buss (2016) believes that women and men both have evolved multiple mating strategies: some of each gender are having casual hook-ups and some committed relationships.   Most educated women are unwilling to settle for men who are less educated, less intelligent, and less professionally successful than they are. The flip side is that men are less exacting on precisely these dimensions, choosing to prioritize, for better or worse, other evolved criteria such as youth and appearance. The good news for those who succeed is that marriages among the educated tend to be more stable, freer of conflict, less plagued by infidelity, and less likely to end in divorce. Educated couples enjoy a higher standard of living as dual professional incomes.

Research shows that males and females exhibit both similarities and differences in what they look for in a marital partner:

- In a 2013 survey of almost 5,500 unattached adults 21 and older, those qualities, attitudes, and expectations illustrate cultural shifts in how singles approach relationships. The online survey of 5,481 individuals was conducted by Market-Tools Inc. Among the findings: 38% would cancel a date because of something they found while doing Internet research on their date; 42% would not date a virgin; 65% would not date someone with credit card debt greater than $5,000; 54% would not date someone with substantial student loan debt; 49% would consider getting into a committed relationship with someone who lived at home with parents.

The survey also asked new questions about technology and social networking. Among those findings: Almost 28% say they've dated someone they met online; 20% met their most recent first date that way; almost half (48%) of gay men and lesbian women have dated someone they met online; 36% have sent a sexy photo or explicit text; 48% of single women and 38% of men research a date on Facebook before the first date; 6% of singles say they have broken up with a significant other due to Facebook; for men it was mostly because of pictures (55%), while for women it was posts on another person's wall (48%).

- Women tend to place a higher value than men on potential partners' socioeconomic status, intelligence, ambition, and financial prospects (Buss, 2015). Women tend to prefer men who are taller than they are with symmetrical features (Alkon, 2010).
- Men consistently show more interest than women in potential partners' youthfulness, good health, and physical attractiveness (Buss, 2015).
- Men prefer wives who are somewhat younger than they are, and women prefer husbands that are somewhat older. However, we are noticing a new trend—as women become more economically independent, they are becoming more interested in selecting younger men as dates and sometimes mates (King, 2014).

GENDER AND YOU

WHAT CHARACTERISTICS DO I DESIRE IN A POTENTIAL MATE?

Following is how a large sample of males and females from a number of different cultures rated the importance of 18 characteristics in a potential mate.

Men's Ranking of Various Traits
1. Mutual attraction—Love
2. Dependable character
3. Emotional stability and maturity
4. Pleasing disposition
5. Good health
6. Education and intelligence
7. Sociability
8. Desire for home and children
9. Refinement, neatness
10. Good looks
11. Ambition and industriousness
12. Good cook and housekeeper
13. Good financial prospect
14. Similar education
15. Favorable social status or rating
16. Chastity
17. Similar religious background
18. Similar political background

Women's Ranking of Various Traits
1. Mutual attraction—Love
2. Dependable character
3. Emotional stability and maturity
4. Pleasing disposition
5. Education and intelligence
6. Sociability
7. Good health
8. Desire for home and children
9. Ambition and industriousness
10. Refinement, neatness
11. Similar education
12. Good financial prospect
13. Good looks
14. Favorable social status or rating
15. Good cook and housekeeper
16. Similar religious background
17. Similar political background
18. Chastity

Source: Buss's Cross-Cultural Findings of Preferences in Mate Selection by David Buss in *Adjustment and Human Relations* by Patricia Alexander (Upper Saddle River, NJ: Pearson Education, 1999).

Mate selection throughout the world. Do people from different countries and different cultures look for the same traits when selecting a mate? The traits that people look for in a marriage vary around the world. In one large-scale study from thirty-seven countries and five islands, people varied in what they considered important in selecting a mate (Buss et al., 1999). Chastity was the most important factor in marital selection in China, India, Indonesia, Iran, Taiwan, and the Palestinian Arab culture. Adults from Japan and Ireland placed moderate importance on chastity. In contrast, adults in Sweden, Finland, Norway, the Netherlands, and Germany generally said that chastity was not important in selecting a marital partner. Researchers were surprised that men and women in the Netherlands, for example, do not care about chastity at all. Neither is virginity valued much in the Scandinavian countries such as Norway and

Sweden. In China, however, virginity is indispensable in a mate—marrying a non-virgin is virtually out of the question. The Chinese also possess less permissive views toward dating and sexuality. Tang and Zuo's (2000) cross-cultural study found that Chinese college students generally possess less open-minded attitudes toward dating, date less frequently, tend to date at an later age, and are less likely to have sex in their encounters than do their American counterparts. Thus, people in cultures in which more conservative norms regarding sexuality are held are less likely to discuss their own sexuality freely. Otherwise they may be seen as promiscuous or dirty (Buss, 2015).

Adults from the Zulu culture in South Africa, Estonia, and Colombia placed a high value on housekeeping skills in their marital preference. By contrast, adults in all Western European countries (except Spain, Canada and the United States) said that housekeeping was not an important trait in their partner.

What about religion? It plays an important role in marital preferences in many cultures. For example, Islam stresses the honor of the male and the purity of the female. It also emphasizes the woman's role in childbearing, childrearing, educating children, and instilling the Islamic faith in their children (Buss, 1999).

Whether we are drawn to people by familiarity, similarity, beauty, or some other quality, mutual attraction sometimes progresses from friendship to the more intense, complex, and mysterious feeling of love.

BECOMING LOVERS

There is a great similarity between love relationships and good-friend relationships. In both of these are high levels of trust, mutual respect, and acceptance. Further, the interactions between the people involved are characterized by high levels of understanding, nurturing, and confiding. Nonetheless, the love relationship with its greater depth of caring and exclusiveness typically generates greater emotion and power. As a result, it can affect individuals more, having the potential to meet a broader sweep of human needs or to cause greater frustration and distress.

What is love? Have you ever looked at someone for the first time and said to yourself, "I think I'm in love"? Is there such a thing as *love at first sight?* Research has found that we do not fall in love—we grow into love. Then, what is love? This is a question people have been asking for years. Mass media, romantic novels, soap operas, and songs have all been attempting to answer this question.

Our lives seem to revolve around this subject. But, does anyone know what love is? Everyone seems to have their own definition of love. When your date says that he or she loves you, what does your date mean? Is it the same as when your mother or father says it to you? What is your definition of love? Before you continue, take a few minutes and write down your definition of love. Share your definition of love with your friends and loved ones. Compare your definition with theirs.

Infatuation is when you think that he's as sexy as Robert Redford, as smart as Henry Kissinger, as noble as Ralph Nader, as funny as Woody Allen, and as athletic as Jimmy Connors. Love is when you realize that he's as sexy as Woody Allen, as smart as Jimmy Connors, as funny as Ralph Nader, as athletic as Henry Kissinger and nothing like Robert Redford in any category—but you'll take him anyway.
—JUDITH VIORST

Love is what's left in a relationship when all the selfishness has been removed.
—CULLEN HIGHTOWER

We have found a definition of *love* that we would like to share with you. When the satisfaction, security, and development of another person is as important to you as your own satisfaction, security, and development, love exists (Barton, 1996). Using this definition of love, you will find that you can measure your love not only for your significant other, but your mother, father, siblings, friends, animals, and even inanimate objects. What do you think?

MYTHS ABOUT LOVE

True or False

T F 1. True love lasts forever.
T F 2. Love can conquer all.
T F 3. Love is a purely positive experience.
T F 4. When you fall in love, you'll know it.
T F 5. When love strikes, you have no control over your behavior.

What are your answers to the above questions? These are some interesting myths about love that many of us have been agonizing over for years. Let us take a look at these myths and dispel some of the confusion regarding them (Weiten et al., 2014).

1. *Does true love last forever?* It would be nice if love would last forever, but most of us have found that it does not. People who believe this myth may pursue love forever, looking for the ideal one that will bring complete happiness. This person will experience a lifetime of frustration. Would we have divorce if love lasted forever? It would be more realistic to view love as a wonderful experience that might be encountered on several occasions throughout life.

2. *Does love conquer all?* Many people believe that love and marriage will allow them to overcome (conquer) all their frustrations and problems in life. A supportive partner will help you solve many of your problems, but it does not guarantee success. Many people jump into relationships for this purpose, only to discover that the relationship creates additional problems.

3. *Is love a purely positive experience?* Mass media, television, movies, and romance novels are creating an unrealistic expectation that love is such a positive experience. In reality it can be a peak experience, but love can also bring intense negative emotions and great pain. As many of you know, a lover is capable of taking us to emotional peaks in either direction.

4. *Do you know when you are in love?* There is no physiological cue to tell us we are in love. So the emotional feeling and the cognitive interpretation is different for each of us. It is a state of confusion that many of us agonize over. It is normal to question our feelings toward another person. Remember, we grow to love someone gradually and usually do not fall in love.

5. *Do you behave irrationally when you fall in love?* Does love take control of your behavior? Some people stop eating, quit studying, are unable to concentrate on their

job and avoid taking responsibility for their actions because they are in love. If you allow your heart to take control of your behavior, you may become vulnerable to irrational decisions about sexual involvement or long-term commitments.

Love is? Love is complex! Love is confusing! Most of you are aware of this. Love is difficult to measure and perplexing. People are yearning for it, will die for it, and even kill for it. But for some reason we have avoided studying it until the last few years. Psychologists are now doing research attempting to discover what love is.

The **triangular theory of love** is a theory of love developed by psychologist Robert Sternberg. In the context of interpersonal relationships, "the three components of love, according to the triangular theory, are an intimacy component, a passion component, and a decision/commitment component":

1. **Intimacy** – Which encompasses feelings of **attachment**, closeness, connectedness, and bondedness.
2. **Passion** – Which encompasses drives connected to both **limerence** [infactuation] and **sexual attraction**.
3. **Commitment** – Which encompasses, in the short term, the decision to remain with another, and in the long term, plans made with that other. (Sternberg, 2004)

"The amount of love one experiences depends on the absolute strength of these three components, and the type of love one experiences depends on their strengths relative to each other" (Sternberg, 2007). Robert Sternberg (2007) has developed a theory of love that includes three distinct components: 1) *passion*, an intense physiological desire for another person; 2) *intimacy*, the feeling that one can share all one's thoughts and actions with another; 3) *commitment*, the willingness to stay with a person through thick and thin, or for better or worse, or in sickness or health. Ideally, marriage is characterized by a healthy amount of all three components. Various com-

> *Love is the word used to label the sexual excitement of the young, the habituation of the middle aged, and the mutual dependence of the old.*
> —JOHN CIARDI

Does true love last forever?

binations of these components result in quite different types of love. Figure 6.1 will demonstrate some of these. For example, Sternberg suggests that romantic love involves a high degree of passion and intimacy, yet lacks substantial commitment to the other person. The passion component of love peaks early in a relationship, and then declines. Intimacy and commitment components build gradually over time. Growth in intimacy and commitment occurs as passion grows weaker, and can sustain a relationship as difficulties arise once passion fades. *Companionate love* is marked by a great deal of intimacy and commitment but little passion. *Consummate love* is the most complete because it includes a high level of all three components. It is the most satisfying because the relationship is likely to fulfill many of the needs of each partner.

David cannot think of anything but Ashley. "She's so wonderful, she's really pretty, I don't think I can live without her." What is David experiencing? Is it love yet? Early in a relationship it may only be passion. When love has only passion (without intimacy or commitment), it is often called "infatuation." We are infatuated with the other person when we cannot stop thinking about them and become physiologically aroused by touching, seeing, or even thinking of them.

Having a lot in common with David, Ashley has a warm comfortable feeling for him. She is concerned about his success and is willing to do whatever she can to help him succeed. Is this the intimacy stage? When love has only intimacy (without passion or commitment), we might be better off calling it "liking." This is when we enjoy being with our partner, respect them, and share with them. Would you call this love?

Does Ashley only like David or could it be something else? Ashley has been thinking more about the relationship recently, as time goes by she's considering the fact that this relationship could last forever. She would stay with David through "thick and thin." Is she getting more serious over the relationship? Is it love yet? When love has only commitment, it is "empty

What things can you do to maintain the components of love?

© Pressmaster/Shutterstock.com

Becoming *Aware*

love." We display empty love when we remain in a relationship from which all passion and intimacy have gone, as unhappy couples do "for the sake of the children." Is this all that Ashley is experiencing?

Wait a minute! There may be more to David's and Ashley's relationship. What's missing? Take a look at the Triangle of Love (Figure 6.1). We notice that their relationship is maturing. There seems to be an equal mixture of intimacy, passion and decision/commitment, and this is called consummate love—an ideal, but difficult to attain relationship. This is the type of relationship we should all be striving to reach. Do all cultures experience this? See Focus on Diversity—Is There a Cultural Influence on Love?

FOCUS ON DIVERSITY

IS THERE A CULTURAL INFLUENCE ON LOVE?

Cultural factors have a strong influence on the value of love. In the United States, love is crucial to a satisfying marriage. In the former Soviet Union, however, only 40 percent of the people say that they married for love; most did so because of loneliness, shared interests, or an unplanned pregnancy (Baron et al., 2012). In research including two individualistic societies (Canada and the United States) and three collectivist societies (China, India, and Japan), romantic love is more likely to be considered an important basis for marriage in individualistic societies than in collectivistic ones. In many Asian societies, the persons getting married are supposed to take into account the wishes of others, especially of parents and other family members. It is not unusual for marriages to be arranged by the respective families on the basis of such factors as occupation and status, not on the basis of love and the lover's free choice. The intense feelings of passionate love and the self-absorption of two lovers would be disruptive to the functioning of the group. In collectivist cultures, such as India and Japan, love is considered less important to a successful marriage than is the ability to resolve family conflicts (Matsumoto, 2007; Dresser, 2005).

A TRIANGULAR MODEL OF LOVE

Sternberg conceptualized love in the form of a triangle with three basic components: intimacy, passion, and decision/commitment. Love may be based primarily on one of these components, on a combination of two of them, or on all three. As shown in the figure, seven different types of relationships are possible, depending on how the components are combined.

Figure 6.1 IS THIS WHAT LOVE IS MADE OF?

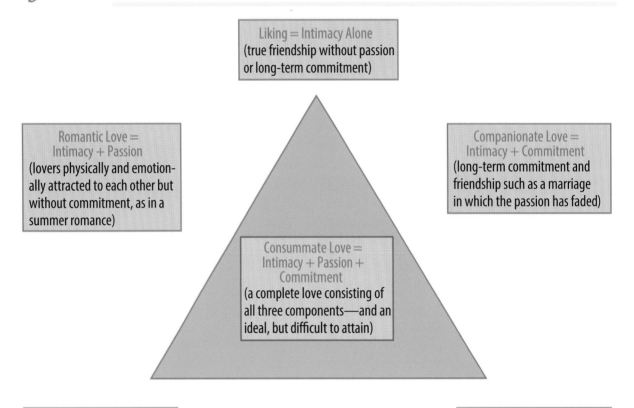

Liking = Intimacy Alone
(true friendship without passion or long-term commitment)

Romantic Love = Intimacy + Passion
(lovers physically and emotionally attracted to each other but without commitment, as in a summer romance)

Companionate Love = Intimacy + Commitment
(long-term commitment and friendship such as a marriage in which the passion has faded)

Consummate Love = Intimacy + Passion + Commitment
(a complete love consisting of all three components—and an ideal, but difficult to attain)

Infatuation = Passion Alone
(passionate, obsessive love at first sight without intimacy or commitment)

Empty Love = Decision/ Commitment Alone
(decision to love another without intimacy or passion)

Fatuous Love = Passion + Commitment
(commitment based on passion but without time for intimacy to develop—shallow relationship such as a whirlwind courtship)

Adapted from Sternberg (2007)

The development of love. Early in a relationship, passion is usually high, which may be one reason new love relationships and affairs are most intense. Intimacy, however, is not as high because the partners have not spent enough time together or shared enough experiences and emotions to be able to understand each other completely. Passionate love without intimacy creates a risk of misunderstanding and jealousy about any other person or activity that seems to interfere with the relationship.

Over time, passion seems to fade while intimacy and commitment grow stronger. According to Sternberg, passion is like an addiction: in the beginning a touch of the hand, a smile, even a mere glance will produce excitement. Gradually, however, one needs a greater dose of stimulation to get the same feeling. We habituate to the passion, and thus to continue this intense feeling for one another, *novel and significant stimuli* must be provided by each of the two individuals.

An understanding of the three components of love and the developmental process will help couples in the building of their relationship. A couple may want to schedule specific times each week, away from children and family, for a period of intimate sharing—a time to discuss problems as well as happy times. You may want to keep the passion burning by scheduling a weekend at the beach, buying your mate a special gift, taking them out to a special dinner, serving them breakfast in bed, etc. What else can you do to maintain the three components of love?

The five love languages. After more than 30 years of marriage counseling, Dr. Gary Chapman (2015), author of *The Five Love Languages*, has concluded that there are basically five emotional love languages—five ways that people speak and understand emotional love. And, it is highly possible that your emotional love language and the language of your spouse may be as different as Chinese is from English. No matter how hard you try to express your love in English, if your spouse understands only Chinese, you will never understand how to love each other. Dr. Chapman believes that love is something you do for someone else; therefore, it is critical to learn to express or respond to the needs of your spouse. Realizing that none of these are gender specific, Dr. Chapman's languages are as follows:

> *Love is patient, love is kind. It does not envy, it does not boast, it is not proud. It is not rude, it is not self-seeking, it is not easily angered, and it keeps no record of wrongs. Love does not delight in evil but rejoices with the truth. It always protects, always trusts, always hopes, and always prevails.*
> —CORINTHIANS 13:4–7

1. **Words of Affirmation.** Some people need verbal appreciation and encouragement in order to feel loved. This may be nothing more than "You look great in that suit," or "You are the best yard guy we've ever had," or "I know you will finish your degree."
2. **Quality Time.** This is more than mere proximity. It's about focusing all your energy on your mate. It's turning off the TV and giving each other quality time—quality listening time, or just doing something together.
3. **Receiving Gifts.** It is one thing to remember birthdays and anniversaries; it's quite more to learn how to give "little" gifts of thoughtfulness throughout the week. Free, frequent, expensive, or rare, if your mate relates to the language of giving gifts, any visible sign of your love will leave him/her feeling happy and secure in your relationship.
4. **Acts of Service.** Sometimes simple chores or tasks around the house that are helpful to another person can be an undeniable expression of love. The task may be to discover what acts performed out of the kindness of your heart—not obligation—will show your love for your spouse.
5. **Physical Touch.** Many mates feel the most loved when they receive physical contact from their partner—a hand on the shoulder, a hug, a kiss, holding hands, a touch on the cheek. Remember, also, that sexual contact, although extremely important, is only one dialect of physical touch.

Perhaps the greatest task is to determine which love language means the most to your spouse, but it is well worth it for a satisfying life together.

> As we look at the relationship of David and Ashley, we find that David finally had the "guts" to ask Ashley out for coffee after class. They discovered

that they have a lot in common (similarities) and have begun to disclose a lot of personal information about themselves to the other person. As their personal disclosure increases, their level of trust increases. Their attraction for one another grows. The flame is lit and the passion becomes more intense. But, wait a minute, what happened to Ashley's boyfriend? Even though Ashley and her boyfriend have dated for more than four years, they really did not have much in common other than school activities. And remember that absence makes the heart grow fonder for someone else (proximity). Remember, Ashley's boyfriend is going to college in another state.

Ashley and David have similar values, religious beliefs, attitudes about life, and the same interests. They are beginning to spend more and more time together and the feeling of intimacy and commitment grows stronger. Ashley is no longer depressed—she is excited about life and her new relationship. She is looking to the future and setting goals. How does David feel about the relationship? Is he committed to the relationship?

Marriage is not a noun; it's a verb. It isn't something you get. It's something you do. It's the way you love your partner every day.
—BARBARA DE ANGELIS

Men vs. women. On the whole, men tend to think they are compatible with their partner before women do. One reason may be that men and women tend to have different attitudes about love. Men are more likely to be "romantics." For example, they are inclined to believe in love at first sight, and to regard true love as magical, impossible to explain or understand.

Women are more likely to be "pragmatists," believing that financial security is as important as passion in nourishing a close relationship and that there are many possible individuals that a person could learn to love. Women tend to be more cautious than men before deciding to take the final step. Researchers say that women seem to do a lot more work when it comes to making a relationship work. What is the next step? Is it marriage or some alternative?

GENDER AND YOU

WHO WORKS HARDER, MALES OR FEMALES?

If you are female and you think you do a lot more of the work when it comes to making your relationship run smoothly—you are right. Researchers say that women have more relationship skills.

- Women are better communicators. They are more comfortable in sharing their feelings and being psychologically intimate (Elder, 2016).
- On the communication score, most men are still playing catch-up with women. For men, actual physical proximity is often as good as intimacy ("I'm here, aren't I?") (Elder, 2016).
- Women are more likely than men to work at improving a relationship (Lawson, 2005).
- Men don't think as often about a relationship's complexities (Lawson, 2005).

Becoming Committed

It is not entirely clear how and when commitment begins. At some time and in some way, two people in a relationship decide that their satisfaction or happiness with each other is significantly greater than in their relationships with other people. Thus, they agree to begin a relatively long-lasting, more intimate relationship that to some extent excludes other close relationships. The couple agrees to depend on each other for the satisfaction of important needs, including companionship, love, and sex. The commitment may or may not include the decision to live together.

Is Love a Feeling or a Decision?

One neglects to see an important factor in love, that of will.

To love somebody is not just a strong feeling—it is a decision, it is a judgment, it is a promise.

If love were only a feeling, there would be no basis for the promise to love each other forever.

A feeling comes and it may go.

How can I judge that it will stay forever, if my actions do not involve judgment and decision?

—ERICH FROMM, PSYCHOANALYST

Making an agreement with another person to enter into a deeper, more exclusive, and lasting relationship is a crucially important life decision that must be made freely and with careful thought. Many individuals, consciously or unconsciously, feel pressured to enter into a relationship that they are not sure is good for them. Many people are not happy in their existing relationship or social situation, be it a bad home environment, an abusive mate, getting too old, being lonely, an alcoholic or addicted mate, etc., so they feel pressured to commit themselves to a new relationship as a means to escape the bad situation. A person who is pushed or pressured into a relationship will discover that their commitment is weaker and less enduring. If the commitment is made in defiance of pressure from parents or peers, the commitment may be very strong. As many of you know, if your parents were to tell you that you *cannot* date a specific person, you will do whatever it takes to make sure you will date them and be more committed to them. This phenomenon is known as *psychological reactance*—the tendency to protect or restore one's sense of freedom or social control, often by doing the opposite of what has been demanded. This is also known as the *Romeo and Juliet effect*, where their love was intensified, not weakened, by their families' opposi-

> Important as it is to choose the right partner, it's probably more important to be the right partner. We focus on changing the wrong person.
> —PATRICIA LOVE

tion. In summation, a commitment is likely to be strongest when it is arrived at freely and when it is cemented by taking action as a result of the commitment.

Should I remain single? Sociologists note that Americans have a rate of marriage—and of remarriage—among the highest in the Western world (Cherlin, 2010). Despite the emphasis on flexibility and freedom in relationships, most emerging adults—at least ninety percent—wish to fall in love, commit, and marry someday. They are just not in a rush to do so (Regnerus & Uecker, 2010). The average age of marriage has risen steadily. According to Census Bureau data (2015), the average age women marry is 27.5 years and for men 29 years. Furthermore, the proportion of people ages 30 to 34 who have never married continues to increase.

Remaining single is becoming a more viable lifestyle. More and more people are remaining single. Furthermore, the negative stereotype of people who remain single, which pictures them as lonely, frustrated, depressed, odd, and unchosen is disappearing.

Studies have shown that married people live longer and are healthier throughout those extra years. Marriage does seem to help both spouses cope better with stress, though men benefit more than women. However, the stress of a bad marriage can undo much of the good that comes along with a happy one (Strong et al., 2014).

It is interesting to note that most studies find that single women are more satisfied with their lives and less distressed than comparable single men, and various lines of evidence suggest that women get along without men better than men get along without women (Stack & Eshleman, 1998; Weiten et al., 2014).

Recent research also shows that overall, Millennials have fewer sexual partners than their parents (the Baby Boomers and Generation X). Granted, the vast majority of young adults are still having sex, but an increasing number appear to be standing on the sidelines (Bahrampour, 2016). Feelings are that delaying sex is not so bad, according to the experts like Stephanie Coontz, director of research at the Council on Contemporary Families. If young people are being intentional about when to have sex it can lead to stronger relationships in the long run. The trend may also reflect women feeling more empowered to say no because they use birth control.

Stephanie Coontz commented that, "As people have gotten much more accepting of all sorts of forms of consensual sex, they've also gotten pickier about what constitutes consent and far less accepting of pressured sex." Some experts are concerned that the drop-off reflects the difficulty some young people are having in forming deep romantic connections. They cite possible negative reasons for putting off sex, including pressure to succeed; social lives increasingly conducted onscreen; unrealistic expectations of physical perfection encouraged by dating apps; and wariness over date rape (Coontz, 2006). On the other hand, it is also possible that more Millennials and iGen'ers will be sexually inactive in early adulthood, given their slower start as teens. With more living with their parents even post-recession (Pew Research Center, 2015), young adults may have fewer opportunities to have sex. In addition, marriage is the traditional outlet for sexuality, and only 26% of Millennials aged 18–32 were married as of 2014, compared to 36% of GenX'ers (born 1965–1979) in 1997 and 48% of Boomers (born 1946–1964) in 1980 (Pew Research Center, 2014).

Noah Patterson, 18, likes to sit in front of several screens simultaneously: a school work project, a YouTube clip, a video game. To shut it all down for a date or even a one-night stand seems a waste. "For an average date you're going to spend at least two hours, and in that two hours I won't be doing something I enjoy." According to the new report, 15 percent of current 20 to 24-year-olds have not had sex since turning 18, up from 6 percent in the early 1990s. And a study last year found that while Millennials are more accepting of non-marital sex than earlier generations, they reported fewer sexual partners than any group since before the sexual revolution—an average of 8, compared to 11 for boomers and 10 for Generation X (Bahrampour, 2016).

The decline seems likely to continue: According to the latest Centers for Disease Control data, the portion of high school students who have ever had sex plunged last year to 41.2 percent after declining steadily from 54.1 in 1991 to 46.8 in 2013. The portion who reported sleeping with multiple partners also plummeted, from 18.7 in 1991 to 15 in 2013 to just 11.5 last year. "Among millennials, the effects are most dramatic among those born in the mid-1990s and later—the first cohort to come of age when smartphones were ubiquitous, this was the group that really started to communicate by screens more and by talking to their friends in person less," said Jean Twenge, lead author of the two studies. So has sex declined because people are not meeting in person? Maybe…. But online life can also affect offline life in more subtle ways—especially when they use a social app on their cellphones and potential mates can disappear forever with a swipe of the thumb (Twenge, 2016).

"It ends up putting a lot of importance on physical appearance, and that I think is leaving out a large section of the population," said Twenge, who teaches psychology at San Diego State University. "For a lot of folks who are of average appearance, marriage and stable relationships was where they were having sex." Unlike in face-to-face meetings where "you can seduce someone with your charm," she said, dating apps are "leaving some people with fewer choices and they might be more reluctant to search for partners at all." It does not help that many Millennials are relatively unfamiliar with the kind of down time it takes to really get to know a partner (Twenge, 2016). Alexandra Wolff, 19, had hoped to find romance in college. In high school, she and her friends were so focused on schoolwork that they didn't date. But as a freshman last year at George Washington University, she found that between meeting new friends, attending classes and participating in extracurricular activities, she still didn't have time. "I don't involve myself in the scene of frat parties and hookup culture…but it seems like every other option is so time consuming and very hard to seek out," said Wolff, who has never had sex. She wants what she calls an "old-fashioned" relationship, leading to marriage and kids. But fellow students are into "very casual one-night stands, going to bars and going home with someone," she said. "It's not like I'm saving myself for anything; it's more like I've been busy." To put another spin on the information "The nature of communication now is anti-sexual," said Norman Spack, associate clinical professor of pediatrics at Harvard Medical School.

"At Tulane University in New Orleans, Wolff's high school classmate Claudia W., 19, feels like Claudia, who didn't want her last name used because "I don't want all my professors reading about how I'm a virgin," said her parents worry. "They always ask me, 'Are you against relationships? Why don't you have a boyfriend?' My mom—she hooked up all the time in college—she's like, 'I would still love you, but are you gay?' But for me it's not anything about chastity or fear of sex… I'm just like, 'eh, it'll happen.'" (Bahrampour, 2016)

In some of the research, Millennials have been called the most cautious generation, the first to grow up with car seats and bike helmets, the first not allowed to walk to school or go to the playground alone. The sense of caution sometimes manifests itself as a heightened awareness of emotional pitfalls. This generation has also grown up in an age in which possible to inflict suffering in ways that are both hidden and horrifyingly public, such as cyberbullying or posting compromising pictures online. In such an environment, young people have developed what some see as necessary defenses and others view as thin skin. "On college campuses you see older people scratching their heads about 'safe spaces,'" Twenge said. "That's about emotional safety, this new idea of words being more harmful," referring to trigger warnings and other terms college-age people use to talk about potentially trauma-inducing stimuli. Meanwhile, in efforts to counteract hookup and drinking culture, some campuses have begun instigating "yes-means-yes" rules stipulating that each step of a sexual encounter require verbal consent. For some, staying away altogether can feel less treacherous. That is Patterson's takeaway. "Third wave feminists seem to be crazy, saying that all men are participating in this rape culture." He opts for porn instead. "It's quicker, it's more accessible, what you see is what you get" (Bahrampour, 2016).

Isn't he curious about actual sex? "Not really," he said. "I've seen so much of it…There isn't really anything magical about it, right?" For his part, Leo Fusco, a 25-year-old construction worker and subcontractor in Oakland, CA has refrained from sex in part because he is repelled by the hookup culture. "I've overheard conversations where every detail was given – 'We were in this position for this long, and then we were in that position' – and that's a major turnoff for me," he said. "There's a lot of people my age who have no filter in terms of how they express themselves in public." Isn't he curious about what sex is like? "I'm curious on a physical level, like I'm curious about how a new sandwich would taste, but it's not like a driving curiosity." Besides, he said, "I don't particularly like not being in control of myself." (Tara Bahrampour, 2016)

Abstinence may not be such a considered choice for everyone, however; there can also be environmental factors. For example, the use of anti-depressants, which doubled between 1999 and 2012, can reduce sex drive. "That's a real problem," Fisher said, adding that antidepressants can also "blunt emotions," making it harder to fall in love. To Spack, that is sad. "Everyone's missing out on a good time," he said. But Fisher is not worried. "It's probably a good thing" she said. Noting that baby boomers were known not only for free love but also for high divorce rates, she added, "I think (taking it slowly) is going to lead to better first marriages" (Bahrampour,2016).

In the end, she predicted, as long as pharmaceuticals don't get in the way, biology will prevail. "Sex is a powerful drive and so is romantic love...The sex system is way below the cortex, it's way below the limbic system" on a level with thirst and hunger. "They'll get to the sex," she said. "I'm positive of that."

It's not that he doesn't like women. "I enjoy their companionship, but it's not a significant part of life," said Patterson, a web designer in Bellingham, Wash.

He has never had sex. "I'd rather be watching YouTube videos and making money." Sex, he said, is "not going to be something people ask you for on your resume."

That attitude does not surprise Helen Fisher, a biological anthropologist at Rutgers University and chief scientific advisor to the dating site Match.com.

"It's a highly motivated, ambitious generation," she said. "A lot of them are afraid that they'll get into something they can't get out of and they won't be able to get back to their desk and keep studying."

Should we live together before marriage? There was a time when "shacking up" was not viewed in a positive light. Today, this is called *cohabitation,* meaning two partners living together as if married, and it's no longer viewed in such a negative light. Cohabitation has undergone considerable changes in recent years (Cherlin, 2004; Oppenheimer, 2003; Seltzer, 2004). The percentage of U.S. couples who cohabit before marriage has increased from approximately 11 percent in 1970 to almost 60 percent at the beginning of the twenty-first century (Bumpass & Lu, 2000).

Cohabitation has become increasingly common, not only in the United States, but also in other industrialized countries. For example, rates are high in Great Britain, Australia, Denmark, Finland, France, and Sweden. In fact, more children in Sweden are born to cohabiting couples than to married couples.

In 2014, for the first time in more than 130 years, adults ages 18 to 34 were slightly more likely to be living in their parents' home than they were to be living with a spouse or partner in their own household (U.S. Census Bureau, 2015). Among young adults, living arrangements differ significantly by gender. For men ages 18 to 34, living at home with mom and/or dad has been the dominant living arrangement since 2009. In 2014, 28% of young men were living with a spouse or partner in their own home, while 35% were living in the home of their parent(s). For their part, young women are on the cusp of crossing over this threshold: They are still more likely to be living with a spouse or romantic partner (35%) than they are to be living with their parent(s) (29%) (Pew Research Center, 2016). It has increased all across socioeconomic, age, and racial groups (Strong, 2014).

Not only do many couples consider cohabitation a prelude to marriage—a trial marriage, they also believe that cohabitation improves the chances of marital success (Wartik, 2005). However, researchers have found an association between premarital cohabitation and increased marital discord and divorce rates (Coontz, 2006). Among

> *Marriage perhaps represents the ideal of human relationships—the setting in which each partner, while acknowledging the need of the other, feels free to be what he or she by nature is, a relationship in which giving and taking are equal, in which each accepts the other, and I confronts Thou.*
> —ERICH FROMM

both men and women aged 15–44 who had ever cohabited and/or married, the largest proportion cohabited before their first marriage. Approximately 28% of men and women cohabited before their first marriage, whereas 23% of women and 18% of men married without ever cohabiting. About 15% of men and women had only cohabited (without ever marrying), and less than 7% of men and women first cohabited after their first marriages ended (Centers for Disease Control and Prevention, 2010). If cohabitation is preceded by an engagement, no previous live-in lovers and no children, the negative effect on a marriage's chances can be less (Luscombe, 2010).

What seems to be the reasons for the higher divorce rate among couples who cohabit? Researchers believe that couples who decide to cohabit are already at a higher risk of divorce than couples who do not, since they tend to be more liberal, sexually experienced, have less traditional attitudes toward marriage, family, and divorce, have slightly lower incomes, and are slightly less religious than non-cohabitants (Smock, 2002; Cherlin, 2010). A lot depends on the individual couple—especially their values.

As more and more people across different backgrounds enter cohabitation relationships, we will learn more concerning whether the *experiences of cohabitation or characteristics of those who cohabit* have greater impact on later marriage.

Why should I marry? People tend to marry out of mixed motives—many of them unclear even to themselves. Now that marriage is no longer necessary for economic survival or the satisfaction of sexual needs, love has become the major rationale for getting married and staying married. Psychologist Harry Stack Sullivan has given us an excellent definition of love—"When the satisfaction, security, and development of another person is as important to you as your own satisfaction, security, and development, love exists."(1968)

Unfortunately, people sometimes marry for the wrong reasons: to become respectable, for money, for a regular sexual outlet, for status, or to make their parents happy. Even cohabiting couples may marry for the wrong reason. Just when the relationship begins to falter, marriage may be sought to save the relationship. It's a temporary "fix," because it does not solve the underlying conflicts.

Ted Huston, Ph.D., a professor of human ecology and psychology at the University of Texas at Austin, has conducted a long-term study of married couples that pierces the heart of social psychological science: the ability to forecast whether a husband and wife, two years after taking their vows, will stay together and whether they will be happy. Huston's work is reported by K. Perina in her *Psychology Today*, article, "The Success of Marriage" (2016). Our culture is also to blame, Huston says, for perpetuating the myth of storybook romance, which is more likely to doom a marriage than strengthen it. He has few kind words for Hollywood, which brings us unrealistic, unsustainable passion. Huston has collected data on 168 marriages since 1979. Huston believes you can learn a lot about a couple's viability from the tempo of their courtship and the sentiments reported while they are dating. Huston found that men who feel uncertain about the relationship when they are "part of a couple, but not committed

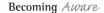

to marriage," are destined for a rocky courtship and marriage. But when women flag similar concerns, there is a "sleeper" effect: Problems usually surface after the honeymoon to wreak havoc on the nascent union. Huston thinks this is because "women are typically more interested in getting married than men, so they'll process their concerns, but they don't want to do anything to disrupt the courtship" (Perina, 2016). So if your new romance starts to resemble a movie script, try to remember: The audience never sees what happens after the credits roll.

The legal and social context of marriage creates barriers to breaking up for opposite-sex partners that may not exist for same-sex partners (Peplau & Beals, 2002; 2004). But in other ways researchers have found that gay and lesbian relationships are similar—in their satisfactions, loves, joys, and conflicts—to heterosexual relationships (Hyde & DeLamater, 2005; Peplau & Beals, 2004). For example, like heterosexual couples, gay and lesbian couples need to find the balance of romantic love, affection, autonomy, and equality that is acceptable to both partners. Lesbian couples especially place a high priority on equality in their relationships (Peplau & Beals, 2004).

There are a number of misconceptions about homosexual couples. Contrary to stereotypes, one partner is masculine and the other feminine in only a small percentage of homosexual couples. Researchers have found that homosexuals prefer long-term, committed relationships (Peplau & Beals, 2004). However, about half of committed gay male couples have an open relationship—one that allows sex outside of the relationship but not affectionate love. Lesbian couples usually do not have this open relationship.

In *Are You the One for Me?*, Barbara De Angelis (2004) reminds readers of some potentially bad love and marriage choices:

- You care more about your partner than he or she does about you.
- Your partner cares more about you than you care about him or her.

What can this couple do to make their marriage last?

Chapter 6: Developing Close Relationships

- You are in love with your partner's potential.
- You are on a rescue mission.
- You look up to your partner as a role model.
- You are infatuated with your partner for external reasons.
- You have partial compatibility—a lot in common in one area—but you ignore the rest of the relationship.
- You choose a partner to be rebellious.
- You choose a partner as a reaction to your previous partner.
- Your partner is unavailable (married or living with someone).

Marriage is a risky proposition. In deciding to get married, people make a long-range projection about the future of their relationship. Obviously, it is difficult to predict 30, 40, or even 50 years of commitment on the basis of one or two years of premarital interaction   Psychologist Harry Stack Sullivan (1986) has given us an excellent definition of love—"When the satisfaction, security, and development of another person is as important to you as your own satisfaction, security, and development, love exists."

One way to determine what may help maintain relationships is to ask couples who have been together for years what they think is important. Robert and Jeanette Lauer (Lauer & Kerr, 1990) in a classic study (if you are headed for graduate school this would be an interesting study to replicate) studied 350 couples who had been married for at least 15 years. It is interesting to note that both husbands and wives, out of 15 choices, listed the same 7 qualities as being important to a successful marriage:

1. My spouse is my best friend.
2. I like my spouse as a person.
3. Marriage is a long-term commitment.
4. We agree on aims and goals.
5. My spouse has grown more interesting.
6. I want the relationship to succeed.
7. Marriage is sacred.

Couples were asked questions about their marriage, ranging from interests, hobbies, sex, money, and attitudes toward their spouses, and reasons why their marriages had lasted.

The most frequently given reason for a lasting marriage is *having a positive attitude toward one's partner*. These individuals see their spouse as their best friend and they like him or her as a person. They are aware that their partner has faults, but their likable qualities more than offset their shortcomings. Many people stated that the present generation takes the marriage vows too lightly and are not willing to work at solving their problems. Marriage is a commitment and takes a lot of work. Both partners have to work at solving their problems. Another key ingredient to a lasting marriage is a mutual agreement about aims and goals of life, such as the desire to make the marriage last. A satisfying sex life is important, but this is not what makes the marriage last. In his *New York Times* best-seller, *The Seven Principles for Making Marriage Work*, John

Marry your best friend as well as your lover. Don't keep secrets or harbor grudges.
—JUDITH LIPTON

Gottman (Gottman & Silver, 2004) believes that the determining factor in whether wives feel satisfied with the sex, romance, and passion in their marriage is, by 70 percent, the quality of the couple's friendship. For men, the determining factor is, by 70 percent, the quality of the couple's friendship.

Marital Adjustment

During courtship, many of us wear *rose-colored glasses.* We tend to ignore or not notice our partner's faults. We tend to focus mostly on pleasurable activities and our partner's positive characteristics. But when people marry, they must face reality and the problems that they will encounter within this new relationship. Suddenly, marriage brings duties and obligations. One is no longer responsible for only oneself but now shares responsibility for two people and perhaps more if children arrive.

> *A happy home is one in which each spouse grants the possibility that the other may be right, though neither believes it.*
> —DON FRASHER

Furthermore, one's identity is changed with marriage. No longer are you simply you— you are now Ashley's husband, or David's wife, or Jon's mother or father. You become interdependent with others in your family and not independent. For some people this loss of independence may become a crisis, but for others this new identity may give them a new lease on life.

The changing nature of male and female roles creates problems for all types of couples as they settle down to live together. Even the most mundane tasks may become a problem. Who pays the bills? Who takes out the trash? Who cooks? Who will stay home and take care of the family? There is no such thing as a problem-free marriage. Successful marriages depend on the couples' ability to handle their problems.

Role expectations. What is the woman's role in married life? Is it different from a man's role? Should gay partners' roles be different? When a couple marry, they assume new roles, that of traditional "husband and wife." We all have developed our own expectations of how a couple should behave in society. These expectations may vary greatly from one person to another. This is sometimes determined by family of origin and even media portrayal. What happens if your expectations are different from your partner's? Sometimes serious problems may occur. The more the two partners work to agree about marital roles, the more likely the marriage will last over a longer period of time.

Where did you learn what the role of a partner should be? Most of us learned this from watching our parents through the process called *modeling (see Chapter Three).* But times are changing and other social forces are having an effect on our roles within a relationship. Careers are changing the timing of marriage and caretaking roles of the family. The women's movement has given women more options and has changed their perception of what their role is in a relationship. Marriage seems to be in a state of transition, and, consequently, most of us are in a state of confusion as to what role we should be playing.

What are your expectations of what married life will be?

© India Picture/Shutterstock.com

It is imperative that couples discuss role expectations in depth before marriage. If they discover that their views are very different, they need to take seriously the potential for problems. Many people ignore gender-role disagreements, thinking they can "straighten out" their partners later on. But as we have all discovered, it is difficult to change our own behavior and more difficult to change someone else's behavior—especially their attitude.

While we are dating, and during the *honeymoon period*, which can be any time from the wedding day to a year or so from that day, many people do not see the people they love as they really are, but rather as they wish (expect) them to be. *We see what we expect to see, we hear what we want to hear—this is a psychological phenomenon of perception that can interfere with the way we perceive the world.* We tend to perceive only the positive characteristics of our partners and ignore the negative characteristics. In essence, a person is in love with their own dreams and ideals and not with the person they marry. Living together day in and day out makes it only a matter of time until each partner is forced to compare ideals with reality.

> **The Honeymoon Is Over.** One morning, after David and Ashley have been married for about a year, Ashley awakens and "realizes" that David is not the same man she married. She accuses him of changing for the worse. He is not as considerate and as kind to her as he was before. He does not pay as much attention to her. He doesn't enjoy going out all the time like they used to. He just wants to stay home. David insists, of course, that he has not changed; he is the same person that she married and he enjoys quiet evenings at home alone with her.

This interaction may be signaling that the *honeymoon* is over for David and Ashley. This stage is very important in most marriages. It usually indicates that the unrealistic, overly high expectations about marriage and one's mate created by "love" are being reexamined. No one can live up to the perfection that is often portrayed in the media or what they think "should" happen in a marriage. Often couples will consult a therapist or take marriage encounter classes to work out some of the issues they have problems with.

In a successful relationship, it means that subjective perceptions are becoming more realistic and more objective. It also means that we are at last coming to know our mate as a real human being rather than as a projection of our expectations. Realizing the humanness of our partner allows us to relax, to be human as well and not feel that we have to live up to our partner's expectations. If my partner can make mistakes and be less than perfect, so can I, thank goodness.

After the *honeymoon period,* intensity diminishes and satisfaction with marriage generally dips, especially for wives. The most commonly cited reason for this change is the arrival of children. For most couples, the time and effort spent on parenting usually takes time away from the partner relationship. Within the past two decades, there does appear to be an increase in married couples making the choice not to have children or at least delay having or adopting children (U.S. Census Bureau, 2011). Some of the reasons often cited are the great costs involved in raising children, the possible conflicts involved with preparation for college and/or career improvements/advancements, loss of autonomy, and the great responsibility of raising children (Belsky, 2010).

What are some of the other issues and problems that a couple may encounter as they begin to face the reality of being married and functioning as a "twosome" rather than an individual? Yes, so many decisions to make!

Marriage, career, and parenthood. As birth control has become common practice, many individuals choose when they will have children and how many children they will raise. Currently, there is a tendency in the United States to have fewer children; the number of one-child families is increasing. People are not only marrying later, but also having children later (Azar, 2003; Grolnick & Gurland, 2001).

What are some of the advantages of having children early or late? Some of the advantages of having or adopting children early (in their twenties) are these: the parents are likely to have more physical energy; for example, they can cope better with getting up in the middle of the night with infants and waiting up until adolescents come home at night. The mother is likely to have fewer medical problems with pregnancy and childbirth. And the parents may be less likely to build up expectations for their children, as do many couples who have waited many years to have children.

There are also advantages to having children later (in their thirties): The parents will have had more time to consider their goals in life, have travelled or saved more money for a family, will be more mature, and will be able to benefit from their experiences to engage in more competent parenting. And the parents will be better established in their careers and have more income for childrearing expenses. This can also be an issue of who gives up their job or cuts back on work if they have children.

> While all couples eventually lose a bit of that "Honeymoon" euphoria, those who remain married don't consider this a crushing blow, but rather a natural transition from "romantic relationship" to "working partnership."
> —DR. TED HUSTON

Parental leave or *family leave* is an employee benefit available in almost all countries except the U.S. (NY Daily News 2011). Hopefully this will be changed in the near future, because, while dual-career couples are the norm today, finances often make the decision regarding childcare. However, resentments and mixed feelings can occur for many couples.

If a woman has to work to help provide for a family, she may feel guilty because she is not at home taking care of the kids. What if she doesn't have to work but prefers to work rather than staying home with the kids? Should she feel guilty for this when this is clearly what makes her happy? What if the woman has the more lucrative career and the decision is made for the man to stay home with the kids? Will he resent his bread-winning wife? Will he maintain his feelings of masculinity when he is not the person who provides money for the family?

Whatever arrangements couples make, Dr. Deborah Siegel (2007) indicates that psychologist Barry McCarthy urges couples to talk about their arrangements in terms of two-year timeframes, agreeing to make a point to check in every six months to see how well the arrangements are working for each individual. Are there other issues to consider? For many working parents, balancing their jobs and their family obligations can be a challenge for the family, "with 14% saying this is very difficult and 42% say it's somewhat difficult. Working mothers (60%) are somewhat more likely than fathers (52%) to say it's difficult for them to balance work and family, and this is particularly the case for mothers who work full time. In fact, one-in-five full-time working moms say balancing the two is *very* difficult for them, compared with 12% of dads who work full time and 11% of moms who work part time" (Pew Research Center, 2015).

The Bureau of Labor statistics for 2015 show that, while the pressures on men to be breadwinners and women to be housewives have been on their way out over the years, they're still far from gone. According to the 2015 American Time Use Study by the U.S. Bureau of Labor Statistics, employed men work an average of 42 minutes per day more than their female counterparts. And, while that's partially due to more women working part-time jobs than men, even among full-time employees men worked 8.2 hours per day compared to women's 7.8 hours. Additionally, 50 percent of women said they did some housework, such as cleaning or laundry, every day, while only 22 percent of men said the same. And 70 percent of women said they prepped or cleaned up food in an average day, while 43 percent of men said the same. Men were slightly more likely than women to participate in yard work—12 percent to 8 percent. On an average day, 85 percent of women and 67 percent of men spent some time doing household activities such as housework, cooking, lawn care, or financial and other household management.

Men's contribution to housework and childcare has almost tripled since 1965, but studies indicate that wives are still doing the bulk of the household chores in America, even when they work outside of the home (Coontz, 2006; Konigsberg, 2011). Employed mothers may very well feel exhausted, so they frequently ask their husbands to help out more with housework and children; this may cause conflicts in the marriage. In a July 2011 report called tellingly, *The New Male Mystique*, the Families and

Work Institute surveyed 1,298 men and concluded that 60 percent of fathers said they were having a hard time managing the responsibilities of work and family compared with only 47 percent of mothers in dual-earner couples (Konigsberg, 2011). As you might expect, men who are better educated or younger tend to be more helpful around the house.

Increasingly, gay and lesbian couples are creating families that include children. Researchers have found that children growing up in gay or lesbian families are

© Diego Cervo/Shutterstock.com

just as popular with their peers, and there are no differences in the adjustment and mental health of children living in these families when they are compared with children in heterosexual families (Anderssen, Amlie, & Ytteroy, 2002; Hyde & DeLamater, 2005). Also, the overwhelming majority of children growing up in a gay or lesbian family have heterosexual orientation

Home or career or both? The question is often a struggle for women.

What other issues and concerns do married couples encounter as they strive to succeed in their marriage?

Marital Conflict

What do most couples argue about? Is it sex, money, children, power, roles and responsibilities, jealousy, or extra-marital affairs? *Money* ranks as the single most common cause of conflict in marriage. Money not only influences a couple's lifestyle but also their feelings of security, self-esteem, confidence, and acceptance by others. Without money, families live in a constant state of stress, fearing the loss of jobs, illness, or household emergencies. Husbands tend to view themselves as poor providers, and their self-esteem may crumble as a result. Dr. Karen Horney most thoroughly discussed the ways people try to attain and maintain a favorable self-image. The clinical writings of Horney, and other psychotherapists as well, document the ways in which people attempt to defend and enhance self-esteem; they also suggest that difficulty maintaining self-esteem, and maladaptive efforts to do so, may be central to a variety of mental health problems.

Neither financial stability nor wealth can ensure marital satisfaction. Even when financial resources are plentiful, money can be a source of marital strain. Quarrels about how to spend money are common and potentially damaging at all income levels. Money is freedom, money is power, and sometimes men and women even lie about it. In fact, Louise Lague (2001) reports in a poll of 1,000 married people, ages 18 and over, half of them men and half women, that the most "hushed-up" issue was how much the respondents paid for something they bought. Couples that tend to be more satisfied with their marriage engage in more joint decisions regarding their finances in comparison to couples that eventually divorce.

Examine the last sentence, and decide what underlies most problems in relationships—be it a marriage, a business relationship, or wherever two or more people interact.

Can a bad relationship be good? Psychologist John Gottman (Gottman & Silver, 2004; Gottman & Declaire, 2007) has been studying love and marriage for over 30 years, with a concentrated 10-year study that has provided valuable research data behind his theories. He believes that some negative emotions used in arguments are more toxic than others: criticism, contempt, defensiveness and stonewalling. *Criticism* involves constantly expressing negative evaluations of one's partner. *Contempt* involves communication of insulting feelings that one's spouse is inferior. *Defensiveness* involves responding to criticism and contempt with obstructive communication that escalates marital conflict. *Stonewalling* involves withdrawing from a discussion, most frequently seen among men. Gottman further indicates that he has learned at least two things from the couples he has studied: *One* is the importance in building and maintaining a friendship in your marriage so that you give your partner the benefit of the doubt when times are tough. This takes constant work. *Second* is that you have a choice every time you say something to your partner. He feels you can say something that will either nurture the relationship or tear it down. In other words, you may win a particular fight with your spouse, but you could lose the marriage in the long run.

Gottman calculates that 69 percent of all marital problems are immutable, arising from basic personality differences between partners. Since behaviors rarely change, what you can change is your perspective (Dixit, 2009). Through all of this, Gottman recommends creating an *emotional bank account* by continuing to make small, everyday sacrifices and by making efforts to notice and appreciate the kindnesses of your partner. He suggests this *emotional bank account* will help sustain couples through more demanding times in which these efforts may fall a bit short (Gottman, 2007).

Gottman contends that many aspects of marriage, often considered critical to long-term success, such as how intensely people fight; whether they face conflict or avoid it; how well they solve problems; how compatible they are socially, financially, even sexually are less important than people and professionals once thought. Gottman believes that none of these things matter to a marriage's longevity as much as maintaining that crucial ratio of five-to-one.

What is this five-to-one ratio? This is the difference between divorce and a positive long-term relationship according to Gottman—it is mind-boggling in its very simplicity. Satisfied couples maintain a five-to-one ratio of positive interactions to negative interactions in their relationship. It is hard to believe that the longevity of your relationship depends primarily on you being five times as nice to your partner as you are nasty to them. This may be surprising to you (Gottman, 1995; Gottman & Silver, 2004).

- Wildly explosive relationships that vacillate between heated arguments and passionate reconciliations can be as happy—and long lasting—as those that seem more emotionally stable. They may even be more exciting and intimate.
- Couples who start out complaining about each other have some of the most stable marriages over time, while those who do not fight early on are more likely to face the road to divorce.
- Fighting, whether rare or frequent, is sometimes the healthiest thing a couple can do for the relationship. In fact, blunt anger, appropriately expressed, "seems to immunize marriages against deterioration." (Gottman, 1996)
- Emotionally inexpressive marriages, which may seem like repressed volcanoes destined to explode, are actually very successful—so long as the couple maintains the five-to-one ratio in what they do express to each other. In fact, too much emotional catharsis among such couples can "scare the hell out of them," says Gottman.
- How warmly you remember the story of your relationship foretells your chances of staying together. In one study that involved couples telling about how their relationship evolved, psychologists were able to predict—with an astonishing 94 percent accuracy—which couples would be divorced within three years.
- Men who do housework are likely to have happier marriages, greater physical health, even better sex lives than men who do not. (Hearing this, men may be running to find the vacuum cleaner.)
- In happy marriages, there are no discernible gender differences in terms of the quantity and quality of emotional expression. In fact, men in happy marriages are more likely to reveal intimate personal information about themselves than women.

> *What counts in making a happy marriage is not so much how compatible you are, but how you deal with incompatibility.*
> —GEORGE LEVINGER

What do you think about the five-to-one ratio? Should we be teaching couples how to apply this to their relationship?

COMMUNICATION PROBLEMS

Successful communication is the cornerstone of any relationship. Such communication must be open, realistic, tactful, caring, and valued. Maintaining this kind of communication is not always easy unless all the people involved are committed to the belief that good communication is important to life and marital satisfaction. This sounds simple, yet couples in marital trouble almost always list failure to communicate as one of their major problems. Basically, communication failures occur because one or perhaps both partners choose not to communicate or because of the lack of communication skills. You may want to refer back to Chapter Five and apply the material discussed in that chapter to improve upon your communication skills.

"The ability of couples to withstand stress, respond to change, and enhance each other's health and well-being depends on their having a relatively equal power balance," reports Carmen Knudson-Martin of Loma Linda University. Equality, psychologists agree, is the world's best antidote to isolation. It's just not easy to attain or to sustain (Marano, 2016). Many couples get so involved in the activities of everyday life—their career, their family activities and their outside interests—that they forget about the needs and interests of their spouse. Even though they spend time with their spouse, they really do not communicate. If this seems to be true of your relationship, you may want to change this by *scheduling a time to communicate*. Tell your mate that you would like to take them out to dinner every Thursday night, even if it is to a fast food restaurant, so you have a time to sit down and talk. This is your time, do not take the kids or anyone else. You may want to write down things you want to talk about during the week so you won't forget about them. Many times a person will get to the scheduled session and say, "There's something I want to talk about, but I forgot what it was." You may want to schedule a weekend away from the family every few months so you can talk and plan for the future. See Consider This . . . Making Up versus Breaking Up, further in the chapter to see the importance of communication in a relationship.

HOW TO HAVE A HAPPY RELATIONSHIP

- **Learn to Calm Down**—Do not let the emotions take control of you. Do not over-react; wait, relax, take a walk, remove yourself from the stress event for a period of time until you have time to calm down and respond logically. Be sure you are ready to not bring up past faults, mistakes, and problems. Once you have calmed down, you can work on the other basic "keys" to improving your relationship.
- **Validate Your Partner**—Validation involves "putting yourself in your partner's shoes and imagining his or her emotional state." Let your partner know that you understand how he or she feels and why, even if you do not agree. You can also show validation by acknowledging your partner's point of view, accepting appropriate responsibility, and apologizing when you are clearly wrong. If this still seems too much of a stretch, at least let your partner know that you are trying to understand, even if you're finding it hard.
- **Learn to Speak and Listen Non-Defensively**—This is tough, Gottman admits, but defensiveness is a very dangerous response, and it needs to be interrupted. One of the most powerful things you can do—in addition to working toward the ideal of listening with empathy and speaking without blame—is to "begin to apply praise and admiration into your relationship." A little positive reinforcement (appreciation) goes a long way toward changing the chemistry between couples.
- **Practice, Practice, Practice**—Gottman calls this "overlearning," doing something so many times that it becomes second nature. The goal is to be able to calm yourself down, communicate non-defensively, and validate your partner automatically—even in the heat of an argument.

Do you agree?

Gottman & Declaire (2007).

FAMILY AND DOMESTIC VIOLENCE

Physical violence is most apt to erupt in families lacking communication skills (Strong et al., 2010). Family violence is difficult to measure and document because most of it occurs in the privacy of the home, away from public view, and also goes unreported. Family violence includes child abuse, violence between spouses, sibling abuse, sexual abuse, and parental abuse by children, especially elderly parents (Duffy & Atwater, 2013).

A survey released by the National Network to End Domestic Violence (NNEDV) reveals telling information about the status of domestic violence services in the U.S. This study is conducted once a year to provide the public with a snapshot of what family violence programs across the U.S. see in their shelters on one particular day. The Centers for Disease Control and Prevention indicates that 1 of 4 women and 1 in 7 men over the age of 18 experiences severe physical violence in their lifetime (Berastain, 2016). On September 16, 2015, 1,752 out of 1,894 (93%) identified domestic violence programs in the United States participated in the 2015 National Census of Domestic Violence Services. During the 24-hour period, domestic violence victim advocates served more than 71,828 adults and children and answered 21,332 emergency hotline calls (nnedv.org/2015census).

Berastain (2016) states that partner abuse also manifests itself in the LGBT community, which experiences domestic violence at equal rates—and sometimes higher—than those of the rest of the population (25 to 33% of the LGBT population experiences domestic violence in their lifetime). Intimate partner abuse in the LGBT population can manifest itself differently from the cisgender pattern, thus presenting specific challenges to recognizing partner abuse and to accessing services. These include: the threat of outing, identity theft, withholding or selling medication, child-custody issues, and the lack of screening to distinguish between abuser and victim and lack of resources, since most shelters are set up for women only. There is also LGBTQ phobia among officials of the court and lack of community awareness, and, finally, LGBT abuse survivors who are closeted might not have friends, family members, faith communities, or other social circles to provide help and support.

If you are in an abusive relationship, it is important to get support. Someone who batters is usually very good at getting their partner isolated away from their family and friends. As a result, victims often begin to feel ashamed and alone and believe that no one would understand. Many survivors have even described feeling as if they did not even know who they were anymore. This makes it even more difficult to survive the abuse, to sort through the feelings, and to make decisions that will be best for you and your children. If you find that you don't have anyone to talk to, consider calling the National Domestic Violence Hotline or a domestic violence program in your area.

It is actually easier than you think to avoid a violent or abusive relationship. Our problem is that we allow our emotions to take control of our behavior and not our common sense and intellect. Recent research has shown that in most relationships where violence has occurred, some form of abuse began during the *dating period.* If a person is abusive while the couple is dating, what are the chances of the person *not* being abusive when they are married? Not very likely! A person does not change overnight or as soon as they sign a marriage license. To the contrary, some people feel that the marriage license is a sign of ownership and they can now do whatever they want to their partner. If you are in an abusive relationship before marriage you may want to "think twice" before making a serious commitment to that person. Abuse can happen from either partner…abuse is gender neutral.

Check this out

Go to www.jacksonkatz.com

Ten Things Men Can Do to Prevent Gender Violence

CODEPENDENCE

> Love creates an "us" without destroying a "me."
> —BITS & PIECES

But, wait a minute, you know you can help that person. They need your help and you love them and you feel you can help them change. If you can get them to marry you it will be easier to help them change. This sounds like the beginning of a *codependent relationship*—where one person has allowed another person's behavior (abuse, chemical addiction, etc.) to affect him or her, and who is obsessed with controlling that person's behavior (Beattie, 2011). Is someone else's problem your problem? If, like so many others, you've lost sight of your own life in the drama of tending to someone else's, you may be codependent. It is natural to want to protect and help the people we care about. It is also natural to be affected by and react to the problems of people around us. As the problems become more serious and remain unresolved, we become more affected and react more intensely to them. Does this sound like anyone you know?

Are you codependent? If you or any of your friends answer yes to the above questions, you may be codependent. Whatever problem the other person has, codependency involves a habitual system of thinking, feeling, and behaving toward ourselves and others that can cause us pain. Codependent behaviors or habits are self-destructive, not only to themselves, but also to all their relationships. Most codependents have been so busy responding to other people's problems that they have not had time to identify, much less take care, of their own problems.

Can a codependent change? Yes, definitely. But as we have already learned, change is not easy—it takes a lot of work and effort on everyone's part. The first step toward change is awareness of the problem, and the second step is acceptance. In order to

CONSIDER THIS

WHAT IS CODEPENDENCY?

- My good feelings about who I am stem from being liked by you.
- My good feelings about who I am stem from receiving approval from you.
- Your struggles affect my serenity. My mental attitude focuses on solving your problems or relieving your pain.
- My mental attention is focused on pleasing you.
- My mental attention is focused on protecting you.
- My mental attention is focused on manipulating you "to do it my way."
- My self-esteem is bolstered by solving your problems.
- My self-esteem is bolstered by relieving your pain.
- My own hobbies and interests are put aside. My time is spent sharing your interest and hobbies.
- Your clothing and personal appearance is dictated by my desires, because I feel you are a reflection of me.
- I am not aware of how I feel. I am aware of how you feel. I am not aware of what I want. I ask you what you want. If I am not aware, I assume.
- The dreams I have for my future are linked to you.
- My fear of rejection determines what I say and do.
- My fear of your anger determines what I say and do.
- I use giving as a way of feeling safe in our relationship.
- My social circle diminishes as I involve myself with you.
- I put my values aside in order to connect with you.
- I value your opinion and way of doing things more than my own.
- The quality of my life is in relation to the quality of yours.
- Have you become so absorbed in other people's problems that you do not have time to identify or solve your own?
- Do you care so deeply about other people that you have forgotten how to care for yourself?
- Do you need to control events and people around you because you feel everything around and inside you is out of control?
- Do you feel responsible for so much because the people around you feel responsible for so little?

become aware of what codependence is, we need to know what the characteristics of a codependent are.

Codependency is many things. It is a dependency on people—on their moods, behavior, sickness or well-being, and their love. It is a paradoxical dependency. Codependents appear to be depended upon, but they are dependent. They look strong but feel helpless. They appear controlling but in reality are controlled themselves, sometimes by a disorder or illness such as alcoholism. If you find yourself in a codependent relationship, you may want to read some of the new literature and self-help books available at your local bookstores or seek professional help through the counseling office or mental health center near you.

During the courtship period and continuing throughout married life, there is an insecure feeling in many individuals when they fear the loss of affection of their partner, especially when they feel threatened by an outside source. That outside source may be a new baby, a new friend, or a new career . Let us take another look at David and Ashley.

David has been working for a law firm for two years now and seems to be doing well. But the job is not as exciting as it originally was for the first two years. David is not considering changing jobs since he still knows that he could be a full partner within five years and that has been his goal for a long time.

On the other hand, Ashley just changed jobs and is extremely excited about the new challenges and the new friends she is getting to know. Ashley is beginning to spend more and more time at work and more time socially with her new friends. Occasionally, she has been working late with a male colleague to complete a major project.

David comes home after work and Ashley is still working. He is used to having her companionship in the evenings. David is beginning to question Ashley about her late evenings and the fact she seems to be so happy recently and excited about life. He seems to be bored with his job and not too happy with the world around him. David is becoming suspicious of Ashley and her friends. What's happening in this relationship?

WHAT'S THE GREEN-EYED MONSTER?

Is David *jealous*? *Jealousy* is an emotion familiar to most of us, if not from direct experience, at least through the experience of friends, from novels, television, and movies. *Romantic jealousy* carries the additional stress associated with the threat of losing an important relationship and often involves feelings of having been betrayed and perhaps deceived. Thus, this feeling of *romantic jealousy* provokes a host of negative feelings focused on the lover, the self, and the perceived rival. And it can be very destructive in relationships (Anderson, 2003).

Gender differences characterize jealousy. Men tend to show strong feelings of sexual jealousy and are especially upset about sexual infidelity. This can motivate them to be very concerned about their partner's faithfulness (Myers, 2015). However, women are often more upset by their partner's emotional infidelity (Buss, 2015).

Is it jealousy or envy? *Jealousy* is defined as the thoughts and feelings that arise when an actual or desired relationship is threatened. *Envy* is defined as the thoughts and feelings that arise when our personal qualities, possessions, or achievements do

> Jealousy is not a barometer by which the depth of love may be read. It merely records the degree of insecurity. It is a negative, miserable state of feeling, having its origin in a sense of insecurity and inferiority.
> —MARGARET MEAD

Becoming *Aware*

not measure up to those of someone relevant to us. In general, society is more accepting of jealousy than envy, understanding the desire to protect lovers from rivals but not the begrudging of a friend's good fortune.

Researchers have suggested that jealousy and envy are rooted in a weak sense of self, low self-esteem or insecurities about self-worth (Marano, 2006). People with poor self-concepts are more likely to fear that the existing relationship is vulnerable to threat. Jealousy is also more likely to occur when people believe they are putting more into a relationship than their partner is; they have serious doubts about their partner's commitment. Men seem to respond differently to jealousy than women. Males seem less likely to admit they feel jealous but are more likely to express anger with themselves or toward the rival; females are more likely to react with depression and with attempts to make themselves more attractive to the partner (Buss, 2003).

Overcoming jealousy is not easy. Anything we can do toward becoming confident, secure individuals will help us cope with our own jealousy. We can try to learn what is making us jealous. What exactly are we feeling and why are we feeling that way? We can try to keep our jealous feelings in perspective. We can also negotiate with our partner to change certain behaviors that seem to trigger our jealousy. Negotiations assume that we too are working to reduce our own unwarranted jealousy. Choosing partners who are reassuring and loving will also help reduce our irrational jealousies. Unfortunately, it is not as easy as it sounds to follow this advice because jealousy is so often irrational, emotional, and unreasonable. Jealousy remains one of the puzzling components of love relationships (Myers, 2015).

> During the last year of David's and Ashley's marriage, we find that David has been spending a lot of his spare time working on their computer, playing games, and learning new programs. Ashley does not like to spend her time playing with some "dumb" computer when she could be exercising or interacting with people. When they first got married, David and Ashley seemed to have a lot in common: tennis, history, same friends and same goals, but now they seem to be growing apart. Ashley has her new job and new friends and David does not seem to be interested in either. All he seems to be interested in is his computer and watching sports on television.

GROWING APART

Is there a point at which you have to admit that it is just not going to work, cut your losses, and walk away? In *Relationship Rescue*, Dr. Phil McGraw (2007) offers two major thoughts for consideration. *First*, do not ever make life-changing decisions in the midst of emotional turmoil. When feelings are running high and language and rhetoric even higher, this is not a time to make decisions that will affect your life and that of your partner and children, if any are involved. Never be in a hurry when making decisions, the consequences of which will be around for a long time. *Second*, if you are going to quit, you earn the right to quit. You don't just get mad; you don't just get your feelings hurt and decide to bail out. You earn the right to quit. Until you can look yourself in the eye in the mirror, until you can look your children in the eye and say I did everything I could to save this relationship and it could not be done, then you have not earned the right to quit.

When considering what it takes to make relationships work, it is useful to look at those who have tried and succeeded as well as those who have tried and failed. Research shows that a few crucial compatibilities make the difference between making up and breaking up. See Consider This . . . Making Up versus Breaking Up.

Who divorces? Tara Parker-Pope, author of *For Better: The Science of a Good Marriage* states, "Modern marriages are getting more and more resilient. With each generation, we're getting a little better about picking mates." The prevailing estimate is somewhere between 40 percent and 50 percent of marriages entered into in a year are likely to become divorces (Parker-Pope, 2010). The vast majority of divorces occur within the first decade, with years seven to ten being somewhat higher. First marriages that end in divorce last a median of about eight years (U.S. Census Bureau, 2011). "In 2013, fully four-in-ten new marriages included at least one partner who had been married before, and two-in-ten new marriages were between people who had both previously stepped down the aisle, according to a Pew Research Center analysis of newly released data from the U.S. Census Bureau." (Pew Research Center, 2014).

The divorce rate in 2015 was 16.9 divorces per 1,000 married women age 15 or older, which is down from 17.6 in 2014 and a peak of almost 23 divorces in 1980. The two measurements are not necessarily related, and it is hard to know why divorce rates are going down, but it could be that living together has become less stigmatized. Marriage rates had been declining for years in part because younger generations have waited longer to get married. But researchers have found that typical marriages still have about a 50% chance of lasting (Adams, 2016).

In addition, divorce rates in the United States are higher than rates elsewhere in the industrialized world (Strong et al., 2010). In *The 7 Principles for Making Marriage Work*, Dr. John Gottman lists the six things that predict divorce. His ability to predict divorce is based in part on his analysis of the 130 newlywed couples who were observed at his "Love Lab" apartment at the University of Washington.

1. **Harsh Startup**. When a discussion leads off with criticism and/or sarcasm (a form of contempt).
2. **Four Horsemen**. Use of criticism, contempt, defensiveness, and stonewalling.
3. **Flooding**. When a partner's negativity is so overwhelming, and so sudden, that it leaves you shell-shocked.
4. **Body Language.** Bodily changes during a conflict discussion (racing heart, hormonal levels).
5. **Failed Repair Attempts.** Analyzing the disagreement pattern they follow .
6. **Bad Memories.** Don't remember the early days of the relationship as positive. (Fulwiler, 2014)

CONSIDER THIS

MAKING UP VERSUS BREAKING UP

Pepper Schwartz (2002), professor of sociology at the University of Washington, analyzed data from the Enrich Couple Inventory involving questions administered to 21,501 couples throughout the country. The researchers compared the answers of the happiest couples to those of the most unhappy and found that the differences between their answers to a few key questions tell a lot about what makes relationships work:

My partner is a very good listener
Unhappy couples 18%   Happy couples   83%

My partner does not understand how I feel
Unhappy couples 79%   Happy couples   13%

We have a good balance of leisure time spent together and separately
Unhappy couples 17%   Happy couples   71%

We find it easy to think of things to do together
Unhappy couples 28%   Happy couples   86%

I am very satisfied with how we talk to each other
Unhappy couples 15%   Happy couples   90%

We are creative in how we handle our differences
Unhappy couples 15%   Happy couples   78%

Making financial decisions is not difficult
Unhappy couples 32%   Happy couples   80%

Our sexual relationship is satisfying and fulfilling
Unhappy couples 29%   Happy couples   85%

We are both equally willing to make adjustments in the relationship
Unhappy couples 46%   Happy couples   87%

I can share feelings and ideas with my partner during disagreements
Unhappy couples 22%   Happy couples   85%

My partner understands my opinions and ideas
Unhappy couples 19%   Happy couples   87%

What do you think about these findings?

What kind of specific marital problems are predictive of divorce? Amato and Previti (2003) found that communication problems, sexual infidelity, jealousy, foolish spending, and substance abuse were the most consistent predictors of divorce.

Your marriage will have a greater chance of lasting if (Strong et al., 2010; Parker-Pope, 2010):

- You marry after the age of 22;
- You grow up in a stable, two-parent home;
- You dated for a long time prior to marriage;
- You are well and similarly educated
- You have a stable income from a job you enjoy;
- You do not cohabit or become pregnant before marriage;
- You are religiously committed;
- You share similar value systems and have mutual life goals;
- You do not have emotional and/or psychological disorders;
- You enjoy spending time together;
- You have "affective affirmation" of each other;
- You are able to communicate and solve problems together.

None of these predictors, by themselves, is essential to a stable marriage, but the more you have, the greater the chance the marriage will last.

Today, marriage partners have a much more flexible view of marriage roles and responsibilities and are likely to expect each other to be a friend, lover, and confidant, as well as wage-earner and care-giver.

> David and Ashley have been married for eight years now. David believes in the "traditional" type of marriage, where there are male and female roles. Ashley believes in the "equalitarian" type marriage, where the responsibilities are shared equally. As you can see, there is beginning to be a lot of conflict within this relationship. David and Ashley no longer seem to have much in common. Ashley has tried to talk to David about their problems, but David does not want to talk about it. He thinks everything is "OK." She's just a complainer.
>
> Ashley decides that it is not worth trying anymore and files for divorce. David gets very upset and feels depressed because he feels that they can save the marriage. He says he will do anything to keep the relationship together, but Ashley says it is too late. Can this marriage be saved?

The impact of divorce. The dissolution of a marriage tends to be a very emotional and traumatic event for most people. Divorced men suffer primarily from loss of *emotional support* and disrupted *social ties* to friends and relatives and sometimes even children (Belsky, 2010). In comparison, divorced women suffer most from *reduced income*.

Men and women differ in how they cope with a failed relationship: women tend to confide in their friends, whereas men tend to start a new relationship as quickly as possible. Some individuals appear to adapt in the early stages of divorce, but show effects later (Hetherington et al., 1998). It takes most people at least two to three years to recover fully from the distress of a divorce, and some have more difficulty than others (Lucas, 2005).

Table 6.1 indicates the steps many people experience as they go through the divorce process.

Table 6.1 STEPS IN DIVORCE GRIEF

- Relief—Moment of no more fussing.
- Shock and surprise—I can't believe this is happening to me.
- Emotional release—How much should I let people see my feelings and how long will I keep crying?
- Physical distress and anxiety—Will I lose my friends?
- Panic—There is something wrong with me; I cannot eat or I eat all the time.
- Two basic emotions in divorce:
  a. Guilt—What did I do wrong?
  b. Rejection—I am not capable of being loved.
- Hostility and projection—I know we are both angry but we are going to end this divorce in a friendly manner.
- Lassitude—Suffering in silence, hard to get anything done.
- Healing—Gradual overcoming of grief and getting on with reality.

For some, divorce can be enhancing. In a healthy divorce, ex-spouses must accomplish three tasks: let go, develop new social ties, and, when children are involved, re-define parental roles (Lucas, 2005).

The first emotional impact of divorce is often that the former spouses become even more angry and more bitter with each other than they were in the marriage. This increased hostility is often followed by and interspersed with periods of depression, disequilibrium, altered patterns of eating and sleeping, drug and alcohol use, along with work and residence change (Kelly, 2004). It is most likely to be the wife who first finds fault with the marriage and files for divorce. In fact, many men are surprised and shocked by the break up, and in the short term, divorce is more devastating to the man than the woman. Over the long term, however, women are more affected, primarily because they are likely to have less money and fewer marriage prospects than divorced men. If they are mothers with custody, the impact of divorce is particularly strong (Duffy & Atwater, 2011).

How does divorce
affect the children?

© Soloviova Liudmyla/Shutterstock.com

What about the children? Divorce may have more of an impact on the children than anyone else. The children have no control in this relationship; they are helpless in this situation. Whatever the kids say or do will not benefit the situation. Generally, no one will listen anyway. Evidence suggests that in the long run it is less damaging to the children if unhappy parents divorce than if the children grow up intact but in a dissension-ridden home (Booth & Amato, 2001).

In *For Better or For Worse: Divorce Reconsidered*, E. Mavis Hetherington (Hetherington & Kelly, 2003), a psychology professor emeritus at the University of Virginia, tracked nearly 1,400 families and more than 2,500 children, some for three decades. Hetherington found that 75 to 80 percent of children of divorce are functioning well, with little long-term damage to their adult lives. She further declared that 25 percent of children from divorced families have social, emotional, or psychological problems, as opposed to 10 percent of kids from intact families. The children's recovery and subsequent adjustment seem to depend primarily on the quality of their relationship with the custodial parent and how well the custodial parent is adjusting to the divorce (Amato & De Buer, 2001). For some children, the effects of divorce tend to show up more as the children reach maturity and struggle to form their own adult relationships.

Though divorce can be hard on the children, psychologists often advise that parents can protect their children and minimize the impact of divorce by taking steps such as the following (Nevid & Rathus, 2010):

- Try, in spite of differences, to agree on how to handle the children
- Help each other maintain important roles in the children's lives
- Do not criticize or disparage each other in front of the children

Becoming *Aware*

Remarriage. Between 70 and 80 percent of divorced people remarry, on the average, within *three to four years* of being divorced (men tend to marry sooner than woman after a divorce). Remarriage is more likely to occur if the divorced person is relatively young, since there seems to be more potential partners still available. There is no guarantee that marriage will be better the second time around; the divorce rate for remarriages is about 65 percent higher than that for first marriages. However, the average duration for second marriages is about the same as for first, about eight to nine years (Kreider, 2005). It may be that some lonely, divorced people marry—too quickly—as they say—"on the rebound." Stepchildren can also be a disruptive factor.

Blended families. An increasing number of remarriages now involve children. Remarriages involving children pose special demands on both the adults as well as the children. In addition to learning how to live with one new person, which can be difficult enough for most people, one or both partners must also become accustomed to a ready-made family. When the children are young, the stepparent has more opportunity to develop rapport and trust with the children. But when there are adolescents involved, it is more difficult for everyone involved. Both parents must make allowances for their stepchildren's initial suspiciousness, jealousy, and resistance. When both parents develop a good working relationship, talking things out and cooperating on discipline and household chores, the blended family may do at least as well as intact families.

As we have previously noted, the traditional model of marriage has been undermined by many different changes within our culture. More and more people are selecting alternatives to marriage. Earlier in the chapter we discussed two alternatives: single life and cohabitation. Another alternative should be mentioned.

Gay/lesbian relationships. The dynamics of a gay/lesbian relationship do not seem to be any different than those in a heterosexual relationship. They are similar in terms of the forces that bring couples together, the factors that predict satisfaction with the relationship, and the problems couples face (Weiten et al., 2012). An increasing number of same-gender couples are rearing children.

The major problem that most gays/lesbians encounter is the negative attitude about homosexuality in our society. Most gay men and nearly all gay women prefer stable, long-term relationships. Promiscuity among gay men is clearly on the decline. Lesbian relationships are generally sexually exclusive. Gay/lesbian relationships are characterized by great diversity. It is not true that gays/lesbians always assume traditional masculine and feminine roles. Both gays/lesbians and heterosexual cohabitants may face some opposition to their relationship from their families, and society in general, and now universally enjoy the legal and social sanctions of marriage in the United States.

Chapter Review

We are motivated not only to seek the company of others, but to form close and lasting relationships. The relationships you have are your greatest assets.

- Relationships evolve, they do not just happen. They take time and effort.
- The three steps involved in a relationship are: 1) **Becoming aware** of the other person—first impression; 2) **Making contact** or getting acquainted; and 3) **Disclosure**.
- Friends play a significant role in our lives. They provide us with *emotional support* and *social ties*. Without friends we experience loneliness.
- We are drawn to people who are similar to us. Research studies have found that similar beliefs and attitudes are the most important aspects of a relationship in order to keep a relationship together over a long period of time.
- In order to find friends, you must go to those places (proximity) where you will find other people who have similar interests and needs.
- The **repulsion hypothesis** indicates that many of us are repulsed by people whom we do not know, and we perceive them as dissimilar to us.
- People with complementary needs tend to be drawn to each other—personality fit.
- The **social exchange theory** states that we measure our actions and relationships on a cost-benefit basis. People maximize their rewards and minimize their costs by employing their resources, either tangible or intangible, to gain the most favorable outcome.
- We tend to like people who like us—reciprocity.
- During the last decade, online matchmaking sites have evolved as a huge industry.
- The most important factors people want in marital selection in China, India, Indonesia, Iran, Taiwan, and the Palestinian Arab culture is chastity. People from the Zulu culture in South Africa, Estonia, and Colombia placed a high value on housekeeping skills.
- Both men and women of many cultures want a mate who possesses qualities of mutual attraction/love, dependable character, and emotional stability/maturity, respectively the highest.
- Men prefer wives who are younger than they are. Women prefer husbands who are somewhat older—but there is an increase in women seeking younger dates and mates.
- Harry Stack Sullivan has given us an excellent definition of love—"When the satisfaction, security, and development of another person is as important to you as your own satisfaction, security, and development, love exists."
- Robert Sternberg has developed a theory of love that includes three components: **passion**—an intense physiological desire for another person; **intimacy**—the feeling that one can share all one's thoughts and actions with another; **commitment**—the willingness to stay with a person through thick and thin.
- According to Sternberg, there are at last seven types of love relationships: liking, romantic, companionate, consummate, infatuation, empty, and fatuous.
- **Psychological reactance** is the tendency to protect or restore one's sense of freedom or social control, often doing the opposite of what has been demanded. This is also known as the Romeo and Juliet effect.
- Although alternatives to marriage are more viable than ever, at least ninety percent of us will marry at least once. Individuals are waiting longer to get married.

- Cohabitation has become increasingly more common throughout the world. Couples who do decide to cohabit are at a higher risk of divorce than couples who do not.
- The dynamics of a gay/lesbian relationship do not seem to be any different than those in a heterosexual relationship. The main problem is the lack of support /negative support they may get if their community does not believe in gay marriage.
- Men and women differ in how they cope with a failed relationship: women tend to confide in their friends, whereas men tend to start a new relationship as quickly as possible. Some individuals appear to adapt in the early stages of divorce, but show effects later.
- Most research indicates that the most important factors in making a marriage last are: be your spouse's best friend; have similar beliefs, values, and attitudes; exhibit a high degree of flexibility; have a positive attitude toward one's partner; and a couple needs to learn to adjust and compromise.
- The more two partners agree about marital roles, the more likely the marriage will last over a longer period of time. It is imperative that couples discuss role expectations in depth before marriage.
- Dr. Gary Chapman indicates there are five love languages: words of affirmation, quality time, receiving gifts, acts of service, and physical touch.
- Successful communication is the cornerstone of any relationship. Such communication must be open, realistic, tactful, caring, and valued. Physical violence is most apt to erupt in families lacking communication skills.
- John Gottman's research indicates that most relationships will be successful as long as the couple maintain the five-to-one ratio of positive responses to negative responses. Gottman also feels that some negative emotions used in arguments are more toxic than others (the "Four Horsemen"): criticism, contempt, defensiveness, and stonewalling.
- Gottman believes 69 percent of all marital problems arise from basic personality differences. He does not feel behavior changes that much, so changing one's perspective is the best advice. He suggests creating an emotional bank account in marriage, meaning to continue to make small, everyday sacrifices, as well as making efforts to notice and appreciate the kindness of your partner.
- A **codependent relationship** is where one person has allowed another person's behavior (abuse, chemical addiction, etc.) to affect him or her, and is obsessed with controlling that person's behavior.
- **Jealousy** is defined as the thoughts and feelings that arise when an actual or desired relationship is threatened, and **envy** as the thoughts and feelings that arise when our personal qualities, possessions, or achievements do not measure up to those of someone relevant to us.
- The prevailing estimate is that somewhere between 40 and 50 percent of U.S. marriages will end in divorce.
- Divorce affects all individuals—parents and children. Parents can help minimize the effect on children by trying to agree on how to handle the children, helping each other to maintain important roles in the children's lives, and not criticizing or making disparaging remarks about each other in front of the children.

Test Review Questions: Learning Outcomes

1. Discuss what is involved in the three steps in the development of a relationship.
2. What are the qualities of a good friend?
3. Explain the importance of similarities, proximity, complementarity, social exchange theory, and reciprocity in the development of friendships.

4. What are the top three mate preferences shared by men and women in Buss's cross-cultural research?
5. Discuss the effective strategies for meeting dates and mates.
6. Discuss the difference between love and infatuation.
7. What is the current estimate of how many marriages will end in divorce?
8. Describe Sternberg's theory of love and explain the seven types of love described in Sternberg's model.
9. Explain the phenomenon known as psychological reactance (the Romeo and Juliet effect).
10. Describe the positive and negative aspects of cohabitation.
11. What makes a happy and successful marriage?
12. Discuss Dr. Gary Chapman's Five Love Languages.
13. What do most couples argue about? Why? What does Gottman say most marital problems arise from?
14. Explain the five-to-one ratio.
15. Explain the four negative emotions John Gottman feels are more toxic than others.
16. What is a codependent relationship?
17. Describe the difference between jealousy and envy.
18. Explain the impact of divorce on the individuals involved, including children. What do psychologists recommend parents can do to minimize the effect on the children?
19. Explain the emotional bank account in marriage. How can it be helpful?
20. Discuss how role expectancies—child care, career, and housework—responsibilities can impact a relationship.
21. Discuss Traits of Friendship categories: Traits of Caring, Traits of Congeniality, and Traits of Integrity, each representing an essential aspect to relational behavior.
22. What is social capital? Why does it matter?

Key Terms

5-to-1 Ratio	Empathy	Marriage
Blended Families	Fatuous Love	Mere Exposure Phenomenon
Codependent Relationship	Friend	Parenthood
Cohabitation	Gay/Lesbian Relationships	Passion
Commitment	Honeymoon Period	Psychological Reactance
Communication	Traits of Caring	Reciprocity
Companionate Love	Traits of Congeniality	Remarriage
Complementary Needs	Traits of Integrity	Repulsion Hypothesis
Confidant	Infatuation	Role Expectations
Consummate Love	Intimacy	Romantic Love
Divorce	Jealousy	Romeo and Juliet Effect
Emotional Bank Account	Liking	Similarities
Empty Love	Love	Singlehood
Envy	Lust	Social Exchange Theory

Reflections: Critical Thinking

1. Explain why we need friends.
2. What is your definition of a good friend? Explain what a good friend is.
3. If you knew someone who was new to town, what would you recommend they do to find new friends?
4. Friendships satisfy needs. Study three relationships (friendships) that you currently have. What needs are they satisfying for you? Explain.
5. How have you used the social exchange theory in your relationships?
6. What is your definition of love? How do you know when you are in love?
7. What are the pros and cons of cohabitation vs. marriage? Explain.
8. What are your experiences with jealousy? How should a person deal with a jealous lover?
9. Explain the role of the male and the role of the female in a heterosexual married relationship. Thinking about heterosexual relationships in your family, are these roles different from how your older-generation relatives viewed their roles within their marriages? Explain.
10. What direct or indirect impact has divorce had on your life?
11. Explain codependence. Have you ever been in a codependent relationship? Discuss the relationship and explain how you could change the situation.
12. Which of the "Five Love Languages" is most important to you?
13. Explain your definition of an Emotional Bank Account in marriage.
14. Which type of lifestyle are you living today? What do you think are its advantages and disadvantages for you? If you could have a different lifestyle, which one would it be? Why?

Web Resources and Web Activity

ACTIVITIES

http://www.artofpeoplebook.com/quiz

Self Assessment Quiz from the book the *Art of People*.

www.gottman.com

Numerous articles related to Gottman's extensive research on making marriage work.

http://www.marriagebuilders.com/

Insightful answers to questions about infidelity, marriage counseling, and divorce.

http://hughson.com/

Named one of the top five Web sites in relation to divorce information. This is an address for individuals contemplating or involved in a divorce.

http://marriage.about.com/cs/communicationkeys/a/lovelanguage.htm

Discussion of five love languages, etc.

Activity: www.authentichappiness.sas.upenn.edu/testcenter.aspx

Close Relationship Questionnaire that measures attachment.

http://www.themachoparadox.com/images/10%20Things%20Flyer.pdf

10 things men can do to Prevent Gender Violence handout.

https://www.usaid.gov/sites/default/files/Violence_in_Womens_Lives.pdf

VIDEOS

http://wapo.st/2aOz3em

The sex lives of Millenials.

http://www.centredaily.com/news/local/article93227647.html

Talk to your doctor about your sexual health.

https://www.youtube.com/watch?v=Ql0Q5uf-AbA

The changing American family (2014) before the 2015 ruling on gay marriages.

https://www.ted.com/talks/helen_fisher_tells_us_why_we_love_cheat

Why we love, why we cheat by Helen Fisher.

https://youtu.be/P3fIZuW9P_M

The person you really need to marry by Tracy McMillan. McMillan answers the question: "Who is the one person you need to marry in order to have a successful relationship? (Yourself)."

http://tedxtalks.ted.com/video/Arranged-Marriages-American-Sty

Arranged Marriages: American Style by Pepper Schwartz, TEDxGatewayArch.

https://www.youtube.com/watch?v=_UoMXF73j0c

The price of invulnerability: Brené Brown at TEDxKC.

https://www.ted.com/talks/mandy_len_catron_falling_in_love_is_the_easy_part

Did you know you can fall in love with anyone just by asking them 36 questions? But … is that real love? Did it last? And what's the difference between falling in love and staying in love?

https://www.youtube.com/watch?v=7vhOAk5T3qA

Can abuse feel good? Kristin Carmichael at TEDxABQWomen.

https://www.ted.com/talks/helen_fisher_studies_the_brain_in_love

Why do we crave love so much, even to the point that we would die for it?

Roles and Expectations

PURPOSE

To discover the roles and expectations people have of themselves and other people in specific categories such as a spouse, parent, student, breadwinner, male, and female.

INSTRUCTIONS

1. Select one of the three alternatives:
    a. Ask four to five married students—may or may not be from the class—to be on a panel. Have the class members ask questions regarding roles and expectations in a marriage.
    b. Divide into groups of approximately four individuals (two females and two males would be ideal).
    c. Each student interviews four or more individuals, from different careers, from different socioeconomic income levels, and/or different ethnic groups.
2. The class may want to create their own questions or ask the questions listed below and then answer the discussion questions.
    a. What career have each of you chosen for yourself? What type of career is selected by the females; by the males? Are the careers sex-role oriented?
    b. What roles do you expect to play at home? Specify the tasks you are willing or not willing to do.
    c. What roles will you take as a parent (full-time parent, half-time, change diapers, and so on)?
    d. What roles will you take as a breadwinner and the financial management of your marriage?
    e. What role expectations did you have of your spouse before marriage?

DISCUSSION

1. Do you see evidence that today's college students subscribe to traditional sex roles or that they are free of such barriers to independent choice? Give examples.

2. What messages did you receive as you were growing up regarding specific expectations or behaviors appropriate to your gender?

3. How do you feel that your life would be different, if at all, if you were a member of the opposite sex? (Imagine, when you wake up tomorrow morning, you are the opposite sex.) What would you do? How would you act? Would others relate to you differently? What would your expectations of yourself be? How would they change?

Are You Compatible?

PURPOSE

To discover whether you and your prospective mate or date are compatible.

INSTRUCTIONS

1. Make a copy and give to your mate.
2. Answer the following questions with the appropriate number.
   1 = Strongly agree   4 = Disagree
   2 = Agree   5 = Strongly disagree
   3 = Neither agree nor disagree
3. Compare, contrast, and discuss responses with mate.
   1. We have similar religious beliefs and values.
   2. We enjoy the same type of leisure activities.
   3. We like each other's friends.
   4. We enjoy each other's sense of humor.
   5. We like to be with each other as much as we can.
   6. We are willing to share whatever we have with each other.
   7. We share our thoughts and feelings about even the most private topics.
   8. We have similar political values and beliefs.
   9. We are willing to listen to each other's problems and help resolve each other's problems.
   10. We tend to agree on how to spend money and how to save money.
   11. We support our partner's interest and activities even if they differ from our own.
   12. Our personal lives, work schedules, sleep habits, outside interests and activities, fit together harmoniously.
   13. We work well together in making decisions.
   14. We are able to resolve conflict situations without getting too emotional or aggressive toward one another.
   15. Our efforts to work out differences usually bring us closer together.
   16. We desire the same level of openness.
   17. We are able to work out a division of tasks and who is responsible for specific responsibilities.
   18. We are both neat or disorderly, etc.
   19. We enjoy the same type of vacations and travel.
   20. We share pleasant feelings and unpleasant feelings about each other and our relationship.

SCORING

Add up your total score. The higher the score the less compatible you seem to be: between 60–80. The lower the score the more compatible you seem to be: between 20–40.

DISCUSSION

After you have completed the rating scale, answer the following questions:

1. Why is it important to have a lot in common with your mate?

2. How can you improve your relationship with your mate to make your relationship more compatible?

3. Do you think that two people who score high on this test could still be compatible? Explain.

What Do You Think of These Trends?

PURPOSE

In 2010, Pew Research Center, in conjunction with *Time* magazine, conducted a nationwide survey of 2,691 adults ages 18 and older to get their opinions on attitudes about the changing American family. See how your judgments compare with those in the survey.

INSTRUCTIONS

1. For each trend, simply place an X in the appropriate column, indicating whether you think the trend is a good thing for society, a bad thing for society, or does not make much difference. Then, compare your attitudes with the responses given in the nationwide survey.
2. Divide into groups of four or five and have small group discussions or have a large class discussion on the discussion questions.

		Good Thing for Society	Bad Thing for Society	Doesn't Make Much Difference
1.	More women not ever having children.	_____	_____	_____
2.	More unmarried couples raising children.	_____	_____	_____
3.	More gay and lesbian couples raising children.	_____	_____	_____
4.	More single women having children without a male partner to help raise them.	_____	_____	_____
5.	More people living together without getting married.	_____	_____	_____
6.	More mothers of young children working outside the home.	_____	_____	_____

SURVEY RESULTS

These were the results calculated as appearing more frequently.

1. 29% bad for society   11% good for society
2. 43% bad for society   10% good for society
3. 43% bad for society   12% good for society
4. 69% bad for society   4% good for society
5. 43% bad for society   9% good for society
6. 37% bad for society   21% good for society

Note: Percentages may not add up to 100% because not all possible response categories are shown. The category of Doesn't Make Much Difference, for example, was added for consideration by the author.

DISCUSSION

1. Why did you mark each trend as you did—good thing, bad thing, or does not matter?

2. What other trends do you feel should have been included in the survey? Why do you feel this way?

3. Were you surprised at any of the survey results? Why or why not?

Rate-A-Mate

PURPOSE

To discover what is important to you and others in selecting a partner. What is important to you in selecting a prospective partner? What is important for other individuals in selecting a partner? How do you think people from other cultures would respond to this survey?

INSTRUCTIONS

1. Make 3 copies of the survey. Then, take the survey individually to see what is important to you in a prospective partner.
2. Give the survey to one of your parents, or someone at least 20 years older than you.
3. As a group or individually, you may want to select individuals from other cultures or different socioeconomic groups, or both.
4. If you are involved in a relationship presently, give this survey to your partner.
5. Take the survey again, but this time, circle the number as you see it relating to you. For example, give yourself a 4 if you feel your health is excellent, a 1 if you are not a good cook or housekeeper, etc.

Circle the number indicating the importance to you.

	INDISPENSABLE OR EXTREMELY IMPORTANT	VERY HIGHLY DESIRED	DESIRED, BUT NOT TERRIBLY IMPORTANT	IRRELEVANT OR UNIMPORTANT
Good health	4	3	2	1
Good cook and housekeeper	4	3	2	1
Attractiveness	4	3	2	1
Pleasing disposition	4	3	2	1
Dependable character	4	3	2	1
Emotional stability and maturity	4	3	2	1
Desire for home and children	4	3	2	1
Refinement	4	3	2	1
Good financial prospect	4	3	2	1
Similar religious background	4	3	2	1
Ambition and industriousness	4	3	2	1
Chastity—No sexual intercourse before marriage	4	3	2	1

Sociable (friendly)	4	3	2	1
Favorable social status	4	3	2	1
Mutual interests	4	3	2	1
Similar educational background	4	3	2	1
Intelligence	4	3	2	1
Complementarity	4	3	2	1

SCORING

Add up your total score. If your score is within 15 points of another individual that took the survey there is a high probability that you will get along well. But, the important aspect to consider is that your score on each individual value is similar to the individuals who are important to you.

DISCUSSION

1. How important is it for partners to have similar values? Can a couple be compatible with many dissimilar values?

2. Are your values different from a person 20 years older than you? What are the differences? Why do you think they have different values?

3. How do your values differ with people from different cultures and different socioeconomic groups? Explain.

4. Do you think it should be important to have a partner whose score is similar to your score as you took the survey the second time (as #5 in the instructions stated)? Explain.

5. What did you learn from this experience?

Name _____ Date _____

Divorce Panel

PURPOSE

To develop an understanding of some key issues to consider when divorce involves children.

INSTRUCTIONS

1. Use class members who are from divorced families as the panel members.
2. Assume the remaining members of the class are all married with children. However, some have already filed for divorce, and some are considering divorce.
3. Therefore, what advice/wisdom from experience would the panel members give to the following questions?

QUESTIONS FOR PANEL MEMBERS

1. What general advice would you suggest in dealing with the children?

2. Should parents stay together for the kids? Why or why not?

3. Did the divorce of your parents have any impact on your personal views of marriage? If so, please explain.

4. Did the divorce have any impact on your dating relationships? If so, please explain.

5. As you think of important events in your life; weddings, for example, how will the divorce impact that event in your life?

6. Did any of you feel that you lost a parent as a result of the divorce? Why or why not?

7. Did any of you feel that you gained a parent figure as a result of a step-parent relationship? Please explain, if possible.

8. Did your relationship with your biological mother or father change as a result of having gained a step-parent?

DISCUSSION

1. What is the reaction from the class members to the Divorce Panel experience?

Why People Get Divorced—Why People Get Married

PURPOSE

- To better understand why people divorce and what it requires to choose to remain married.
- To get a better understanding of why people stay married.
- To discover if unmarried individuals perceive the reasons for divorce differently than divorced individuals.
- To discover whether unmarried, married, and divorced individuals have similar perceptions of why people stay married.

INSTRUCTIONS

1. Interview four to six people who have been divorced, 4 to 6 people who have never been married, and 4 to 6 people who are married to find out why they feel divorce generally occurs. (You may want to use the form available on page 297.)
2. Ask them what they would consider the major reason (in order of importance) for the high divorce rate in this country. (Ask the divorced individuals to make this judgment based on their own experiences.)
3. Ask them what they would consider the major reasons (in order of importance) for staying married.
4. Divide into small groups or have a large class discussion.

DISCUSSION

1. Do any individuals consider unrealistic romantic expectations to be a contributing factor for getting divorced? If so, what are they?

2. Do the divorced and the never-married people respond differently? If so, how would you characterize these differences? If not, why do you think people agree on the basic causes even when they have had very different experiences?

3. What seem to be the major reasons for divorce?

4. What seem to be the major reasons for staying married?

5. What could we do to prevent the high number of divorces in our society?

6. Did the exercise stimulate your thinking about yourself, your interpersonal style, and your relationships to your fellow group members? Why or why not?

Name _____ Date _____

Marital Status _____ Age _____

1. What would you consider the major reasons are for the high divorce rate in this country? (List in order of importance.) Note: Divorced individuals will need to make this judgment based on their own experiences.

2. What would you consider the major reasons are for staying married? (List in order of importance.)

3. What do you think could be done to decrease the divorce rate in the United States?

Name _____ Date _____

Developing Close Relationships

LEARNING JOURNAL

Select the statement below that best defines your feelings about the personal value or meaning gained from this chapter and respond below the dotted line.

I learned that I . . .   I was surprised that I . . .

I realized that I . . .   I was pleased that I . . .

I discovered that I . . .   I was displeased that I . . .

....

Chapter 7
Resolving Interpersonal Conflict

Life will punch you, right in the gut. It will feel just like
that time you fell off the swing in 3rd grade and
the ground knocked the air out of you.
Life will knock the air out of you, but don't stop breathing.
Heartbreak will find you and it will crush you.
You'll lay in bed with a heart as broken as the
mirror that fell off your wall in college. But
do not be fooled—a broken mirror is still a mirror.
And a broken heart is still a heart.
It will continue to beat just like that old clock on your
grandma's wall that's been there for what looks like
centuries.

Life will get tough. Mama always said, "when it rains
it pours." And you will find out again: Mama is always right.
You'll get caught in the rain and soon you will
find yourself trying to cross a river of disappointment
so when those floods come, put on your
rain boots. Those rivers may be scary, but you are
stronger than they are. You may be as innocent as a sheep,
but be as courageous as a lion.
Always remember that people will let you down, so
stop letting them hold you down, but never

stop caring for them. Do not let yourself become bitter.
Bitterness is cancer and it will destroy from the
inside out.

Life will get tough and some days you will feel the weight
of the world on your back. Don't feel bad if you have to slow
down and take a load off. Rest. You need it.
But never let the weight of life's disappointments hold you
back. Keep your head up.

Life will get tough and your arms will never be long enough
to hug all the people who are hurting, but don't let that
stop you from trying. You can't save the world, but don't
let that stop you from trying either.
Never give up. Never give in.

Wake up each day and smile at yourself. The most beautiful
person in the world is the one staring back at you.
Take that smile and give it away to everyone you
walk by, because smiles are the best medicine.
Most importantly, be good. Do good, despite how
bad the world seems. I promise you there is good in
this world. You just have to look, and, sometimes,
you have to be the good. You have to be the stars
shining in the darkest nights. You can do it.

Carry on.

Used with permission Colton Snead, MHR Norman, OK, 2016

Think About This...

Have you ever found yourself in one of the following situations?
- Your parents have really been yelling at you. They do not understand you, and you do not understand them.
- You and your roommate cannot seem to divide the chores equally. Is there any hope for this living arrangement?
- You and your best friend had a major argument. You left mad and hurt.
- You and your co-workers have been squabbling and productivity is down. The boss is really angry.

Actually, the list could go on and on, but the fact is clear: when two or more people live or work closely together, for any length of time, a degree of conflict will be generated (O'Neill & Chapman, 2007). Furthermore, the greater the emotional involvement and day-to-day sharing, the greater the potential for conflict. Although it is impossible to eliminate conflict, there are ways to manage it effectively. There is hope for healthier, stronger, and more satisfying relationships.

What Is Conflict?

The word *conflict* comes from the Latin roots *com* meaning "together," and *figere* meaning to "strike." Common synonyms of conflict emphasize words like "struggle," "fight," "clash," and "sharp disagreements." Using these thoughts, Joyce Hocker and William Wilmot (2010) provide an interesting definition of conflict. Their idea is that **conflict** is an expressed struggle between at least two people who perceive the situation differently and are experiencing interference from the other person in achieving their goals.

What causes these struggles, interferences, and perceptions?

> *Everything that irritates us about others can lead us to an understanding of ourselves.*
> —CARL JUNG

What Causes Conflict?

Conflicts occur between people because people are different, think differently, and have different needs and wants. In fact, social psychologist Morton Deutsch (Deutsch et al., 2006) believes that conflicts usually involve any of six basic types of issues: *1) control over resources, 2) preferences and nuisances, 3) values, 4) beliefs, 5) goals*, and *6) the nature of the relationship between the partners.*

Perhaps the key word is *differentness,* because this is what causes conflict in human relationships. Differentness is a reality to reckon with, and the reality is that people enter relationships with differences in socioeconomic and cultural backgrounds, sex-role expectations, levels of self-esteem, ability to tolerate stress, tastes and preferences, beliefs and values, interests, social and family networks, and capacity to change and grow. And, add to these differences that many people are deficient in communication and conflict resolution skills and frequently have misunderstood styles of conflict management (Tannen, 2001). Therefore, it is easy to understand why *differentness* leads to disagreement and conflict.

The Realities of Conflict

Even though conflict is inevitable, it can have positive as well as negative effects. Thomas Gordon (2000), noted author and psychologist, explains this clearly:

> A conflict is the moment of truth in a relationship—a test of its health, a crisis that can weaken or strengthen it, a critical event that may bring lasting resentment, smoldering hostility, psychological scars. Conflicts can push people away from each other or pull them into a closer and more intimate union; they contain the seeds of destruction and the seeds of greater unity; they may bring about armed warfare or deeper mutual understanding.

In our society, conflict is often viewed negatively: It is "bad" to show anger, to disagree, or to fight. Some people look at conflict as something to avoid at all costs; but conflict is not necessarily bad—it exists as a reality of any relationship. It would truly be a rare relationship if over a period of time one person's needs did not conflict with the other's needs. In school and in the workplace clashes can happen. Since conflict is inevitable, coping with confrontations is one of the most critical of social skills. It's not the degree of conflict that sinks relationships, but the ways people resolve it. We must remember that conflict needs to be viewed from a problem-solving perspective. Often, solutions bring about change, and changes in a relationship should not be feared. Human relationships are dynamic and reflect the changes that accompany personal growth. Disagreements, if handled well, can help people know themselves better, improve language skills, gain valuable information, and cement their relationships (Marano, 2000).

Constructive ways for resolving conflict will be discussed later in the chapter.

We will now discuss in more detail three common benefits of constructive conflict resolution (Dubrin, 2010).

A quarrel between friends, when made up, adds a new tie to friendship, as experience shows that the callosity formed round a broken bone makes it stronger than before.
—ST. FRANCIS DE SALES

Conflict is not only inevitable, it's good. It means that two people have different perspectives.
—LAURIE PUHN

POSITIVE EFFECTS OF CONFLICT

Promotes growth in a relationship. People who work through their conflicts can develop a stronger and more intimate relationship. They take the time to learn about each other's needs and how they can be satisfied. They take the time to clarify their feelings. They take the time to share, and in so doing, realize that dealing with problems can be an opportunity to know each other better.

Allows for healthy release of feelings. When conflicts are resolved in constructive ways, both parties are able to air their feelings and leave the situation free of anger and hostility. For example, in a family conflict, unresolved anger and hostility can affect a person's performance at work or school. Likewise, unresolved anger and hostility in a work-related conflict is frequently brought home and may interfere with family and even social relationships. Talking things out and sharing what is going on are marvelous ways to relieve tension and anxiety (Weiten et al., 2014).

Increases motivation and self-esteem. When you have been able to resolve a personal conflict, or make a difficult decision, you naturally feel stronger and more motivated to tackle other struggles and difficult times. There is a real sense of pride and freedom when you join others and show respect for your rights and the rights of others. As a result, self-esteem is enhanced, and you are more motivated to take other interpersonal risks.

Conflicts can be turned into creative opportunities for more positive relationships.

D.W. Johnson found that research shows that if you are a conflict positive person you can enrich yourself:

First, conflicts can focus attention on problems that need to be solved.

Second, conflicts generate the energy, focus, and motivation needed to solve the problems.

Third, conflicts stimulate curiosity, interest, and information search.

Fourth, conflicts facilitate the understanding of other people's perspectives on the problems.

Fifth, conflicts can clarify your identify (who you are and what you stand for), what you care about and are committed to, and values.

Sixth, conflicts provide an arena for the full and active use of your skills and abilities, allowing you to test yourself and assess your abilities.

Seventh, conflicts may promote cognitive, social, moral and even physical development. Conflicts can stimulate change and growth. It is through conflicts, for example, that dysfunctional patterns of behavior that need to be changed can be identified.

Eighth, conflicts can release anger, anxiety, insecurity, and sadness that, if kept inside, make you mentally and physically sick.

Ninth, conflicts may keep your relationships clear of irritations and resentments and strengthen your confidence that you and your friends can resolve conflicts constructively (Johnson, 2015).

> *Not everything that is faced can be changed, but nothing can be changed until it is faced.*
> —JAMES BALDWIN

NEGATIVE EFFECTS OF CONFLICT

How we view conflicts and how we manage them can cause destructive outcomes. DeCenzo and Silhanek (2002) outline two negative effects:

The manner in which we approach interpersonal conflict. People generally view conflict with a belief that there must be a winner and a loser. It is human nature to want to win, just like it is human nature to not want to lose. When people approach a conflict situation with attitudes of winning and losing, a "tug of war" is often proclaimed. The net result is often one of disaster.

Larger problems and deeper personal resentments may occur. Just because you avoid a conflict or fail to resolve a conflict does not mean the conflict is forever gone. It is likely to return again with much greater intensity. You may be less willing to cooperate if you have leftover anger or "bad" feelings from a previous confrontation. Failure to deal with conflict constructively can even "rob" you of a potentially satisfying relationship.

So far, we have been discussing the positive and negative realities of conflict. The question now is: when faced with a conflict, how do you handle it?

How did your parents manage conflicts?

What Is Your Style of Conflict Management?

© Monkey Business Images/Shutterstock.com

You are probably thinking that your style of conflict management depends on the conflict and who is involved. Although that is probably true, most people have developed a characteristic style of managing conflicts. This style has emerged from our unique personality traits, as well as from what we learned growing up.

Think for a moment about how your parents managed conflicts. If your mother cried, sulked, or avoided confrontations, you may find yourself imitating her behavior. If your father yelled, intimidated, and dominated others with his anger, you may see some of these traits in your own pattern of conflict management. The question then is: How is your style of conflict management like and unlike those of your parents?

Actually, most of us go through life responding to conflict in a natural way that feels good to us. We may be unaware of our particular style and of even what methods we use to resolve interpersonal conflict. We may continue to use our approach whether it is appropriate or not.

Before we discuss the ways of responding to conflict, it might be beneficial to identify some rights that each person has in interpersonal interactions, whether conflictual or not. Based on the writings of Smith (2000), and Davis et al. (2008), the Consider This below lists a sample of these Basic Human Rights.

CONSIDER THIS

BASIC HUMAN RIGHTS

1. The right to say no to a request without feeling guilty
2. The right not to give people reasons for every action you take
3. The right to ask other people to listen to your point of view
4. The right to ask others to correct errors they made that affect you
5. The right to change your mind
6. The right to ask other people to compromise rather than get only what they want
7. The right to ask others to do things for you
8. The right to persist in making a request if people will not respond the first time
9. The right to be alone if you wish
10. The right to maintain your dignity in relationships
11. The right to evaluate your own behavior and not just listen to evaluations that others offer
12. The right to make mistakes and accept responsibility for them
13. The right to avoid manipulation by other people
14. The right to have and express your own feelings and opinions
15. The right to get what you pay for
16. The right to ask for information from professionals
17. The right to choose not to assert yourself
18. The right to set your own priorities
19. The right to be successful
20. The right to be treated with respect

Smith (2000); Davis et al. (2008).

Now that you know some rights that each person has in interpersonal interactions, what would your answers be to these questions: Is it difficult for you to make your wishes known to others? Are you sometimes pushed around by others because of your own inability to stand up for yourself? Do you ever push others around to get what you want? Do you speak your thoughts and feelings in a clear, direct manner, without judging or dictating to others? The answers to these questions characterize your behavior style in responding to conflict.

Behavior Styles

Now, we will return to our earlier question: How do you respond to conflict?, Elizabeth Scott (2016), an authority on conflict resolution and communication skills, has indicated that poor communication can weaken bonds, creating mistrust and even contempt! George Bach (1989) felt that dirty fighting techniques can weaken relationships and cause much pain, resentment, and hostility.

There are basically **three behavior styles** we use in handling opposition and responding to conflict. These have been classified as *passive* (also known as nonassertive), *aggressive*, and *assertive*.

Assertive is where you want to be… We will discuss the behaviors, belief systems, advantages, disadvantages, and when it might be appropriate to use each style.

MISTAKES TO AVOID

Elizabeth Scott (2016) believes that communication is the best way to avoid conflict. This is her list of mistakes to avoid.

1. **Avoid Conflict Altogether.** Rather than discussing building frustrations in a calm, respectful manner, some people just don't say anything to their partner until they're ready to explode, and then blurt their frustrations out in an angry, hurtful way.
2. **Being Defensive.** Denying responsibility may seem to alleviate stress in the short run, but it creates long-term problems when partners don't feel listened to and unresolved conflicts continue to grow.
3. **Overgeneralizing.** Avoid starting sentences with "You always" and "You never," as in, "You always come home late!" or "You never do what I want to do!" Stop and think about whether or not this is really true.
4. **Being Right.** It's damaging to decide that there's a "right" way to look at things and a "wrong" way to look at things, and that your way of seeing things is right.
5. **Mind-Reading.** This creates hostility and misunderstandings. It's important to keep in mind that we all come from a unique perspective and work hard to assume nothing; really listen to the other person and let them explain where they are coming from.
6. **Forgetting to Listen.** Don't underestimate the importance of really listening and empathizing with the other person! These listening skills are important to bear in mind.
7. **Playing the Blame Game.** Some people handle conflict by criticizing and blaming. Instead, try to view conflict as an opportunity to analyze the situation objectively, assess the needs of both parties, and come up with a solution that helps you both.
8. **Trying to "Win" the argument.** The point of a relationship discussion should be mutual understanding and coming to an agreement or resolution that respects everyone's needs.

9. **Making Character Attacks.** Sometimes people take any negative action from a partner and blow it up into a personality flaw. Remember to respect the person, even if you don't like the behavior.

10. **Stonewalling.** When one partner wants to discuss troubling issues in the relationship, sometimes people defensively stonewall, or refuse to talk or listen to their partner.

Passive/Nonassertive Style of Conflict Resolution

You may respond to conflict situations by **avoidance**. That is, you may remove yourself from the situation by leaving, shutting up, placating, concealing your feelings, or postponing a confrontation until a better time (Hocker & Wilmot, 2010).

Behavior description: When you behave passively, sometimes referred to as *submissively*, you are usually emotionally dishonest, indirect, and self-denying. You are likely to listen to what has been said and respond very little. Because you do not express your honest feelings, needs, values, and concerns, you actually allow others to violate your space, deny your rights, and ignore your needs. More importantly, you actually demonstrate a lack of respect for your own needs and rights.

Belief system: The message of a passive/nonassertive person is, "I should never make anyone uncomfortable or displeased except myself. I'll put up with just about anything from you; my needs and my feelings don't matter, you can take advantage of me."

Advantage: You usually do not experience direct rejection or get blamed for anything. Others may view you as nice, selfless, and easy to get along with. This approval from others is extremely important to you.

Disadvantage: You are taken advantage of and may *store up a heavy load of resentment and anger*. You do not get your needs met and other people do not know what you want or need. Consequently, passive people lack deep and enduring friendships. They frequently lose the love and respect of the people they were busy making sacrifices for.

> *Are there genuinely nice, sweet people in the world? Yes, and they get angry as often as you and I. They must—otherwise, they would be full of vindictive feelings, which would prevent genuine sweetness.*
> —THEODORE RUBIN

Aggressive Style of Conflict Resolution

You may respond to conflicting situations by *fighting*. That is, you **move against** another with the intent to hurt. In his book *Human Aggression*, Green (2001) refers to the aggressive style as **domination**.

Behavior description: You may literally or verbally attack another person. Typical examples of aggressive behavior are fighting, blaming, accusing, threatening, and generally stepping on people without regard for their feelings, needs, or ideas. You may be loud, abusive, rude, and sarcastic. You are in this world to intimidate and to overpower other people.

Belief system: The message of an aggressive person is, "I have to put others down in order to protect myself; I must exert my power and control over others. This is what I want; what you want is of lesser importance or of no importance at all."

Advantage: Other people do not push the aggressive person around, so they seem to wind up getting what they want. They tend to be able to protect themselves and their own space. They *appear* to be in control of their own life and even the lives of others.

Disadvantage: In the process of your gaining control, the other person in the interaction frequently feels humiliated, defensive, resentful, and usually hurt. Others do not want to be around you, and you wind up with an accumulation of enemies. This causes you to become more vulnerable and fearful of losing what you are fighting for: power and control over others. Therefore, you may create your own destruction.

Assertive Style of Conflict Resolution

You may respond to conflicting situations by *moving toward*. That is, you move toward your opposition until you are either closer together or on the same side. In *The Encyclopedia of Conflict Resolution*, Heidi and Guy Burgess (1997) indicate this style is used in **cooperative (collaborative) problem solving**, with some negotiation and compromise along the way.

Behavior description: You behave assertively when you stand up for yourself, express your true feelings, and do not let others take advantage of you. However, you are considerate of others' feelings. Actually, assertion is a manner of acting and reacting in an appropriately honest manner that is direct, self-respecting, self-expressing, and straightforward. You defend your rights and personal space without abusing or dominating other people. Joseph Telushkin (1998), in his powerful book, *Words That Hurt, Words That Heal,* expresses these thoughts:

> In a dispute with someone, you have the right to state your case, express your opinion, explain why you think the other party is wrong, even make clear how passionately you feel about the subject at hand. But these are the only rights you have. You do not have a moral right to undercut your adversary's position by invalidating him or her personally. It is unethical to dredge up past information about the person—information with which you're most likely familiar because of your formerly close association—and use it against that person.

Becoming *Aware*

Belief system: The message of the assertive person is, "I respect myself, and I have equal respect for others, too. I am not in this world to conform to others' expectations of me, and likewise, they are not in this world to conform to my expectations."

The Great Dishwashing Controversy

Two roommates had a problem: One of them (A) often left dirty dishes in the sink rather than cleaning them up at once. This infuriated B, who felt disrespected. For a long time, B suffered in silence.

Eventually, however, B confronted A. B was astounded when A stoutly maintained that it was B's refusal to let A do the dishes on A's own schedule that was rude and disrespectful.

Now that A and B were talking, however, they discovered they both had unstated beliefs about when dishes should be done—beliefs they had simply assumed the other person knew and had chosen to ignore. They were finally able to work out a compromise, though, when they realized that expectations are useless (and even detrimental) until you communicate them.

Advantage: You generally get more of what you want without making other people mad. You do not have to feel wrong or guilty because you vented your feelings—you left the door to communication open. Consequently, effective confrontation is mutually acceptable. From this, you develop more fulfilling relationships. Also, because you exercise the power of choice over your actions, you are in a much better position to feel good about yourself. In *Asserting Yourself,* Sharon and Gordon Bower (2004) remind readers: "The extent to which you assert yourself determines the degree of your confidence and self-esteem."

Disadvantage: As you become more open, honest, and direct, you also take some real risks in how others will perceive you. Some people have difficulty with these kinds of exchanges; therefore, you may experience some hurts and disappointments in some of your relationships.

> *Sarcasm is dirty fighting.*
> —GEORGE BACH

Now that we have discussed the three styles, it might be helpful to note the behaviors exhibited by the three styles in various situations. Table 7.1 lists these behaviors. Then, we will look at the three styles in action. The *passive/nonassertive, aggressive,* and *assertive* styles are illustrated in the following examples of a woman who wants help with the house.

Table 7.1 BEHAVIORS EXHIBITED BY ASSERTIVE, AGGRESSIVE, AND NONASSERTIVE PERSONS

SITUATION	ASSERTIVE	AGGRESSIVE	NONASSERTIVE
In conflict situations	Communicates directly	Dominates	Avoids the conflict
In decision-making situations	Chooses for self	Chooses for self and others	Allows others to choose
In situations expressing feelings	Is open, direct, honest, while allowing others to express their feelings	Expresses feelings in a threatening manner; puts down, inhibits others	Holds true feelings inside
In group meeting situations	Uses direct, clear "I" statements: "I believe that . . ."	Uses clear but demeaning "you" statements: "You should have known better . . ."	Uses indirect unclear statements: "Would you mind if?"

Adapted from Reece & Brandt (2010).

The Styles in Action

Passive/nonassertive style:

> **Margret:** Excuse me, but would you be a sweetie and pick up your clothes in the bathroom?
>
> **Charles:** I'm reading the paper.
>
> **Margret:** Oh, well, all right.

Analysis: The statement "Oh, well, all right" only rewards Charles for postponing Margret's request. Margret certainly does not get what she wants. She probably feels sorry for herself and may pay him back by giving him the "silent treatment" over dinner.

Aggressive style:

> **Margret:** I've got another thing to tell you. I've had it with picking up after you and trying to keep this house straight. You either pitch in or help me, or I'm quitting this nonsense.
>
> **Charles:** Now, calm down, I'm reading the paper.
>
> **Margret:** Did your mother just "wait" on you and treat you like a king? You don't give a flip about anything around this house, as long as you get to read the daily news whenever you want.
>
> **Charles:** Now, don't start in on me about my mother.

Margret: All you do is come home and relax in the easy chair and grab the paper.

Charles: Shut up! What's wrong with you?

Analysis: The opening statement is an attack, and Margret "relives" hostilities of earlier annoyances. Interactions such as this clearly have no winner, because aggressive behavior hurts another person, creates resentment, and guarantees resistance to change.

Assertive style:

Margret: I would like for you to pick up your clothes in the bathroom.

Charles: I'm reading the paper.

Margret: I would feel much better if we shared in keeping the house straight. You can read the paper when we're done straightening the house.

Charles: I'm almost finished with the sports section.

Margret: Well, I can start the wash. Will you help me when you are through reading the sports section?

Charles: Sure!

Analysis: Assertive behavior does not aim to injure but to solve an interpersonal problem. Assertive requests include a specific goal and the willingness to negotiate a mutually agreeable plan to solve the problem.

It would be unreasonable to expect people to use assertive behavior exclusively. There are times when it is wise to be passive and just give in to others; there are times when it is necessary to aggressively defend your rights; there are times when being assertive does not succeed in obtaining its goal.

Jay Heinrichs (2013) believes whether you believe it or not arguments surround you and play with your emotions, change your decisions, and are attitude changers.

We do not have to always win and being assertive lets you get your way more often than not without arguing and hurting others.

Learning to Be Assertive

> *I'm going to let what you just said season a bit before responding.*
> —KATHLEEN REARDON

The main goal of assertiveness training is to help people express their thoughts, feelings, and rights in a way that respects those of others. As you learn to do this, it is important that you become aware of the different types of assertive expressions (Atwater & Duffy, 2010).

Basic assertion is learning to stand up for your rights or express your feelings, such as saying, "Pardon me, I'd like to finish what I was saying."

Another type of assertiveness is *learning to express positive feelings,* such as, "I really liked the way you cleaned the car." Do you have difficulty in giving compliments, as well as receiving them? Some people do.

You may have to use an *escalating type of assertion when people fail to respond to your earlier request.* An example here would be, "This is the third time I'm going to tell you. I don't want to change insurance companies."

Then, there are occasions when you need to express *negative feelings.* The *"I" message,* frequently referred to as the focal point of learning to be assertive, is a way of expressing yourself effectively before you become angry and act in self-defeating ways.

The "I" message. According to Thomas Gordon (2000), an "I" message has four parts: 1) an objective, nonjudgmental description of the person's behavior in specific terms, 2) how I feel about this, 3) the concrete effects on me, and 4) a request and an invitation to respond. Let us look at each part.

1. **An objective, nonjudgmental description of the person's behavior in specific terms.** There are four guidelines to help you deliver an effective behavior description.

    First, describe the person's behavior in specific terms, rather than fuzzy, unclear words. For example,

Specific	Fuzzy
When you frequently call after 11 o'clock at night . . .	When you frequently call me late at night . . .

    The person you are angry with may have a different idea of what late means. Therefore, if you want your needs to be met, you will need to give the exact time you consider too late to receive a phone call.

    Second, do not add your thoughts and perceptions about the other person's motives, attitudes, character, and so on. It is human nature to describe another person's behavior by stating what you think the other person intended. This causes defensiveness, whereas describing what a person actually did creates an atmosphere for further communication.

    Third, make your behavior description an objective statement, rather than a judgment. Assertion messages avoid character assassinations, blame, sarcasm, and profanity.

    Fourth, behavioral descriptions should be as brief as possible. The longer your message is, the more likely you will not be heard and understood. Also, there are fewer

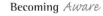

tendencies for others to judge and evaluate when you keep your message simple. One sentence is ample.

2. **How I feel about this.** Once you have identified what your real feelings are, you must take the responsibility for your own feelings. This means you say, "I feel angry or disappointed," rather than "You made me feel angry or disappointed." Continuing with the late-night calls as an example, we now have the following:

> When you call me after 11:00 o'clock at night, I feel angry.

3. **The concrete effects on me.** People may not be aware of how their behavior is affecting you. In most instances, they are not deliberately trying to annoy or frustrate you. Once they become aware of how their behavior affects you, they are usually more considerate. Our example now becomes:

> When you call me after 11:00 o'clock at night, I feel angry, because I am awakened by your calls at least twice a week.

4. **A request and an invitation to respond.** Simply stated, this means that you use "I" messages and tell others what behavior you would like for them to substitute the next time a similar exchange occurs. Be sure and express your request in one or two simple sentences. It is important to be firm, specific, and kind. Then, give the person an invitation to respond to your request. Also, where possible, give a positive response for the agreement. Some examples might be: "We'll have more time together . . ."; "We'll have a neater house . . ."; "We'll save money . . ."; "I'll be able to get my work in on time . . ."; I'll be less tired and more fun to be with . . .'; and so on. Our example now looks like this:

> When you call me after 11:00 o'clock at night, I feel angry, because I am awakened by your call at least twice a week. I'd like you to call before 10:00 o'clock, except in an emergency. Will you agree to that? Then, we can have a much more pleasant conversation.

To be sure that you understand each part of the "I" message, review the examples in Table 7.2. You will notice that these "I" messages do not attack or blame the other person.

SUGGESTIONS FOR DELIVERING AN ASSERTIVE "I" MESSAGE

Alberti and Emmons (2008) offer three suggestions for improving the success of assertive "I" messages.

Write and practice your message before delivering it. This will give you an opportunity to review two important questions: 1) Is it likely to arouse defensiveness in the other person? 2) Are you likely to get your needs met with this assertion?

> Assertiveness is not about aggression But rather a display of the confidence one has in their knowledge, beliefs or abilities.
> —TOM OLDS

Table 7.2 EXAMPLES OF "I" MESSAGES

NONJUDGMENTAL DESCRIPTION OF PERSON'S BEHAVIOR	MY FEELINGS ABOUT IT	CONCRETE EFFECTS ON ME	A REQUEST AND AN INVITATION TO RESPOND
1. When you call me after 11:00 o'clock at night . . .	I feel angry . . .	because I am awakened by your calls at least twice a week.	I would like you to call before 10:00 o'clock, except in an emergency. Will you agree to that? If so . . .
2. When you are late picking me up from work. . .	I feel frustrated . . .	because I waste a lot of time waiting for you.	I would like to be picked up on time. Will you agree? If so . . .
3. When you do not put your dirty clothes in the hamper . . .	I feel irritated . . .	because it makes extra work for me when I do the wash.	I would like you to put your dirty clothes in the hamper each day. Will you agree to that? Then . . .
4. When you borrow my car and bring it home on "empty" . . .	I feel annoyed . . .	because I have to get gas before I can go to work.	I would like you to refill the tank with as much gas as you use. Will you? If so . . .

Remember: You can arrange the four parts of the "I" message in a way that is natural and fits your personal style. For example, *I feel irritated when you do not put your dirty clothes in the hamper because it makes extra work for me when I do the wash. I would like you to put your dirty clothes in the hamper each day. Will you agree to that? Then, we will have more time together.*

Develop assertive body language with your "I" message. In order to assure that your verbal message is congruent with your nonverbal behavior, you will need to (Review Chapter Five for more details):

- Maintain direct eye contact
- Maintain an erect body posture
- Speak clearly, firmly, and with sufficient volume to be heard
- Emphasize your message with appropriate gestures and facial expressions
- Do not whine or have an apologetic tone to your voice.

Peace cannot be kept by force. It can only be achieved by understanding.
—ALBERT EINSTEIN

Don't be sidetracked by the defensiveness or manipulation of others. This can be accomplished by using the ***broken-record technique***—calmly repeating your point without getting sidetracked by irrelevant issues. Some examples might be:

- Yes, but . . .;
- Yes, I know, but my point is . . .;
- I agree, but . . .;
- Yes, but I was saying . . .;
- Right, but I'm still not interested.

Remember, persistence is one of the keys to effective assertion. One of the main reasons why people do not get their needs met when they assert is because they give up or give in after the first defensive or manipulative response of the other person (Communication Research Associates, 2012).

HOW TO SAY NO WITHOUT FEELING GUILTY

There is a rampant myth in our culture that to be considered nice, you have to say *yes* all the time. Perhaps you don't want to hurt someone's feelings or you don't want another person to be upset with you. When we keep saying *yes*, resentment and anger build. It is possible to develop the skills to say *no* with confidence, kindness, and peace of mind. And, you can have more time, more space, more efficiency, and control over your life. In *How to Say No without Feeling Guilty: And Say Yes to More Time, More Joy, and What Matters Most to You*, Patti Breitman et al. (2001) give these pointers:

- **Start small.** Practice saying *no* in nonthreatening encounters, where little is at stake and success is almost assured.
  Examples: Tell your best friend you don't want to go to her favorite restaurant . . . then suggest another. Tell your son he can't have more ice cream before bedtime.
- **Keep it simple.** The most effective *"nos"* are the least complicated. The more details you supply, the more likely the other person will try to change your mind.
  Furthermore, if you supply too many details, the other person may feel your "excuse" isn't good enough.
  Examples: Say *no* to requests for money in simple language, without offering a reason—I wish I could, but I can't. Say *no* to someone who wants to change shifts with you by simply saying, I have plans.
- **Buy time** when responding to requests. It relieves pressure when you're not sure how to say *no* diplomatically . . . or simply need more time to make a decision.
  Examples: I'll check my calendar and get back to you . . . Let me ask my wife, husband, friend, etc., about their plans for that day.
- **Remain generous.** Saying *no* without guilt is much easier when it is done in the context of generosity. This means being helpful and available to family, friends, and coworkers whenever you can—as long as it doesn't cause you significant stress or inconvenience.
  Examples: I'm sorry I can't go shopping with you this weekend. Give me a call again. I can't help you with the fundraiser this time, but perhaps I can next time.
- **Understand your Yes.** You will feel most confident saying *no* if you have a strong vision of what to say *yes* to. Why are you saying *no* to a particular request? What obligation or priority are you trying to make room for?

Remember, once you stop investing the better part of yourself doing things you don't want to do or being with people you don't want to see, you can focus your actions on your core beliefs, priorities, and passions. Margo Maine (2005), co-author of *The Body Myth*, has a thought-provoking comment, *I finally found a way to be nice: by saying yes—to myself.* Remember, *No* is a complete sentence. And, saying *no* is a powerful form of assertive behavior.

So far, we have discussed the passive, aggressive, and assertive behavior styles used in interpersonal conflict. Added to these different behavior styles are two powerful variables that affect the way people manage conflict: gender and culture. We will now discuss each of these factors.

Gender and Conflict Management

You will recall that, in Chapter Five, we discussed the different communication styles that men and women use. We indicated that males are likely to speak and understand a language of "status and independence," while females are likely to speak and understand a language of "connection and intimacy." These different communication styles obviously lead to different approaches in dealing with conflict.

> *We meet naturally on the basis of our sameness and grow on the basis of our differentness.*
> —VIRGINIA SATIR

Gender differences. Actually, these differences can be seen in childhood. For example, males are more likely to be aggressive, demanding, and competitive, while females are more cooperative. Boys try to get their way by ordering each other around. In contrast, girls like to make proposals for action: "Let's go let's ask her" or "What do you think?"

Male children make light of aggressive demands and are competitive, while females are more cooperative as children from preschool through early adolescence. In later years, adolescent men are described as being concerned with power and more interested in content than relational issues. Teenage boys often engage in verbal showdowns, and many engage in physical fights. Adolescent girls also use aggression and conflicts, but their methods are usually more indirect than boys'.

Gender differences start at a young age—females tend to be more cooperative.

© *spass/Shutterstock.com*

Becoming *Aware*

Teenage girls more often use gossip, backbiting, and social inclusion to fight.

Phrases that people use to describe male conflict include "men don't worry about feelings"; they think men are more direct. Phrases used about women's conflict styles include: "women are better listeners," "women try to solve problems without controlling the other person," and "females are more concerned with others' feelings" (Weitan et al., 2014). Deborah Tannen (2001) views this difference in childhood language as reflecting the different social structures of girls and boys, and women and men.

GENDER AND YOU

WHO MAKES THE DECISIONS AT HOME?

- Of the 1,260 individuals surveyed in 2008—either married or living together—women wield more decision-making power at home.
- In 43 percent of the couples, women made more decisions—almost twice as many as men—in the four areas Pew surveyed: planning weekend activities, household finances, major home purchases, and TV watching.
- The survey also found that 43 percent of men don't have the final say in any of those decisions; they either share the decision making or defer to their partners.
- As for household finances, the Pew study found that couples disagree on who has the greater influence. About 45 percent of women surveyed said they manage the family's money; 37 percent of the men say they manage it.
- Older couples are more likely than younger couples to make a decision together, the study found. More than a third of those 65 or older said they share in the decision making in at least three or four areas.

Pew Research Center (2008).

In the hierarchical order that boys and men find or feel themselves in, status is indeed gained by telling others what to do and resisting being told what to do. But girls and women find or feel themselves in a community that is threatened by conflict, so they formulate requests as proposals rather than orders, to make it easy for others to express other preferences without provoking a confrontation. If a man struggles to be strong, a woman struggles to keep the community strong.

These differences often persist into adulthood. M. J. Collier's (1991) survey of college students revealed that, regardless of cultural background, men and women view conflicts in contrasting ways. From this study, female students described men as being concerned with power and more interested in content than relational issues. By contrast, women were described as being more concerned with maintaining the relationship during a conflict. Do you agree or disagree with what the college students said?

A look at the entire body of research on gender and conflict suggests that the differences in how the two sexes handle conflict are actually rather small. Although men and women may have characteristically different conflict styles, the individual style of each communicator—regardless of gender—and the nature of the relationship are more important than gender in shaping the way he or she handles conflict (Adler & Proctor, 2014).

Benjamin Seider (2010), graduate student in psychology, University of California, Berkeley did a laboratory study of 154 couples and noted that couples who use the pronoun *we* behave in more positive ways during disagreements. Couples who regularly talk about their conflicts by saying *we*, *our*, and *us* show more affection and less anger during arguments. Couples who tend to use pronouns that express separateness—such as *I*, *you*, and *me*—have lower levels of marital satisfaction. Using the word *we* during arguments may help couples align themselves on the same team.

Learning flexibility. Tannen (2001) suggests that when one's habitual style is not working, trying harder by doing more of the same will not solve problems. She advises men and women to adopt some flexibility in their styles. For example, women who avoid conflict at all costs would be better off if they learned that a little conflict will not kill them. And, men who habitually take oppositional stances would be better off if they broke their addiction to conflict. After all, because people are different, not only in gender but in cultural background, differences in attitudes toward verbal opposition will persist among friends, lovers, and fellow workers. Frustration can be reduced by simply realizing that what seems like unfair or irrational behavior may just be the result of a different style in approaching conflict.

> *We find comfort among those who agree with us—growth among those who don't.*
> —FRANK CLARK

Culture and Conflict Management

Different cultures often define and deal with conflict in different ways. When individuals from different cultures face a conflict, their normal, habitual communication patterns may not blend smoothly. An example of the challenge faced by an American husband and his Chinese wife is illustrated on the following page (Fontaine, 1999). What do you think this couple can do to more effectively deal with conflict? With their cultural differences, will they be able to find a conflict style that is comfortable for them both?

Ting-Toomey and Oetzel (2002) suggest that the way in which people manage conflict varies depending on their cultural background. That is, high-context and low-context cultures manage conflict quite differently.

HOW WOULD YOU HANDLE THIS CULTURAL CONFLICT?

An American husband would typically confront his Asian wife verbally and directly (as is typical in the United States) leading her to generally withdraw completely from the discussion. She on the other hand, would indicate her displeasure by changes in her mood and eye content (typical for Asian culture) that were either not noticed or uninterpretable by her husband. Thus neither "his way" nor "her way" was working and they could not see any realistic way to "compromise" Fontaine (1999).

CROSS CULTURAL RELATIONSHIPS

The loyalty we often feel toward our own culture and traditions can sometimes mean we find it difficult to understand another's cultural signals. In a relationship situation where two people have differing beliefs, it is these feelings that can be pushed to the forefront, overwhelming the individual feelings they have for one another. Making families mesh and understand one another when they come from two completely different backgrounds isn't always the easiest thing.**But having conversations about the topic of culture and how it plays into your relationship and how to deal with others prejudices is something you need to do together.** One way to appreciate each other's culture is to learn how to express love (and other stuff) in different languages (Kruschewsky, 2014).

High-context cultures. These cultures value self-restraint, avoid confrontation, rely heavily on nonverbal systems, and give a great deal of meaning to the relationships between communicators. Preserving and honoring the face of the other person is a prime goal, and communicators go to great lengths to avoid any communication that might risk embarrassing a conversational partner. The Japanese, Chinese, Asian, and Latin American cultures are examples of high-context cultures. Japanese, for example, are reluctant to say "no" to a request. They will probably respond with, "Let me think about it for a while," which anyone familiar with Japanese culture would recognize as a refusal (Adler & Proctor, 2014).

Low-context cultures. These cultures use more explicit language, are more direct in their meanings, rely less on nonverbal systems, and stress goals and outcomes more than relationships. Examples include the German, Swedish, American, and English cultures. Individuals in low-context cultures manage conflict more directly. They are more confrontational and more goal oriented rather than being relationally focused, and they are less concerned about "saving face." Therefore, conflict in low-context cultures is more open, volatile, and threatening than high-context conflict (Gudykunst, 2005).

Let's get back to our example of the American husband and the Chinese wife. The husband from a low-context culture and the wife from a high-context culture were simply responding to their cultural learning of how to deal with conflict. For example, when indirect communication (that used by the wife) is a cultural norm, it is unreasonable to expect more straightforward approaches to succeed (that used by the husband). Can the husband learn to be cautious in his straightforward approach and more attuned to his wife's nonverbal signals? Can the wife be more verbally direct without relying so much on her nonverbal signals to express her real feelings?

One thing is for sure, a mutual understanding about their cultural attitudes toward verbal conflict may result in less frustration in the future. Yes, conflicts will still arise, but at least they can be arguing about real conflicts of interest rather than fighting styles.

STRATEGIES FOR HANDLING CONFLICT

When you approach a conflict situation, you can choose to *avoid* the situation, *fight* with use of power and force, or *move toward,* using negotiation skills (Adler & Rodman, 2011). Most research indicates that in deciding how to handle conflict, two distinct factors come into play: **assertiveness**; the degree to which you want to have your own way or satisfy your own interest and **cooperativeness**; the degree to which you are concerned about maintaining the relationship or satisfying the concerns of others (Rahim & Magner, 1995).

Therefore, depending on the levels of assertiveness and cooperativeness, there are five general strategies for handling conflict: avoiding, accommodating, competing/forcing, compromising, and collaborating (Hocker & Wilmot, 2010). See Table 7.3.

Avoiding strategy (lose-lose). In this approach, individuals attempt to passively ignore the conflict rather than resolve it. They may avoid the conflict by refusing to take a stance, physically leaving it, or escaping the conflict by mentally leaving the conflict. Often, people who use this strategy hope that ignoring the problem will make it go away. If the relationship is not very important or the conflict is very minor, it may just be wise to avoid the confrontation. However, if the relationship is important or the conflict is much greater, avoiding the conflict generally results in greater misunderstandings, resentments, hurt feelings, and more conflicts. Unfortunately, avoiders have a low concern for self and others, and a lose-lose situation is created because the conflict is not resolved.

> *Hatred is never ended but by love, and a misunderstanding is never ended by an argument but by tact, diplomacy, conciliation, and a sympathetic desire to see the other person's viewpoint.*
> —BUDDHA

> *Behavior is a mirror in which everyone shows his image.*
> —GOETHE

Becoming *Aware*

Table 7.3 THE THOMAS-KILMAN CONFLICT MODEL

COMPETING FORCING (Win–Lose)		COLLABORATING (Win–Win)
Confrontational and aggressive. Must win at any cost. Also called Passive-Aggressive		Needs of both parties are legitimate and important. High respect for mutual support. Assertive and cooperative.
COMPROMISING (Partial Lose–Lose)		
Important all parties achieve some goals and maintain good relationships. Assertive but cooperative.		
AVOIDING (Lose–Lose)		ACCOMMODATING (Lose–Win)
Nonconfrontational. Ignores or passes over issues.		Agreeable, non-assertive behavior.
Denies issues are a problem.		Cooperative even at the expense of personal goals.
These are the five conflict strategies or styles of conflict management. Each has a different level of assertiveness and cooperation. Which strategy do you most commonly use?		

Adapted from Lamberton & Minor (2010).

Accommodating strategy (lose-win). When using this strategy, individuals attempt to resolve the conflict by passively giving in to the other party. The accommodating approach is unassertive and cooperative. Individuals who use this strategy prefer harmony to conflict, desire to be liked, and believe that conflict is damaging to relationships. If you don't have strong preferences or feelings about a particular situation or issue, occasional accommodating is appropriate. However, if you often find yourself "giving in" just to please the other person, you will probably have feelings of resentment and are increasingly taken advantage of by the other person. This approach represents a low concern for self and a high concern for others, thus resulting in a lose-win situation.

Passive Aggressive (win-lose or maybe even lose-lose). This strategy is characterized by the use of aggressive behavior, an uncooperative attitude, and an autocratic attempt to satisfy one's own needs at the expense of others, if necessary. When maintaining close supportive relationships is not critical, this strategy is sometimes used. And, there are times when a legitimate authority figure has to make a difficult decision knowing others will not like it. Since this win-lose approach to conflict involves a high concern for self and low concern for others, deep feelings of resentment and hostility often result. In some instances, feelings of wanting to get even and compete on a deeper level may even result in a lose-lose situation.

Compromising strategy (partial lose-lose). This approach is used with attempts to resolve the conflict through assertive give-and-take concessions or cooperation. Compromisers value harmony as well as individual satisfaction and often will try to work out the situation so nobody gets all he or she wants, but everyone gets something. Compromising is a constructive way to resolve conflicts because neither side experi-

If you want
to go fast, go
alone, but if
you want to go
far, go together.
—MANDINKA
PROVERB

ences a total loss and both sides experience some sense of winning, thereby resulting in a partial lose-lose outcome. The advantage of this strategy is that the conflict is resolved, and relationships are maintained.

Collaborating strategy (win-win). Using this strategy, parties attempt to jointly resolve the conflict with the best solution agreeable to all parties. Since collaborating involves a high degree of assertiveness and a high degree of cooperation, it is also called the problem-solving strategy. Collaborating encourages openness and honesty and stresses the importance of criticizing or critiquing ideas rather than the persons involved. Because there is a high concern for self and others, collaborating tends to produce a climate of trust and respect in a win-win situation. Research shows if you participate in coming up with a solution, you are much more likely to comply with it (Puhn, 2010).,

Mastering Interpersonal Conflict

As we have noticed, it is highly possible to resolve conflict constructively. Here are a few general suggestions and guidelines to remember (Lerner, 2002; Verderber et al., 2009):

- Choose your battles carefully. Is this a minor, moderate, or major conflict? Think about the conflict before you react.
- Be calm, no yelling or speaking in harsh, loud tones. Avoid loaded words that may hurt or harm others—no "put downs."
- Don't blame the other person or make accusations. Tell the other party how you feel. Rather than, "You make me mad . . .", or "It's all your fault . . ." say, "I am angry . . .", or "I like it when we cook dinner together."
- Do not demand. Remember to request. Rather than, "You should . . ." or "You ought to . . ." say, "I would appreciate your watering the yard."
- Do not bring up the past. Doing so will only kindle old resentments and get in your way of dealing with the current problem.
- Avoid categorical statements like "You *always* . . ." or "You *never* . . ." These statements will only put the other person on the defensive.
- Take responsibility for your actions. Stop wanting to be right. Do not be afraid to say, "I made a mistake. I am sorry. Please forgive me." It is often amazing how many hours are spent avoiding just saying, "I was wrong."
- Listen without judging by showing respect for the other person and his/her position. Try to emphasize and understand his/her frame of reference.
- Learn to say you are sorry.

Cooperation is
the thorough
conviction that
nobody can get
there unless
everybody gets
there.
—VIRGINIA
BURDEN

The pillow method. When it seems impossible to gain empathy and understand another position and frame of reference, it might be helpful to remember the *pillow* *method.* Author and poet Paul Reps (1967) describes how a group of Japanese school children created it to remind people that a problem can be viewed from four different angles (*like the four corners of a pillow*). And, it just might be possible to form a new conclusion based on your new view of the issue, which is the *middle* of the pillow. This technique is now taught in business schools throughout the world (Punches, 2010). Here are the angles or positions to consider:

Position 1: "I am right and you are wrong." This position is easy and comfortable since we generally see the strengths in our position and find fault with anyone who disagrees with us.

Position 2: "You are right, and I am wrong." This is the hard part. Now, think about the other person's frame of reference. Put yourself in the other person's shoes and imagine how the person feels about the situation. What justification does this person have to feel the way he or she feels?

Position 3: "We're both right, and we're both wrong." In this position, you try to identify common ground. What are the strengths and weaknesses of each side? There is merit in both views. Be fair and even-handed as you evaluate both sides.

Position 4: "The issue is not as big as I was making it." In this position you consider that when compared to everything else you could be concerned about, you may be blowing the issue out of proportion. You may want to ask yourself, "Is this really where I want to focus my time and attention? Is the issue really as important as I had originally thought?"

Conclusion: There is truth in all perspectives. How do you think and feel about the issue now? What will you do about it? After you have looked at an issue from these different perspectives, you may not change your mind or even solve the problem. However, you will definitely gain new insights, increase your tolerance for the other person's position, and improve the overall communication climate with this individual.

STEPS FOR WIN-WIN CONFLICT RESOLUTION

Let us now look more closely at the exact steps used in the win-win approach to interpersonal conflict resolution.

Many authorities have written on the no-lose or win-win approach to conflict resolution. However, win-win problem solving works best when it follows a seven-step approach, based on the writings of Douglas Stone et al. (2010) and Thomas Gordon (2000). The steps are:

1. **Define the Problem in Terms of Needs, Not Solutions.** This is the critical point where you need to decide what it is you want or need. We generally define a problem in terms of solutions—what will satisfy our need. This really leads to win/lose results—one person gets what he or she wants, and the other loses what he or she wants. For example, let's consider this exchange between David and John.

David: I need the car to go to the library and study.
John: I need the car to go to the out-of-town basketball game.

David and John have both defined their goal in terms of solutions. They each want to get what they want—the car. Actually, David and John both had a need for transportation, and the family car was the solution.

A useful key to identify a *need* is to fill in the following blank "I need . . ." with a statement of the goal, not the solution. For example, "I need some kind of transportation" (the goal), "but I do not have to use the family car" (John and David's original solution).

Sometimes your needs may not be as clear as the example above. In these cases, either think about your *needs* alone before approaching the other person, or talk to a third party who may be able to help you separate your thoughts. Do not forget to explore all the reasons you are dissatisfied as well as the relational issues that may be involved.

2. **Share Your Problem and Unmet Needs.** Once you have defined your problem and unmet needs, it is time to share them with the other person. Remember, no one can be expected to meet your needs unless they know why you are upset and what you want. There are two guidelines to remember in this step:

First, *be sure to choose a time and place that is suitable.* Frequently, destructive fights often start because the initiator confronts the other person who is not ready. Unloading on a tired, busy person is likely to result in your concerns not being heard or given much attention. Furthermore, it is important that you are calm and have time to discuss what is bothering you. Bringing up issues of concern when you are angry, overly upset, or in a hurry frequently causes you to say things you really do not mean. Making a date to discuss what is bothering you increases the likelihood of a positive outcome. You might say, "Something's been bothering me. When would be a convenient time for us to talk about it?"

Second, *be sure and use "I" messages and the assertive techniques* you have already learned in this chapter. You will remember that the most important part of the "I" message is to describe how your partner's behavior affects you—not attach blame or labels.

The final part of this step is to confirm your partner's understanding of what he or she heard.

3. **Listen to the Other Person's Needs.** Once you are sure the other person understands your message, it is now time to find out what he or she needs to feel satisfied about the issue. Remember, if you expect some help in meeting your needs, it is only fair that you be willing to help the other person meet his or her needs. Thinking back about the exchange between David and John, John might say, "Now that I've told you that I need a way to go to the library to study, tell me what you need to feel okay about this situation with the family car." David might say, "I also need a way to the out-of-town basketball game." Be sure to review the listening skills discussed in Chapter Five and be prepared to listen actively to your partner. It is

also important to check your understanding of your partner's needs before going any further. You might say, "Now, do I understand correctly that you need . . .?"

You are now ready to arrive at a shared definition of the problem that expresses *both needs*. Try to state both sets of needs in a one-sentence summary of the problem. For example, David and John might conclude, "We both need a way to go where we want or need to go, and we only have one car."

4. **Brainstorm Possible Solutions.** Once the problem is adequately defined, the search for possible solutions begins. You might suggest, "What are some things we might do?"

   Roger Fisher and William Ury (2011), two Harvard law professors, give some important guidelines to assist in the brainstorming session:
   - *Seek quantity rather than quality.* Think of as many solutions as possible. Do not evaluate, judge, or belittle any of the solutions offered. This will come in the next step.
   - *Avoid ownership of a solution.* It is important to not get involved with your solution and my solution. Build upon each other's solutions by adopting an attitude: These are *our* solutions.
   - *List every possible solution.* The final result should be a long list of possible ideas and solutions. Since each idea needs to be considered, it is advisable for all solutions to be written down. Otherwise, a good idea may get lost.

5. **Evaluate the Possible Solutions and Choose the Best One.** *Check Possible Consequences.* Now it is time to evaluate the solutions in terms of how they best meet the mutually-shared goals. You want to evaluate how each solution meets each partner's needs and then arrive at a final understanding of which solution satisfies the most goals. However, sometimes it is easier and less time-consuming to initiate these four guidelines:
   - Ask the other person which solution he or she feels best solves the mutual shared goal. Be sure his or her needs are met.
   - State which solution looks best to you. Be sure your needs are met.
   - See which choices match with yours and the other person's.
   - Together, decide on one or more of the solutions. If you took the time to carefully examine each other's needs when you began your conflict resolution, several of the same solutions will generally be selected by both people.

   It is extremely important that each person be satisfied with the final solution. Remember, people are generally more motivated to work on resolving a problem if they are not manipulated or pressured into deciding on the best solution.

   The final aspect of this step is to *consider the possible consequences of your final solution or combination of solutions.* Sometimes it is helpful to ask, "What is the worst thing that could happen by choosing this solution?"

6. **Implement the Solution.** It is extremely important that you agree on exactly how the solution will be implemented. Your solution will be effective only if you mutually agree *on who does what and by when.*

> Unless both sides win, no agreement can be permanent.
> —JIMMY CARTER

> The normal life span of a quarrel is two or three days. If a person hurts or offends you, you are entitled to be upset with him for that long. (We are talking about routine arguments and misunderstandings here, not major offenses.) If the bitter feelings extend into a fourth day, it is because you are choosing to hold on to them. You are nursing a grievance, keeping it on artificial life support, instead of letting it die a natural death.
> —HAROLD KUSHNER

Because people are forgetful, it is usually desirable to write out the agreement that was reached, being sure to include the details of *who will do what by when.* The written agreement should be viewed as a reminder to both parties about exactly how the solution will be implemented.

7. **Evaluate the Solution at a Later Date.** Just as you made a date to begin talking about your problem and unmet needs, it is also important to make a date to review the progress of your final solution. This is an opportunity to "check back" with each person to see how the solution is working for each person. Is the mutually shared goal being met? If changes need to be made, now is the time to discuss what is on your mind.

Personal problem solving. It is important to note here that a modification of the win-win approach to interpersonal conflict resolution can also be used in personal problem solving. Hammond (2002) and his colleagues provide these steps:

*   Identify and define the conflict-problem.
*   Generate a number of possible solutions.
*   Evaluate the alternative solutions.
*   Decide on the best solution.
*   Evaluate the solution at a later date.

Ken Watanabe (2009), author of *Problem Solving 101*, summarizes personal problem solving by saying, *"Problem solving is easy when you know how to set a clear goal, figure out how to reach it, and follow through while reviewing your progress and making changes to your plan as necessary."*

When people join together and take the time to find a solution acceptable to both, most problems that occur between them can be resolved with a high degree of success. However, the win-win approach to conflict resolution is not a panacea for all life's problems. There are some occasions when this method will not work, or when another approach is more fitting.

When Conflicts Cannot Be Resolved

Sometimes, the most well-thought-out plans do not always work. Despite your best intentions and most dedicated efforts, not all conflicts can be worked through. In *Beyond Blame,* Jeffrey Kottler (2003), a professor of counseling and educational psychology, describes three occasions when conflicts may not be resolved: differences in basic beliefs, values, and past issues; struggles where there is no solution; and situations out of our control. The author would like to add one more—when things have to be a certain way. Let's look more closely at these.

Differences in basic beliefs, values, and past issues. There are times when two people are so different in their basic beliefs and values, and in the ways they perceive the world, that conflict between them is unavoidable, no matter what they do. Is there a person in your life with whom you have to work or associate with frequently who has completely different political or religious orientations from you? Or, what about some unresolved family issues with a relative from the past that can never really be laid to rest completely? Perhaps you have tried and tried to see each other's point of view, but you still disagree, and each party leaves feeling angry or hurt. You may just have to face a reality of life: agree to disagree when you discuss certain topics.

> *Maturity begins when we're content to feel we're right about something, without feeling the necessity to prove someone else is wrong.*
> —SIDNEY J. HARRIS

Struggles where there is no solution. The reality of life is that there is no guarantee that any particular human struggle has a solution, and certainly not a "best" one that can be determined easily. Look at this example:

> Maria has just received the call from the doctor. Her mother has a progressive case of Alzheimer's disease and now must move in with Maria and her husband, Hector. The sick mother is verbally abusive and demanding to Hector, and oftentimes even to Maria. There are no other family members to help with the sick mother, and finances are tight, making it impossible to send the mother elsewhere. Added to these difficulties are cultural values related to taking care of aging parents. They have no choice but to all live together, knowing that harmony among them is out of the question.

What can Hector and Maria do? They can partition off the house as much as possible, giving them and the sick mother as much privacy as possible. Hector and Maria can support one another as they try to enforce some limits. However, they still have to live with a certain degree of conflict in their home. There is no solution to this situation other than to learn to endure the situation in such a way that they minimize its effect on their relationship.

Situations out of your control. Have you ever had to deal with a situation in which you believed that if only you worked harder, if you knew more, or were more highly skilled, you could make things better? What would you do in the following situation?

> After 25 years of a stable, happy marriage, Jenny started drinking heavily. Their only child had finished college and was financially independent. George had talked to Jenny about her problem, and they had been to numerous counseling sessions. Jenny said she wanted to quit drinking, but she did little to help herself. So, the drinking continued. George had been an extremely responsible father and husband and felt that he could, or should, be able to do something to help Jenny with her problem. Divorce was the last thing George wanted to consider.

Is there anything that George can do to "fix" the problem? In life, it is critical to recognize realistically what is within your power to change and what is not. George needs to come to accept that not everyone really wants to change, no matter what they might say. Sometimes the payoffs of a person's dysfunction and behavior are too unattractive, or they just do not want to do the hard work that is involved. Rather than blaming Jenny or himself for the situation, George can take inventory of all the things that he has tried that have not worked, and rather than repeating them, try something else. Perhaps George may need to separate himself from Jenny for a period of time and let Jenny decide what she wishes to do for herself. George can choose to take up a new hobby, or interest, with friends who can be supportive of him during this time. He can build a new life for himself; George cannot "fix" Jenny's problem—only Jenny can.

When things have to be a certain way. Have you ever wanted someone to change to meet wants or expectations you believe are important? "If only they would . . . things around here would be so much better." Consider the following situation, assuming you are the roommate who wants "things around here to be better."

> There is growing tension between you and your roommate. She has an 8:00 class and gets up before you do and eats a breakfast muffin and orange juice at your kitchen table. Your roommate continues to leave her dirty plate, glass, and crumbs on the table. You clean your side of the table and put your dishes in the dishwasher when you leave for school. This is just essential—the way it is supposed to be! You are irritated and decide to discuss this with your roommate, knowing that she is quite good about cleaning her side of the table when she gets in from class and sharing in the other chores around the apartment. Your roommate listens to your concerns and indicates a willingness to change. However, the problem continues, and you become more and more irritated.

What are your options? You can clean up her side and run the risk of having to do more of the cleaning chores around the apartment, you can get another roommate, you can decide to live by yourself, or you can decide to not let the dirty dishes bother you so much.

When you live and work with other people, it is only natural that differences in the *way some things should be done* can create problems. The reality of life is, however, that if you want *some things* to be a *certain* way, then it is unrealistic to think that other people will necessarily do what you believe is *essential*. Thinking otherwise is a guarantee for conflict and stress to exist. In our example, the problem is yours—your roommate is happy and just trying to get to class on time. In other words, the person who is bothered by the problem is the person who needs to correct the problem.

Review the options discussed above and decide what to do, but remember—*when you believe something must be done a certain way and at a certain time, these beliefs may create some unnecessary stress in your life.* Sometimes, we all need to learn to live with less than what we want! Chapter Eight will discuss in more detail the stress involved in placing unrealistic demands and expectations on other people.

Chapter Review

When any two people live or work closely together, conflict is bound to occur just because people are different, think differently, and have different needs and wants that sometimes do not match.

- **Conflict** is an expressed struggle between at least two people who perceive the situation differently and are experiencing interference from the other person in achieving their goals.
- Conflicts usually involve any of six basic types of issues: 1) control over resources, 2) preferences and nuisances, 3) values, 4) beliefs, 5) goals, and 6) the nature of the relationship between the partners.
- Constructive resolution of conflicts can promote growth in a relationship, allow for a healthy release of feelings, and increase motivation and self-esteem.
- Two negative effects of conflict can be: the manner in which we approach interpersonal conflict (believing there must be a winner and a loser), and larger problems with deeper personal resentments may occur.
- The three behavior styles used in handling opposition and responding to conflict are: 1) **passive**—also known as nonassertive, 2) **aggressive**, and 3) **assertive**. The assertive approach is generally the most appropriate, effective, and constructive way of responding to conflict.
- There are several types of assertive expressions: basic assertion, learning to express positive feelings, and an escalating type of assertion when people fail to respond to your earlier request.
- The **"I" message** is frequently referred to as the focal point of learning to be assertive—expressing yourself effectively before you become angry and act in self-defeating ways. The four parts of the "I" message are: 1) an objective, nonjudgmental description of the person's behavior in specific terms; 2) how I feel about this; 3) the concrete effects on me; and 4) a request and an invitation to respond, with positive consequence.
- When delivering an assertive "I" message, it is helpful to remember these suggestions: Write and practice your message before delivering it, develop assertive body language with your "I" message, and do not be sidetracked by the defensiveness or manipulation of others.
- When we keep saying yes, resentment and anger build. Some pointers in learning to say no are: start small, keep it simple, buy time, remain generous, and understand your yes.
- Making families mesh and understand one another when they come from two completely different backgrounds isn't always the easiest thing
- Added to the different behavior styles used in interpersonal conflict are two powerful variables that affect the way people manage conflict: gender and culture. Regardless of cultural background, men and women view conflicts in contrasting ways. Likewise, high- and low-context cultures manage conflict quite differently.
- Research shows that couples who use we, our, and us show more affection and less anger during arguments. And, couples who use I, you, and me during disagreements have lower levels of marital satisfaction.
- Most research indicates that in deciding how to handle conflict, two distinct factors come into play: assertiveness and cooperativeness.
- The **pillow method** helps a person view a conflict from four different angles and possibly reach a new conclusion.
- **Win-win problem solving** works best when it follows a seven-step approach: 1) define the problem in terms of needs, not solutions; 2) share your problem and unmet needs; 3) listen to the other person's needs; 4) brainstorm possible solutions; 5) evaluate the possible solutions and choose the best one—check possible consequences; 6) implement the solution; and 7) evaluate the solution at a later date.

- Personal problem solving can be facilitated with the following steps: 1) identify and define the conflict, 2) generate a number of possible solutions, 3) evaluate the alternative solutions, 4) decide on the best solution, and 5) evaluate the solution at a later date.
- There are some occasions when the win-win approach to conflict resolution may not work. Possible occasions can include: differences in basic beliefs, values, and past issues; struggles where there is no solution; situations out of our control; and when things have to be a certain way.
- The list of mistakes in conflict: 1) Avoiding Conflict Altogether, 2) Being Defensive, 3) Overgeneralizing, 4) Being Right, 5) Mind-Reading, 6) Forgetting to Listen, 7) Playing the Blame Game, 8) Trying to "Win" the Argument, 9) Making Character Attacks, and 10) Stonewalling

How you resolve your interpersonal conflicts is the single most important factor in determining whether your relationships will be healthy or unhealthy, mutually satisfying or unsatisfying, friendly or unfriendly, deep or shallow, or intimate or cold.

Test Review Questions: Learning Outcomes

1. Define conflict and what causes conflict.
2. Why is conflict generally viewed negatively?
3. What are the positive and negative effects of conflict?
4. What are the three behavior styles used in handling opposition and responding to conflict? Explain the behavior description, belief system, advantages, and disadvantages of each style.
5. What are at least five suggestions given for mastering interpersonal conflict?
6. List at least ten Basic Human Rights.
7. Explain the behaviors exhibited by the assertive, aggressive, and nonassertive person in conflict situations and in situations expressing feelings.
8. What is the focal point of learning to be assertive? List and write an example of each of the four parts of an "I" message.
9. When delivering an "I" message, what three suggestions should you remember?
10. Explain the pointers given for learning to say no. Is no a complete sentence?
11. What are at least three different ways in which men and women view and deal with conflict?
12. Explain the different approaches high- and low-context cultures use in conflict resolution.
13. What two factors come into play when deciding how to handle a conflict?
14. List and give examples of the three methods you can use in conflict resolution.
15. Explain the pillow method. What different positions are involved?
16. What are the seven steps to use in win-win conflict resolution? What does research show about the level of commitment often demonstrated when one participates in coming up with a solution to a problem?
17. What are the steps to be used in personal problem solving?
18. Explain possible occasions when conflict may not be resolved.
19. Explain the differences between genders regarding conflict resolution.
20. What do laboratory studies reveal about couples who use the pronouns we, our, us, I, you, and me during disagreements?
21. Can all conflicts be resolved? Explain.

Key Terms

Accommodating Strategy
Aggressive
Assertiveness
Avoidance
Avoiding Strategy
Broken-Record Technique
Collaborating Strategy
Collaborative Problem Solving

Competing/Forcing Strategy
Compromising Strategy
Conflict Management
Cooperativeness
Domination
Gender Differences
High-Context Culture
"I" Message

Low-Context Culture
Partial Lose-Lose
Passive/Nonassertive
Pillow Method
Stonewalling
Win-Lose
Win-Win

Reflections: Critical Thinking

1. What kinds of differentness in others cause you the greatest interpersonal conflict?
2. What situations do you find most difficult to respond to with assertive behavior?
3. Generally speaking, have your conflicts made your relationships stronger or weaker? Why?
4. Which one of the parts of the "I" message is most difficult for you to remember to use?
5. Discuss any personal experiences you have had with the different approaches high- and low-context cultures use in conflict resolution.
6. Do you agree that men and women view and deal with conflict differently? Why or why not?
7. Do you disagree with any of the Basic Human Rights? If so, explain.
8. Is the win-win approach to conflict resolution too good to be true?
9. With whom is it most difficult for you to say no? With whom is it most difficult for you to be assertive?
10. What is your preferred strategy for resolving conflict?
11. Do you think it is possible to resolve conflict with the pillow method? Why?
12. Discuss gender differences in interpersonal conflict.

Web Resources

ACTIVITIES

http://stress.about.com/od/relationships/a/conflict_res.htm

Conflict skills for healthy relationships.

http://www.crinfo.org/

Links to Internet resources and information about publications and organizations on conflict resolution.

http://helpguide.org/mental/eq8-conflict-resolution.htm

Learn how to manage and resolve conflict in your work and family relationships.

www.communicationandconflict.com/skills.html

Reviews the skills involved in practicing both effective communication and effective conflict resolution.

http://www.peacemakers.ca/bibliography/bib50resolution.html

Conflict transformation and peacebuilding: A selected bibliography.

https://www.verywell.com/conflict-resolution-

Conflict resolution mistakes to avoid.

https://www.mindtools.com/pages/article/Assertiveness.htm

Mindtools: Essential skills for an excellent career: Assertiveness training.

http://ggia.berkeley.edu/

Greater good in action: Science-based practices for a meaningful life.

VIDEOS

https://www.ted.com/talks/julian_treasure_how_to_speak_so_that_people_want_to_listen?language=enn

How to speak so that people want to listen.

https://www.youtube.com/watch?v=V5MIUGjyC-M

Leo Buscaglia - Born for Love.

https://www.youtube.com/watch?v=xBp1hkxz_Ow

Rejection on Social Media - It Hurts! By Guy Winch, PhD.

https://www.youtube.com/watch?v=KY5TWVz5ZDU

Conflict resolution.

https://www.youtube.com/watch?v=o97fVGTjE4w

Conflict – Use It, Don't Defuse It, by CrisMarie Campbell and Susan Clarke, TEDxWhitefish

https://www.youtube.com/watch?v=_l5GowKNXpU

The Pillow Method: A Tool for Building Empathy. https://www.youtube.com/watch?v=ibmqUz6g8PU

Shifting Perspectives: Pillow method planning wedding.

https://www.ted.com/talks/amy_cuddy_your_body_language_shapes_who_you_are?language=en

Body language affects how others see us, but it may also change how we see ourselves. By social psychologist Amy Cuddy.

http://www.ted.com/talks/william_ury

The walk from "no" to "yes" by William Ury, a mediator, writer, and speaker who works with conflicts ranging from family feuds to boardroom battles to ethnic wars. He's the author of *Getting to Yes*.

https://www.youtube.com/watch?v=cFdCzN7RYbw

Reciprocity.

The Assertiveness Inventory

PURPOSE

To assess your strengths and weaknesses in being assertive and to establish goals for improvement.

INSTRUCTIONS

1. Respond to the following questions by drawing a circle around the number that describes you best.

   For some questions, the assertive end of the scale is at 0, for others at 4.
   Key:
   0   means no or never
   1   means somewhat or sometimes
   2   means average
   3   means usually or a good deal
   4   means practically always or entirely

1. When a person is highly unfair, do you call it to their attention?	0 1 2 3 4
2. Do you find it difficult to make decisions?	0 1 2 3 4
3. Are you openly critical of others' ideas, opinions, behavior?	0 1 2 3 4
4. Do you speak out in protest when someone takes your place in line?	0 1 2 3 4
5. Do you often avoid people or situations for fear of embarrassment?	0 1 2 3 4
6. Do you usually have confidence in your own judgment?	0 1 2 3 4
7. Do you insist that your spouse or roommate take on a fair share of household chores?	0 1 2 3 4
8. Are you prone to "fly off the handle"?	0 1 2 3 4
9. When a salesperson makes an effort, do you find it hard to say "No" even though the merchandise is not really what you want?	0 1 2 3 4
10. When a latecomer is waited on before you are, do you call attention to the situation?	0 1 2 3 4
11. Are you reluctant to speak up in a discussion or debate?	0 1 2 3 4
12. If a person has borrowed money (or a book, garment, thing of value) and is overdue in returning it, do you mention it?	0 1 2 3 4
13. Do you continue to pursue an argument after the other person has had enough?	0 1 2 3 4
14. Do you generally express what you feel?	0 1 2 3 4
15. Are you disturbed if someone watches you at work?	0 1 2 3 4
16. If someone keeps kicking or bumping your chair in a movie or a lecture, do you ask the person to stop?	0 1 2 3 4

17. Do you find it difficult to keep eye contact when you are talking to another person? 0 1 2 3 4

18. In a good restaurant, when your meal is improperly prepared or served, do you ask the waiter/waitress to correct the situation? 0 1 2 3 4

19. When you discover merchandise is faulty, do you return it for an adjustment? 0 1 2 3 4

20. Do you show your anger by name calling or obscenities? 0 1 2 3 4

21. Do you try to be a wallflower or a piece of the furniture in social situations? 0 1 2 3 4

22. Do you insist that your property manager (mechanic, repairman, janitor) make repairs, adjustments, or replacements which are his or her responsibility? 0 1 2 3 4

23. Do you often step in and make decisions for others? 0 1 2 3 4

24. Are you able openly to express love and affection? 0 1 2 3 4

25. Are you able to ask your friends for small favors or help? 0 1 2 3 4

26. Do you think you always have the right answer? 0 1 2 3 4

27. When you differ with a person you respect, are you able to speak up for your own viewpoint? 0 1 2 3 4

28. Are you able to refuse unreasonable requests made by friends? 0 1 2 3 4

29. Do you have difficulty complimenting or praising others? 0 1 2 3 4

30. If you are disturbed by someone smoking near you, can you say so? 0 1 2 3 4

31. Do you shout or use bullying tactics to get others to do as you wish? 0 1 2 3 4

32. Do you finish other people's sentences for them? 0 1 2 3 4

33. Do you get into physical fights with others, especially with strangers? 0 1 2 3 4

34. At family meals, do you control the conversation? 0 1 2 3 4

35. When you meet a stranger, are you the first to introduce yourself and begin a conversation? 0 1 2 3 4

2. **Analyzing Your Results:** When you complete the Inventory, you'll probably be tempted to add up your total score. Don't! It really has no meaning, since there is no such thing as a general quality of assertiveness. The authors of the inventory suggest the following steps for analysis of your responses to the Assertiveness Inventory:

   a. Look at individual events in your life, involving particular people or groups, and consider strengths and shortcomings accordingly.

   b. Look at your responses to questions 1, 2, 4, 5, 6, 7, 9, 10, 11, 12, 14, 15, 16, 17, 18, 19, 21, 22, 24, 25, 27, 28, 30, and 35. These questions are oriented toward nonassertive behavior. Respond to these questions: Do your answers to these items tell you that you are rarely speaking up for yourself? How do you feel about what you have learned about yourself?

   c. Look at your responses to questions 3, 8, 13, 20, 23, 26, 29, 31, 32, 33, and 34. These questions are oriented toward aggressive behavior. Respond to these questions: Do your answers to these questions suggest you are pushing others around more than you realized? How do you feel about what you have learned about yourself?

DISCUSSION

Most people confirm from completing these three steps that assertiveness is situational in their lives. No one is nonassertive all the time, aggressive all the time, assertive all the time! Each person behaves in each of the three ways at various times, depending upon the situation. It is possible that you have a characteristic style that leans heavily in one direction. Reread each question on the Inventory and carefully analyze your answers. Look specifically at four aspects (situations, attitudes, obstacles, and behavior skills) of the information and respond to the questions below:

1. What *situations* give you trouble? Which can you handle easily?

2. What are your *attitudes* about expressing yourself? For example, do you feel you have a "right" to be assertive? Why or why not?

3. What *obstacles* are in the way of your assertions? For example, are you frightened of the consequences, or do other people in your life make being assertive especially difficult? Who?

4. Are your *behavior skills* (eye contact, facial expression, body posture) intact? Can you be expressive when you need to?

5. What specific goals do you need to set for yourself in learning to be more assertive?

Understanding the Passive, Aggressive, and Assertive Styles

PURPOSE

To practice composing passive, aggressive, and assertive responses to real-life situations.

INSTRUCTIONS

1. After each situation, compose a passive, aggressive, and assertive response.
2. Then, share your responses in an open class discussion or divide into small groups of four students.
    a. You have just paid for your dinner at one of your favorite restaurants. However, you suddenly realize that your change is a dollar short.

    Passive Response:

    Aggressive Response:

    Assertive Response:

    b. You are relaxing with the paper after a long day. Your spouse rushes in and hands you a list of food items and says, "I never thought you would get here. Quick, pick these up from the store."

    Passive Response:

    Aggressive Response:

    Assertive Response:

    c. Your teacher lost the test you handed in and says you must take the test again.

    Passive Response:

Aggressive Response:

Assertive Response:

d. Your roommate has not been doing his or her share of chores around the apartment.

   Passive Response:

   Aggressive Response:

   Assertive Response:

e. While you wait patiently for the clerk to finish with the customer ahead of you, another customer comes in and the clerk waits on him before you.

   Passive Response:

   Aggressive Response:

   Assertive Response:

DISCUSSION

1. Which responses were the most difficult for you to compose: the passive, aggressive, or assertive?

2. Would others who know you well say you are more passive, aggressive, or assertive in dealing with conflicts and problem solving? Explain.

3. Do you think there are gender differences in certain styles?

Say It with "I" Messages

PURPOSE

To learn how to construct an assertive "I" message in order to express your feelings and get your needs met.

INSTRUCTIONS

1. Respond to each of the following situations by writing an appropriate "I" message. Each "I" message should include the following five key phrases: Remember, you can rearrange the phrases in a way that is natural and fits your personal style.

When you . . .

I feel . . .

Because . . .

I'd prefer or like . . . Will you . . . ?

So that . . . or, If so . . . or Then . . .

Sample Situation

Your sister, brother, or friend borrowed your new coat and returned it dirty.

"I" message: **When you** borrow my coat and return it dirty,

I feel angry,

because now I will have to take it to the cleaners before I can wear it.

I'd like you to return my coat clean the next time you borrow it. Will you agree to that?

If so, you can borrow it again.

a. **Situation:** Your co-worker has been asking you to change shifts with him/her. You only have two or three hours' notice of the desired shift change.

   "I" message:

b. **Situation:** Your best friend is to meet you at the movie, and he/she is late *again*. This time he/she shows up 40 minutes late.

   "I" message:

c. **Situation:** Your group is working on a class project. Other people in the room are talking so loudly that you can't hear what your group is saying.
"I" message:

d. **Situation:** The teacher had promised to return your test on Monday. It is now Friday and you still don't know how you did.
"I" message:

e. **Situation:** A friend borrows your English book and promises to return it the next day. She doesn't bring it back.
"I" message:

f. Make up a situation and make an "I" Message to go with it.
Situation:

"I" message:

2. Now, divide into groups of four and share your assertive messages. Members of the group will give each person feedback on his or her assertive messages.
3. Correct any errors in your assertive messages and try to practice giving "I" messages during the next week.

Discussion

1. What errors, if any, did you find in your assertive messages?

2. Do you think you will be able to practice any of these assertive messages in the next week? Explain how.

3. What will your biggest problem be in learning to be assertive?

4. How do you plan to overcome this problem?

The Pillow Method—Developing Empathy

OBJECTIVE

To gain a greater understanding and empathy for another person's perspective on a situation when it is different from your own and is causing problems in your relationship with that person.

INSTRUCTIONS

1. Identify a situation in which you and someone important to you have different conflicting viewpoints. This might be a husband-wife issue, a friend-friend issue, a parent-child issue, a teacher-student issue, a brother-sister issue, an employer-employee issue, etc. Describe the issue and why the issue has evolved into such a great disagreement.

2. Review the discussion of the Pillow Method. Then, identify the reasons, facts or examples that support each position.
    a. I am right and you are wrong.

    b. You are right and I am wrong.

c. We're both right and we're both wrong.

d. This issue is not as big as I am making it.

e. Conclusion: There is truth in all four positions.

DISCUSSION

1. What new insights about the conflict or areas of disagreement have you gained?

2. How do you think and feel about the issue now, and what will you do about it?

Name _____ Date _____

A Critical Decision

PURPOSE

To give students an opportunity to participate in a critical family decision.

INSTRUCTIONS

1. Participants will read the following case history and arrive at an individual decision.
2. Small groups of five members will be formed and will be asked to arrive at a group (family) decision.
3. A spokesman from each group will be selected to reveal the group's decision to the entire class.
4. While reading the following case history, bear in mind that you are a member of Mr. Smith's family.

Mr. Smith, age 63, has been physically disabled for almost 13 years. This disability has been due to 8 major surgeries, 2 of which were the successful removal of malignant tumors. Furthermore, Mr. Smith has a very severe case of emphysema, which has caused tremendous damage to his lungs. However, for the last 3 years, Mr. Smith has been experiencing excellent health—considering his known difficulties. Nevertheless, Mr. Smith enters the hospital today for an endoscopic exam of his esophagus. This was due to the passing of blood during the past week.

The exam revealed a large tumor toward the bottom of the esophagus. The chest specialist stated the tumor was definitely malignant and that the cancer had probably spread into the lymph glands. She advised that surgery be done immediately. However, she did state that there was probably only a 5 percent chance that the tumor could be removed and that—at most—Mr. Smith would have only one year to live. If surgery was not done, Mr. Smith would choke to death. However, if surgery was done, Mr. Smith's chances of tolerating the 5-hour surgery and anesthesia, due to his severe emphysema and damaged lungs, would be "nip and tuck." In other words, his chances of dying on the operating table were very great.

Mr. Smith, not knowing all of the above details, stated that if surgery had to be done—it had to be done—but he would like to wait a week or two. However, he would do whatever the family members thought best.

5. Now, consider that you are a member of Mr. Smith's family and you and the other family members will make this critical decision. (Your instructor will reveal what actually happened.)

6. Questions to consider:
   a. What is the problem involved?

   b. What are the alternatives?

   c. What are the consequences and responsibilities involved for each alternative?

   d. What is the preferred solution of each family member and why?

   e. What emotional or logical factors contributed to your solution?

   f. Was there any interpersonal conflict with the family members?

DISCUSSION

1. Have any of you ever been involved in a decision such as this? How did you feel?

Name _____ Date _____

Resolving Interpersonal Conflict

LEARNING JOURNAL

Select the statement below that best defines your feelings about the personal value or meaning gained from this chapter and respond below the dotted line.

I learned that I . . .   I was surprised that I . . .

I realized that I . . .   I was pleased that I . . .

I discovered that I . . .   I was displeased that I . . .

....

Chapter 8
Managing Stress and Wellness

We are never presented with lessons until we are ready to learn them. So, life always gives exactly the teacher we need at every moment. This includes every mosquito, every misfortune, every red light, every traffic jam, every obnoxious supervisor (or employee), every illness, every loss, every moment of joy or depression, every addiction, every piece of garbage, every breath.

—Charlotte Joko Beck,
Zen teacher and author

I try to take one day at a time, but sometimes several days attack me at once.
—Jennifer Yane

Think About This...

> Stress is like spice—in the right proportion it enhances the flavor of a dish. Too little produces a bland, dull meal; too much may choke you. The trick is to find the right amount for you.
> —DONALD TUBESING

Did this story "put life into perspective" for you? Certainly it is true that fewer health, financial, family, work, or social problems would make life more secure and satisfying. However, not having any problems or any stress would leave you with no choices in life, which would be dull and uninteresting. A certain number of problems and stresses can be stimulating. While some stress is good and necessary, excessive stress can create physical problems and/or behavioral changes.

Do you know that you have the power within yourself to modify both the amount of stress in your life and your reaction to it? Some of you may need to make only a few minor adjustments in your daily life for stress to become more constructive and manageable. Some of you will have to make some radical external changes (for example, change jobs) or internal changes (such as change some of your social requirements and/or attitudes).

Most people, who with courage and support undertake such changes, have only one regret: that they did not make the changes sooner. We would like to encourage you to begin considering what adjustments you may need to make in your daily life for stress to become more constructive and manageable.

Let's begin by discussing what stress is and what causes it.

What Is Stress?

Stress has become such an ingrained part of our vocabulary and daily existence that it is difficult to believe that our current use of the term originated only a little more than 50 years ago, when it was essentially "coined" by Hans Selye (Rosch, 2016). Even though there is no widely accepted definition of stress, the following viewpoints are worthy of consideration. Hans Selye studied stress for over 50 years. He considered stress to be the demand made on an organism to adapt, cope, or adjust. Selye defines *stress* as the rate of wear and tear within the body. Stress has also been defined as the anxious or threatening feeling that comes when we interpret or appraise a situation as being more than our psychological resources can adequately handle (Lazarus, 2006).

Which of the following would you call stressful?

1. Building a new home
2. Being audited by the IRS
3. Getting a promotion
4. Sitting in a dentist's chair
5. Getting married
6. Taking an exam

All of these six life events are stressful because they require us to adapt and change in response to them, which taxes our mental and physical adaptive mechanisms. Because positive or pleasurable events, such as getting a new home, can require as much adaptation on our part as negative or painful events, like being audited by the IRS, they can all be stressful. Living a stress-free life is just not reality.

TYPES OF STRESS

Hans Selye in his classic book (1974), *Stress without Distress*, has described and labeled four basic types of stress:

1. *Eustress* is defined as moderate or normal psychological stress. This type of stress strengthens us for immediate physical activity, creativity, and enthusiasm. It is characterized as short-lived, easily identified, externalized, and positive. Two examples would be an individual who experiences short-term stress by psyching up for the hundred-yard dash and an individual who is really excited about be-

> *Successful activity, no matter how intense, leaves you with comparatively few "scars." It causes stress but little distress.*
> —HANS SELYE

ginning a new project at work. The secret of positive stress is a sense of control. When we can make choices and influence the outcome of a situation, we meet the challenge successfully and return to a normal level of functioning relatively quickly. This is the happy feeling of "I did it!"

2. *Distress* is negative or harmful stress that causes us to constantly readjust or adapt. Distress occurs when we feel no control over outcomes; we see few or no choices; the source of stress is not clear; the stress is prolonged over a period of time; or several sources of stress exist simultaneously. However, not all negative events cause psychological distress. According to Richard Lazarus (2000), distress arises only when the stressor makes demands on the individual that exceed the individual's ability to cope. Therefore, distress is accompanied by feelings of tension, pressure, and anxiety rather than the concerted energy of eustress.

Even positive or pleasurable events can be very stressful.

© bikeriderlondon/Shutterstock.com

3. *Hyperstress* or overload occurs when stressful events pile up and stretch the limits of our adaptability. An example would be an individual who goes through a divorce, loses a parent, and then has a serious illness, all in the same year. It is when we have to cope with too many changes at once or adapt to radical changes for which we are not prepared that stress can become a serious problem.

4. *Hypostress* or underload occurs when we are bored, lacking stimulation, or unchallenged. This type of stress frustrates our need for variety and new experiences. For example, having a job that does not have new challenges can cause constant frustration. This is considered negative stress. Hans Selye believes that people who enjoy their work, regardless of how demanding it may be, will be less stress-ridden than people who are bored with a job that makes few demands or is too repetitive. It is not the stress itself that is enjoyed but instead the excitement or stimulation of the anticipated rewards. If you are involved in something you like, you are much more likely to handle frustration, pressure, or conflict effectively (**Rosch, 2016**). This kind of stress is just not as "stressful."

Stress is like a violin string. If there's no tension, there's no music. But if the string is too tight, it breaks. You want to find the right level of tension for you—the level that makes harmony in your life.
—ALLEN ELKIN, PHD

Becoming *Aware*

We have seen that some stress is necessary to give our lives variety and to challenge us to grow and expand our abilities; but too much stress, or the wrong kind, or at the wrong time, becomes debilitating.

As important as it is to understand what stress is, it is even more important to understand where the stress originates. When you determine what stress means for you, you have a choice of dealing with it more effectively or eliminating it completely. The key to reducing stress is to prevent it. Getting enough sleep, a proper diet, avoiding excess caffeine and other stimulants, and taking time out to relax may be helpful in this regard. We will be discussing prevention later in the chapter.

CAUSES OF STRESS

Is it other people, your job, too many things to do, your financial situation, pressure, illness? **Stress** consists of an event, called a *stressor*, plus how we feel about it, how we interpret it, and what we do to cope with it.

Common stressors include:

- The setting in which we live
- Other people
- Places we go
- Our daily routine
- Family members
- Our job
- Time—too little, too much
- Money
- School
- Dating
- Our given health condition
- A spoken word
- A certain event
- A simple thought

What about college students and their degree of stress? "Young Americans between 18 and 33 years old—the so-called Millennials—are more stressed than the rest of the population, according to a new report from the American Psychological Association. On a scale of 1 to 10, the millennial generation stands at 5.4 stress-wise, significantly

> Exercise relieves stress. Nothing relieves exercise.
> —TAKAYUKI IKKAKU

The daily routine is a common stressor.

© dotshock/Shutterstock.com

higher than the national average of 4.9, the association found after surveying more than 2,000 Americans.

'Clearly there are a number of pressures facing young people that might account for this increase in stress,' said Norman Anderson, CEO of the American Psychological Association. 'These individuals are growing up in an era of unprecedented economic upheaval. This coincides with the time they are finishing school and trying to establish themselves in society.' What's stressing them out? 'Jobs and money mostly,' said Anderson" (APA, 2016).

Life events. Two words best relate to the actual cause of stress: *change* and *threat*. Either or both can disturb the psyche. When workers lose their jobs, that job-loss is a significant change and usually a threat to their ego, self-esteem, and even the material aspects of their life. Similarly, the loss of a spouse is a major change and may pose many different threats.

On the other hand, there are positive events such as marital reconciliation and retirement, which can also create changes and threats that must be faced. The changes that result from positive events, however, are generally not as difficult to cope with as the changes that result from negative ones.

Changes and threats often fall into three possible categories (Taylor & McGee, 2000):

1. **Anticipated Life Events.** Examples might be graduation from high school and entering college, a job promotion, marriage, birth, and retirement.
2. **Unexpected Life Events.** Some examples might be a serious accident, separation from a spouse or someone we love, sudden death of a loved one, divorce, and financial problems.
3. **Accumulating Life Events.** This would include a dead-end job, traffic, deadlines and pressures, and ongoing conflict with friends or family members.

As you can see, some of the changes and threats above are major and some may be described as just the everyday circumstances of life. What about the daily hassles of living?

Daily hassles. Some health psychologists believe information about daily problems provide a better clue to the effects of stress than major life events (Bottos & Dewey, 2004). Richard Lazarus (2006), a leading psychologist who studies emotions and stress, calls these irritating and frustrating incidents that occur in our everyday transactions with the environment—***daily hassles***.

What about your own life? What are the biggest hassles? Are any of the following everyday problems or nuisances stressful for you: misplacing or losing things, having too many tasks to do, wasting time, or worrying about meeting high achievement standards?

While traumatic life events, such as the death of a loved one or the loss of one's job, are stressful and exert adverse effects on health, the minor hassles of daily life—

> *Have you ever felt that it's the little things in life that get you down? Daily hassles may have a greater effect on our moods and health than do the major misfortunes of life.*
> —RICHARD LAZARUS

> *If you want creative workers, give them enough time to play.*
> —JOHN CLEESE

perhaps because of their frequent, repetitive nature—may sometimes pile up until they eventually overwhelm you (Almeida, 2005). Whatever their relative importance, both traumatic life events and daily hassles are important sources of stress for many individuals. Remember, stress eventually adds up.

Now, consider this question: What causes some people to be devastated and others motivated by the same event? After all, change by itself does not necessarily lead to stress reactions in all individuals (Nairne, 2013).

Cognitive appraisal. Modern stress theory agrees that what causes us stress is not what happens, but how we perceive or *appraise* the situation. To feel stress, it is necessary to: 1) perceive there is some kind of demand or threat present, and 2) conclude that you may not have adequate resources available to deal with that threat (Lazarus, 2006). For example, your first reaction to potentially stressful situations, such as waiting in line, dealing with a sloppy roommate, making a public speech, taking an exam, seeing a vicious animal, or being in a car accident, is to appraise the situation in terms of whether it harms, threatens, or challenges your physical or psychological well-being. The secret lies in knowing that you have choices about how you look at external events, how you define them, how you attribute meaning to them, and how you react to them mentally and emotionally (Gallwey et al., 2009).

Remember, identical environmental events can lead to two very different stress reactions, depending on how the event is interpreted. Consider an upcoming exam: everyone in the class receives the same test, but not everyone will feel the same amount of stress. Those people who are prepared for the exam—the people like you who studied—are likely to feel less stress. Again, you perceive the threat, but you have adequate resources to deal with it.

If you break your neck, if you have nothing to eat, if your house is on fire—then you got a problem. Everything else is inconvenience.
—ROBERT FULGHUM

Play is the highest form of research.
—ALBERT EINSTEIN

If attitudes towards rest and relaxation do not change, the next generations will see an even greater risk for illnesses and addiction.
—BONNIE PERUTTZI

Think About This...

Common Daily Hassles
 1. Anxiety over tests and grades
 2. Troubling thoughts about the future
 3. Difficulty relaxing
 4. Concern about health
 5. Not getting enough sleep
 6. Concern about physical appearance
 7. Misplacing or losing things
 8. Not enough time to do the things you need to do
 9. Being lonely
10. Interpersonal relationship problems
11. Traffic delays
12. Financial status
13. Home maintenance chores, shopping, and preparing meals
14. Job dissatisfaction and/or concerns about job security
15. Wasting time in lines at the store, restaurant, or for appointments
Which one/s are hassles for you? What else represents a hassle for you?

CONSIDER THIS

INTERNALLY CREATED PRESSURES

- Do you expect problem-free living?
- Are you pessimistic and expect the worst from life?
- Do you compare your achievements, or lack of them, to those of others?
- Do you worry about situations you cannot control?
- Are you a perfectionist? Do you expect too much of yourself or others?
- Are you competitive and seem to turn every encounter into a win/lose situation?
- Are you a victim of "hurry sickness" and constantly expect yourself to perform better and faster?
- Are you self-critical? Do you focus on your faults, rather than your strengths?
- Do you expect others, rather than yourself, to provide your emotional security?
- Do you assume you know how others feel and what they want from you, instead of asking them?
- Do you feel powerless and fail to see your available choices?
- Do any of these sound familiar to you?

> *We cannot control the parade of negative thoughts marching through our minds. But we can choose which ones we will give our attention to. Picture your thoughts as people passing by the front of your home. Just because they're walking by doesn't mean you have to invite them in.*
> —GLADYS EDMUNDS

Often, our greatest source of stress is the tremendous pressure and anxiety that we create internally with our thoughts and feelings. Do you often feel powerless and fail to see your available choices? Do you often worry about situations you cannot control?

Trying to control things that are outside our control is enormously stressful—yet many of us unwittingly do this. When you feel stressed, consider . . . *What don't I control here? What am I trying to control here? What could I control here that I'm not currently controlling?* Confronting these questions can help us focus on things that we can accomplish and reduce our stress over things that we cannot (Gallwey et al., 2009).

Since the way we interpret and label our experiences can serve either to relax or stress us, you will learn how to deal with stressful thoughts and feelings later in this chapter. However, one helpful technique seems appropriate to discuss at this time.

We can control our thoughts, so we would be wise to practice *thought-stopping* techniques in stressful situations. **Thought stopping**, developed by Joseph Wolpe, a noted behavior therapist, involves concentrating on the unwanted thoughts and, after a short time, suddenly stopping and emptying your mind. The command *stop* is generally used to interrupt the unpleasant thoughts. Negative thoughts are sometimes so strong that they sap our energy and drain our motivation, making us feel physically tired and even sickly. However, with a little practice at thought-changing, anyone can break free of negative thought patterns for good (Seguin, 2015) Then, it is time to substitute thoughts that are reassuring and self-accepting. This technique, called **cognitive restructuring**, can turn off some of the negative chatter (Jacobs, 2004). For example, you say, "I know I am going to survive this divorce," rather than, "I will never make it without Joe." One positive thought at a time can gradually shift the balance of your thinking from negative to positive.

Now, let's see what happens to the body when stressful events and thoughts arise.

I Am Your Master

I can make you rise or fall. I can work for you or against you.

I can make you a success or failure.

I control the way that you feel and the way that you act.

I can make you laugh . . . work . . . love. I can make your heart sing with joy . . . achievement . . . elation. . . .

Or I can make you wretched . . . dejected . . . morbid. . . .

I can make you sick . . . listless. . . .

I can be as a shackle . . . heavy . . . attached . . . burdensome . . . lost forever unless captured by pen or purpose.

I can be nurtured and grown to be great and beautiful . . . seen by the eyes of others through action in you.

I can never be removed . . . only replaced.

I am a THOUGHT

Why not know me better?   —Robert Conklin

THE EFFECTS OF STRESS

Dr. Hans Selye, in his years as a stress researcher, found that the body has a three-stage reaction to stress. He termed this chain of stress reaction the ***general adaptation syndrome*** (Rosch, 2016):

Stage 1—Alarm,
Stage 2—Resistance, and
Stage 3—Exhaustion

We will discuss each of these reactions.

The alarm stage. Your body recognizes the stressor and prepares for fight or flight, which is done by a release of hormones from the endocrine glands. These hormones cause an increase in the heartbeat and respiration, elevation in the blood sugar level, increase in perspiration, dilated pupils, and slowed digestion. According to Dr. Walter B. Cannon of the Harvard Medical School, you then choose whether to use this burst of energy for fight or flight.

The resistance stage. This is a period of recovery and stabilization, during which the individual adapts to the stress. Consequently, the individual does what he or she can to meet the threat. Although it is true that the level of bodily arousal is not as high as it was in the alarm stage, it does remain higher than usual. This is nature's way of giving us greater protection against the original stressor. Coping responses are often strongest at this point. Because the individual attempts to do what is necessary to meet the threat, the most effective behavior of which the person is capable often comes forth. Often, people are so overwhelmed in the alarm stage that they simply cannot function. However, if there is effective functioning, it occurs in the resistance stage.

The exhaustion stage. Stress is a natural and unavoidable part of our lives, but it becomes a problem when it persists and becomes long term. Continuous stress will not enable the important *resistance* step to take place, and you will go from step one, *alarm*, directly to step three, **exhaustion**. When you remain exhausted because of continual exposure to stress, you become more receptive to physiological reactions and behavioral changes.

The immune system. The ***immune system*** is the body's defense and surveillance network of cells and chemicals that fight off bacteria, viruses, and other foreign or toxic substances (Plotnik, 2014). Have you ever gotten a cold, strep throat, or some other bacterial or viral infection after a stressful period, such as when final exams are over? This rather common experience of "coming down with something" illustrates how prolonged stressful experiences can decrease the effectiveness of your immune system. The primary weapons of the immune system are *lymphocytes*, which are specialized white blood cells that attack and destroy most of these foreign invaders. Stress can lower the immune response by either decreasing the number of lymphocytes in the bloodstream or by somehow suppressing the response of the lymphocytes to foreign substances that have invaded the body.

It is important to note that short-term stress, under most circumstances, actually boosts the immune system, functioning as an adaptive response for injury or infection. "It's extreme, constant stress over a long period of time that impairs the immune system," explains Monika Fleshner, a neuroimmunopsychologist at the University of Colorado in Boulder (Raeburn, 2006).

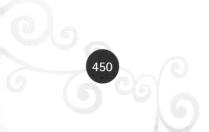

Physical Effects of Stress

In various ways, stress takes a heavy toll on our well-being. For example, more than three out of every five doctor's office visits are for stress-related problems, and up to 90 percent of reported illness and disease is stress-related (Duffy & Atwater, 2014). According to Heidi Hanna in Stressaholic, 5 Steps to Transform Your Relationship with Stress, chronic multitasking and increasing demands on our time and energy have caused a neurochemically based dependence on sources of stress and stimulation. As a result, modern society is tired and wired, suffering from physical exhaustion while mentally amped up, and unable to get adequate rest (Hanna, 2014). **Hanna has developed a strategy called the Sharp solution to** help make changes to your **bad stress** habits. Addiction to stress is one of the results of not balancing our brain with rest and **we need to take the time to** recharge it. By engaging our brain, we can strategically re-wire how we operate, become more focused and productive, flexible and resilient **(Hanna 2013).**

The Sharp Solution: A Brain-Based Approach for Optimal Performance

"Increasingly, medical research links stress, including work-related forms such as job strain, to a range of serious health effects, such as obesity, diabetes, certain types of cancers, and heart disease. One of the main hormones released in response to stress is cortisol" (Rudolph et al., 2016). Chronic stress can contribute to higher risks for heart disease, increased progress of cancer and increased speed at which cancer may return, more susceptibility to develop a prediabetic condition, memory problems and Alzheimer's, irritable bowel syndrome, peptic ulcers, and more (Hall, 2008).

Yet, before these more serious health problems can develop, your body has a natural way of telling you there is too much stress and tension in your life. Furthermore, most of us have a special physical organ or target area that lets us know when the stress is too great. Do you know what your special target is? Once you have learned to tune into your own signals, you will be able to recognize stress when it starts, before it takes a toll on your body. Review Table 8.1 for some of the physical effects of stress.

BEHAVIORAL EFFECTS OF STRESS

Another measuring tool for you to help recognize excessive stress in yourself and others is through behavioral changes. Review these changes in Table 8.1, Effects of Stress.

Table 8.1 EFFECTS OF STRESS

PHYSICAL		
Headaches	Rapid heart rate	Excessive sweating
Dermatitis	Impotence	Dizziness
Ulcers	Indigestion	Muscle spasms
Asthma	Diarrhea	Hypertension
Colitis	Stomach aches	Blurry vision
Common colds	Fatigue	Burning stomach
Skin rashes	Aching back and limbs	Vomiting
Allergies	Neck and shoulder tension	Delayed menstruation
Hyperventilation		
BEHAVIORAL		
Nervous tics	Clammy skin	Nail biting
Door slamming	Withdrawal	Grinding of teeth
Fist clenching	Depression	Temper tantrums
Insomnia	Irritability	Apathy
Tears	Acts of violence	Changed smoking habits
Frowning	Impatience	Worry
Hair twisting	Changed eating habits	Boredom
Jaw tightening	Changed drinking habits	Visible fears

Davis et al. (2008).

> *How do I cope with stress? I clean and organize.*
> —SANDRA LEE

Evaluate this list in relationship to your own life and add any other physical or behavioral changes you may experience that are not included here. This list can help you recognize imbalance and disharmony within and without, and that recognition is necessary if you are to effect a positive change for yourself.

Now that you know how to recognize physiological and behavioral effects of stress, is there anything else you need to be aware of? Albert Ellis found that change is hard for most people and they do not want to do what is difficult even if it is in their best interest (Ellis, 2002). So you may find it hard to change your behavior.

PERSONALITY TYPES

Are you a stress seeker or a stress avoider? How do you perform under pressure? Is it possible to respond to the normal pressures and stress of life with vitality, meaning, and joy? What kind of lifestyle do you prefer to live: rushed, relaxed, or somewhere in between?

Research has indicated that there are basically three personality types in relation to stress, with each type differing in their abilities to handle stress effectively. These types

Becoming *Aware*

are *Type A, Type B,* and a combination of *Type A* and *Type B*. What behavioral characteristics do these types have?

Type A. There has been a tremendous amount of research directed toward determining the correlation between heart disease and emotional stress. Among the findings is evidence that there is an association between coronary artery and heart disease and a complex of emotional reactions, which have been designated as the *Type A behavioral pattern* by Friedman and Rosenman (1982). Limitations of the original 1982 study involve problems with external validity. Because the study used an all-male sample it is unknown if the results could be generalized to a female population (McLeod, 2014).. These researchers found that almost all of their cardiac patients had in common a competitive, aggressive, ambitious, and stressful lifestyle (McLeod, 2014).

Research on the link between Type A personality behavior and coronary disease indicates that the lethal core of the Type A personality is not time urgency. Attention is focusing on *hostility and anger-prone tendencies,* which fuel an aggressive, reactive temperament (Smith & Ruiz, 2002; Rayl, 2007; McLeod, 2014). The Type A personality type's behavior makes them more prone to stress-related illnesses such as raised blood pressure. Such people are more likely to have their "flight or fight" response set off by things in their environment. As a result, they are more likely to have the stress hormones present, which over a long period of time leads to a range of stress-related illnesses. Researchers found that more than twice as many Type A people as Type B people developed coronary heart disease. When the figures were adjusted for smoking, lifestyle, etc. it still emerged that Type A people were nearly twice as likely to develop heart disease as Type B people.

Here are some other characteristics of the ***Type A*** behavioral pattern (Kleinke, 2002):

- A drive to succeed, coupled with impatience, irritability, and aggressiveness
- Trouble relaxing and is restless
- Perfectionist and seeks results *now*
- Feelings of pressure even when relaxed
- A constant clock watcher
- Ignores fatigue while doing strenuous work
- Thrives on stress; his or her work is never done
- Only happy with a vigorous, fast-paced lifestyle
- Time pressures frequently create frustration and sometimes hostility
- May appear nervous, scattered, and hyper
- Eats fast, walks fast, and talks fast

Type B. This behavior pattern is the opposite of the Type A (Friedman & Rosenman, 1982). People with ***Type B behavioral pattern*** tend to be more tolerant of others, are more relaxed than Type A individuals, more reflective, experience lower levels of anxiety and display higher level of imagination and creativity (McLeod, 2014). ***Type B*** people are seldom harried by the need to be involved in an ever-increasing series of activities in a continually decreasing amount of time. Here are some other characteristics of Type B people (Kleinke, 2002):

> *One striking thing we have discovered is that there are two main types of human beings: "race-horses" and "turtles."*
> —HANS SELYE

> *The greatest weapon against stress is our ability to choose one thought over another.*
> —WILLIAM JAMES

© Phovior/Shutterstock.com

- Serious but easy going
- Patient and relaxed
- Enjoy leisure and opportunities to experiment and reflect
- Prefer a peaceful, steady, quiet, and generally tranquil lifestyle
- Not easily irritated
- Are less competitive than A's
- Slower paced; feel no need to hurry
- May appear lethargic, sluggish, and bored
- Are stress avoiders; may avoid new challenges
- Speak slowly, walk slowly, eat slowly
- Sometimes lack the excitement, enthusiasm, and dynamism needed to perform at peak levels under pressure

Every night, I have to read a book, so that my mind will stop thinking about things that I stress about.
—BRITNEY SPEARS

The time to relax is when you don't have the time for it.
—THE BEST OF BITS & PIECES

Type B people may have a tremendous drive, but they may not take the risks necessary for big rewards. When they do take the risks, their drive is coupled with time to ponder leisurely and weigh alternatives. It may sound like Type B people do not have a lot of stressors. However, if they are in a Type A environment that requires a great deal of structure, this can be very stressful to them. Studies carried out on women have not shown such a major difference between Type A and Type B and subsequent health. This may suggest that different coping strategies are just as important as personality. The study was able to control for other important variables, such as smoking and lifestyle. This is good as it makes it less likely that such extraneous variables could confound the results of the study (McLeod, 2014).

Which type are you? Most of us are either Type A or Type B, with varying degrees of Type A and B. It is estimated that about 40 percent of the population is Type A and 60 percent is Type B (Paulus et al., 2000).

You will be given an opportunity to complete a personality type inventory at the end of this chapter. Like most stress inventories, this one is somewhat flawed because it does not give enough weight to individual differences. Be sure and take this into consideration when you look at your scores.

Are you …

a racehorse   a turtle

or somewhere in between?

What kind of lifestyle do you prefer to live: rushed, relaxed, or a balance between the two?

Actually, each of us is really the best judge of ourselves, and we can gradually develop an instinctive feeling that tells us whether we are running above or below the stress level that suits us best. Do you know what your normal stress endurance level is? We encourage you to examine your own behavior in relation to stress, because the key to effective stress management is recognizing when stress becomes more debilitating than stimulating.

In the following section, we will discuss some negative and debilitating techniques of coping with stress.

PTSD, Negative, and Defensive Coping

How people behave under stress depends to some extent on the level of stress experienced. For example, survivors of traumatic events such as rape, military combat, medical emergencies, witnessing a death or near-death, major accidents, and terrorist attacks may cope well at the time of the trauma, but months later experience a delayed emotional reaction known as *posttraumatic stress disorder (PTSD)*. Posttraumatic stress disorder is a severe anxiety disorder characterized by symptoms of intense fear, anxiety, and avoidance behavior, resulting from an unusually distressing event (Duffy & Atwater, 2014). Furthermore, PTSD is a prolonged maladaptive reaction to a traumatic event, and it may last for years or even decades afterward.

Coping refers to active efforts to master, reduce, or tolerate the demands created by stress (Weiten et al., 2014). When we cope, we consciously think and make a decision

> *The best years of your life are the ones in which you decide your problems are your own. You do not blame them on your mother, the ecology, or the president. You realize that you control your own destiny.*
> —ALBERT ELLIS

to deal with the problems we face. However, we may cope in negative ways. We may drink too much, eat too much, worry too much, or even abuse medication and drugs.

Sometimes the stress, frustration, and conflict of dealing with these problems interferes with our ability to maintain a healthy self-concept. We become extremely sensitive to threats to our ego. We will do almost anything to avoid, escape, or shield ourselves from the anxieties elicited by these threats.

In order to protect our feelings of self-esteem and self-respect, we may unconsciously resort to various distortions of reality, frequently referred to as ***defense mechanisms*** (Freud, 1936).

Defense mechanisms do not eliminate the problems that are the cause of anxiety, but they help us to hide or disguise our feelings and temporarily deal with anxiety or stress. Defense mechanisms have two primary characteristics. *First, they distort and deny reality. Second, they operate unconsciously, so that we are unaware that we are using them.* See Table 8.2 for some examples of commonly used defense mechanisms.

Defense mechanisms are designed to help us escape the pain of anxiety in stressful situations. Most of us would have difficulty maintaining our mental health without resorting to such defenses. However, the trouble is that these defenses can become common patterns of behavior for reacting to problems and stress.

Do you have a habit of using any of these defense mechanisms? Think of it like this: the more aware you are of the defense mechanisms you use and why you use them, the more likely will be your attempts to face your stressful situations in an open and honest manner. It is important for you to remember that, although defense mechanisms offer you short-term relief, your discomfort quickly returns. Why? Your problem has not been solved!

Table 8.2 EXAMPLES OF COMMONLY USED DEFENSE MECHANISMS

DEFENSE MECHANISM	DEFINITION
Rationalization	When the explanations offered are reasonable, rational, and convincing, but not real reasons.
Projection	When we attribute our own feelings, shortcomings, or unacceptable impulses to others.
Reaction Formation	When impulses are not only repressed, they are also controlled by emphasizing the opposite behavior.
Denial	When we refuse to recognize or acknowledge a threatening situation.
Repression	When we exclude painful, unwanted, or dangerous thoughts and impulses from our conscious mind.
Sublimation	When we direct our basic desires toward a socially valued activity.
Regression	When we psychologically return to a form of behavior characteristic from an earlier stage of development.
Displacement	When we redirect strong feelings from one person or object to another that seems more acceptable and less threatening.

Adapted from Pastorino & Doyle-Portillo (2011); Nairne (2010).

Speaking of problems for a moment, is there a difference in how men and women cope with problems and the normal stresses of living? Does cultural background have any influence on what events are perceived as most stressful? Let us look further at these two questions.

GENDER, CULTURE, AND STRESS

As we have already discussed, individuals have different levels of tolerance for stress. Some seem to thrive in situations in which others feel uncomfortably stressed. Also, some individuals actually seem to seek out stressful situations. As a result of these differences, methods of coping with stress vary accordingly.

Gender and stress. One of the major differences between men and women is how they cope with stress. Researchers have found that while men are more likely to fight or flee when stressed, women show a different response to stress, called *tend* and *befriend*, which involves nurturing and seeking social support (Taylor, 2004). Also, men tend to become increasingly focused and withdrawn, while women tend to become increasingly overwhelmed and emotionally involved. These differences in coping styles can lead to friction in relationships. Review Gender & You below for a classical example of differences in coping styles.

> *Rationalization may be defined as self-deception by reasoning.*
> —KAREN HORNEY

GENDER AND YOU

When Tom comes home, he wants to relax and unwind by quietly reading the newspaper. He is stressed by the unsolved problems of his day and finds relief through forgetting them.

His wife, Mary, also wants to relax from her stressful day. She, however, wants to find relief by talking about the problems of her day. The tension slowly building between them gradually becomes resentment. Tom secretly thinks Mary talks too much, while Mary feels ignored.

How do you deal with the problems of your day?

Without understanding their differences, Mary and Tom will grow farther apart. Often, when a man has problems, or is under stress and cannot find a solution, he copes by doing something else to disengage his mind from the problems of the day, like reading the newspaper, playing a game, or tinkering with his car. He will focus on solving his problems at a later date, and during this time, he temporarily loses awareness of everything else. However, when a woman becomes upset, or is stressed by her day, to find relief, she may cope by seeking out someone she trusts and then talk in great detail about the problems of her day or whatever potential problems she may see on the horizon. Through exploring her feelings in this process, she gains a greater awareness of what is really bothering her. Although she would like to talk with her husband, she frequently finds that he attempts to help her find a solution to her problems. After all, that is what he would do, solve his problem himself.

In *You Just Don't Understand*, Deborah Tannen (2001) suggests that men just listen to women's problems, without giving advice. Remember, talking is a woman's natural and healthy way of reacting to stress, and if she feels she is being heard, her stress will seem much less. On the other hand, women need to let men disengage and ponder their own problems, and when they have discovered the solution for themselves, they will then share some of "what has been going on with them" and possibly even report their personal solution(s). Remember, quiet concentration, without an immediate need to talk, is often a man's natural and healthy way of reacting to stress.

Getting back to Mary and Tom, do you think Mary can learn to let Tom have a little time to unwind from the day before she tries to talk with him? Do you think Tom can learn to just *listen* and try to *understand* Mary's problems?

Culture and stress. Who you are is a factor in what you may find stressful and how stressed you feel. For example, in 1995, Judith Pliner and Duane Brown surveyed 229 students (123 females and 106 males) from four ethnic groups (Caucasian, African American, Hispanic, and Asian American) who were asked to estimate how stressful they would expect to find events in three different domains: academic, financial, and personal (**Rosch, 2016**). Responses to the survey, summarized in Focus on Diversity, indicate that an individual's ethnic background is associated with what that person appraises as stressful.

FOCUS ON DIVERSITY

Four ethnic groups—Caucasian, African American, Hispanic, and Asian American—estimate how stressful they would expect to find events in three different domains:

Academic Domain: Older African Americans and Hispanics perceived more academic stress than older Asian Americans. Older Hispanics perceived significantly more academic stress than older Caucasians.

Financial Domain: Both African American and Hispanic individuals felt more stress in meeting financial events than did either Caucasian or Asian American individuals.

Personal Domain: African American men perceived greater stress in the personal domain than did African American women. Young Caucasian women perceived more stress in this domain than did older Caucasian women.

(Rosch, 2016)

Does ethnicity-related stress have harmful effects on individuals' mental and physical health? Researchers are showing increased interest in exploring the stress experienced by members of various ethnic groups in at least the following areas: 1) discrimination or perceived discrimination, 2) concern that their behavior might be interpreted as characteristic of derogatory stereotypes, and 3) pressure to not abandon their cultural heritage. (Weiten et al., 2014).

Perhaps it is now time to answer this question: How can I cope when I have so many problems and so many stressors?

WHAT AFFECTS THE WAY INDIVIDUALS COPE WITH STRESS?

It seems that some individuals are stress resistant and others are more susceptible to the harmful effects of stress. What accounts for the difference in the way different individuals cope with stress? Dr. Lyle Miller and Dr. Alma Smith (1994) give an interesting view in their book, *The Stress Solution*:

> People are quite different from one another in their susceptibility to stress. Some are like horses, and some are like butterflies. The horses tolerate great amounts of stress without faltering or breaking stride; the butterflies fall apart under the slightest demand or pressure. Whether you're a horse or a butterfly depends on several ingredients: your physical constitution, how well you take care of yourself, and your resources for coping with stress. The tougher you are, the more you can take. If you have a stress-prone constitution, are lazy about exercise, eat poorly, abuse stimulants, don't get enough sleep, or don't use your coping resources, you don't stand much chance against stress.

Hardiness. One characteristic that seems to distinguish stress-resistant people from those who are more susceptible to its harmful effects is known as **hardiness**. Actually, this term refers to a cluster of characteristics rather than just one. Stress researcher S. R. Maddi's (2006) findings suggest that hardy people seem to differ in attitudes from others in three respects:

- **Commitment** (rather than alienation)—they have deeper involvement in their jobs and other life activities.
- **Control** (rather than powerlessness)—they believe that they can, in fact, influence important events in their lives and the outcomes they experience.
- **Challenge** (rather than threats)—they perceive change as a challenge and an opportunity to grow rather than as a threat to their security.

One thing seems fairly certain: stress-hardy people manage their lives by managing themselves—they control their own attitudes and coping tendencies. Without a doubt, there are resilient individuals who bounce back from stressful experiences quickly and effectively. As a matter of fact, they use humor, positive emotions, cognitive flexibility, cognitive reappraisal, social support, and optimism to cope with adversity (Southwick

A pleasure a day keeps stress away.
—ETHEL ROSKIES

Of all the forces that make for a better world, none is so indispensable, none so powerful, as hope. Without hope people are only half alive. With hope they dream and think and work.
—CHARLES SAWYER

How can I cope when I have so many problems and so many stressors?

et al., 2005). It is important to remember that individuals can and do experience personal growth during adverse times (Duffy & Atwater, 2014).

Some of these findings point to the role of an optimistic outlook in stress tolerance (Nairne, 2010).

Afterward: If I Could Live It Over

If I had to live my life over again, I'd dare to make more mistakes next time.

I'd relax.

I would limber up.

I would be sillier than I have been this trip.

I would take more chances.

I would take more trips. I would climb more mountains, swim more rivers.

I would eat more ice cream and less beans.

I would perhaps have more actual troubles, but I'd have fewer imaginary ones.

You see, I'm one of those people who live seriously and sanely hour after hour, day after day.

Oh, I've had my moments. And if I had it to do over again, I'd have more of them.

Becoming *Aware*

In fact, I'd try to have nothing else, just moments, each after another, instead of living so many years ahead of each day.

I've been one of those persons who never goes anywhere without a thermometer, a hot water bottle, a raincoat and a parachute.

If I had it to do over again, I would travel lighter than I have.

If I had to live my life over, I would start barefoot earlier in the spring and stay that way later in the fall.

I would go to more dances.

I would ride more merry-go-rounds.

I would pick more daisies.

—NADINE STAIR

(This delightful perspective of life was written at age 85.)

Optimism or pessimism. *Optimism* is defined as a general tendency to envision the future as favorable. In contrast, *pessimism* may be defined as a general tendency to envision the future as unfavorable. Research suggests that optimists cope with stress in more adaptive ways than pessimists (Bernstein, 2010). For example, optimists are more likely to engage in action-oriented, problem-focused coping. They are more willing than pessimists to seek social support, and they are more likely to emphasize the positive in their appraisals of stressful events. David Armor, an assistant professor of psychology at Yale, notes, "Positive assumptions about the future may allow us to tolerate stressful situations that would otherwise be unbearable" (Paul, 2011). For the person who expects to achieve success, stress may be viewed as an obstacle to be overcome rather than as an obstacle that cannot be hurdled. Consequently, pessimists are more likely to deal with stress by giving up or engaging in denial. Studies show that optimists are better at coping with the distress associated with *everything* from menopause to heart surgery (Newman, 2000).

Are you a horse or a butterfly? Do you believe you can influence important events in your life and the outcomes you experience? Do you perceive change as a challenge or a threat to your security? What choices do you have when confronted with stressful events and situations?

> *Pessimists calculate the odds. Optimists believe they can overcome them.*
> —TED KOPPEL

Are you a horse or a butterfly? . . .

Three coping options. Actually, we have three different options when we are confronted with stressful events and situations. According to Taylor and McGee (2000), we can:

1. **Change Environments.** We might choose to move to another city, change jobs, separate from our spouse, and so on.
2. **Change the Environment.** We can often work to improve the situation that is causing us so much stress.
3. **Change Me (Improve My Coping Skills).** William James once said, "The greatest discovery of our generation is that men can alter their lives by altering the attitudes of their mind." This is especially important to remember in relation to stress because, as we stated earlier, *it is not really the event that causes stress, it is our reaction to it—our attitude.*

> The Chinese word for crisis means opportunity with danger. In the middle of every difficulty lies opportunity.
> —ALBERT EINSTEIN

Our reaction to any event, stressful or not, depends on our thoughts and feelings about what happened or what should have happened. Earlier in this chapter, we stated that, most often, the greatest source of stress is the tremendous pressure and anxiety we create internally with our own thoughts and feelings. We also indicated that we would discuss how to deal with stressful thoughts and feelings. We are now ready to do this.

DEALING WITH STRESSFUL THOUGHTS AND FEELINGS

Have you ever said, "I can't help the way I feel"? You want to feel calm when taking tests, but you still get butterflies in your stomach. You want to feel confident when talking to your teacher about a "bad" grade, but you still feel nervous. You do not want to be afraid of heights, but you cannot keep yourself from feeling scared. It is almost like you have no control over your feelings. These feelings are just automatic responses to certain stressful events and people in your life.

Consequently, you may say that these events or people cause you to feel the way you do. After all, touching your hand to a hot burner causes pain, so why can't people and certain events cause you stress? Let us diagram two events and see what is happening.

Activating Event	•	Causes	•	Consequences or Feelings
Touching your hand to a hot burner		•		Physical pain
Talking to your teacher		•		Stressful, tense feelings

By now, you are still convinced that certain events and other people cause you to feel the way you do. The author will not argue with you that touching your hand to a hot burner really does cause pain. However, I cannot agree that talking to your teacher really causes you to have tense, stressful feelings. Here's why!

THE POWER OF SELF-TALK

Rational emotive therapist Albert Ellis (2001), who died at the age of 93 in 2007, indicated that the event of talking to your teacher does not cause you to feel tense and stressed. Instead it is your beliefs, or what you say to yourself *(self-talk)* about talking to your teacher that causes you to feel tense, nervous, and stressed.

Ellis (2001) believed that a great deal of our stress is unnecessary, and that it really comes from faulty conclusions we have made about the world. It is really our interpretations, *what we say to ourselves about our experiences,* which creates the debilitating emotions of anxiety, anger, and depression, as discussed in Chapter Four.

> *In a real sense, through our own self-talk, we are either in the construction business or the wrecking business.*
> —DOROTHY CORKVILLE

Let us examine the theory of Dr. Ellis by looking at an example he frequently gave at the Institute for Rational-Emotive Therapy in New York:

> Assume you walk by your friend's house, and he sticks his head out the window and calls you a bunch of nasty names. You would probably become angry and upset with your friend.

> Now let's imagine that you were walking by a mental hospital, rather than your friend's house, and your friend is a patient in the hospital. This time, he yells at you, calling you the same ugly names. What would your feelings be? Would you be as angry and upset now that you know he is not normal and does not live in his house? Probably not!

Actually, the activating event (being called nasty names) was identical in both cases, but your feelings were very different because you were saying something very different to yourself.

In the first example, you were probably saying things like, "He shouldn't call me those nasty names! That's really awful! I'll pay him back!"

> *People feel disturbed not by things, but by the views they take of them.*
> —EPICTETUS

However, in the second example, you might be telling yourself something like, "Poor sick John. He can't help what he is doing." Instead of feeling angry, you were probably feeling a degree of sympathy for your friend.

It is easy to see that your *different beliefs (interpretations and thoughts)* about the events determined your feelings. Let us look at the diagram of your two emotional experiences: A + B = C.

A	+	B	=	C
ACTIVATING EVENT	+	THOUGHTS OR BELIEFS	=	CONSEQUENCES OR FEELINGS
Being called names		My friend shouldn't do this		Angry, upset
Being called names		My friend must be sick		Pity, sympathy

Ellis (2003) and cognitive therapist Aaron Beck (Beck et al., 2006) stress that our extreme, debilitative, and stressful emotions are due largely to our *irrational beliefs*—what we say to ourselves. This is also called **cognitive reappraisal**. Remember that cognitive reappraisal is an emotion response strategy that involves changing the way we respond to stress by reinterpreting the meaning of the emotional stimulus. Have you ever failed a series of tests and thought negatively about yourself? If you did, your self-talk might be defeating. Or, you could be positive and not engage in defeating self-talk.

Self-talk is one of the most simple and powerful ways we can change our attitudes. Think about it: what we think determines how we feel, which in turn determines what we do, which is what defines us. So short circuit the negative self-talk and learn how to be your own hero. Mary Mueller (2001), author of *Taking Care of Me*, suggests we work on replacing some of our negative self-talk with the following:

- "I should" with "I want . . ."
- "I can't" with "I haven't yet . . ."
- "I'll try" with "I'll do my best . . ."
- "He/she makes me . . ." with "I feel _____ when . . ."

What Is the Difference in Irrational and Rational Beliefs—Self-Talk?

> *Your most important irrational pathway is musturbation—or you're devoutly following the tyranny of the shoulds.*
> —ALBERT ELLIS

Sometimes, **self-talk**, what we say to ourselves about an event or situation, is irrational. It does not even make sense, but we believe that it is true. *The ingredient that makes a belief irrational is that it cannot be scientifically verified. There is no empirical evidence or proof to support the belief.*

Irrational beliefs (self-talk) result in inappropriate emotions, behaviors, and more stress. Inappropriate emotions and behaviors are those that are likely to thwart an

Becoming *Aware*

individual's desired goals. Consequently, the individual feels stressed. An example of this cycle is **must**urbation, a term coined by Albert Ellis to refer to demandingness about the self, others, or the world. "**I must do…**"

On the other hand, ***rational beliefs (self-talk)*** are those beliefs that result in appropriate emotions and behaviors. Appropriate emotions and behaviors are those that are likely to help an individual attain desired goals. Consequently, the individual feels less stress. It is important to remember that even negative emotions (such as disappointment, concern, etc.) can be appropriate. *The ingredient that makes a belief rational is that it can be scientifically verified. There is empirical evidence or proof to support the belief.*

We will now examine the characteristics of irrational and rational self-talk: What makes sense and what doesn't? What objective evidence can be provided to support your self-talk—your beliefs?

Characteristics of Irrational and Rational Self–Talk

Almost all irrational self-verbalizations include Should Statements, Awfulizing Statements, and Overgeneralizations. David Burns (2006) refers to these irrational self-verbalizations *as a twisted form of absolutist thinking*. We will now look at these individually.

Should statements. These are absolutistic demands or moral imperatives that the individual believes must occur. Individuals tend to express their shoulds in three areas: *I should, you should, and the world should. Should statements also contain words such as ought, have to, and must.*

> Have you ever made statements similar to the ones below?
> Helen **should not** be so inconsiderate.
> John **should** be a better teacher.
> People **ought** to be at meetings on time.
> I **have to (must)** make an "A" on the next test. *Do not "should" on yourself.*

> *The way one interprets and evaluates reality is the key to one's emotional and mental health.*
> —ALBERT ELLIS

These statements all imply that other people and things in your world need to be as you want them to be. This is really unreasonable.

True, it would be more pleasant if Helen were more considerate; it would be helpful if John were a better teacher; it would be beneficial if people were at meetings on time; it would be nice to make an "A" on the exam.

Think about it like this: Does it really make sense that a person *should* or *should not* do something? Where can you find objective proof that a person *should* or *should not* do something? Is not it reasonable that people can actually do or choose not to do whatever they want? What evidence or proof can you provide that you *must* make an A on the test? Are you going to die if you do not make an A?

It is perfectly rational for us to wish that people would behave differently and that things in our world would be as we want them to be. It is even okay to change what can be changed and accept those things that cannot be altered. It is unreasonable, however, for you to expect that other people or the world will ever meet your unrealistic expectations. Reality is reality! Failure to accept this reality can result in your life being filled with disappointments and *more stress.* Albert Ellis (2003), author of *How to Stubbornly Refuse to Make Yourself Miserable about Anything—Yes, Anything,* has an interesting insight:

"You mainly make yourself needlessly and neurotically miserable by strongly holding absolutist irrational beliefs, especially by rigidly believing unconditional shoulds, oughts, and musts, and ruminating them over and over again..." (Ellis, 2003)

Awfulizing statements. Generally, when we say that the world, ourselves, or someone *should* be different, we imply that it is *awful* or *terrible* when they are not different. Have you ever made any of the following statements? If so, ask yourself, "Where can I find the proof or evidence to support these beliefs?"

> What she did to me is just **awful!**
> It is just **terrible.**
> I just can't **stand it.**
> I can't **bear** it.

It is true that things in our world could be improved and that events that happen to us are unfortunate. However, when you consistently talk about how *terrible* or *awful* something is, you will eventually convince yourself that what you are thinking and saying is right. This kind of *self-talk* causes you to feel angry, depressed, and, therefore, stressed.

In some instances, something is so *terrible* or *awful* that you convince yourself that *you can't stand it* or *you can't bear it.* As cold and callous as it may sound, if you are alive and conscious, you are *standing it, you are bearing it.*

Would not it be far less stressful and certainly more rational for your self-talk to be:

> "This situation is going to be difficult for me, but I will work hard and use my positive attitude and abilities to be as successful as I can be."

Overgeneralizations. We often make overgeneralizations based on a single incident or piece of evidence, and we ignore everything else that we know about ourselves and others. Cue words that indicate you may be overgeneralizing are: *all, every, none, never, always, everybody,* and *nobody.* Overgeneralizations frequently lead to human worth statements about ourselves and other people. And, these statements do not even make sense. Think about these statements!

You Were Fired: I'll never get another job—I'm a complete failure.

Your Spouse Left You: No one will ever want to marry me now—I must be unlovable.

First of all, *never* and *ever* mean a long time. Just because you lost your job, does that prove that no one else will ever hire you and that you are a *complete* failure? To be a *complete* failure, you would have to fail 100 percent of the time. This is unrealistic. Oh yes, have you forgotten that you have had other jobs besides the one you just lost? Just because your spouse left you, does that *prove* that you are unlovable? Think about it: Who else in your life cares about you? Surely, someone else does.

Sometimes we use overgeneralizations when we exaggerate shortcomings of others. For example:

You **never** listen to me.

You **never** do anything for me.

The chances are highly probable that "they" can remember and prove to you at least one time they listened and at least one time they did something for you.

Statements such as these lead to anger, resentment, alienation from other people, and more stress. Would not it be more accurate to say:

Sometimes you do not listen to me.

You have done some nice things for me.

Disputing Irrational Beliefs

How do you avoid these irrational beliefs that create feelings of stress? Ellis and MacLaren (2005) recommend these steps:

1. **Monitor Your Emotional Reactions.** Try to describe what you are *feeling* as accurately as possible. Say, "I feel angry, depressed, fearful, hurt, jealous, sad, worried." Because it is possible to experience more than one negative emotion at the same time, be sure to write down all the unpleasant feelings that you are having.
2. **Describe the Activating Event.** Write down your perception of the event or whatever seemed to trigger the events that led to your unpleasant feelings and your present stressful condition. It may be something that someone did; it may be something you need to do but are afraid of doing; it may be a series of several small unpleasant happenings, and you have just had too much!

3. **Record Your Self-Talk.** What are you saying to yourself that is causing you to feel angry, depressed, and so on? What are you thinking or what is going through your head? What are you worried about? When you think about . . . (the activating event), how do you make yourself depressed or angry? Becoming aware of your self-talk may be difficult at first, but with practice, you can learn to do so.

4. **Dispute Your Irrational Beliefs.** It is now necessary for you to go back to step 3 and do three things: 1) decide whether each statement is a rational or an irrational belief, 2) explain why the belief does or does not make sense, and 3) write some different statements that you can say to yourself in the future to prevent yourself from having such debilitative emotions and experiencing such stress. For example, let us say that you are the type of person who overgeneralizes about the consequences of failing a test. You think such irrational thoughts as:

"Why do I always mess up?"

"This is going to be terrible."

Some effective coping statements might include:

"I'm not going to think about failing."

"I'm going to concentrate on being successful; that's better than getting nervous."

"I'm going to take three deep breaths, relax, calm down, and practice positive thinking; then I'll start to work on the exam."

Now that you know how to identify and dispute the irrational beliefs that have been causing you stress, we will now discuss some additional ways of managing stress.

Tips for Managing Stress

Following is a list of several suggestions that may help you live with stress, whether it is an occasional mild upset, which most of us experience, or one that is more lasting and severe.

- **Identify Your Causes of Stress.** Monitor your state of mind throughout the day. If you feel stressed, write down the cause, your thoughts, and your mood. Once you know what's bothering you, develop a plan for addressing it. That might mean setting more reasonable expectations for you and others or asking for help with household responsibilities, job assignments, or other tasks. List all your commitments, assess your priorities, and then eliminate any tasks that are not absolutely essential.

- **Build strong relationships.** Relationships can be a source of stress if they are not healthy. But strong, mutually supportive relationships can reduce stress.
- **Work Off Stress.** If you are angry or upset, try to do something physical such as running, gardening, playing tennis, or cleaning out the garage. Working the stress out of your system will leave you much better prepared to handle your problems.
- **Have Fun.** Do something each day that you really enjoy, whether it is reading your favorite book or magazine, having lunch with a friend, watching your favorite TV program, taking a walk, playing your musical instrument, or having fun with some kiddie-toy collection. Authorities agree that people who preserve their sense of fun are better equipped to solve problems, think creatively, and manage stress.
- **Talk It Out.** When something is bothering you, talk it out with someone you trust and respect, such as a friend, family member, clergyman, teacher, or counselor. Sometimes another person can help you see a new side to your problem and, thus, a new solution.
- **Focus on Gratitude.** It is physiologically impossible to be stressed and thankful at the same time. Two thoughts cannot occupy our mind at the same time. If you are focusing on gratitude, you can't be negative (Brown, 2012).
- **Do Something for Others.** If you find that you are worrying about yourself all the time, try doing something for somebody else. This helps get your mind off yourself and can give you a sense of well-being.
- **Have Some Real Close Friends.** Having true friends that you do not need to fear criticism from, and whom you can talk freely to, is important. Friends who are accepting are not a threat to your ego. Without at least one such friend, a person is forced into emotional isolation, which in itself is a stress, and one that usually produces adverse responses.

> *Experience is not what happens to a man. It is what a man does with what happens to him.*
> —ALDOUS HUXLEY

> *I have been sustained throughout my life by three saving graces—my family, my friends and a faith in the power of resilience and hope.*
> —ELIZABETH EDWARDS

© Izf/Shutterstock.com

Work off your stress with some physical activity!

- **Eat Sensibly.** Try to have balanced meals and pay close attention to the habit of eating "junk foods." Do not starve yourself to lose weight. Watch excessive sugar and caffeine. Think of your body as a car. If you do not put oil, gas, and water in your car frequently, it will quit running. So will your body if you abuse it with improper eating habits.

- **Get Organized.** Plan, schedule, take notes, and keep good files. Organizing the daily nitty-gritty of life reduces stress. Save your memory for more creative and pleasurable things (Dembling, 2006).

- **Rehearse.** When you are facing a situation that you know will be stressful to you, rehearse it. Either mentally or with a friend, anticipate what might occur and plan your response. Being prepared reduces stress.

- **Overcome Procrastination.** One of the simplest and most effective solutions is to just get started—anywhere on a task. The moment you think "I'll feel more like doing this later" or "I work better under pressure," recognize that you're just about to procrastinate—to give in to feel good (Pychyl, 2011).

- **Learn to Say "No."** Say no when your schedule is full, to activities you do not enjoy, to responsibilities that are not really yours, to emotional demands that leave you feeling drained, to other people's problems that you cannot solve.

- **Learn to Accept What You Cannot Change.** Remember the words of the philosopher, Epictetus: "Happiness and freedom begin with a clear understanding of one principle: Some things are within your control, and some things are not. It is only after you have faced up to this fundamental role and learned to distinguish between what you can and cannot control that inner tranquility and outer effectiveness become possible."

- **Understand Worry.** You can think about your problems or you can worry about them, and there is a vast difference between the two. Worry is thinking that turned *toxic. . . .* Thinking works its way through problems to conclusions and decisions.

- **Avoid Self-Medication.** There are many chemicals such as alcohol and other drugs that can mask stress symptoms, but they do not help you adjust to stress itself. Also, many are habit-forming and can cause more stress than they solve; consult your doctor before you decide to use them. It is important, too, that the ability to handle stress come from within you, not from externals.

- **Live a Balanced Life.** Make time for what is important to you. Work and school are important, but they are not the only important areas in your life. What about time with your family and friends? What about time for a hobby? Stop and ask yourself, "Am I spending too much time on one important area of my life and forgetting the others?"

- **Get Enough Sleep and Rest.** Lack of sleep can lessen your ability to deal with stress by making you more irritable. If stress continually prevents you from sleeping, you should inform your doctor.

- **Write in a Journal or Diary.** Studies confirm the value of expressing stressful thoughts to others or getting them down on paper—even if you never tell anyone (Stone et al., 2000).

- **Shun the "Perfect" Urge.** Some people expect too much from themselves and are in a constant state of worry and anxiety because they think they are not achieving as much as they should.

- **Develop a Regular Exercise Program.** A sensible exercise program can begin with a short daily walk that is gradually increased. To avoid excess physical stress, you need to develop your own program gradually and then maintain it constantly. There is increasing evidence that regular, sensible exercise causes a number of important chemical changes in the body. It helps to eliminate depression. It helps to alleviate anxiety. Sensible, enjoyable exercise is nature's antistress reaction remedy. Experts consider aerobics to be an excellent release.
- **Take Care of Yourself.** If you do not, no one else will. Don't say, "I don't have time." You have got all the time there is—24 hours a day—so begin today by choosing some stress reduction techniques that will divert your attention from whatever is causing you stress. Take a leisurely day off from your routine.
- **Learn to Relax.** You can learn to counteract your habitual reaction to stress by learning to relax. Relaxation gives you more energy and normalizes your physical, mental, and emotional processes. Consequently, you are more equipped to handle the stresses in your life (Underwood, 2005). Consider having a relaxing massage.

> *Positive attitudes—optimism, high self-esteem, an outgoing nature, joyousness, and the ability to cope with stress—may be the most important bases for continued good health.*
> —HELEN HAYES

Play

Play is a critical element of holistic wellness. What better way to beat stress! Dr. Stuart Brown is a psychiatrist, clinical researcher, and founder of the National Institute for Play. Dr. Brown is also the author of *Play: How it Shapes the Brain, Opens the Imagination and Invigorates the Soul* (2010). He has found that play shapes our brain, helps us foster empathy, helps us navigate complex social groups, and is at the core of creativity and innovation. Dr. Brown argues that play is not optional. He writes, "The opposite of play is not work—the opposite of play is depression." He explains, "Respecting our biologically programmed need for play can transform work. It can bring back excitement and newness to our job. Play helps us deal with difficulties, fights stress, provides a sense of expansiveness, promotes mastery of our craft, and is an essential part of the creative process. Most important, true play that comes from our inner needs and desires is the only path to finding lasting joy and satisfaction in our work. In the long run, 'work does not work without play.'"

The Relaxation Response

Would you like to try a deep breathing and relaxation exercise now? One of the best studied stress relievers is the relaxation response, first described by Harvard's Herbert Benson close to 20 years ago (Benson, 2001). Its great advantage is that it requires no special posture or place. You can use this relaxation response even if you are stuck in traffic, when you're expected at a meeting. Or, you can use this response if you are having trouble falling asleep because your mind keeps replaying over the events of the day. Are you ready?

- Sit or recline comfortably. Close your eyes if you can, and relax your muscles.
- Breathe deeply. To make sure that you are breathing deeply, place one hand on your abdomen, the other on your chest. Breathe in slowly through your nose, and as you do you should feel your abdomen (not your chest) rise.
- Slowly exhale. As you do, focus on your breathing. Some people do better if they silently repeat the word *one* as they exhale; it helps clear the mind.
- If thoughts intrude, do not dwell on them; allow them to pass on and return to focusing on your breathing. Although you can turn to this exercise any time you feel stressed, doing it regularly for 10 to 20 minutes at least once a day can put you in a generally calm mode that can see you through otherwise stressful situations. Was Dr. Benson correct? Do you feel more relaxed?

Obviously, not all of these coping strategies and stress-management techniques are applicable to everyone. So take a long, hard look at your own personal lifestyle, and try to make a good evaluation as to what factors are adding stresses to your life, particularly negative stress. Perhaps you will even find yourself falling into the category of Type A behavior. Then, select the specific strategies that fit your personal situation and make a commitment to do whatever is necessary to reduce the negative stress in your life or at least learn to cope with it more effectively.

Things usually turn out best for people who make the best of the way things turn out.
—ART LINKLETTER

For fast-acting relief try slowing down.
—LILY TOMLIN

Chapter Review

Even if it were possible to go through life without stress, we really would not want to, because stress is what prepares us to handle things we are unfamiliar with, or things that appear to threaten us. Without a doubt, some stress challenges us to think creatively and to find innovative solutions to problems.

- **Stress** is the rate of wear and tear within the body.
- There are four basic types of stress: **eustress** (good or short-term stress), **distress** (negative or harmful stress), **hyperstress** (overload), and **hypostress** (underload).
- Stress consists of an event, called a **stressor**, plus how we feel about it, how we interpret it, and what we do to cope with it.
- Two words best relate to the actual cause of stress: **change** and **threat**. Changes and threats often fall into three possible categories: 1) anticipated life events, 2) unexpected life events, and 3) accumulating life events.
- **Daily hassles**—irritating and frustrating incidents that occur in our everyday transactions with the environment—may sometimes pile up until they eventually overwhelm us.
- Modern stress theory agrees that what causes us stress is not what happens to us but how we perceive what happens to us.
- When you feel stress because of control issues, three questions you can ask yourself are: what don't I control here?, what am I trying to control here?, and what could I control here that I'm not currently controlling?
- The opposite of play is not work—the opposite of play is depression.
- Relaxation done regularly helps you feel less stressed.
- Irrational self-verbalizations include should statements, awfulizing statements, and overgeneralizations.
- Prolonged stressful experiences can decrease the effectiveness of your immune system. Various illnesses can result. Short-term stress generally boosts the immune system.
- The body has a three-stage reaction to stress: alarm, resistance, and exhaustion. These stages of a chain reaction to stress are called the **general adaptation syndrome**.
- Stress can be a problem because it is linked to a number of illnesses. There are both physical and behavioral effects of stress.
- Research has indicated that there are basically three personality types in relation to stress—**Type A**, **Type B**, and a **combination** of Type A and Type B.
- How people behave under stress depends to some extent on the level of stress experienced. Some individuals who have experienced severe cases of trauma may later experience a delayed emotional reaction known as **posttraumatic stress disorder**—PTSD.
- There are both negative and defensive techniques of coping with stress. Some commonly used defense mechanisms in coping with stress are: rationalization, repression, projection, reaction formation, sublimation, displacement, regression, and denial.
- Although some events are inherently stressful for everyone, many other events are appraised as stressful or not according to an individual's culture, gender, and conditioning.
- Hardy people seem to deal more effectively with stress. They are more likely to demonstrate the attitudes of commitment, control, and challenge when dealing with stressful situations. Optimistic people are more likely to cope with stress in more adaptive ways than pessimists.

- Three options, when confronted with stressful events and situations, are: 1) change environments, 2) change the environment, and 3) change me—improve my coping skills.
- One of the most effective ways of dealing with stressful thoughts and feelings is to watch or change our self-talk—what we say to ourselves about our experiences or what is happening to us.
- Our extreme, debilitative, and stressful emotions are due largely to our **irrational beliefs**—what we say to ourselves.
- If you are focusing on gratitude, you can't be negative.
- **Self-talk** can be irrational, resulting in inappropriate emotions, behaviors, and more stress. Self-talk can also be rational, resulting in appropriate emotions, behaviors, and less stress.
- Almost all irrational self-verbalizations contain should statements, awfulizing statements, and overgeneralizations.
- Irrational beliefs that create feelings of stress can be improved by using a four-step process: 1) monitoring your emotional reactions, 2) describing the activating event, 3) recording your self-talk, and 4) disputing the beliefs which are irrational.
- There are numerous strategies for learning to live with stress. It is important to select the specific strategies that fit your personal situation and to which you can make a commitment for coping and dealing with the stress in your life.
- **Play** shapes our brain, helps us foster empathy, helps us navigate complex social groups, is at the core of creativity and innovation, and helps reduce stress.

Handled well, stress is a positive force that strengthens us for future situations. But handled poorly, or allowed to get out of hand, stress becomes harmful and can lead to physical, mental, or emotional problems.

Therefore, it is extremely important not only that we recognize stress, but that we learn how to handle it, live with it, and make it work for us.

Test Review Questions: Learning Outcomes

1. What is stress? Give examples of the four basic types of stress.
2. Define the term stressor, and explain what else stress consists of.
3. What two words best relate to the actual cause of stress? Explain the three categories that changes and threats often fall into.
4. What Is the difference between irrational and rational beliefs—self-talk?
5. Explain what your daily hassles consist of.
6. In relation to the power of our thoughts, what causes some people to be devastated and others to be motivated by the same event?
7. When you feel stressed over issues about personal control, what three questions would be good for you to ask yourself?
8. Explain the three-stage reaction to stress.
9. Explain the relationship between the immune system and prolonged stressful experiences.
10. How does stress affect you physically as well as behaviorally?

11. Why do these cue words indicate that you may be overgeneralizing: *all, every, none, never, always, everybody,* and *nobody*?

12. Explain the characteristics of the Type A and Type B personality behavior patterns. Which personality type are you?

13. List and define some of the more commonly used defense mechanisms. What are the two primary characteristics of defense mechanisms? What is PTSD?

14. In relation to stress, explain the different coping styles of men and women.

15. Explain the extent that Caucasian, African American, Hispanic, and Asian American cultures perceive stressful events which might be in the academic, financial, and personal domains.

16. List and explain the three characteristics of hardy people. How do optimistic and pessimistic people differ in their reaction to stressful events? Explain resilience (hardiness) in relation to stress.

17. Explain the three options possible when confronted with stressful events and situations.

18. Name and give examples of the three self-verbalizations frequently found in irrational beliefs—self-talk. How could these same examples be worded into rational beliefs—self-talk?

19. How could you rephrase the following negative self-talk statements to make them more positive? "I should," "I can't," "I'll try," "He/she makes me . . ."

20. Identify and explain the four-step process for disputing irrational beliefs.

21. List at least 10 tips for managing stress.

22. According to Albert Ellis, what is the correct equation in relation to the cause of stressful feelings and emotions?

23. What has caused a neurochemically based dependence on sources of stress and stimulation to provide fuel for our chaotic lifestyles?

Key Terms

Alarm Stage	Hardiness	Reaction Formation
Awfulizing Statements	Hyperstress	Regression
Cognitive Reappraisal	Hypostress	Relaxation Response
Cognitive Restructuring	Immune System	Repression
Coping	Irrational Beliefs	Resistance Stage
Daily Hassles	Optimism	Self-Talk
Defense Mechanisms	Overgeneralizations	Stressor
Denial	Pessimism	Sublimation
Displacement	Posttraumatic Stress Disorder	Thought Stopping
Distress	(PTSD)	Type A Behavioral Pattern
Eustress	Projection	Type B Behavioral Pattern
Exhaustion Stage	Rational Beliefs	
General Adaptation Syndrome	Rationalization	

Reflections: Critical Thinking

1. What is your personal definition of stress?
2. Discuss the types of situations that are most stressful to you.
3. What are some examples of daily hassles in your environment?
4. What can you do to alleviate some of the stress, as well as daily hassles, in your life?
5. Have you ever gotten a cold, strep throat, or some other bacterial or viral infection after a stressful period? What do you think contributed to your getting sick?
6. How does stress affect you physically, as well as behaviorally?
7. Discuss this statement: Modern stress theory agrees that what causes stress is not what happens to us but how we perceive what happens to us.
8. In relation to stress, how do Type A and Type B personalities create difficulties in relationships with others?
9. Discuss the differences in the way men and women cope with stress.
10. What techniques do you personally use to manage stress?
11. How do optimistic and pessimistic people differ in their reaction to stressful events?
12. Which defense mechanism do you more commonly use? Why?
13. Explain PTSD from the viewpoint of anyone you have personally known who may have struggled with this diagnosis.
14. Discuss any areas of personal control you currently struggle with.
15. Describe the relaxation response. Does it work for you?

Web Resources and Web Activities

www.youmeworks.com/optimisminterview.html

Information on a healthy balance between optimism and pessimism.

http://stress.about.com/

Various links on dealing with stress.

http://www.stress.org

The site for the American Institute for Stress.

http://cogbtherapy.com/cbt-blog/2014/5/4/hhy104os08dekc537dlw7nvopzyi44

Improve your cognitive reappraisal.

www.authentichappiness.sas.upenn.edu/testcenter.aspx

The Gratitude Survey measures appreciation about the past.

VIDEOS

https://www.youtube.com/watch?v=Iw3sDgaoBeA

21 Ways to Stop Worrying by Dr Albert Ellis, 1991

https://www.youtube.com/watch?v=_rwkU8BfVgk

How to Deal with Difficult People (Albert Ellis, PhD)

https://www.youtube.com/watch?v=KuWKWjVXcwo

Brené Brown, Fear: A culture of not enough.

https://www.youtube.com/watch?v=_UoMXF73j0c&t=15s

The price of invulnerability: Brené Brown at TEDxKC.

https://www.youtube.com/watch?v=7XFLTDQ4JMk

Getting stuck in the negatives (and how to get unstuck) by Alison Ledgerwood, TEDxUCDavis.

https://www.youtube.com/watch?v=v-t1Z5-oPtU

How stress affects your body by Sharon Horesh Bergquist.

https://www.youtube.com/watch?v=RcGyVTAoXEU

Kelly McGonigal: How to make stress your friend.

https://www.youtube.com/watch?v=yEh3JG74C6s

What causes wellness by Sir Harry Burns, TEDxGlasgow.

https://www.youtube.com/watch?v=wmdp7tr8UFc

A journey of a worrier to a warrior by Colleen Lightbody, TEDxHyderabad.

https://www.youtube.com/watch?v=Awd0kgxcZws

Settle Down, Pay Attention, Say Thank You: A How-To by Kristen Race at TEDxMileHighWomen.

www.mentalhelp.net/psyhelp/chap4

This site examines aspects of behavior such as procrastination, self-control, and managing loss of control or relapse.

Name _____ Date _____

Where Does the Stress Come from in Your Life?

PURPOSE

To discover where the sources of stress are in your life.

INSTRUCTIONS

1. You need to keep track of any stressful event that occurs in your life for a one-week period of time. Each day at approximately 10:00 A.M., 6:00 P.M., and 10:00 P.M. write down each of the stressful events that occurred to you during the previous period of time.
2. Use the following form:

DAY	TIME	STRESSFUL EVENT	TYPE OF STRESS (INDICATE WHETHER THE EVENT INVOLVES CONFLICT, HASSLE, CHANGE, FRUSTRATION, OR SOME COMBINATION.)	YOUR REACTION

3. Complete the following questions at the end of the week:

    a. Is there a specific type of stress that is most frequent in your life? Explain.

    b. Is there a specific location or set of circumstances that produce a great deal of stress for you? Explain.

    c. What specific reaction to the stressful events did you display? Give examples.

    d. What could you do to reduce the amount of stress in your life?

Name _____ Date _____

How Much Can You Take?

PURPOSE

To help you become more aware of stress-producing events in your life, whether negative or positive, and to demonstrate the correlation between cumulative stress and possible major health changes.

INSTRUCTIONS

1. Each participant is to individually fill out the Social Readjustment Rating Scale by transferring to the "Your Event" column, the EXACT NUMBER assigned for each stressful event you have experienced in the past 12 months. For example, if you have been fired from your job, you would place 47 in "Your Event" column. Then, total "Your Event" column.
2. In evaluating your scores, pay very close attention to Discussion Questions 3 and 4.
3. Become aware of what your chances are of experiencing a major health change in the next two years:

    0–150 points   =   1 in 3 chance
    150–300 points   =   50–50 chance
    Over 300 points   =   almost 90 percent chance

4. Divide into groups of four or five to discuss the results of each individual's scale.

SOCIAL READJUSTMENT RATING SCALE

LIFE CHANGES	VALUE	YOUR EVENT
FAMILY:		
Death of a spouse	100	_____
Divorce	73	_____
Marital separation	65	_____
Death of a close family member	63	_____
Marriage	50	_____
Marital reconciliation	45	_____
Major change in health of family member	44	_____
Pregnancy	40	_____
Addition of new family member	39	_____
Major change in arguments with spouse	35	_____
Son or daughter leaving home	29	_____
Trouble with in-laws	29	_____
Spouse starting or ending work	26	_____
Major change in family get-togethers	15	_____

PERSONAL:

Detention in jail	63	_____
Major personal injury or illness	53	_____
Sexual difficulties	39	_____
Death of a close friend	37	_____
Outstanding personal achievement	28	_____
Start or end of formal schooling	26	_____
Major change in living conditions	25	_____
Major change in personal habits	24	_____
Changing to new school	20	_____
Change in residence	20	_____
Major change in social activities	19	_____
Major change in church activities	19	_____
Major change in sleeping habits	16	_____
Major change in eating habits	15	_____
Vacation	13	_____
Christmas	12	_____
Minor violations of the law	11	_____

WORK:

Being fired from work	47	_____
Retirement from work	45	_____
Major business adjustment	39	_____
Changing to a different line of work	36	_____
Major change in work responsibilities	29	_____
Trouble with boss	23	_____
Major change in working conditions	20	_____

FINANCIAL:

Major change in financial state	38	_____
Mortgage or loan for major purchase (home, etc.)	31	_____
Mortgage foreclosure	30	_____
Credit card dept. or loan of more than $5,000	17	_____
	Total Points	_____

Holmes, T. H., & Rahe, R. H. "The Social Readjustment Rating Scale," from *Journal of Psychosomatic Research*, No. 227. Reproduced by permission from Pergamon Press Ltd., Headington Hill, Oxford, England.

DISCUSSION

1. Did you already have an awareness of the amount of stress in your life or were you surprised? Which area (family, personal, work, or financial) presented more stress-producing events?

2. What are some things you could do to lessen or control stress-producing events in your life?

3. Remember, positive changes may be stressful, but they are less of a hassle than negative changes. Have most of the changes and threats you experienced (listed) been more positive or negative? Why?

4. Hans Selye has said that "all the stress inventories are flawed because they fail to give enough weight to individual differences" (Epstein, 1999). Also, stress inventories often do not take into account how individuals perceive a given change, much less how they cope with it. How do you feel about these statements as you evaluate your score?

Name _____ Date _____

Type A and Type B Behavior

PURPOSE

To help you identify individual personality characteristics that would indicate Type A or Type B behavior.

INSTRUCTIONS

1. Rate yourself as to how you typically react in each of the situations listed below by circling one response for each question.
2. Find your total score by adding together the circled number response of each question.
3. Determine whether your behavior is primarily Type A or Type B according to the following scale:

1–47	Extreme Type B
48–94	Type B
95–141	Both Type A and Type B
142–188	Type A
189–235	Extreme Type A

    In general, a score greater than 120 is Type A and a score less than 120 is Type B.

	ALWAYS	FREQUENTLY	SOMETIMES	SELDOM	NEVER
1. Are you punctual?	5	4	3	2	1
2. Do you work under constant deadlines?	5	4	3	2	1
3. Do you indulge in competitive hobbies?	5	4	3	2	1
4. Do you like routine household chores?	5	4	3	2	1
5. Do you prefer to do a task yourself because others are too slow or can't do it as well?	5	4	3	2	1
6. Do you work while you are eating, in the bathroom, etc.?	5	4	3	2	1
7. Do you walk fast?	5	4	3	2	1
8. Do you eat hurriedly?	5	4	3	2	1
9. Are you patient and understanding?	5	4	3	2	1
10. Do you carry on several lines of thought at the same time?	5	4	3	2	1

	ALWAYS	FREQUENTLY	SOMETIMES	SELDOM	NEVER
11. Do you interrupt others when they talk about subjects that don't interest you?	5	4	3	2	1
12. Do you pretend to listen to others when they talk about subjects that don't interest you?	5	4	3	2	1
13. How often does time seem to pass rapidly for you?	5	4	3	2	1
14. How often do you look at your watch?	5	4	3	2	1
15. Do you feel vaguely guilty when you relax and do absolutely nothing for several hours/days?	5	4	3	2	1
16. How often do you become exasperated when standing in line at movies, restaurants, etc.?	5	4	3	2	1
17. Do you ever find that you cannot recall details of the surroundings after you left a place?	5	4	3	2	1
18. How often are you preoccupied with getting materialistic things?	5	4	3	2	1
19. Do you use a relaxed, laid back speech pattern?	5	4	3	2	1
20. How often do you attempt to schedule more and more in less and less time?	5	4	3	2	1
21. How often do you feel aggressive, hostile, and compelled to challenge people who make you feel uncomfortable?	5	4	3	2	1
22. Do you accentuate your speech, talk fast?	5	4	3	2	1
23. How often do you gesture by clenching your fists, banging your hand on the table, pounding one fist into the palm of the other hand, clenching your jaw, grinding your teeth, etc.?	5	4	3	2	1
24. Do you prefer respect and admiration to affection?	5	4	3	2	1
25. Do you listen well and attentively?	5	4	3	2	1
26. Do you evaluate the activities of yourself and others in terms of numbers (e.g., minutes, hours, days, dollars, age)?	5	4	3	2	1
27. How often do you play to win?	5	4	3	2	1

	ALWAYS	FREQUENTLY	SOMETIMES	SELDOM	NEVER
28. How often do you stay up late to socialize?	5	4	3	2	1
29. How often are you angry?	5	4	3	2	1
30. Do you go out of your way to conceal your anger?	5	4	3	2	1
31. How often are you dissatisfied you're your present position or promotional progress?	5	4	3	2	1
32. Do you daydream a lot?	5	4	3	2	1
33. Do you participate in numerous organizations?	5	4	3	2	1
34. Did you ever attend night school?	5	4	3	2	1
35. How often do you go to a doctor?	5	4	3	2	1
36. Do you ever "sigh" faintly between words?	5	4	3	2	1
37. How often do you come to work even when you are sick?	5	4	3	2	1
38. How often is your laughter a grim, forced chuckle?	5	4	3	2	1
39. Do/would you avoid firing people?	5	4	3	2	1
40. How often are you genuinely open and responsive to people?	5	4	3	2	1
41. How often do you go to bed early?	5	4	3	2	1
42. If you smoke, do you prefer cigarettes as opposed to a pipe or cigar?	5	4	3	2	1
43. How often do you salt your meal before tasting it?	5	4	3	2	1
44. How often do you exercise?	5	4	3	2	1
45. Do you ever combine vacations with business?	5	4	3	2	1
46. How often do you work late?	5	4	3	2	1
47. How often do you hum, fidget, or drum your fingers while not involved in an activity?	5	4	3	2	1

Total Points _____

Mirabal, Thomas E. "Identifying Individual Personality Characteristics." Reproduced by permission from Synergistic Training Systems, Inc., Dallas, TX.

DISCUSSION

1. Did the results of this exercise make you aware of any Type A behavior pattern in your own personality? Were you surprised?

2. What are some of the dangers of Type A behavior?

3. Is it possible to change from Type A to Type B? How?

4. Would you want to change your behavior patterns if you could?

Irrational and Rational Self-Talk

PURPOSE

To focus on how irrational and rational self-talk can be used in common, practical events and situations.

INSTRUCTIONS

1. For each situation below, consider how you would feel and what you might say to yourself. Then, write an irrational and a rational belief about each situation.
2. Be prepared to share your responses in a class discussion or in small groups of four or five students.

SITUATION	IRRATIONAL SELF-TALK	RATIONAL SELF-TALK
1. You have to give a 5-minute speech in your college class (Example)	1. This is terrible. I just can't bear having to give this speech.	1. This is going to be difficult. I will work hard and be as successful as I can be.
2. You didn't meet a very important work deadline.	2.	2.
3. A friend cancelled a date with you.	3.	3.
4. You are criticized publicly in class or at work.	4.	4.
5. You're having a final exam in your most difficult class.	5.	5.
6. You have just had a major "blow-up" with your fiancé/fiancée.	6.	6.
7. You were laid off from your job.	7.	7.
8. Write your own situation.	8.	8.

DISCUSSION

1. Was it easier for you to write the irrational or the rational self-talk and beliefs? Why?

2. How many times did you use *should, should not, must, ought, have to?*

3. How many times did you write awfulizing statements?

4. How many times did you make overgeneralizations?

5. How do you think irrational self-talk contributes to a common situation becoming more stressful?

Coping with Stress Inventory

PURPOSE

To analyze how you currently manage your stress.

INSTRUCTIONS

Listed below are some common ways of coping with stressful events. Mark those that are characteristic of your behavior or that you use frequently.

_____	1.	I ignore my own needs and just work harder and faster.
_____	2.	I seek out friends for conversation and support.
_____	3.	I eat more than usual.
_____	4.	I engage in some type of physical exercise.
_____	5.	I get irritable and take it out on those around me.
_____	6.	I take a little time to relax, breathe, and unwind.
_____	7.	I smoke a cigarette or drink a caffeinated beverage.
_____	8.	I confront my source of stress and work to change it.
_____	9.	I withdraw emotionally and just go through the motions of my day.
_____	10.	I change my outlook on the problem and put it in a better perspective.
_____	11.	I sleep more than I really need to.
_____	12.	I take some time off and get away from my working life.
_____	13.	I go out shopping and buy something to make myself feel good.
_____	14.	I joke with my friends and use humor to take the edge off.
_____	15.	I drink more alcohol than usual.
_____	16.	I get involved in a hobby or interest that helps me unwind and enjoy myself.
_____	17.	I take medicine to help me relax or sleep better.
_____	18.	I maintain a healthy diet.
_____	19.	I just ignore the problem and hope it will go away.
_____	20.	I pray, meditate, or enhance my spiritual life.
_____	21.	I worry about the problem and am afraid to do something about it.
_____	22.	I try to focus on the things I can control and accept the things I can't.

Evaluate your results: The **even-numbered** items tend to be constructive tactics and the **odd-numbered** items tend to be less constructive tactics for coping with stress.

From *Relaxation & Stress Reduction Workbook*, 6th edition. Reprinted by permission of New Harbinger Publications.

Congratulate yourself for the even-numbered items you checked. Summarize or list those below.

Think about whether you need to make some changes in your thinking or behavior if you checked any odd-numbered items. Summarize or list below.

DISCUSSION

1. Of the even-numbered items you haven't tried before, which ones do you think might be options for you to try?

2. What other positive ways of coping with stress do you think might be an option for you?

Practice laughter techniques and exercises.

LAUGHTER EXERCISES

- **Humming Laughter Sounds:** Laugh as you hum, mouth closed. Play with the pitch, up and down the scale, feeling the vibrations resonate through your body. As you get more adept at feeling the resonation, try to move it deliberately, through your chest, your jaw, your nose, your sinus cavities, your forehead, the top of your head, then back down again.
- **Laughter Breath:** Inhale deeply, then exhale in a combination of first quick bursts of air coming out and finishing with vocal laughter. Repeat 5-7 times.

From the Laughter University online, where they have many more…http://www.laughteronlineuniversity.com/exercises/

Managing Stress and Wellness

LEARNING JOURNAL

Select the statement below that best defines your feelings about the personal value or meaning gained from this chapter and respond below the dotted line.

I learned that I . . .   I was surprised that I . . .

I realized that I . . .   I was pleased that I . . .

I discovered that I . . .   I was displeased that I . . .

....

Chapter 9
Values, Ethics, and Choices

© Rawpixel.com/Shutterstock.com

Make your commitments to enduring values and institutions—honesty, integrity, trust, confidence, family, and other matters of the heart. Go ahead and challenge the status quo, but you must also decide what lasts—what really counts—what no one can take away from you. These are your values, and they will accompany you wherever you work and wherever you live.

—Jack D. Rehm, Business leader

Think About This...

What wisdom would you impart to the world if you knew it was your last chance? At many colleges, professors are asked to give a hypothetical final talk called "The Last Lecture." In this talk, they ruminate on what matters most to them. In 2007, Randy Pausch, a professor in the computer science department at Carnegie Mellon University, agreed to give a last lecture. A few weeks later, he learned that he had only months to live—he was dying of pancreatic cancer.

A month after learning that his cancer was terminal, Randy Pausch gave his 76-minute speech, "Really Achieving Your Childhood Dreams." He talked about what his childhood dreams had taught him about life and the lessons he had learned along the way, such as to show gratitude, don't complain, and don't give up when faced by challenges, which he calls "brick walls." He also discussed enabling the dreams of others, having fun, asking for what you want, daring to take a risk, looking for the best in everybody, dreaming big, making time for what matters, and living with integrity and joy. At the end, Pausch tells the audience that his talk isn't for them—it's for his kids. The lecture isn't about dying—it's about living. Ten months after giving the lecture, Randy died at the age of 47.

Randy Pausch's last lecture has become an Internet sensation, a bestselling book, and inspiration to others who are going through cancer or other tough situations. As Randy said, "We cannot change the cards we are dealt, just how we play the hand."

So, if you had to vanish tomorrow, what would you want to leave as your legacy?

Randy Pausch (2008).

> *It's important to understand the difference between Guilt and Shame. Guilt = I Did Something Bad. Shame = I Am Bad. Guilt is about our behaviors – shame is about who we are.*
> —BRENÉ BROWN

We face a rapidly changing world in which old values give way to new ones or to none at all. Today, people are trying to make sense of the world in which we find ourselves. Many who are fortunate enough to achieve power, fame, success, and material comfort nevertheless experience a sense of emptiness. It is no surprise that people are asking more value questions: What is the good life for me? What is really important to me? What is life all about? What are my personal ethics? How can I find meaning and purpose in life? In order to begin to find answers to these questions, we need first of all to be able to identify what values are.

What Are Values?

The Merriam Webster dictionary has two definitions we might want to consider:

> 1. the regard that something is held to deserve; the importance, worth, or usefulness of something. Such as "your support is of great value." 2. a person's principles or standards of behavior; one's judgment of what is important in life. Such as "they internalize their parents' rules and values."

Or we could roll them both together and say "A value is the degree of importance we attach to various beliefs, ideas, objects, or things" and our personal goals (Mynatt & Doherty, 2013).

For just a few minutes, consider the following analogy: If you were going to build a new home, one of the first considerations would be to decide upon your house plan.

After having carefully studied your house plan and having made the necessary adjustments, you would have your house plan converted into a blueprint. This blueprint would serve as a guide for the construction of your new home. For example, the choices and decisions concerning the layout of the kitchen, the placement of doors and windows, the design of electrical outlets, and so on, would be in accordance with this blueprint—the plan or guide for your new home.

Could it be possible that we also have a blueprint or guide concerning the choices and decisions we make in our way of living? Is there a relationship between this *blueprint* or *guide* and our values?

Authors have written extensively about the meaning of the term value(s). For example, *a value is the degree of importance we attach to various beliefs, ideas, objects, or things* (Mynatt & Doherty, 2013). Hunter Lewis (2007) defines *values* in this way:

> Although the term value(s) is often used loosely, it should be synonymous with personal beliefs about the "good," the "just," and the "beautiful," personal beliefs that propel us to action, to a particular kind of behavior and life.

We could conclude then that our values give rise to our personal goals and tend to place limits on the means we shall use to reach them (Rathus & Nevid, 2013).

Because we have many values, it is therefore appropriate to speak of our set of values or our *value system*. A *set of values* is more than just a set of rules and regulations. Instead, it is *the underlying system of beliefs about what is important in life to a person*. Actually, our value system represents the blueprint or guideline for the choices and decisions we make throughout our life. Still true today, Kluckhohn (1956) explains these choices and decisions:

> Every individual operates according to a system of values, whether it is verbalized and consistently worked out or not. In selecting goals, in choosing modes of behavior, in resolving conflicts, he is influenced at every turn by his conception of what is good and desirable for him. Although everyone's value system is in some degree unique, an individual's values are usually grounded in the core values of his culture. . . . Depending on his conception of what is desirable and good in human life, he selects certain goals over others and patterns his behavior according to standards of what he believes to be right and worthwhile. The way a man carries on his business activity, the kind of relationships he has with his wife and children and with his friends, the degree of respect he has for other individuals (and for himself), his political and religious activity—all these reflect the individual's values, though he may scarcely have thought them through.

Types of Value Systems

In 1928, Eduard Spranger, a German philosopher and psychologist, defined six different types of people based on their types of value systems, or their frameworks for de-

Things have the value that we ourselves have the capacity to give them.
—NIKOS KAZANTZAKIS

What is a value system? First of all, it is yours, and it is unique because you are one-of-a-kind. It is your code of ethics by which to live. It is your "behavior-bible." It is what guides your life.
—HELEN JOHNSON

One's philosophy is not best expressed in words; it is expressed in the choices one makes... and the choices we make are ultimately our responsibility.
—ELEANOR ROOSEVELT

It is easier to fight for one's principles than to live up to them.
—ALFRED ADLER

veloping their own beliefs (Lamberton & Minor, 2014). Do you fit into any of **Spranger's Six Value Systems?**

1. *The Theoretical Person.* This individual seeks *to discover truth*.
2. *The Economic Person. Personal needs, production, marketing, credit, and wealth are more important to this type of person than are social or artistic values*
3. *The Aesthetic Person. Beauty, form, and harmony* are most important to this type of individual.
4. *The Social Person. Loves other people.* Kindness and unselfishness are very important values.
5. *The Political Animal.* This type is *very power motivated.* Their values center on influence, fame, and power.
6. *The Religious Person. Believes that the highest value is unity.* They try to understand the universe as a whole and relate to it meaningfully.

Most people don't identify with just one single type since a combination of two or more is often more accurate and descriptive. Which value system/s do you think are more closely related to your own personal value system?

How Do Values Develop?

Throughout your life, you have, in all probability, heard many *life messages:* "Life is . . .," "Success is . . .," "The most important thing is . . ." transmitted to you by parents, peers, and society in general.

We are not born with values, but we are born into cultures and societies that promote, teach, and impart their values to us. We learn to be what we are.

Shoulds and should nots. Most psychologists concur that we first acquire the cognitive understanding of *right and wrong by observing the behavior of the people most important to us,* usually (and hopefully) our parents (Begley & Kalb, 2000). Actually, our first goals and ambitions will be drawn from this frame of reference. During the first few years of our life, we lack the knowledge and maturity to evaluate our value orientation (Freiberg, 2009/2010).

As we entered school, however, parental influence was combined with the influence of peers, teachers, and public media. We had one set of *shoulds* and *should nots* from our parents. The church often suggested a second. Our friends and "peer group" offered a third view of values. Recent research indicating that many young people spend 30 to 40 hours a week in front of the TV set and the Internet has fueled continuing great concern about the influence of television, Internet and social media, and advertising claims on values formation (Reece & Brandt, 2014). A 2012 Pew survey by Amanda Lenhart found that only 35% of 12 to 17 year olds regularly socialized face to face anymore. This compared to 63% of teens who said they communicated mostly via text messages and averaged 167 texts a day. "Will this next generation not be as social face to face and value social media relationships more? This is troubling because research has found that we can get physically and psychologically ill without real meaningful human contact." (Lenhart 2012). It seems the igeneration values technology. Kardasras stated "We now know that those iPads, smartphones and Xboxes are a form of digital drug." (Kardaras, 2016).

With all of this additional information, we began to question and reevaluate our original value orientation. Much of this questioning was revealed through testing the

© Monkey Business Images/Shutterstock.com

shoulds and *should nots*. Therefore, actual experience became very real in the forming of our value system. For some people, this reevaluation period occurred during the adolescence period, early adulthood, or maybe even later.

Were your parents the biggest influence on your value system?

Individuation. How old were you when you reevaluated your original value system? Were you 18, 20, 25, or . . .? Regardless of the exact time, examining and acquiring your personal set of values was, or is, the birth of your own individuality. In fact, Carl Jung (1923), one of the early psychoanalysts, called the process of becoming an individual—individuation. Although individuals may accept many of their parents' values, to genuinely individuate they must choose these values freely rather than automatically incorporating them into their personality because they "should."

Individuation refers to the separation from our family system and the establishing of our identity based on our own experiences, rather than merely following our parents' dreams. Although individuals may accept many of their parents' values, to genuinely individuate they must choose these values freely rather than automatically incorporating them into their personality.

Life is not measured by the number of breaths we take, but by the moments that take our breath away.
—MAYA ANGELOU

The values we place upon different aspects of our environment have an effect upon how we view things and how we function. In other words, an act viewed as right or wrong, moral or immoral will depend upon the frame of reference of the perceiver. As a result, something that one person considers worthwhile and desirable may appear exactly the opposite to another person. Do we, therefore, tend to judge other people's actions by our own standards—our values?

What else influences the development of our values?

THE INFLUENCE OF OTHER FACTORS

Other important factors are influential in the formation of our value system. Some of these are religious beliefs, attitudes, prejudices, and stereotypes.

Religious beliefs. What is a belief? A ***belief*** is the acceptance of some thought, supposition, or idea that a statement is true or that something exists. This belief may be in a God, or in Gods, or even in some form of spirituality. Studies show that most Americans want spirituality, but perhaps not in religious form. Lifeway Christian Resources did a survey in 2010 of 1,200 18- to 29-year-olds and found that 72 percent say they're really more spiritual than religious (Grossman, 2010). In the United States, for example, women are more likely than men to say religion is "very important" in their lives (60% vs. 47%), according to a 2014 Pew Research Center survey. And by many measures, Millennials are much less likely than their elders to be religious. Data on religious beliefs and practices come from international Pew Research Center surveys of the general population in 84 countries conducted between 2008 and 2015. Based on these wide-ranging and comprehensive datasets, Pew researchers found that, "globally, women *are* more devout than men by several standard measures of religious commitment. An estimated 83.4% of women around the world identify with a faith group, compared with 79.9% of men" Pew Research Center, Religion and Public Life (March 2016).

For nearly 40 years, Dr. Vern Bengtology (Professor of Sociology and Gerontology at the University of Southern California) has overseen the Longitudinal Study of Generations, which has become the largest study of religion and family life conducted across several generational cohorts in the United States. When Bengtson noticed the growth of nonreligious Americans becoming increasingly pronounced, he decided in 2013 to add secular families to his study in an attempt to understand how family life and intergenerational influences play out among the religionless. He was surprised by what he found: High levels of family solidarity and emotional closeness between parents and nonreligious youth, and strong ethical standards and moral values that had been clearly articulated as they were imparted to the next generation. "Many nonreligious parents were more coherent and passionate about their ethical principles than some of the 'religious' parents in our study," Bengston told me. "The vast majority appeared to live goal-filled lives characterized by moral direction and sense of life having a purpose" (Zuckerman, 2016).

Roughly three-quarters of Millennials feel a strong sense of gratitude or thankfulness at least weekly (76%). And 51% say they feel a deep sense of spiritual peace and well-being at least once a week (Alper, 2015). In fact, M. Scott Peck (2003), in *The Road Less Traveled,* notes that he likes to speak of *spirituality* rather than *religiosity.* Peck goes on to indicate that every major religion of the world has similar ideas of love, the same goal of benefiting humanity through spiritual practice, and the same effect of making their followers into better human beings. However, in an interview with Robert Epstein (2002) for *Psychology Today,* Peck reminded readers that one person's experience with spirituality would be different from another person's experience.

In some form or another, religion and established moral codes are found in all cultures and societies. A commitment to a chosen moral code helps individuals gain a sense

> *Wherever I go meeting the public... spreading a message of human values, spreading a message of harmony, is the most important thing.*
> —DALAI LAMA

> *It is never too late to be who you might have been.*
> —GEORGE ELLIOT

of meaning and purpose in their lives, and thus, plays an integral part in shaping their value system (Compton, 2005). David Brooks in his 2016 book, *The Power of Altruism*, explains that there are two lenses people use to look at the world …the moral lens and the economic lens. When someone offers money to do something "instead of following their natural bias toward reciprocity, service and cooperation, you encourage people to do a selfish cost-benefit calculation. They begin to ask, 'What's in this for me?'"(Brooks, 2015). Ricard (2016) feels "there's an altruism revolution underway, and it just may be the saving grace for the 21st century."

Attitudes. *Attitudes* are positive or negative orientations toward a certain target. For example, you have attitudes toward specific persons (parents, children, teachers), as well as toward groups of people (blacks, whites, male ministers, female ministers). You also have attitudes toward things or targets such as food, movies, holidays, or marriage.

Values

Values come from many sources.

What source has had the greatest influence in the development of your value system?

The attitudes you have today have been acquired throughout your life. How did you acquire them? You may have acquired some of your attitudes by hearing parents, family, friends, and teachers express positive or negative attitudes toward certain issues or people. The mass media, including advertising, may also be responsible for shaping some of your attitudes. The attitudes you have formed through your own direct experience are strongest, however, and they are also more resistant to change (Compton, 2005). You can learn to make choices that create happiness and decrease suffering by learning to pay more attention to your goals, attitudes, and feelings of self, and spending less time attempting to rescue, control, and manage others (Hetherington, 2008). Brooks (2016) said to be a good worker or citizen, you often make an altruistic commitment.

The meaning of things lies not in the things themselves, but in our attitude towards them.
—ANTOINE DE SAINT EXUPÉRY

More than likely, your positive attitudes are a result of positive experiences, and your negative attitudes are a result of negative experiences. Whatever you learned in these experiences is likely to take the form of *expectations* later in life. It is just natural to expect the same or similar results from similar situations. Consider these statements:

I'm not going to get married again; if I did, it would just probably end in another divorce.

Tom's mother is so different from Frank's mother—certainly not what I expected from a mother-in-law.

I'm sure I can work for Mrs. Jones; I've worked for another female, and we got along just great.

As you can see in these examples, the attitudes were formed from prior *experiences* and *expectations.* Is it possible that your prior experiences and expectations are shaping the attitudes and values you presently hold? If so, do you need to reevaluate these attitudes and values? Remember, the stronger an attitude is, the more difficult it is to change. Why? Because your emotions are involved.

While it is true that we discussed prejudice and stereotypes in Chapter One as they relate to meeting people and forming perceptions about people, we want to briefly review prejudice and stereotypes as they relate to how we form our beliefs/values and act on these beliefs/values.

- **Prejudices.** A *prejudice* is a **preconceived opinion, feeling, or attitude**, either positive or negative, that is formed without adequate information. For example, you may have a negative prejudice toward the African American English teacher who is going to teach your class next semester. Although you have not had this teacher before, you have heard statements made by other students, and you have already formed your opinion. It is only when you are actually in this teacher's class that you can make a justified opinion. Why? Prejudices are often unjustified attitudes. And, sometimes these attitudes extend to entire groups of people. The word "prejudice" can literally be broken down into "pre-" and "judgment." Aptly, much of prejudice stems from our pre-judging other people's habits, customs, clothes, ways of speaking, and values. We often do this with no basis for the judgment other than the fact that they (the customs, values, food, etc.) are different from our own (Rodolfo Mendoza-Denton, 2011).

Actually, there are three components to a **prejudice** (Myers, 2013). They are as follows:

- To hold **certain *beliefs* against members of a group**—*Indians are mostly alcoholics.*
- To *feel* **negatively toward them**—*I despise Jews.*
- To be inclined **to *act* negatively** toward them—*I wouldn't hire a Mexican.*

It is interesting to note that our strongest negative emotions are often reserved for groups rather than individuals. As Gordon W. Allport (1979) commented in his classic book, *The Nature of Prejudice,* "anger is customarily felt toward individuals only, whereas hatred may be felt toward whole classes of people." If we included multiculturalism early in life so children can learn about others and make friends of many cultures we would not have as much hatred and misinformation about others. Starting Small produced by the Teaching Tolerance Project of the Southern Poverty Law Center has many ideas and resources for others to use (2008). Many examples of prejudice involve in-group and out-group processes and often the belief that the members of "the other group" are taking too much of whatever is valuable (e.g., good jobs, land, clean water) for their less-deserving group. One hope is that by learning about the psychological processes that underlie prejudice in general and the specific nature of any particular prejudice in a context, we can better understand and more effectively reduce prejudice. Even a small reduction will make this a worthwhile option. Reducing prejudice and stereotyping will take time so that prejudice against specific groups, such as women and girls, the elderly, gays and lesbians, people with disabilities, and other groups will be helped also (Dovidio, Glick, & Rudman, 2005).

Stereotypes. When we allow our prejudiced attitudes to make *generalizations* by categorizing an object, person, or situation, we are guilty of **stereotyping**. As psychologist Jack Dovidio of Yale University notes in 2014: "we create stereotypes to explain why things are the way they are and stereotypes don't have to be true to serve a purpose." For example:

Women are emotional.

Latin Americans are a hot-headed race.

Mothers-in-law are bossy and interfering people.

There are just a bunch of hypocrites at that church.

According to these examples, if you are a woman, a Latin American, a mother-in-law, or if you go to *that* church, you have now been given a label. You are not thought of as an individual—you are a member of the group and, of course, you have *their* similar characteristics.

- Pause for a minute and just ask yourself these questions: What prejudices and stereotypes do I have? What are they based on? Do I really want to have these values?

At this point, you may find it helpful to review Focus on Diversity—Breaking Down Barriers, for some suggestions on dealing with prejudices, bias, and stereotypes.

> *All I've ever tried to tell anyone is that I'm not a black man or a white man or anything else. All I've been was American.*
> —GEORGE FOREMAN

> *Be a rainbow in someone else's cloud.*
> —MAYA ANGELOU

FOCUS ON DIVERSITY

BREAKING DOWN BARRIERS

To reduce your prejudices and use of stereotypes, these steps may be helpful:

1. Admit your prejudices and biases and try to understand them.
2. Identify the stereotypes that reflect your prejudices and attempt to modify them.
3. Identify the actions that reflect your prejudices and modify them.
4. Avoid judging differences; view diversity as a strength.
5. Attempt to learn about cultures that differ from your own. Try to understand their values.
6. We need to recognize and battle our own bias, racism, and privilege.
7. Think about white privilege and how you can discuss it and confront it without hurting others; it can be hard to hear and understand another's point of view.
8. By demonstrating that you respect and care about others, you increase the chances that you can open the door to relationships in which you learn from others just as they learn from you.

Johnson (2008); Corey & Corey (2008); Henslin (2015); Coleman (2016); Johnson (2014)

Are you willing to test, adapt, and change your perceptions? Do the readings, quizzes, and watch the videos at the end of the chapter for further insight.

What Are My Values?

At the present time, what things are most important to you in your life? Is your career of primary importance? How about your school work and/or the training for your future career? How about the time you spend with your family? Do you have outside leisure interests, community activities, or volunteer work?

© gorillaimages/Shutterstock.com

Actually, what you value most often determines how you will spend your time. When you decide to work late on a repeated basis rather than go home to dinner, this is a value decision. If you gave up a movie in order to study for a test, this is also a value decision. When you decide to go out with some friends rather than attend your son's baseball game, this is another value decision.

You are always making value decisions, and an awareness of what values are most important to you can help you to live a more harmonious and less stressful life. When you know which values have a higher priority, you can more easily make life's major and minor decisions.

GENDER AND YOU

TOP SIX PERSONAL VALUES

In human relations/psychology of adjustment classes at Tarrant County College, Northeast Campus, 1,151 students—51 percent females and 49 percent males—reveal their top personal values:

Males
1. Close family and friends
2. Happiness
3. Stable marriage
4. A fulfilling career
5. Financially stable
6. Good health

Females
1. Close family and friends
2. Stable marriage
3. Happiness
4. Good health
5. Financially stable
6. A fulfilling career

What are your top values? How do your top six values compare with what the male and female students said?

ROBERT LOUIS STEVENSON'S DAILY DOZEN

The most interesting thing about any human being is the values by which he or she lives. Unfortunately, most of us never take the time to sit down and really think through the moral precepts that consciously or unconsciously guide our lives.

The following "daily dozen" constitute the personal creed of writer Robert Louis Stevenson (1850–1894).

1. Make up your mind to be happy. Learn to find pleasure in simple things.
2. Make the best of your circumstances. No one has everything, and everyone has something of sorrow intermingled with the gladness of life. The trick is to make the laughter outweigh the tears.
3. Don't take yourself too seriously. Don't think that somehow you should be protected from misfortunes that befall others.
4. You can't please everybody. Don't let criticism worry you.
5. Don't let your neighbor set your standards. Be yourself.
6. Do the things you enjoy doing, but stay out of debt.
7. Don't borrow trouble. Imaginary things are harder to bear than the actual ones.
8. Since hate poisons the soul, do not cherish enmities, grudges. Avoid people who make you unhappy.
9. Have many interests. If you can't travel, read about new places.
10. Don't hold postmortems. Don't spend your life brooding over sorrows and mistakes. Don't be one who never gets over things.
11. Do what you can for those less fortunate than yourself.
12. Keep busy at something. A very busy person never has time to be unhappy.

From the more commonly mentioned values, the final results on the previous page actually reveal the top six prioritized values. You will also be given an opportunity to complete this activity, and you might want to compare your results with these findings.

Do values change? Your values do change as you go through the various life stages. As children, your highest value might have been play and having fun; as adolescents, perhaps it was peer relationships; as young adults, it may be relationships with the opposite sex; and as adults your highest value may be your family and the work you do. For many older people, service to others and enjoying leisure time are often the highest values.

If you are currently seeking some change in your career or lifestyle, it may be due in part to the fact that some of your values may have changed. This is called **values clarification** and it is discussed below. What was important to you in the past may be less important now. You may want to devote greater attention in your life to new things or to some of the things you did not have as much time for in the past.

Do you see any changes in your personal set of values over the past five or ten years? Has there been any change in the kinds of values you consider to be important in your life? You will be given several opportunities in the activities at the end of this chapter to review your values—past and present.

We have already stated that because we are unique individuals, something that one person considers a value might not be a value to another person. For example, we all want a feeling of security. However, your idea of what makes you feel secure may differ remarkably from that of other people. Some people may equate security primarily with money; others may equate security with education, religion, or close family relationships. Sometimes combinations of all these types of security are desired. The order of importance then becomes a matter of value (Coontz, 2016).

CONSIDER THIS

YOUR VALUES—SOME HARD QUESTIONS

You probably do not have the answers to these questions on the tip of your tongue. They require some thought and discussion. They will lead you to a better understanding of your values.

1. If you were independently wealthy, what would you do with your life?
2. What issues are of deep concern to you regarding your home, campus, community, church, state, country, or world?
3. If you were independently wealthy, to what causes would you contribute?
4. After your death, what would you like people to say about you? How would you like to be remembered?

Clarifying Your Personal Values

Clarifying our values is a crucial aspect of self-development (Rathus & Nevid, 2012). Sometimes important choices in life are made on the basis of peer pressure, unthinking submission to authority, or the power of propaganda. We may even guide our lives by what others expect of us, instead of what we truly believe is right. Many times, thoughts and expectations of society and others largely influence our value system. Thus, our value orientation becomes other-directed rather than self-directed. The obvious result is a feeling of being very insecure and easily threatened in our valuing process.

Are you a people-oriented person?

> By assuming that people are selfish, by prioritizing arrangements based on selfishness, we have encouraged selfish frames of mind. Maybe it's time to upend classical economics and political science. Maybe it's time to build institutions that harness people's natural longing to do good.
>
> —DAVID BROOKS

When we become conscious of our own personal value system and how it functions, we can begin to manage our own value system rather than allowing others to manage it for us. Hunter Lewis (2007), in his thought-provoking book, *A Question of Values*, emphasizes the importance of managing our own value system:

> People need to think about their own values, think hard about them, think for themselves. Personal values really do matter. Without functioning values, we can hardly live at all, much less lead a purposeful and satisfying life.

How do we discover what our true values are?

Values clarification is a process that helps people arrive at an answer. Howard (2016) shares this thought:

It is not concerned with an ultimate set of values (that is for you to decide), but it does stress a method to help you determine the content and power of your own set of values. It is a self-audit, and an inventory of soul and spirit. It is a tool to help you freely decide between alternatives or among varied choices. It is a methodology to help you make a decision, to act, to determine what has meaning for you.

To describe a man's philosophy is to say how he orients himself to the world of his experiences, what meanings he finds in events, what values he aspires to, what standards guide his choices in all that he does.
—ABRAHAM KAPLAN

According to Howard (2016), the process of clarifying values involves choosing, prizing, and acting, as seen in the How To above.

Before something can be a *full,* true value, it must meet all seven of the following criteria. Howard (2016) suggests that there are three levels involved in the criteria: ***choosing*** relies mainly on the cognitive or thinking area; ***prizing*** relies on the affective or feeling area; and ***acting*** relies on the behavioral areas. When we have a ***full value***, our thoughts, feelings, and actions are in agreement; what we think, say, feel, and do are in agreement and are evident in our lives.

Let us look at the seven criteria a little more closely.

It is our choices... that show what we truly are, far more than our abilities.
—J. K. ROWLING

Choosing freely means we consciously and deliberately make the choice ourselves. There is no pressure to believe what our parents taught us. An example of choosing freely would be when you have been raised and taught that there is only one religion worthy of your belief, and you later decide that your beliefs are more in line with another religious faith. Even if you end up choosing the same religious faith which your parents hold, that becomes a full value for you because you make the personal choice to follow that faith.

Choosing from alternatives means there are options. If there are no alternatives, there is no freedom of choice. For example, you really cannot value breathing, of itself, because there is no choice involved; a person must breathe to live. However, you can value mountain air, or a special breathing technique, such as yoga.

Choosing after considering the consequences means you ask yourself, "What would be the result of the alternatives to my choice?" This gives you the opportunity to choose with thoughtful consideration, and not on impulse. Many of the problems which we have are the result of impulsive, poorly thought-out decisions, or action taken without regard for ourselves or others. For example, sometimes people impulsively decide to get a divorce and then later realize they are not happy with their "quick" decision.

Cherishing and feeling happy about the choice means that it influences your behavior in some way, and you do not mind spending your time on this value. For example, if you value being thrifty and you need to buy a new multi-media device, you will spend a considerable amount of time researching and comparing prices. When you finally get your multi-media device, you will be satisfied and content that you "got the best buy."

Publicly affirming a value means you are willing to tell others about it. Some people even crusade for their values. For example, if you value a particular political ideology, you may be seen campaigning for the politician who holds the same value. Remember, you have the right to publicly affirm your values, but you do not have the right to impose your values on others. This interferes with their freedom of choice.

Doing something about a value means taking action. Full values are those things which we work for, do something about, and take action on. Thus, what a person does reflects his or her values. For example, you will read literature that supports your values; you will join clubs or organizations whose members share your values and whose goals correspond to your values.

Acting repeatedly means there is a life pattern that is evident, and the stronger the value, the more it influences your life. There is a consistency of action which manifests itself in all aspects of your life: in dress, in friends selected, in the place you live, in leisure time, in what you read, in your career, in the selection of your spouse, and how you spend your time and money.

In summary, a value that is freely chosen from alternatives whose consequences have been thoughtfully considered, of which we are proud and happy to the point that we publicly take a stand, and that we act upon with repetition and consistency is a full value. What about those values we simply say are important to us?

> *When you walk your talk, people listen.*
> —GERMAN PROVERB

VALUE INDICATORS

Most of us have partial values that are in the process of being formed. Partial values, or *value indicators*, include desires, thoughts not acted on, opinions, interests, aspirations, goals, beliefs, attitudes, feelings, convictions, activities, day-dreams (Rokeach, 2000). For example, we may say that we have a certain goal, but we are not working toward it. Also, we may say that we have an interest in learning to play bridge, but we have never taken the time to act on that interest.

We have already stated that the way we use our money and time is a strong value indicator. For example, John may say he values very highly the importance of reading and keeping up in "his thinking." However, if you asked him how much time he spends reading each week or when he last bought a good book, you may be surprised to discover that he does not even remember. It has been said before that a simple process in determining the strength of a value is to ask a person or family to describe how they spend their money. Generally speaking, the more money they spend on something, the greater the value is to people.

> *If you can bring your actions and the time you spend in your life more into harmony with your values, you will feel more in control of your life and more satisfied with the decisions you make.*
> —FRED HECKLINGER

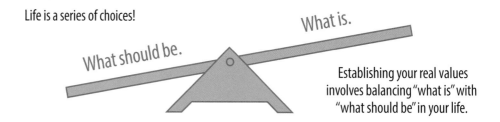

Life is a series of choices!

What should be.

What is.

Establishing your real values involves balancing "what is" with "what should be" in your life.

It is easy to see that we can find out what our real values are by examining our *actual behaviors—the way in which we invest our time, money, energies, and resources.* Consequently, in order to better understand your real values, you might want to apply the following four tests to your value orientation (Rokeach, 2000):

1. **The Choice Test.** What do I do in situations involving a choice?
2. **The Time Test.** How much time and energy am I willing to spend on the value?
3. **The Sacrificial Test.** What satisfaction am I willing to forego on behalf of the value?
4. **The Emotion Test.** How much satisfaction or guilt do I experience when I am true to my value or when I violate it?

The most important thing to remember is that to claim a value, you must act in accordance with what you say you believe. Otherwise, you will be on a seesaw, going up and down and back and forth between "what is" and "what should be" in your life.

WE LEARN TO VALUE WHAT WE SUFFER FOR

We write our own destiny . . . we become what we do. —MADAME CHIANG KAI-SHEK

Why does a child who has to work to earn money value his or her bicycle more than the child who is given a bicycle? Why are members of cults so dedicated to their organizations? These questions and many others may be answered by taking a look at cognitive dissonance, the mental pain of inconsistency, and justifying a sacrifice.

Cognitive dissonance. What is cognitive dissonance, and how does it affect our values, beliefs, and attitudes? The Merriam Webster dictionary defines it as the state of having inconsistent thoughts, beliefs, or attitudes, especially as relating to behavioral decisions and attitude change. We are all motivated to maintain consistency within ourselves. We do not normally hold values, beliefs, or attitudes that are mutually incompatible or dissonant with each other, nor do we behave in ways contradictory to our values or attitudes. Although people differ in the amount of inconsistency they can tolerate, a basic assumption of ***cognitive dissonance theory*** is that inconsistency is intolerable to an individual.

If you do not live the life you believe—you will believe the life you live. —STEPHEN COVEY

The concept of cognitive dissonance was introduced by Leon Festinger in 1957, to account for reactions to inconsistencies in attitudes and beliefs. According to this theory, when two or more cognitions such as beliefs, opinions, and the things we know about various types of behavior, people, objects, or circumstances are in disagreement (dissonance), a state of tension results. This inconsistency (dissonance) motivates the individual to adjust these cognitions so as to reduce the dissonance and thereby reduce the tension (Aronson et al., 2012).

Becoming *Aware*

The mental pain of inconsistency. When there is dissonance between attitudes and behavior, the individual may modify attitudes rather than behavior.

To illustrate these points, suppose that a cigarette smoker is aware of the dangers of smoking to his or her health but continues to smoke. The individual is faced with two dissonant cognitions: "I enjoy smoking, or smoking is harmful." The *dissonance theory* predicts that such an inconsistency would produce an uncomfortable state that would motivate the individual either to give up smoking or change his or her ideas about the risks involved in continuing to smoke. In cases such as this, we typically find the individual expressing one of the following ideas:

- "I enjoy smoking and it is worth it."
- "No one in our family has ever had cancer."
- "A person can't always avoid every possible dangerous situation and still continue to live an enjoyable life."
- "Perhaps if I stopped smoking I would put on weight, which is equally as bad for one's health."

Thus, Festinger suggests that continuing to smoke is consistent with the person's ideas about smoking.

Although the individual may have stated that he or she would like to give up smoking, the person's inability to do so resulted in rationalizing some facts to support his or her belief system and to match the person's behavior. Now the tension is somewhat relieved. However, it has been suggested by some authorities that the individual may have to deal with his or her true feelings and behavior again.

Can you think of ways cognitive dissonance and the mental pain of inconsistency might apply to difficulties in losing weight or in breaking a substance abuse habit?

Justifying a sacrifice. To answer the questions asked earlier, as we have observed through cognitive dissonance, an individual is motivated to justify his or her behavior. A child who has to work to earn money to buy a bicycle will value it more because he or she put more effort into getting it. Club members, just as other members of groups and organizations, will generally experience some type of initiation process that will take a lot of effort on the individual's part. After putting in all this effort, the individual has to justify why he or she suffered or worked so hard in order to be a member of the club or organization. As a result of all this, the individual will generally become a very dedicated member of this group as a means of justifying why he or she went through this process.

As a student, most of you would admit that you value a class you succeeded in that took more effort than a class you succeeded in that was considered "easy." As you can see from these examples, *we learn to value what we suffer for* (Aronson, 2013). A value that is freely chosen from alternatives whose consequences have been thoughtfully considered, of which we are proud and happy to the point that we publicly take a stand, and that we act upon with repetition and consistency is a full value. What about those values we simply say are important?

> *It's important for people to know what you stand for. It's equally important that they know what you won't stand for. Above all, you better not compromise yourself; it is all you got.*
> —JANIS JOPLIN

Although individuals may accept many of their parents' values, to genuinely individuate they must choose these values freely rather than automatically incorporating them into their personality because they "should."

Making Ethical Choices

This is a confusing world to live in. At every turn, we are forced to make choices about how to live our lives. Consider these questions: **What is your philosophy of life?** What would be included in your system of **personal ethics?** What do you do when you are confronted with confusion and conflicts regarding your **values and ethics?** How do your decisions affect your **character and integrity?** As you think about these questions, one thing is certain; your personal system of ethics is based on the values and attitudes you practice in your daily living. Actually, your system of **personal ethics** becomes an attempt to reconcile what *ought to be* with *what is*. Each of us, relying on our set of personal ethics, must decide what is *right or wrong* for us. There are many alternatives, but each of us can *choose* our direction in life

Character and ethics. Stephen Covey (2004), in his highly popular book, *The 7 Habits of Highly Effective People,* is concerned about some of the choices currently being made. He indicates that prior to World War I, people governed their lives by values like "integrity, humility, fidelity, temperance, courage, justice, patience, industry, simplicity, modesty, and the Golden Rule." He calls these attributes the *character ethic* because they are basic principles of effective living, and true success depends on integrating these principles into one's character. Covey is concerned that we have made a distinct shift away from the character ethic toward the *personality ethic*, where success is based more on image, personality, technique, appearance, and having a positive mental attitude. Covey says:

We have become so focused on building ourselves up we have forgotten the foundation that holds it up is that of **character** and **integrity.** Many are focused on reaping the goods without the need to sow the fields. And, if there is no **integrity**, the challenges of life will reveal one's true **character. (2006)**

Former U. S. senator Al Simpson said, "If you have character, that's all that matters; and if you don't have character, that's all that matters, too." So what is character? *Character* is composed of personal standards of behavior, including honesty, integrity, and moral strength (Reece & Brandt, 2014). Can this be learned?

The *Six Pillars of Character* is a framework for teaching good character and is composed of six ethical values (characteristics) everyone can agree upon: **Trustworthiness; Respect; Responsibility; Fairness; Caring; and Citizenship.** Each of the six character traits are used within the CHARACTER COUNTS! Program to help instill a positive learning environment for students and a "culture of kindness," making schools a safe environment for students to learn. The Six Pillars of Character values are not political, religious, or culturally biased. In fact, every year for over 20 years the program has been officially recognized and endorsed by the U.S. Senate and the president of the United States. Ethics educator Michael Josephson (1994) of the Character Counts Coalition has developed a *Character Counts!* model for educational institutions and organizations throughout the country to teach the *six pillars of character*: 1) trustworthiness, 2) respect, 3) responsibility, 4) fairness, 5) caring, and 6) citizenship The Character Counts coalition has developed the following list of 10 key guidelines as a foundation for character development: (You will have an opportunity to evaluate your own standing on these character traits in an exercise at the end of the chapter—see Guidelines for Character Development.)

> *Character is a by-product; it is produced in the great manufacture of daily duty.*
> —WOODROW WILSON

- **Be honest.** Tell the truth; be sincere; do not mislead or withhold information in relationships of trust; do not steal.
- **Demonstrate integrity.** Stand up for your beliefs about right and wrong; be your best self; resist social pressure to do wrong.
- **Keep promises.** Keep your word and honor your commitments; pay your debts and return what you borrow.
- **Be loyal.** Stand by family, friends, employers, community, and country; do not talk about people behind their backs.
- **Be responsible.** Think before you act; consider consequences; be accountable and "take your medicine."
- **Pursue excellence.** Do your best with what you have; do not give up easily.
- **Be kind and caring.** Show you care through generosity and compassion; do not be selfish or mean.
- **Treat all people with respect.** Be courteous and polite; judge all people on their merits; be tolerant, appreciative, and accepting of individual differences.
- **Be fair.** Treat all people fairly; be open minded; listen to others and try to understand what they are saying and feeling.
- **Be a good citizen.** Obey the law and respect authority; vote; volunteer your efforts; protect the environment.

Andrew Dubrin (2014) defines **character trait** as an enduring characteristic of a person that is related to moral and ethical behavior that shows up consistently. For example, if an individual has the character trait of being untruthful, he or she will lie in many situations. However, the character trait of honesty leads to behaving honestly in most situations. It is believed by Dubrin that if you develop, or already have, the ten character traits, it will be easy for you to behave ethically in your dealings with others.

> There is a choice you have to make,
> In everything you do.
> And you must always keep in mind,
> The choice you make, makes you.
> —AUTHOR UNKNOWN

TEN ESSENTIAL CHARACTER TRAITS FOR A HAPPIER LIFE

1. Be Humble
2. Be Courageous
3. Be Grateful
4. Be Tolerant
5. Be Loving
6. Be Forgiving
7. Be Selfless
8. Be Honest
9. Be Persistent
10. Be Expectantly Patient

Ken Wert, *Meant to be Happy* (2016)

Ethics and the professions. Many businesses have a code of ethics for their employees to follow in dealing with customers and clients. Likewise, many professions have ethical training and a code of ethics required for continued licensure and/or certification. For example, accounting classes may explore how it's unethical to "cook the books," and public relations classes could examine how students would feel about promoting a client with an unhealthful product. See Figure 9.1 for the Gallup survey on honesty and ethics in professions.

Integrity and ethics. If you are ever in doubt when trying to understand the ethics of a situation and find the proper solution, it might be helpful to review and consider your responses to the following questions (Vandeveer & Menefee, 2009):

> You are born with three things: intelligence, endurance, and the opportunity to build integrity. You decide how much intelligence and endurance you are going to use. You build integrity every single day with the choices you make.
> —BOB KERREY

1. Is it legal?
2. How do I feel about this? Am I feeling unusually anxious? Am I fearful?
3. Will any rules, policies, or regulations be violated?
4. Is the proposed action consistent with past practice?
5. Does my conscience bother me?
6. How would I feel if the details of this situation appeared on the front page of the local newspaper?
7. Does the situation require that I lie about the process or the results?
8. Do I consider this to be an extraordinary situation that demands an unusual response?
9. Am I acting fairly? Would I want to be treated this way?
10. Would I be able to discuss the proposed situation or action with my immediate supervisor, my family, my minister, my closest friends, my company's clients, or the president of the company?
11. What would I tell my child, sibling, young relative, or close, valued friend to do in this situation?
12. Will I have to hide or keep my actions secret? Has someone warned me not to disclose my actions to anyone?

Becoming Aware

While you may not need to ask yourself all 12 questions in every situation, your honest answers to perhaps even half of the questions may give you guidance in difficult situations.

Figure 9.1 HONESTY/ETHICS IN PROFESSIONS

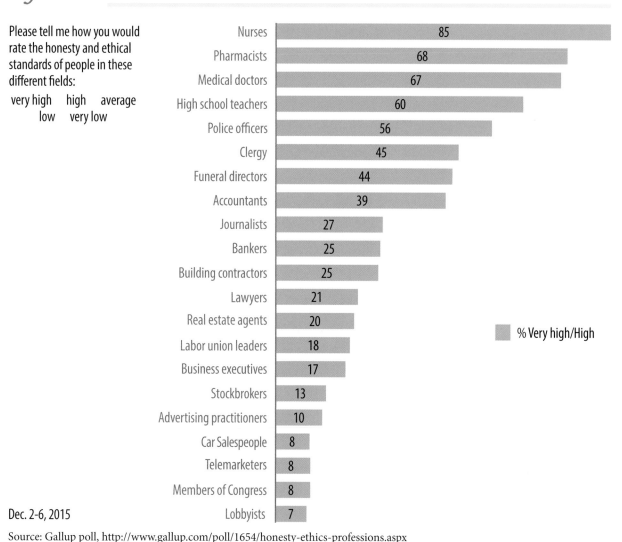

Please tell me how you would rate the honesty and ethical standards of people in these different fields:

very high   high   average   low   very low

Nurses	85
Pharmacists	68
Medical doctors	67
High school teachers	60
Police officers	56
Clergy	45
Funeral directors	44
Accountants	39
Journalists	27
Bankers	25
Building contractors	25
Lawyers	21
Real estate agents	20
Labor union leaders	18
Business executives	17
Stockbrokers	13
Advertising practitioners	10
Car Salespeople	8
Telemarketers	8
Members of Congress	8
Lobbyists	7

■ % Very high/High

Dec. 2-6, 2015

Source: Gallup poll, http://www.gallup.com/poll/1654/honesty-ethics-professions.aspx

Classic psychologist Lawrence Kohlberg, best known for his theory of stages of moral development, reminds us that "the highest level of moral functioning requires us to use ethical principles to define our own moral standards and then to live in accord with them." Ideally, our choices will be made on the basis of our values and ***ethics***— our standards of conduct or behavior—what we do (DeCenzo & Silhanek, 2002). In short, ethics determines where you draw the line between right and wrong.

It is important to note that ***integrity*** is exhibited when you achieve congruence between what you know, what you say, and what you do. When your behavior exhibits your beliefs, you have integrity. When you say one thing but do something else, you lack integrity. When your behavior is in tune with your professed standards and values—when you practice what you believe in—you have integrity (Reece & Brandt, 2014).

Moral development. Morality includes a set of principles or ideals that help a person distinguish right from wrong and act on this distinction. Even when we do the "wrong thing," we usually know what the "right thing" is. For many years, Kohlberg (1981) studied how individuals make moral judgments. He was interested in the process by which people arrive at moral choices—what kind of reasoning makes something right or wrong. He proposed three levels of moral development—the knowledge of right and wrong behavior. See Table 9.1 for a summary of these levels and examples of each type of thinking.

Table 9.1 KOHLBERG'S THREE LEVELS OF MORAL DEVELOPMENT

LEVEL OF MORALITY	HOW RULES ARE UNDERSTOOD	EXAMPLE
Preconvention morality (typically very young children)	The consequences determine morality; behavior that is rewarded is right; that which is punished is wrong.	A child who steals a toy from another child and does not get caught does not see that action as wrong.
Conventional morality (older children, adolescents, and most adults)	Conformity to social norm is right; nonconformity is wrong.	A child criticizes his or her parent for speeding because speeding is against the stated laws.
Postconventional morality (about 20 percent of the adult population)	Moral principles determined by the person are used to determine right and wrong and may disagree with societal norms.	A reporter wrote a controversial story goes to jail rather than reveal the source's identity.

Adapted from Ciccarelli & Noland (2014); Kohlberg (1981).

Confusion and conflict. Being human, sometimes we may experience confusion and conflict and, we may even have a value conflict, a clash between values that encourage opposing actions (Wyer, 2004).

Perhaps one of the most difficult things to do is to establish for ourselves a consistent set of values (Pojman, 2012). If we go against a value, we feel bad. Inconsistencies in our values make us unhappy; they make us feel guilty. If we usually live up to our values, we are happy, satisfied people with consistent value systems.

It is true that we cannot always satisfy our values; many compromises must be made, because value conflicts are likely to appear when two or more people get together. Therefore, we need to learn when we can afford to give up and compromise values and when we cannot. It is best not to compromise values of high priority. Values that are not so important may be compromised without destroying our self-concept, as well as our personal ethics. Actually, satisfied, happy people are people who do not compromise their most important values but are willing to compromise their less important values.

Perhaps the question is really—*What is most important to me?* In making value compromises, therefore, it is very important that we understand our priorities. It is this understanding that helps us define our purpose and gives meaning to our life. Controversial radio icon Dr. Laura Schlessinger puts it quite simply: "Ultimately, we decide the course of our lives by the ethical decisions we make."

Conflicts in values are also seen with social media use today. So many issues arise with social media that everyone has to contemplate how they feel about them and educate themselves. In 2014 78% of Americans felt that, in many ways, the U.S. social media had "opened doors and minds" on issues that often people are afraid to discuss. The Pew Research Center has an August 2016 survey that shows that Americans are increasingly turning to social media for news and political information. Like in the 1960's and 70's when integration and women's equal rights were being discussed, protested, and values were changing, the television was the medium that spread information. Times are changing, according to Pew Research; in 2016 social media also served as important valid venues, where groups with common interests came together to share ideas and information just like television was in the 1960's and 70's. Today, you must check for the validity of social media news. In the 2016 presidential election, news was created by foreign newscasters that was not true. And a number of people felt it changed the results of the presidential race (CBS NEWS, Nov, 2016). Instagram, Twitter, Facebook, and other social media sites can help users bring greater attention to issues through their collective voice if we monitor and verify sources. Some researchers and activists credit social media with propelling racially focused issues to greater national attention (Anderson & Hitlin, 2016).

Other factors influencing the formation of our value system include religious beliefs, attitudes, prejudices, and stereotypes. The three components to a prejudice are: to hold certain beliefs against members of a group, to feel negatively toward them and to be inclined to act negatively toward them. Because we live and work in a multicultural world, it is extremely important that we be willing to view diversity as a strength and to test, adapt, and change our perceptions as we interact with others.(Tolerance.org)

People share a common social understanding of the stereotypes that are pervasive in our culture, and this knowledge can foster implicit bias even if a person does not necessarily endorse the cultural stereotype (Devine, 1989; Fazio, Jackson, Dunton, & Williams, 1995). One explanation is that people implicitly make associations and evaluations based on cultural knowledge in a way that "may not be available to introspection and may not be wanted or endorsed but is still attitudinal because of its potential to influence individual perception, judgment, or action" (Nosek, 2007, p. 68).

Character is what you are in the dark.
—DWIGHT MOODY

The Importance of Meaning and Purpose

Viktor Frankl, a European psychiatrist, dedicated much of his professional life to the study of meaning in life. According to Frankl (1997), what distinguishes us as humans is our **search for purpose**. The striving to find meaning in our lives is a primary motivational force. Humans are able to live and even die for the sake of their ideals and values. Frankl (1997) is fond of pointing out the wisdom of Nietzsche's words: **"He who has a why to live for can bear with almost any how."** Drawing on his experiences in the death camp at Auschwitz, Frankl asserts that inmates who had purpose or a meaningful task in life had a much greater chance of surviving than those who had no sense of mission (Corey & Corey, 2008).

Someone might reasonably ask what having a sense of meaning and purpose gives to a person. Crystal Park (2013) defines *meaning* as simply "perceptions of significance." She argues that meaning gives life significance. Irwin Yalom (2000) reviewed a number of studies of the role of meaning in people's lives and described the following results:

- A person's lack of a sense of meaning in life is related to the existence of emotional and behavioral disorders; the less the sense of meaning, the greater the degree of personal disturbances.
- A positive sense of meaning in life is associated with having a set of religious beliefs.
- A positive sense of meaning is associated with possessing values relating to the betterment of humanity and an interest in the welfare of others.
- A positive sense of meaning is associated with a dedication to some cause and with having a clear set of life goals.
- Meaning in life is not to be seen as a static entity but should be viewed in a developmental perspective. The sources of meaning differ at various stages in life, and other developmental tasks must precede the development of meaning.

In *Tuesdays with Morrie* (Albom, 2002), the dying Morrie shared a thought worth reflecting upon: "Learn how to die, and you learn how to live." Morrie makes some perceptive comments that go to the heart of finding purpose and meaning in life:

> So many people walk around with a meaningless life. They seem half-asleep, even when they're busy doing things they think are important. This is because they're chasing the wrong things. The way to get meaning into your life is to devote yourself to loving others, devote yourself to community around you, and devote yourself to creating something that gives you purpose and meaning.

Dr. Barry Schwartz (2000), professor of psychology at Swarthmore College, in his review of social psychologist David G. Myer's book, *The American Paradox: Spiritual Hunger in an Age of Plenty*, discusses additional insights about the importance of meaning and purpose. He notes that in some respects freedom and opportunity have simply made us more miserable than ever. For example, even though wealth is at an all-time high, we have less happiness, more depression, more fragile marital relationships, less communal contentment, more crime (even after the recent decline), and more demoralized children. It seems that we walk aimlessly through life—searching, searching, searching for "what's the meaning" (Rogers, 2005). Incidentally, we will discuss more research on happiness in the next chapter.

Corey and Corey (2008) summarize the importance of meaning and purpose:

> Humans apparently have a need for some absolutes in the form of clear ideals to which they can aspire and guidelines by which they can direct their actions.

Do you have clear ideals to which you can aspire and guidelines by which you can direct your actions? Do you have meaning and purpose in your life? Alex Pattakos (2010) reflects on the work of Victor Frankl and writes about not being a prisoner of our thoughts and believes that we need to exercise the ***freedom to choose our attitude.***

As human beings, it is our challenge and our task to create our own meaning and attitude. No one can do this for us.

Each man must look to himself to teach him the meaning of life. It is not something discovered; it is something molded.
—ANTOINE DE SAINT-EXUPÉRY

I fought all my life for women to make their own choices, in their personal and professional lives. I made mine.
—HILLARY CLINTON

Chapter Review

A well-defined value system is basic to personal motivation, self-determination, and a life with meaning. Actually, our value system should be the control point of our life, helping us to choose the direction and course we will take.

- A **value** is the degree of importance we attach to various beliefs, ideas, objects, or things.
- Eduard Spranger, a German psychologist, defined six different types of people based on their types of values systems: the theoretical, economic, aesthetic, social, religious, and political.
- We are not born with values, but we are born into cultures and societies that promote, teach, and impart their values to us. We first gain our value orientation from the "significant others" in our lives, with the years of adolescence being extremely important for the learning and development of values. During this time, we test the shoulds and should nots coming from peers, school, media, and advertising influences.
- **Individuation** is the separation from our family system and the establishment of our own identity based on our own experiences and values.
- Other factors influencing the formation of our value system include religious beliefs, attitudes, prejudices, and stereotypes. The three components of a **prejudice** are: to hold certain beliefs against members of a group, to feel negatively toward them, and to be inclined to act negatively toward them.
- Because we live and work in a multicultural world, it is extremely important that we be willing to view diversity as a strength and to test, adapt, and change our perceptions as we interact with others.
- Our values do change as we go through various stages of our life.
- **Values clarification** is a process that helps individuals discover their true values. The process of clarifying values involves choosing freely from alternatives, **prizing** or affirming the choice publicly, and acting repeatedly in some pattern of life.
- Since many Americans value social media, there is potential for social media to increase worker productivity and connect to many other places in the world, but workplaces are realizing that they need to make rules for all workers—not just younger users, about inappropriate social media use at the office.
- **Value indicators** or partial values are values still in the process of being formed. How we use our time and money are often strong value indicators. Four tests to apply to your value orientations include: 1) the choice test, 2) the time test, 3) the sacrificial test, and 4) the emotion test.
- According to the **cognitive dissonance theory**, when two or more cognitions such as beliefs, opinions, and the things we know about various types of behavior, people, or circumstances are in disagreement (dissonance), a state of tension results. This inconsistency (dissonance) motivates the individual to adjust these cognitions so as to reduce the dissonance and thereby reduce the tension. Often, attitudes, rather than behavior, are modified. Quite simply, we are motivated to justify our behavior. We frequently learn to value what we suffer to obtain.
- A person's lack of a sense of meaning in life is related to the existence of emotional and behavioral disorders; the less the sense of meaning, the greater the degree of personal disturbances.
- One of the most difficult tasks we face is living with our values—there are so many choices to make. Since World War I, there has been a focus on behavior and personality—the **personality ethic**—having the right kind of personality defined by the right techniques. Prior to World War I, there was a focus on the **character ethic**—a style of living based first and foremost on prioritized principles and values.
- The six pillars of character are trustworthiness, respect, responsibility, fairness, caring, and citizenship.

- According to Pew Research (2016) social media also can serve as an important venue where groups with common interests come together to share ideas and information.
- Character is composed of personal standards of behavior, including honesty, integrity, and moral strength.
- Ten essential character traits for a happier life are: 1) Be Humble, 2) Be Courageous, 3) Be Grateful, 4) Be Tolerant, 5) Be Loving, 6) Be Forgiving, 7) Be Selfless, 8) Be Honest, 9) Be Persistent, 10) Be Expectantly Patient.
- A **character trait** is an enduring characteristic of a person that is related to moral and ethical behavior that shows up consistently.
- Some guidelines for character development are to be honest, demonstrate integrity, keep promises, be loyal, be responsible, pursue excellence, be kind and caring, treat all people with respect, be fair, and be a good citizen.
- Humans apparently have a need for some absolutes in the form of clear ideals to which they can aspire and guidelines by which they can direct their actions.
- Nurses continue to outrank other professions in Gallup's annual honesty and ethics survey.
- **Ethics** is our standards of conduct or behavior—what we do.
- **Integrity** is exhibited when you achieve congruence between what you know, what you say, and what you do.
- **Morality** includes a set of principles or ideals that help a person distinguish right from wrong and act on this distinction.
- Psychologist Lawrence Kohlberg proposed three levels of moral development—preconventional morality, conventional morality, and postconventional morality.
- In making value compromises, it is extremely important that we remember our priorities.
- Rogers (2005) believes that, even though wealth is at an all-time high, we have less happiness, more depression, more fragile marital relationships, less communal contentment, more crime (even after the recent decline), and more demoralized children. It seems that we walk aimlessly through life—searching, searching, searching for "what's the meaning."
- Pattakos (2010) reflects on the work of Victor Frankl and writes about not being a prisoner of our thoughts and believes that we need to exercise the ***freedom to choose our attitude.***

Test Review Questions: Learning Outcomes

1. Explain what the term "value" means.
2. Name and explain Spranger's six value systems.
3. Explain how we develop values. Define the term individuation and explain its significance in the development of our value system.
4. List and give examples of the three components of a prejudice.
5. Explain at least three things you can do to break down barriers in dealing with prejudices and stereotypes.
6. Define character.
7. Name and discuss character traits for a happier life.
8. Define values clarification, and explain the process of clarifying values.

9. List and give examples of the four tests to apply to your value orientations. Explain at least two strong value indicators.

10. Define character trait and discuss the 10 guidelines for character development.

11. What are the 12 questions to ask yourself when trying to understand the ethics in difficult situations?

12. Explain the cognitive dissonance theory, using a personal example, if possible. How does justifying a sacrifice relate to the concept of cognitive dissonance?

13. Distinguish between the personality ethic and the character ethic.

14. What are the six pillars of character?

15. Define and discuss what contributes to a person having integrity.

16. What profession continues to outrank other professions in Gallup's annual honesty and ethics survey?

18. Name and explain Kohlberg's three levels of moral development.

19. What is the most important thing to remember when considering whether to make value compromises?

20. Explain the role and significance of meaning in an individual's life.

21. What are your values?

22. Why do individuals have a need absolutes in the form of clear ideals to which they can aspire and guidelines by which they can direct their actions?

23. Social media influences and permeates many aspects of daily life for Americans today, and the workforce is no exception. Discuss.

24. Conflicts in values are also seen with social media use today. There are so many issues, in fact, that everyone has to contemplate how they feel about them and educate themselves. In 2014 78% of Americans felt that, in many ways, the U.S. social media has "opened doors and minds" on issues that often people are afraid to discuss.

Key Terms

Acting
Attitudes
Belief
Character
Character Ethic
Character Trait
Choosing Freely
Cognitive Dissonance Theory
Ethics
Full Value

Individuation
Integrity
Morality
Personality Ethic
Prejudice
Prizing
Spranger's Six Value Systems
Stereotyping
The Aesthetic Person
The Economic Person

The Political Animal
The Religious Person
The Social Person
The Theoretical Person
Value
Value Indicators
Value System
Values Clarification

Reflections: Critical Thinking

1. What have been some of the factors that have influenced the development of your value system? Which factor has been of the greatest significance?
2. What are some differences between your value system of today and that of 5 or 10 years ago?
3. Two strong value indicators were discussed: how we spend our money and how we spend our time. Which one is a greater indicator?
4. Discuss any prejudices and stereotypes you have personally experienced.
5. How can we minimize prejudice and stereotyping in our society? How would you compare prejudicial attitudes today compared to 10–20 years ago?
6. What is your perception of the value assessment survey of college students discussed in this chapter? Take the test at the following link. What did you learn about yourself with this test? https://implicit.harvard.edu/implicit/takeatest.html
7. What are some of your partial values or value indicators which are in the process of being formed?
8. Have you ever applied the cognitive dissonance theory to one of your stated values? If so, explain how you changed your belief system to "match" your behavior.
9. How would you describe your personal ethics? How would you describe your philosophy of life?
10. Some social observers believe that our nation is in moral decline. How do you feel about this?
11. What are your thoughts about the six pillars of character being taught in the schools?
12. Can you think of other questions to consider when contemplating the ethics of difficult situations?
13. How would you personally define morality?
14. What are the top three ethical professions in the U.S.?

Web Resources and Web Activities

ACTIVITIES

www.josephsoninstitute.org

Various links on creating a world where decisions and behaviors are guided by ethics.

www.character.org

Numerous articles on developing character education in companies and schools.

www.globalethics.org

Dedicated to promoting ethical action in a global context.

http://www.globaldialoguecenter.com/collections/frankl/index.shtml

Numerous articles on Viktor Frankl and the importance of meaning and purpose.

www.authentichappiness.sas.upenn.edu/testcenter.aspx

Meaning in Life Questionnaire measures meaningfulness.

http://www.beliefnet.org

What do you believe?

http://www.coe.uga.edu/workethic/

Work ethic: where do you stand?

http://greatergood.berkeley.edu/ei_quiz/

How well do you read other people?

https://implicit.harvard.edu/implicit/takeatest.html

Project Implicit (The IAT) measures the strength of associations between concepts (e.g., black people, gay people, disabilities) and evaluations (e.g., good, bad) or stereotypes (e.g., athletic, clumsy). The main idea is that making a response is easier when closely related items share the same response key. When doing an IAT you are asked to quickly sort words into the left and right hand side of the computer screen by pressing the "e" key if the word belongs to the category on the left and the "i" key if the word belongs to the category on the right. The IAT has five main parts.

http://serendip.brynmawr.edu/playground/pd.html

Go to the following site and play the game. What did you learn? How does this relate to human relations? This is an interactive site that illustrates the classic prisoner's dilemma negotiation strategy.

World population

http://www-popexpo.ined.fr/english.html

https://www.nwabr.org/sites/default/files/ValuesActivities.pdf

Ethics and values activities.

http://ethicsed.org/activities

The School for Ethical Education.

https://www.scu.edu/ethics/ethics-resources/

Markkula Center for Applied Ethics.

http://education.wm.edu/centers/ttac/documents/articles/statementofbeliefactivity.pdf

Statement of belief activity.

http://www.tolerance.org/module/anti-bias-framework-unpacking-identity

The Anti-Bias Framework: Unpacking Identity.

http://www.tolerance.org/article/racism-and-white-privilege

Racism and white privilege.

http://greatergood.berkeley.edu/article/item/how to_avoid_picking_up_prejudice_from_media

Readings: How to Avoid Picking Up Prejudice from the Media

By Amanda Sharples and, Elizabeth Page-Gould, September 7, 2016.

http://greatergood.berkeley.edu/article/item/top_10_strategies_for_reducing_prejudice

Readings: The Top 10 Strategies for Reducing Prejudice

By Rodolfo Mendoza-Denton, January 3, 2011.

http://greatergood.berkeley.edu/article/item/the_chauffers_dilemma

Readings: The Chauffeur's Dilemma

By Arlie Hochschild, September 1, 2005. The rich are getting richer and the poor are getting left behind. Why don't more people stick up for fellow citizens facing hard times? Because, argues Arlie Hochschild, empathy is being squeezed from the American way of life.

http://greatergood.berkeley.edu/article/item/why_you_should_share_your_struggles_on_facebook

Readings: Why You Should Share Your Struggles on Facebook

By Kira M. Newman, March 14, 2016.

VIDEOS

https://www.youtube.com/watch?v=3_t4obUc51A

Introduction to Ethics from the Academy of Ideas.

https://www.youtube.com/watch?v=ji5_MqicxSo

Randy Pausch (2008) Last Lecture: Achieving Your Childhood Dreams.

https://www.youtube.com/watch?v=MIeAnU7_7TA

The Way We Never Were: American Families and the Nostalgia Trap

https://www.youtube.com/watch?v=XEtaaW3UFZA

A Date With Your Family: 1950's American Family Values.

https://www.youtube.com/watch?v=n5Q5FQfXZag

Implicit Association Test.

https://www.youtube.com/watch?v=-8H7eeMNfLw

How I Learned to Love Unconscious Bias, by Kristin Maschka, TEDxPasadenaWomen.

https://www.youtube.com/watch?v=Fr8G7MtRNlk

Implicit Bias: How it affects us and how we push through by Melanie Funchess, TEDxFlourCity.

http://www.latimes.com/opinion/opinion-la/la-ol-video-secular-parenting-moral-kids-without-god-religion-premiumvideo.html

Can kids be good without God? Watch our video chat with columnist Patt Morrison and Phil Zuckerman, author of "Living the Secular Life."

Name _____ Date _____

Self-Inventory

PURPOSE

To understand and evaluate your value system for personal goal setting.

INSTRUCTIONS

1. For each statement below, indicate the response that most closely identifies your beliefs and attitudes. Use this code:

    5 = Strongly agree
    4 = Agree in most respects
    3 = Undecided
    2 = Disagree in most respects
    1 = Strongly disagree

    _____ 1. Because of the demands and expectations of others, it is difficult for me to maintain a true grasp of my own identity.
    _____ 2. At this particular time, I have a sense of purpose and meaning that gives me direction.
    _____ 3. I have evaluated and questioned most of the values I now hold.
    _____ 4. Religion gives a source of meaning and purpose to my life.
    _____ 5. I generally live by and proclaim the values I hold.
    _____ 6. I have a close idea of who I am and what I want to become.
    _____ 7. I let others influence my values more than I'd like to admit.
    _____ 8. The majority of my values are similar to those of my parents.
    _____ 9. Generally, I feel clear about what I value.
    _____ 10. My values and my views about the meaning of life have changed a great deal during my lifetime.
    _____ 11. The way I use my time right now reflects my personal values.
    _____ 12. I have a clear picture of "my philosophy of life."
    _____ 13. I must admit that I have some prejudices and stereotypes that are currently part of my value system.
    _____ 14. The way I spend my money right now reflects my personal values.
    _____ 15. The values that I presently believe in are the ones I want to continue to live by.

2. Responses may be shared in small groups or just viewed as a personal inventory.

DISCUSSION

1. Would you like to change your responses to any of the questions? Which ones, and to what numerical degree?

2. What goals would you like to set to ensure that the desired responses occur?

Guidelines for Character Development

PURPOSE

To determine how you rate on guidelines suggested by Michael Josephson of the Character Counts Coalition as a foundation for character development (1994).

INSTRUCTIONS

1. Rate yourself with a check mark (✓) as either completely satisfied, moderately satisfied, or needs improvement on the following character traits:

    1. **Be honest.** Tell the truth, be sincere, do not mislead or withhold information in relationships of trust, do not steal.

        Completely satisfied _____   Moderately satisfied _____   Needs improvement _____

    2. **Demonstrate integrity.** Stand up for your beliefs about right and wrong, be your best self, resist social pressure to wrong.

        Completely satisfied _____   Moderately satisfied _____   Needs improvement _____

    3. **Keep promises.** Keep your word and honor your commitments, pay your debts and return what you borrow.

        Completely satisfied _____   Moderately satisfied _____   Needs improvement _____

    4. **Be loyal.** Stand by family, friends, employers, community, and country; do not talk about people behind their backs.

        Completely satisfied _____   Moderately satisfied _____   Needs improvement _____

    5. **Be responsible.** Think before you act, consider consequences, be accountable and "take your medicine."

        Completely satisfied _____   Moderately satisfied _____   Needs improvement _____

    6. **Pursue excellence.** Do your best with what you have, do not give up easily.

        Completely satisfied _____   Moderately satisfied _____   Needs improvement _____

    7. **Be kind and caring.** Show you care through generosity and compassion, do not be selfish or mean.

        Completely satisfied _____   Moderately satisfied _____   Needs improvement _____

8. **Treat all people with respect.** Be courteous and polite; judge all people on their merits; be tolerant, appreciative, and accepting of individual differences.

Completely satisfied _____ Moderately satisfied _____ Needs improvement _____

9. **Be fair.** Treat all people fairly, be open-minded, listen to others and try to understand what they are saying and feeling.

Completely satisfied _____ Moderately satisfied _____ Needs improvement _____

10. **Be a good citizen.** Obey the law and respect authority, vote, volunteer your efforts, protect the environment.

Completely satisfied _____ Moderately satisfied _____ Needs improvement _____

2. Now make a list of those traits where you feel improvement is needed.

DISCUSSION

1. What do you think you can do to improve the traits you checked as needing improvement?

2. Do you agree that if you have developed all of the above character traits it will be easy for you to behave ethically in your dealings with others? Why or why not?

Name _____ Date _____

Moral Dilemma

Purpose

To review your moral reasoning in a situation that pits two opposing moral values against each other.

Instructions

1. Read the following scenario, adapted from a classic ethics test developed by psychologist Lawrence Kohlberg over 50 years ago (1956).
2. Then individually answer the discussion questions below.
3. Your instructor may choose to divide the class into small groups or have a large class discussion after the discussion questions have been individually answered by the class members. (This was the moral dilemma that Kohlberg originally used with Chicago kids to determine the six stages of morality. Kohlberg was not really interested in whether the subject says "yes" or "no" to this dilemma but in the reasoning behind the answer—so in your groups think about that as you discuss.)

   In Europe, a woman was near death from a special kind of cancer. There was one drug that the doctors thought might save her. It was a form of radium that a druggist in the same town had recently discovered. The drug was expensive to make, but the druggist was charging ten times what the drug cost him to make. He paid $400 for the radium and charged $4,000 for a small dose of the drug. The sick woman's husband, Heinz, went to everyone he knew to borrow the money and tried every legal means, but he could only get together about $2,000, which is half of what it cost. He told the druggist that his wife was dying, and asked him to sell it cheaper or let him pay later. But the druggist said, "No, I discovered the drug and I'm going to make money from it." So, having tried every legal means, Heinz gets desperate and considers breaking into the man's store to steal the drug for his wife.

Individual questions to prepare for the group discussion

1. Should Heinz steal the drug?

   1a. Why or why not?

2. Is it actually right or wrong for him to steal the drug?

   2a. Why is it right or wrong?

3. Does Heinz have a duty or obligation to steal the drug?

   3a. Why or why not?

4. If Heinz doesn't love his wife, should he steal the drug for her? Does it make a difference in what Heinz should do whether or not he loves his wife?

   4a. Why or why not?

5. Suppose the person dying is not his wife but a stranger. Should Heinz steal the drug for the stranger?

   5a. Why or why not?

6. Suppose it's a pet animal he loves. Should Heinz steal to save the pet animal?

   6a. Why or why not?

7. Is it important for people to do everything they can to save another's life?

   7a. Why or why not?

8. It is against the law for Heinz to steal. Does that make it morally wrong?

   8a. Why or why not?

9. In general, should people try to do everything they can to obey the law?

   9a. Why or why not?

   9b. How does this apply to what Heinz should do?

10. In thinking back over the dilemma, what would you say is the most responsible thing for Heinz to do?

    10a. Why?

GROUP DISCUSSION

1. Do you agree that the husband's behavior was excusable under the circumstances? Why or why not?

2. Should Heinz have been arrested for theft? Why or why not?

3. If you were Heinz, would you have stolen the drug? Why or why not?

4. If you were Heinz, what would you have done instead of stealing the drug?

Name _____ Date _____

Personal Value Assessment

PURPOSE

To identify your values through priority ranking.

INSTRUCTIONS

1. The following is a list of personal values. Go through this list and rate the personal values in terms of their importance to you. Place a check (✓) mark in the category that best represents your feelings about how important the personal value is to you. (Exercise continues through the next 3 pages.)

PERSONAL VALUE	VERY IMPORTANT	MODERATELY IMPORTANT	SOMEWHAT IMPORTANT	NOT IMPORTANT
Good health				
Having close friendships				
Having a close family				
A fulfilling career				
A long life				
A stable marriage				
A financially comfortable life				
Independence				
Being creative				
Participating in an organized religion				
Intimacy with another				
Having children				
A variety of interests and activities				
Freedom to create my own lifestyle				
Having a house				
A happy love relationship				
Fulfilling careers for me and my spouse				
Contributing to my community				
Abundance of leisure time				
Happiness				

Ability to move from place to place				
A life without stress				
Strong religious values				
A chance to make social changes				
To be remembered for my accomplishments				
Helping those in distress				
Freedom to live where I wish				
A stable life				
Time to myself				
Enjoyment of arts, entertainment and cultural activities				
A life without children				
A life with many challenges				
Opportunity to be a leader				
Opportunity to fight for my country				
A chance to make a major discovery that would save lives				
A good physical appearance				
Opportunity to establish roots in one place				
Opportunity for physical activities				
An exciting life				
A chance to get into politics				
To live according to strong moral values				
Opportunity to teach others				
To write something memorable				
A chance to become famous				
To help others solve problems				
To make lots of money				

Others:

Fred Hecklinger and Bernadette Black, *Training for Life* (Dubuque, IA: Kendall Hunt Publishing Company, 2012). Used with permission.

2. In the space below, list at least 10 of your most important personal values from your Personal Values Assessment.

1. _____

2. _____

3. _____

4. _____

5. _____

6. _____

7. _____

8. _____

9. _____

10. _____

3. In the space below, list your top 5 personal values in order of priority, with number one as the most important.

1. _____   first priority

2. _____   second priority

3. _____   third priority

4. _____   fourth priority

5. _____   fifth priority

DISCUSSION

1. Does your life right now reflect your values? Is the time you spend consistent with your priorities?

2. If the time you spend in your life right now does not reflect your personal values, how can you change your life so that the time you spend is more in keeping with your values?

3. Are there some parts of your life that you would like to change but that you cannot right now? If so, what is your timetable for bringing your lifestyle more into harmony with your values?

Values in Eight Broad Areas of Life

PURPOSE

To help you identify your values in eight broad areas of life.

INSTRUCTIONS

Below are 16 items. Rate how important each one is to you on a scale of 0 (not important) to 100 (very important). Write the number 0–100 on the line to the left of each item.

Not Important				**Somewhat Important**					**Very Important**	
0	**10**	**20**	**30**	**40**	**50**	**60**	**70**	**80**	**90**	**100**

_____ 1. An enjoyable, satisfying job.

_____ 2. A high-paying job.

_____ 3. A good marriage.

_____ 4. Meeting new people, social events.

_____ 5. Involvement in community activities.

_____ 6. My relationship with God/my religion.

_____ 7. Exercising, playing sports.

_____ 8. Intellectual development.

_____ 9. A career with challenging opportunities.

_____ 10. Nice cars, clothes, home, etc.

_____ 11. Spending time with family.

_____ 12. Having several close friends.

_____ 13. Volunteer work for not-for-profit organizations like the cancer society.

_____ 14. Meditation, quiet time to think, pray, etc.

_____ 15. A healthy, balanced diet.

_____ 16. Educational reading, TV, self-improvement programs, etc.

Below, transfer the numbers for each of the 16 items to the appropriate column, then add the two numbers in each column.

	Professional	Financial	Family	Social
	1. _____	2. _____	3. _____	4. _____
	9. _____	10. _____	11. _____	12. _____
Totals	_____	_____	_____	_____
	Community	Spiritual	Physical	Intellectual
	5. _____	6. _____	7. _____	8. _____
	13. _____	14. _____	15. _____	16. _____
Totals	_____	_____	_____	_____

The higher the total in any area, the higher the value you place on that particular area. The closer the numbers are in all eight areas, the more well-rounded you are.

DISCUSSION

1. Think about the time and effort you put forth in your top three values. Is it sufficient to allow you to achieve the level of success you want in each area? If not, what can you do to change?

2. Is there any area in which you feel you should have a higher value total? If yes, which, and what can you do to change?

Multicultural Panel Discussion

PURPOSE

To learn to value and respect fundamental differences among cultures and ethnic groups.

INSTRUCTIONS

Using the diverse populations within your classroom, your instructor will select multicultural, ethnic, and gender-mixed members from the class to participate in a panel discussion of the topics below. Instructors are encouraged to allow time for questions from the class members.

TOPICS

1. Attitudes, beliefs and values concerning:
   Dating/personal relationships
   Marriage (within culture, outside of culture, interracial marriage)
   Divorce
   Family life (including extended families)
   The purpose and meaning of life
   Education
   Work/careers
   Social involvement
   Religion, worship, spirituality, moral codes
   Death and funerals
   Government enforced laws
   Leisure time
   Male roles/female roles

2. Customs and practices about:
   Holiday celebrations (religious and other)
   Weddings and funerals
   Appearance (clothing, shoes, or other attire)
   Gift giving and charity
   Food, alcohol, or drugs (differences in types, use or misuse of)

3. Miscellaneous concerns:
   What would you like the class members to understand most about your culture or ethnic group?

Discussion

1. What did you learn as a result of this panel discussion?

2. Explain any prejudices or stereotypes you may have previously held that you perceive differently as a result of this panel discussion.

3. Are there any questions that you would have liked to ask but didn't feel comfortable asking? If so, what are the questions?

Values and Ethics

LEARNING JOURNAL

Select the statement below that best defines your feelings about the personal value or meaning gained from this chapter and respond below the dotted line.

I learned that I . . .   I was surprised that I . . .

I realized that I . . .   I was pleased that I . . .

I discovered that I . . .   I was displeased that I . .

. . . .

Chapter 10
Life Planning

© Rawpixel.com/Shutterstock.com

Advice for Graduates

If you're sitting out there now with a nice, neat little outline for the next ten years, you'd better be careful. Life may have other plans. Life will present you with unexpected opportunities, and it will be up to you take a chance, to be bold, to have faith and go for it.

—*JOHN GRISHAM, Writer*

Think About This...

Compare your journey through life to a train trip. You are constantly moving ahead, with stops along the way. With every mile and every new passenger, the train changes just a small amount. For every new person you meet or new experience you have, you change a bit. Just as the train will take on new passengers, employees, and supplies and will eventually let them go, so will you take on new interests, friends, and skills. Some of them you will choose to keep and others you will let go. But just as the train keeps going, remaining basically the same, so do you keep going. You are changed by your experiences, but you always come back to you and you must make the decisions that significantly alter your journey through life.

Just as a train goes through tunnels, around curves, and encounters bumpy tracks, slowdowns and detours, your journey through life will be marked by both smooth and rough travel. At times the direction in which you are headed may not seem very clear. But a course is there, just as the train tracks are there. You may end up going in circles at times, but you still keep moving. Whenever you come to a junction and have to decide which track to take, you must make a decision. Some of these decisions can significantly alter the direction of your life. You run your life, just as an engineer runs a train. You will be responsible for making many decisions. You must invest time and energy on this journey, but the rewards should be well worth your investment (Hecklinger & Black, 2012).

You are now on your journey and have already been through many stations or experiences on the way. Do you like the direction that your life is taking? Do you feel that you have control over where you are going? You must decide whether to take charge of your trip and be the engineer or simply be a passenger on your train, letting others make the critical decisions for you. This vignette is talking about living in the present and being mindful.

The authors believe you have the right and power to make choices about your life. Furthermore, the authors believe that your long-range happiness is guaranteed when you decide to direct and plan your own life. "But, isn't this all just a little bit frightening?" you might ask. Yes, but so often challenging and fun!

> *Nobody can go back and start a new beginning, but anyone can start today and make a new ending.*
> —MARIA ROBINSON

Learning to Take Risks

If you are ever going to get serious about life planning, you will have to take risks. There is simply no way you can grow without taking chances, because everything you really want in life involves taking a risk. To live a creative, interesting, challenging, and successful life, you have to gamble, take some risks, and experiment (Johnson, 2008).

Psychiatrist David Viscott (2003) defines *risk* in this way:

> To risk is to loosen your grip on the known and the certain and to reach for something you are not entirely sure of but believe is better than what you now have, or is at least necessary to survive.

Basic law of life. One-half of knowing what you want in life is knowing what you are willing to give up to have what you want. This translates into a basic law of life:

For everything you get in life, you also have to give up something. (Figler, 2013)

Take a risk!

© nullplus/Shutterstock.com

Think about the truth of this. For example, if you go to college to further your education and career opportunities, you have to give up some time for study and going to class; you may have to accrue a large amount of debt, if you have no college savings, scholarship, or job; if you take a job promotion in another state, you have to give up the security of your friends and familiar places; if you get married, you have to give up some of your independence; if you decide to have children, you have to give up some of your personal time; if you decide to lose some weight, you have to give up some of your high-calorie snack foods; and if you decide to retire from the world of work, you have to give up a higher paycheck. <u>Take a risk!</u>

As you can see, in every risk, there is some unavoidable loss, something that has to be given up to move ahead. However, life is full of many risks and changes. Dr. Spencer Johnson (2002), author of the best-seller *Who Moved My Cheese?* reminds readers: "Change isn't everything; it's the only thing. Embrace change, don't fight it."

Many people are terrified by any possible loss and try to avoid all risks. However, this is really the surest way of losing. Why would you lose if you didn't take risks?

Dr. David Viscott (2003) gives us the answer:

> If you do not risk, risk eventually comes to you. If a person postpones taking risks, the time eventually comes when he will either be forced to accept a situation that he doesn't like or to take a **risk** unprepared. . . . If you continually shun any risk, you become comfortable with fewer and fewer experiences. . . . Your world shrinks and you become rigid. . . . Your life has no direction but is only a reaction to what the world presents to you.

When your dreams include service to others—accomplishing something that contributes to others—it also accelerates the accomplishment of that goal. People want to be part of something that contributes and makes a difference.
—JACK CANFIELD

Therefore, the purpose of life planning is not to eliminate risks but to be certain that the risks you take are the right ones, based on careful thought (Boles, 2005). The question then becomes, how can I find direction for my life? ***Intelligent risk-taking*** means having a process for making good risk decisions—think about these steps.

HOW TO TAKE RISKS EFFECTIVELY

- **Know your motivations.** What do you really want to achieve? Why? Don't take major chances on something you're not enthusiastic about. You'll work harder on goals that are important to you. Failure at something trivial may make you reluctant to try something really important to you.
- **Define success at the start.** Figure out what you want to achieve in specific, measurable terms. You don't have to account for every variable, but you should have a solid idea of the results you're looking for.
- **Look at the best and worst outcomes.** To evaluate risks and rewards, try to determine what the worst-case scenario would look like, whether the payoff is worth that risk, and how you could prevent it from happening. Consider the best-case scenario as well: How will you recognize success? What will you do next? This helps you prepare for contingencies.
- **Consider your timetable.** Do you have to take this risk right now? How quickly do you need results? Don't rush if you don't have to. Breaking your plan down into individual segments can help you minimize risks and learn what's needed to succeed.
- **Focus on benefits, not dangers.** Keep the hazards in mind, but don't let them overwhelm you. Think about the potential outcome, and you'll be able to stay the course even when the road gets rocky.
- **Get started.** You can make all the plans you want, but ultimately you have to take the leap. Don't turn preparation into a full-time activity. You'll feel more energized when you're in the midst of the struggle than when you're just getting ready.
- **Do what matters most to you.** Taking a risk to please or impress someone else will not produce the gratification or results that you had hoped for. MacKay (2015)

MacKay's Moral: No risk, no success. Know risk, know success.

What Motivates You?

There's so much pressure—especially in today's hypercompetitive and hyper-informed society—for people to be something they're not. You get it from parents, from friends, from teachers, from television, from the Internet, from magazines, from advertisements you pass in the street, from nearly everything you see and do in any given day. The old saying "Where there's a will, there's a way" means that if you want—really want—to do something, you will find a way to do it. In other words, you must be **motivated** to act. The stronger your motivation, the more likely you are to accomplish your purpose. The weaker your motivation, the less likely you are to reach your goal.

What is it that causes a person to consider getting a college degree, becoming more financially responsible, seeking the company's sales award, or planning the direction of their life? Let us look at the impact of needs and drives.

Needs and drives. A *need* is a condition that exists when we are deprived of something we want or require. When a need exists, it creates a *drive* that pushes (motivates) us to satisfy the need. Therefore, it is appropriate to say that when you're motivated, you are in a state of tension. To relieve this tension, you engage in activity. The greater your tension, the greater your drive to bring about relief (Drafke & Kossen, 2008).

If all the air were suddenly sucked out of the room you are in right now, what would happen to your interest in reading the remaining pages of this chapter for your final exam? You would not care about reading and studying for a final exam and getting a credit in your last college course; you would not care about anything except getting air. Survival would be your only motivation.

But now that you have air, it does not motivate you. Stephen Covey (2005) calls this one of the greatest insights in the field of human motivation: *Satisfied needs do not motivate. It's only the unsatisfied need that motivates.*

Psychologists have said that there is a reason for everything a person does. Therefore, what are some of the needs that lead people to different types of action?

Fundamental human needs. In *First Things First,* Stephen Covey (2005) discusses the essence of human needs being captured in the phrase: *to live, to love, to learn, and to leave a legacy.* Specifically, these four human needs are

1. *To live* is our *physical* need for such things as food, clothing, shelter, economic well-being, and health.
2. *To love* is our *social* need to relate to other people, to belong, to love, to be loved.
3. *To learn* is our *mental* need to develop and to grow.
4. *To leave a legacy* is our *spiritual* need to have a sense of meaning, purpose, personal congruence, and contribution.

Although we will refer to these needs again when we discuss what goals you would most want to accomplish, these needs are believed to be fundamental to human fulfillment. If these basic needs are not met, we feel empty and incomplete.

> Motivation is not a matter of will-power; it's a matter of want-power.
> —PAUL KARASIK

> Gratitude is the single most important ingredient to living a successful and fulfilled life.
> —JACK CANFIELD

Maslow's Hierarchy of Needs

With all of the pressure that exists in today's hypercompetitive, hyper-informed society, how does one truly accept oneself holistically? As Abraham Maslow (1998), a classic psychologist highlighted, we all follow our own paths; it matters only how completely we dedicate ourselves to achieving the personal and psychological greatness that lies at the top. At the top of the self-acceptance ladder lies the concept of self-actualization. It might help us to understand Maslow's theory of human motivation by referring to how we reach the top of a ladder—*one step at a time*. With self-actualization, you achieve expert control of your creativity, spontaneity, and problem-solving skills. You have assumed a comfortable and sensible morality. You operate with the ability to separate fact from fiction, while eliminating prejudice. It is, in its own way, the clearest definition of what it means to be enlightened as a person. Maslow feels that before we can "blossom" and grow toward self-actualization, the top of the ladder, we progress through certain steps. The problem is that self-actualization doesn't have anything to do with the people around you. Notice the "self" part of the term. The only thing that matters is **your** progress, not the progress of others. If you hope to self-actualize—or at least get on the path to self-actualization—you must stop gauging yourself against other people's accomplishments. His theory of the stepladder, better known as *Maslow's Hierarchy of Needs*, might look something like Figure 10.1.

Basically, Maslow believes that there are certain survival needs that must be met before we can become concerned with the satisfaction of other needs. We will now examine *Maslow's Hierarchy of Needs*.

Physiological needs. These biological needs include food, water, and air, which are essential to our physical well-being. Hence, they are often referred to as our *primary needs* because they keep us alive.

Safety and security needs. When our physiological needs have been satisfied, the safety needs are the next most important step on the hierarchy. Safety and security needs include a reasonably orderly and predictable way of life, a savings account, shelter, insurance policies, etc.

Figure 10.1 **MASLOW'S HIERARCHY OF NEEDS**

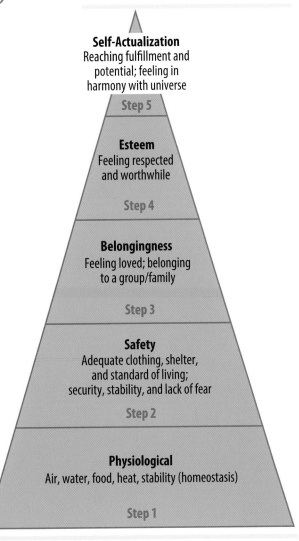

Self-Actualization
Reaching fulfillment and potential; feeling in harmony with universe

Step 5

Esteem
Feeling respected and worthwhile

Step 4

Belongingness
Feeling loved; belonging to a group/family

Step 3

Safety
Adequate clothing, shelter, and standard of living; security, stability, and lack of fear

Step 2

Physiological
Air, water, food, heat, stability (homeostasis)

Step 1

© wavebreakmedia/Shutterstock.com

Love and belonging needs drive us to seek meaningful relationships with others.

Love and belonging needs. If our physiological needs are satisfied and our safety needs have been reasonably fulfilled, needs for love, affection, and belonging are the next step on the hierarchy. Love and belonging needs drive us to seek meaningful relationships with others. We seek acceptance, approval, and a feeling of belonging in our social relationships. Companionship and friendship are very important in satisfying this need to love and be loved.

Esteem needs. Maslow believes that if people have their survival, safety, and affection needs met, they will develop a sense of appreciation for themselves. This sense of appreciation may be nothing more than the development of self-confidence, which strengthens our self-esteem—our self-worth. We need to experience some degree of success to feel that we have achieved something worthwhile.

Self-actualization needs. The last step on the hierarchy represents the fullest development of our potentialities. Some writers believe that ***self-actualization*** is the need for self-fulfillment—to fulfill oneself as a creative, unique individual according to his or her own innate potentialities. Self-actualization does not require any tricks or tools. To reach the next rung, you need only to accept who you are and then take the steps necessary to become the best version of you that you can be. Once you are totally comfortable with who you are, who you've surrounded yourself with, you may complete your journey towards self-actualization. As you see who you are becoming, adopt an attitude that you're not afraid to go against the grain. Stop adapting to societal ideals and start being you. The empowerment that results will astonish you. There are degrees of achievement of self-actualization. One person might feel that complete fulfillment is being the ideal partner. Another person might satisfy this need by setting a career goal and reaching it. Actually, self-actualization is a matter of interpretation, and we have the right to decide what constitutes our own satisfaction of this top step on the hierarchy.

Where are you on the ladder? It is important that we realize that this stepladder of needs is somewhat flexible. All people do not fulfill their needs in the same order that Maslow gives; there are some exceptions. For example, some people may feel that self-esteem is more important than belonging and love. Furthermore, many of us move around on the ladder, as we strive to satisfy several needs together.

1. **Stop measuring yourself against others.**
2. **Learn to accept yourself holistically.**
3. **Understand that *you* are in control.**
4. **Don't stop growing.**

From Green (2013) 4 Steps to Self-Actualization and Becoming the Best Version of You

How do you go about satisfying the needs and wants in your life?

Plan Your Life Like You Would a Vacation

Richard Boles (2011), in his workshops on Life Planning, frequently refers to our lives being divided into three periods. The first period is that of *getting an education;* the second period is that of *going to work and earning a living or working in the home and community;* and the third and last period is that of *living in retirement.*

One of Boles's concerns is that these periods have become more and more isolated from each other. He makes a statement you may find somewhat surprising:

> Life in each period seems to be conducted by those in charge without much consciousness of . . . never mind, preparation for . . . life in the next period.

Why plan? Setting goals gives you long-term vision and short-term <u>motivation</u>. It focuses your acquisition of knowledge, and helps you to organize your time and your resources so that you can make the very most of your life. The dictionary says a ***goal*** is an aim or purpose—a plan. You would not think of going on a vacation without some plans or goals for your trip. After all, you might get lost. Are you trying to play the game of life without goals by moving from different periods of your life without any plans or any direction?

In short, we might say that goals give purpose and meaning to our lives; they give us something to aim for, something to achieve.

Osman Abraham (2016) sums this up well: "Goals are what take us forward in life; **they are the oxygen to our dreams.** They are the first steps to every journey we take and are also our last. It's very important that you realize the significance and importance of goal-setting and apply this knowledge in your life." Osman, A. (2016)

What Is A Goal?

According to Wikipedia the exact definition of a goal is:

> A desired result a person or a system envisions, plans, and commits to achieve. A personal or organizational desired end-point in some sort of assumed development. Many people endeavor to reach goals within a finite time by setting deadlines.

In other words, any planning you do for the future, regardless of what it is, **is a goal**. So the next time you are planning on doing the weekly chores or decide on watching that really cool action movie after work, always keep in mind that these small tasks count as goals, and, while seemingly insignificant, you are goal setting.

5 Reasons Why Goal Setting Is Important

1. Goals Give You Focus

Imagine having to shoot an arrow without being given a target. Where would you aim? And say you did aim at some random thing (out of sheer perplexity). Why would you aim there? And what would the purpose be? You get the idea… This is a literal example of what life is like without a goal or target in mind. **It's pointless and a waste of energy and effort.**

You can have all the potential in the world but *without focus* your abilities and talent are useless. Just like how sunlight can't burn through anything without a magnifying glass focusing it, you can't achieve anything unless a goal is focusing your effort. At the end of the day *goals are what give you direction in life.* By setting goals for yourself you give yourself a target to shoot for. This sense of direction is what allows your **mind to focus** on a target, and, rather than waste energy shooting aimlessly, allows you to hit your target and reach your goal.

> *If you aim at nothing, you will hit it every time.*
> —ZIG ZIGLAR

2. Goals Allow You To Measure Progress

By setting goals for yourself you are able to measure your progress because you always have a fixed endpoint or **benchmark to compare with**. Take this scenario for example:

David makes a goal to write a book with a minimum of 300 pages. He starts writing every day and works really hard but along the way he loses track of how many more pages he has written and how many more he needs to write. So rather than panicking David simply counts the number of pages he has already written and he instantly determines his progress and knows how much further he needs to go.

3. Goals Keep You Locked In And Undistracted

By setting goals you give yourself mental boundaries. When you have a certain end point in mind you **automatically stay away** from certain distractions and stay focused towards the goal. This process happens automatically and subtly but according to research does happen.

To get a better idea, imagine this. Your best friend is moving to Switzerland and the flight takes off at 9:00 PM. You leave right after work at 8:30 PM and you know it's a 20-minute walk to get to the airport. So you make it a goal to reach the airport in 15 minutes by jogging so that you can have more time to say your goodbyes. Would you get distracted by "anything" along the way? Would you stop for a break or a snack? Would you stop by your house before going to the airport?

I bet you answered no for each question and at the end of the day this is what a goal gives you, **FOCUS**. No matter who you meet along the way or what you see (assuming nothing is out of the ordinary) your goal allows you to stay locked in. You subconsciously keep away from distractions and your focus remains only on the goal. And by the way if you didn't know yet this is how you become successful, you set a goal, you lock it in, and then give it your 100%.

4. Goals Help You Overcome Procrastination

When you set a goal for yourself **you make yourself accountable to finish the task.** This is in complete contrast with when you do things based on a whim and it doesn't matter whether you complete them or not. Goals tend to stick in your mind and if not completed they give you a **"Shoot! I was supposed to do that_____ today!"** reminder. These reminders in the back of your head help you to overcome procrastination and laziness.

But keep in mind that long-term goals actually promote procrastination. Most people aren't good with deadlines 3 months away. So whenever you're given a long-term goal, break it down into a several short-term goals so you can complete a chunk of the larger long-term goal every week or even every day.

5. Goals Give You Motivation

The root of all the **motivation or inspiration** you have ever felt in your entire life is goals. Goal setting provides you with the foundation for your drive. By making a goal **you give yourself a concrete endpoint to aim for and get excited about.** It gives you something to focus on and put 100% of your effort into and this focus is what develops motivation. (Abraham, 2017)

The responsibility is yours. Psychologist Angela Duckworth in her 2016 book, called *Grit*, found in her research that passion and perseverance made high achievers get what they wanted in life. They often had a determination that made them resilient and hardworking. They also knew passionately what and where (a direction) they were going. It is your responsibility to build the road to your own enrichment; you must lay the foundation. David Campbell (2007), in his thought-provoking book, *If You Don't Know Where You're Going, You'll Probably End Up Somewhere Else,* likens life to a never-ending pathway, which has many side roads or paths in the form of options which confront us along that road; these side roads or paths have gates which are open or

© CandyBox Images/Shutterstock.com

Prepare yourself so you have the tools needed to reach your goals.

closed to us. When we come to each new option, there are two factors that determine whether we continue on the same path or take a new direction: one is *credentials*, and the second is *motivation*.

If you have the credentials (such as education, training, skills), you do have an option available to you and may choose or not choose to take a new path. If you do not have the credentials, the gate remains closed at that point even if you are extremely motivated. In other words, no matter how much you may want that option, if you have not prepared for it, it is not going to be available to you.

Where will you be in 5/10/20 years? You may not know, but you probably have some dreams and ideas. Planning today will help you to go where you want to go, just like you want to get to your vacation destination, rather than drift along relying on luck or fate. Remember, do not forget to keep your options open.

Without a doubt, goals help us control the direction of change in our lives. We may have to ask ourselves quite often, "Where am I now? What are my goals? What are my plans for reaching these goals?"

Setting Your Goals: What Do You Want?

What do you want to achieve? It is important that you get to the "heart of yourself" and answer this question. Whatever is satisfying and worthy can be a goal for you

> *Planning is bringing the future into the present so that you can do something about it.*
> —ALAN LAKEIN

> *Since we are changing, having goals is a way for us to direct that change. Since we have no choice but to be older, we can choose how we intend to grow older. We can also choose to have better health or worse, more freedom or less, greater income or less, more relationships or fewer.*
> —JAMES FELDMAN

to accomplish. Therefore, no goal is *too insignificant* if it contributes to your sense of achievement. It cannot be small; only you can make it small. Living each day fully is just as important as writing a book. At any rate, you, not anyone else, must be impressed with the goals you set for your life. Richard Boles (2017) confirms this statement:

> You have got to know what it is you want, or someone is going to sell you a bill of goods somewhere along the line that can do irreparable damage to your self-esteem, your sense of worth, and your stewardship of the talents that God gave you.

Authors Covey (2013), Roger-John and McWilliams (2004), and Ziglar (2000) write of at least seven different kinds of goals:

- physical
- financial
- spiritual
- career
- family
- mental
- social

Do you have any needs, wants, or desires that could be worked on in any of the seven goal areas? Think about some of these possibilities:

- Would you like to lose some weight or improve your appearance in some way? Would you like to start a personal physical fitness program?
- Would you like to meet some new people? Would you like to do some volunteer work for non-profit organizations or become more involved in your community?
- Are you satisfied with your spiritual life? If not, what could you do to improve that element in your life?
- Have you been thinking of further developing your skills and capacities? What would you like to accomplish?
- Do you need to spend more time with your family? Do you need to reestablish a relationship with a distant family member?
- Is your financial management what it needs to be to provide for necessities and some of your wants? How can you save to buy that new car next year?
- Would you like an enjoyable, satisfying job? Have you thought of planning to make an appointment with a counselor at your school and begin some serious career counseling?

As you can see, the list of possibilities is just endless. You know what some of your wants and needs are. Are you ready to select one or more of the seven goal areas and begin to establish some serious goals? When? What is wrong with today? Do not procrastinate. There will never be a completely convenient time.

All I know is that the first step is to create the vision—that creates the <u>want</u> *power.*
—ARNOLD SCHWARZEN-EGGER

HOW TO SET SUCCESSFUL GOALS

1. **Belief.** The first step to goal setting is to have absolute belief and faith in the process. If you don't believe you can absolutely transform your life and get what you want, then you might as well forget about goal setting and do something else. If you are in doubt, look around you. Everything you can see began as a thought. Make your thoughts turn into reality.

2. **Visualize what you want.** Think of what you deeply desire in your life or where you want to be a year from now. What changes have to take place? What do you need to know or learn? What spiritual, emotional, personal, financial, social or physical properties need to be addressed? The clearer you are with each of these dimensions will bring your vision into sharp focus. The clearer you are, the easier it will be to focus on making it happen.

3. **Get it down!** Writing down your goals is key to success. By writing down your goals, you become a creator. Failure to write down your goals often means you will forget them or won't focus on them. Have them written down where you can see them every day.

4. **Purpose.** Knowing why you want to achieve your goals is powerful. Identifying the purpose of your goal helps you instantly recognize why you want that particular goal and whether it's worth working toward. Knowing why you want something furnishes powerful motivation to see it through to the finish. After all, if the purpose of earning a million dollars is to put it in the bank for a rainy day, you probably won't be as motivated as you will if you need it to pay for your child's cancer treatment.

5. **Commit.** This might sound obvious to you but it's a step that has disastrous consequences when it's taken lightly. Write a few pages about why and how you are committing to each goal; why it's important to you, what it means to you, why the outcome is necessary and what are you going to do to make it happen. Without strong commitment you aren't likely to follow through.

6. **Stay focused.** By focusing on your goals, you manifest. You may not know how you'll reach your goals but when you make a daily practice of focus, they become easier to reach. Having your goals written down somewhere where you will see them each day is a good idea. Your mind will notice that there is a discrepancy between where you are now and where you want to be which will create pressure to change. If you lose focus you can always bring it back. Without a regular practice of focusing on your goals you may be distracted by something.

7. **Plan of action.** Being really clear about what you want, knowing your purpose, writing your goals down, committing to them, and staying focused gives you the power of clarity to write down a list of action steps. You may not know all the steps ahead of time but you will know the next steps that take you in that direction. Having goals without a plan of action is like trying to complete a complex project without a project plan. There is too much going on, it's too disorganized, you miss deadlines and you don't have priorities. Eventually you get frustrated and the project/goal fails or collapses under its own weight.

8. **No Time Like the Present.** To show how committed you are to your goals, think of something you can do right now that will get you moving toward fulfilling your goals. Even if it's just making a phone call, do it now. You will be surprised how this simple step reinforces all the previous steps and gets you motivated and moving toward what you desire. If you are not motivated to do something right now, how are you going to get motivated tomorrow?

9. **Accountability.** To push through when things get tough, you have to hold yourself accountable unless you bring in outside help like a coach who provides it for you. It makes sense to have someone beside yourself who can provide valuable feedback at critical junctures, like a friend or a mentor. Telling your friends and family about your goals may give you the accountability your need.

10. **Review.** Make it part of your day to review your goals and take action. This keeps your goals alive and top of mind. It's a good time to convert the overall plan into discrete action steps that you can take throughout the week. It will also help you be aware if one goal feels stuck and you are over compensating on another goal.

By following these steps and practicing your goals each day, you have all the elements you need to succeed and achieve your goals. It isn't always easy to push through. Some days will be easier than others but if you keep focused on your goals you will be amazed at the progress you will make. Remember, almost everything begins as a thought. You can be what you imagine if you follow these simple steps. (Foster, 2015)

Independence

*Time = Life,
Therefore,
waste your time
and waste your
life, or master
your time and
master your
life.*
—ALLEN
LAKEIN

The idea of what it means to become "independent" has evolved significantly in recent generations, and new research from North Carolina State University finds that the concept of being either dependent or independent doesn't apply to almost half of young adults in the United States. Dr. Anna Manzoni (2016) found that young people fell into one of four groups—only one of which had all of the indicators of independence. That "independent" group accounted for 28 percent of young people. At the other extreme was the "dependent" group, which included people who received financial support from parents and were least likely to live on their own or think of themselves as independent. The dependent group made up 23 percent of young people. A third group, the "independent non-adults," was made up of people who were independent in terms of the objective residential and financial indicators, but who did not think of themselves as independent adults. Independent non-adults made up 24 percent of young people. The last group, called "residential dependents," were financially independent and thought of themselves as independent adults, but still lived with their parents. Residential dependents made up 25 percent of young people (Manzoni, 2016).

Contributors to Success

There are countless definitions of what success really is. **Success** has often been referred to as the progressive realization of a worthwhile, predetermined personal goal (McCullough, 2005). For example, some people define success in terms of money and material possessions. Others may feel success is found in personal relationships. Then, there are some people who believe that developing their potential in work or some particular interest defines success. We might conclude that *success* is setting a goal and achieving that goal, whatever that goal may be.

What actually contributes to success?

A sense of direction.   Your first step is accepting your true self, but the second part understands that the journey has no end point. To **self-actualize**, you must always strive to expand your horizons as a human being. To achieve success, you must always seek it. If we do not know where we are going, we will certainly end up elsewhere. There will, no doubt, be conflicting wants and needs (Green, 2013). However, we need to establish priorities and make choices. **A philosophy of life**—or rules for living and values in life—is basic to the direction we choose. Successful people know the direction in which they are moving, and why they are going there.

A feeling of self-confidence. If we desire to be successful, a belief in our abilities and our worth as a human being is extremely essential. Most of our actions, feelings, behavior, and even our abilities are consistent with the degree of self-confidence we have. Surely, we have all experienced failures, as well as successes in life. However, if we allow our failures to rule our life, we will never be able to realize our full potential. We are all imperfect. To be successful, we must learn to accept that our blunders, as well as our successes, are a part of us. Our blunders should only be remembered as guides to learning. Johnson (2012) makes this profound statement:

> A basic tenet of all individuals who wish to succeed in any endeavor is "I have to be willing to fail." You cannot learn, you cannot improve your interpersonal effectiveness, you cannot build better relationships, and you cannot try new procedures and approaches unless you are willing to accept your mistakes. You need the ability to fail. Tolerance for failure and the ability to learn from it are very specific characteristics of any highly successful person.

Certainly, feelings of successful achievement are the greatest motivation for continued success. We have all heard the statement that we can do whatever we think we can. Thus, we will never experience success unless we have confidence in ourselves. Because your performance is directly tied to the way you see yourself, real confidence in yourself is always demonstrated by action.

> *If your success is not on your own terms; if it looks good to the world but does not feel good in your heart, it is not success at all.*
> —ANNA QUINDLEN

> *It's a misnomer that our talents make us a success. They help, but it's not what we do well that enables us to achieve in the long run. It's what we do wrong and how we correct that ensures our long-lasting success.*
> —BERNIE MARCUS, FOUNDER OF HOME DEPOT

> *Maybe your life is not falling apart; maybe it's falling together. Don't fearfully hold on to what needs to end. The familiar life crumbles so the new life can begin.*
> —BRYANT MCGILL

HOW TO ACHIEVE SUCCESS

If you want to be successful, you have to take 100 percent responsibility for everything that you experience in your life. This includes the level of your achievements, the results you produce, the quality of your relationships, the state of your health and physical fitness, your income, your debts, your feelings—everything.

—JACK CANFIELD, The Success Principles (2006)

The traditional version tells us that there are two things you need to succeed: talent and hunger, or drive. I have added a third thing, and that is optimism. You can have all the talent in the world, but if you don't believe you can overcome failure, if you do not mentally rehearse success, then your talent and drive will come to nothing once you have been knocked down.
—MARTIN SELIGMAN

A healthy mental attitude. The one word that influences our life more than any other is *attitude*. This word actually controls our environment and our entire world. Actually, our life is what our thoughts make it.

Certainly, a healthy mental attitude does not imply a Pollyanna attitude toward all our problems. It simply means that we approach our problems and goals with a positive attitude. A negative attitude defeats us before we even start to work on our goals. On the other hand, a positive attitude enables us to take action toward facing our problems and obtaining our goals. Mamie McCullough (2005), author and motivational speaker, defines a positive and a negative attitude in this way: "A positive attitude says, *I can;* a negative attitude says, *I can't* or *I won't.*" Behavioral researcher Shad Helmstetter (2011) offers this thought-provoking statement:

> "No one, not one single person who was ever born on the face of this earth, was born to fail—or to automatically succeed. Through life—we tend to make choices to fail or succeed."

© *Minerva Studio/Shutterstock.com*

Do you have a positive mental attitude?

A belief in perseverance. In the game of life, you have to put something in before you can take anything out. After all, is not this what you also have to do with your checking account? Successful people *itch* for a lot in life, but they are willing to *scratch* for what they want. Therefore, we must determine how much time we are willing to give and what sacrifices we are willing to make toward the attainment of our goals. The magic word to success has been referred to as *work*—working hard and long to accomplish goals (Doskoch, 2005).

We need to remember that to give up is to invite complete defeat. Some people *quit* before they have given themselves a chance to succeed. People with a true belief in perseverance work toward their goals when encouraged and work harder when discouraged. It is very easy to give up, but much harder to continue, especially when "the going gets rough." However, nothing worthwhile has ever been accomplished the easy way.

CONSIDER THIS

The value of courage, persistence, and perseverance has rarely been illustrated more convincingly than in the life story of this man (his age appears in the column on the right):

Failed in business	22
Ran for Legislature—defeated	23
Again failed in business	24
Elected to Legislature	25
Sweetheart died	26
Had a nervous breakdown	27
Defeated for Speaker	29
Defeated for Elector	31
Defeated for Congress	34
Elected to Congress	37
Defeated for Congress	39
Defeated for Senate	46
Defeated for Vice President	47
Defeated for Senate	49
Elected to President of the United States	51

That's the record of Abraham Lincoln!

> *If we think happy thoughts, we will be happy. If we think miserable thoughts, we will be miserable. If we think sickly thoughts, we will be ill. If we think failure, we will certainly fail. Successful people succeed because they think they can attain their goal.*
> —AUTHOR UNKNOWN

> *Experience is simply the name we give our mistakes.*
> —OSCAR WILDE

> *My life has been a trade-off. If I wanted to reach the goals I set for myself, I had to get at it and stay at it every day.*
> —SAM WALTON

An understanding of others.   More than likely our goals will involve other people. As a matter of fact, it is dangerous to make goals without carefully considering the effects they could have on your family. Remember, *you do have to work around and with these folks.* Furthermore, you want to take them with you down the road to your successes.

It is important, therefore, that we learn to understand what their needs are, how they feel, and how to interact with them. Learning the art of human communication is vitally important to achieving success. Successful people rarely make it completely on their own; they have generally been encouraged by others.

Learn the lesson.   What did you do right, and what could you have done better? Take the time to review and assess the obstacles you overcame and the goals you accomplished on your journey.

In essence, people who are successful in reaching their goals have *direction, dedication, discipline, and a super-positive attitude, with realism included.*

But, will you have enough time to develop these qualities of success?

The Time in Your Life

Time presents a problem to all of us. Alec Mackenzie (2009), a time-management expert, offers some interesting insights:

> You can't save it and use it later.
> You can't elect not to spend it.
> You can't borrow it.
> You can't leave it. Nor can you retrieve it.
> You can't take it with you, either.

For example, you have been told that to be successful you must *learn to manage your time.* This is impossible. You cannot *manage time.* It is frustrating to think you can manage something over which you have absolutely no control. But you can learn to manage *yourself.*

Another false assumption is saying, "I don't have time to do that." That is probably not so. You have the time. You just do not choose to spend it in that manner. It is probably an unpleasant task that you would rather not do. That's okay. But why blame time?

Or how about, "She has more time than I do." Everybody has the same amount of time. But everybody spends it doing different things by choice or habit. David Allen, in his 2015 book, *Getting Things Done: The Art of Stress-Free Productivity,* believes "a new paradox has emerged in this new millennium: people have enhanced quality of life, but at the same time they are adding to their stress levels by taking on more than they have resources to handle."(2015, pg 4)

Becoming *Aware*

Time management is really self-management. There are several ways of looking at exactly how much time we have. For example, each of us has *twenty-four hours—1,440 minutes a day, 10,080 minutes a week, or 8,760 hours a year* to spend, invest, or fritter away. We spend time doing the maintenance tasks of life—working, eating, sleeping, and so on. We invest time in learning, creating, or loving. These time "investments" continue to pay dividends in personal satisfaction, career advancement, or fond memories. Sometimes we fritter away valuable time in activities we do not really enjoy and soon forget. Often, this is caused by our inability to say "No!" (Lakein, 2008).

Remember, you should be the master of time and not let it master you. Discovering your *time wasters* is the key to managing yourself in relation to time. The word *time waster* can be defined to mean anything preventing you from achieving your objectives most effectively. Most time wasters are self-generated. For example, do you ever procrastinate—put things off until it's too late or no longer matters? You might be surprised to learn that *procrastination* is one of the most common time management problems, or time wasters.

Establishing priorities. Take a moment and reflect on this question: What one thing could you do in your personal and professional life that, if you did it on a regular basis, would make a tremendous positive difference in your life? Now, reflect on this question: How much time are you spending in this area or on this activity?

People who accomplish the most do so not because they have more time, but because they use their time more wisely. They know that planning and goal setting are the keys to successful time management.

Stephen Covey (2013), author of the best-seller, *The 7 Habits of Highly Effective People,* teaches participants in personal leadership training groups that the essence of effective time and life management is to organize and execute around *balanced priorities.* Covey then asks his participants to consider the following: If you were to fault yourself in one of three areas, which would it be:

What are your time wasters?

1. The inability to *prioritize*
2. The inability or desire to *organize* around those priorities
3. The lack of *discipline* to execute around them, to stay with your priorities and organization

Covey says that most people believe that their main fault is *discipline.* However, Covey believes the basic problem is that people's *priorities have not become deeply planted in their hearts and minds.* In *First Things First,* Covey (1994) summarizes the importance of priorities with these words:

> *Perhaps the most valuable result of all education is the ability to make yourself do the thing you have to do when it ought to be done, whether you like it or not. It is the first lesson that ought to be learned and is probably the last lesson a person learns thoroughly.*
> —THOMAS HUXLEY

© 2013, jciphotography, Shutterstock, Inc.

Putting first things first is an issue at the very heart of life. Almost all of us feel torn by the things we want to do, by the demands placed on us, by the many responsibilities we have. We all feel challenged by the day-to-day and moment-by-moment decisions we must make regarding the best use of our time.

Decisions are easier when it's a question of "good" or "bad." We can easily see how some ways we spend our time are wasteful, mind-numbing, even destructive. But for most of us, the issue is not between the "good" and the "bad," but between the "good" and the "best." So often, the enemy of the best is the good.

$86,400

If you had a bank that credited your account each morning with $86,400, carried over no balance from day to day, allowing you to keep no cash in your account, canceling all unused funds at the end of each day, what would you do?

You have such a bank. It's called time.

Every morning, each person's account is credited with 86,400 seconds. Every night, each second not put toward a good purpose is canceled. Time carries no balance forward. Nor does time allow us to borrow against future allocations.

We can only live on today's deposit and invest our time toward the utmost health, happiness, and success.(2013, pg12)

80–20 principle. People who effectively manage their time have learned to structure their lives so that they focus most of their time and energy on what is most important to them and minimize the time they spend on activities that they do not value. They realize that the quality of their lives is enhanced when they are able to do a few things well, instead of trying to find time to do a little of everything.

You may be thinking to yourself: "All of my responsibilities are important; I can't simply drop some of them to do what I please." Have you heard of the ***80–20 principle***? Vilfredo Pareto, an Italian economist, noted that 20 percent of what we do yields 80 percent of the results. Conversely, 80 percent of what we do yields 20 percent of the results. This principle can be applied to many areas of life. For example, about 20 percent of the newspaper is worth your while to read. You are better off just skimming the rest of it. A good 80 percent of most people's mail is junk and best not read at all. Just about 80 percent of your housework can wait almost indefinitely, while 20 percent of it, if not done, would soon make your home uninhabitable (Covey, 2013 pg 164).

Becoming *Aware*

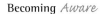

HOW TO WASTE TIME

- Procrastination
- Personal disorganization
- Lack of planning
- Poor communication
- Commuting and/or traffic delays
- Lack of self-discipline
- Not setting deadlines
- Inability to say no!
- Playing video games
- Meetings
- Excessive errands
- Watching TV
- Talking on the telephone or cell phone
- Attempting too much at once
- Leaving tasks unfinished
- Drop-in visitors
- Texting
- Facebook/Internet

Which of these time wasters create a problem for you? Which do you have control over?

> Anything less than a conscious commitment to the important is an unconscious commitment to the unimportant.
> —STEPHEN COVEY

Using time effectively is dependent on *your daily identification of priorities of the important things you have to do or want to do* (Lock, 2005 pg). You must decide what the important objectives are in your life and then establish priorities every day in relation to these objectives.

Culture and the Organization of Time

Let us assume that you have arranged to meet one of your friends for lunch at 12:30 P.M. The friend has not arrived at 12:45, 1:00, or even 1:15. Now, answer these questions: What time did you arrive? Were you "on time"? How long would you wait for your friend before you started to feel worried or annoyed?

In most parts of the United States and Canada, you would have been there pretty close to 12:30 and not waited much past 1:00. That is because these countries, along with northern European nations, are what Edward T. Hall calls **monochronic cultures**: Time is organized into linear segments in which people do one thing "at a

> What, of all things in the world, is the longest and the shortest, the swiftest and the slowest, the most neglected, and the most regretted, without which nothing can be done: TIME.
> —VOLTAIRE

time." Actually, the day is divided into appointments, schedules, and routines, and because time is a precious commodity, people do not like to "waste" time . In such cultures, therefore, it is considered the height of rudeness (or status) to keep someone waiting(Hall,ET,1959).

However, the farther south you go in Europe, South America, and Africa, the more likely you are to find **polychronic cultures**. In these cultures, time is organized along parallel lines. People do many things *at* once, and the demands of friends and family supersede those of the appointment book. As a matter of fact, people in Latin America and the Middle East think nothing of waiting all day, or even a week, to see someone. The idea of having to be somewhere "on time," as if time were more important than a person, is unthinkable. Cohen notes that "Traditional societies have all the time in the world. The arbitrary divisions of the clock face have little saliency in cultures grounded in the cycle of the seasons, the invariant pattern of rural life, community life, and the calendar of religious festivities" (Cohen, 1997, p. 34).

The differences in time orientation between the two cultural styles is summarized in Focus on Diversity—Time Orientation.

CONSIDER THIS

TIME ORIENTATION

Monochronic People	Polychronic People
Do *one* thing at a time	Do *many* things at once
Take time commitments seriously	*Consider time* commitments an objective to be achieved, if possible
Give the *job* first priority	Give *people* first priority
Adhere religiously to plans and schedules	*Change* plans and schedules often and easily
Emphasize promptness	*Care less* about own promptness than other people's needs; are almost never "on time"
Saving time *is* good	Saving time *not as* important

Which time orientation do you prefer?   Hall,Edward T. (1959)

Creating Harmony in Your Life

Think about the last time you heard a symphony orchestra play and then answer these questions: Just by chance, was there one instrument that was given so much emphasis the others simply were not heard? Was there one instrument that seemed *out of sync*? Or, were all the instruments playing in a harmonious melody?

What does a symphony orchestra have to do with your life? The important areas in your life, to which you devote your time and energy, do not exist in isolation but are very much like a symphony orchestra playing. Individual instruments (like work) sound fine, but when combined into a symphony (your life), the effect on your whole life is then multiplied. Could it be possible that you have not found a harmonious melody to play with all of the important areas in your life? Could it be possible that you might have one important "instrument" that has been given so much emphasis, that there is no way for the others to be heard? Balance is important with our lives, as with a symphony orchestra.

Stephen R. Covey, son of the late Stephen Covey, recently published a book of writings and thoughts of his father, The 12 Levers of Success.(2016) He explains that his dad, Stephen R. Covey, believed there were only two ways to experience life: primary greatness or secondary greatness. The intrinsic rewards of primary greatness are integrity, responsibility, and contribution. His father felt that primary greatness far outweighed the extrinsic rewards of secondary greatness which is money, popularity, and the self-absorbed, pleasure-ridden life that some people consider "success."(Covey, 2016 pg xviii.). He discusses the "12 Levers of Success" that you need to work on starting with integrity. (2016, pg. 51)

Your chair of life. Someone once said that each individual has a ***chair of life***. This chair contains four legs, each representing an extremely valuable part of our life. For example, the four legs might be: 1) Vocation, 2) Family and friends, 3) Avocation—interests and hobbies, and 4) Spirituality.

If we are experiencing contentment in each of these areas, we must be contributing some quality time to each of these areas. In short, *our chair of life is in balance*—there is a harmonious melody in our life. However, if one of the legs becomes longer or shorter than the others because of too much time or too little time, we feel uncomfortable, stressed, and oftentimes dissatisfied. In short, *our chair of life is out of balance*—a harmonious melody does not exist in our life.

If it is difficult for you to relate to a symphony orchestra, then find a chair with four legs and sit down for just a moment. Label each leg of the chair with the important areas of your life. To give you an example, 1) Work, 2) Family, 3) School, 4) Playing tennis with friends. Let's assume that by the time you go to school and work and spend some time with your family, you are finding little time for your favorite stress-relieving hobby—playing tennis with your friends. As a result, you are beginning to feel a little cheated. Get several books and place them under the leg of the chair representing this very important leisure activity. Now, sit down in the chair. How do you feel? Off-balance, right! Are you afraid you are going to fall over?

> One who every morning plans the priorities of the day and follows out that plan carries a thread that will guide one through the most busy life. But, where no plan is laid, where the disposal of time is surrendered merely to the chance of incidents, chaos soon reigns.
> —VICTOR HUGO

What would your chair of life look like?

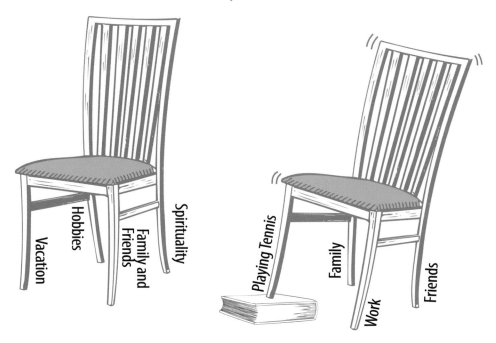

Would it be in balance or out of balance?

This is the true picture of what goes on in our life when we either direct too little or too much time to the important areas in our life. Something is "out of synch." You notice yourself getting really irritated or even depressed.

This illustration can even be used to describe a person who is so committed to the World of Work that there is little time for family life or anything else. Is the pursuit of a career worth losing the respect and admiration of your family? You will have to decide that, but here is a view from Mary Kay Ash (2008), the founder of Mary Kay Cosmetics:

> It's most fulfilling to build a successful career, but if you lose your spouse and family in the process, then, I think you have failed. Success is so much more wonderful when you have someone to share it with. It's no fun to come home and count your money by yourself.

The important thing is to learn to recognize when your chair of life is getting out of balance and take immediate action to balance your time and energy on all the important aspects of your life. Otherwise, you may lose a major portion of one or more legs of your chair of life. When this happens, your whole life is out of balance. M. Scott Peck (2003) makes a thought-provoking statement:

Mature mental health demands an extraordinary capacity to flexibly strike and continually restrike a delicate balance between conflicting needs, goals, duties, responsibilities, etc. The essence of this discipline of balancing is "giving up." ... As we negotiate the curves and corners of our lives, we must continually give up parts of ourselves since the loss of balance is ultimately more painful than the giving up required to maintain balance.

In essence, in life there are tradeoffs. There is a price to pay for what is important to you. You and you alone must decide what your trade-offs will be.

> *You need to live with a clock and a compass. The clock helps you deal with the routine issues of life. The compass sets the direction for your life and gives you a vision. It drives you to your goals.*
> —STEPHEN COVEY

RECIPE FOR SUCCESSFUL LIFE PLANNING

- Know what you want.
- Know what you are willing to give up to have what you want.
- Have a game plan.
- Go to work consistently each day on your game plan.

Effective Life Planning: It's All Up to You!

The key to successful life planning is the *willingness to take responsibility for ourselves.* It is indeed possible for us to take control of our lives in the midst of the forces around us. In a life situation, we have three choices: *change it, enjoy-tolerate it, or leave it.* To *change it,* we must change our behavior, goals, or circumstances. If we choose to *enjoy it*, we must recognize that it is our choice to stay with it, for whatever set of reasons. Then, if we choose to *leave our life situation,* we must find another environment for our energies. We must remember that feeling forced to stay with our life situation and hating it is not a viable and productive alternative.

> *Fear is a question. What are you afraid of and why? Our fears are a treasure house of self-knowledge if we explore them.*
> —MARILYN FRENCH

There are many opportunities for us to grow, to find interesting work, and to vary our lives. Actually, the freedom and opportunity to realize our potential are relatively rich and available to a relatively large proportion of people. However, we must choose to actively pursue the possibilities we do have. We cannot wait for "good things" to happen to us; we have to make them happen.

Because goals give direction and purpose to our life, goal setting should be a continuous activity throughout our lifetime. What happens in life planning is that we pause frequently to reevaluate ourselves, our goals, and our performances. As we improve in the understanding of ourselves, our wants, needs, and goals may change.

With this thought in mind, there are some questions you may want to ask yourself about the arena of life and work planning: *Who Am I? What Am I Up To Right Now? Where Am I Going? And What Difference Does It Make Anyhow?* (Corey & Corey, 2008). If we, from time to time, apply these questions to our personal objectives, our lives will be more effective, satisfying, and of course, more in balance.

But, what exactly makes a person feel satisfied and fulfilled? Have you ever asked yourself these questions: "Is there a secret to happiness?" "What would really make me happy?" We will conclude this chapter with a discussion of happiness and well-being.

Happiness and Well-Being

The question of what makes a person happy has been the subject of much speculation and increasingly more research studies. Americans have a peculiar relationship to happiness. On the one hand, we consider happiness a right, and we do everything in our power to try to possess it, most particularly in materialistic form. However, materialistic comforts by themselves have not led to lasting happiness. Having reached that conclusion, often do not see another way and retreat into our comforts, barricading ourselves from what appears to be a hostile and threatening world. And, we continue to crave a happiness that seems both deserved and yet out of reach.

What is happiness? Psychiatrist Dr. Mark Epstein (2016) believes that one reason we have so much trouble attaining happiness is that we do not even know what it is. For example, the very ways in which we seek happiness actually block us from finding it. Our first mistake is in trying to wipe out all the sources of displeasure in our lives. Ac-

What is happiness to you?

© ESB Professional/Shutterstock.com

tually, pleasure and displeasure are two sides of the same coin. We cannot have one without the other, and trying to split them off from each other only mires us more deeply in our own dissatisfaction (Kaplin, 2010). Furthermore, Harvard psychologist Daniel Gilbert discovered a deep truth about happiness: Things are almost never as bad—or as good—as we expect them to be (Flora, 2016).

Perhaps we need a neutral midpoint of emotional health. "What is that?" you may be wondering. Andrew Weil, MD, the founder and director of the Arizona Center for Integrative Medicine at the University of Arizona, defines **contentment** as an internal state of well-being that's relatively impervious to life's transient ups and downs, and is independent of what you have or don't have (Weil, 2011). For example, if you hitch your moods to something external—getting a raise, a new car, a new lover—then what happens if that goes away? Contentment, on the other hand, is an inner feeling of calm; it's not dependent on external circumstances, possessions, or an episode of good fortune. Dr. Mark Epstein believes the cultivation of mindfulness or contemplative practice is not done as much as we need to pursue happiness because *there's never enough time for contemplative practice, there's always more pressing things to attend to. The concerns of daily life are like the waves in the ocean; there are an infinite number of them, wherever you are (2016).*

 **Check this out** HOW HAPPY ARE YOU?

HOW HAPPY ARE YOU?

The Satisfaction with Life Scale was devised by University of Illinois psychologist Edward Diener, a founding father of happiness research. Since then, the scale has been used by researchers around the world (Pavot & Diener, 2008).

Indicate your agreement with each item using the following 1 to 7 scale. Total your score.
7—Strongly agree; 6—Agree; 5—Slightly agree; 4—Neither agree nor disagree; 3—Slightly disagree; 2—Disagree; 1—Strongly disagree.

_____ In most ways, my life is close to my ideal.
_____ The conditions of my life are excellent.
_____ I am satisfied with my life.
_____ So far I have gotten the important things in life.
_____ If I could live my life over, I would change almost nothing

_____ **Total Score**

Scoring
31–35—Extremely satisfied; **26–30**—Very satisfied; **21–25**—Slightly satisfied; **20**—Neutral; **15–19**—Slightly dissatisfied; **10–14**—Dissatisfied; **5–9**—Extremely dissatisfied

Most Americans score in the **21–25** range. A score above **25** indicates that you are more satisfied than most Americans are.

> *Always live your life with one dream to fulfill. No matter how many of your dreams you have realized in the past, always have a dream to go. Because when you stop dreaming, life becomes a mundane existence.*
> —SARA HENDERSON

Social psychologist David G. Myers reviews thousands of recent studies conducted worldwide in search of the key to happiness in his book, *The Pursuit of Happiness*. Dr. Myers and Pavot (2008) define **happiness** in this way: "It is a 'pervasive' sense that life is good—a state of well-being that outlasts yesterday's moment of elation, today's buoyant mood, or tomorrow's feeling of sadness." It is contentment.

Psychologists and researchers frequently refer to happiness as **subjective well-being (SWB)** and are exploring it in their labs. SWB refers to how people experience the quality of their lives and includes both emotional reactions and cognitive judgments. Psychologists have defined **happiness** as a combination of life satisfaction and the relative frequency of positive and negative affect (Myers, 2014). One discovery is that happy people show more electrical activity in the left frontal lobe of the brain, while those who tend toward sadness or depression show more right frontal lobe activity (Myers, 2014). University of Minnesota researchers Lyken and Csikszentmihalyi (2001) indicate that about 50 percent of one's satisfaction with life comes from genetic programming.

Myths and Truths about Happiness

Additional work needs to be done in refining and redefining studies of who has SWB, who does not, and why, and how to help those who do not have enough. In the process, researchers are overturning many cherished myths and coming up with surprising new findings:

- **Happiness is not an illusion or a delusion.** SWB can be measured on finite scales and is just as real as its opposite number, depression. People who define themselves as satisfied are supported in their belief by friends and family who concur. Happiness is evident in practically everything they do.
- **Happiness and marriage may go together.** Some people are happier married than divorced or single says Dr. Ed Diener (2003), researcher from the University of Illinois. Married people appear to be happier because they generally are less lonely and have roles as spouse and parent that enhance self-esteem and happiness.
- **Happiness knows no gender.** An analysis of 146 SWB studies showed a less than one percent difference in happiness between the sexes (Myers, 2014). This contradicts the popular belief that women are sadder than men. Although it is true that women are twice as likely as men to suffer from depression and anxiety, men have five times their rate of alcoholism and antisocial personalities—which evens out the happiness equation.
- **Happiness doesn't depend on age.** No particular stage of life is less happy than any other; not the tumultuous teenage years, not the "midlife crisis" period, not even the waning decades of old age. However, in face-to-face interviews with around 28,000 people ages 18 to 88, Yang (2008), a University of Chicago sociologist, in-

dicates that it does appear that people are most content between ages 60 and 86—a time when most are focusing less on achievements and more on enjoying life and relationships. Researchers from the University of Basel examined the self-reported emotions of thousands of 13- to 89-year-olds and discovered trends in how we evaluate ourselves over the lifespan. The overall forecast revealed—the older, the happier (Schreiber, 2011).

- **Wealth does not beget happiness.** Money does buy happiness, but only up to the point where it enables you to live comfortably. Beyond that, more cash doesn't boost your well-being (Kashdan, 2016).

GENDER AND YOU

QUALITY-OF-LIFE ENHANCERS

In a survey of the *Forbes* 100 wealthiest, Dr. Diener found that the privileged are not much happier, overall, than working-class folk. Money may become an avenue for something bigger and better—a way to keep score and compare. For example, you may have a lovely home, but if it sits next door to a neighbor's mansion, it may be a more a source of dissatisfaction than of happiness. Even striking it rich does not seem to have the effect of boosting a person's happiness. Studies of lottery winners reveal that the sudden euphoria experienced upon winning quickly wears off and many people want your money. What is important, though, is having enough money to buy life's necessities (Diener, 2003).

Who Is Happiest?

Drs. Diener (2003), Myers (2014), and their fellow SWB researchers have pinpointed a number of traits that seem to be shared by happy people:

> There are no small parts, only small actors.
> —CONSTANTIN STANISLAVSKI

- **Self-Esteem.** Happy people like themselves. A healthy self-esteem is positive yet realistic and provides a less fragile foundation for enduring joy. Hand in hand with self-esteem go personal identity and having a sense of purpose, accomplishment, and achievement.
- **Optimism.** Happy people are hope filled and are confident they can make things better, even when they have failed or experienced rejection in some endeavor. People who expect the best are the happiest, and they are also healthier and less vulnerable to illness.
- **Extroversion.** Happy people are more outgoing, more cheerful, and high-spirited. Extroverted people are more involved with people, have a larger circle of friends,

engage in rewarding social activities, experience more affection, and enjoy greater social support.

- **Personal Control.** Happy people believe that they choose their own destinies. You will recall from our discussion in Chapter Three, individuals with an "internal locus of control" participate in determining the contents of their lives and live more happily. Summarizing the University of Michigan's nationwide surveys, Angus Campbell (2007) commented that "having a strong sense of controlling one's life is a more dependable predictor of positive feelings of well-being than any of the objective conditions of life we have considered."

Other ingredients to happiness. Having a strong spiritual faith; having close, supportive friendships and marriages; and having work and other activities that enhance our identity and absorb us appear to be additional ingredients to happiness (Garcia, 2005). Being really happy, according to psychologist Mihaly Csikszentmihalyi (2016) is ***living in a state of flow***—that is, being totally absorbed in an activity, whether at work or play. Complete immersion in an experience could occur while you are singing in a choir, dancing, playing bridge, or reading a good book. If you <u>love</u> your job, it could happen during a complicated surgical operation or a close business deal. It may occur in a social interaction, when talking with a good friend, or while playing with a baby. Moments such as these provide flashes of intense living against the dull background of everyday life. *Flow* goes beyond mere contentment; it entails active participation, a sense of mastery, and the use of all or most of your skills. Using too few skills generates boredom, which Dr. Csikszentmihalyi warns, may be the biggest threat to happiness.

Of all the things we do, interaction with others is the least predictable. At one moment we experience flow, the next apathy, anxiety, relaxation, or boredom. Over and over, however, our findings suggest that people get depressed when they are alone, and that they revive when they rejoin the company of others. The strong effects of companionship on the quality of experience suggest that investing energy in relationships is a good way to improve life (Csikszentmihalyi, 2016).

Ways to Be Happy

Have you ever thought, I will be happy when this semester is over and I make an "A" in my Human Relations class, or when I get a new job, or meet the perfect someone with whom to share my life? But, would you like to start making happiness a habit right now? In her book, *Simple Abundance,* Sarah Breathnach (2009), writes of our need to adopt a new state of mind about happiness. She encourages us to stop thinking that things outside our control will bring us happiness.

Certainly, the semester being over and making an "A" in Human Relations, getting a new and exciting job, or finding that special someone can make us feel—at least momentarily—happier. But the magic seeds of contentment are planted deep within us—our outlook on life (McGowan, 2005). Although the pursuit of happiness is an inalienable right guaranteed by the Declaration of Independence, we have to be willing to pursue it.

In *Notes on How to Live in the World and Still Be Happy*, Hugh Prather (2011) says, "You must make the effort—the struggle to be happy now—and not first gain what you need in order to be happy." Dr. Myers (2008) agrees by saying, "happiness is less a matter of getting what you want—money, possessions, success, etc.—than of wanting what you have." He offers 10 steps to happiness, culled from his own and other psychologists' observations of how happy people live.

Ultimately, genuine happiness can only be realized once we commit to making it a personal priority in our lives.

Bonnie Ware worked in palliative care, spending time with patients who had only a few months to live. The most common regret that they expressed to her was, "I wish I'd had the courage to live a life true to myself, not the life others expected of me" (Haden, 2016).

WHAT OTHER PEOPLE THINK—ESPECIALLY PEOPLE YOU DON'T EVEN KNOW—DOES NOT MATTER. WHAT OTHER PEOPLE WANT YOU TO DO DOESN'T MATTER.

In *Life is So Good*, George Dawson (2002), who died at the age of 103, tells of how he became bored with fishing at the age of 98 and found time to do the one thing he was never able to in his younger days—he learned to read. "Don't worry about what someone else thinks," Dawson writes in his autobiography. "Just do the right thing and take pride in yourself."

Martin Seligman, founder of the "Positive Psychology" movement, which focuses on strengths rather than weaknesses, asserts that it is not happiness we should be seeking, but a "life of well-being." In Dr. Seligman's (2004; 2011) books, *Authentic Happiness* and *Flourish*, he believes a life of well-being has four parts: 1) *a pleasant life*—a life that successfully pursues the positive emotions about the present, past, and future, 2) *a good life*—using your strengths to obtain abundant gratification in the main realms of your life, 3) *a meaningful life*—using your strengths and virtues in the service of something much larger than you are, and 4) *a life of fostering good, important relationships*.

Perhaps the words of Dr. Russ Harris (2008) in his book, *The Happiness Trap*, are worth remembering:

If you are not living according to your values, you will not be happy, no matter how much you are achieving.

My advice is to live your life. Allow that wonderful inner intelligence to speak through you. The blueprint for you is to be your authentic self lies within. In some mystical way the microscopic egg that grew to be you had the program for your physical, intellectual, emotional, and spiritual development. Allow the development to occur to its fullest; grow and bloom. Follow your bliss and be what you want to be. Don't climb the ladder of success only to find it's leaning against the wrong wall. Do not let your age limit your future growth as a human being.
—BERNIE SIEGEL, 2011

Success is not to be pursued; it is to be attracted by the person we become.
—JIM ROHN

TIPS FOR HAPPINESS

Jeff Haden writes that, when planning your life, remember the bottom line—you want your plan to reflect your own vision of happiness!

Good news and bad news: Unfortunately, approximately 50 percent of your happiness, your "happiness set-point," is determined by personality traits that are largely hereditary. Half of how happy you feel is basically outside your control.

Bummer.

But, that means 50 percent of your level of happiness is totally within your control: relationships, health, career, etc. So even if you're genetically disposed to be somewhat gloomy, you can still do things to make yourself a lot happier.

Like this:
1. **Make good friends.** It's easy to focus on building a professional network of partners, customers, employees, connections, etc., because there is (hopefully) a payoff.
   But there's a way to making real (not just professional or social media) friends. Increasing your number of friends correlates to higher subjective wellbeing; doubling your number of friends is like increasing your income by 50 percent in terms of how happy you feel.
2. **Actively express thankfulness.** According to one study, couples that expressed gratitude in their interactions with each other resulted in increases in relationship connection and satisfaction the next day--both for the person expressing thankfulness and (no big surprise) for the person receiving it. (In fact, the authors of the study said gratitude was like a "booster shot" for relationships.) Of course the same is true at work. Express gratitude for an employee's hard work and you both feel better about yourselves.
3. **Actively pursue your goals.** Goals you don't pursue aren't goals; they're dreams, and dreams make you happy only when you're dreaming. Pursuing goals, though, does make you happy. According to David Niven, author of *100 Simple Secrets of the Best Half of Life*, "People who could identify a goal they were pursuing were 19 percent more likely to feel satisfied with their lives and 26 percent more likely to feel positive about them."
4. **Do what you do well.** Everyone has at least a few things they do incredibly well. Find ways to do those things more often. You'll be a lot happier. And probably a lot more successful.
5. **Give.** While giving is usually considered unselfish, giving can also be more beneficial for the giver than the receiver. Providing social support may be more beneficial than receiving it.
6. **Don't single-mindedly chase "status."** Money is important. Money does a lot of things. (One of the most important is to create choices.) But after a certain point, money doesn't make people happier. After about $75,000 a year, money doesn't buy more (or less) happiness, just many things. Chase a few experiences instead.
7. **Live the life you want to live.**

(Jeff Haden, 2016)

Breathe Easy

We have all been told to "take a deep breath." Andrew Weil, MD, recommends we take that one step further with this exercise: "4–7–8 breath." "Doing this daily will induce a feeling of serenity," says Dr. Weil (2011). Dr. Weil also adds, "Over time, it will give you greater emotional resilience—especially in hard moments."

- **Step 1.** Rest the tip of your tongue on the mouth, behind your top teeth.
- **Step 2.** Exhale completely through your mouth, with your lips slightly pursed, to make a whoosh sound.
- **Step 3.** Close your mouth and inhale deeply and slowly through your nose to a silent count of 4.
- **Step 4.** Keep your mouth closed and gently retain your breath for a silent count of 7.
- **Step 5.** Exhale slowly through your open mouth for a count of 8, making the same whoosh sound.
- **Step 6.** Repeat steps 3, 4, and 5 for a total of four breaths. Perform this twice daily for optimal results.

https://www.drweil.com/videos-features/videos/the-4-7-8-breath-health-benefits-demonstration/

> *I've learned that if you pursue happiness, it will elude you. But if you focus on your family, your friends, the needs of others, your work, and doing the very best you can, happiness will find you.*
> —AUTHOR UNKNOWN

Chapter Review

If you are going to get serious about life planning, you will have to take risks. The purpose of life planning is to be certain that the risks you take are the right ones, based on careful thought.

- **Intelligent risk taki**ng involves knowing your motivations, defining success, looking at best and worst outcomes, making a timetable, focusing on benefits, getting started, and doing what matters to you.

- Needs and drives cause us to consider life planning. A **need** is a condition that exists when we are deprived of something we want or require. When a need exists, it creates a drive that pushes (motivates) us to satisfy the need. One of the greatest insights in the field of human motivation is that satisfied needs do not motivate. It's only the unsatisfied need that motivates.

- Four fundamental human needs, according to Stephen Covey, are to live, to love, to learn, and to leave a legacy.

- Abraham Maslow's **Hierarchy of Needs** is based on the principle that there are certain survival needs that must be met before we can become concerned with the satisfaction of other needs. The hierarchy of needs encompasses: physiological, safety and security, love and belonging, self-esteem, and self-actualization, the fullest development of our potentialities.

- Our lives are divided into three periods: 1) getting an education, 2) going to work and earning a living or working in the home and community, and 3) living in retirement. It is important that we consider each period when we consider life planning. A **plan** is a goal or aim for satisfying the needs and wants of your life. In short, **goals** give purpose and meaning to our lives.

- Authorities generally write of at least seven different kinds of goals: physical, financial, spiritual, career, family, mental, and social.

- Some guidelines or criteria for identifying personal goals and making them work are: your goals must be your own, the goal must not be in conflict with one's personal value system, goals need to be specific and written down, start with short-range goals, goals must be realistic and attainable, and goals should contain specific time deadlines.

- **Success** might be defined as the progressive realization of a worthwhile, predetermined personal goal. Contributors to success are: a sense of direction, a feeling of self-confidence, a healthy mental attitude, a belief in perseverance, an understanding of others, and learn the lesson.

- A basic tenet of all individuals who wish to succeed in any endeavor is "I have to be willing to fail." And, the magic word to success has been referred to as "work"—working hard and long to accomplish goals.

- You cannot manage time, but you can learn to manage yourself within the time you have. Discovering your **time wasters**—anything preventing you from achieving your objectives most effectively—is the key to managing yourself in relation to time. The essence of effective time and life management is to organize and execute around balanced priorities. When we either direct too little or too much time to the important areas in our life, our chair of life is out of balance.

- The **80-20 principle** states that 20 percent of what we do yields 80 percent of the results; and conversely, 80 percent of what we do yields 20 percent of the results.

- In **monochronic cultures**, time is organized sequentially, and schedules and deadlines are valued over people. In **polychronic cultures**, time is organized horizontally, and people tend to do several things at once and value relationships over schedules.

- The key to successful life planning is the willingness to take responsibility for ourselves. As we take control of our lives in various situations, we have three choices: change it, enjoy/tolerate it, or leave it.

- Four questions to ask yourself about the arena of life and work planning are: 1) Who am I? 2) What am I up to? 3) Where am I going? and 4) What difference does it make anyway?
- One mistake people commonly make in seeking happiness is to try to wipe out all the sources of displeasure in their life, but we cannot have one without the other. Happiness is a sense that life is good—a state of well-being that outlasts yesterday's moment of elation, today's buoyant mood, or tomorrow's feeling of sadness. It is **contentment**.
- Psychologists have defined **happiness** as a combination of life satisfaction and the relative frequency of positive and negative affect.
- Several truths about happiness are: happiness is not an illusion or a delusion, happiness and marriage may go together, happiness knows no gender, happiness does not depend on age, and wealth does not beget happiness.
- Several traits that seem to be shared by happy people are: self-esteem, optimism, extroversion, and personal control. Having a strong spiritual faith; having close, supportive friendships and marriages; and having work and other activities that enhance our identity and absorb us into the flow appear to be additional ingredients to happiness. Living in a state of **flow** is being totally absorbed in an activity, whether at work or play, with a sense of mastery, and the use of all or most of one's skills.
- We can learn to adopt a new state of mind about happiness: making the effort to be happy now, rather than first gaining what we want or need in order to be happy.
- Contentment is the goal.
- Seligman says a **life of well-being** has four parts: a pleasant life, a good life, a meaningful life, and a life of fostering good, important relationships.
- **Breathe Easy** is an exercise suggested by Dr. Andrew Weil to induce a feeling of serenity.

Test Review Questions: Learning Outcomes

1. Explain what the Basic Law of Life means and how it applies to risk taking.
2. Explain how needs and drives cause us to consider life planning or take various directions for our life. In the field of human motivation, which needs motivate, and which needs do not motivate?
3. Explain the four fundamental human needs, as outlined by Stephen Covey.
4. Explain the concept of Maslow's Hierarchy of Needs. List and discuss the needs at each level in the hierarchy.
5. According to Richard Boles, into what three periods are our lives divided? Explain how these three periods should be considered in life planning. Discuss the purpose of goal setting.
6. List at least five different kinds of goal areas, as discussed in the text.
7. Discuss the guidelines or criteria for identifying personal goals and making them successful.
8. Explain the contributors to success. What is the magic word to success?
9. Identify and explain the significance of the basic tenet of all individuals who wish to succeed in any endeavor.
10. Explain why it is impossible to manage time. What is the essence of effective time and life management? Explain the chair of life concept. Is your chair of life in balance or out of balance—why?
11. Discuss the meaning of the 80-20 principle as it applies to establishing priorities in one's life.
12. Distinguish between monochronic and polychronic cultures in relation to the way time is organized.

13. Identify and explain the key to successful life planning. What three choices do we have as we learn to take control of our lives in various situations?

14. Discuss four questions you can ask yourself about the arena of life and work planning.

15. Define happiness, and discuss why pleasure and displeasure are "two sides of the same coin."

16. Intelligent risk taking involves which steps?

17. Explain the term, "living in a state of flow," as it relates to happiness.

18. Explain how we can learn happiness.

19. Define contentment.

20. Discuss Seligman's parts of a life of well-being. What is SWB? Define it.

21. What is the purpose of the Breathe Easy exercise suggested by Dr. Andrew Weil?

22. List three (3) characteristics of intelligent risk-taking.

Key Terms

Basic Law of Life

Chair of Life

Contentment

Drive

Esteem Needs

Flow (Living in a state of)

Goal

Happiness

Intelligent Risk Taking

Love and Belonging Needs

Maslow's Hierarchy of Needs

Monochronic Cultures

Need

Physiological Needs

Polychronic Cultures

Risk

Safety and Security Needs

Self-Actualization Needs

Success

SWB

Time Waster

80-20 Principle

Reflections: Critical Thinking

1. What risks are you afraid of taking right now in your life?

2. What are you going to have to give up to have what you want?

3. What do you think are the basic needs and wants of human beings?

4. Identify some of the needs and wants you have established right now in your life. What are you doing now to satisfy them?

5. Of Maslow's five basic needs, which one seems most important for you to satisfy right now?

6. What does success mean to you?

7. What determines success in our society?

8. Discuss this statement: Each of us becomes what we think about.

9. What is your greatest time waster? How much of your time do you spend on this activity?

10. Diagram and discuss your chair of life. Is it in balance? If not, why?

11. Discuss, giving examples, how the 80-20 principle has applied to your life.

12. What is your definition of happiness?

13. Discuss this statement: if you can't appreciate what you have, your achievements will feel hollow.
14. What would a life of well-being look like to you?
15. What is your definition of contentment?
16. What motivates you?
17. What is intelligent risk-taking?
18. What is SWB?
19. Why learn a breathing exercise?

Web Resources and Web Activities

http://greatergood.berkeley.edu/

Greater good in Action Science-based Practices for a Meaningful Life.

www.motivation123.com/

A psychological view of motivation and happiness.

http://www.mapnp.org/library/prsn_prd/decision.htm

A site designed by an expert who guides you through step-by-step decision making.

http://angeladuckworth.com/grit-scale/

The Grit Survey measures the character strength of perseverance.

The Work-Life Questionnaire measures work-life satisfaction.

http://www.ted.com/read/ted-studies/psychology

Psychology: Understanding Happiness.

www.authentichappiness.sas.upenn.edu/testcenter.aspx

Authentic Happiness Inventory measures overall happiness.

VIDEOS

http://www.upworthy.com/researchers-studied-the-ways-spending-money-can-affect-happiness-e-results-are-eye-opening?c=upw1&u=781e1b682edf6d11d917cd528b9824421641e9e5

Researchers studied the ways spending affects our happiness. The results are eye-opening.

http://www.ted.com/read/ted-studies/psychology

Psychology: Understanding Happiness TED Studies, ... study and coursework includes: positive psychology.

http://www.npr.org/2012/05/02/151881205/the-pursuit-of-happiness

"TED Radio Hour: Understanding Happiness": Being happy is a universal human yearning, but this simple goal often eludes us. If we're truly able to attain happiness, then how do we find it? Three TED speakers offer some big ideas for achieving happiness.

http://www.ted.com/talks/robert_waldinger_what_makes_a_good_life_lessons_from_the_longest_study_on_happiness/transcript?language=en

What makes a good life? Lessons from the longest study on happiness.

http://links.upworthy.mkt5937.com/ctt?kn=8&ms=MTIyNjkyNzQS1&r=NzM1NjU0NTc2NTcS1&b=0&-j=NTgzNjM3Njk0S0&mt=1&rt=0

Here are 5 things you may regret at the end of your life, from a nurse who works with the dying.

https://www.ted.com/speakers/angela_lee_duckworth

Angela Duckworth explains her theory of Grit.

http://www.upworthy.com/science-found-4-categories-of-independence-in-young-adults-where-do-you-belong?c=upw1&u=781e1b682edf6d11d917cd528b9824421641e9e5

Science found 4 categories of independence in young adults. Where do you belong?

https://www.youtube.com/watch?annotation_id=annotation_385315229&feature=iv&src_vid=NUslk-3jiooU&v=yux_m8AdzwY

Personal goal setting video: How to set SMART goals to boost confidence and achieve your dreams.

http://www.ted.com/talks/emilie_wapnick_why_some_of_us_don_t_have_one_true_calling

Career coach Emilie Wapnick celebrates the "multipotentialite": those of us with many interests, many jobs over a lifetime, and many interlocking potentials.

https://www.youtube.com/watch?v=HTfYv3IEOqM

Daniel Goleman on Focus: The secret to high performance and fulfillment.

http://www.ted.com/read/ted-studies/psychology

https://www.drweil.com/videos-features/videos/the-4-7-8-breath-health-benefits-demonstration/

Breathing exercise for better health

Name _____ Date _____

Your Life's Activities

PURPOSE

To demonstrate how your activities make up your life.

INSTRUCTIONS

1. Divide the circle on the left, as a pie, into parts that represent your current life. Label each part: for example, home life, work, personal, education, leisure, and whatever else represents your current life.
2. Divide the circle on the right into parts that represent your life three years ago. Use the same labeling as in the first circle or add others as needed.
3. For the third circle, divide it in a way that represents the ideal way you'd like your life to be. Label each part as in previous circles.

Current Life

Three Years Ago

Ideal Life

4. Complete the answers to the questions below and be prepared to discuss them in small groups.

DISCUSSION

Let us compare and contrast the three circles.

1. What is keeping your present circle of activities from being like the ideal circle?

2. What can you do within the next six months to make the ideal circle like your real life?

3. Is your ideal circle realistic for you? Why or why not?

4. What did you learn about yourself from this activity?

Name _____ Date _____

What Do You Want?

PURPOSE

To establish three sets of goals and to examine what you are really working toward accomplishing.

INSTRUCTIONS

1. Write down what goals you would like to accomplish in the following areas. If you do not have a goal in a particular area, that is okay. You decide.

    FAMILY:

    a.

    b.

    PHYSICAL:

    a.

    b.

    MENTAL:

    a.

    b.

    SOCIAL:

    a.

    b.

    SPIRITUAL/RELIGIOUS:

    a.

    b.

    FINANCIAL:

    a.

    b.

    CAREER:

    a.

    b.

2. Next, select the three things you want most to accomplish within the next six months.

    a.

    b.

    c.

3. Now, select from your goals the three things you want most to accomplish in the next year.

    a.

    b.

    c.

4. Now, select your three most important life goals.

    a.

    b.

    c.

5. Write down why you want to achieve the goals. List all the ways you will personally benefit from achieving the goals.

    a.

    b.

    c.

6. Now, write down anything, large or small, you have done within the past month to accomplish any of these goals.

DISCUSSION

1. Are you presently working toward what you say is important to you? If not, why?

2. Do you really want these things?

3. Review the seven areas of possible goals and write down what goals you really want to start working on now.

Lifeline

PURPOSE

To take a look at where you have been, where you are, and where you want to go.

INSTRUCTIONS

1. If done in class, on a piece of heavy poster board or construction paper, start with the year in which you were born and depict the significant experiences and people who have helped shape your life.
2. Your lifeline will be dated in terms of the years these significant experiences or people appeared in your life.
3. Make notations above or below each year to remind you of exactly what occurred.
4. When completed, your lifeline will appear like a graph: "highs and lows," "hills and valleys," and "steady" periods of your life. You may use pictures, words, or whatever you wish to depict these significant time periods in your life.
5. The last dot on your lifeline should be on a "hill," a high point in the future. Fantasize and jot some words down to describe what you would like to have happen in your life in the next five or ten years. What will you be doing, where will you be, and who will be with you?
6. After you have completed your lifeline, you will divide into small groups and explain your lifeline. Be prepared to give a 3 to 5 minute presentation.

DISCUSSION

1. How do you feel about the quality of your life at the present time?

2. What experiences are primarily responsible for where you are today?

3. What experiences are primarily responsible for what you want to accomplish in the future?

4. What goals are implied as you picture yourself 5 to 10 years in the future?

My Future Autobiography

PURPOSE

To think about the quality of your life and to demonstrate that you still have a life ahead with which to do whatever you choose.

INSTRUCTIONS

1. In the space below, write at least a two or three paragraph autobiography for yourself. Include things that you would like to have said or written about you near the end of your life. Write about things that you would like to accomplish and what contributions you want to make. Write about what character strengths you want to have and what qualities you want to develop.

2. Have someone else read your autobiography and complete the first discussion question.

DISCUSSION

1. What long-range goals are implied in this autobiography? Write them below, even if they are vague.

2. Do you see any similarity in the goals implied here and in the goals you listed in the previous activity?

Goal Development

PURPOSE

To further understand yourself and to define your goals.

INSTRUCTIONS

1. List your strengths, based on questionnaires, personal assessments, assignments, and personal experiences gained in or out of class this term.

2. List your weaknesses, based on questionnaires, personal assessments, assignments, and personal experiences gained in or out of class this term.

3. Re-evaluate your responses to the exercises in this chapter and what you now know about yourself. List the five most important things in your life at the present time.

    a.

    b.

    c.

    d.

    e.

4. Review your lifeline and what you know about yourself and list at least three peak experiences that have been meaningful to you.

   a.

   b.

   c.

5. What other peak experiences would you like to have in the future?

6. Review your autobiography and your lifeline and list the tentative goals implied in each activity.

7. Review your responses to the activity "What Do You Want?" and your responses to the previous questions in this activity and write down at least three goals that you want to start working on now.

   MY GOALS:

   a.

   b.

   c.

Name _____ Date _____

Goal Project

PURPOSE

To develop a plan of action for what you want to accomplish.

INSTRUCTIONS

1. From the previous exercise, select two goals and develop a plan of what you can do this next year to achieve these goals.

Goal Number One

1. I want to

2. What obstacles must I overcome?

3. How do I plan to overcome these obstacles? Be specific.

4. What behaviors must I change?

5. How do I plan to change these behaviors? Be specific.

6. When will I achieve this goal? Be specific.

Goal Number Two

1. I want to _____

    _____

2. What obstacles must I overcome?

3. How do I plan to overcome these obstacles? Be specific.

4. What behaviors must I change?

5. How do I plan to change these behaviors? Be specific.

6. When will I achieve this goal? Be specific.

DISCUSSION

1. How do you feel about the goal project you have just completed?

Name _____ Date _____

Life Planning

LEARNING JOURNAL

Select the statement below that best defines your feelings about the personal value or meaning gained from this chapter and respond below the dotted line.

I learned that I . . .   I was surprised that I . . .

I realized that I . . .   I was pleased that I . . .

I discovered that I . . .   I was displeased that I . .

....

Glossary

5-to-1 Ratio A five-to-one ratio of positive interactions to negative interactions is vital to a happy relationship.

80-20 Principle 20 percent of what we do yields 80 percent of the results; and conversely 80 percent of what we do yields 20 percent of the results.

Accommodating Strategy A lose-win strategy where individuals attempt to resolve the conflict by passively giving in to the other party.

Acting A process of clarifying values, whereby an individual follows a pattern of taking action on a chosen value.

Active Listening Seeing the expressed idea or problem from the speaker's point of view.

Advising Response Responding to others by offering a solution.

Agreeableness One of the "big five" dimensions of personality: ranges from good-natured, cooperative, trusting at one end to irritable, suspicious, uncooperative at the other.

Aggression Any behavior that is intended to hurt someone, either verbally or physically.

Aggressive Moving against another with an intent to hurt.

Alarm Stage The stage where the body recognizes the stressor and prepares for fight or flight, which is done by a release of hormones from the endocrine glands.

Anger The feeling of extreme displeasure, usually brought about by interference with our needs or desires.

Annoyance A mild form of anger.

Anxiety An unpleasant, threatening feeling that something bad is about to happen; the basis of the fear is not generally understood.

Assertiveness Response to conflict situations that involves standing up for yourself, expressing your true feelings, and not letting others take advantage of you; however, assertiveness involves being considerate of others' feelings.

Assume or Assumptions in Communication To accept as fact without any evidence of proof.

Attentive Listening One of the four levels of normal listening; paying attention and focusing energy on the words that are being said.

Attitudes Positive or negative orientations toward a certain target.

Attribution Error The tendency to overemphasize internal explanations of other people's behavior.

Attribution Theory An explanation that suggests we frequently overestimate the influence of an individual's personality and underestimate the impact of his or her situation.

Autonomy vs. Doubt Erikson's psychosocial crisis at the second stage of the human life cycle; the two- and three-year-old develops independence and self-reliance in proportion to positive parental encouragement and consistency of discipline.

Avoidance Response to conflict situations that involves being passive and removing yourself from the conflict.

Avoiding Strategy A lose-lose strategy where individuals attempt to passively ignore the conflict rather than resolve it.

Basic Law of Life For everything you get in life, you also have to give up something.

Behavioral Contract An agreement (commitment) made to change your behavior.

Belief The acceptance of some thought, supposition, or idea.

Blended Families A family system consisting of stepchildren and stepparents.

Blind Area of Johari Window Information about you of which you are unaware but is easily apparent to others.

Body Leakage Where body postures rather than the face leak the truth.

Broken-Record Technique Calmly repeating your assertive message without getting sidetracked by irrelevant issues.

Categorizing Placing people into groups—by race, sex, physical attractiveness, height, etc.

Catharsis An emotional release through talking.

Chair of Life An analogy, representing four valuable parts of life. The "chair" (our life) can either be in balance or out of balance, based on the amount of time we devote to each of these important parts of life.

Character Composed of personal standards of behavior, including honesty, integrity, and moral strength.

Character Ethic A style of living based on principles and values rather than on techniques.

Character Trait An enduring characteristic of a person that is related to moral and ethical behavior and shows up consistently.

Choosing Freely Consciously and deliberately making a value choice without any pressure from significant others.

Classical Conditioning A type of learning in which a neutral stimulus acquires the capacity to evoke a response that was originally evoked by another stimulus.

Closed Questions Questions that often result in yes, no, or a very short response.

Codependent Relationship A dependency on people—on their moods, behavior, sickness, well-being, and their love.

Cognitive Dissonance A concept (theory) that accounts for reactions to inconsistencies in attitudes and beliefs.

Cognitive Restructuring The process of modifying thoughts, ideas, and beliefs.

Cognitive Theory Our mental processes turn our sensations and perceptions into organized impressions of reality.

Cohabitation A situation in which couples live together outside of marriage.

Collaborating Strategy A win-win strategy where parties attempt to jointly resolve the conflict with the best solution agreeable to all parties.

Collaborative Problem Solving The win-win approach to conflict resolution whereby conflicts are resolved with no one winning and no one losing. Both win because the solution must be acceptable to both.

Collectivism Putting group goals ahead of personal goals and defining one's identity in terms of the groups to which one belongs.

Commitment A joint decision to begin a relatively long-lasting, more intimate relationship that to some extent excludes other close intimate relationships.

Communication The process of conveying feelings, attitudes, facts, beliefs, and ideas between individuals, either verbally or nonverbally, and being understood in the way intended.

Communication Barriers Things that stop, block, prevent, or hinder the communication process.

Communication Channels The medium through which a message passes from sender to receiver.

Communication Process A process involving three parts: 1) a sender of the message, 2) a receiver of the message, and 3) the content of the message.

Companionate Love Commitment and intimacy, but no passion.

Compensation This involves efforts to overcome imagined or real inferiorities by developing one's abilities.

Competing/Forcing Strategy A win-lose strategy where an individual uses aggressive behavior to satisfy one's own needs at the expense of the other person.

Complementary Needs One person's strengths compensate for the others' weaknesses.

Compromising Strategy A lose-lose strategy that attempts to resolve the conflict through assertive give-and-take concessions or cooperation.

Conditioned Response (CR) A learned reaction to a conditioned stimulus that occurs because of previous conditioning.

Conditioned Stimulus (CS) A previously neutral stimulus that has, through conditioning, acquired the capacity to evoke a conditioned response.

Confidant A significantly close personal friend with whom one can safely share one's deepest concerns and joys.

Conflict An expressed struggle between at least two people who perceive the situation differently and are experiencing interference from the other person in achieving their goals.

Conflicting Stimuli Things that are in conflict with your beliefs and values.

Conscientiousness One of the "big five" dimensions of personality: ranges from well organized, careful, responsible at one end to disorganized, careless, unscrupulous at the other.

Consequences The results of your behavior—positive reinforcement, negative reinforcement, or punishment.

Consummate Love Commitment, intimacy, and passion.

Contentment An internal state of well-being that's independent of what you have or don't have, or life's ups and downs.

Cooperativeness The degree to which one is concerned about maintaining the relationship or satisfying the concern of others in conflict resolution.

Coping Refers to active efforts, either positive or negative, to master, reduce, or tolerate the demands created by problems and/or stress.

Cultural Display Rules in Emotions Norms about when, where, and how much individuals from different cultures should show emotions.

Daily Hassles Irritating and frustrating incidents that occur in our everyday interactions with the environment.

Debilitative Emotions Emotions that prevent a person from functioning effectively.

Decoding The process in which a receiver attaches meaning to a message.

Defense Mechanisms Behavior patterns used to protect one's feelings of self-esteem and self-respect.

Delight The earliest pleasant reaction (emotion), appearing in the form of smiling, gurgling, and other babyish sounds of joy.

Denial A defense used when we refuse to recognize or acknowledge a threatening situation.

Desensitization Method of behavioral modification whereby the individual's fear of an object or person is replaced by relaxation.

Displacement A defense used when the person redirects strong feelings from one person or object to another that seems more acceptable and less threatening.

Distress Negative or harmful stress that causes a person to constantly readjust or adapt.

Divorce A complete, legal breaking up of a marriage.

Domination An aggressive technique of resolving conflict, characterized by moving against another with the intent to hurt.

Door Openers Short responses inviting the other person to share his/her ideas, judgments, or feelings.

Double Bind in Communication A situation in which the nonverbal message contradicts the verbal message.

Drive An internal tension or force that pushes (motivates) us to satisfy a need.

Ego The rational, logical, and realistic part of the personality that attempts to maintain balance between the id and superego.

Emotional Attachments Feelings that there is someone around to take care of us or help us out.

Emotional Bank Account Continuing to make small, everyday sacrifices and making efforts to notice and appreciate the kindness of your partner.

Emotional Debt A condition of imbalance in which feelings are trapped instead of expressed.

Emotional Intelligence The ability to monitor, access, express, and regulate one's own emotions; the capacity to identify, interpret, and understand others' emotions; and the ability to use this information to guide one's thinking and actions.

Emotion-Packed Phrases Phrases that, when combined with different mood levels, can cause an individual to verbally react in inappropriate ways.

Emotions Feelings that are experienced.

Empathetic Listening The fifth level, known as the highest form of listening to others; listening with the intent to understand. (See Active Listening and the Understanding Response.)

Empathy An active process in which you try to learn all you can about another person rather than having only a superficial awareness.

Empty Love A form of love that includes commitment, but no intimacy or passion.

Encoding The process of putting thoughts into symbols—most commonly words.

Envy The thoughts and feelings that arise when our personal qualities, possessions, or achievements do not measure up to those of someone relevant to us.

Esteem Needs The need to feel worthwhile, which is often satisfied by maintaining a healthy self-image, through status, prestige, a good reputation, or titles; also referred to as one of Maslow's Hierarchy of Needs.

Ethics Our standards of conduct or behavior.

Eustress Good stress or short-term stress that strengthens individuals for immediate physical activity, creativity, and enthusiasm.

Exhaustion Stage In a three-stage reaction to stress, the stage in which continuous stress will not enable the important resistance step to take place, and an individual will go from step one, alarm, directly to step three, exhaustion.

Expectations The perceived possibilities of achieving a goal.

Explanatory Style The story you construct about why things happen.

Exposure Effect A phenomenon that states the more we are exposed to novel stimuli, a new person, or a new product, our liking for such stimuli increases.

External Locus of Control A characteristic of individuals who see their lives as being beyond their control; they believe what happens to them is determined by external forces—whether it be luck or fate, or other people.

External Noise Includes such elements in the physical environment as temperature, a show on television, music on a stereo, loud traffic, or any other external event or distracting influences.

Extraversion One of the "big five" dimensions of personality: ranges from sociable, talkative, fun-loving at one end to sober, reserved, cautious at the other.

Extraversion (E) or Introversion (I) A preference on the MBTI covering how you get energized as a person.

Facilitative Emotions Emotions that contribute to effective functioning.

Fatuous Love Commitment and passion, but no intimacy.

Fear The feeling associated with expectancies of unpleasantness.

Feedback The process by which the sender clarifies how his or her message is being received and interpreted.

First Impressions One of the factors that seems to influence our social perceptions. (See Social Perceptions.)

Flow (living in a state of) Being totally absorbed in an activity, whether at work or play, with a sense of mastery, and the use of all or most of one's skills.

Forgiveness A healing process involving six stages, whereby painful past experiences are put into perspective and one gets on with life, unencumbered by excess emotional baggage.

Friend A person attached to another by respect or affection.

Full Value A value that meets all of the criteria that have been established by Value Clarification theorists.

Gay/Lesbian Relationships Homosexual relationships.

General Adaptation Syndrome The stages of a chain of reactions to stress.

Generativity vs. Self-Absorption Erikson's psychosocial crisis at the seventh stage of the human life cycle; conflict between concern for others and concern for self.

Genuineness This means being honest and open about one's feelings, needs, and ideas—being what one really is without front or facade.

Goal An aim or purpose—a plan.

Good Grief The process of working through the stages of grief so that it becomes a positive growth experience.

Grief and Bereavement To be deprived of someone or something very important; sometimes referred to as mourning.

Grief Work The process of freeing ourselves emotionally from the deceased and readjusting to life without that person.

Guilt The realization of sorrow over having done something morally, socially, or ethically wrong.

Happiness A sense that life is good—a state of well-being that outlasts yesterday's moment of elation, today's buoyant mood, or tomorrow's feeling of sadness.

Hardiness A cluster of characteristics that seem to distinguish stress-resistant people from those who are more susceptible to its harmful effects. These characteristics are commitment, control, and challenge.

Hate May be thought of as intense anger felt toward a specific person or persons.

Hearing The physiological sensory process by which auditory sensations are received by the ears and transmitted by the brain.

Hidden Agenda Entering a conversation or situation with a special interest in mind, a grudge that we are wanting to bring into the open, or even a "chip on our shoulder."

Hidden Area of Johari Window Information and personal feelings that you keep hidden from others.

High-Context Culture Those cultures that value self-restraint, avoid confrontation, rely heavily on nonverbal systems, and give a great deal of meaning to the relationships between communicators. Examples are the Japanese, Chinese, Asian, and Latin American cultures.

Honeymoon Period Any time from the wedding day to a year or so from that day.

Hostility A mild form of anger/hate directed to a specific person or group.

Hyperstress An overload that occurs when stressful events pile up and stretch the limits of a person's adaptability.

Hypostress An overload that occurs when a person is bored, lacking stimulation, or unchallenged.

"I" Message A message that describes the speaker's position without evaluating others.

Id The part of the personality composed of the basic biological drives that motivate an individual.

Identity vs. Role Confusion Erikson's psychosocial crisis at the fifth stage of the human life cycle, in which the 12- to 18-year-old adolescent must integrate his experiences to develop a sense of ego identity.

Ignoring while Listening One of the four levels of general listening, better known as not really listening at all.

Immune System The body's defense and surveillance network of cells and chemicals that fight off bacteria, viruses, and other foreign or toxic substances.

Impression Management Our conscious efforts to present ourselves in socially desirable ways.

Individualism Putting personal goals ahead of group goals and defining one's identity in terms of personal attributes rather than group memberships.

Individuation The establishment of one's identity, based on experiences, rather than following parents' dreams.

Industry vs. Inferiority Erikson's psychosocial crisis at the fourth stage of the human life cycle; the 6- to 11-year-old whose curiosity is encouraged develops a sense of industry, as opposed to the child whose curiosity is disparaged and who develops a sense of inferiority.

Infatuation An irrational feeling or passion for someone or something. Passion, but no commitment or intimacy.

Inferiority Complex A concept that underlies and motivates a great deal of human behavior. A striving for superiority is a universal drive to adapt, improve oneself, and master life's challenges.

In-Group—Out-Group Bias Refers to our tendency to perceive people differently depending on whether they are members of our in-group or out-group.

Initial Response Level Every response of the targeted behavior that occurs within a specific period of time prior to conditioning.

Initiative vs. Guilt Erikson's psychosocial crisis at the third stage of the human life cycle; the 4- or 5-year-old either is encouraged to go out on his own or is restricted in his activities.

Integrity This is exhibited when you achieve congruence between what you know, what you say, and what you do.

Integrity vs. Despair Erikson's psychosocial crisis at the eighth stage of the human life cycle; a response that depends on how an old person remembers his life.

Intense Emotions Emotions that are debilitative—they disrupt our overall functioning.

Interactional Possibilities Considering the situation and the possible options before making a response.

Internal Locus of Control The state in which individuals who feel that what happens to them and what they achieve in life is due to their own abilities, attitudes, and actions.

Internal Noise Includes such things as a headache, lack of sleep, daydreaming, preoccupation with other problems, or even a preconceived idea that the message is going to be unimportant or uninteresting.

Internal Psychological Filter A filter through which all information received is processed. This filter consists of prejudices, past experiences, hopes, and anxieties.

Interpersonal Relations Our interactions with others—how they relate to us and how we relate to them.

Interpretative Response A response in which the receiver tries to tell the sender what his or her problem really is and how the sender really feels about the situation.

Intimacy The feeling that one can share all of one's thoughts and actions with another.

Intimacy vs. Isolation Erikson's psychosocial crisis at the sixth stage of the human life cycle; the young adult either is able to relate to others or feels isolated.

Intimate Distance One of Hall's four distance zones, ranging from skin contact to 18 inches.

Irrational Beliefs Beliefs that result in inappropriate emotions and behaviors.

Jealousy The state of demanding complete devotion from another person; being suspicious of a rival or of one believed to enjoy an advantage.

Johari Window A model that describes the relationship between self-disclosure and self-awareness.

Judging Response A response that shows that the receiver is making a judgment about the motive, personality, or reasoning of the sender.

Judgment (J) or Perception (P) A preference on the MBTI covering the kind of lifestyle you prefer to live.

Kinesics The science of study of nonverbal communication.

Law of Effect Behaviors followed by possible consequences are more likely to be repeated and behaviors followed by negative consequences are less likely to be repeated.

Learned Helplessness The assumption—based on past failures—that one is unable to do anything to improve one's performance or situation and gives up.

Learned Optimism A learned way of explaining both good and bad life events that in turn enhance our perceived control and adaptive responses to them.

Learning A relatively permanent change in behavior as a result of experience or practice.

Liking A fondness or preference for someone or something. Intimacy, but no commitment or passion.

Listening An intellectual and emotional process that integrates physical, emotional, and intellectual inputs in a search for meaning and understanding.

Listening with the Third Ear Listening to what is said between the lines and without words, what is expressed soundlessly, and what the speaker feels and thinks.

Living Together Loneliness (LTL) The results of a discrepancy between expected and achieved contact.

Loneliness A feeling of longing and emptiness, which is caused by the lack of emotional attachments and/or social ties.

Lose-Lose An approach to conflict resolution whereby neither party is happy with the outcome.

Lose-Win The result of the accommodating strategy in conflict resolution, with low concern for self and a high concern for others.

Love When the satisfaction, security, and development of another person is as important to you as your own satisfaction, security, and development (Harry Stack Sullivan); also referred to as the desire to see another individual become all they can be as a person—with room to breathe and grow.

Love and Belonging Needs The need to feel loved, included, and accepted; this need usually assumes importance after the safety and survival needs have been met; also referred to as one of Maslow's Hierarchy of Needs.

Low-Context Culture Those cultures that use more explicit language, are more direct in their meanings, rely less on nonverbal systems, and stress goals and outcomes more than relationships. Examples are the German, Swedish, American, and English cultures.

Lust An intense physiological attraction for another person.

Marriage A close union of two people who decide to share their lives, dreams, and goals with each other.

Maslow's Hierarchy of Needs The arrangement of needs in order of basic importance as established by Abraham Maslow: physiological needs, safety needs, belongingness and love needs, esteem needs, and self-actualization needs.

Matching Hypothesis A concept that proposes that people of similar levels of physical attractiveness gravitate toward each other.

Mere-Exposure Effect The more familiar we become with someone or something the more accepting we will become.

Microexpressions Fleeting facial expressions that last only a fraction of a second.

Mid-Life Crisis Occurring somewhere between the ages of 40 and 45; may be characterized by a painful and disruptive struggle with one's identity and satisfaction of personal needs.

Mid-Life Transition Stage One of Levinson's developmental stages occurring between the ages of 40 and 45; characterized as the period when individuals realize their life is half over and they reevaluate their life and what they want out of the remainder of their life.

Mild Emotions Emotions that are facilitative—they assist us in preparing for the future, solving problems, and in doing what is best for us.

Minimal Encourages Brief indicators to the speaker indicating that the receiver is still listening.

Mixed Emotions Emotions that are combinations of primary emotions. Some mixed emotions can be expressed in single words (that is awe, remorse), whereas others require more than one term (that is, embarrassed and angry, relieved and grateful).

Modeling Imitating a behavior one observes.

Monochronic Cultures Cultures in which time is organized sequentially; schedules and deadlines are valued over people.

Moods A general feeling tone.

Morality Includes a set of principles or ideals that help a person distinguish right from wrong and act on this distinction.

Move Against Being aggressive and responding to conflicting situations with the intent to hurt.

Moving Toward Responding to conflicting situations by moving toward your opposition until you are either closer together or on the same side.

Mutual Reward Theory (MRT) States that a relationship between two people is enhanced when there is a satisfactory balance of rewards between them.

Myers-Briggs Type Indicator (MBTI) A questionnaire consisting of 16 basic personality types and four dimensions.

Narcissism The tendency to regard oneself as grandiosely self-important.

Need A condition that exists when we are deprived of something we want or require.

Negative Reinforcement Anything that increases a behavior by virtue of its termination or avoidance.

Neurotic Anxiety Anxiety experienced when the quality of the threatening experience is blown out of proportion to the actual danger posed, and to the point that the anxiety hinders daily functioning.

Neuroticism One of the "big five" dimensions of personality: ranges from calm, secure, and self-satisfied at one end to anxious, insecure, self-pitying at the other.

Neutral Stimulus (NS) Classical conditioning begins with a stimulus that does not elicit a response. The neutral stimulus will eventually become the conditioned stimulus (CS).

Noise Anything that interferes with communication and distorts the impact of the message.

Nonverbal Communication Messages expressed by other than linguistic means.

Novel Stimuli People, places, or things that are new, different, unique, or original.

Observational Learning Learning that occurs when an individual's behavior is influenced by the observation of others—modeling.

One-Way Communication Communication in which a receiver provides no feedback to a sender.

Open Area of Johari Window An area that represents information, feelings, and opinions that you know about yourself and that others know about you.

Open Communicator One who is willing to seek feedback from others and to offer information and personal feelings to others.

Openness Trust and mutual sharing of information and feelings.

Openness Trait One of the "big five" dimensions of personality: ranges from imaginative, sensitive, intellectual, at one end to down-to-earth, insensitive, crude at the other end.

Open Questions Questions that provide space for the speaker to explore his or her thoughts.

Operant Conditioning Conditioning based on the principle of reinforcement; the consequences of a response determine whether that response will persist.

Operant Level The number of responses prior to conditioning or baseline of behavior prior to conditioning.

Optimism A general tendency to envision the future as favorable.

Optimistic Explanatory Style Using external, unstable, and specific explanations for negative events.

Paralinguistics Nonlinguistic means of vocal expression: tone, rate, pitch, and so on.

Paraphrase Stating the essence of the other person's spoken words in your own words.

Parenthood The role of being a mother or father.

Parroting To repeat exactly the speaker's words.

Partial Lose-Lose The result of the compromising strategy in conflict resolution, where nobody gets all that he or she wants, but everyone gets something.

Parts of a Communication Transaction Six steps commonly referred to as the idea, encoding, transmission, receiving, decoding, and understanding.

Passion An intense physiological desire for another person.

Passive Avoiding or removing yourself from the conflicting situation by leaving, shutting up, placating, concealing your feelings, or postponing a confrontation until a better time.

Passive Listening See One-Way Communication.

People Perception The study of how we form impressions of others.

Perceptual Awareness Process The means by which we interpret or misinterpret the world around us.

Personal Distance One of Hall's four distance zones, ranging from 18 inches to 4 feet.

Personality Ethic A style of living based on having the right image and doing the right things, defined by the right kind of special techniques and a positive mental attitude.

Personality Fit The process of being attracted to another person because the differences in one person's strengths compensate for the other person's weaknesses.

Personal Self-Image The part of the self that includes physical, behavioral, and psychological characteristics that establish uniqueness.

Pessimism A general tendency to envision the future as unfavorable.

Pessimistic Explanatory Style Using internal, stable, and global explanations for negative events.

Physical Attractiveness Our perception of the beauty of another person.

Physiological Needs Our most basic and fundamental needs, such as food, water, sleep, clean air to breathe, exercise, and sex; also called our primary or survival needs; also referred to as one of Maslow's Hierarchy of Needs.

Pillow Method A technique used to gain empathy and understanding of another's position and frame of reference when disagreements exist.

Polychronic Cultures Cultures in which time is organized horizontally; people tend to do several things at once and value relationships over schedules.

Positive Reinforcement Anything that increases a behavior by virtue of its presentation.

Pot of Self-Worth Virginia Satir's view of how much self-worth we have at any given time; the amount in the pot is constantly changing based on the different experiences we have, as well as the feedback we get from others.

Prejudice A preconceived opinion, feeling, or attitude, either positive or negative, which is formed without adequate information.

Preparation Anxiety Anxiety that helps individuals get energized to deliver their best, such as mild tension before going for a job interview.

Pretending while Listening One of the four levels of normal listening. Some examples are "Yeah. Uh-huh. Right."

Primacy Effect Occurs when the first impression carries more weight than subsequent information.

Primary Emotions Basic emotions identified by R. Pluchick as joy, acceptance, fear, surprise, sadness, disgust, anger, and anticipation; identified by Gary Emery and James Campbell as mad, sad, glad, and scared.

Primary Reinforcers Reinforcers to which we respond automatically, without learning (food, drink, heat, cold, pain, physical comfort or discomfort).

Prizing Cherishing and being happy with the choice (value), as well as being willing to affirm the choice (value) publicly.

Projection A defense mechanism used when an individual attributes their own feelings, shortcomings, or unacceptable impulses to others.

Proximity Geographical nearness, location.

Psychological Reactance The tendency to protect or restore one's sense of freedom or social control, often by doing the opposite of what has been demanded.

PTSD A severe anxiety disorder characterized by symptoms of intense fear and avoidance behavior, resulting from an unusually distressing event.

Public Distance One of Hall's four distance zones, ranging outward from 12 feet.

Punishment Anything that decreases a behavior by virtue of its presentation.

Questioning Response A response that indicates that the receiver wants to probe the sender for additional information and to discuss the issue further.

Rage Uncontrolled, intense anger and implies that the anger is expressed through violent physical activity.

Rational Beliefs Beliefs that result in appropriate emotions and behaviors.

Rationalization A defense mechanism consisting of reasonable, rational, and convincing explanations, but not real reasons.

Reacting to Others A situation in which the emotional, feeling, and irrational characteristics of a person are communicated.

Reaction Formation A defense mechanism in which impulses are not only repressed, they are also controlled by emphasizing the opposite behavior.

Real Self The person you really are, not who you think you are; a situation in which the belief system is accurate, rather than distorted.

Reciprocal Determinism The interacting influences between, person, behavior, and environment.

Reciprocity The tendency to like individuals who tend to like us.

Regression A defense used when we psychologically retreat to a form of behavior characteristic of an earlier stage of development.

Reinforcement The effect of applying reinforcers.

Reinforcers Pleasant or unpleasant stimuli that strengthen behavior.

Remarriage Marrying for the second, third, or subsequent time.

Repression A defense mechanism consisting of the exclusion of painful, unwanted, or dangerous thoughts and impulses from the conscious mind.

Repulsion Hypothesis People are initially, spontaneously repulsed by strangers who are very dissimilar to themselves.

Resentment Chronic anger resulting from unresolved anger at an injustice.

Resistance Stage The period of recovery and stabilization, during which the individual adapts to the stress.

Responding Reflectively Paraphrasing the essence of the speaker's content and mirroring back to the speaker the emotions which he/she is communicating.

Responding to Others A situation in which the rational, thinking, logical part of a person is communicated.

Risk To reach for something you are not entirely sure of but believe is better than what you now have, or is at least necessary to survive (David Viscott).

Role Confusion An uncertainty experienced by individuals during the ages of 12 and 18 about who they are and where they are going.

Role Expectations Beliefs about a man and woman's roles in marriage.

Romantic Love A form of love that includes intimacy and passion, but no commitment.

Romeo and Juliet Effect Same as psychology reactance—when love is intensified, not weakened, by their families' opposition.

Safety and Security Needs The need to protect oneself from danger and to keep safe from harm; on a psychological level, safety needs might relate to safety and security, such as finding and keeping a job; also referred to as one of Maslow's Hierarchy of Needs.

Search for Meaning Viktor Frankl's idea that our task in life is to create a life that has meaning and purpose.

Secondary Reinforcers Stimuli to which we have attached positive or negative value through association with previously learned conditioned reinforcers.

Selective Listening One of the four levels of normal listening, known as hearing only certain parts of the conversation.

Self-Actualization The fulfillment of one's own completely unique potential.

Self-Actualization Needs The need for self-fulfillment; the need to become all that one is capable of becoming; also referred to as one of Maslow's Hierarchy of Needs.

Self-Awareness The capability to reflect and decide and become aware of our responsibility for choosing the way we live and thus influence our own destiny.

Self-Change Program A five-step program to self-change.

Self-Control A person's sense of their ability to control their own behavior.

Self-Disclosure The process of deliberately revealing information about oneself that is significant and that would not normally be known by others.

Self-Discovery The process of getting to know yourself as a person—the person within yourself.

Self-Efficacy Our belief about our ability to perform behaviors that should lead to expected outcomes.

Self-Esteem An overall evaluation of oneself, whether one likes or dislikes who one is, believes in or doubts oneself, and values or belittles one's worth.

Self-Evaluation How you compare yourself with others.

Self-Fulfilling Prophecy A prediction or expectation of an event that makes the outcome more likely to occur than would otherwise have been the case.

Self-Image A mental blueprint of how we see ourselves and how we feel about ourselves.

Self-Perception How you evaluate your "self"—physically and psychologically.

Self-Serving Bias A person's tendency to evaluate their own behavior as worthwhile, regardless of the situation.

Self-Talk A person's beliefs or what they say to themselves.

Self-Theory Carl Rogers' theory, defining the development of the self in terms of self-actualization.

Self-Validation Disclosing information with hopes of obtaining the other person's approval.

Self-Worth Virginia Satir's idea that our individual worth is our perception of what happens between people and inside people.

Semantics The study of the meaning and changes of meaning in words.

Sensing (S) or Intuition (N) A preference on the MBTI covering what you pay attention to when you gather information.

Shame A painful emotion caused by consciousness of guilt, shortcomings, or impropriety.

Shyness The feelings, physical reactions, and thoughts that create a state of anxiety, discomfort, and inhibition.

Significant Others The important people in our lives.

Significant Stimuli Anything directly related to another person's needs, wants, interests, and desires.

Similarities The process of selecting friends because of comparable interests, income level, educational beliefs, and so on.

Singlehood The decision not to marry.

Situational Shyness Specific environmental circumstances that develop feelings, physical reactions, and thoughts that create a state of anxiety, discomfort, and inhibition.

Social Comparison How a person evaluates themself in relation to others.

Social Control Revealing personal information may increase your control over other people and sometimes over the situation.

Social Distance One of Hall's four distance zones, ranging from 4 to 12 feet.

Social Exchange Theory We measure our actions and relationships on a cost-benefit basis. People maximize their rewards and minimize their costs by employing their resources to gain the most favorable outcome.

Social Learning Theory The theory that suggests that personality development occurs through observational learning.

Social Perception The way we perceive, evaluate, categorize, and form judgments about the qualities of people we encounter.

Social Ties The feeling that we are part of a group or have an identity.

Spranger's Six Value Systems Relates to six different types of people based on their types of value systems, or their frameworks for developing their own beliefs.

Stages of Psychosocial Development Eight stages of Erikson's human life cycle; the stages are trust vs. mistrust, autonomy vs. doubt, initiative vs. guilt, industry vs. inferiority, identity vs. role confusion, intimacy vs. isolation, generativity vs. self-absorption, and integrity vs. despair.

Stepfamilies Remarriages involving children from one or both spouses.

Stereotyping A process of making generalizations by categorizing an object, person, or situation.

Strengths-Based Psychology Focusing more on what's right with people rather than focusing more on people's shortcomings.

Stress The nonspecific response of the body to any demand placed on it, whether that demand be real, imagined, pleasant, or unpleasant.

Stressor A stressful event.

Sublimation A defense whereby an individual redirects their basic desires toward a socially-valued activity.

Success The outcome of setting a goal and achieving that goal, whatever that goal may be.

Superego The part of the personality that consists of our values, morals, religious beliefs, and ideals of our parents and society; sometimes referred to as our conscience.

Supportive Response A response that shows the receiver's intent is to reassure, comfort, or minimize the intense feelings of the sender.

Suppression A defense mechanism in which people are conscious of their emotions, but deliberately control rather than express them.

Symbols in Communication Such things as the selection of words, tone and pitch of voice, nonverbal method, or even types of supportive materials.

Sympathy An involuntary feeling—the passive experience of sharing another person's fear, grief, anger or joy.

Target Behavior The goal you have set for yourself—your behavioral goal.

The Aesthetic Person Beauty, form, and harmony are most important to this type of individual.

The Economic Person Personal needs, production, marketing, credit, and wealth are more important to this type of person than are social or artistic values.

The Political Animal This type of person is very power motivated, with values centered on influence, fame, and power.

The Religious Person To this individual, the highest value is unity; he or she tries to understand the universe as a whole and relates to it meaningfully.

The Social Person This person values and loves other people, with kindness and unselfishness as very important values.

The Theoretical Person This individual seeks to discover truth and observes happenings and thinks them through, trying whenever possible to put ideas into a system.

Thinking (T) or Feeling (F) A preference on the MBTI covering how you make decisions.

Thought Stopping Concentrating on the unwanted thoughts and, after a short time, suddenly stopping and emptying the mind of all stressful thoughts.

Time Waster Anything preventing you from achieving your objectives most effectively.

Trait A relatively stable and consistent personal characteristic.

Trust vs. Mistrust Erikson's psychosocial crisis at the first stage of the human life cycle; the subsequent response of a person to the way he is treated as an infant.

Two-Way Communication An exchange of information in which the receiver deliberately provides feedback to a sender.

Type A Behavioral Pattern A behavioral pattern characterizing individuals who live a competitive, aggressive, ambitious, and stressful lifestyle.

Type B Behavioral Pattern A behavioral pattern characterizing individuals who live a more relaxed and less hurried lifestyle.

Unconditional Positive Regard The situation in which love is given freely and does not depend on any specific aspects of behavior.

Unconditioned Response (UCR) An unlearned reaction to an unconditioned stimulus that occurs without previous conditioning.

Unconditioned Stimulus (UCS) A stimulus that evokes an unconditioned response without previous conditioning.

Understanding Response This response indicates that the receiver is seeking to fully understand what the sender is actually saying. This is the most effective way of responding to others and requires the skills of active listening, sometimes referred to as empathetic listening. (See active listening and empathetic listening).

Unknown Area of Johari Window Information about you that is unknown to self or others.

Value The personal worth placed on an object, thought, or idea.

Value Indicators Partial values, such as desires, thoughts not acted on, opinions, interests, aspirations, goals, and so on, which are in the process of being formed.

Value System The personal blueprint or guidelines for one's life, based upon one's values.

Values Clarification A process that helps people distinguish between full values and partial values.

Verbal Communication The expression of words; language.

Win-Lose An approach to conflict resolution whereby one person gets his or her way, and the other does not.

Win-Win An approach to conflict resolution whereby conflicts are resolved with no one winning and no one losing. Both win because the solution must be acceptable to both.

"You" Messages Messages creating a feeling of blame and accusation.

References

CHAPTER 1

Aberson, C., Healy, M., & Romero, V. (2000) Ingroup bias and self-esteem: A meta-analysis. *Personality and Social Psychology Review,* 4, (2): 157-173.

Adler, R., & Proctor, R. (2014). *Looking Out Looking In*. Boston, MA: Wadsworth.

Allan, G. (2008). Flexibility, friendship, and family. *Personal Relationships*, 15, 1–16. doi: 10.1111/j.1475-6811.2007.00181.x

Aronson, E., Wilson, T., & Akert, R. (2015). *Social Psychology*. Upper Saddle River, NJ: Pearson Education, Inc.

Asatryan, K. (2016). *Stop Being Lonely: Three Simple Steps to Developing Close Friendships and Deep Relationships.* Novato, CA: New World Publishing

Baron, R., Branscombe, N., & Byrne, D. (2012). *Social Psychology*. New York: Allyn & Bacon.

Baumgarte, R. (2002). Cross-gender friendship: The troublesome relationship. In R. Goodwin & D.Cramer (Eds.). *Inappropriate Relationships* (pp.103-124). Mawah , NJ: Lawrence Erlbaum Associates.

Berscheid, E. (2000). Attraction. In A. Kazdin (Ed.), *Encyclopedia of Psychology*. Washington, DC and New York: American Psychological Association and Oxford University Press.

Berscheid, E., & Reis, H.T. (2000). Attraction and close relationships. In D.T. Gilbert, T. Fiske, & G. Lindsey (Eds.), *The Handbook of Social Psychology* (4th ed.), vol. 2. Boston, MA: McGraw Hill, 193–281.

Bolton, E. (2014). AAUW: What we can do to combat stereotypes and bias. http://www.aauw.org/2014/08/13/why-stereotypes-are-bad/

Brown, B. (2010). *The Gifts of Imperfection*: Center City, MN: Hazelden.

Bryant, J. (2009). *Love Leadership: The New Way To Lead In A Fear-Based World.* San Francisco: Jossey-Bass.

Buscalia, L. (1982). *Living, Loving and Learning:* New York: Ballantine.

Byers, E. S., & Demmons, S. (2010). Sexual satisfaction and sexual self-disclosure within dating relationships. *Journal of Sex Research, 36*, 180-189. doi:10.1080/00224499909551983

Carducci, B., & Zimbardo, P. (2016). The cost of shyness. *Psychology Today.*

Carducci, B. (2000). *Shyness—A Bold New Approach*. New York: Perennial.

Carducci, B., & Zimbardo, P. (2016). Are you shy? *Psychology Today,* 28, 6.

Casriel, E. (2007). Stepping out. *Psychology Today,* 40, 69–75.

Christakis, N.A. & Fowler, J.H. (2009*). Connected: The surprising power of our social networks and how they shape our lives.* New York, NY: Little, Brown and Company.

Creole, H. (2016). *Overcoming Depression and Loneliness.* Self published.

Davis, E. (2014). *Connected: Curing the Pandemic of Everyone Feeling Alone Together.* Nashville, TN: B&H Publishing.

DuBrin, A. (2013). *Human Relations for Career and Personal Success.* Upper Saddle River, NJ: Pearson Education, Inc.

Duckworth, A. (2016). *Grit: The Power of Passion and Perseverance.* NY: Scribner.

Duffy, K. (2007/2008). *Annual Editions: Personal Growth and Behavior.* Dubuque, IA: McGraw Hill Contemporary Learning Series.

Duffy, K., & Atwater, E., et al (2013). *Psychology for Living.* Upper Saddle River, NJ: Pearson.

Fehr, B. (1999). *Friendship Processes.* Thousand Oaks, CA: Sage Publications.

Fisk S., Cuddy, A., Glick, P., & Xu, J. (2002). A model of (often mixed) stereotype content: competence and warmth respectively follow from perceived status and competition. *Journal of Personality and Social Psychology*, 82 (6), 878–902.

Fiske, S. (2014). *Social Beings* (4th ed.). New York: Wiley.

Fiske, S. (2012). Social structures and neural maps of inter-group processes. *British Journal of Social Psychology*, 70, 491–512.

Fiske, S. T., Lin, M., & Neuberg, S. L. (1999). The continuum model. In S. Chaiken & Y. Trope (Eds.), *Dual-Process Theories in Social Psychology.* New York: Guilford Press.

Flora, C. (2004). Snap judgments. *Psychology Today,* May/June, 60–66.

Gale, T. (2007). *Prejudice in the Modern World Reference Library.* Detroit, MI: UXL.

Giddens, A. (2005). *Sociology.* Cambridge, UK: Polity Press.Gosling, S. (2016). Mixed signals. *Psychology Today*, 42, 61–71.

Gudino, O., & Lau, A. (2010). Parental cultural orientation, shyness, and anxiety in Hispanic children: An exploratory study. *Journal of Applied Developmental Psychology* 31, 3: 202-210.

Gudykunst, W., & Ting-Toomey, S . (1991). *Culture and Interpersonal Communication.* Newbury Park, CA: Sage.

Hafen, B.Q., Karren, K.J., Frandsen, K.J., & Smith, N.L. (2005). *Mind/Body Health.* Boston, MA: Allyn & Bacon.

Hanna, S., Suggett, R., & Radke, D. (2008). *Person to Person–Positive Relationships Don't Just Happen.* Upper Saddle River, NJ: Pearson.

Henderson, G., & Long, W. (2016). *Introduction to Human Relations Studies.* Springfield, IL: Charles Thomas Publisher LTD.

Hewstone, M., Rubin, M., & Willis, N. (2002). Intergroup bias. *Annual Review of Psychology*, 53, 575–604.

Huong, B. T. (2010). 'Let's talk about sex, baby': Sexual communication in marriage in contemporary Vietnam. *Culture, Health &S exuality, 12,* S19-S29. doi:10.1080/13691050903072025

Hutson, M. (2009). Best face forward. *Psychology Today*, 42, 20.

Hutson, M. (2016). Relationships: Best face forward. *Psychology Today*, 42, 20.

Karbo, K. (2016). Friendship: The laws of attraction. *Psychology Today,* 39, 91–95.

Kansas Health Foundation, (2016). Community Toolbox. University of Kansas: http://communityhealth.ku.edu/publications/pdf/R16.pdf retrieved 10/11/16

Kilmartin, C. (2010). *The Masculine Self.* Cornwall-on-Hudson, NY: Sloan Publishing.

Kleman, E. (2007). *Journaling for the world to see: A proposed model of self disclosure intimacy in blogs.* Paper presented at the annual meeting of the National Communication Association, Chicago, IL.

Kraus, L.A., Davis, M.H., Bazzini, D., Church, M., & Kirchman, C.M. (1993). Personal and social influences on loneliness: The mediating effect of social provisions. *Social Psychology Quarterly,* 56, 37–53.

Lamberton, L. (2014). *Human Relations – Strategies for Success.* New York: McGraw Hill.

Leahy, R.L. (2006). *The Worry Cure: Seven Steps to Stop Worry from Stopping You.* New York: Three Rivers Press.

Loehr A. (2016). *Eight Quick Tips for Interpersonal Communication and Relationship Building.* Huffington Post blog US edition: April 12.

Lynch, C., & Daniels, V. (2000). *Patterns of Relationships.* https://www.sonoma.edu/users/d/daniels/lynch.html

Monsour, M. (2002). *Women and Men as Friends.* Mahwah, NJ: Erlbaum.

Myers, D.G. (2013). *Social Psychology.* New York: Worth.

Nelson, S. (2016). *Frientimacy: How to Deepen Friendships for Lifelong Health and Happiness.* Berkeley, CA: Seal Press.

Nevid, J. (2015). *Essentials of Psychology: Concepts and Applications.* New York: Houghton Mifflin Co.

National Institutes of Health. (2009). *News in Health Newsletter.*

Nicholaisen, M., Thorsen, K, (2016). What are friends for? Friendships and loneliness over the lifespan--From 18 to 79 years, *International Journal of Aging and Human Development,* 84, 126-158.

Norris, A.R. (2011). Impression management: Considering cultural, social, and spiritual factors. *Inquiries Journal,* 3 (7): 1.

O'Connel, A., & O'Connel, V. (2005). *Choice and Change.* Upper Saddle River, NJ: Prentice Hall.

Pelusi, N. (2007). The privacy paradox. *Psychology Today,* 40, 68–69.

Plous, S. (2003). *Understanding Prejudice and Discrimination.* New York: McGraw Hill.

Punches, B. (2010). *What You Say and Do Next Matters!* Dubuque, IA: Kendall Hunt Publishing Co.

Reeder G.D. (2013). Attribution as a gateway to social cognition. *Journal of Personality and Social Psychology,* 69.

Reiss, I. L. (2006). *An Insider's View of Sexual Science since Kinsey.* Lanham, MD: Rowman & Littlefield.

Rodgers, J. (2006). Altered ego. *Psychology Today,* 39, 72–75.

Rosen, L. (2011). Is Constant "Facebooking" Bad for Teens? Research presented at the American Psychological Association meeting, Washington DC, August 5, 2011.

Rosenthal, R., & Jacobson, L. (2003). *Pygmalion in the Classroom.* Norwalk, CT: Crown Publishing Co.

Santrock, J. (2006). *Human Adjustment*. New York: McGraw Hill.

Schafer, J. (2015). Self-disclosures increase attraction: Talking about yourself is not always a bad thing. *Psychology Today* blog. https://www.psychologytoday.com/blog/let-their-words-do-the-talking/201503/self-disclosures-increase-attraction

Sheldon, P. (2008). The relationship between unwillingness to communicate and students' Facebook use. *Journal of Media Psychology, 20,* 67-75.

Sheldon, P. (2013). Examining gender differences in self-disclosure on Facebook versus face-to-face. *The Journal of Social Media in Society* 2(1).

Shenk, J.W. (2009). What makes us happy? *The Atlantic Magazine,* June 1.

Smock, A. D., Ellison, N. B., Lampe, C., & Wohn, D. Y. (2011). Facebook as a tool-kit: A uses and gratification approach to unbundling feature use. *Computers in Human Behavior, 27,* 2322-2329.

Stein, M., & Walker, J. (2009). *Triumph over Shyness and Social Anxiety*. New York: McGraw Hill.

Vitelli, R. (2013). Painfully shy: Can shyness lead to problems with depression and anxiety? *Psychology Today,* 12, 23.

White, V., & Demarais, A. (2005). *First Impressions: What You Don't Know About How Others See You*. New York: Bantam.

Wills, T. A., & Ainette, M. G. (2012). Social networks and social support. In A. Baum, T.A. Revenson & J. Singer (Eds.), *Handbook of Health Psychology* (2nd ed.). New York, NY: Psychology Press.

Wilson, J. (2008). The conflation of public and private identity: The notion that privacy is a "right" is likely lost on the Millenial. *Psychology Today*, Dec 2008.

Wilson, R. (2007). Loneliness increases risk of dementia. *Bottom Line Personal*, 28, 15.

Winch, G. (2013). Together but still lonely. *Psychology Today*. June 2013

Wiseman, H., Mayseless, O., & Sharabany, R. (2006). Why are they lonely? Perceived equal quality of early relationships with parents, attachment, personality, predispositions and loneliness in first-year university students. *Personality and Individual Differences, 40,* 237–238.

Wood, J.T. (2017). *Communication Mosaics*. Belmont, CA: Wadsworth.

Wood, W., Wood, E., & Boyd, D. (2013). *Mastering the World of Psychology*. New York: Pearson.

Worchel, S., Cooper, J., Goethals, G., & Olson, J. (2000). *Social Psychology*. Belmont, CA: Wadsworth.

Yum, Y., & Hara, K. (2005). Computer-mediated relationship development: A cross-cultural comparison. *Journal of Computer-Mediated Communication,11*(1). Retrieved from http://jcmc.indiana.edu/vol11/issue1/yum.html.

Zimbardo, P. (1990). *Shyness, What It Is, What to Do about It*. Reading, MA: Addison-Wesley.

Zhou, X., Sedikides, C., Wildschut, T., Gao, D.-G. (2008). Counteracting loneliness: On the restorative function of nostalgia. *Psychological Science 19* (10), 1023–9. doi:10.1111/j.1467-9280.2008.02194.x. PMID 19000213.

CHAPTER 2

Adler, A. (1998). *What Life Could Mean to You*. Boston, MA: Little Brown.

Adler, R., & Proctor, R. (2011). *Looking In Looking Out.* Boston, MA: Wadsworth.

Bandura, A. (2001). Failures in self-regulations: Energy depletion or selective disengagement. *Psychological Inquiry, 7,* 20–24.

Bandura, A. (2004). *Toward a Psychology of Human Agency.* A paper presented at the meeting of the American Psychological Society, Chicago, IL.

Branden, N. (2007). *The Psychology of Self-Esteem.* New York: John Wiley & Sons.

Brody, N., & Erhlichman, H. (1998). *Personality Psychology: The Science of Individuality.* Upper Saddle River, NJ: Prentice Hall.

Bronson, P. (2007). How not to talk to your kids: The inverse power of praise. *New York Magazine,* August 3.

Cloninger, S. (2013). *Theories of Personality.* Upper Saddle River, NJ: Prentice Hall.

Cole, M., Field, H., & Harris, S. (2004). Student learning motivation and psychological hardiness: Interactive effects on students' reactions to a management class. *Academy of Management Learning and Education,* March, 64–85.

Davidson, T. (2014). STRENGTH: A system of integration of solution-oriented and strength-based principles. *Journal of Mental Health Counseling,* 36, 1-17.

Dweck, C. (2007). *Mindset: The New Psychology of Success.* NY: Random House

Dweck, C. (2012). *Mindset: How You Can Fulfill Your Potential.* Penn: Robinson Publishing

Eder, R.A., & Mangelsdorf, S.C. (1997). The emotional basis of early personality development Implications for the emergent self-concept. In R. Hogan, J. Johnson, & S. Briggs (Eds.), *Handbook of Personality Psychology.* San Diego: Academic Press, 209–324.

Elliott, C. (2004). Putting your best face forward. *Psychology Today,* May/June, 49–50.

Erikson, E. (1993). *Childhood and Society.* New York: W.W. Norton.

Feldman, R.S. (2013). *Development Across the Life Span.* Upper Saddle River, NJ: Prentice Hall.

Festinger, L. (1954). A theory of social comparison processes. *Human Relations,* 7, 117–140.

Flora, C. (2005). The measuring game: Why you think you'll never stack up. *Psychology Today,* 38, 42–50.

Frankl, V.E. (2006). *Man's Search for Meaning.* New York: Washington Square Press.

Freud, S. (1965). *New Introductory Lectures on Psychoanalysis.* New York: W.W. Norton.

Gibbs, N. (2005). Midlife crisis? Bring it on. *Time,* May 16, 53–63.

Helgoe, L. (2010). Revenge of the introvert. *Psychology Today,* 43, 54-61.

John, O.P., & Srivastava, S. (2008). The big five-trait taxonomy: History, measurement, and theoretical perspectives. In L.A. Pervin, & O.P. John (Eds.), *Handbook of Personality: Theory and Research* (3rd ed.). New York: Guilford Press, 102–138.

Kassin, S., Fein, S., Markus, H. (2016). *Social Psychology.* Boston: Cengage Learning.

Keirsey, D. (1998). *Please Understand Me II.* Del Mar, CA: Prometheus Nemesis Book Company.

Kerpin, D. (2016). *11 Simple Skills That Will Get You Everything You Want.* New York: Crown Publishing Random House.

Kimmel, M., & Aronson, A. (2011). *Sociology Now.* Boston, MA: Pearson.

Krueger, J., & Vohs, K. (2003). Does high self-esteem cause better performance, interpersonal success, happiness, or healthier lifestyles? *Psychological Science in the Public Interest*, 4, 1–44.

Krueger, R., & Johnson W. (2008). Behavioral genetics and personality. In O.P. John, R.W. Robbins, & L.A. Pervin (Eds.), *Handbook of Personality Theory and Research*. New York: Guilford, 287–310.

Langer, E. (2014). *Mindfulness 25th Anniversary edition*. Boston: DaCapo Press.

Larsen, R., & Buss, D. (2014). *Personality Psychology Domains of Knowledge about Human Nature*. Upper Saddle River, NJ: Prentice Hall.

Levinson, D. (1986). A conception of adult development. *American Psychologist*, 41, 3–13.

Marano, H. (2008). The making of a perfectionist. *Psychology Today,* 41, 81–86.

Matsumoto, D. (2007). Culture, context and behavior. *Journal of Personality*, 75, 1285–1320.

McCrae, R.R., & Costa, P.T., Jr. (2005). *Personality in Adulthood*. New York: The Guilford Press.

McCrae, R.R., & Costa, P.T., Jr. (2008). A five-factor theory of personality. In L.A. Pervin, & O.P. John (Eds.), *Handbook of Personality: Theory and Research* (3rd ed.). New York: The Guilford Press, 139–153.

McGraw, P. (2003). *Self Matters*. New York: Free Press.

McKay M., & Fanning, P. (2000). *Self-Esteem*. Oakland, CA: New Harbinger.

Mischel, W. (2007). *Introduction to Personality*. New York: Wiley.

Myers, D.G. (2013). *Psychology*. New York: Worth.

Myers, I., & Myers, P. (1995). *Gifts Differing*. Palo Alto, CA: Consulting Psychologist Press.

Nevid, J., & Rathus, S. (2012). *Psychology and the Challenges of Life*. New York: Wiley.

Nier, J. (2004). Why does the above average effect exit? *Teaching of Psychology,* 31, 53–54.

Pastorino, E., & Doyle-Portillo, S. (2012). *What is Psychology?* Belmont, CA: Wadsworth.

Pollard, M.W., & McKinney, C. (2016). Parental physical force and alcohol use in emerging adults: Mediation by psychological problems. *Journal of Interpersonal Violence*. 2016, Jul 25. pii: 0886260516659654

Rath, T. (2007). *StrengthsFinder 2.0*. New York: Gallup Press.

Rogers, C. (1995). *On Becoming a Person: A Therapist's View of Psychotherapy*. Boston, MA: Houghton Mifflin.

Rosenberg, M. (1965). *Society and the Adolescent Self-image*. Princeton, NJ: Princeton University Press.

Sanford, L., & Donovan, M. (1993). *Women and Self Esteem*. New York: Penguin Books.

Satir, V. (1988). *New Peoplemaking*. Palo Alto, CA: Science and Behavior Books.

Satir, V. (2001). *Self Esteem*. Berkeley, CA: Ten Speed Press.

Schacter, D., Gilbert, D., Wegner, D. (2011). *Psychology* (2 ed.). New York, NY: Worth Publishers.

Sheehy, G. (2006). *Passages: Predictable Crises of an Adult Life*. New York: Ballantine Books.

Sullivan, H.S. (1968). *The Interpersonal Theory of Psychiatry*. New York: Norton.

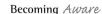

Tallon, R., & Sikora, M. (2004). *Awareness to Action: The Enneagram, Emotional Intelligence and Change*. Scranton, PA: University of Scranton Press.

Weiten, W., Dunn, D., & Hammer, E. (2014). *Psychology Applied to Modern Life*. Belmont, CA: Wadsworth.

Chapter 3

Aamodt, M., & Raynes, R. (2001). *Human Relations in Business*. Belmont, CA: Wadsworth.

Ackerman, J., Goldstein, J., Shapiro, J., & Bargh, J. (2009). You wear me out: The vicarious depletion of self-control. *Psychological Science*, 20, 326-332.

Allen, David M. (2014). Mindfullness or Mindlessness? Stress tolerance skills are great, but why remove the source of stress? *Psychology Today* online , February.

Aronson, E., Wilson, T., & Akert, R. (2013). *Social Psychology*. Upper Saddle River, NJ: Pearson Education, Inc.

Bandura, A. (2008). *Self-efficacy in Changing Societies*. West Nyack, NY: Cambridge University Press.

Buscaglia, L. (1985). *Living, Loving and Learning*. New York: Ballantine Books.

Cline, F., & Fay, J. (2000). *Parenting with Love and Logic: Teaching Children Responsibility*. Carol Stream, IL: Tyndale House Publishers.

Deaner, R.O., Geary, D.C., et al (2012). A sex difference in the predisposition for physical competition: Males play sports much more than females even in the contemporary U.S. *U.S. PLoS ONE,* 7(11), e49168. doi:10.1371/journal.pone.0049168

Duckworth, A.L., Peterson, C., Mathews, M.D. & Kelly, D.R. (2007). Grit:Perseverance and passion for long- term goals. *Journal of Personality and Social Psychology,* 92(6), 1087–1101.

Flora, C. (2016). You 2.0. *Psychology Today,* June 9.

Gardner, R. (2002). *Psychology Applied to Everyday Life*. Belmont, CA: Wadsworth.

Goldberg, S. (2002). The 10 rules of change. *Psychology Today*, 35, 38–42.

Hockenbury, D.H., & Hockenbury, S.E. (2013). *Psychology*. New York: Worth.

Judge, T. A., & Bono, J. E. (2001). Relationship of core self-evaluations traits—self-esteem, generalized self-efficacy, locus of control, and emotional stability—with job satisfaction and job performance: A meta-analysis. *Journal of Applied Psychology*, 86, 80-92.

Kormanik, M.B., Rocco, T. S. (2009). Internal versus external control of reinforcement: A review of the locus of control construct. *Human Resource Development Review*, 8, 4, 463-483.

Leahy, R. (2006). *The Worry Cure*. New York: Three Rivers Press.

Martin, G., & Pear, J. (2015). *Behavior Modification*. Upper Saddle River, NJ: Prentice Hall.

Mischel, W. (2004). Toward an integrative science of the person. *Annual Review of Psychology*, 55, 1–22.

Moscovici, S., & Markova, I. (2006). *The Making of Modern Social Psychology*. Cambridge, UK: Polity Press.

Neimark, J. (2007). The optimism revolution. *Psychology Today,* 40, 88–94.

Newman, J. (2001). Sailing through the blues. *Reader's Digest,* January, 145–148.

Pychyl, T. (2008). Procrastination: A strategy for change. *Psychology Today* online.

Pychyl, T. (2010). Implementation intentions facilitate action control: One of the most effective anti-procrastination strategies I know. *Psychology Today.* Posted Jan 21, 2010.

Roden, J. (2004). Revisiting the health belief model. *Nursing Health and Science,* 6, 1–10.

Rotter, J.B. (1990). Internal versus external control of reinforcement: A case study of a variable. *American Psychologist,* 45, 489–491.

Santrock, J. (2006). *Human Adjustment.* New York: McGraw Hill.

Scheier, M., Carver, C., & Bridges, M. (1994). Distinguishing optimism from neuroticism (and trait anxiety self-mastery, and self-esteem.): A re-evaluation of the life orientation test. *Journal of Personality and Social Psychology,* 67, 1063–1078.

Scholtz, U., Gutierrez-Dona, B., Sud, S., & Schwarzer, R. (2002). Is perceived self-efficacy a universal construct: Psychometric findings from 25 countries. *European Journal of Psychological Assessment,* 18(3), 242–251.

Schultz, D., & Schultz, S. (2013). *Theories of Personality.* Belmont, CA: Wadsworth.

Seligman, M.E.P. (2006). *Learned Optimism.* New York: Knopf.

Skinner, B.F. (2002). *Beyond Freedom and Dignity.* New York: Hackett Publishing.

Vaughan, S. (2000). Optimists live better lives than pessimists. *Bottom Line,* December 15, 13–14.

Wargo, E. (2009). Resisting temptation: Psychological research brings new strength to understanding willpower. *Observer,* 22, 10-15.

Watson, D.L., & Tharp, R.G. (2014). *Self-Directed Behavior.* Belmont, CA: Wadsworth.

Webber, R. (2010). Make your own luck. *Psychology Today,* 43, 63-68.

Weiten, W., Dunn, D., & Hammer, E. (2012). *Psychology Applied to Modern Life.* Belmont, CA: Wadsworth

Worchel, S., Cooper, J., Goethals, G., & Olson, J. (2000). *Social Psychology.* Belmont, CA: Wadsworth.

CHAPTER 4

Adler, R., & Proctor, R. (2014). *Looking Out Looking In.* Boston, MA: Wadsworth.

Aiken, M. (2016). *The Cyber Effect: A Pioneering Cyberpsychologist Explains How Human Behavior Changes Online.* New York: Spiegel & Grau.

Amen, D. (2015). *Change Your Brain, Change Your Life : The Breakthrough Program for Conquering Anxiety, Depression, Obsessiveness, Lack of Focus, Anger, and Memory Problems.* New York: Harmony Publishers.

Anderson, C.A., Gentile, D.A., & Buckley, K.E. (2007). *Violent Video Games Effects on Children and Adolescents: Theory Research and Public Policy.* New York: Oxford University Press.

Bandura, W. (2008). *Self-efficacy in Changing Societies.* West Nyack, NY: Cambridge University Press.

Baskin, T.W., & Enright, R. D. (2004). Intervention studies on forgiveness: A meta-analysis. *Journal of Counseling and Development,* 82, 79-90.

Brown, B. (2012). *Daring Greatly*. New York: Avery.

Brown, B. (2007). *I Thought It Was Just Me (but it isn't): Telling the Truth about Perfectionism, Inadequacy and Power*. New York: Gotham Publishers.

Burns, D. (2008). *Feeling Good: The New Mood Therapy*. New York: William Morrow and Co.

Buscaglia, L. (1996). *Love: What Life is all About*. New York: Holt, Rinehart and Winston.

Carlson, R. (2007). *Don't Sweat the Small Stuff . . . and it's all small stuff*. New York: Hyperion.

Cline, F.W., & Fay, J. (2006). *Parenting with Love and Logic: Teaching Children Responsibility* (CD). Evergreen, CO: Love and Logic Press.

Cose, E. (2005). *Bone to Pick: Of Forgiveness, Reconciliation, Reparation and Revenge*. New York: Atria.

Dienes, K.A., Torres-Harding, S., Reinecke, M.A., Freeman, A., Sauer, A. (2011). Cognitive therapy. In S. B. Messer and A. S. Gurman (Eds.), *Essential Psychotherapies: Theory and Practice* (3rd ed.). New York, NY: The Guilford Press. pp. 143–160.

Dickenson, G., & Leming, M. (2014). *Annual Editions: Dying, Death, and Bereavement*. New York: McGraw Hill/Dushkin.

Duffy, K. (2007/2008). *Annual Editions: Personal Growth and Behavior*. Dubuque, IA: McGraw Hill Contemporary Learning Series.

Duffy, K., & Atwater, E. (2014). *Psychology for Living: Adjustment, Growth and Behavior Today*. Englewood Cliffs, NJ: Prentice Hall.

Ellis, A. (2000). *How to Control Your Anxiety Before it Controls You?* North Hollywood, CA: Wilshire Books.

Ellis, A. (2001). *Feeling Better, Getting Better, Staying Better*. New York: Impact Publishers.

Ellis, A., & Harper, R. (1998). *A Guide to Rational Living*. New York: Impact Publishers.

Emery, G. (2000). *Overcoming Depression*. Oakland, CA: New Harbinger Publications.

Enright, R. (2001). *Forgiveness Is a Choice: A Step-by-Step Process for Resolving Anger and Restoring Hope*. Chicago, IL: American Psychological Association.

Evans, C., & Chapman, M. (2014). Bullied youth: The impact of bullying through lesbian, gay, and bisexual name calling. *American Journal of Orthopsychiatry*, 84, (6) 644–652.

Felmlee, D., & Faris, R. (2016). Toxic ties: Networks of friendship, dating, and cyber victimization. *Social Psychology Quarterly*, 79(3), 243–262.

Feuerman, M, (2016). *21 Warning Signs of an Emotionally Abusive Relationship*. World of Psychology psychcentral.com

Foltz-Gray, D. (2002). Anger with no hurt. *Reader's Digest*, July, 130–135.

Freeman, S. (2005). *Grief and Loss. Understanding the Journey*. Belmont, CA: Brooks/Cole.

Fromm, E. (2006). *The Art of Loving*. New York: Perennial.

Gardner, R. (2002). *Psychology Applied to Everyday Life*. Belmont, CA: Wadsworth.

Gibbs, N. (2001). The EQ factor. *Time*, 2, 60–68.

Ginott, H. (2003). *Between Parent and Child*. New York: Three Rivers Press.

Goldsmith, D.J., & Fulfs, P.A. (1999). You just don't have the evidence: An analysis of claims and evidence in Deborah Tannen's you just don't understand. In M.E. Roloff (Ed.), *Communication Yearbook 22.* Thousand Oaks, CA: Sage, 1–49.

Goleman, D. (2006). *Emotional Intelligence: 10th Anniversary Edition—Why It Can Matter More Than IQ.* New York: Bantam Books.

Goleman, D. (2007). *Social Intelligence: The New Science of Human Relationships.* New York: Bantam Books.

Goleman, D. (2011). *The Brain and Emotional Intelligence: New Insights* (1st ed.). Northampton, MA: More than Sound.

Gorman, C. (2002). The science of anxiety. *Time,* June 10, 45–53.

Greenberg, M. (2003). Good grief: The different ways to cope after loss. *Psychology Today,* 36, 44.

Gudykunst, W.B., & Young, Y.K. (2003). *Communicating with Strangers.* New York: McGraw Hill.

Howie, P. (2015). *Meditations for Angry People.* www.pearlescapes.co.uk.

John-Roger, & McWilliams, P. (1994). *Life 101.* Wilton, CT: Consolino & Woodward.

Jung, C.G. (1923). *Psychological Types.* New York: Harcourt Brace.

Kagan, J. (2009). *What is Emotion? History, Measures and Meanings.* New Haven, CT: Yale University Press.

King, L. (2014). *The Science of Psychology.* New York: McGraw Hill.

Kübler-Ross, E. (1997). *Death: The Final Stage of Growth.* New York: Simon & Schuster.

Kushner, H. (2004). *When Bad Things Happen to Good People.* New York: Anchor.

_____(2007). *Overcoming Life's Disappointments.* Portmoody, BC: Anchor.

Larsen, E. (1992). *From Anger to Forgiveness.* New York: Ballantine Books.

Lazarus, R. (2000). Reason and our emotions: A hard sell. *The General Psychologist,* 35, 16–20.

Leahy, R. (2005). The way of the worrier. *Psychology Today,* 38, 68–72.

Lerner, H.G. (2005). *The Dance of Anger.* New York: Harper Collins.

Luskin, F. (2007). *Forgive for Love.* New York: Harper.

Mayer, J., & Salovey, P. (2004). *Emotional Intelligence: Key Reading on the Mayer and Salovey Model.* Port Chester, NY: Dude Publishing.

Mayer, J., Salovey, P., & Caruse, D. (2009). Emotional intelligence: New ability or eclectic traits. *American Psychologist,* 63, 503–517.

Nay, W. (2010). Overcoming anger. *Psychology Today Blog,* Jan. 31, 2010.

Ng'andu, J. (2015). Life long success starts with social – emotional learning. *Edutopia, December.*

Parker, H. (2008). *Anger, Rage and Relationship: An Empathic Approach to Anger Management.* New York: Routledge.

Plutchik, R. (2003). *Emotions and Life: Perspectives from Psychology, Biology, and Evolution.* Washington, DC: American Psychological Association.

Preidt, R. (2016). *HealthDay;US News and World Report*

Reiner, A. (2016). Teaching men to be emotionally honest. *New York Times,* April 10.

Rogers, C. (1995). *On Becoming a Person: A Therapist's View of Psychotherapy.* Boston, MA: Houghton-Mifflin.

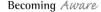

Rolls, G. (2010). *Women Can't Park, Men Can't Pack: The Psychology of Stereotypes*. London, England: Hodder & Stoughton.

Rosenthal, A. (2009). Shame on me. *Psychology Today*, 42, 16.

Schmidt, B. (2002). Fear not. *Psychology Today*, 35, 46–54.

Silk, S., Goldman, B. (2016). We've all been there, stumbling for words at a bedside or funeral. The ring theory helps you know what to say. *Los Angeles Times*, April 20.

Simon, S. (2005). The lion tamer. *Psychology Today*, 38, 54–60.

Simon, S., & Simon, S. (1991). *Forgiveness: How to Make Peace with Your Past and Get on with Your Life*. New York: Warner Books.

Simonini, R. (2011). The terminator. *Psychology Today*, 44, 28–29.

Sisemore, B. (2009). Lessons in forgiveness. *The Dallas Morning News*, August 8, 2009.

Smedes, L. (2007). *Forgive & Forget: Healing the Hurts We Don't Deserve*. New York: Harper Collins Paperback.

Spencer Scott, P. (2016). Feeling awe may be the secret to health and happiness. *Parade*, October 17.

Tavris, C. (1989). *Anger: The Misunderstood Emotion*. New York: Simon & Schuster, Inc.

Viscott, D. (1990). *The Language of Feelings*. New York: Pocket Books.

Walton, D. (2013). *Emotional Intelligence: A Practical Guide*. New York: MJF Books.

Weiten, W. (2013). *Psychology-Themes and Variations*. Pacific Grove, CA: Brooks/Cole.

Welshons, J., & Dyer, W. (2012). *Awakening from Grief: Finding the Road Back to Joy*. Novato, CA: New World Library.

Westburg, G. (2004). *Good Grief*. Minneapolis, MN: Augsburg Publishers.

Wood, S., & Wood, E. (2014). *Mastering the World of Psychology*. Needham Heights, MA: Allyn & Bacon.

Ybarra, M., & Mitchell, K. (2006). Cyberbullies increasingly target peers online. *APA Monitor*, 37, No. 9.

CHAPTER 5

Adler, R., Rosenfeld, L., & Proctor, R. (2015). *Interplay—The Process of Interpersonal Communication*. New York: Oxford University Press.

Atkinson, D.R. (2004). *Counseling American Minorities*. New York: McGraw Hill.

Barker, L., & Watson, K. (2000). *Listen Up: How to Improve Relationships, Reduce Stress, and Be More Productive by Using the Power of Listening*. New York: St. Martin's Press.

Baruth, L.G., & Manning, M.L. (2011). *Multicultural Counseling and Psychotherapy: A Lifespan Perspective*. Englewood Cliffs, NJ: Prentice Hall.

Blanchard, K. (2006). *Putting the One Minute Manager to Work: How to Turn the Three Secrets into Skills*. New York: William & Morrow.

Bolton, R. (1986). *People Skills*. New York: Simon and Schuster, Inc.

Burgoon, J., Guerrero, L.K., & Floyd, K. (2016). *Nonverbal Communication*. New York: Routlege.

Burgoon, J., & Levine, T. (2010). Advances in deception detection. In S.W. Smith, & S.R. Wilson (Eds.), *New Directions in Interpersonal Communication Research*. Thousand Oaks, CA: Sage.

Carnegie, D. (2010). *How to Win Friends and Influence People*. New York: Simon & Schuster.

Ciaramicoli, A. (2001). *The Power of Empathy: A Practical Guide to Creating Intimacy, Self-understanding and Lasting Love*. New York: Dutton.

Cline, F.W., & Fay, J. (2006). *Parenting with Love and Logic: Teaching Children Responsibility* (CD). Evergreen, CO: Love and Logic Press.

Communication Research Associates. (2016). *Communicate! A Workbook for Interpersonal Communication*. Dubuque, IA: Kendall Hunt Publishing Co.

Covey, S.R. (1998) First Things First. Franklin Covey NY Simon Shuster

Covey, S.R. (2005). *Principle-Centered Leadership* (CD-Audiobook). Prince Frederick, MD: Your Coach in a Box.

Covey, S.R. (2013). *The Seven Habits of Highly Effective People* (CD). New York: Free Press.

Dean, A. (1996). *Caring For The Family Soul*. New York: USA Penguin Group Inc., pg 97.

De Vito, J.A. (2012). *The Interpersonal Communication Book*. Reading, MA: Addison Wesley.

Drago, E. (2015). The effect of technology on face-to-face communication. *The Elon Journal of Undergraduate Research in Communications.*

Dresser, N. (2005). *Multicultural Manners: New Rules of Etiquette for a Changing Society*. New York: John Wiley & Sons, Inc.

Eckman, P. (2007). *Emotions Revealed: Recognizing Faces and Feelings to Improve Communication and Emotional Life*. New York: Owl Books.

Emanuel, R., et al. (2008). How college students spend their time communicating. *Interpersonal Journal of Listening*, 22, 13–28.

Englander-Golden, P., & Satir, V. (1991). *Say It Straight*. Palo Alto, CA: Science and Behavior Books, Inc.

Fisher-Sykes, J. (2005). Bite your tongue! 10 ways to be an effective listener. *Living Magazine*, June, 54–58.

Gordon, T. (2000). *Parent Effectiveness Training*. New York: Three Rivers Press.

Groder, M. (1997). All about criticism. *The Bottom Line,* 18, 13–14.

Hall, E.T. (1992). *The Hidden Dimension*. Garden City, NY: Anchor Books.

Hamilton, C. (2014). *Communicating for Results*. Belmont, CA: Wadsworth.

Hamilton, C. (2014). *Essentials of Public Speaking*. Belmont, CA: Wadsworth.

Hanna, S., Suggett, R., & Radtke, D. (2008). *Person to Person*. Upper Saddle River, NJ: Prentice Hall.

Heslin, R., & Alper, T. (1983). Touch: A bonding gesture. In J.M. Wiemann, & R.P. Harrison (Eds.), *Nonverbal Interaction*. Beverly Hills, CA: Sage Publishing Co.

Horn, S. (1997). *Tongue Fu! How to Deflect, Disarm and Defuse Any Verbal Conflict*. New York: St. Martins Press.

Internet Activities. (2009). *Pew Internet and American Life Project*, January 6.

Johnson, D. (2014). *Reaching Out*. Needham Heights, MA: Allyn & Bacon.

Kassian, M. (2014). *Conversation Peace*. Nashville, TN: LifeWay Press.

Kirwan Institute. (2016). *Implicit Bias Report* http://kirwaninstitute.osu.edu

Knapp, M., & Hall, J. (2014). *Nonverbal Communication in Human Interaction*. New York: Wadsworth Publishing Co.

Lerner, H. (2002). *The Dance of Connection*. New York: HarperCollins.

MacGeorge, E., Graves, A., Feng, Gilliham, S., & Burleson, B. (2004). The myth of gender cultures. *Sex Roles*, 50, 143–175.

Marano, H. (2016). Love interruptus. *Psychology Today*, July/August, 58-59.

Matsumoto, D. (2004). Paul Ekman and the legacy of universals. *Journal of Research in Personality*, 38, 45–51.

Menninger, K., & Holzman, P. (Eds.). (2010). *Theory of Psychoanalytic Technique*. Northvale, NJ: Jason Aronson.

Milliken, M.E. (2011). *Understanding Human Behavior*. Albany, New York: Dalmar Publishers, Inc.

Nonviolent Communication. (2017). https://www.cnvc.org/ retrieved 3/17/17

O'Neill, S., & Chapman, E. (2008). *Your Attitude Is Showing: A Primer on Human Relations*. Englewood Cliffs, NJ: Pearson.

Pachter, B. (2006). *When the Little Things Count . . . and They Always Count*. Cambridge, MA: De Capo Press.

Perina, K. (2006). Distinct emotional dialects. *Psychology Today*, 39, 5.

Perina, K. (2011). Secrets of special agents. *Psychology Today*, 44, 56–73.

Piercy, F., Sprenkle, D. Wetchler, J., et al. (1996). *Family Therapy Sourcebook*.

Reece, B., & Brandt, R. (2014). *Effective Human Relations in Organizations*. Boston, MA: Houghton Mifflin Co.

Rogers, C. (1957). The necessary and sufficient conditions of personality change. *Journal of Counseling Psychology*, 22, 95–110.

Rogers, C. (1995). *On Becoming a Person: A Therapist's View of Psychotherapy*. Boston, MA: Houghton Mifflin.

Rosenberg, M. (2005). *Nonviolent Communication*. Encinitas, CA: Puddledancer Press.

Santrock, J. (2006). *Human Adjustment*. New York: McGraw Hill.

Satir, V. (1992). *Making Contact*. Millbrae, CA: Celestial Arts.

Tannen, D. (2007). *You Just Don't Understand*. New York: Ballantine Books.

Tavris, C., & Wade, C. (2011). *Invitation to Psychology*. Englewood Cliffs, NJ: Prentice Hall.

Turkle, S. (2012). *Alone Together: Why We Expect More from Technology and Less from Each Other*. New York: Basic Books.

Turkle, S. (2016). *Reclaiming Conversations: The Power of Talk in the Digital Age*. New York: Penguin Publishing.

Wing Sue, D. (2010). Racial microaggression in everyday life: Is subtle bias harmless? *Psychology Today* blog, October 5.

Wing Sue, D. (2010). *Racial Microaggressions in Everyday Life: Race, Gender and Sexual Orientation*. Hoboken, NJ: John Wiley & Sons.

Wood, J. (2013). *Gendered Lives*. Boston, MA: Wadsworth.

CHAPTER 6

Abrams, A.(Nov 17, 2016). Divorce rate in U.S. drops to nearly 40-year low. *Time Magazine USA Time.com* retrieved March 10, 2017.

Alkon, A. (2010). The truth about beauty. *Psychology Today*, 43, 54–65.

Amato, P.R., & De Buer, D.D. (2001). The transmission of marital instability across generations: Relationship skills or commitment to marriage? *Journal of Marriage and Family*, 63, 103–1051.

Amato, P.R., & Previti, D. (2003). People's reasons for divorcing: Gender, social class, the life course, and adjustment. *Journal of Family Issues*, 24, 602–626.

Anderson, M. (2015). For teens, phone calls are reserved for closer relationships. Pew Research Center.

Anderson, R.E. (2003). Envy and jealousy. *American Journal of Psychotherapy*, 56, 455–479.

Azar, S.T. (2003). *Adult development and parenthood*. In: Demick J, (Ed.), Adult Development. New York: Sage.

Bahrampour, T. (2016). *Why more millennials are avoiding sex: 'There isn't really anything magical about it'* Washington Post, Aug. 2.

Baron, R., Branscombe, N., & Byrne, D. (2012). *Social Psychology*. Boston, MA: Allyn & Bacon.

Beattie, M. (2011). *Co-Dependent No More Workbook*. New York: HarperCollins.

Belsky, J. (2013). *Experiencing the Lifespan*. New York: Worth Publishers.

Berastain, P. (2016). Domestic Violence in LGBT Communities: *US edition Huffington Post* February 2.

Booth, A., & Amato, P.R. (2001). Parental pre-divorce relations and offspring post-divorce well-being. *Journal of Marriage and Family*, 63, 197–212.

Bordens, K., Horowitz, I. (2013). *Social Psychology, Fourth Edition*. Solon, OH: Academic Media Solutions.

Brown, B. (2007*). I thought it was just me (but it isn't); Making the journey from what will people Think to I am enough*. New York: Penguin Random House.

Bumpass, L., & Hsien-Hen L. (2000). Trends in cohabitation and implications for children's family contexts in the U.S. *Population Studies*, 54, 29-41.

Bureau of Labor Statistics. (2015). *American Time Use survey-2015 results*, A BLS News Release Friday, June 24, 2014.

Buss, D.M., et al. (1999). International preferences in selecting mates: A study of 37 cultures. *Journal of Cross Cultural Psychology*, 21, 5–47.

Buss, D.M. (2003). *The Evolution of Desire*. Jackson, TN: Basic Books.

Buss, D.M. (2015). *Evolutionary Psychology*. Boston, MA: Allyn & Bacon.

Buss, D.M. (2016). *The Mating Crisis Among Educated Women*. Edge.Com

Buss, D.M., Shackelford, T.K., Kirkpatrick, L.A., & Larsen, R.J. (2001). A half century of mate preferences: The cultural evolution of values. *Journal of Marriage and Family*, 63, 491–503.

Centers for Disease Control and Prevention. (2010). *Cohabitation*. Atlanta, GA: Author.

Chapman, G. (2015). *The Five Love Languages*. Northfield, MN: Northfield Publishing.

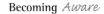

Chatterjee, C. (2016). Can men and women be friends? *Psychology Today,* June 9, 61–67.

Cherlin, A. (2010). Demographic Trends in the United States: A Review of Research in the 2000s. *Journal of Marriage and Family,* 72, 1-17.

Cherlin, A. (2010). *The Marriage-Go-Round: The State of Marriage and the Family in America Today.* New York: Vintage.

Coontz, S. (2006). *Marriage, a History: How Love Conquered Marriage.* New York: Penguin Group.

Daugherty, J., & Copen C. (2016). Trends in attitudes about marriage, childbearing, and sexual behavior: United States, 2002, 2006–10, and 2011–13. National Health Statistics Reports, no. 92. Hyattsville, MD: National Center for Health Statistics.

De Angelis, B. (2004). *Are You the One for Me?* (CD). New York: Macmillan Audio.

Degges-White S. (2015). The 13 essential traits of good friends. *Psychology Today,* March.

Dixit, J. (2009). Driving me crazy. *Psychology Today,* 42, 66–74.

Dresser, N. (2005). *Multicultural Manners: New Rules of Etiquette for a Changing Society.* New York: John Wiley & Sons, Inc.

Duffy, K., & Atwater, E. (2013). *Psychology for Living.* Upper Saddle River, NJ: Pearson.

Elder, S. (2016). The Emperor's new woes. *Psychology Today,* June.

Evans, F. Barton (1996). *Harry Stack Sullivan: Interpersonal Theory and Psychotherapy.* London: Routledge.

Fry, R. (2016). *For First Time in Modern Era, Living With Parents Edges Out Other Living Arrangements for 18- to 34-Year-Olds.* Pew Research Center.

Fry, R. (2016). *The evolving landscape of young adult living arrangements.* Pew Research Center.

Fulwiler, M. (2014). *The Six Things that Predict Divorce.* The Gottman Institute Blog, October.

Godek, G. (1997). *Love.* Markham, ON: Sourcebooks Trade.

Gottman, J. (1995). *Why Marriages Succeed or Fail.* New York: Simon and Schuster, Inc.

Gottman, J., & Carrere, S. (2000). Welcome to the love lab. *Psychology Today,* 23, 42–47.

Gottman, J., & Declaire, J. (2007). *Ten Lessons to Transform Your Marriage.* New York: Three Rivers Press.

Gottman, J., & Silver, W. (2004). *The Seven Principles of Making Marriage Work* (CD). London: Orion.

Grolnick, W.S., Gurland, S.T., DeCourcey, W., & Jacob, K. (2002). Antecedents and consequences of mothers' autonomy support: An experimental investigation. *Developmental Psychology,* 38, 143-155.

Hetherington, E., & Kelly, J. (2003). *For Better or For Worse: Divorce Reconsidered.* New York: W.W. Norton.

Hetherington, E.M., et al. (1998). The role of individual differences and family relationships in coping with divorce and remarriage. In P.A. Cowan, & E.M. Hetherington (Eds.), *Family Transition.* Hillsdale, NJ: Erlbaum.

Hyde, J., & DeLamater, J. (2014). *Human Sexuality.* New York: McGraw Hill.

Katz, J. (1999). Ten Things Men can do to Prevent Gender Violence. www.jacksonkatz.com

Katz, J. (2015). Engaging men in prevention of violence against women. In Johnson, H., Fisher, B., Jaquier, V., *Critical Issues on Violence Against Women: International Perspectives and Promising Strategies*, London: Routledge, 233–243.

Katz, J. (2006). *The Macho Paradox: Why Some Men Hurt Women and How All Men Can Help.* Naperville, IL: Sourcebooks.

Kelly, J. (2004). Divorce: The adult perspective. In B.B. Wolman (Ed.), *Handbook of Developmental Psychology.* Englewood Cliffs, NJ: Prentice Hall.

Konigsberg, R. (2011). Chore wars. *Time,* August 8, 2011.

Kreider, R. (2005). *Number, Timing, and Duration of Marriages.* 2001 U.S. Census Bureau, Household Economic Studies. Washington, DC: Department of Commerce.

Lague, L. (2001). How honest are couples really? *Reader's Digest,* August, 2001, 88–99.

Lawson, W. (2005). Newlyweds: How deep is your love. *Psychology Today,* 38, 32.

Livingston,G. (2014). *Four-in-Ten Couples are Saying "I Do," Again Growing Number of Adults Have Remarried.* Pew Research Center.

Lucas, R. (2005). Time does not heal all wounds; a longitudinal study of reaction and adaptation to divorce. *Psychological Science,* 16, 945–950.

Luscombe, B. (2010). What's it good for? *Time,* 176, 47–56.

Marano, H. (2006). Relationships. *Psychology Today,* 39, 48–49.

Marano, H. (2016). Love and Power. *Psychology Today, June 9.*

Matsumoto, D., & Juang, L. (2013). *Culture and Psychology.* Florence, KY: Wadsworth.

McGraw, P. (2007). *Relationship Rescue.* New York: Hyperion.

Myers, D.G. (2015). *Exploring Social Psychology.* New York: McGraw Hill.

Nevid, J., & Rathus, S. (2013). *Psychology and the Challenges of Life.* Hoboken, NJ: John Wiley & Sons, Inc..

NNEDV.org/census. (2010) *National Domestic Violence Counts,.*

NNEDV.org/census(2015). *National Domestic Violence Counts,.*

O'Meara, J. D. (1989). Cross-sex friendships: Four basic challenges of an ignored relationship. *Sex Roles,* 21, 525-543.

Overstreet, L. (2007). *Gaining Perspective.* Dubuque, IA: Kendall Hunt Publishing Co.

Parker-Pope, T. (2010). *For Better: The Science of a Good Marriage.* New York: Dutton Adult.

Parker, K. (2015). *Raising Kids and Running a Household: How Working Parents Share the Load.* Pew Research Center.

Perina, K. (2016). The Success of a Marriage. *Psychology Today,* June 9.

Pew Internet & American Life Project. (2007). *Online dating.* April 29, 2007, Washington, DC.

Pew Research Center. (2014). *Millennials in adulthood: Detached from institutions, networked with friends.* Retrieved March, 7, 2014 from http://www.pewsocialtrends.org/2014/03/07/millennials-in-adulthood/.

Pew Research Center. (2015). *More Millennials living with family despite improved job market.* Retrieved July 29, 2015 from http://www.pewsocialtrends.org/2015/07/29/more-millennials-living-with-family-despite-improved-job-market/.

Pew Research Center. (2016). *15% of American Adults Have Used Online Dating Sites or Mobile Dating Apps.*

Pew Research Center. (2016). *Millennials Overtake Baby Boomers as America's Largest Generation.*

Regnerus, M., & Uecker, J. (2010). *Premarital Sex in America: How Young Americans Meet, Mate and Think about Marrying.* Oxford, England: Oxford University Press.

Pew Research Center Staff. (2009). *Survey: Working moms wish for part-time jobs.* Pew Survey, people-press.org.

Rodrigues, A., Hal, J., & Fincham, F. (2006). *What predicts divorce and relationship dissolution?* In M.A. Fine, & J.H. Harvey (Eds.), *Handbook of Divorce and Relationship Resolution.* Mahwah, NJ: Erlbaum.

Rosen, L. (2010). Welcome to the iGeneration. *Psychology Today.*

Sapadin, L.A. (2014). Birds of a feather? Not when it comes to sexual permissiveness. *Journal of Social and Personal Relationships,* 31, 93-113.

Schwartz, P. (2002). Love is not all you need. *Psychology Today,* 35, 57–62.

ScienceDaily (2008, June 4). Are People More Likely To Become Friends Based on Proximity Or Shared Values and Interests? Retrieved July 11, 2016 from www.sciencedaily.com/releases/2008/06/080602163842.htm

Seltzer, J. A. (2004), Cohabitation in the United States and Britain: Demography, kinship, and the future. *Journal of Marriage and Family*, 66, 921–928. doi:10.1111/j.0022-2445.2004.00062.x

Siegel, D. (2007). Two people, one breadwinner. *Psychology Today,* 20, 46–48.

Smith A., (2016). *15% of American Adults Have Used Online Dating Sites or Mobile Dating Apps.* Pew Research Center.

Smock, P. (2000). Cohabitation in the United States: An appraisal of research themes, findings, and implications. *Annual Review of Sociology*, 26.

Stack, S., & Eshleman, J. (1998). Marital status and happiness: A 17-nation study. *Journal of Marriage and the Family,* 60, 527–536.

Sternberg, R.J. (2004). A Triangular Theory of Love. In H.T. Reis, C. Rusbult, *Close Relationships.* New York: Psychology Press, p. 258 .

Sternberg, R.J. (2007). Triangulating love" In T.J. Oord, (Ed.,) *The Altruism Reader: Selections from Writings on Love, Religion, and Science.* West Conshohocken, PA: Templeton Foundation, p. 332.

Strong, B., DeVault, C., Sayad, B., & Cohen, T. (2014). *The Marriage and Family Experience.* Belmont, CA: Wadsworth.

Sullivan, H.S. (1968). *The Interpersonal Theory of Psychiatry.* New York: Norton.

Tang, S. M., & Zuo, J. P. (2000). Dating attitudes and behaviors of American and Chinese college students. *The Social Science Journal,* 37, 67-78. doi:10.1016/S0362-3319(99)00066-X

Taylor, S.E., & Peplau, L.A. (2009). *Social Psychology.* Upper Saddle River: NJ: Prentice Hall.

U.S. Bureau of the Census. (2015). *Median Age of First Marriage:1890-2015.* Washington, DC: U.S. Government Printing Office.

Twenge J., Sherman, R.A., Brooke, R., & Wells B.E. (2017). Sexual inactivity during young adulthood is more common among U.S. millennials and iGen: Age, period, and cohort effects on having no sexual partners after age 18, *Arch Sex Behav,* 46, 433. doi:10.1007/s10508-016-0798-z

Wartik, N. (2005). The perils of playing house. *Psychology Today,* 38, 42–52.

Weiten, W., Dunn, D., & Hammer, E. (2014). *Psychology Applied to Modern Life.* Belmont, CA: Wadsworth.

Wood, S., Wood, E., & Boyd, D. (2014). *Mastering the World of Psychology.* New York: Pearson.

CHAPTER 7

Adler, R., & Proctor, R. (2014). *Looking Out Looking In.* Boston, MA: Wadsworth.

Adler, R., & Rodman, G. (2011/2014). *Understanding Human Communication.* Fort Worth, TX: Harcourt Brace.

Alberti, R.E., & Emmons, M.L. (2008). *Your Perfect Right: A Guide to Assertive Living* (6th ed.). San Luis Obispo, CA: Impact Publishers, Inc.

Atwater, E., & Duffy, K. (2013). *Psychology for Living: Adjustment, Growth and Behavior Today.* Englewood Cliffs, NJ: Prentice Hall.

Baskin, T.W., & Enright, R. D. (2004). Intervention studies on forgiveness: A meta-analysis. *Journal of Counseling and Development, 82,* 79-90.

Bolton, R. (1986). *People Skills.* New York: Simon & Schuster, Inc.

Bower, S.A., & Bower, G.H. (2004). *Asserting Yourself.* Philadelphia, PA: DeCapo Press.

Breitman, P., Hatch, C., & Carlson, R. (2001). *How to Say No without Feeling Guilty: And Say Yes to More Time, More Joy, and What Matters Most to You.* New York: Broadway.

Burgess, H., & Burgess, G. (1999). *Encyclopedia of Conflict Resolution.* Santa Barbara, CA: ABC-Clio.

Buscaglia, L. (1994). *Born for Love.* New York: Ballantine.

Collier, M.J. (1991). Conflict competence within African, Mexican, and Anglo-American friendship. In S. Ting-Toomey, & F. Korzenny (Eds.), *Cross-Cultural Interpersonal Communication.* Newbury Park, CA: Sage.

Communication Research Associates. (2012). *Communicate! A Workbook for Interpersonal Communication.* Dubuque, IA: Kendall Hunt Publishing Co.

Davis, M., Eshelman, E., & McKay, M. (2008). *The Relaxation and Stress Reduction Workbook.* Oakland, CA: New Harbinger Publications.

DeCenzo D., & Silhanek B. (2002). *Human Relations Personal and Professional Development.* Upper Saddle River, NJ: Prentice Hall.

Deutsch, M., Coleman, P., & Marcus, E. (2006). *Handbook of Conflict Resolution.* New Haven, CT: Yale University Press.

Dubrin, A. (2010). *Human Relations for Career and Personal Success.* Upper Saddle River, NJ: Prentice Hall.

Fememenia, N., & Warner, N. (2015). *The Silent Marriage: How Passive Aggression Steals Your Happiness.* New York: Creative Conflict Resolution Inc.

Fisher, R., & Ury, W. (2011). *Getting to Yes: Negotiating Agreement without Giving In.* New York: Simon & Schuster Audio.

Fontaine, G. (1999). Cultural diversity in intimate intercultural relationships. In D.D. Cahn (Ed.), *Conflict in Intimate Relationships*. New York: Guilford.

Green, R. (2001). *Human Aggression*. Pacific Grove, CA: Brooks/Cole.

Gordon, T. (2000). *Parent Effectiveness Training*. New York: New American Library.

Gudykunst, W. (2005). *Theorizing About Intercultural Communication*, Thousand Oaks, CA: Sage Publications.

Hammond, J., Keeney, R., & Faiffa, H. (2002). *Smart Choices: A Practical Guide to Making Better Decisions*. Cambridge, MA: Harvard Business School Press.

Harrison, D.D. (1978). *Some Things Are Better Said in Black and White*. Fort Worth, TX: Branch Smith, Inc.

Heinrichs, J. (2013). *Thank You For Arguing*. New York: Three Rivers Pres.s

Hocker, J., & Wilmot, W.W. (2010). *Interpersonal Conflict*. New York: McGraw Hill.

Johnson, D.W. (2014). *Reaching out: Interpersonal effectiveness and self-actualization* (12th ed.). Boston: Allyn & Bacon.

Johnson, D.W. (2015). Are you a conflict positive person? Research shows benefits of being conflict positive. *Psychology Today*. December edition.

Kottler, J. (2003). *Beyond Blame*. San Francisco: CA: Jossey-Bass.

Lamberton, L., & Minor, L. (2014). *Human Relations: Strategies for Success*. New York: McGraw Hill.

Kruschewsky, G.(2014). 14 Beautiful Experiences That Make Your Cross-Cultural Relationship Truly Special. *http://www.huffingtonpost.com/2014/02/19/inter-cultural-relationship_n_4800492.html*. Feb 19, 2014

Lerner, H.G. (2002). *The Dance of Connection*. New York: HarperCollins.

Maine, M., & Kelly, J. (2005). *The Body Myth: Adult Women and the Pressure to be Perfect*. Hoboken, NJ: Wiley.

Marano, H. (2000). The eight habits of highly popular people. *Psychology Today,* 33, 78.

Morin, R. (2008). Who Makes the Decisions in Your Home? Pew Research Center. Washington, DC.

O'Neill, S., & Chapman, E. (2008). *Your Attitude Is Showing: A Primer on Human Relations*. Englewood Cliffs, NJ: Prentice Hall.

Phelps, S., & Austin, N. (2002). *The Assertive Woman: A New Look*. San Luis Obispo, CA: Impact Publishers.

Puhn, L. (2010). *Fight Less, Love More: 5-Minute Conversations to Change Your Relationship without Blowing Up or Giving In*. New York: Rodale Books.

Punches, B. (2010). *What You Say and Do Next Matters!* Dubuque, IA: Kendall Hunt Publishing Co.

Rahim, M., & Magner, N. (1995). Confirmatory factor analysis of the styles of handling interpersonal conflict. *Journal of Applied Psychology,* 80, 122–132.

Reece, B., & Brandt, R. (2010). *Effective Human Relations in Organizations*. New York: Houghton Mifflin Co.

Reps, P. (1967). *Pillow Education in Rural Japan. Square Sun, Square Moon*. New York: Tuttle.

Scott, E. (2016). Confllict Resolution Mistakes to Avoid. VeryWell.com

Seider, B. (2010). Couples who use the pronoun we. *Bottom Line*, June 15, 2010.

Smith, M. (2000). *When I Say No I Feel Guilty: For Managers & Executives*. New York: A Train Press.

Stone, D., Patton, B., & Heen, S. (2010). *Difficult Conversations*. New York: Penguin Putnam.

Tannen, D. (2001). *The Argument Culture: Stopping America's War of Words*. New York: Ballantine Books.

Tannen, D. (2001). *You Just Don't Understand*. New York: Ballantine Books.

Telushkin, J. (1998). *Words that Hurt, Words that Heal*. New York: William Morrow and Company, Inc.

Ting-Toomey, S.T., & Oetzel, J. (2002). *Managing Intercultural Conflict Effectively*. Thousand Oaks, CA: Sage Publications.

Verderber, K., Verderber, R., & Berryman-Fink, C. (2013). *Inter-Act: Interpersonal Communication Concepts, Skills and Contexts*. New York: Oxford University Press.

Watanabe, K. (2009). *Problem Solving 101*. London, England: Penguin Books.

Weiten, W., Dunn, D., & Hammer, E. (2014). *Psychology Applied to Modern Life*. Belmont, CA: Thompson Wadsworth.

CHAPTER 8

Almeida, D. (2005). Resilience and vulnerability to daily stressors, assessed via diary methods. *Current Directions in Psychological Science, 14*, 64–68.

American Psychological Association Report (retrieved September (2016). http://www.apa.org/helpcenter/stress.aspx. David S. Krantz, PhD, Beverly Thorn, PhD, and Janice Kiecolt-Glaser, PhD,

Beck, A., Freeman, A., & Davis, D. (2015). *Cognitive Therapy of Personality Disorders*. New York: The Guilford Press.

Benson, H. (2001). *The Relaxation Response*. New York: Harper Collins.

Bernstein, A. (2016). *The Myth of Stress*. Tampa, FL: Free Press.

Bernstein, E. (2016). Steps to turn off the nagging self-doubt in your head most of us lose time to negative thoughts; reframe your thinking and feel more positive. *The Wall Street Journal*, June 13.

Bottos, S., & Dewey, D. (2004). Perfectionist's appraisal of daily hassles and chronic headache. *Headache, 44*, 772–779.

Brown, B. (2012). *Daring Greatly: How the Courage to Be Vulnerable Transforms the Way We Live, Love, Parent, and Lead*. New York: Gotham.

Brown, S., & Vaughn, C. (2010). *Play: How it Shapes the Brain, Opens the Imagination, and Invigorates the Soul*. New York: Penguin Press.

Burns, D. (2006). *The Feeling Good Handbook*. New York: William Morrow and Co.

Burns, D. (2007). *When Panic Attacks: The New Drug-Free Anxiety Therapy That Can Change Your Life*. New York: Random House.

Castillo, L. G., Schwartz, S. J. (2013). Introduction to the special issue on college student mental health. *Journal of Clinical Psychology, 69*(4), 291-297

Ciaramicoli, A. (2016). *The Stress Solution: Using Empathy and Cognitive Behavioral Therapy to Reduce Anxiety and Develop Resilience*. Novato, CA: New World Library.

Davis, M., Eshelman, E.R., & McKay, M. (2014). *The Relaxation and Stress Reduction Workbook*. Oakland, CA: New Harbinger Publications.

Dembling, S. (2006). The do's and don'ts of tackling stress. *The Dallas Morning News*, January 3.

Duffy, K., & Atwater, E. (2014). *Psychology for Living*. Upper Saddle River, NJ: Pearson.

Ellis, A. (2001). *Overcoming Destructive Beliefs, Feelings and Behaviors: New Directions for Rational Emotive Behavior Therapy*. New York: Prometheus Books.

Ellis, A. (2002). *Overcoming Resistance: A Rational Emotive Behavior Therapy Integrated Approach*. New York: Springer Publishers.

Ellis, A. (2003). *How to Stubbornly Refuse to Make Yourself Miserable about Anything—Yes, Anything*. New York: Carol Publishing Group.

Ellis, A., & MacLaren, C. (2005). *Rational Emotive Therapy: A Therapist's Guide*. New York: Impact Publishers.

Epstein, R. (1999). On the real benefits of eustress: A conversation with Hans Selye. *Psychology Today Reader*. Dubuque, IA: Kendall Hunt Publishing Co.

Freud, S. (1936). *The Problems of Anxiety*. New York: Norton.

Friedman, M., & Rosenman, R.H. (1982). *Type A Behavior and Your Heart*. New York: Fawcett.

Gallwey, W., Hanzelik, E., & Horton, J. (2009). *The Inner Game of Stress*. New York: Random House.

Hall, K. (2008). The hidden truth threat. *Bottom Line, 29*, 1–2.

Hanna, H. (2014). *Stressaholic: 5 Steps to Transform Your Relationship to Stress*. Hoboken, NJ: Wiley.

Hanna, H. (2013). *The Sharp Solution: A Brain-Based Approach for Optimal Performance*. Hoboken, NJ: Wiley.

Jacobs, G. (2004). How to stay upbeat and stay healthy. *Bottom Line*, March 1, 12–13.

Kadison, R. & DiGeronimo, T.F. (2004). *College of the overwhelmed: The campus mental health crisis and what to do about it*. San Francisco, CA: Jossey-Bass.

Kleinke, C. (2002). *Coping with Life Challenges*. Pacific Grove, CA: Brooks/Cole Publishing Co.

Lazarus, R.S. (2000). Toward better research on stress and coping. *American Psychologist, 55*, 665–673.

Lazarus, R.S. (2006). *Stress and Emotion*. New York: Springer Publishing.

Maddi, S. R. (2006). Hardiness: The courage to grow from stresses. *Journal of Positive Psychology.* 1 (3), 160–168. doi:10.1080/17439760600619609

McLeod, S. (2014). *Type A Personality.* Retrieved from www.simplypsychology.org/personality-a.html

Mueller, M. (2001). *Taking Care of Me: The Habits of Happiness*. Sevierville, TN: Insight, Inc.

Nairne, J. (2013). *Psychology: The Adaptive Mind*. Belmont, CA: Wadsworth/Thomas Learning.

Newman, J. (2000). Sailing through the blues. *Health*, September.

Orma, S. (2016). *Stop Worrying and Go to Sleep*: *How to Put Insomnia to Bed for Good*. eBook. https://drorma.com/overcome-insomnia/

Pastorino, E., & Doyle-Portillo, S. (2012). *What is Psychology?* Belmont, CA: Thompson Wadsworth.

Paul, A. (2011). The uses and abuses of optimism. *Psychology Today*, Nov./Dec., 5–63.

Paulus, P., Seta, C., & Baron, R. (2000). *Effective Human Relations: A Guide to People at Work*. Needham Heights, MA: Allyn & Bacon.

Peale, N.V. (2003). *The Power of Positive Thinking*. New York: Simon and Schuster.

Peruttzi, B L. (2016). *Transition House Wellness Newsletter*, Fall edition.

Pliner, J., & Brown, D. (1995). Helpers among students from four ethnic groups. *Journal of College Student Personnel*, 26, 147–157.

Plotnik, R. (2014). *Introduction to Psychology*. Pacific Grove, CA: Wadsworth.

Pychyl, T. (2011). Oops, where did the day go? *Psychology Today*, Sept./Oct., 58–61.

Raeburn, P. (2006). A case for double-edged optimism. *Psychology Today,* 39, 74–79.

Rayl, A. (2007). The price of a broken heart. *Psychology Today,* 40, 96–102.

Reetz, D. R., Barr, V., & Krylowicz, B. (2013). The Association for University and College Counseling Center Directors Annual Survey. Washington, D.C.: AUCCCD.

Rosch, P. (2016). The American Institute of Stress. Young Adults Are Most Stressed Generation: Survey. Retrieved from http:www.stress.org

Rudolph, K., Sánchez, B., Stuart, E., Greenberg, B., Fujishiro, K., Wand, G., Shrager, S., Seeman, T., Diez Roux, V. & Golden, S. Job strain and the cortisol diurnal cycle in MESA: Accounting for between- and within-day variability. *American Journal of Epidemiology*, 183(5), 497–506.

Sifferlin, A. (2013). The Most Stressed Out Generation? Young Adults. Retrieved from Healthland.Time.com/2013

Schultz, D., & Schultz, S. (20092010). *Psychology and Work Today*. Upper Saddle River, NJ: Prentice Hall.

Scott, E. (2016). Attitude, Self Talk and Stress. Retrieved from https:www.VeryWell.com

Seguin, A. (2015). *Negative Thoughts: Discover How to Stop Negative Thoughts by Changing the Way You Think*. Lexington, KY: Miafn, LLC.

Smith, T., & Ruiz, J. (2002). Psychological influences on the development and course of coronary heart disease: Current status and implications for research and practice. *Journal of Consulting and Clinical Psychology,* 70, 548–568.

Southwick, S., Vythilingam, M., & Charney, D. (2005). The psychobiology of depression and resilience to stress. *Annual Review of Clinical Psychology,* 1, 255–291.

Stone, A., Smith, J., Kaell, A., & Hurewitz, A. (2000). Structured writing about stressful events. *Health Psychology*, 19, 619–624.

Surveys.ap.org (2008). College students' degree of stress is high. A survey conducted Feb. 28–March 6 by Edison Media Research.

Tannen, D. (2007). *You Just Don't Understand: Women and Men in Conversation*. New York: Harper Collins.

Taylor, D., & McGee, D. (2000). *Stress Management Workshop Series*. Arlington, TX: Metro-McGee Associates, Inc.

Taylor, S.E. (2004). Commentary in Taylor takes on fight-or-flight. *American Psychological Society,* 17, 21.

Underwood, A. (2005). The good heart. *Newsweek*, October 3, 49–55.

Weiten, W., Dunn, D., & Hammer, E. (2014). *Psychology Applied to Modern Life*. Belmont, CA: Wadsworth.

Wolpe, J. (1992). *The Practice of Behavior Therapy*. Elmsford, NY: Pergamon Press.

CHAPTER 9

Albom, M. (2002). *Tuesdays with Morrie*. New York: Broadway.

Allport, G.W. (1979). *The Nature of Prejudice*. Reading, MA: Perseus.

Alper, B. (2015). *Millenials are less religious than older Americans, but just as spiritual*. Pew Research Center: Nov. 23, 2015 FactTank

Anderson, M., & Hitlin, P. (2016). *Social Media Conversations About Race*. Pew Research Center.

Aronson, E. (2012). *The Social Animal*. New York: Worth Publishers.

Aronson, E., Wilson, T., & Akert, R. (2013). *Social Psychology*. Upper Saddle River, NJ: Pearson Education, Inc.

Brooks, D. (2016). The power of alturism. *New York Times,* July 8.

Begley, S., & Kalb, C. (2000). Learning right from wrong. *Newsweek*, March 13, 30–32.

Ciccarelli, S., & Noland, J. (2014). *Psychology*. Upper Saddle River, NJ: Pearson.

Cohen, R. (2004). *Negotiating Across Cultures: International Communication in an Interdependent World* (rev. ed.). Washington, DC: United States Institute of Peace.

Coleman, P. (2016). Racism and Violence in America, What are white allies to do? Online The Five Percent blog

Coontz, S. (2016). *The Way We Never Were: American Families and the Nostalgia Trap*. New York: Basic Books.

Compton, W. (2005). *An Introduction to Positive Psychology*. New York: Wadsworth.

Corey, G., & Corey, M. (2008). *I Never Knew I Had a Choice*. Pacific Grove, CA: Brooks Cole Publishing Co.

Covey, S.R. (2004). *The Seven Habits of Highly Effective People*—Anniversary Edition. New York: Free Press

Covey, S.R. (2006). *The Speed of Trust-The One Thing that Changes Everything*. New York: Free Press.

DeCenzo, D., & Silhanek, B. (2002). *Human Relations: Personal and Professional Development*. Upper Saddle River, NJ: Prentice Hall.

Devine, P. (1989). Stereotypes and prejudice: Their automatic and controlled components. *Journal of Personality and Social Psychology*, 56, 680-690.

Dovidio, J. F., Glick, P. S., & Rudman, L. A. (2005). *On the Nature of Prejudice: Fifty Years After*. Allport. Malden, MA: Blackwell Pub.

Dubrin, A. (2014). *Human Relations for Career and Personal Success*. Upper Saddle River, NJ: Prentice Hall.

Epstein, R. (2002). M. Scott Peck wrestling with God. *Psychology Today,* 35, 68–73.

Fazio, R., Jackson, J., Dunton, B., & Williams, C. (1995). Variability in automatic activation as an unobtrusive measure of racial attitudes: A bona fide pipeline? *Journal of Personality and Social Psychology*, 69, 1013-1027.

Festinger, L. (1957). *A Theory of Cognitive Dissonance*. Stanford, CA: Stanford University Press.

Frankl, V.E. (1997). *Man's Search for Meaning.* New York: Washington Square Press.

Freiberg, K. (2009/2010). *Annual Editions: Human Development.* Dubuque, IA: Mc-Graw Hill/Dushkin.

Grossman, C. (2010). 72% of millennials more spiritual than religious. *USA Today,* April 27, 2010.

Hall, E.T. (1959). *The Silent Language.* New York: Doubleday.

Hecklinger, F., & Black, B. (2012). *Training for Life.* Dubuque, IA: Kendall Hunt Publishing Co.

Henslin, J. (2015). *Essentials of Sociology.* New York: Pearson.

Hetherington, C. (2008). *Choose Happiness: Pay Attention to Co-Dependent Patterns.* Iowa City, IA: Hetherington and Associates.

Howard, P. (2016). *The Values Toolkit: Application Manual for the Owner's Manuel for Values at Work.* Charlotte, NC: CentACS Press.

Humbert, P. (2016). Living a great life from Goal Setting 101 Manual. http://www.philiphumbert.com/index.htm

Johnson, D. (2008). *Reaching Out.* Needham Heights, MA: Allyn & Bacon.

Johnson, D. (2014). *Reaching Out: Interpersonal Effectiveness and Self-Actualization.* Boston: Pearson.

Josephson, M. (1994). Does character still count? *USA Weekend,* September 23–25, p. 20.

Jung, C.G. (1923). *Psychological Types.* New York: Harcourt Brace.

Kardaras, N. (2016). *Glow Kids: How Screen Addiction Is Hijacking Our Kids-and How to Break the Trance.* New York: St. Martins Press.

Kardaras, N. (2016). It's digital heroin: How screens turn kids into psychotic junkies. http://nypost.com/2016/08/27/its-digital-heroin-how-screens-turn-kids-into-psychotic-junkies/

Kluckhohn, F. (1956). Value orientations. In R.R. Grinker, Sr. (Ed.), *Toward a Unified Theory of Human Behavior: An Introduction to General Systems Theory.* New York: Basic Books, Inc.

Kohlberg, L. (1981). *The Philosophy of Moral Development: Moral Stages and the Idea of Justice.* San Francisco, CA: Harper and Row.

Lamberton, L., & Minor, L. (2014). *Human Relations: Strategies for Success.* New York: McGraw Hill.

Lenhart, A. (2012). Teens, smartphones and texting. http://www.pewinternet.org/2012/03/19/teens-smartphones-texting/

Lewis, H. (2007). *A Question of Values.* New York: Harper and Row.

Myers, D.G. (2013). *Psychology.* New York: Worth.

Mynatt, C., & Doherty, M. (2013). *Understanding Human Behavior.* Upper Saddle River, NJ: Pearson Education.

Nosek, B. (2007). Implicit-explicit relations. *Current Directions in Psychological Science,* 16, 65-69

Olmstead, K., Lampe, C., Ellison, N. (2016). Social Media in the Workplace. Pew Research Center, June.

Park, C. (2013). The meaning making model: A framework for understanding meaning, spirituality, and stress-related growth in health psychology. *European Health Psychologist,* 15, 40-17.

Pattakos, A. (2010). *Prisoners of Our Thoughts.* San Francisco, CA: Berret-Kohler Publishers, Inc.

Pausch, R. (2008). *The Last Lecture.* New York: Hyperion Books.

Peck, M. (2003). *The Road Less Traveled,* 25th Anniversary Edition. New York: Simon & Schuster.

Pew Research Center, Religion and Public Life (March 2016) *Gender gap in worship service attendance differs between Muslim-majority and Christian-majority countries.*

Pojman, L.P. (2012). *Ethics: Discovering Right and Wrong.* Belmont, CA: Wadsworth.

Rathus, S., & Nevid, J. (2013). *Psychology and the Challenges of Life.* New York: Wiley.

Reece, B., & Brandt, R. (2014). *Effective Human Relations in Organizations.* Boston, MA: Houghton Mifflin Co.

Ricard, M. (2015). *Altruism: The Power of Compassion to Change Yourself and the World.* New York: Little Brown Publishers.

Rogers, M. (2005). The book that changed my life. *Fort Worth Star Telegram,* September 19.

Rokeach, M. (2000). *Understanding Human Values.* New York: The Free Press.

Schwartz, B. (2000). Waking up from the American Dream. *Psychology Today,* 32, 74.

Spranger, E. (1928). *Types of Men.* New York: Harcourt Brace Jovanovich (Johnson Reprints).

Stahl, L. (2010). SMU moves to emphasize ethics in all fields of study. *Dallas Morning News,* December 25, 2010.

Tolerance.org A project of the Southern Poverty Law Center retrieved 3/14/17

Values. (n.d.). *Dictionary.com Unabridged.* Retrieved August 17, 2016 from Dictionary.com website http://www.dictionary.com/browse/values

Vandeveer, R., & Menefee, M. (2009). *Human Behavior in Organizations.* Upper Saddle River, NJ: Pearson.

Wert, K. (2016). *Ten Essential Character Traits for a Happier Life.* Retrieved from Meant to be Happy.com website

Wyer, N. (2004). Value conflicts in intergroup perception: A social cognitive perspective. In G.V. Bodenhausen, & A.J. Lambert (Eds.), *Foundation of Social Cognition.* Mahwah, NJ: Erlbaum.

Yalom, I.D. (2000). *Momma and the Meaning of Life.* Dunmore, PA: HarperCollins.

Zuckerman, P. (2016). LA Times Op-Ed: How secular family values stack up. *LA Times* Sept. 18.

Chapter 10

Allen, D. (2015). *Getting things Done: The art of Stress Free Productivity.* New York: Penguin Press.

Ash, M.K. (2008). *The Mary Kay Way: Timeless Principles from America's Greatest Woman Entrepreneur.* New York: Wiley.

Boles, R.N. (2005). *How to Find Your Mission in Life.* Berkeley, CA: Ten Speed Press.

Boles, R.N. (2017). *What Color Is Your Parachute?* Berkeley, CA: Ten Speed Press.

Breathnach, S. (2009). *Simple Abundance.* New York: Warner Books.

Campbell, A. (2007). *The Sense of Well-Being in America.* New York: McGraw Hill.

Campbell, D. (2007). *If You Don't Know Where You're Going, You'll Probably End Up Somewhere Else.* Niles, IL: Thomas More Press.

Canfield, J. (2006). *The Success Principles.* New York: Collins Living.

Corey, G., & Corey, M. (2008). *I Never Knew I Had a Choice.* Pacific Grove, CA: Brooks Cole Publishing Co.

Covey, S.R. (2015). *The 12 Levers of Success.* New York: Simon and Schuster.

Covey, S.R. (2014). *The Leader in Me.* New York: Simon & Schuster.

Covey, S.R. (2013). *The Seven Habits of Highly Effective People.* New York: Simon & Schuster.

Covey, S.R., Merrill, A.R., & Merrill, R. (1996). *First Things First.* New York: Fireside edition Simon and Schuster.

Csikszentmihalyi, M. (2016). Finding flow. *Psychology Today,* June edition.

Davis, M., Eshelman, E., & McKay, M. (2008). *The Relaxation & Stress Reduction Workbook.* Oakland, CA: New Harbinger Publications, Inc.

Dawson, G., & Glaubman, R. (2002). *Life Is So Good.* New York: Penguin USA.

Diener, E. (2003). *Frequently Asked Questions (FAQs) about Subjective Well-Being (Happiness and Life Satisfaction).* Champaign, IL: Department of Psychology, University of Illinois.

Doskoch, P. (2005). The winning edge. *Psychology Today, 38,* 42–52.

Drafke, M., & Kossen, S. (2008). *The Human Side of Organizations.* Upper Saddle River, NJ: Pearson Education, Inc.

Duckworth, A. (2016). *Grit: The Power of Passion and Perseverance.* New York: Simon and Schuster.

Epstein, M. (2016). Opening up to happiness. *Psychology Today* June edition online.

Figler, H. (2013). *The Complete Job Search Handbook.* New York: Owl Books.

Flora, C. (2016). The pursuit of happiness. *Psychology Today, 42,* 60–69.

Foster, B. (2015). 10 steps to successful goal setting: *Huffington Post – The Blog.* Retrieved July 14, 2016 from http:/www.huffingtonpost.com/Bradley-foster/how-to-set-goals-b3226083ihtml

Garcia, L. (2005). Happiness Is . . . *The Dallas Morning News,* May 24.

Gasca, P. (2015). *Become a Better Leader With These 5 Cultural-Awareness Tips.* Entrepreneur.com

Green, K. (2013). *4 Steps to Self-Actualization and Becoming the Best Version of You.* Huffington Post.

Gullebeeau, C. (2016). *Born for this: How to find the work you were meant to do.* New York, NY: Penguin Random House LLC

Haden, J. (2014). Seven things to remarkably happy people do more. Inc.com blog, March 24.

Harris, R. (2008). *The Happiness Trap.* Boston, MA: Trumpeter.

Hecklinger, F., & Black, B. (2012). *Training for Life.* Dubuque, IA: Kendall Hunt Publishing Co.

Helmstetter, S. (2011). *Who Are You Really, and What Do You Want.* New York: Park Avenue Press.

John-Roger, & McWilliams, P. (2004). *Do It.* Los Angeles: Prelude Press.

Johnson, D. (2012). *Reaching Out.* Needham Heights, MA: Allyn & Bacon.

Johnson, S. (2002). *Who Moved My Cheese?* New York: G. P. Putnam's Sons.

Kaplan, J. (2010). Buddhism and psychotherapy: An interview with Dr. Mark Epstein. *Psychology Today,* October edition.

Kashdan, T. (2016). Three ways culture shapes happiness and well-being. *Psychology Today,* February edition online.

Lakein, A. 2008). *How to Get Control of Your Time and Your Life.* New York: New American Library.

Lock, C. (2005). 26 simple steps to make your life easier and get more done in a day. *Living Magazine,* August, 44–46.

Lyken, D., & Csikszentmihalyi, M. (2001). Happiness—stuck with what you've got. *Psychologist,* 14, 470–472.

Mackenzie, A. (2009). *The Time Trap.* New York: AMACOM (Division of American Management Association).

MacKay, H. (2015, June 1). How to take risks effectively. Posted to Unexpress Blog http://www.unexpress.com/harvey-mackay/

Manzoni, A. (2016). Conceptualizing and measuring youth independence: A multi-dimensional approach using latent class analysis. *Acta Sociologica,* June 29.

Maslow, A. (1998). *Maslow & Management.* New York: John Wiley & Sons.

McCullough, M. (2005). *Rules for Success: Time Tested Keys for Developing Excellence in Your Life.* Colorado Springs, CO: River Oak Publishing.

McGowan, K. (2005). The pleasure paradox. *Psychology Today,* January/February, 52–53.

Myers, D.G. (2008). *The American Paradox: Spiritual Hunger in an Age of Plenty.* New Haven, CT: Yale University Press.

Myers, D.G. (2014). *Myers Psychology for AP.* New York: Worth Publishing.

Osman, A. (2016). *5 powerful reasons why goalsetting is important.* Retrieved from http://www.codeofliving.com

Pavot, W., & Diener, E. (2008). The Satisfaction With Life Scale and the emerging construct of life satisfaction. *Journal of Positive Psychology,* 3, 137–152

Peck, M.S. (2003). *The Road Less Traveled,* 25th Anniversary Edition. New York: Simon & Schuster, Inc.

Prather, H. (2011). *Notes on How to Live in the World and Still Be Happy.* Boston, MA: RedWheel/Weiser.

Schreiber, K. (2011). Ego in full bloom. *Psychology Today,* 44, 18.

Seligman, M.E. (2004). *Authentic Happiness: New Positive Psychology to Realize Your Potential for Lasting Fulfillment.* New York: Free Press.

Seligman, M.E. (2011). *Flourish.* New York: Free Press.

Seigel, B. (2011). *Love, Medicine and Miracles: Lessons Learned about Self-Healing from a Surgeon's Experience with Exceptional Patients* (Kindle Edition). New York: William Morrow Paperbacks.

Viscott, D. (2003). *Finding Your Strength in Difficult Times.* New York: McGraw Hill.

Weil, A. (2011). *Spontaneous Happiness.* New York: Little Brown & Co.

Worchel, S., Cooper, J., Goethals, G., & Olson, J. (2000). *Social Psychology.* Chicago, IL: Nelson-Hall.

Yang, Y. (2008). Social inequalities in happiness in the United States. *American Sociological Review,* 73, 204–226.

Yu, W. (2011). How to become a happier person. *Inform,* August, 10–11.

Ziglar, Z. (2000). *See You at the Top.* Nashville, TN: Thomas Nelson Publishers.

Index

NOTE: Page references in *italics* refer to figures and tables.

attribution error, 35
attribution theory, 35
Authentic Happiness (Seligman), 579
autonomy, doubt *versus,* 78
aversive events, learned helplessness and, 141–144
aversive racism, 265
avoidance, 399
avoiding strategy of conflict (lose-lose), 412, *413*
awe, feeling, 218–219
Awfulizing Statements, 465–467

B

Bach, George, 398
balance
 life planning for, 570–573
 managing stress with, 470
Bandura, Albert, 97, 151–155, 203
barriers, to communication, 262, *263*
barriers, to listening, 285–288
"Basic Human Rights" (Smith; Davis), 397
Basic Law of Life, 550–551
Beck, Aaron, 464
behavior
 behavioral contract, 162
 behavior styles, in interpersonal conflict, 398–399
 stress and, 451–452, *452*
 values and, 514
beliefs, 504–505
Bengtson, Vern, 504
Benson, Herbert, 471–472
bereavement, 209–211
Berger, Ann, 19
Better (Parker-Pope), 364
Beyond Blame (Kottler), 418
bias
 defined, 72
 implicit bias, 72, 292
 self-serving bias, 107
Big Five (personality theory)
 "Big Five" Test (Activity), 121–123
 overview, 83–84
 personality factors, *83*
birth order, 77
bisexuality, defined, 72
blame, 228, 398
Blanchard, Kenneth, 270
blended families, 369
Blind Area (Johari Window), 10

body leakage, 264
body movement, 268–269, *269*
Body Myth, The (Maine), 407
Boles, Richard, 556
Bolton, Robert, 292–293, 297
brainstorming, 417
Branden, Nathaniel, 113
Breathnach, Sarah, 578
Breitman, Patti, 407
broken-record technique, 406
Brooks, David, 505
Brown, Brené, 207–208
Brown, Stuart, 471
Bryant, John Hope, 3
bullying
 cyberbullies targeting peers online, 204–206
 defined, 205
 victims of, 42–43, 206–208
Bureau of Labor Statistics, 354
Burgess, Guy, 400
Burgess, Heidi, 400
Burns, David, 465–467

C

Cain, Susan, 88
calm, emotion and, 358
Campbell, David, 558–559
Cannon, Walter B., 450
Carducci, Bernardo, 22, 25, 26
career
 ethics and the professions, 518–519, *519*
 marriage, parenthood, and, 353–355
caring
 ethics and, 516–517
 as friendship trait, 324
Carlson, Richard, 192–193
Carnegie, Dale, 299–300
categorizing, 32–33
catharsis, 6
Cattell, Raymond, 83
cellphones, using, 279, 281
Center for Nonviolent Communication, 259
Centers for Disease Control, 345
chair of life, 571, 572
challenge, stress and, 459
channels, of communication, 261
Chapman, Gary, 341–342

domestic violence, 359–360

domination, 399

Donovan, Mary Ellen, 113

Don't Sweat the Small Stuff (Carlson), 193

door openers, for listening, 293–294

double bind, of communication, 263

doubt, autonomy *versus,* 78

Dovidio, Jack, 265

Drago, Emily, 282

Dubrin, Andrew, 517

Duckworth, Angela, 158, 558

duration, of emotions, 197

Dweck, Carol, 84–86, 158

E

Economic Person (Spranger's Six Value Systems), 502

"egalitarian" marriage, 366

ego, 76

80-20 principle, 568

Ellis, Albert, 194, 463–468

Emery, Gary, 194–195, 197, 221

Emmons, Michael L., 405–407

Emotional Intelligence (Goleman), 217

emotions, 191–255. *see also* nonverbal communication

    bullying victims, 206–215

    calming down, 358

    characteristics of, 193–195

    cyberbullies targeting peers online, 204–206

    dealing with, 221–224

    defined, 192–193

    development of, 215–216

    effects of conflict and, 394 (*see also* interpersonal conflict; marital conflict)

    emotion, defined, 193

    emotional attachment in relationships, 18–21

    emotional bank account, 356

    emotional debt, 221

    emotional intelligence, 192–193, 216–221

    emotion-packed phrases, 280

    emotion wheel, *197*

    expressing feelings and, 224–227

    forgiveness and healing process, 227–230

    overview, 191–192

    problem emotions, 198–204

    summarized, 231–234

    types of, *196*, 196–198, *197*

    Web Resources and Web Activities about, 234–236

Activities

    Am I Emotionally Intelligent?, 237–238

    Anger Inventory, 245–247

    Dealing with Emotions, 255

    Develop a "Wellness Toolbox" to Deal with Mental Health, 251–252

    Do Women Express More Emotions than Men?, 249–250

    Emotional Expressivity Scale, 239–240

    How I Express My Feelings, 243–244

    Identifying Feelings, 241–242

    Learning to Forgive, 253–254

empathy

    empathetic listening, 292–297

    friendship and, 324

    for overcoming shame, 208

    for person-to-person communication, 298–299

    Pillow Method-Developing Empathy (Activity), 435–436

    "walking in another's shoes" and, 15

empty love, 339

encoding, 260

encouragement, to speakers, 294

Encyclopedia of Conflict Resolution, The (Burgess, Burgess), 400

Englander-Golden, Paula, 290

Enright, Robert, 229

environment

    physical environment as subliminal message (non-verbal communication), 272–273

    reciprocal determinism and, 98–99

    self-control and, 143–144

    stress and, 462

envy, 362–363

Epstein, Mark, 574, 575

Epstein, Robert, 504

Erikson, Erik, 76, 78–81

esteem needs, 554

ethics. *see also* values

    character and, 516–517

    confusion and conflict about, 520–521

    Guidelines for Character Development (Activity), 533–534

    moral development and, 519–520, *520*

    Moral Dilemma (Activity), 535–537

    professions and, 518–519, *519*

    Values and Ethics (Activity), 547

ethnicity, stress and, 458–459. *see also* culture

eustress, 443–444

evaluation, for conflict management, 418

evaluative response, 288–289, 296–297

"Everyone Has a Story" (Snead), 278

exercise, 471

exhaustion stage (general adaptation system), 449–450

expectations

    for relationships, 18–21

    self-fulfilling prophecy, 36–37, *37*

explanatory styles

    Are You an Optimist or a Pessimist? (Activity), 175–176

    for health, happiness, and success, 148–149

    learned optimism, 149–150

    optimistic, 147–148

    pessimistic, 147–148

external locus of control

    defined, 146

    internal *versus,* 139–140, *144*

external noise, 261–262

extroversion (Myers-Brigg Type Indicator), 86

extroversion (OCEAN personality trait), 83, *83*

extroversion, making friends and, 577–578

eye contact, 266–267

Eysenck, Hans, 83

F

face, loss of, 203

facial expression, 266–267

facilitative emotions, 198

fairness, 516–517

Families and Work Institute, 354–355

family and domestic violence, 359–360

family leave, 354

Faris, Robert, 206

fatuous love, *340*

faults, listing, 111

Fay, Jim, 156

fear

    facing, 200

    of getting acquainted (shyness), 21–27

    growth *versus,* 111

    overview, 198–199

feedback, in communication process, 261

feeling (Myers-Brigg Type Indicator), 87

feelings. *see also* emotions

    dealing with stressful feelings, 462–463

    Emotional Expressivity Scale (Activity), 239–240

    expressing, 224–227

    feeling *versus* acting, 223

    How I Express My Feelings (Activity), 243–244

    Identifying Feelings (Activity), 241–242

    release of, 394

    words for feelings, when needs are not satisfied, 277

    words for feelings, when needs are satisfied, 276

Fehr, Beverly, 18

Felmlee, Diana, 205, 206

Festinger, Leon, 514–515

financial domain, stress and, 458

first impressions

    First Impressions (Activity), 57–58

    overview, 29–30, 32

First Impressions (White, Demarais), 39

First Things First (Covey), 553, 567

Fisher, Helen, 346–347

Fiske, Susan, 32

Five Dominant Patterns of Relationships, 13–15

Five Love Languages, The (Chapman), 341–342

five-to-one ratio, 356–357

Fleshner, Monika, 450

flexibility, 410

Flourish (Seligman), 579

flow, living in a state of, 578

focus, goals for, 557, 558

For Better or For Worse (Hetherington), 368

Forgive for Love (Luskin), 229

forgiveness

    Learning to Forgive (Activity), 253–254

    overview, 227–230

Forgiveness (Simon, Simon), 227

Forgiveness Is a Choice (Enright), 229

Frankl, Viktor, 92, 522, 523

Freud, Sigmund, 75–76, 81

friendship

    challenges of, 327–331

    developing new relationships, 40–45, *42*

    end of a friendship, 296

    extroversion and, 577–578

    importance of, 469

    loneliness and, 15, 17–18

    between men and women, 325, 326–327

    need for, 325–327

    overview, 323–324

    as protection for bullying, 207

    reciprocity, 331

    social exchange theory, 331

Becoming *Aware*

relaxation
>breathing for, 581
>
>importance of, 471
>
>relaxation response, 471–472

religion
>dating and mate selection, 335
>
>religious beliefs and values, 503–504

Religious Person (Spranger's Six Value Systems), 502

remarriage, 369

repression, as defense mechanism, *456*

repression of emotions, 219–220

repulsion hypothesis, 330

resentment, 202

resistance stage (general adaptation system), 449–450

respect, 298, 516–517

responding style, 288–292
>active and empathetic listening, 292–297
>
>advising, 289–290
>
>evaluative or judging, 288–289
>
>implicit bias and, 292
>
>interpretive, 290
>
>overview, 288
>
>questioning, 290–291
>
>responding reflectively, 294–296
>
>Rogers on, 296–297
>
>supportive, 290
>
>understanding, 291

responsibility, 5, 143, 516–517

Ring Theory, 210–211

risks
>intelligent risk-taking, 552
>
>learning to take risks, 550–552
>
>self-control for, 143

Road Less Traveled, The (Peck), 504

Rogers, Carl, 90–91, 101, 106, 288, 296–297, 298, 325

role confusion, identity *versus,* 79

role expectations, in marriage, 351–353

role models, 151

romantic jealousy, 362–363

romantic relationships. *see* close relationships

Romeo and Juliet effect, 343

Rosen, Larry, 24

Rosenberg, Marshall, 259

S

sacrifices, values and, 514–516

sadness, 195. *see also* depression

safety and security needs, 554

Salovey, Peter, 216

same-sex relationships/marriage. *see also* LGBTQ (lesbian, gay, bisexual, and transgender)
>gender roles in marriage and, 355
>
>marital conflict in gay/lesbian relationships, 369

Sanford, Linda, 113

Sapadin, Linda, 327

Satir, Virginia, 92–93, 258–259, 290

Schlessinger, Laura, 521

Schwartz, Barry, 522–523

Schwartz, Pepper, 331

Scott, Elizabeth, 398

Scott, Peter Spencer, 218–219

scripted relationships, 14–15

search for meaning, 92

secondary reinforcers, 156–157

Seider, Benjamin, 410

Seidman, Gwen, 29

self
>nature of, 100–101
>
>"possible selves," 100
>
>public *versus* private self, 3
>
>real self, 102–104
>
>"The Person That Is Me" (Krause), 100–101

self-absorption, generativity *versus,* 79–80

self-actualization
>defined, 555
>
>Maslow's Hierarchy of Needs, *554,* 554–556
>
>Rogers on unconditional positive regard, 90–91

self-awareness, 69–135
>Adler's individual psychology theory, 76–78
>
>cognitive and social theories, 97–101, *98*
>
>cognitive theories, overview, 94–96, *96*
>
>Erikson's eight stages of psychosocial development, 78–81
>
>finding real self for, 102–104
>
>Frankl on search for meaning, 92
>
>for growth and change, 113
>
>individualism *versus* collectivism, 104–105, *105*
>
>overview, 69–70
>
>personality development, 75–76
>
>personality types, *83,* 83–89
>
>Rogers' self-theory-humanistic approach, 90–91
>
>Satir on self-worth, 92–93
>
>self-esteem and, 104–113, *107*
>
>"self-image" development, 70–75
>
>strengths-based psychology, 89–90, *90*

These are Human Relations students' hands that are in an OU class called The Wellness Project. The class has the vision to empower personal well-being, improve mental wellness, and increase life joy.

Teaching them positive wellness skills that will help and support them to be stronger individuals in life.

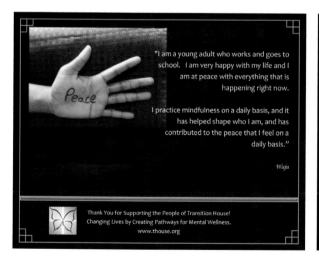

"I am a young adult who works and goes to school. I am very happy with my life and I am at peace with everything that is happening right now.

I practice mindfulness on a daily basis, and it has helped shape who I am, and has contributed to the peace that I feel on a daily basis."

Waju

Thank You for Supporting the People of Transition House!
Changing Lives by Creating Pathways for Mental Wellness.
www.thouse.org

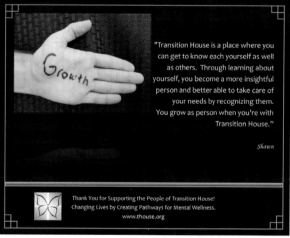

"Transition House is a place where you can get to know each yourself as well as others. Through learning about yourself, you become a more insightful person and better able to take care of your needs by recognizing them. You grow as person when you're with Transition House."

Shawn

Thank You for Supporting the People of Transition House!
Changing Lives by Creating Pathways for Mental Wellness.
www.thouse.org

All images courtesy of Bonnie Peruttzi.

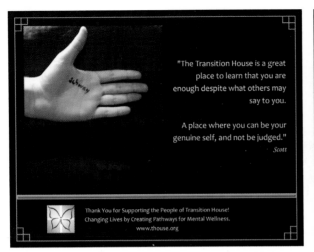

"The Transition House is a great place to learn that you are enough despite what others may say to you.

A place where you can be your genuine self, and not be judged."
— *Scott*

Thank You for Supporting the People of Transition House!
Changing Lives by Creating Pathways for Mental Wellness.
www.thouse.org

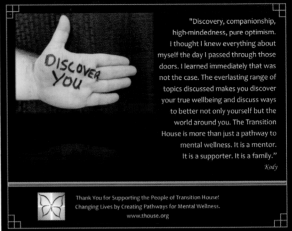

"Discovery, companionship, high-mindedness, pure optimism. I thought I knew everything about myself the day I passed through those doors. I learned immediately that was not the case. The everlasting range of topics discussed makes you discover your true wellbeing and discuss ways to better not only yourself but the world around you. The Transition House is more than just a pathway to mental wellness. It is a mentor. It is a supporter. It is a family."
— *Kody*

Thank You for Supporting the People of Transition House!
Changing Lives by Creating Pathways for Mental Wellness.
www.thouse.org

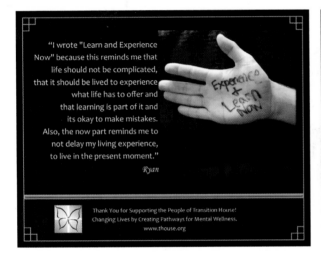

"I wrote "Learn and Experience Now" because this reminds me that life should not be complicated, that it should be lived to experience what life has to offer and that learning is part of it and its okay to make mistakes. Also, the now part reminds me to not delay my living experience, to live in the present moment."
— *Ryan*

Thank You for Supporting the People of Transition House!
Changing Lives by Creating Pathways for Mental Wellness.
www.thouse.org

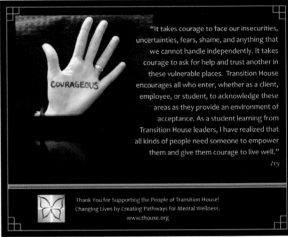

"It takes courage to face our insecurities, uncertainties, fears, shame, and anything that we cannot handle independently. It takes courage to ask for help and trust another in these vulnerable places. Transition House encourages all who enter, whether as a client, employee, or student, to acknowledge these areas as they provide an environment of acceptance. As a student learning from Transition House leaders, I have realized that all kinds of people need someone to empower them and give them courage to live well."
— *Ivy*

Thank You for Supporting the People of Transition House!
Changing Lives by Creating Pathways for Mental Wellness.
www.thouse.org

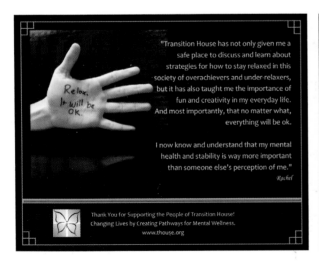

"Transition House has not only given me a safe place to discuss and learn about strategies for how to stay relaxed in this society of overachievers and under-relaxers, but it has also taught me the importance of fun and creativity in my everyday life. And most importantly, that no matter what, everything will be ok.

I now know and understand that my mental health and stability is way more important than someone else's perception of me."
— *Rachel*

Thank You for Supporting the People of Transition House!
Changing Lives by Creating Pathways for Mental Wellness.
www.thouse.org

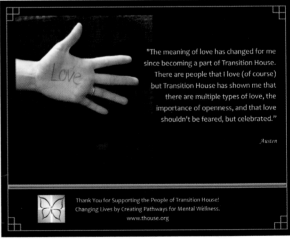

"The meaning of love has changed for me since becoming a part of Transition House. There are people that I love (of course) but Transition House has shown me that there are multiple types of love, the importance of openness, and that love shouldn't be feared, but celebrated."
— *Austen*

Thank You for Supporting the People of Transition House!
Changing Lives by Creating Pathways for Mental Wellness.
www.thouse.org

Becoming *Aware*